Off White

Off White

Readings on Race, Power, and Society

Michelle Fine, Lois Weis,
Linda C. Powell, and L. Mun Wong,
Editors

ROUTLEDGE
New York • London

Published in 1997 by
Routledge
29 West 35th Street
New York, NY 10001

Published in Great Britain by
Routledge
11 New Fetter Lane
London EC4P 4EE

Printed in the United States of America on acid-free paper.

Library of Congress Cataloging-in-Publication Data

Off white : readings on society, race, and culture / by Michelle Fine
. . . [et al.].
        p.   cm.
    Includes bibliographical references and index.
    ISBN 0–415–91301–2 (hc : alk. paper). — ISBN 0–415–91302–0 (pbk.
: alk. paper)
    1. Whites—United States—Race identity.   2. Racism—United
States.   3. Social classes—United States.   4. United States—Race
relations.   5. Race awareness—United States   I. Fine, Michelle.
E184.A1034   1996
305.8′00973—dc20
                                                    96–25153
                                                      CIP

Contents

Preface

Michelle Fine, Linda C. Powell, Lois Weis, and L. Mun Wong

High in the tower, where I sit above the loud complaining of the human sea, I know many souls that toss and whirl and pass, but none there are that intrigue me more than the Souls of White Folk.

Of them I am singularly clairvoyant. I see in and through them. I view them from un-usual points of vantage. Not as a foreigner do I come, for I am native, not foreign, bone of their thought and flesh of their language. Mine is not the knowledge of the traveler or the colonial composite of dear memories, words and wonder. Nor yet is my knowledge that which servants have of masters, or mass of class, or capitalist of artisan. Rather I see these souls undressed and from the back and side. I see the working of their entrails. I know their thoughts and they know that I know. This knowledge makes them now em-barrassed, now furious! They deny me my right to live and be and call me misbirth! My word is to them mere bitterness and my soul, pessimism. And yet as they preach and strut and shout and threaten, crouching as they clutch at rags of facts and fancies to hide their nakedness, they go twisting, flying by my tired eyes and I see them ever stripped—ugly, human.

———W. E. B. Du Bois

Within the past ten years we have witnessed a flurry of scholarship on multiculturalism, but across these texts there rings out a consistent silence, a silence on questions of whiteness which Du Bois flagged some 75 years ago.

Scholars of multiculturalism, critical gender and race theory, and subaltern discourses have spent considerable energy centering the voices of those historically excluded and marginalized. Voices of those positioned at the "margins" or "on the edge" are being heard within and across all disciplines, contributing to a reformation of what constitutes "knowledge." While we do not mean to overstate the transformative success, it is indeed the case that significant challenge has taken place in academic canons and that these challenges at least partially reflect the intellectual and community-based movements of women and men of color, as well as white women, gays, les-bians and bisexuals, persons with disabilities, and the working class and poor. As we make our voices heard in the academy, therefore, a single white coherent and male, heterosexual, and elite narrative no longer characterizes any of our fields.

Strikingly absent from even these critical debates and scholarship, however, has been atten-tion to the question of whiteness; whiteness as race, as privilege, as social construction. While recent collections pluralize our understandings of color through biography and history, few have sought to unravel the very raced hierarchies that shape our schools, communities, social research, political movements, and our sexual lives. Although theorists and researchers includ-ing Nancy Hartsock, Dorothy Smith, Leslie Roman, Judith Rollins, Patricia Collins, bell hooks, and Toni Morrison have argued persuasively for research on privileged standpoints, few studies have taken up this challenge. White standpoints, privileged standpoints, are still generally taken as the benign norm or, in some cases, the oppressive standard—either way escaping serious scrutiny.

This volume, *Off White: Essays on Race, Power, and Society*, tries to fill this space. In it we place "whiteness" front and center of the analysis in order to subject it to the kind of scrutiny that rouses it off of unmarked space. As Ruth Frankenburg has recently argued, "to speak of whiteness . . . refers to a set of locations that are historically, socially, politically and culturally produced and, moreover, are intrinsically linked to unfolding relations of domination. Naming whiteness displaces it from the unmarked, unnamed status that is itself an effect of dominance. Among the effects on white people both of race privilege and of the dominance of whiteness are their seeming normativity, their structured invisibility." Using Frankenburg, Du Bois, Morrison, Roediger, and others as our intellectual base, we are, in this volume, focusing squarely on this prismic site of constructed dominance. The lively set of essays which follow are crafted in the languages of critical theory, postcolonialism, feminist thought, queer theory, and critical race theory. Our task is to provide colorful conversation about whiteness, prying it open and wedging it off of its unexamined center.

Our contributors were selected, primarily, from the two fields of psychology and education. Both fields have harvested vexing and debilitating internal contradictions within race studies. Each has a long history of scholarship on topics of race, racism, and ethnicity, and each has contributed to what Sandra Harding would call the "racial ordering of society."

Psychology, the home of I.Q. testing, special education, multicultural studies, cross-cultural psychology, intergroup relations, and stereotyping research, has spawned studies of personality, I.Q., motivation, achievement, and other measures of "merit" and competence that have camouflaged the ever-raced biases for ordering the world. So, too, education, the site for democratic inquiry, heterogeneity, and exposure to and celebration of "difference," has become a foundational space within which children of differing races, ethnicities, social class, language backgrounds, and genders "learn their place" in the broader culture. A great deal of research within the past twenty years has shown explicitly how schools, in spite of intentions to the contrary, serve to sort children along social class, race, and gender lines, contributing to massive inequalities in educational and, later, occupational outcomes. Indeed, the school has been shown to be a primary site for such sorting, in spite of the good will of large numbers of teachers, administrators, and associated professionals. The frameworks and research of psychology have been complicit in encouraging this ordering.

Through these two fields, whiteness has come to be more than itself; it embodies objectivity, normality, truth, knowledge, merit, motivation, achievement, and trustworthiness; it accumulates invisible supports that contribute unacknowledged to the already accumulated and bolstered capital of whiteness. *Rarely, however, is it acknowledged that whiteness demands and constitutes hierarchy, exclusion, and deprivation.* The production and maintenance of white privilege is not an easy task, therefore. The very academic frameworks and practices of education and psychology have worked hard to prop up racial hierarchies, securing the place of select groups within these hierarchies for many years now. A trenchant analysis of the "propping up" function of these fields is long overdue.

As profoundly as psychology and education are implicated in the production of whiteness, however, and its rigid emergence as norm, it is also the case that within both disciplines there is a bubbling and emergent set of scholars who have dared to analyze critically the categories that underlie the very structuring of racial categories and hierarchies. By interweaving race/ethnicity with gender, colonialism, nation, social class, and sexuality, and by analyzing the ways in which social institutions carry and voice multiple discourses of race, these researchers have begun to unravel the ways in which race operates through and with gender, social class, and sexuality. The authors in this volume, while not taking all these issues into account, are among those who seek to understand the ways in which race and racial hierarchies work with and through other forms of lived identity and institutional life to produce and sustain power inequities.

On Beginnings

As with all genesis stories, the idea for *Off White* must be credited widely. All four of us have been worrying and writing about whiteness, and its obvious absence in psychological and educational research, for a long time. Mun wrote and taught on the topic in 1992, Linda has been teaching about whiteness as power for years, and in the data that Lois and Michelle have been collecting in both Buffalo and Jersey City, from poor and working-class young adults of diverse racial/ethnic groups, the pains and privileges, the "deflation" and disappointments, of whiteness have been hyper-apparent. Even before angry white men made it to the covers of *Time* and *Newsweek*, we knew it was time to analyze that which had been both invisible and dominant.

While the analytic study of whiteness defines, for all of us, both our work and intimate lives, we have found ourselves with few intellectual resources upon which to rely. Early on Peggy McIntosh, Adrienne Rich, Marilyn Frye, bell hooks, George Lipsitz, and David Roediger offered us road maps. But few in education or psychology, theorists or researchers, were willing to enter this space. Indeed, both conservatives and liberals within psychology and education have so fetishized "people of color" as the "problem to be understood" that whiteness, in all its glistening privilege, has evaporated beyond study. One of the ironies of white power is the ability to escape social and intellectual surveillance.

And so this book is testimony to the urgency, richness, and necessity of studying whiteness as a system of power and privilege, as a group, an identity, a social movement, a defense, an invention. The essays in this collection speak through the kind of *heteroglossia* which might make even Bakhtin cringe. We intentionally invited folks who would disagree, who would stake out positions that contrast or are irrelevant to one another. We did so to declare this field as territory for bold, compelling, and provocative theory and research, not as intellectually foreclosed positions floating above the empirical world.

Organizing *Off White*

This book is organized into five parts. In the opening section, *Theorizing Whiteness*, we display a set of eye-opening, provocative essays which split open, that is, explode the notion of whiteness, both theoretically and empirically, as it is embodied and as it is institutionalized. We offer this set of essays early in the book to break any illusions of coherence for the volume, to force readers to reconcile our virtual ignorance about whiteness and the fertile ground upon which this invisible privilege has prospered. In this section, we hear from Linda Powell on the unconscious forces of whiteness in producing "Black underachievement"; Deborah Britzman, who opens a psychoanalytic cut into whiteness as identity, biography, and relationship; Jill

Morawski on the buried history of whiteness in psychological research, and Howard Winant on the contemporary proliferation of white social movements.

Part Two, *White Performances,* includes perhaps some of our most tortured essays. Tortured because the writers have "outed" their institutions, schools in many cases, in order to conduct a close and embedded analysis of how racism travels like a virus through institutional structures, policies, practices, relationships, fights, and identities. By so doing, these authors have rendered themselves and their colleagues vulnerable—to assault, to misinterpretation, to denial and to defensiveness. While each of these essays walks carefully and cautiously into taboo territory, each is particularly bold and compelling. For if we do not dare to analyze the very institutions in which we work and the ways in which we and colleagues are implicated in the reproduction of racism and the propping up of whiteness, then how can we move beyond theory at its most hollow? How can we move toward transformation?

We note, in this light, that each author chose to "analyze" his/her institution not because they believed their institution to be particularly noxious on the grounds of racism, but because they believed their institutional analyses to be unfortunately, if provocatively, typical of the institutional dynamics that most of us contend with, and ignore, in our own home sites. In each of these essays, academics have boldly decided to contest business as usual. Each unpacks and unravels the raced and colonial hierarchies that are embedded within institutions: a high school in the South (Michelle Fine); a progressive private school (Virginia Chalmers); a boarding school for Native Americans (Dennis Carlson); a predominantly white teacher education program in the Northeast (Rosenberg); a set of universities bent on hiring, and then marginalizing, women of color faculty (Cook), and an Alaskan institution of higher learning, working with Native students (Gilmore and associates). In this section, too, we have institutional travel stories, from William Tierney who moves "diversity struggles" through fiction; Michael Apple who journeys internationally in his analysis of production, reproduction, and consumption; and Bill Ayers who patterns autobiography on the social history of race relations and political movements in the second half of the 20th century. In each essay, these writers have broken a silence and they have paid a price. We worry about the complications of institutionalized "outing" and how profoundly "unprofessional" it is perceived to be. But we worry far more about institutional complicity and our own "professional" silences.

In part three we move into essays on *Living Whiteness,* analyzing how it is that whiteness is embodied, psychologized, refracted in our professional work, and embedded in colonizing practices of work and intimacy. Ann Phoenix forces us to listen to white adolescents who both deny and indulge their white skins and the associated privileges; Robert Carter enables readers to hear the many ways that white adults can "wear" their white identities and consciousness; Michael Billig playfully unravels the construction of the White Queen of England in working-class narratives; Sam Gaertner and associates expose the subtle workings of pro-white racism; Faye Crosby reveals the race, gender, and class stories of her familial and intellectual biography; through the narratives of white working-class men, Lois Weis, Amira Proweller and Craig Centrie provide us with some explanations of the white male backlash at this historical moment; and Louise Kidder painfully reminds us of the deep, nuanced, but not at all subtle discourse of everyday white colonialism, near impossible to interrupt, cementing the talk of white colonials in India. Through these essays we see and hear the ways in which whiteness defines social identities and cross-racial relations as profoundly as it is denied.

In part four, *White Screens,* we go to the movies, watch TV, read stories, and analyze the implications of whiteness in multiple media. Across the essays we hear the sharp scalpel of cultural analysis prying open mass media, documenting messages portrayed, messages subdued, messages received as they blanket audiences with representations of whiteness, color and what Corinne Squire calls "images of miscegenation." These pieces are authored by Pat Macpherson, who tracks the emergence of white girl sexuality peaking across the 50s and 60s, blossoming as "colored" sexuality remains in shadows; Cameron McCarthy and colleagues who analyze the production of the "discourse of resentment" emergent in and through contemporary films of urban violence; Leslie Roman, whose piece cautions white feminist writers about the appropriation, if not invention, of historic heroines of color, writing through a redemptive discourse; Corinne Squire, who documents the perverse representations of Whites and Blacks littering contemporary daytime talk shows; James Jones, who analyzes sharply the grossly divergent and raced understandings of the recent "O.J. verdict"; and Liz Ellsworth, who, through C. Carr's biography, analyzes the representations and pedagogical implications of the double binds of whiteness. These essays offer a complex rendering of representations and their internalizations, resistances, and structured silences. These essays ask "At Whose Expense?" some representations of race are fronted, while others are quietly "whited out."

In part five, *White Politics: Coalitions and Borderlands,* we end the volume with a set of essays of possibility that stretch toward transformative visions of multiracial/ethnic work. Deborah Neumair and Medria Williams write on the racial, gendered, and sexual dynamics between them in their rich and fertile collaboration. Two essays, one by Aida Hurtado and Abby Stewart and the other by Brinton Lykes and Amelia Mallona, open up the pleasures and dangers of doing collaborative research in which researchers and participants are deeply committed to excavating race, power, and subjectivities. A fourth chapter, coauthored by Beverly Tatum and Sandra Lawrence, asks a similar set of questions about collaborative educational practices and professional development among African American and white teachers. With a similar analysis, Nancie Zane probes some devastating and then hopeful insights about the institutional constructions and personal embodiments of whiteness held and narrated by a group of corporate-elite white men. Finally, Becky Thompson writes with and for a collection of white, antiracist activist women who commit in their professional, political, and personal lives to the undoing, that is, e-racing, of insidious structures of racism.

Across the five sections of the book, the essays draw upon and snatch from critical race theory, feminist thought, psychoanalytic writings, organizational theory, cultural studies, postcolonial critique, and queer theory, thus contributing to a wonderful (re)thinking within education and psychology. From these very distinct groundings, a shocking display of analyses has emerged, forcing readers and writers to contend with the many fragments of whiteness that saturate social consciousness, scaffold racial hierarchies, and season personal identities. Together these essays expose the perversions of racial formations that appear to be "natural," with whiteness sitting at the glistening top, and, too, they suggest possibilities for researching race/ethnicity and power, weaving community, scholarly work, intimate life, and social movements with democratic engagement and "difference."

WORRIES

As for our worries for the volume, yes, we have a few. We worry that in our desire to create spaces to speak, intellectually and empirically, about whiteness, we may have reified whiteness as a fixed category of experience and identity; that we have allowed it to be treated as a monolith, in the singular, as an "essential something." We despair that a terrifying academic flight toward something called white studies could eclipse the important work being done across the range of race, postcolonialism, ethnicity, and "people of color"; that research funds could shift categories; that understanding whiteness could surface as the new intellectual fetish, leaving questions of power, privilege, and race/ethnic political minorities behind as an intellectual "fad" of the past.

We worry, therefore, that there will follow a spate of books on whiteness when, in part, we (arrogantly? narcissistically? greedily? responsibly?) believe that maybe this should be the last book on whiteness, that we should get back to the work of understanding and dismantling the stratified construction of race/colors, rather than one group at a time. We worry that white writers will indulge in what Susan Stanford Friedman calls a narrative of guilt, accusation, or denial, and by so doing will dispense with the real work of organizing for racial justice and engaging in antiracism pedagogies.

And yet we are also delighted that undergraduates and graduate students now have a text from which to draw smart theory, vivid research, and powerful pedagogies, so they can struggle with whiteness as a pivotal feature of what Winant and Omi have called the racial formation. We are thrilled that we have been able to gather together such an array of writers, diverse by discipline, theoretical spin, political orientation, race, ethnicity, language, and sexuality, in one colorful site.

We thank Philip Rappaport, once an editor at Routledge, for inspiring us and Jayne Fargnoli for sustaining us.

Theorizing Whiteness

The Achievement (K)not:
Whiteness and "Black Underachievement"

ONE

Linda C. Powell

Linda C. Powell is an educator, psychotherapist and organizational consultant. She is President of Resources For Change, Inc., a Philadelphia-based research and consulting firm. She is currently Lecturer on Education at the Graduate School of Education, Harvard University.

INTRODUCTION

The extensive literature on black academic underachievement has a very specific focus. The research looks either at the stresses and conditions of individual Black students in a racist society (see for example Howard, 1985; Steele, 1993; Fordham, 1993, 1988) or at the ways in which schools could be more effective for these students (Comer, 1988; Edmonds, 1979, 1986). On rare occasions, the exploration of this phenomenon turns itself on its head to examine black excellence (Hilliard and Delpit, 1995). Occasionally, researchers will also investigate the organizational dynamics of schools that combine to "create" academic achievement (notably Fine, 1990; Lightfoot, 1990; Guinier, Fine, Bartow, et al., 1993; and Mack, 1995).

While efforts to understand and reverse the failure experience of minority students have been intense and sustained, the phenomenon of "black underachievement" is stubborn, pervasive, and extraordinarily complex. We know a great deal about what is effective for Black students, their schools, and families; yet it remains extremely difficult to mobilize the resources and will required to make a systemic difference in their lives.

What may be missing from this literature and from various interventions is a better understanding of the role that whiteness plays in the knot of minority student failure. This essay explores the hypothesis that "black underachievement" is not a simple knot tied within and among the Black community, but is actually composed of many strands of differently weighted rope, some of them black and some white. The white strands are woven into the black in a convoluted way that can passively prevent the knot from loosening. Thinking of the entire knot as a whole—using group-as-a-whole theory (Wells, 1985; Smith and Berg, 1987)—may provide an additional lens in the consideration of this phenomenon; if we can begin to identify a dynamic relationship between whiteness and the phenomenon that is then labeled "black underachievement" we might find additional levers for change in Black children's lives.

The centerpiece of this essay is a partial description of a class experience about whiteness from the perspective of the instructor; it is incomplete and intended to be heuristic and evocative. Any complete exploration would include the reflections of the students and the three teaching assistants and the group relations conference staff on a wide range of topics.[1] I frame the case with

4

two experiences, from almost thirty years ago, and from the present, which I carried into the classroom.

THE HISTORIC KNOT

In 1968, I was a high school senior planning to attend college. By virtue of SAT scores I was both a State Scholar (one of the top students in the state) and a National Achievement Semifinalist (a student of African American descent). I received recruitment letters from colleges around the country. One of the most prestigious universities in my state sent me two letters. The first was addressed to the State Scholar, and assured me that I was among the best and the brightest; they were delighted to consider offering me admission, and it would be their honor to train me for the leadership that I would (inevitably) provide for my community and my country. This letter falls squarely into what I will call the *discourse of potential*. The second letter was addressed to the National Achievement scholar; it focused on what a wonderful university it was, how fortunate I would be to have the chance to attend and how many remedial and supportive programs were in place to help me when I (inevitably) ran into difficulty at this world-class university. This letter was a perfect example of the *discourse of deficit*.

Many White people laugh nervously when I tell this story, and rush to mistakenly compare it with the cases of young White people offered admission to prestigious colleges if they are thought to be Black yet denied admission if they are White. Upon examination, these cases are not comparable at all. That selection decision raises a question about the equitable distribution of scarce resources. The *existence* of two letters raises questions about institutional racism and its expression.

There are at least three ways of understanding this episode. First, it was simply a computer error and without further meaning. This explanation often accompanies the laughter I get following this story. Just a glitch of little import. It isn't meaningful to these listeners that this university didn't recognize that one could be *both* African American and a top student in the state. Perhaps the organization unconsciously wanted me to see both letters (or didn't care enough to prevent it), so that I might understand my place and be assured that I was not leadership material.

Another hypothesis is that the incident is a coded discourse on competence. Perhaps the university could not simply send the first letter because it was deeply conflicted about educating a talented African American woman at the close of the 1960s. It was simply too painful for a "world class university" to admit that it might be incapable of preparing me for leadership.

The psychological mechanisms of splitting and projection may play important roles in this incident. Obviously every student has both potential and developmental needs. It is the task of education to recognize both in every student. Rather than admit that the social and political changes of the 1960s were making the task of education increasingly complex and that there was concern in the university about its ability to effectively educate all people, the worry about incompetence is projected into students of color, via the discourse of deficit. While this diminishes the potential of these students and privileges their deficits, it preserves the university's sense of value. The students become the only ones with possible incompetence. Likewise, White students are supported, empowered, and affirmed, via the discourse of potential (as though they had no deficits) and it just feels like "they earned it." Black students, their families, and their communities are burdened with the "rumor of inferiority" (Howard, 1986) in a subtle and stifling way. White students remain unfettered by the complexities of race and their whiteness, believing that meritocracy must be real because it has always rewarded *their* hard work. Black students are keenly aware of un-fairness, expected to keep silent and continue to perform if they seek the benefits that the White world offers.

Under normal circumstances, White students get the "white" letter and never know that the second letter exists, while Black students are absolutely clear that theirs is a race-coded letter. Black and White students meet at the same college in the same classes but with fundamentally different messages about their right and ability to be there. In this way, Black students carry a burden of awareness and clarity about race on behalf of all.[2]

The Knot—Live and in Living Whiteness

I offered a new course[3] at a graduate school of education to explore leadership and authority in urban schools. There was a special emphasis on the challenge of change in these institutions and on the issues of race, poverty, and power. The design of the course was drawn from the tradition of laboratory learning that provides insight and practice for leadership (see Heifetz, 1995; Schall, 1995). Unlike many courses that are highly structured with regard to classroom dynamics, this class was not organized to be "safe" in the popular sense or to help students (or faculty) feel comfortable. The course was designed with much of the ambiguity and dynamic of "real-life." In previous courses, I had discovered that students and I would enact in real time the content-related material; process often *was* content when race and power were under study. The task in this class was to attend closely to what actually happens in the here-and-now and make meaning from it.

The course was also an example of my change-oriented professional development efforts in urban public schools (Powell, Barry, and Davis, 1996; Powell and Barry, 1995; Powell, 1993). Professional development with adults involved in systemic change efforts must be designed with four key attributes. With *experiential learning,* experiences and values must be engaged by paying increasing attention to the "here and now." With *parallel process,* dynamics in class can give us valuable clues to the experiences of those working in urban schools. With *holding environment,* individuals and groups need psychological support to experience and work through the predictable conflicts that arise during this kind of learning; and with the *strategic use of theory,* the utility of research can be greatly enhanced by placing it squarely within the context of immediate experience and application.

The seventeen Black, White, and biracial students enrolled in the course created a microcosm of the academic community; all areas of the school were represented, as well as one other graduate school in the area. Most students were connected to schools during the course, although only one of them was a full-time teacher in an urban school. The teaching staff included two doctoral students and a recent alumna, all of whom had taken similar classes and worked with me previously. The Lead Teaching Fellow (African American male) took primary responsibility for the administrative and logistic issues of the course. The two other teaching staff (White French male and Japanese-American female) supported the task of interpreting our experience over time during the semester.

A central learning experience in this course was a two-day group relations conference (Rice, 1965; Rioch, 1975; Banet and Hayden, 1977; Powell, 1996). This experiential conference focused student attention on the exercise of leadership and followership and the difficulties encountered in the exercise of authority. Group relations conferences give an actual experience of splitting, projection, introjection. This is qualitatively and quantitatively different from reading about these mechanisms and can be extremely disorienting. This intense and unusual experience was later evaluated by most of the students in the class as an incredibly powerful—if unexpected—learning experience.[4]

The conference served as an intervention in the class' ability to express and explore conflict. Prior to the conference, the predictable conversation about race used students of color to express strong feelings about race while White students responded to them. While this response was often honest, tortured, and searching, it still veiled whiteness in the potential discourse while the Black students spoke from the pain of the deficit discourse. The racial identity of the White students (Carter and Helms) often seemed less developed as whiteness was solely defined as a reaction to color. It was always individual (no racial group identity) and ahistoric (in this moment in time.) The relative inability of White students to talk about their own racial identity was covered by their discovery of and interest in the issues raised by students of color.

During the group relations conference, some students were surprised to discover that they held ideas and values about race (and gender, age, and authority) that remained outside of their immediate awareness but were potent nonetheless. Students of all racial backgrounds discovered that they had feelings about their own race as well as about the race of others. This process of discovery seemed both enlivening and confusing.

Because of, or despite, the innovative teaching methods, I chose to base the course grade on two academic papers with explicit criteria for grading. I also required weekly memos. These communications were not required to take any particular form nor were they graded. Students were free to choose their style and content. Most took the memos as an opportunity to communicate a wide range of ideas, experiences, and reactions to the class. The memos informed me that every student wrote and thought clearly; no one seemed hesitant to say what they thought. I felt certain that, regardless of the material, they would all be able to demonstrate their learning and do well in the class.

This was not true. After grading the midterm papers on their conference experiences, I noticed that there was a wider range of grades than I had ever given, from A's to a C–. The lower graded papers were similar in that they were not carefully prepared; sentences were left unfinished, complex thoughts were not explained. Most had not been spell-checked. Very important ideas were presented in their most strongly felt and least digested form. I was compelled by the raw power of their ideas and by a respect for their experience, but I was working much too hard to understand these papers.

Many students reported great difficulty writing this paper. Perhaps there had been an unconscious expectation that anything taught by a Black woman would be easy. I certainly didn't appreciate the impact of the return of repressed material that normally stays unconscious on the traditional task of writing an academic paper. What I didn't realize was that this assignment may have exacerbated the traditional split between thinking and feeling. Students admitted later that they struggled with doing "good" academic writing, writing that is by definition bloodless, heady, and disconnected.[5] Conflict, passion, and values were cut in the ruthless search for some imagined objectivity. This writing assignment may have increased the traditional split of feeling and thinking, leaving Black students holding the feelings which had been devalued by the task (and thereby having their thinking impaired) and White students more free to do the thinking in the heady academic assignment.

While reviewing the papers, the Lead Teaching Fellow literally swore out loud and asked I had I noticed the grading pattern? The African American students had gotten the lowest grades. The Japanese-American woman on the teaching staff noticed what neither of us as African Americans could bear to see: the biracial and lightest skinned Black people had earned the highest grades within that group. A "pigmentocracy" had emerged among the students who were not white.

Stunned, I reread all the papers, looking carefully at the distribution of grades. Knowing from the memos that all my students wrote well, my immediate hypothesis was that this pattern revealed something flawed and shameful about me as a teacher and as an African American. I reread the papers, looking for unreliability or a pattern of bias. I compared the papers to previous memos, which were not formally evaluated. When I felt confident that the grade distribution was not "natural," I was left with an ethical dilemma.

I had offered this class with the explicit understanding that our experience was a source of learning about urban schools (parallel process). I had provided a theoretical perspective that group behavior could be understood as organic, with individual members taking on roles on behalf of the whole (group-as-a-whole theory). I had provided a capacity for interpretation of complex experience (holding environment). With this in place, we had reproduced the most relentless feature of urban schools yet the data was entirely "in" the teaching staff. Could we bring this up for discussion? *Should* we bring it up? Since grades might be considered private property, did we have the right to "out" students' grades without their permission, even in a group-oriented course? What would be the productive outcome of such a discussion?

Colleagues I consulted admitted that this racial grading pattern occurred in their classes as well, and that they had no strategy for dealing with it. They suggested various actions, all of which had to do with my relationships to the *Black* students. "Doing something" with and for them was the consistent theme: Why not meet with them individually and give constructive feedback with the opportunity to redo the paper? Or why not get them together as a subgroup so as not to "shame" them publicly, airing *our* dirty laundry.

This didn't feel right. How could I teach a theory about the group as a whole, without at least considering the involvement of *all* students in the creation of this outcome? What would happen if we included the White students in the analysis? I realized how few White students had been directly angry at me. Difficult experiences with the larger institution and with me as its representative had been publicly expressed by the students of color. The intense conversations about race had been led by students of color. Perhaps they had also been organized to protect and shield the fragility and incompetence of whiteness while fronting the confusion, passion, and hurt of Black students.

I consulted several students of color, seeking their reaction to the possibility of class discussion. None of them seemed especially surprised by the grade distribution and several were curious about the possibility of a class conversation. Heartened by the reaction of these students (whom we still mistakenly thought had the most at risk), the teaching staff decided to present the grade distribution as opening data for a conversation in class. We were far from certain that it was the right thing to do; it was too important not to discuss.

This conversation was not based on the scientific method of moving toward a single right answer. Instead, we employed the interpretive stance (Shapiro and Carr, 1991) to build an understanding of what had happened, "moving from uncertainty to uncertainty." As a group, the class worked together to generate "mutually exclusive and alternative explanations" (Wells, 1985) of the grading distribution; we also tried to understand what our experience might mean in urban schools and in the larger societal context. In retrospect, I believe our ability to have this conversation, to work through ambiguity, discomfort, and rage, was a powerful demonstration of what had been learned in the class.[6]

The simplest explanations looked at the individual: the individual Black students' backgrounds talents, skills, and motivations somehow interacted to create their low grades. Or the hard-working, well-organized White students worked hard for their deservedly high grades. Or, my own self-hatred emerged in the grading; as a sell-out of Black people, I was functioning in a gatekeeper role to assure that none of my Black students would succeed, thereby solidifying my position as "one of the few."

More complex hypotheses centered around subgroup behavior. Perhaps the Black students as a group were testing me: would I really hold them to the published grading standards? Would I risk affirming their competence by refusing to accept less than excellent work? I wondered if the Black students had withheld their best work to prevent me from feeling successful as a teacher. Their "underachievement" might be a way to act out rage—projecting their own feelings of incompetence and confusion so that I might know precisely what life in this organization feels like for them (Kahn, 1993).

The White students as a subgroup seemed less encumbered by conflicts about authority and were better able to use me in my role as professor. White students who were overwhelmed and unable to finish the paper asked for an extension. Several of them took an extra 24 hours and turned in A papers, receiving an A–. Black students also reported lack of time as a major difficulty in completing the paper; however, none of them considered asking for an extension, which as one Black woman said, 1) would put *me* in an awkward situation and 2) would feel like "asking for welfare."

These ideas were quite useful, but felt partial. One of the most explosive and painful moments in a generally intense discussion came as a White woman expressed her sense that she had "worked hard and deserved" her grade; she resented the implication that she was in any way involved with or responsible for the Black students' work. This same woman also spontaneously reported that she had been furious at me for several weeks. I had forgotten an appointment to meet with her; when she arrived at my office, I was involved in something else and asked might we reschedule? Although she reacted casually, she had actually gone to great inconvenience and expense to keep the appointment. She repressed this anger at me. Once she got fully in touch with it, she later reported developing a very unusual writer's block.

When this student was "unaware" of her anger at me, where had it "gone"? One hypothesis is that it is borne by those with a greater and more complex experience about race. These strong feelings are projected into students of color, who then hold and express them on behalf of all, leaving White students free for "raceless" work.

A single experience of unfairness or disrespect with a person of another race (and with greater authority) had an impact on this student; lacking the inoculation of a lifetime of the racial discourse of deficit, the experience with me was painful and her response to it may have affected her performance. If bearing the full complexity of race, including rage and the experience of disrespect and inequity, affects students' ability to perform, then it is not surprising that Black students "underachieve."

After further reflection on this moment, I developed a more complex hypothesis influenced by McCollum's (1991) theory of group development. Placing task, leadership, and environment in a dynamic interaction might yield the following: A Black leader/"colored" teaching staff in a White organization is likely to increase the already tremendous anxiety that is generated by the study of the "evaded curriculum" (AAUW, 1992) of race, power, authority. Any evaluation task that splits affect and cognition may differentially enable student performance, when students of color are holding more of this anxiety about race.

There is a covert and unacknowledged conversation about stigma occurring in the absence of a candid public conversation about whiteness. This may allow White people to use Black people as receptacles for their concerns about deficit, while holding on to their grip on the discourse of potential.[7]

THE KNOT TIGHTENS

Last fall, I found myself in an all-White community in the heartland evaluating a program in the local high school. This school had won state awards for excellence in academics and sports and had a dropout rate of less than 10 percent. No children were lost; even those few who failed to graduate could be traced: they were working at local stores and gas stations. The school was almost completely White, with fewer than 5 percent minority students and faculty of color.

This school also had every "at-risk" program known to humankind, including some extraordinary role shifts for a public school: food programs, clothes closets, and an ongoing support group for students in abusive relationships. When I asked school personnel how these unusual programs had come about, they said simply that the kids needed them to be successful in school. In a late-night phone call to an East Coast colleague, I was perplexed: why did they do all of this at-risk stuff when the dropout rate was so low? My friend pointed out that I had the equation reversed: there were so few dropouts because the supports were there for students to succeed.

The students in this school did not get labeled—were not required to enter the discourse of deficit—in order to receive this support. They did not have to present themselves for the projections of "needy" or "at risk"; they remained simply (White) students, formed and supported within the discourse of potential. Teachers acknowledged their inability to continue "business as usual," admitted their professional limitations; but where did their anxieties and concerns about change and competence go?

Why did this picture differ so strikingly from the urban scenes with which I was more familiar? How had this organization freed itself from the tremendous conflicts that urban teachers have when confronting similar dilemmas? How could these teachers simply see the students as valuable and respond to their needs? One clue came during a public meeting when a speaker mentioned the "really troubled" Black families who lived in the state capital; *they* had difficult problems. But here, the argument went, everything was basically fine; their community was not like *that*. The unnamed, unknown Black people 150 miles away were convenient vessels for anxiety about change or meeting students' needs. This projection freed this community to do more of whatever was necessary—no matter how innovative or expanded the role for public schools—for the success of their children. This was projection on a societal level. Urban schools get filled with these projections of deficit and take up the role of the "violent, hopeless" schools (as if this was all they are), freeing other organizations to be more responsive and creative (as if they have no similar problems). No wonder, then, that urban schools have tremendous difficulty making needed changes; they have become the symbolic containers for all of our difficulties. We "need" them to fail, for if not, all schools would be required to examine their own difficult experiences about race (including whiteness), change and achievement.

LOOSENING UP

Although extremely difficult, the class conversation about grades was worth the risk because something very important shifted. Their final papers were uniformly fabulous: creative, passionate, beautifully written. On a hopeful note, perhaps we reproduced this situation in order to understand and possibly change it; this would parallel the phenomenon in psychotherapy that clients often repeat a difficult or maladaptive experience in order to understand and perhaps master it.

Although I was nervous about evaluation, the final grades were all high primarily because the papers *as a group* were stronger. Several interracial pairs emerged to work together on projects, using the lenses from the class to explore real-world questions.

James Baldwin said not every problem faced can be solved, but no problem can be solved until it is faced. Our experience in this course suggests that we need to open a far deeper conversation about academic achievement, which acknowledges how whiteness uses blackness as a receptacle for fragility and conflict. The evasion of an authentic conversation about whiteness in specific and race in general may have a disproportionate impact on the performance of Black students. This evasion may lower our ability to tackle complex problems of equity and change.

This case highlights many serious dilemmas about teaching for social change. What is the place of controversial classroom work? I had taken every possible precaution regarding holding environment, theory, relationships, provision of a teaching staff/student ratio of 1/6, etc. If I couldn't responsibly open up this conversation, then it simply can't be had—and it must be had often if we are to improve the academic achievement of Black students. Some believe that doing work involving the unconscious in an academic environment is irresponsible. On the other hand, to continue to teach as though everything important lies in our awareness is also irresponsible. Finally, "casualty " is not simply a word used to identify someone psychologically hurt in group work; if children are suffering and dying at alarming rates in this country, maybe the benefits we would accrue toward change would be worth the risk of psychological discomfort in our classrooms. Kids are already taking the risks. Maybe educators could take more.

The ongoing conversation in this culture about race is sometimes notable in its silences or its perversions, but it is always in progress by virtue of each of our physical embodiment and identity development. Regardless of what we intend to teach or learn we each import our part of this conversation into our classrooms. That conversation must be directly engaged, as in the class we may miss the remarkable possibilities of stronger work, of deeper collaboration, of actually making change.

A new visual metaphor of black underachievement would be a knot with many strands in both black and white. There are tiny intermediate twists which have been in place for many years and are hard and tight. Some of the twists are brand new and have been tied over the old. The black strands and the white operate like a hoist, holding each other in place. Pulling at the black strands alone will not untie the knot, and may actually tighten it. The white strands must loosen as well. This loosening will inevitably involve pain and learning for Whites as they explore their privilege, incompetence, and profound interrelatedness with people of color; they will need to explore their own discourse of deficit. Blacks will also need to explore our dangerous ability to lead, creating and owning our discourse of potential. We must also face those areas of fear of and collusion with the larger social system that we both love and hate. Teachers have the privilege and responsibility of creating new conversations in our classrooms which go beyond a description of risk and capacity, to actually demonstrate and develop them.

REFERENCES

AAU Report: *How Schools Shortchange Girls*. (1992) Wellesley College Center for Research on Women, Washington, D.C.: American Association of University Women.

Banet, A., and Hayden, C. (1977). The Tavistock Primer. In J. E. Jones and J. W. Pfeiffer (eds.), *The 1977 Annual Handbook for Group Facilitators*. CA: University Associates, Inc.

Carter, R. T., and Helms, J. E. (1990). White Racial Identity Attitudes and Cultural Values. In J. E. Helms (ed.) *Black and White Racial Identity: Theory, Research and Practice*. Westport, CT: Greenwood Press.

Comer, James, School Power: A Model for Improving Black Student Achievement. In W. O. Smith and E. W. Chunn (eds.) Black Education: A Quest for Equity and Excellence.

Edmonds, R. (1986). Characteristics of Effective Schools. In Neisser, U. (ed.) The School Achievement of Minority Children: New Perspectives. 93–104. Hillsdale, NJ: Lawrence Erlbaum Associates.

Edmonds, R. (1979). Effective Schools for the Urban Poor. Educational Leadership (37). October, 15–24.

Fine, M. (1990). *Framing Dropouts: Notes on the Politics of an Urban High School.* Albany: State University of New York Press.

Fordham, S. (1988). Racelessness as a Factor in Black Students School Success: Pragmatic Strategy or Pyrrhic Victory. *Harvard Educational Review, 58(1)*, 54–84.

Fordham, S. (1993). Those Loud Black Girls: (Black) Women, Silence, and Gender "Passing" in the Academy. *Anthropology and Education Quarterly, 24(1)*, 3–32.

Guinier, L., Fine, M., Balin, J., Bartow, A., and Stachel, D. L. (1994). Becoming Gentlemen: Women's Experiences at One Ivy League Law School. *University of Pennsylvania Law Review*, 143 (1), 1–110.

Heifetz, R. A. (1994). *Leadership Without Easy Answers.* Cambridge, MA: Belknap Press of Harvard University.

Hilliard, A., and Delpit, L. (1995). Panel Presentation, "Black Excellence in Education." Annual Convention, American Educational Research Association.

Howard, J. (1985). *Rumors of Inferiority.* Atlantic Monthly Press, August.

Kahn, W. (1993). Facilitating and Undermining Organizational Change: A Case Study. *The Journal of Applied Behavioral Science, 29(1)*, 32–55.

Mack, C. (1995). "Leadership and Improving Student Performance in a Multi-Ethnic, Cultural, and Linguistic Public School District: There's going to be Bedlam if We Get 'Em." Unpublished manuscript.

Menzies, I. E. P. (1975). A Case-Study in the Functioning of Social Systems as a Defense against Anxiety. In A. D. Colman and W. Harold Bexton (eds.), *Group Relations Reader 1*. Washington, D.C.: A. K. Rice Institute.

McCollum, M. (1990). Reevaluating Group Development: A Critique of the Familiar Models. In J. Gillette and M. McCollom (eds.) *Groups in Context: A New Perspective on Group Dynamics*. Reading, MA: Addison-Wesley Publishing Co.

Powell, L. C. (1994). Interpreting Social Defenses: Family Groups in an Urban Setting. In M. Fine (ed.), *Chartering Urban School Reform: Reflections on Public High Schools in the Midst of Change*. New York: Teacher's College Press.

Powell, L. C. (1996). Authority, Leadership and Organizational Change. *A Group Relations Conference in the Tavistock Tradition*. Harvard University Graduate School of Education.

Powell, L., and Barry, M. (1995). Professional Development for Change: A Working Paper. Resources for Change, Philadelphia, PA.

Powell, L. C., Barry, M., and Davis, G. (in press). Facing Reality in Urban Public Schools: Using Racial Identity Theory in Family Group. *Racial Identity Theory: Applications for Individual, Group and Organizational Interventions*. Lawrence Erlbaum Associates.

Rice, A. K. (1965). *Learning for Leadership: Interpersonal and Intergroup Relations.* England: Tavistock Publications.

Rioch, M. (1975). All We Like Sheep. In A. D. Coleman and W. H. Bexton (eds.), *Group Relations Reader I*. Washington, D.C.: A. K. Rice Institute.

Schall, E. (1995). Learning to Love the Swamp: Reshaping Education for Public Service. *Journal of Policy Analysis and Management, 14(2)*, 202–220.

Shapiro, E. R., and Carr, A. W. (1991). *Lost in Familiar Places.* New Haven: Yale University Press.

Smith, K. and Berg, D. (1987). *Paradoxes of Group Life: Understanding Conflict, Paralysis, and Movement in Group Dynamics.* San Francisco, CA: Jossey Bass.

Steele, C. (1992). Race and the Schooling of Black Americans. *Atlantic 269(4)*, 68–73.

Wells, L. (1989). *"On the Praxis of Group-Taking: Consultants as Nautical Navigators."* Unpublished manuscript. Howard University, Washington, D.C.

Wells, L., (1985). A Group-as-a-Whole Perspective and Its Theoretical Roots. In A. D. Coleman and M. H. Geller (eds.), *Group Relations Reader 2*. Washington, D.C.: A. K. Rice Institute.

NOTES

1. I repressed this entire experience until Michelle Fine and Emily Style drew it out in conversation twenty years later. An understanding of power and a sense of support are important for the recovery of these memories. Without community or interpretation, we repress these experiences because there is no environment that is prepared to hear it.
2. Other key issues that emerged were poverty and spirituality. I have invited students and teaching staff to collaborate on an extended examination of the course and its impact on their change agent efforts in urban schools.
3. The development of this course was made possible by a faculty fund which supports teaching and curriculum innovation.
4. Colleagues from the Kennedy School of Government, Harvard University, and from the New York and Boston Centers of the AKRI volunteered their time to make this conference possible. More information on group relations conferences is available from the A. K. Rice Institute, P. O. Box 1776, Jupiter, FL, 33468-1776.
5. Students found Kahn's (1993) article tremendously helpful as a demonstration of the powerful use of personal experience in scholarly writing.
6. Beyond the earliest moments of this class, I cannot create a linear reconstruction of what followed. The discussion was tightrope walking without a net; I entered an altered state unlike teaching in any previously experienced sense and more like group relations consulting (Wells, 1989). I certainly assume that others present might recall the ninety minutes very differently. And as Shapiro and Carr have noted, we are all "right," offering different parts of a complex picture.
7. The two people in class who defined their racial identity outside the black-white dichotomy played important roles. The discussion seemed greatly helped by a woman who did not describe herself as either black or white, using her bicultural identity as a position to take leadership in this discussion. She uttered the unspeakable and contributed to a holding environment that enabled difficult positions to be expressed and faced. Another biracial woman felt victimized by what she identified as an exclusive black-white conversation, feeling silenced since her experience was not directly named. Group-as-a-whole theory suggests that Blacks and Whites may be working on behalf of an increasingly complex culture to sort out a fundamental question about achievement and merit. While they are not the "only" groups to have these concerns, Blacks and Whites may have been unconsciously nominated to hold this split on behalf of the larger culture. In that case, those groups would *both* need help to work as well as a reminder of our status as representatives, not sole stakeholders.

Many thanks to my students who encouraged me to write about the class experience; to the teaching staff who contributed: Leon Braswell, Francois Guillieux, and Betsy Hasegawa; and to the colleagues who commented on drafts at various stages: Anne Scheibner, Kito Peters, Debra Noumair, William Kahn, Gwendolyn Davis, Margaret Barry, Lola West, Donelda Cook, Scott Barg, and Laure Cassidy.

White Experimenters, White Blood, and Other White Conditions: Locating the Psychologist's Race

Jill G. Morawski

TWO

Jill G. Morawski is Professor of Psychology and Women's Studies at Wesleyan University. She works on the psychology of gender and is author of *Practicing Feminisms, Reconstructing Psychology: Notes on a Liminal Science* (University of Michigan, 1994). She also is engaged in studies of the history of psychology and has edited *The Rise of Experimentation in American Psychology* (Yale, 1988). She currently is involved in two projects: a study of the cultural politics of reproductive technologies and a history of laboratory practices in twentieth-century American psychology.

The contours of America's long-standing obsession with race have been mirrored in psychologists' studies of race. Scientific psychology has not simply reflected dominant cultural understandings of race but has reconfigured race through the discipline's evolving theoretical commitments. In an era of research fascinated by individual differences, for instance, race conveniently stood as a "natural" category for comparing differences, whereas in a research climate attuned to social problems, race comprised a crisis to be rectified. In the spirit of laboratory practices, psychologists literally experimented with race, alternately designating it a conceptual category, a variable, a genetic entity, a methodological problem, or a cognitive process.

Among these changing foci of scrutiny was the occasional consideration of the scientist's race. There exist writings, spanning nearly 75 years, which examine the race of scientists, be they acting as examiners, testers, interviewers, observers, or experimenters. Having encountered several instances where psychologists observed their own racial identities, I suspected that much could be learned from these cases but it soon became apparent that they were anomalies. Aside from approximately 100 studies devoted to the subject, few research reports published during the period even mention the investigator's race. Save a minuscule subset, then, experimental psychology reports, including over 90 percent of the research on race indicate no race of experimenter (Graham, 1992; McLoyd, 1991).

Logic and facts reined and reigned in on my initial project. Indeed, during the period there were but a few gestures of researchers' serious self-reflection on their race. Moreover, the predominant tendency in these studies was to deflect self-appraisal away from the experimenter and away from examining whiteness. Over time, the experimenter's race was routinely treated as a discrete variable or a factor of secondary interest. Routinization of this issue had become a tactical means to shift and manage scientific visions and identities, not to interrogate them. Toni Morrison has described the dismissal of race matters in American literature "as a kind of trembling hypochondria always curing itself with unnecessary surgery" (1992, p. 13). Most of the interrogations of the experimenter's race look like such unnecessary surgery, removing once and for all some ambiguous race from nearly abstracted and careless experiments.

The foremost finding of my historical analysis, then, is that the matter of the experimenters' race has been deferred to a politics of epistemology. The epistemic commitment to an abstracted, formless observer preponderated. Questions about the observer's identity have been overshadowed by this prevailing commitment. A second finding of the historical analysis is related to this quiet dismissal of the race of experimenter issue. In the process of taking up and ultimately rejecting consideration of the experimenter's race, these studies transferred scientific attention to the race of the subjects. The subjects' racial status, skin color, degree of "white blood," racial psychology, or attitudes eventually gained primary consideration. In the end, the vast majority of race of experimenter studies have been about the *other*, not the self of the investigator. Gazing outward and not inward, these studies have sustained a focus on the raced subject—the broad subject of race and/or the particular racialized subjects who participate in experimentation.

Until very recently, race research comprised a psychology of the "other" wherein nonwhite races were the targets of investigation. That research presumed, but did not interrogate, a normative psychology of whiteness. Instead, it demonstrated a keen regard for the nature of otherness, all the while largely neglecting the meanings and implications of whiteness. Studies on the race of experimenter, while sporadic in occurrence, nevertheless correspond to this dominant approach to race in North American psychology. Given this correspondence, the chapter proceeds from a survey of conventional conceptions of race to an examination of how and when the experimenter's race was acknowledged. Awareness of experimenter's race was not a random event, but tended to arise at junctures when the political implications of psychological research became particularly pronounced. For many psychologists, the objective observation of experimenter's race represented efforts to ensure that truly scientific data—objective and value-free facts—were brought to these political concerns. For a few psychologists, analyzing the experimenter's race was expressly intended as a means to examine the politics of science. Regardless of psychologists' specific motivations, the general outcome of these studies was the erasure of politics, either by ignoring, minimizing, or forgetting the experimental problem.

"RACE" IN AMERICAN PSYCHOLOGY

To claim that race has been one preoccupation of psychology in America over the last century comprises a fair statement, one readily supported by historical evidence. To claim that race is difficult to locate, even that it has been invisible, in experimental work in that time span also would stand as credible even as it seems to contradict the first claim. Race in psychology, if viewed from a historical vantage point, has a now-you-see-it-now-you-don't quality. The simultaneity of prominence and invisibility is neither illusion nor happenstance, but is the product of the variegated intellectual traditions and political inclinations which have influenced American experimental psychology. German psychophysics, developed in the mid-nineteenth century, aimed to discover universal laws of mental life. These laws would govern *all* minds regardless of people's cultural or individual particularities. By contrast, a concomitant engagement with individual difference research ensued from Darwinism thinking and its presupposition of evolutionary determinism, chance variation, and selection of particular mental attributes. From its inception Darwinism was applied to race, deeming it a natural variation readily accessible to assessment and comparison. American psychology was not shaped only by these two traditions: it also matured with an indigenous aspiration to be a useful science, to be practicable in the everyday world. Race has been one of those practical problems for psychology, emerging most frequently in response to policy issues of immigration, education, social welfare, and integration.

The confluence of these intellectual traditions has had two notable effects on the treatment of race in psychology. One peculiar effect has been the aforementioned feature of race as at once visible and invisible within psychology. The introspection movement of the early twentieth century, for instance, paid little attention to race matters in its search for universal qualities of the mind, whereas the concurrent work on intelligence testing quickly identified race as a possible determinant of group differences in mental ability. In the present, research on cognition and memory rarely features considerations of race, whereas studies of school achievement and addiction research routinely assess race differences. A second effect of psychology's plural traditions has been the mobility, even mutability, of the concept. At various times and in various investigative venues race has been taken to be a natural, kind, genetic entity, personal attribute, attitude, or an interpersonal perception. Some of these these variations in the meaning of race in research transpired sequentially (i.e., the change from early twentieth-century interests in race differences to studies of prejudice by the early 1940s), but they also have coexisted within a single time frame. Thus, current studies of the genetic bases of race coincide with investigations of the social bases of race and racism. The resultant conceptual confusions are substantial and are described in recent recommendations for clarifying the notion of race and distinguishing it from concepts of genetics, ethnicity, and culture (Betancourt and López, 1993; Helms, 1992; Yee, Fairchild, Weizmann, and Wyatt, 1993; Zuckerman, 1990).

The alterations and multiplicity of race concepts complicate the construction of any simple historical narrative of the psychology of race, yet some overarching patterns in research can be discerned. Evident over the last 75 years are three trends: a shift in emphasis from bodily and material phenomena to mental (cognitive) phenomena; a primary focus on African Americans as racial others; and an unremitting preoccupation with methodology (Gaines and Reed, 1995; Henriques, 1984; Samelson, 1978).

Intellectual commitments, then, guided psychological investigations of race. However, these commitments along with the general interest in race were configured through sociopolitical concerns. Interest in race waxed and waned with changes in the cultural climate. The fact that African Americans have been the predominant racial group studied (Jones, 1991), the minority which is most often the subject of political debate, intimates the motivations underguiding research. The personal and political attitudes of individual scientists further attest to linkages between race research and sociopolitics (Pastore, 1949; Samelson, 1978; Tucker, 1994). The fact that these sociopolitical matters were at odds with a chief edict of psychology's scientific epistemology—that the rational scientists put aside politics and identity matters, including their race—may be the source of an intriguing duality of vision. That is, many research programs harbor a dual model of persons: at least when the experimenter is white, the race of *experimenter* is held to be unrelated to his or her cognitions, whereas the race of the *subject* is held to possibly affect his or her cognitions.

Locating the Problem: Epistemology or Methodology?

Empiricism holds that the social status of the observers, given adequate training, is irrelevant to scientific practice. Epistemological traditions like empiricism, however, are historical and social products: Just as objectivity has had different meanings at different historical moments, so have conceptions of the objective scientist or scientific observer. Our modern understanding of objectivity, fashioned in the nineteenth century, is based on aspirations for censuring the personal (subjective) and eliminating the observer's presence as well as on the ideals of precision, sustained scrutiny, and sensory acuity. Objectivity thus defined guided the mundane tasks of scientific work, but it also constituted "a profoundly moralized vision, of self-command triumphing over the temptations and frailties of flesh and spirit" (Daston and Galison, 1992, p. 83).

Psychologists' considerations of experimenters' race need to be viewed in terms of the then-current conceptions of scientific observers—scientists' construals of scientists. However, while the observer's status and capabilities constitute epistemological concerns, in scientific practice they often have been translated into methodological problems. The race of the experimenter was treated as one such problem. Before considering its treatment as a methodological concern, the general beliefs about the experimenter's status as objective observer warrant review.

By the end of the nineteenth century, science was conceived not just as a means to acquire a certain kind of knowledge or as a profession but also as a moral enterprise (Hollinger, 1989). Karl Pearson, in his popular 1892 philosophy of science text, captured this conception in claiming that "Modern science, as training the mind to an exact and impartial analysis of the facts, is an education specially fitted to promote sound citizenship" (1892/1937, p. 9). Pearson claimed that while the "savage" deifies trees and water to account for natural events, the "civilized man" expresses "his emotional experience in works of art and his physical and mental experience in the formulae or so-called laws of science" (p. 36). Pearson's description aims to depict a universal attitude, but in actuality it casts the scientist as a distinct personality, one associated with a specific social class. In most depictions of the era, the scientist was educated, broad-minded, serious, and manly. The writings of the first generation of experimental psychologists mirror this image of the scientist. Edward Titchener described the necessity of "long-training" to overcome the "ignorance" that he observed in the untrained mind (1910, p. 350). E. W. Scripture encouraged the "education of men, instead of bookworms and mummies" (1894, p. 570). To G. S. Hall, research training "emancipates the mind from error and superstition" and, above all, "gets the mind into independent action, so that men can become authorities and not echoes" (1910, p. 350). George Trumbell Ladd wrote that "It is not arrogant to claim that the trained psychologist *understands* not only the child, the idiot, the madman, and the hypnotic subject, but also the artist, the scientist, the statesman, and the thinker, as psychological beings, far better than any of these classes understand each other, or even themselves" (1894, p. 21). Robert Woodworth observed in 1910 that "members of the inferior races" were suitable, indeed, "admirable subjects for the psychologist," providing that the psychologist understood that he should not try to secure "elaborate" responses from them (introspections being one such elaborate response). Instead, "If tests are put in such form as to appeal to the interests of the primitive man, he can be relied on for sustained attention" (p. 179). The desirable scientific observer shared cultural ideals of manliness and middle-class professionalism (Rotundo, 1993), along with certain qualities of the late-Victorian gentleman.

The experimenter's status, one privileged by gender and race as well as education, was just one of the myriad problems in race research which initiated methodological discussions. Whether it be the establishment of group norms, statistical methods to account for variance, control of dialect effects, representative sampling, or test-norming, race research generated methodological disputes. Some areas of race research have become virtually ongoing contestations over methodological issues. For instance, the now nearly century-long investigation of race differences in intelligence looks like an ongoing pattern of confrontations over a series of methodological problems, from attaining representative sampling to constructing culture-free tests. Likewise, the classic studies of doll preference, conducted by the Clarks and used in the *Brown vs. Board of Education* decision, initiated many alterations in procedure, evoking numerous questions about methodology (for example, Banks, 1976). Among the sciences and social sciences alike, the discipline of psychology has a long-standing reputation for its intense concern with methods, even a "method fetish" (Toulmin and Leary, 1985), but the fixation on methodological matters in race research exceeds even this reputation.

Two specific methodological concerns relating to the race of the experimental actors emerged during this century and have perplexed the design, as well as the interpretation of experiments. The first problem entails the subjects (now usually called participants) in research. In particular, the problem concerns the fact that subjects' racial status has been recorded and examined in relatively few studies beyond those expressly investigating race. Even when this status has been reported, it has been done in an inconsistent manner. The simplest solution to this problem has been to include subjects of more than one race (white) and to report these data routinely. Assessments of the presence of African-American participants in psychology journal articles over the last three decades concur that the percentage is somewhere between 3.6 and 5 percent (Graham, 1992; Jones, 1983; McLoyd and Randolph, 1986). Related to this representation problem is the larger concern about whether inclusion is done in order to conduct race-comparative or race-homogeneous studies. Graham's (1992) analysis of selected APA journal articles which were published between 1970 and 1989 found approximately three times as many articles devoted to race comparisons as to race homogeneous investigations. In these considerations of the race of subjects, what might be held as simple matters of inclusiveness or even simply representative sampling can be seen upon closer inspection to be guided by metatheoretical commitments. Such methodological issues are tied, on the one hand, to beliefs about whether race is related to psychological experiences and processes, and on the other hand, to questions about whether race itself or the differences among races warrant attention.

A second methodological concern that has figured in the race research enterprise is the race of the investigator. On first appearance this problem might resemble that of the race of subject: it might well be conceived as a problem requiring greater attention to representativeness, inclusiveness, and comparisons of investigators. But, both the historical and epistemological conditions of the researcher problem do not parallel those of subjects. Neither do the solutions. The history of race in America has been such that while there has been no shortage of subjects of differing races, researchers have been overwhelmingly, at times exclusively white (Guthrie, 1976; Wispe et al., 1969). The practical consequences of this labor problem, however, mostly have gone unappreciated, perhaps because they have been overshadowed by a troublesome epistemological dilemma. In the empiricist tradition to which modern psychology has cleaved itself (a tradition which is kept alive in the sciences), the social status of the observer is held to be irrelevant: with appropriate training in the scientific method, any person can observe the world, and observe it in the same way. Objectivity requires removal of the subjective or personal and can be practiced by any appropriately trained observers, regardless of their particular social status. Suggesting that different sorts of persons, i.e., persons of different genders, ages, nationalities, or races, observe differently violates the epistemological premises of empiricism (Harding, 1986) and the attendant goal of objectivity. Acknowledging the observer's racial status also increases the pressure to address other identity differentials, thus potentially producing an unending list of qualifiers, such as ethnicity, age, economic status, attractiveness, gender, etc. Such admissions thus complicate the research process just as they necessarily implicate a subjectivity of the researcher that has been long denied in psychology.

These two lingering methodological issues, the race of subjects and the race of investigators, then, have not methodology at their roots but history, metatheory, and epistemology. Nevertheless, these problems routinely have been rendered as mere (albeit often debated) technical difficulties. Conceptualized as methodological matters, these problems obscure the more substantial "methodological horrors" (Woolgar, 1988) of the scientific practice they represent. Woolgar's term, methodological horrors, refers to the realization that we, as observers, have no final assurance that our representations of objects in the world accurately reflect those objects in the world. One such real horror is reflexivity, that back-and-forth process whereby our representation depends on pre-existing knowledge of what that representation refers to and vice versa. In the human sciences reflexivity is even more complex because the objects of inquiry are humans or human activities; representations thus refer back to the observer as well as to others who are being observed. Reflexivity, in the end, is a self-referential activity (Morawski, 1994). Yet, scientific practices are structured to hide methodological horrors such as reflexivity. Strategies for doing so include construing the horrors as a mere technical difficulties or presenting the problem as a problem for others, for instance as a problem of the subjects but not the researcher (Woolgar, 1988). As a consequence of the latter strategy, the psychologist and the ordinary person are taken to be different, again perpetuating a dual model of persons. One introductory textbook candidly depicted this duality in racial terms by drawing an analogy between Robinson Crusoe's relationship with his man Friday and the psychologist's relationship with his "other-one" (Meyer, 1921).

Psychological studies of the race of experimenter constitute an example of research strategies created to mask the problems associated with reflexivity. Researchers' self-awareness of their own racial membership, or their self-construals of race more generally, could open the way for intentional (and productive) reflexive analysis, but the studies on experimenter's race reveal, at most, minimal self-awareness. These studies have deflected self-appraisal by making a transference: the problem of the experimenter's race is and has been conceptualized as a problem of the participants. Transferred to the participants, that problem is then construed either as a technicality (experimental artifact) to be controlled if not eliminated and/or an enduring psychological attribute of the participants. Of course, given changes in psychological theorizing about race and in psychology's investigative procedures, interpretations of the race of experimenter problem have varied across the century. Despite these variations, the deflection of self-appraisal has persisted, and the problem of the experimenter's race has been perceived as technical and/or as residing with the subjects.

These omissions, obscurations, and transferences of the researcher's race have notable implications for theory as well as for empirical findings. Most obvious of these consequences is the subterranian existence of our understandings of whiteness and an accompanying fixation on racial "others" and their "differences." Whiteness is buried. Likewise sacrificed are the generative possibilities for reflexive practices on the part of researchers. We have, for instance, not developed ways through which *I*, as an interrogator of the racial identities of earlier psychologists, can begin to assess the meaning of my own whiteness for these interrogations (or *vice versa*).

EXPERIMENTAL DRAMAS: EARLIER STUDIES

Twentieth-century psychology proceeded with an epistemic commitment that served to deflect attention from the social identities of observers. Yet it also thrived on an attitude of empirical curiosity in which the game permitted, even encouraged, the manipulation and control of variables to ascertain previously unknown outcomes. As a discipline replete with theoretical debate, empirical studies were the chief means to resolve such conflicts as well as to explore hunches (later formalized as hypotheses). The possibility that the race of the investigator influenced research results was one such hunch. To date, my research assistant Jessica Smock and I have located 86 empirical studies that address this hunch. The exact number of such studies is difficult to ascertain as it is undoubtedly the case that there is other research in which the race of experimenter was an auxilliary interest; such studies would go undetected since we used subject indices, titles, and citations to locate our cases. Our analysis of the 86 studies indicates a long history of awareness *and* evasion.

The first report on race of experimenter did not appear until 1916. Although the account was published in a major journal, the author chose anonymity. However, timeliness and authorship become moot points in light of the comprehensiveness and prescience of this brief report that carried the understated title "Some suggestions relative to study of the Mental Attitude of the Negro." The article opens with a quote from Nietzsche on the erroneous tendency of persons to treat the unknown as "strange" and as warranting study. According to Nietzsche, the reality of the matter of strangeness is actually the reverse because "The known is the accustomed, and the accustomed is the most difficult of all to understand, that is to say, to perceive as a problem, to perceive as strange, distant, outside of us" (quoted in anon., 1916, p. 201). With Nietzsche's reflexive reversal of the relations of self and other, known and unknown, the author undertook a sweeping appraisal of race psychology that moves from an inquiry into the definition of race to a psychological analysis of experimenters—white and negro experimenters alike. The typical question of "who is the negro" is usually answered by some likely social-scientific responses, ranging from "anyone who is not a Caucasian" to the estimation of relative degrees of white and negro blood. On the problem of explaining race differences in intelligence, the author noted the impossibility of any adequate experimental controls to test the nature-nurture alternatives. Such a definitive experiment would require control of all environmental conditions, and if for no other reason, it would be impossible because "where are we to find a negro and a white child who have had even approximately the same environment, one a member of the ruling race, the other kept in subjection?" (p. 201).

The crucial dilemma posed in the article entails yet another problem: the scientist. To the author, "the most serious objection to the present methods of investigation is based on the fact that white people conduct the investigation; especially is there danger if the investigator is a stranger" (anon., 1916, pp. 201–202). The mere presence of the white investigator, even a "friendly" one, is shown to elicit certain attitudes from negro subjects. These attitudes include the negro's determination "not to let a white person know anything about him" (p. 202), as well as the way that the negro subject is "proficient in interpreting the moods of the overlord and in devising ways and means to placate him" (p. 202). The investigator too brings other relational dynamics to the research setting. The general tendency of people, including scientists, to want to confirm their suspected beliefs is augmented in this case by an "unconscious mental bias"—toward a belief that negroes are of inferior intelligence. The author concluded that it is impossible for members of the "white race" to conduct fair studies.

This short essay foreshadows the variety of explanations that would be given to the race of experimenter issue over the remainder of the century. The author named what some other investigators would later describe: the potential psychological reactions of the negro subject (although not the white subject) and the limitations of both black and white investigators. With impressive prescience, the author also attempted to move beyond these problems of racialized roles to imagine a solution in the form of a collaborative objectivity wherein scientists of different racial memberships "each could supply what the other lacked." Albeit through the notion of "each," the author broached an account of whiteness.

Within the decade following this essay, several relevant articles were published. Each article engaged one of two types of treatments of the experimenter's race. The first type of treatment can be referred to as "rhetorical disregard," for it entailed recognition and then dismissal of concerns about the experimenter. Sometimes rhetorical dismissal entailed a direct claim that the matter of the experimenter's race is a concrete methodological problem. In one of the earliest studies to discuss how subjects of different races may react differently to test situations, that is, to acknowledge the "white" context of testing, authors Pressey and Teter (1919) noted that "the tests were given by white examiners, to colored children in a school showing no adaptation to the particular needs of this race, and in communities where there is sufficient race consciousness for the colored people to be a distinct class by themselves" (p. 278). Through the application of logic, however, the problem was dismissed because "certain of the differences found seem to be too marked to be explainable as the result of such factors alone" (p. 278). Seemingly satisfied with noting implications of the scientist's race, none of these experimenters put their observations of observers to an empirical test.

A second type of treatment of the race of experimenter problem entailed empirical, rather than simply rhetorical, work. In 1927, Horace Bond reported a study of negro children's intelligence that was conducted by a negro investigator. The results diverged significantly from most race comparison studies of intelligence: Not only did negro children display a wide distribution of I.Q. scores, but a fair number tested in the "exceptional" range. Bond's data were challenging, but his framing of the study and its results were even more so. His study ensued not simply from a methodological worry but from a unique appraisal of the entire program of race psychology research. That program was portrayed as a rule-bound "game":

> First one must have a *white* examiner; a group of *Negro* children; a test standardized for *white* children tested by *white* examiners; and just a few pre-conceived notions regarding the nature of "intelligence," the degree with which Negro children are endowed, if at all, with this faculty and the *fact* that the social status of Negro children need not be considered as an extra allowance for scores different from whites. (p. 257)

The game includes special logic rules, especially the axiom that high-scoring white children come from high social status families because the family was highly intelligent (and, therefore, intelligence is inherited). Another rule is one that states that examiners must carefully establish "rapport" with white subjects "[b]ut for some reason, perhaps the docility of the Negro subjects, or the innate superiority of the race to which the examiner belongs, this caution is not to be regarded in Negro children" (p. 257). Bond sarcastically confessed that he broke a rule in surmising that "as white investigators are able to gain fullest *rapport* with white children, the same thing might be true of Negro testers with Negro children" (p. 258). In the end, Bond's insider/outsider status as a trained psychologist and a negro enabled him to construct a radically different and multiple framing of the experimental situation.

Exercises of critique such as Bond's and the aforementioned 1916 critique may have been only that—exercises. They appeared in a period of expansion and professional legitimation during which psychologists were struggling to certify their scientific status and to find markets for their products (Camfield, 1970; O'Donnell, 1985; Sokal, 1987). White psychologists' understandings of themselves as scientists were infused with ideals of middle-class professionalism, including implicit assumptions about race. In this atmosphere of professional progress, the 1916 anonymous review might well have gone unheeded. Readers who held the dominant image of the magnanimous, objective scientist would logically reject the appeal to reflect on their conceptions of "others." After all, given objective training which would allow one to see the world clearly and at a distance, such reflection would be unnecessary. Bond's critique and nonconforming data most likely received quite different responses. For one thing, it appeared not in a mainstream psychology journal but in *The Crisis*, a negro intellectual journal created and edited by W. E. B. Du Bois (Guthrie, 1976). The actual responses of white investigators are unknown, for it appears that only black researchers replied to it in print. What would it mean to a white psychologist, familiar with the plentiful findings about the inferiority of negro intelligence, to hear about discordant data—and to hear it from a negro psychologist? Just as Bond's study reported anomalous results about negro intelligence, so did his racial identity make him conspicuous in a crowd of psychologists whose scientific identity covered their race.

METHODOLOGICAL AND SOCIAL SOPHISTICATION: THE 1930S AND 40S

During the first four decades of this century, psychology rapidly accrued intricate methodological norms and eventually moved toward exploring social-psychological, as well as psychological dimensions, of thought and action. Among the methodological advances made by the late 1930s was procedural attention to the psycho-social dynamics of the experimental situation. The use of confederates, Rosenzweig's identification of "experimental artifacts," and various forms of experimenter bias were among the discovered dynamics (Suls and Rosnow, 1988). The first experiment (using systematic manipulation of variables) to test the notion that the race of investigator influenced the experimental outcome appeared in 1936. Inspired by the anonymous 1916 article and by Bond's analysis, Herman Canady (1936) conducted a study in which a race comparison of children's intelligence was coupled with a race comparison of the experimenter's influence on the testing results. By this time, making the problem of the experimenter's race a variable was a logical procedural step mandated by empirical research. Adhering to these mandates, Canady reasoned that the influence "can be determined only by recourse to facts, and until the present time the problem has been discussed wholly as a matter of opinion" (pp. 210–211). The opinions previously voiced in the literature had been about the (white) experimenter's influence on negro children, but Canady included white subjects in his sample because he logically inferred that if white examiners could not establish adequate rapport with negro subjects, then it also might be true that a negro examiner could not gain the full cooperation of white children. One negro and twenty white examiners were used, and each child was tested by a negro and a white examiner (the sequence was varied). The subjects were unaware that the experiment was about "rapport" (p. 211). The study was qualified with the caveat that the subjects were from (relatively) integrated Evanston, Illinois, and not the South with its "race friction" (p. 218) and its separation between the two races "as though they lived on different continents" (p. 211). The results, too, were qualified. With a negro examiner the negro children's I.Q. increased an average of six points and the white children's I.Q. decreased by approximately the same amount of points; the change was reported as "haphazard rather than progressive upward and downward" (p. 219). The results were not quite unequivocal: Canady found that there were effects, but they did not neatly confirm the unexplicated hypothesis of "rapport."

Rapport became perceived as a problem of race research: although the word was rarely defined, it soon became an unproblematic concept, a buzz word, in the psychological literature. The term was used without elaboration in several early discussions of I.Q. testing situations, was described at some length in Klineberg's 1935 *Race Differences*, and thereafter acquired the status of a known phenomenon. It generally was taken for granted that rapport was a problem when the subject was not white, a belief following from a tacit assumption that experimenters were white. The rare instances when writers imagined otherwise, that the experimenter was not white, had a sensational impact. For example, in his social psychology text Britt fortifies the concept by asking the assumed (white) reader, "Would it make any difference in your performance if an intelligence test were administered to you, a white person, by a very dark Negro?" (Britt, 1941, p. 433).

The rising concerns with rapport indicate several changes in investigative practices which took place by the late 1930s. In keeping with the general transition from the study of race differences to race prejudice (Samelson, 1978), the race of experimenter issue too became a social-psychological phenomenon. Likewise, consistent with the growing efforts to cover concrete problems that threatened the validity of human experimentation (primarily by making them technical problems) the experimenter's race came to be considered a methodological matter. Two significant reconfigurations accompanied this transition to the social and technical domains. First, emphasis on the experimenters themselves was transferred from the experimenter as an individual to the social interaction; only a few psychologists continued to note the problem of the possible assumptions of racial superiority on the part of white scientists (i.e., Gilliland and Clark, 1939, p. 184). Second, as rapport came to be a code word for the complex racial dynamics of the experimental situation, it was transfigured into a variable, a technical detail that was related as much or more to the subjects as to the experimenters. Both reconfigurations transposed the experimenter's attributes or actions onto those of the subjects.

These reconfigurations occurred amid an atmosphere of reformism: many psychologists shared the optimistic cultural belief that social injustices to minority groups and the underprivileged should and can be removed. There was considerable faith that such amelioration could be effected largely through education of minorities and the majority alike. It was at this moment of its identification as a specific experimental concern that the race of experimenter was reduced to a variable of minor methodological concern. Transfigured into a social-psychological phenomenon, the concern then was transferred to the minds of the subjects, who, after all, were the targets of eventual remediation in order to improve race relations in America.

The Social as Complex: Post World War II

The interest in race prejudice, along with studies of the experimenter's race, continued on a steady course until the early 1960s. The research produced during this period yielded further refinements both in the social psychology of race perceptions and in the technicalities of experimental procedures (methods). Above all, what had been tacitly conveyed through the term rapport was fashioned into intricate accounts of the dynamics of racial interaction. In so refining models of racial interaction, whatever problems had been associated with the race of experimenters were largely transferred to the subjects. Placing the weight not only of the experimenter's race but of the subjects' race as well in the subjects' heads yielded a new and remarkably coherent victim psychology. Although it would be another decade before the structure and implications of victim psychology were identified (Ryan, 1971), much of the postwar research converged to conceptualize minorities in general, and black subjects in particular, as the cause of their own problems. In victim psychology the victim's stigma or problem is seen as environmentally determined, but "the stigma, the defect, the fatal difference—though derived in the past from environmental forces— is still located *within* the victim, inside his skin" (p. 7).

As rapport and related racial interactions were addressed, the social situation was more precisely located in the subjects. Even while rapport was systematically examined, the homogeneity of researchers (in their class, age, sex, and race) was seen as advantageous; to one methodologist, the exception was the problem of "the reluctance of Negroes to express their opinions freely to whites" (Hyman, 1954, p. 159). Anxieties accompanying the very subject of race were rapidly becoming a problem residing with the subjects. Thus, the reported "fears" that the study of racial attitudes cause anxiety or socially desirable responses (MacKenzie, 1948; Reynolds, 1949) were submitted to empirical scrutiny. Between 1945 and 1965 at least 16 studies explored the race of experimenter effect, most of them producing significant results. And the effect was no longer a problem for intelligence research alone but also was found in numerous subject areas, including TAT, frustration-aggression, GSR, and verbal tasks; it became a concern of polling researchers, interviewers, and psychotherapists as well as of experimenters and test examiners (Bernstein, 1965; Heine, 1950; Katz, Robinson, Epps, and Waly, 1964; Rankin and Campbell, 1955; Riess, Schwartz, and Cottingham 1950; Trent, 1954; Williams, 1964; Williams and Cantril, 1945; Winslow and Brainerd, 1950). During this period the problem also earned a place in review articles (Dreger and Miller, 1960; Katz, 1964; Masling, 1960; Shuey, 1958).

The studies include both majority and minority psychologies to explain the persistence of prejudice and discrimination, often suggesting that members of both races had to change in order to reduce race conflict. However, the growing fascination with the minority personality tipped the balance of attention, which had already been slanted by the methodological focus on subjects and not experimenters. Herman aptly described the overarching theme of the postwar period: "If white attitudes were in need of change, black personalities were the proof that change was both mandatory and long overdue" (1995, p. 183). Posited in an era when psychoanalysis occasionally was comingled with social psychology, the depiction of the negro subject as ego-defended and anxious was an amenable one. Most of the empirical studies concurred in surmising that negro subjects not only had less rapport with white experimenters than with negro experimenters, but negro subjects also tended to be fearful, defensive, withholding, and ingratiating such mixed-race experimenters (Williams and Cantril, 1945). Textbooks of the period elaborated on this interpretation, weaving it into the new theories of prejudice. By "growing up in the shadow of race," as two textbook authors described the origins of prejudice, negro youth develop defense mechanisms to protect themselves from the discrimination they must endure (Sargent and Williamson, 1958, p. 654). In presenting this new minority psychology, Sargent and Williamson simply designated the race of experimenter as a *variable*, a "complicating" one (p. 656). By confining a victim psychology with methodological language focused on experimental situations and subjects, whiteness and white experimenters faded from the analysis.

From 1945 to the 1960s, researchers from a variety of specialties seemed to concur on the problem of race in psychology studies, yet this emerging consensus that the problem resided with the subjects (and to some extent with black researchers) was not shared universally. A few investigators differed in their assessments, pointing to the possible effects of personality which could trigger experimenter bias or to the conditions of social reality. In a study of the Negro Version of the TAT, Schwartz, Reiss, and Cottingham (1951) considered both of these factors. Based on their study using negro and white subjects, negro and white test administrators, and negro and white TAT cards, they emphatically concluded that "We do not believe that skin color replaces the more important factors of social reality in determining, facilitating, or impeding the reactions of Negroes and whites to Negro and white cards and to Negro and white examiners" (p. 400). In an era in which investigators were intrigued by cognitive or intrapsychic processes and victim psychology, the idea of a social and material reality was not to flourish.

CIVIL RIGHTS IN THE LAB: THE 1960S AND BEYOND

The question of the race of experimenter continued and, by the mid-1960s, became one of a host of race issues receiving attention from psychologists. The civil rights movement, underway in the 1950s, soon influenced psychological research in multiple ways: most importantly, it offered an opportunity for psychologists to utilize their expertise in policy-making. Research on black psychology and race conflicts scrutinized the family, masculinity, and urban life to uncover what eventually became known through the 1965 Moynihan report as a "tangle of pathology." Psychological experts were persuasive in their demonstrations of the psychological bases of social problems, convincing policy-makers, citizens, and activists alike that the psychological realm needed adjustment.

Sensitivity to race matters, and to their psychological dynamics in particular, also was manifested in the escalated concern with the race of experimenter. Between 1966 and 1975, 46 studies on the subject were published; in the following decade, 1976–1985, 26 studies appeared. Despite this increased regard, the matter of the experimenter's race was neither resolved nor illuminated. Approximately 20 percent of the studies report no significant effects of the race of investigator. Several of these studies submit that purported race effects are really due to some other characteristics of the examiner, notably social class, personality, or personal bias (Williams, Best, and Boswell, 1975; Womack and Wagner, 1967). Others suggest that characteristics of subjects (other than race), or a combination of such charateristics of subjects and those of experimenters, are more influential in the experimental setting (Samuel, 1977; Sattler and Theye, 1967). Something is amiss in the experiment, these studies deduced, but it is not race.

During the 25-year period 1965–1990, a significant majority of the studies reported a race of experimenter effect. These studies yield no simple assessment of the race of experimenter effect because they vary substantially in methodology: they differ in races examined, subject and experimenter variables, and dependent measures. What is probably more important is that, although the studies rely on diverse explanation of race effects, they nevertheless tend to converge in emphasizing the subjects' psychological processes or reactions to the experimenter (and not the experimenter's actions or reactions). Against and above a methodological cacophany, then, one apparent message is clear: the subjects and not the experimenters are the source of interest. If the race of experimenter is an effect, it is not being examined in the experimenter but in the subject.

During this period psychological depictions of the nonwhite (still typically African-American) subject were modified. Earlier portrayals of the resistant—withholding yet ingratiating—negro subject were altered to accommodate political and cultural awareness of black identity. The black subject was coming to be recognized as having a unique heritage and as living in a duplicitous world. Negro students and patients were no longer only seen as deprived and excluded but also as "oppressed" (Smith, 1967). Hence, the black subject of psychological analysis was ascribed with an apparent degree of agency and a positive identity. Pettigrew, who in 1964 had written extensively about the negro "role," including his or her role in research, with its defenses of withholding, stupidity, and slowness, reconsidered this role in light of subsequent events. In 1970 he stated that "the Negro's own protests and assertion of civil rights, his increasing educational and economic opportunities, the findings of social science, and the emergence of proud new African nations all have salved the old wounds" (Pettigrew, 1970, p. 151). The emergence of a visible black intelligentsia, a group deeply concerned about race, fostered historical and cultural exploration of black identity (Goodman, 1976; Guthrie, 1976; Jones, 1972).

With these changes in the model black subject, the experimenter's race faded even more. Empirical studies emphasized the cognitive and affective processes of subjects, deflecting analysis from the experimenter. The technical detailing of experimental artifacts, indeed, the very relegation of race to the category "artifact," further diminished the experimenter's self-awareness, and deflected attention away from the investigator in general. Rendering race an experimental "condition" made it all seem ephemeral or at least mobile, hence movable and removable. Continued focus on the minority psyche, even through a proactive identity politics, served to detract critical regard away from the investigator. So successful were these transferences of gaze that only occasionally did more conservative researchers need to argue that the race of experimenter did not matter (Jensen, 1980, pp. 596–603).

CONCLUSION

The experimental method, adopted from neighboring sciences, provided psychology with a protocol for work as well as for professional legitimation. Psychologists took that method to be a genuinely liberating practice. The experiment permitted the researcher to control the messiness of human life in order to locate its underlying causal mechanisms. It also provided a place where researchers could perfect *acts of self-control*—where they could conduct observations cleansed of personality, biases, and expectations. As such, the human psychology experiment constituted a new form of social relations in which authority and abilities were differentially named and distributed. Many of the risks of experimentation which such social relations consequently imposed upon subjects have been identified and addressed in an elaborate code of ethics. Regarding the investigators, these experimental social relations and their consequences have received less attention.

There are now plentiful studies, however, demonstrating that what psychologists have taken to be an interesting experimental phenomena, and how they perceived those phenomena, have been shaped by their culture. The experimenter's race has been one such experimental phenomenon that has changed dramatically in response to the political and social climate. In the early years of the century, the need for psychologists to establish a market for their skills encouraged them to investigate salient social concerns such as the race aspects of schooling, reform, and immigration. During the interwar years, changes in the population of psychologists (namely, the increase in émigrés from Europe), along with the liberalized politics of the depression, fostered new interests in improving human relations. After World War II, psychologists were able to expand their place in policy-making, persuasively demonstrating that race, along with other social matters, was a psychological problem. Throughout these involvements, psychologists' conceptions of race were transfigured through changing sentiments and politics.

The presence (or absence) of African-American psychologists also has been influential in the history of seeing (or not seeing) the experimenter's race. While psychologists of diverse races addressed the matter of the effect of the experimenter's race, African-American psychologists (despite their near invisibility in the profession) were the first to produce a comprehensive critical analysis (Bond, 1927) and a systematic experiment designed to assess the effect (Canady, 1936). More recent theoretical work has led some social scientists, particularly feminist and minority investigators, to a new quandary related to the experimenter's race. These researchers self-critically acknowledge the identity of the experimenter. Thus, reluctant to abandon the scientific epistemology that denies the observer as a particular, historically situated person, they are equally resistant to dismissing their own personal and political attributes.

The race of the investigator, in the end, simultaneously reveals and conceals the race (whiteness) of psychologists. The epistemic project to create a position of nowhere from which to observe human life at once illustrates the vibrant dualism of secularism and anxiety, democracy and class privilege, progressive reformism, and ethnocentricity. Yet, investigations of the race of the experimenter also have concealed much. Study of these studies is revealing: it shows how we as investigators become educated to step out of our skin (or other features of our bodies), how we conceptualize the skin of others and how we confine our self-reflections—ignoring our positions as cultural actors and segregating our "lived" experiences from our "experimental" ones. These acts of concealment may be as telling about whiteness as our invention of the objective observer.

REFERENCES

Anonymous (1916). Some Suggestions Relative to a Study of the Mental Attitude of the Negro. *Pedagogical Seminary, 23*, 199–203.

Banks, W. C. (1976). White Preference in Blacks: A Paradigm in Search of a Phenemenon. *Psychological Bulletin, 83*(6), 1179–1186.

Bernstein, A. S. (1965). Race and Examiner as Significant Influences on Basal Skin Impedance. *Journal of Personality and Social Psychology, 1*(4), 346–349.

Betancourt, H., and Lopez, S. R. (1993). The Study of Culture, Ethnicity, and Race in American Psychology. *American Psychologist, 48*(6), 629–637.

Bond, H. M. (1927). Some Exceptional Negro Children. *The Crisis*, 257–259.

Britt, S. H. (1941). *Social Psychology of Modern Life*. New York: Rinehart and Company, Inc.

Camfield, T. M. (1970) *Psychologists at War: The History of American Psychology and the First World War*. Ph.D. dissertation, The University of Texas at Austin.

Canady, H. G. (1936). The Effect of "Rapport" on the I.Q.: A New Approach to the Problem of Racial Psychology. *Journal of Negro Education, 5*, 209–219.

Datson, L., and Galison, P. (1992). The Image of Objectivity. *Representations, 40*, 81–128.

Dreger, R. M., and Miller, K. S. (1960). Comparative Psychological Studies of Negroes and Whites in the United States. *Psychological Bulletin, 57*(5), 361–402.

Gaines, S. O., and Reed, E. S. (1995). Prejudice: From Allport to Du Bois. *American Psychologist, 50*(2), 96–103.

Gilliland, A. R., and Clark, E. L. (1939). *Psychology of Individual Differences*. New York: Prentice-Hall.

Goodman, J. (1976). Race, Reason, and Research. In L. M. King, V. J. Dixon, and W. W. Nobles (Eds.), *African Philosophy: Assumptions and Paradigms for Research on Black Persons*. Los Angeles: Fanon Center Publication.

Graham, S. (1992). "Most of the Subjects Were White and Middle Class": Trends in Published Research on African Americans in Selected APA journals, 1970–1989. *American Psychologist, 47*(5), 629–639.

Guthrie, R. V. (1976). *Even the Rat Was White: A Historical View of Psychology*. New York: Harper and Row.

Hall, G. S. (1894). The New Psychology as a Basis of Education. *Forum, 17*, 713.

Harding, S. (1986). *The Science Question in Feminism*. Ithaca, NY: Cornell University Press.

Heine, R. W. (1950). The Negro Patient in Psychotherapy. *Journal of Clinical Psychology, 6*, 373–376.

Helms, J. E. (1992). Why is There No Study of Cultural Equivalence in Standardized Cognitive Ability Testing? *American Psychologist, 47*(9), 1083–1101.

Henriques, J. C. (1984). Social Psychology and the Politics of Racism. In J. C. Henriques, C. Hollway, C. Urwin, C. Venn, and C. Walkerdine (Eds.), *Changing the Subject: Psychology, Social Regulation, and Subjectivity*. London: Methuen.

Herman, E. (1995). *The Romance of American Psychology: Political Culture in the Age of Experts*. Berkeley, CA: University of California Press.

Hollinger, D. A. (1989). Inquiry and Uplift: Late Nineteenth-Century American Academics and the Moral Efficacy of Scientific Practice. In T. L. Haskell (Eds.), *The Authority of Experts: Studies in History and Theory* (pp. 142–156). Bloomington: Indiana University Press.

Hyman, H. H. (1954). *Interviewing in Social Research*. Chicago: University of Chicago Press.

Jensen, A. R. (1980). *Bias in Mental Testing*. New York: The Free Press.

Jones, J. M. (1983). The Concept of Race in Social Psychology. In L. Wheeler and P. Shaver (Eds.), *Review of Personality and Social Psychology* (pp. 117–150). Beverly Hills, CA: Sage.

Jones, J. M. (1991). Psychological Models of Race: What Have They Been and What Should They Be? In

J. D. Goodchilds (Ed.), *Psychological Perspectives on Human Diversity in America* (pp. 5–46). Washington, D.C.: American Psychological Association.

Jones, R. L. (Ed.) (1972) *Black Psychology*. New York: Harper and Row.

Katz, I. (1964). Review of Evidence Relating to Effects of Desegregation on the Intellectual Performance of Negroes. *American Psychologist, 19*, 381–399.

Katz, I., Robinson, J. M., Epps, E. G., and Waly, P. (1964). The Influence of Race of the Experimenter and Instructions Upon the Expression of Hostility by Negro Boys. *Journal of Social Issues, 20*(2), 54–59.

Klineberg (1935). *Race Differences*. New York: Harpers and Brothers.

Ladd, G. T. (1894). *Primer of Psychology*. New York: Scribner.

MacKenzie, B. K. (1948). The Importance of Contact in Determining Attitudes Toward Negroes. *Journal of Abnormal and Social Psychology, 43*, 417–441.

Masling, J. (1960). The Influence of Situational and Interpersonal Variables in Projective Testing. *Psychological Bulletin, 57*, 65–85.

McLoyd, V. C. (1991). What is the Study of African American Children the Study of? In R. L. Jones (Eds.), *Black Psychology* (pp. 419–429). Berkeley, CA: Cobb and Henry.

McLoyd, V. C., and Randolph, S. M. (1986). Secular Trends in the Study of African-American Children: A Review of Child Development, 1936–1980. In A. B. Smuts and J. W. Hagen (Eds.), *History and Research in Child Development: Monographs for the Society of Research in Child Development*. Chicago: University of Chicago Press.

Meyer, Max F. (1921) *Psychology of the other-one, an Introductory Text-book of Psychology*. Columbia, MO: The Missouri Book Company.

Morawski, J. G. (1994). *Practicing Feminisms, Reconstructing Psychology: Notes on a Liminal Science*. New Haven: Yale University Press.

Morrison, T. (1992). *Playing in the Dark: Whiteness and the Literary Imagination*. New York: Vintage Books.

O'Donnell, J. (1985). *The Origin of Behaviorism: American Psychology, 1870–1920*. New York: New York University Press.

Pastore, N. (1949). *The Nature-Nurture Controversy*. New York: King's Crown Press.

Pearson, K. (1937). *The Grammar of Science*. New York: Meridian Books.

Pettigrew, T. F. (1964). *A Profile of the Negro American*. Princeton: D. Van Nostrand Company, Inc.

Pettigrew, T. F. (1970). The Role and its Burden. In R. V. Guthrie (Ed.), *Being Black: Psychological-Sociological Dilemmas* (pp. 146–155). San Francisco: Canfeld Press.

Pressey, S. L., and Teter, G. F. (1919). A Comparison of Colored and White Children by Means of a Group Scale of Intelligence. *Journal of Applied Psychology, 3*, 277–282.

Rankin, R. E., and Campbell, D. T. (1955). Galvanic Skin Response to Negro and White Experimenters. *Journal of Abnormal and Social Psychology, 51*, 30–33.

Reynolds, R. T. (1949). Racial Attitudes Revealed by a Projective Technique. *Journal of Consulting Psychology, 13*(1), 396–399.

Riess, B. F., Schwartz, E. K., and Cottingham, A. (1950). An Experimental Critique of Assumptions Underlying the Negro version of the TAT. *Journal of Abnormal and Social Psychology, 45*, 700–709.

Ryan, W. (1971). *Blaming the Victim*. New York: Vintage Books.

Rotundo, E. A. (1993). *American Manhood: Transformations in Masculinity from the Revolution to the Modern Era*. New York: Basic Books.

Samelson, F. (1978). From "Race Psychology" to "Studies in Prejudice": Some Observations on the Thematic Reversal in Social Psychology. *Journal of the History of the Behavioral Sciences, 14*(3), 265–278.

Samuel, W. (1977). Observed IQ as a Function of Test Atmosphere, Tester Expectation, and Race of Tester: A Replication for Female Subjects. *Journal of Educational Psychology, 69*(5), 593–604.

Sargent, S. S., and Williamson, R. C. (1966). *Social Psychology: An Introduction to the Study of Human Relations* (2nd ed.). New York: Ronald Press Company.

Sattler, J. M., and Theye, F. (1967). Procedural, Situational, and Interpersonal Variables in Individual Intelligence Testing. *Psychological Bulletin, 68*(5), 347–360.

Schwartz, E. K., and Riess, B. F. (1951). Further Critical Evaluation of the Negro Version of the TAT. *Journal of Projective Techniques*, *15*, 394–400.

Scripture, E. W. (1894). Methods of Laboratory Mind-Study. *Forum*, *17*, 558–570.

Shuey, A. M. (1958). *The Testing of Negro Intelligence*. London: Holborn Publishing Company.

Smith, D. H. (1967). The White Counselor in the Negro Slum School. *The School Counselor*, 268–272.

Sokal, M. M. (Ed.). (1987). *Psychological Testing and American Society, 1890–1930*. New Brunswick, NJ: Rutgers University Press.

Suls, J. M., and Rosnow, R. L. (1988). Concerns About Artifacts in Psychological Experiments. In J. G. Morawski (Ed.), *The Rise of Experimentation in American Psychology* (pp. 163–187). New Haven: Yale University Press.

Titchener, E. B. (1910). *A Textbook of Psychology*. New York: MacMillan.

Toulmin, S., and Leary, D. E. (1985). The Cult of Empiricism in Psychology and Beyond. In S. Koch and D. E. Leary (Eds.), *A Century of Psychology as Science* (pp. 594–617). New York: McGraw-Hill.

Trent, R. D. (1954). The Color of the Investigator as a Variable in Experimental Research with Negro Subjects. *Journal of Social Psychology*, *40*, 281–287.

Tucker, W. H. (1994). *The Science and Politics of Racial Research*. Urbana: University of Illinois Press.

Williams, F., and Cantril, H. (1945). The Use of Interviewer Rapport as a Method of Detecting Differences Between "Public" and "Private" Opinion. *Journal of Social Psychology*, *22*, 171–175.

Williams, J. A. (1964). Interviewer-Respondent Interaction: A Study of Bias in the Information Interview. *Sociometry*, *27*, 335–352.

Williams, J. E., Best, D. L., and Boswell, D. A. (1975). The Measurement of Children's Racial Attitudes in the Early School Years. *Child Development*, *46*, 494–500.

Winslow, C. N., and Brainerd, J. E. (1950). A Comparison of the Reactions of Whites and Negroes to Frustration as Measured by the Rosenzweig Picture-Frustration Test. *American Psychologist*, *5*(7), 297.

Wispe, L., Ash, P., Awkward, J., Hicks, L. H., Hoffman, M., and Porter, J. (1969). The Negro Psychologist in America. *American Psychologist*, *24*, 142–149.

Womack, W. M., and Wagner, N. N. (1967). Negro Interviewers and White Patients: The Question of Confidentiality and Trust. *Archives of General Psychiatry*, *16*, 685–692.

Woodworth, R. S. (1910). Racial Differences in Mental Traits. *Science*, *31*(788), 171–186.

Woolgar, S. (1988). *Science: The Very Idea*. New York: Tavistock.

Yee, A. H., Fairchild, H. H., Weizmann, F., and Wyatt, G. E. (1993). Addressing Psychology's Problems with Race. *American Psychologist*, *48*(11), 1132–1140.

Zuckerman, M. (1990). Some Dubious Premises in Research and Theory on Race Differences: Scientific, Social, and Ethical Issues. *American Psychologist*, *45*(12), 1297–1303.

Author's Note

Jessica Smock assisted in coding and analysis of the race of experimenter studies. Scott Plous and Karl Scheibe gave insightful comments on a draft of the chapter. Michelle Fine and Mun Wong's encouragement made the project happen. To all these people I give thanks.

Difference in a Minor Key:
Some Modulations of History, Memory, and Community

Deborah P. Britzman is Associate Professor in the Faculty of Education with graduate appointments in Social and Political Thought, Psychology, and Women's Studies at York University, Canada. Her research interests are in the area of psychoanalysis and education.

Freud offers a rather curious category in *Civilization and Its Discontents* to ponder the inclination toward aggressive hatred between social groups. The term "narcissism of minor differences" describes as a problem how individuals imagine themselves as members of a particular collectivity. The problem is not so much that people join together as it is what must be also done in the name of group distinction. In Freud's words: "It is always possible to bind together a considerable number of people in love, so long as there are other people left over to receive the manifestations of their aggressiveness" (1975: 51). The examples Freud offers are noteworthy in that he rehearses the hostilities among various European people: those who may share the same space of nation and language, those of different nations, and, then, the Jews' long history of Christianity's aggressions toward them.

Freud's naming of this dynamic as "minor" or "small" is not to suggest that histories of subordination, group hatred, and nationalist imperialisms are trivial. He is examining the social and psychic grounds of these histories as a problem for inquiry and for argument (LaCapra, 1994; Young-Bruehl, 1993). The term "minor" or "small" is only meant to signify the idea that there is no biological ground to the cultural dynamics and hatreds between communities. Both love and hatred, for Freud, are psychic demands elaborated socially and historically. The narcissism Freud worries about concerns the aggressive intensification and social costs of an excessive self-regard. Michael Ignatieff's (1995) thoughts about narcissism as prohibiting an acknowledgement of the dignity of the other offers a way into this concept:

> The facts of difference themselves are neutral. It is narcissism that turns difference into a mirror. In this mirror, a narcissist does not see the others in and for themselves; he sees them only as they reflect upon or judge himself. What is different is rejected if it fails to confirm the narcissist in his or her own self-opinion. (p. 19)

Part of what the narcissist cannot tolerate is her or his own inner conflict or difference; what is intolerable is projected elsewhere, onto the other.

Freud's concern, then, is with the psychic investments of distinguishing the self from the other that leave the self no other strategy than to place difference into the other's identity. He is also interested in how aggression becomes the grounds for bonding within a community. Moreover, in questioning love, and by placing the conflict of love with the demand for social esteem into the realm of the ego—itself an effect of history—Freud can then refuse the dominant essentialist discourses on race, namely eugenics, biology, and heredity, the European anchorage points or props for various modern racisms (Foucault, 1990; Gilman, 1991, 1993).

Such an operatic shift—from the so-called scientific empiricism of race as a biological law to the murky and contradictory interpretations called history and psychic structure—was, of course, in the Jewish Freud's own interests. By the late nineteenth century, Freud's generation had become the Jewish object that crystallized popular, legal, and scientific racism within Europe. "The Jewish Problem" was a racial problem and with this racialization came "The Jewish Look." In medical, anthropological, and race science writing, the "Jew" became construed as a historical throwback or anachronism in need of explication, containment, and ultimately, annihilation. As a race, they were represented in this literature as capable of tricking (because at first glance they looked like anyone else) and contaminating (because their blood was dirty) white Christian Europeans. But Freud was unsatisfied with scientific theories of heredity and degeneration. So he dismissed the category of "race" as being capable of explaining anything and instead studied the affective and imaginary dynamics of individuals and their dreams (de Certeau, 1988; Foucault, 1978; Gilman, 1992). In refusing to ground its study of human suffering in the eugenics of science, psychoanalysis can be considered as one of the first antiracist sciences in Europe.[1]

But why begin with Freud when this discussion investigates the ways particular communities form themselves and relate to others? Why pose these dynamics as a problem of love? To bring to bear on the field of antiracist pedagogy the psychoanalytic question of narcissism of minor differences allows us to consider as a problem the conditions for identification and disassociation that divide and trouble the self and the other. This ambivalence is the Freudian sense of love; the romance with domination and mastery and the problem of what love must suffer to be socially tamed and named as proper. Throughout this discussion, I will be troubling the sentimental consolation that separates love from aggression and suggest that attention to those minor differences within and between communities permits a different kind of argument for the field of antiracist pedagogy; one that can attend to questions of how communities are fashioned, one that admits the relations between ethics and cultural memory, and one that figures the conflicts of love. The pedagogical problem developed in this chapter, then, is twofold. How might anybody come to be called—in the name of community—to the service of the self/other divide? How might the field of antiracist pedagogy rethink the problem of community in ways that allow community to be more than a problem of repudiating others through those narcissisms of minor differences?

This discussion, then, focuses on the historical constructions of Jewishness as a race and what such a history suggests when North American Jews and African Americans dialogue between and among each other. I consider how the category of race has been conceptualized in anti-Semitic race writing and how this history modulates present discussions. But rather than view each community as an undifferentiated mass or as mutually exclusive in its experiences, categories, and demands, this chapter considers how differences within communities fashion relations between communities. This strategy is meant to illustrate a particular dilemma typically ignored when educational efforts focus on questions of race and racism. It has to do with how the category of "race" works to articulate sex and gender. To consider this complication, I offer the example of race writing by Jewish lesbians.

A short study of selected Jewish lesbian writing challenges the academic distinctions that position identity markers such as "race," "sex," and "gender" as capable of being separable and as standing alone. The writing discussed in this chapter suggests that the body is not lived in installments and that taken together, markers of the body such as race, gender, and sex act upon each other in ways that seem both unpredictable and surprising. To state the obvious, Jewish lesbians do not live in a vacuum: larger historical dynamics shape how Jewish lesbians engage within and between social, cultural, political, and institutional communities. Jewish lesbians are not reducible to an identity of either this or that and so their discussions complicate the field of antiracist pedagogy in two important ways. One has to do with what Stuart Hall (1988: 29) terms as "the new politics of representation [that crosses] questions of racism irrevocably with questions of sexuality." As we will see in this chapter, the history of Jewish racialization suggests that racist constructions of the body require that the body also be constructed through gender and sexuality in order for the category of race to be intelligible. What may not be so obvious is that even those who write against racism are not immune from excluding large segments of their community from representation. The other way Jewish lesbian writing complicates antiracist pedagogy has to do with how questions of cultural memory are engaged. In this writing, memory is not limited to a template that records one's past experiences. Rather, memory becomes more like a method, a strategy to organize and make new desires. Thus in this writing, memory can complicate itself with events, questions, and histories never directly experienced. Such an orientation should be quite central to educational efforts for education is, after all, a means to extend the self with experiences that can only be engaged through the other. To view the modulations of memory and its forgettings opens the field of antiracist pedagogy to the argument that bodies are more complicated than the first glance can bear to acknowledge and that first glance is often organized by those naracissims of minor differences.

My concern is to think discursively along with a few conversations within a rather small and often ignored imagined community, Jewish lesbians. Their writing will be juxtaposed with mainstream discussions of Jewishness and race. It is a rather curious montage that may reveal more about the kaleidoscopic fractures of "the new politics of representation"—those minor keys—than an explication of the social structures that incite whiteness. All of the writers I discuss begin with the problematic of social power as it pertains to racial inequalities. But unlike those who discuss the term "white privilege" as if it were monolithic, ahistoric, and unambivalent in experience, debates within Jewish lesbian communities and between Jews and African Americans lend themselves to historical nuance. They suppose that identity is not the sum of singular and conscious acts but is rather a social relation caught up—even as it catches itself—in the detours of history, memory, and communities.

Many of the arguments between North American Jews and African Americans engage the question of whether expanding cultural memory can allow for the dignity of solidarity between groups of people and hence exceed those narcissisms of minor differences. In mainstream debates between African Americans and Jews, tensions are examined when Jewishness is collapsed into the imperatives of whiteness. In debates within Jewish lesbian writing, there is the additional refusal of collapsing Jewishness into the imperatives of masculinity and heterosexuality.[2]

Still, to hold to such dissonance, such differences, remains quite tricky, particularly if one moves to both mainstream literature on Jewish racialization and the literature, over the last thirty years, that addresses relations between Blacks and Jews in the United States. Part of the problem may be that the category of "Jew," as with the category of "Black," does not signal its own internal differences of gender, sex, and class. Another part of the problem, as many have pointed out, is that "Black" and "Jew" are not mutually exclusive.[3] And, in a curious detour that renders discussions of racialization even more unwieldy, Paul Gilroy (1993: 212) recounts how W. E. B. Du Bois, while traveling in Eastern Europe during the Dreyfus Affair, "puzzled over the meaning of being mistaken for a Jew while travelling." Du Bois was dropped off at a Jewish inn after he answered "yes" when asked by the carriage driver if he was a Jew. Finally, we can complicate even further by bringing to bear on this discussion the history of Eastern and Western European Jewish racialization. Given the *Shoah*, the idea of the Jew as "white" in both North America and

Europe is barely fifty years old.[4] In North America, persistent memories of what Joan Nestle (1987) calls "a restricted country" and the contemporary resurgence of the New Right's Christian fundamentalist commitment to anti-Semitism and racism bother any seamless capacity or desire for many Jews to enmesh Jewishness with whiteness.

But if one can begin from the vantage point that the social meanings of race, sex, and gender are cacophonous in their historicity, the noise, in Sander Gilman's (1991) study *The Jew's Body*, is made for and by men. Chapters are organized by how European science imagined as problematic and in need of explanation the various body parts of male Jews, including "scientific" examination of "the Jewish foot," "the Jewish nose," "the Jewish voice," and "the Jewish psyche." Such features of anti-Semitic writing—cloaked in the authority of scientific discourse—legitimized the mythic but irreversible modern social fact of the Jew as other to white. Thus as modern white supremacy was distinguishing itself from the Other, whiteness required a gender and a sex: in this context whiteness became a synecdoche for normality and masculinity. The "[male] Jew" became a metonymy for deviancy and femininity (Mayer, 1982).

The grounds upon which racism is built in this anti-Semitic literature challenges current educational definitions of racism as merely performing the commonly taught formula that racism equals prejudice plus power, and that race is a natural category somehow distorted by racism. As well, the history of European Jewry challenges notions of white privilege as an instant, transparent, and unitary accessory to the body. Such ahistoric conceptualizations are more an effect of essentialized discourses of race and perhaps the educational desire to simplify the complex histories of racism in the name of certainty and correction. These conceptualizations must forget what Foucault (1990: 89) has termed as "the mechanisms" of power, "ensured [not] by right but by technique, not by law but by normalization, not by punishment but by control." The normalization of race—as with the normalization of gender and sex—as an obvious, visible, and predictive feature of the body is thus a discourse that gestures to the problem of how mechanisms of power produce proper and improper bodies.[5]

The problem is that, as a discourse, racism installs a rarified naturalism into the body. Then, one's nature—regardless of conduct and actions, and indeed, actions in this discourse are read as only confirming nature—can never be altered (Bauman, 1991). It is precisely this fixity—this unchanging, ahistoric nature—that can then be read, interpreted, counted, classified, categorized, contained, and rendered as visible. Within the Nazi imaginary, Jewishness, as opposed to Judaism, is a problem of blood, not an effect of conscience, desire, practice, or community. The elaboration of racial eugenic sciences and the practices of "racial betterment," then, fashioned upon that which could not be seen, a science of visibility organized to imagine the proper body. And in the process of bestowing appearance to what could not be distinguished, race—for the Jew—became a secret to be spoken and a truth to be found. Thus, "the Jewish look."

Fifty years later, speaking of North American Ashkenazi Jews, Sander Gilman (1991: 170) asks, "Are Jews white? and what does 'white' mean in this context. . . . How has the question of racial identity shaped Jewish identity in the Diaspora?" We can complicate this question with a parenthetical remark pertaining to early twentieth-century discussions about Jews that Gilman (1993: 8) makes in another of his studies: "(The very term 'Jew' is as much a category of gender, masculine, as it is a category of race.)"[6] The problem seems to be twofold: what do race and gender mean in terms of the shaping of difference within Jewish identities? And, if the term "Jew" is coded as masculine, and indeed, the mainstream debates between African Americans and Jews are largely debates between middle-class men about middle-class men (Melnick, 1993), and the term "Jew" is also coded historically as "not white," what are the dynamics of racialization and engenderment for diasporic Jewish lesbians?

Here, a slight detour is in order in that Jewish women may also be stereotyped through behavior which in turn constitutes "a look." Being pushy, loud-mouthed, and fussy, the Jewish woman's body is overbearing, bossy, and insatiable. Jewish men have a different economy of visibility. Culturally, as Jews, they are obligated to mark—indeed, to cut—their male body. Nothing is comparable for Jewish women, even though, in the first instance, Jewishness is matriarchically bestowed. Publicly, religious Jewish males may wear a kippa to identify as Jews whereas religious Jewish females are only obligated to signify their relation to heterosexual marital status.[7] Within and beyond Jewish sociality, the very common complaint about looking (and sounding) too Jewish or not looking (and sounding) Jewish enough plays differently in terms of gender, sex, race, and geography. These modulations of Jewish difference signify, as well, questions of assimilation and Jewish self-hatred. Sander Gilman's (1991: 235) comment is pertinent: "The desire for invisibility, the desire to become "white," lies at the center of the Jew's flight from his or her own body."

James Baldwin recognized this desire for invisibility when, in the late 1960s, he wrote complexly about the antagonistic relations between African Americans and Jews and the incapacity to generalize or transfer sufferings as the claim for understanding.

In the American context, the most ironical thing about Negro anti-Semitism is that the Negro is really condemning the Jew for having become an American white man—for having become, in effect, a Christian. The Jew profits from his status in America, and he must expect Negroes to distrust him for it. (p. 37)

Baldwin engages a double problem: the refusal of a certain historicity—a particular ethicality—that Jewish (male) difference could reference and the perception that, in North America, light-skinned Jews can assimilate and, indeed, many have tried to assimilate into an unmarked whiteness that forecloses Jewish difference.

Years later, in what is perhaps now known as one of the most sustained meditations on racism and anti-Semitism by a Jewish lesbian of Eastern European decent, Elly Bulkin (1984) holds the tension that one's history of oppression is no guarantee of any kind of social sensitivity or insight into anyone's difference, including one's own. Perhaps in reversing Baldwin's equation, Bulkin examines her own contradictory anger in holding to the assumption that

[one's] gut-level experience of their own oppression will provide them with a ready store of empathy for others. When, for instance, I am dyke-baited on my block by teenagers, white and Black, I am, in total defiance of logic, angrier at the Black kids than at the white ones: *they*, I mutter to myself, should know better! (p. 150)

But what is being claimed by the claim "they should know better?" Baldwin's essay renders this familiar problem as uncanny:

If one blames the Jew for not having been ennobled by oppression, one is not indicating the single figure of the Jew but the entire human race, and one is also making a quite breathtaking claim for oneself. (p. 41)

There is, then, a significant tension within the observations of both Baldwin and Bulkin, and this has to do with the question of everyone's cultural memory in the matter of racism and with turning one's expectations for the conduct of another back upon the self. At stake becomes the ethicality required for dialogue. This returns us to those narcissisms of minor differences and the conflicts—indeed the betrayals—that emerge when one thinks of the other as "a mirror," or at least as having the obligation to "know better." Then, as Baldwin and Bulkin turn this obligation back to the self, something more significant can be examined, namely the ethical and interminable problem of knowing others and of being known in terms that refuse excessive self-regard and subordination.

But refusing to be subordinated does not guarantee that one will not subordinate another. This tension works differently in one of the first anthologies of Jewish lesbian writing, *Nice Jewish Girls: A Lesbian Anthology*. Today, one might read it as largely testimonial. It offers firsthand accounts of the desire for recognition on one's own terms even as one seeks group affinity and affirmation. Many contributors sketch the geography of anti-Semitism, homophobia, and racism in North America and Europe and write against the disavowals of these dynamics within feminism, leftist politics, and mainstream Jewish communities. Then, we see more clearly how narcissism of minor differences works within groups where individuals imagine each other as similar but not so much so that they may be claimed as members.

The awkwardness of imagining that all Jewish lesbians face the same dilemmas or even that Jewish lesbianism means something similar to those who claim this identity is analyzed by Pauline Bart (1984) in her essay "How a Nice Jewish Girl Like Me Could." She describes a trip to Amsterdam where, during a heated discussion on lesbian separatism, she meets another Jewish lesbian. Afterwards, Bart asks her how she survived World War II:

> . . . she tells me that she was sent from Christian family to Christian family. I mention that she does not look Jewish. She says, "Of course not. If I looked Jewish I'd be dead." She gets a terrible headache and I feel guilty and stupid. We return to her apartment where I learn of her role in the founding of Israel's gay liberation movement. She left after finding it impossible to live openly as a lesbian. In Israel she was in *galut* because she was a lesbian and in Amsterdam she is in *galut* because she is a Jew. (p. 61)

The economy of guilt is quite complicated here and very different histories of the Jewish Diaspora are at stake. Perhaps Bart remembers the shame of being shut out of one's community and bothers this memory by repeating this exclusion with the mythic "Jewish look." Like Bulkin, Bart might berate herself for not knowing better and for thinking that her own experiences of exclusion are comparable enough to shed a modicum of insight into the exclusions of another. But neither identity nor history is as stable as one's memory remembers. The modulations of historical geographies and genealogies of Jewish racialization and sexualization make both memory and community a question, not an extension of imagined similitude.

In many of these essays, there is no tidy agreement on the meanings and effects of racialization, or even how Jewishness might be commonly understood. *Nice Jewish Girls* has a section called "Jewish Identity: A Coat of Many Colors," where differences of geography, generation, and the meanings of race within and between Jewish communities are discussed. There are questions as to hierarchies within Jewishness in terms of the dominant definition of who can claim Jewishness within religiosity and within secular contexts where light-skinned Jews assimilate as white and hence not Jews. These writers try to sort through those narcissisms of minor differences.

But transposing racial terms to describe differences between Jewish lesbians effects new discussion. Elly Bulkin's essay published a few years later argues with some of the racial formulations of *Nice Jewish Girls*. In a rather long footnote, Bulkin reprints a criticism from Rita Arditti, who writes in part:

It seems to me [that Jews of color is] a broad term that derives from the North American division between white people in this country and blacks. . . . [Jews of color] seems to lump together all the Jews who are not "white." And who are "white Jews"? (p. 201)

Arditti then asks how Ashkenazic, Sephardic, Ethiopian, and Latin American Jews would be racially categorized and which criteria hold in which places. The rejoinder to the term "Jews of color" raises the question of when racial classification becomes significant to Jews as Jews, particularly given that modern diasporic Jewishness exceeds racial and national boundaries and that at least since 1492 the expulsion of Jews from their country of birth is precisely because of their Jewishness.[8]

Still, as Arditti points out, in North America the matter of whiteness matters for those secular Jews with light skin. Bulkin analyzes her recollection of being seen as white and her forgetting that, encountered as a stranger, she is seen as white. She remembers going out for ice cream with a group of women who attended the 1981 National Women's Studies Conference on racism. She happens to be standing alongside a Black woman, who, upon entering the restaurant says to herself "Here I come, white folks!" Bulkin is embarrassed at her own

unpreparedness for this particular venture into white America. The moment I wandered through the door, *my* skin color did not grab the attention of the white person sitting over a sundae. . . . A few hours after I had been on a panel on racism in the lesbian community, I could imagine going out for an ice cream as a simple and uncomplicated act. (p. 143)

But acts of identity are neither simple nor conscious and much of the writing by lesbians of any positionality concerns examination of the thousand tiny slights bodies accrue and offer in daily life. Such accountings are made in order to enlarge the accountability of memory and to consider identity as a social relation.

To complicate Bulkin's ice cream memory, consider Leslie Feinberg's (1993) *Bildungsroman*, *Stone Butch Blues*, a novel about the life of a working-class, Jewish, transgendered person.[9] Our protagonist, Jess Goldberg, is a battlefield on two legs. From the cruel gaze of the normative glance that reads the body as a literal confirmation of gender, Jess's body is read as transgressing the intelligibility of both femininity and masculinity. Jess identifies as white, but in the world of strangers, this marker does not effect public normalization. Instead, the dominant discourse of the properly gendered body pushes Jess out. Walking into that same ice cream store, Jess would face the hostility that accrues across the small and seemingly insignificant acts of going to the public toilet to the gendered greeting workers are required to make in dealing with customers. The hostility is dual: it has to do with Jess becoming angry at being mistaken and the hostility people feel when they get something wrong. But even these kinds of dismissals do not grant Jess any immunity from participating in racist discourses. The Buffalo gay bars of the 1950s and 1960s were, for the most part, segregated by race and class and this history visits Jess's friendships without an invitation.

For Jess, the refusal of racism is troubled by an interracial friendship with Edwin, who gives Jess a copy of W. E. B. Du Bois's *The Souls of Black Folk* and forces Jess to consider their differences as lesbians. Jess tells someone: "You know, I always fall back on assuming [what] Ed and I deal with every day as butches is pretty much the same. . . . Ed reminded me about what she faces everyday that I don't" (p. 129). This acknowledgment occurs the day after the assassination of Martin Luther King and the racial tensions within white and black lesbian communities over the meaning of his death. But it was not until years later that Jess actually reads Du Bois's text and finds the passage Edwin marked on "this double-consciousness, this sense of always looking at one's self through the eyes of others"(p. 178) and begins to think about the psychic structure of living without the alibi of gender, race, and sex.

But can the body be without an explanation? In perhaps one of the most provocative attempts by a Jewish lesbian artist to engage this question, Jyl Lynn Felman (1993) transgresses the obvious with the imaginary geography of "the erotic," one of the most volatile sites of narcissism of minor differences. Felman begins "De Vilde Chayes—The Wild Beasts":

> This is about the erotic. My erotic. About when you see me my erotic. And when you don't. This is about the erotic. My white non-white ethnic white erotic self. And when I'm seen and when I'm not. Seen at all. This is about my erotic. And my sisters erotic. Our *sephardic ashkenazic mizrachic* erotic. When you think you are seeing our *sephardic ashkenazic mizrachic* white non-white ethnic white erotic selves. And what you don't see. When you think you are seeing me. If you are seeing me. At all. Are you seeing a luscious wild *vilde chaye* a *zaftig svelt kayn aynhoreh* stunning *vilde chaye?* Or are you seeing loud pushy money lender big nose zionist oppressor that you want to fuck? In the ass. This is about the erotic. My erotic. My white non-white erotic self. About when I'm seen as white and when I'm not.

Such a fantasy refuses to tidy the ambivalence called love. There are no offers of apology and explication, no comfort of experience and identity claims, just the force of desires arguing with the other, becoming other to the pull toward self-mastery and composure. There is no proper body and the piece demands from its readers something other than moral outrage. This concatenation of desire is not within the realm of rationality or representation because it posits the view that multiple and conflictive histories of bodies haunt desire thereby making the distinction between love and aggression difficult to maintain. Indeed, engagement with the phantoms of *De Vilde Chayes* returns us, perhaps more insistently, to Freud's curious category of "narcissism of minor differences," where history fashions desire and desire may both dismiss and engage the modulations of its own otherness. This may be the "double consciousness" of Eros. The meeting of the look is an erotic and haunted relation and in this space, racial matters are indivisible from matters of desire and cultural memory.[10]

What, then, might come of an antiracist pedagogy unafraid of examining the question of love and with what social bonding means when agression becomes part of its dynamic? What would actually become a question if the stability of race as capable of speaking for itself was called into question? One possibility resides, I think, in the acknowledgment that the historical constructions that allow race to become the grounds of racism have both a material and psychic cost. And while antiracist pedagogies have been astute in analyzing the structures of inequality, the problem of narcissism of minor differences that tolerate such inequality is rarely broached. Examination into the discourses that render race as intelligible may complicate any facile gesture to reduce the question of racism to the sole terrain of individual psychology, ignorance, or to the educational solution of supplying the correct representations. If these problems and repairs are offered as consolations, the writers discussed here would have no place in the classroom or in antiracist pedagogy. But, if antiracist pedagogy is to be more than a consolation, it must make itself inconsolable by engaging with what it excludes, namely the complex and contradictory debates within communities over how communities are imagined and are made subject to their own persistent questions. The move is not towards a new inclusivity, although opening the stakes of identification and learning from the conflicts within community should trouble what is imagined as a normal race or, more pertinently, as a normal representation of race. But the demand is one that centers community as a question of difference as having the potential to modulate the ethics of cultural memory.

When it comes to examining the history of race, and the writers discussed here render this concern as the beginning, antiracist pedagogies must unapologetically explore the operatic fields of sexualities, of Eros, and of those narcissisms of minor differences, not because suffering ennobles, or is comparable, or even because a knowledge of suffering installs the proper guilt. Rather, its appeal must be to incite identifications and enlarge the geography of memory in order for memory to engage the modulations of its own otherness. In studying as a problem that difficult relation called love—itself the grounds of community—categories like race, sex, and gender can be thought of as matters that require more than one look, indeed, as social and psychic matters that require an education that can bear an ethical renunciation of representation as mastery and as mirror, as self-aggrandizement and as the grounds for excessive self-regard.

REFERENCES

Baldwin, James. "Negroes are anti-Semitic because they're anti-white." Reprinted in *Blacks and Jews: Alliances and Arguments*. Edited by Paul Berman, pp. 31–41. New York: Delacorte Press, 1994.

Bauman, Zygmut. *Modernity and the Holocaust*. Ithaca: Cornell University Press, 1989.

Beck, Evelyn Torton, ed. *Nice Jewish Girls: A Lesbian Anthology*. Watertown: Persephone Press, 1982.

Bulkin, Elly, Pratt, Minnie Bruce, and Smith, Barbara. *Yours in Struggle: Three Feminist Perspectives on Anti-Semitism and Racism*. Brooklyn: Long Haul Press, 1984.

de Certeau, Michel. *The Writing of History*. Translated by Tom Conley. New York: Columbia, 1988.

Feinberg, Leslie. *Stone Butch Blues: A Novel*. Ithaca: Firebrand Books, 1993.

Felman, Jyl Lynn. "De Vilde Chayes-The Wild Beasts." In *The Body of Love*. Edited by Tee A. Corinne, pp. 9–13. Austin: Banned Books, 1993.

Foucault, Michel. *The History of Sexuality: An Introduction*. New York: Vintage, 1990.

Freud, Sigmund. *Civilization and Its Discontents*. Translated by Joan Riviere. London: Hogarth Press, 1975.

Gilman, Sander. *The Jew's Body*. NY: Routledge, 1991.

Gilman, Sander. *Freud, Race and Gender*. Princeton: Princeton University Press, 1993.

Gilroy, Paul. *The Black Atlantic: Modernity and Double Consciousness*. Cambridge: Harvard University Press, 1993.

Goldberg, David Theo. *Racist Culture: Philosophy and the Politics of Meaning*. Cambridge: Blackwell, 1993.

Hall, Stuart. "New Ethnicities." *Black Film and British Cinema*. ICA Documents, London, 1988.

Ignatieff, Michael. "Nationalism and the Narcissism of Minor Differences." *Queens Quarterly* 102, 13–26.

LaCapra, Dominick, *Representing the Holocaust: History, Theory, and Trauma*. Ithaca: Cornell University Press, 1994.

Mayer, Hans. *Outsiders: A Study in Life and Letters*. Translated by Denis M. Sweet. Cambridge:, M.I.T. Press, 1982.

Melnic, Jeffrey. "Black and Jew Blues." *Transitions* 62, 106–121.

Nestle, Joan. *Restricted Country*. Ithaca: Firebrand Books, 1987.

Young-Bruehl, Elizabeth. "Discriminations." *Transition: An International Review* 60, 53–69.

NOTES

1. It must be noted that in the Fin de Siecle, Jewish professionals were quite divided as to how to think about the category of Jewish racialization. For a study of Jewish scientists' resistance to nineteenth- and early twentieth-century racism where the category of race is maintained but in some ways reinflected with a

positivity for Jewish definitions of Jewishness, see John M. Efron, *Defenders of the Race: Jewish Doctors and Race Science in Fin-de-Siecle Europe*. New Haven: Yale University Press, 1994.

2. Writing by Jewish lesbians on questions of identity and social difference is quite extensive. I note only a partial list. See, for instance, Jyl Lynn Felman, "If Only I Had Been Born a Kosher Chicken," *Tikkun* (Summer 1994); "Jewish Women," *Fireweed* (Spring 1992); Marilyn Hacker, *Winter Numbers: Poems*, NY: Norton, 1994; Judith Katz, *Running Fiercely Toward a High Thin Sound*, Ithaca: Firebrand Books, 1992; Melanie Kay/Kantrowitz, *The Issue Is Power: Essays on Women, Jews, Violence and Resistance*, San Francisco: Aunt Lute, 1992; Melanie Kay/Kantrowitz and Irena Klepfisz, eds. *The Tribe of Dina: A Jewish Women's Anthology*, Boston: Beacon Press, 1989; Irena Klepfisz, *Dreams of an Insomniac: Jewish Feminist Essays, Speeches and Diatribes*, Portland: The Eighth Mountain Press, 1990; Andrea Freud Lowenstein, *This Place*, Boston: Pandora Press, 1984; Joan Nestle, *Restricted Country*, Ithaca, NY: Firebrand Books; Sara Schulman, *My American History: Lesbian and Gay Life During the Reagan/Bush Years*, New York: Routledge, 1994; Muriel Rukeyser, *Breaking Open*, New York: Random House, 1973; and Jo Sinclair, *Wasteland*, Philadelphia: Jewish Publication Society, 1987.

3. In the context of North America, see, for example, the discussions of bell hooks, "Keeping a Legacy of Shared Struggle," in *Blacks and Jews: Alliances and Arguments*, edited by Paul Berman, pp. 229–238, New York: Delacorte Press, 1994; Abraham Lavender, ed., *A Coat of Many Colors: Jewish Subcommunities in the United States*. Westport, CT: Greenwood Press, 1977; Julius Lester, *Lovesong: Becoming a Jew*. New York: Henry Holt and Company, 1988; and Josylyn Segal, "Interracial Plus," in *Nice Jewish Girls: A Lesbian Anthology*. edited by Evelyn Torton Beck, pp. 55–58, Watertown: Perspehone Press, 1982. Such discussions concern the fact that Jews constitute many races. But also see Ellen Willis, "The Myth of the Powerful Jew," in Berman, pp. 183–209. Willis argues that the term "Jew" is not a racial term.

From a very different vantage, two of the most interesting discussions of the interrelations between "Blacks" and "Jews" that address the notion of cultural memory can be found in Paul Gilroy, *The Black Atlantic: Modernity and Double Consciousness*. Cambridge: Harvard University Press, 1993; and Joe Wood, "The Problem Negro and other Tales," in Berman, pp. 97–128.

4. Here, the concept of "race" is used not in terms of phenotype but in terms of what David Theo Goldberg (1993: 47) calls "racialized discourse," which he defines as "not consist[ing] simply in descriptive representations of others. It includes a set of hypothetical premises about human kinds (e.g. the 'great chain of being,' classificatory hierarchies, etc.) and about the differences between them (both mental and physical). It involves a class of ethical choices (e.g. domination and subjugation, entitlement and restriction, disrespect and abuse)."

5. To constitute discourses of "the visible" as an imagined category is not to deny the material effects of racism. Indeed, the "visible" is quite central to the operation and maintenance of everyday racism for African Americans. See, for example, Regina Austin, " 'A Nation of Thieves': Consumption, Commerce, and the Black Public Sphere." *Public Culture* 15 (1994): 225–248.

6. Earlier in this paper, I described how in anti-Semitic writing, the "Jew" is coded as feminine. In that literature, femininity is a code for a failed masculinity or, in slightly different terms, an effeminate/homo masculinity. It may be that the term "Jew" was masculinized by Jewish men in order to renunciate anti-Semitic representations of themselves. But in masculinizing the term "Jew" and in generalizing Jewish male experience onto an entire people, much of the contemporary writing by Jewish men then forgets sexual difference within Jewish communities in its assertion of masculine heterosexual experience as universal.

7. To complicate the matter a bit more, Art Spiegelman, the author of *Maus: A Survivor's Tale*, drew for the cover of the February 14, 1993 Valentine issue of *The New Yorker* a kiss between what appeared to be a Hasidic man and an African American woman. This illustration provoked significant debates and appears again on the cover of a the edited work *Blacks and Jews: Alliances and Arguments*. Editor Paul Berman rehearses some of the issues involved in the preface to the volume. In the illustration, while the man could be coded as "Jew" the only marker available to the woman was "race."

8. For a very different discussion of racialization and the historical shifts of hierarchical power within Jewish history among Jews of different nations, see Alain Finkielkraut, *The Imaginary Jew*, translated by Kevin O'Neill and David Suchoff, Lincoln: University of Nebraska Press, 1994, particularly section II, "The Visible and the Invisible."

9. This novel can be placed within the tradition of secular Jewish proletariat novels such as Michel Gold's *Jews Without Money* and Jo Sinclair's *The Changeling*. (Problematically, and speaking parenthetically of yet another example of narcissism of those minor differences, writing by gay and lesbian Jews is not claimed by mainstream Jewish scholars as contributing to and, indeed, perhaps being capable of revitalizing the field of Jewish secular literature.) Our protagonist Jess, for example, runs away from an abusive Jewish family. Given her/his transgendered desires, Jess feels most at home in gay and lesbian communities and in labor union struggles.

10. Questions of racializing sexuality and the ambivalence of the erotic have been explored quite explicitly by such gay writers of color as Melvin Dixon, *Vanishing Rooms*, New York: Plume Books, 1992; Kobena Mercer, "Skin Head Sex Thing: Racial Difference and the Homoerotic Imaginary"; and Richard Fung, "Looking for My Penis: The Eroticized Asian in Gay Video Porn," in *How Do I look? Queer Film and Video*, ed. Bad Object-Choices. Seattle: Bay Press, 1991; Derrick Scott, "Jungle Fever? Black Gay Identity Politics, White Dick, and the Utopian Bedroom," *GLQ* 1, 2(1994): 299–322; and in the films of Isaac Julian, such as "Looking for Langston" and "The Attendant."

Behind Blue Eyes:
Whiteness and Contemporary U.S. Racial Politics

FOUR

Howard Winant

Howard Winant is Professor of Sociology at Temple University. He is the author of several books: *Racial Conditions: Politics, Theory, Comparisons* (1994); *Racial Formation in the United States*, with co-author Michael Omi (2nd ed., 1994); and *Stalemate: Political Economic Origins of Supply-Side Policy* (1988). He has also written extensively on comparative racial politics and theory, with particular reference to Latin America and Brazil. At present he is working on a project analyzing global racial politics and the resurgence of the right.

INTRODUCTION

At an urban college campus in California, whites and blacks, Latinos and Asians, sit side-by-side in the overcrowded classroom, and in their own separate groups in the cafeteria. As they drive home to their segregated neighborhoods, they pump the same high-volume hip-hop sounds through their car speakers. A few miles up the interstate, neo-Nazis train at a private ranch. A few miles the other way, a multiracial garment workers' union is being organized; a majority of the workers in the bargaining unit are Asians and Latinos, but there are some whites. Among the organizers, one of the most effective is a young white woman who speaks good Spanish.

Clearly, there are many varieties of "whiteness." This essay examines racial politics and culture as they shape the status of whites. I begin from the premise that it is no longer possible to assume a "normalized" whiteness, whose invisibility and relatively monolithic character signify immunity from political or cultural challenge. An alternative perspective is demanded, one which begins from a recognition of *white racial dualism*. The discussion of this theme, in the next section of this essay, is an extension to whites of the Du Boisian idea that in a racist society the "color line" fractures the self, that it imposes a sort of schizophrenia on the bearers of racialized identities, which forces them to see themselves simultaneously from within and without. Du Bois of course intended this analysis to explain problems of black politics and culture at the turn of the twentieth century; it was a time when few publically questioned the normalization of whiteness. His idea can be extrapolated to whites at the end of the twentieth century; today, I suggest, whiteness has been deeply fissured by the racial conflicts of the post–civil rights period. Since the 1960s contemporary racial discourse has been unable to function as a logic of racial superiority and justified exclusion. Therefore it has been forced into *re*articulations, *re*presentations, *re*interpretations of the meaning of race and, perforce, of whiteness.

In the following section of this paper I analyze the *new politicization of whiteness* which has taken shape particularly in the post–civil rights era—the period since the ambiguous victory of the civil rights movement in the mid-1960s. Here I discuss the reasons why, contrary to the racially egalitarian thrust of the civil rights "revolution," the significance of white identity was reinterpreted and repoliticized—largely in a reactionary direction—in the wake of the 1960s.

Next, I analyze the range of *white racial projects* that the contemporary politics of racial dualism generates. How do interpretations of the meaning of whiteness link to political positions, policies, and programs? I discuss a series of racial projects that span the political continuum, and develop some critical perspectives on the "left" or "progressive" projects.

In the final section, I focus on *the future of whiteness* in the United States and sketch out some elements of what a potential antiracist politics for whites might look like.

WHITENESS AS RACIAL DUALISM

Once, U.S. society was a nearly monolithic racial hierarchy, in which everyone knew "his" place. Today, nobody knows where he or she fits in the U.S. racial order.

Thirty years after the enactment of civil rights legislation, agreement about the continuing existence of racial subordination has vanished. The meaning of race has been deeply problematized. Why? Because the legacy of centuries of white supremacy lives on in the present, despite the partial victories of the 1960s. Because the idea of "equality," it turned out, could be reinterpreted, rearticulated, reinserted in the business-as-usual framework of U.S. politics and culture. Because that framework is extremely resilient and able to absorb political challenges, even fundamental and radical ones. Because the outlawing of formal discrimination, which was a crucial and immediate objective of the 1960s movements, did not mean that informal racist practices would be eradicated, or indeed even that antidiscrimination laws would be seriously enforced.

And yet it would be inaccurate to say that the movement failed. In virtually every area of social life, the impact of the postwar racial mobilizations is plain to see (Jaynes and Williams, 1989). Although in some sectors, like housing desegregation, massive efforts to transform an entrenched and complex pattern of racial discrimination were largely (though not entirely) defeated (Massey and Denton, 1993), in other areas—for example the desegregation of the armed forces (Moskos, 1988; Butler, 1980)—really remarkable change occurred.

Therefore, not only blacks (and other racially identified minorities), but also whites, now experience a division in their racial identities. On the one hand, whites inherit the legacy of white supremacy, from which they continue to benefit. But on the other hand, they are subject to the moral and political challenges posed to that inheritance by the partial but real successes of the black movement (and affiliated movements). These movements advanced a countertradition to white supremacy, one which envisioned a radicalized, inclusive, participatory democracy, a substantively egalitarian economy, and a nonracial state. They deeply affected whites as well as blacks, exposing and denouncing often unconscious beliefs in white supremacy, and demanding new and more respectful forms of behavior in relation to nonwhites. Just as the movements partially reformed white supremacist institutions, so they partially transformed white racial consciousness. Obviously, they did not destroy the deep structures of white privilege, but they did make counterclaims on behalf of the racially excluded and subordinated. As a result, white identities have been displaced and refigured: they are now contradictory, as well as confused and anxiety-ridden, to an unprecedented extent. It is this situation which I describe as white racial dualism.[1]

THE NEW POLITICIZATION OF WHITENESS

What are the implications of post–civil rights era racial dualism for contemporary politics? There seems little doubt that the new politicization of whiteness plays a crucial role in determining the direction of U.S. politics today. Many analysts have pointed to the significance of race as a "wedge issue" that divides the Democratic Party, inducing large numbers of working- (or middle-) class whites to vote Republican (Greenberg, 1985; Edsalls, 1992). Of course, this "wedge" has been there for a long time: it operated under slavery, flourished in the late-nineteenth-century populist era, and problematized the New Deal Coalition. It threatened to split the Democratic Party in 1948. It did in fact split the party after the 1960s.

Since that time the meaning of whiteness has been cast into doubt: does it signify privilege or is it merely one identity—one form of "difference"—among others? To what extent is race still a salient marker of social position and status, and to what extent is it a relic of the past in a society now determined to be "color-blind"? In some respects, the crisis of "whiteness" does reflect the greater racial egalitarianism of the post–civil rights period. In other ways this crisis is merely the latest defense of white supremacy, which now covers itself with the fig leaf of a formal egalitarianism. The contemporary crisis of whiteness—its dualistic allegiances to privilege and equality, to color consciousness and color-blindness, to formally equal justice and to substantive social justice—can be discerned in the contradictory character of white identity today.

There were three new developments which set the stage for the new politicization of whiteness. First, the *erosion of white ethnicity* in the post–WW II period meant that a more uniform racial identity, that of "Euro-American," became available to whites. Second, *class politics lost much of its resonance* in a postindustrial economy characterized by capital flight and downsizing; as a result standards of living stagnated and opportunities for political mobilization along class lines faded. Third, the limited reforms achieved by the black movement and its allies in the 1960s were susceptible to reinterpretation by the right, making a *de facto racial reaction* ideologically palatable to the political center.

* * *

Thus from the late 1960s on, white identity has been reinterpreted, rearticulated in a dualistic fashion: on the one hand egalitarian, on the other hand privileged; on the one hand individualistic and "color-blind," on the other hand "normalized" and white.

Nowhere is this new framework of the white "politics of difference" more clearly on display than in the reaction to affirmative action policies of all sorts (in hiring, university admissions, federal contracting, etc.). Assaults on these policies, which have been developing since their introduction as tentative and quite limited efforts at racial redistribution (Johnson, 1967, but see also Steinberg, 1995), are currently at hysterical levels. These attacks are clearly designed to effect ideological shifts, rather than to shift resources in any meaningful way. They represent whiteness as *disadvantage*, something which has few precedents in U.S. racial history (Gallagher, 1995). This imaginary white disadvantage—for which there is almost no evidence at the empirical level—has achieved widespread popular credence, and provides the cultural and political "glue" that holds together a wide variety of reactionary racial politics.

WHITE RACIAL PROJECTS

Both the onset of white racial dualism and the new politicization of whiteness in the post–civil rights era reflect the fragmentation of earlier concepts of white racial identity and of white supremacy more generally. In their place, a variety of concepts of the meaning of whiteness have emerged. How can we analyze and evaluate in a systematic fashion this range of white racial projects?

As I have argued elsewhere (Winant, 1994; Omi and Winant, 1994), the concept of racial pro-jects is crucial to understanding the dynamics of racial formation in contemporary society.

Existing racial projects can be classified along a political spectrum, according to explicit crite-ria drawn from the meaning each project attaches to "whiteness." Such a classification will nec-essarily be somewhat schematic, since in the real world of politics and culture ideas and meanings, as well as social practices, tend to overlap in unpredictable ways. Nevertheless, I think it would be beneficial to attempt to sort out alternative conceptions of whiteness, along with the politics that both flow from and inform these conceptions. This is what I attempt here, focusing on five key racial projects, which I term *far right, new right, neoconservative, neoliberal,* and *new aboli-tionist.*

The Far Right Racial Project

On the far right the cornerstone of white identity is belief in an ineluctable, unalterable racialized difference between whites and nonwhites. Traditionally, this belief has been biologically grounded, and in many respects it remains so today. But a distinct modernizing tendency exists on the far right as well. It is thus necessary to distinguish between explicitly fascist and "neofascist" currents within the far right racial project.

Explicitly fascist elements on the far right can be identified by two features: their frank belief in the biological superiority of whites over nonwhites (and Jews), and their insurrectionary pos-ture vis-a-vis the state. Although their accounts of the nature and sources of racial difference vary, often relying on religious doctrine, as in the case of the so-called "Christian Identity" movement, which identifies blacks and Jews as "mud people" whose origins are different from those of "Aryans," a biologistic element is always present. Explicitly fascist groups on the far right openly admire Nazi race-thinking, fantasize about racial genocide, and dream of establishing an all-white North American nation, or, failing that, seceding from the United States to establish such a na-tion, possibly in the Northwest (Ridgeway, 1990; Diamond, 1995; Novick, 1995; Southern Poverty Law Center, 1995).

While acts of racial and anti-Semitic terror continue and even increase, and the elaboration of fascist doctrine continues as well, significant modernizing currents have appeared on the far right in the past decade, leading me to assert that the "neofascist" dimension of the far right's racial project has gained considerable ground. These tendencies occupy an intermediate position be-tween the explicit fascism I have discussed and the more mainstream *new right* racial project which I address in the following section.

"Neofascists" generally have an ultraright provenance—a history of association with the KKK or Nazi groups—but they now actively seek to renovate the far right's traditions of white racial nationalism (Walters, 1987) and open advocacy of white supremacy. Largely as a result of the challenges posed by the 1960s, the far right, no less than other U.S. political currents, has been forced to rearticulate racial meanings, to reinterpret the content of "whiteness" and the politics that flows from it.

"Neofascism's" response has been political mobilization on racial grounds: if blacks have their organizations and movements, why shouldn't whites? The various activities of David Duke ex-emplify the new trend: his electoral campaigns, his attempts at student organization (for exam-ple his effort to create white student unions on college campuses), and his emblematic National Association for the Advancement of White People.[2]

In the far right's view, the state has been captured by "race mixers" and will have to be recap-tured by white racial nationalists in order to end the betrayal of "traditional values" that a

racially egalitarian and pluralistic national politics and culture would portend. Whether this reactionary objective could happen by peaceful means, or whether an armed insurrection would be
required to achieve it, remains a matter of dispute. Whether a rhetoric of absolute racial difference (*a la* the explicitly fascist currents on the far right) will be most effective in accomplishing
this, or whether a rhetoric of white victimization and white rights (*a la* the renovated neofascist
currents on the far right) will work better in the post–civil rights era, is also in question. But on
one objective both currents of the far right project are united: the United States must remain a
white man's country.

The New Right Racial Project

The contemporary new right has its origins in resistance to the black movement of the 1950s and
60s; with the Wallace campaign of 1968 (Edsalls, 1992), this resistance crystallized as a national,
electorally oriented, reactionary social movement. The Wallace campaign drew large numbers of
far right activists, Klansmen, and neo-Nazis into electoral politics for the first time in the postwar
period (Diamond, 1995; Ridgeway, 1990; Novick, 1995). Although his initial 1964 run for the
presidency had emphasized southern intransigence, states' rights, and explicit resistance to racial
reform in general, by 1968 Wallace had formulated a right-wing populism which went well beyond mere resistance to racial integration.

Like the far right, the new right seeks to present itself as the tribune of disenfranchised whites.
But the new right is distinguished—if not always sharply—from the far right by several factors.
First, rather than espouse racism and white supremacy, it prefers to present these themes subtextually: the familiar "code-word" phenomenon. Second, it wholeheartedly embraces mainstream
political activity, rather than abjuring it or looking at it suspiciously. Third, it can accept a measure
of nonwhite social and political participation, and even membership (think of Alan Keyes, for instance), so long as this is pursued on a "color-blind" basis and adheres to the rest of the authoritarian, nationalist formula. For the far right in general, "color-blindness" is race mixing and
therefore *verboten*. For the new right, suitably authoritarian versions of "color-blindness" are fine.

The new right diverges from neoconservatism (discussed below) in its willingness to practice
racial politics subtextually, through coding, manipulation of racial fears, etc. *De facto*, it recognizes the persistence of racial difference in U.S. society. The new right understands perfectly well
that its mass base is white, and that its political success depends on its ability to interpret white
identity in positive political terms. Precisely because of its willingness to exploit racial fears and
employ racially manipulative practices, the new right has been effective in achieving much of its
agenda for political and cultural reaction and social structural recomposition. These were crucial
to the new right's ability to provide a solid base of electoral and financial support for the Republican Party and the Reagan "revolution." The demagoguery employed by George Bush in the
1988 Willie Horton campaign ads, or by Pete Wilson or Phil Gramm in their contemporary attacks on immigrants and affirmative action, shows this strategy is far from exhausted. Neoconservatism has not, and could not, deliver such tangible political benefits, and in fact lacks an
equivalent mass political base.

The Neoconservative Racial Project

Neoconservative discourse seeks to *preserve* white advantages through denial of racial difference.
For neoconservatism, racial difference is something to be overcome, a blight on the core United
States values—both politically and culturally speaking—of universalism and individualism.

The doctrine of natural rights frames the liberal view of citizenship that in turn informs the neo-conservative vision of race. It is visible in the dissent of Justice Harlan from the *Plessy* decision in 1896. It is visible in "the American creed" which Myrdal claimed as a universalizing and individuating tendency that would ultimately sweep away irrational race prejudice and bigotry in the United States (Myrdal, 1962 [1944]). It is visible in the founding documents of U.S. neoconservatism, such as Glazer's essay on "the American ethnic pattern" (Glazer, 1978). And it is visible in the basic antistatism and laissez-faire attitude of neoconservatives, in regard to racial matters.

Besides its fundamental suspicion of racial difference, which it also seeks to equate (or reduce) to ethnicity (Omi and Winant, 1994, 14–23), the neoconservative project has cast doubt on the tractability of issues of racial equality, tending to argue that the state cannot ameliorate poverty through social policy, but in fact only exacerbates it (Williams, 1982). These positions indicate the substantial distance the neoconservative project has traveled from the liberal statism, and indeed the racial pluralism, with which its chief spokespeople once identified, for example in Glazer and Moynihan's *Beyond the Melting Pot* (1970 [1963] but see also Steinberg, 1995).[3]

The appeal to universalism—for example in terms of social policy or critical educational or literary standards—is far more subtle than open or coded appeals to white racial fears, since it has far greater capacity to represent race in apparently egalitarian and democratic terms. Indeed the very hallmark of the neoconservative argument has been that, beyond the proscription of explicit racial discrimination, every invocation of racial significance manifests "race-thinking," and is thus suspect:

> In the phrase reiterated again and again in the Civil Rights Act of 1964, no distinction was to be made in the right to vote, in the provision of public services, the right to public education, on the ground of "race, color, religion, or national origin." Paradoxically, we then began an extensive effort to record the race, color and (some) national origins of just about every student and employee and recipient of government benefits or services in the nation. . . . This monumental restructuring of public policy . . . , it is argued by Federal administrators and courts, is required to enforce the laws against discrimination. . . . It is a transitional period, they say, to that condition called for in the Constitution and the laws, when no account at all is to be taken of race, color and national origin. But others see it as a direct contradiction of the Constitution and the laws, and of the consensus that emerged after long struggle in the middle 1960s. (Glazer, 1978, p. 4)

Yet a refusal to engage in "race-thinking" amounts to a defense of the racial *status quo*, in which systematic racial inequality and, yes, discrimination as well, are omnipresent.[4]

Thus the neoconservative perspective is not as inclusionary as it superficially appears. Indeed, neoconservatism suffers from *bad faith*. It may serve for some as a rationalizing formula, a lament about the complexities of a social world in which the traditional verities, and indeed the traditional speakers, writers, and political actors, have come under challenge from a host of "others," but as soon as it advances beyond critique to proposals for action its pious professions of universality and liberality are quickly replaced by advocacy of laissez-faire social policies, and hence of the status quo.

The Neoliberal Racial Project

Neoliberal discourse seeks to *limit* white advantages through denial of racial difference. The overlap with neoconservatism is, of course, hardly accidental. Yet there are significant differences in political orientation between the two projects.

Neoliberalism recognizes the cross-cutting and competitive dynamics of race- and class-based forms of subordination in the postindustrial, post–civil rights era. It seeks systematically to narrow the differences which divide working- and middle-class people as a strategy for improving the "life-chances" of minorities, who are disproportionately poor. It thus attempts to appeal to whites with arguments about the medium- and long-term consequences upon their living standards of downward mobility and greater impoverishment of nonwhites. The neoliberal racial project can thus be described as social democratic, focused on social structure (as opposed to cultural representation *a la* the various right-wing racial projects), and somewhat class reductionist in its approach to race.

The most effective, as well as controversial, spokesperson for the neoliberal racial project has undoubtedly been William Julius Wilson. In a series of prominent scholarly works and political interventions, Wilson has argued for the use of class-based criteria (and consequently, against the use of racial logics) in formulating social policy aimed at achieving greater substantive equality in U.S. society. He has contended that this reorientation of social policy priorities is both better suited to the contemporary dynamics of capitalist development, and more politically strategic in ways that explicit, racially oriented policies are not.

A similar argument has been proposed by Michael Lind, who argues that "the American elites that subsidize and staff both the Republican and the Democratic parties have steadfastly waged a generation-long class war against the middle and working classes" (Lind, 1995a, p. 35) using race, as well as other divisions, to achieve unprecedented levels of power and concentrated wealth.

Both Wilson and Lind call for a nationalism of the left, a populist alliance of the have-nots, regardless of race, against the haves. Lind's version is perhaps more radical and certainly more explicitly nationalist: he proposes specific measures to tax corporate flight, restrict immigration, and establish a "common high-wage trading bloc." Like Wilson, he proposes to eliminate affirmative action, which he would replace with a

transracial America . . . , [where] a color-blind, gender neutral regime of individual rights would be combined with government activism promoting a high degree of substantive social and economic equality. (Lind, 1995b, p. 15)

The neoliberal project actively promotes a pragmatic vision of greater substantive equality, linking class and race, and arguing for the necessity of transracial coalition politics. These themes seem to me worthy of support, and receive more discussion below in this essay's concluding section.

For the present I wish simply to register some of my unease with the neoliberal project in respect to its treatment of race. Most specifically, I question the argument that race-specific policies should receive less attention in a progressive political agenda (Wilson, 1987, 10–12). Despite protestations that the neoliberal approach is more hardheaded, more willing to face up to the difficult questions of the supposed "rise of social pathologies in the ghetto," it is also noteworthy that the neoliberal project tends to deny, sometimes explicitly and sometimes implicitly, the ongoing relevance of white supremacy to ghetto and barrio poverty. It tends to deemphasize the "dirty little secret" of continued racial hostility, segregation, and discrimination of all sorts.

Powerful as some of Wilson's, Lind's, and others' arguments are, they do not succeed in demonstrating the demise of racism or white privilege. They largely fail to recognize the ongoing racial dualism that prevails in the contemporary period, perceiving post–civil rights era conflicts between whites and racially defined minorities merely as strategic problems, and paying less attention to the deep-seated *structural* racial conflicts endemic to U.S. society.

This weakness is more noticeable in some areas than others, for example in respect to residential segregation or criminal justice issues, which simply cannot be understood as outcomes of "color-blind" capitalist development imperatives or deindustrialization, and are certainly not the product of affirmative action. Rather, the imperviousness of these problems to political reform testifies to the continuing viability of old-fashioned white supremacy, and to the competitive advantages whiteness still has to offer.

What drops out of the neoliberal project, then, is precisely the cultural and moral dimensions of white supremacy. The neoliberal project does not challenge whites on their willingness to receive a "psychological wage," which amounts to a tangible benefit acquired at the expense of nonwhites (Du Bois, 1977 [1935]; Roediger, 1991; Harris, 1993). Indeed, the neoliberal project does not challenge whites to abjure the *real* wage subsidies, the artificially low unemployment rates, or the host of other material benefits they receive by virtue of their whiteness (Lipsitz, 1995).

Nevertheless, the neoliberal project does undertake a crucial task: the construction of a transracial political agenda and the articulation of white and minority interests in a viable strategic perspective. This is something which has been missing from the U.S. political scene since the enactment of civil rights legislation thirty years ago.

The New Abolitionist Racial Project

The new abolitionist project stresses the "invention of whiteness" as a pivotal development in the rise of U.S. capitalism. Advocates of this view have begun a process of historical reinterpretation which aims to set race—or more properly, the gestation and evolution of white supremacy—at the center of U.S. politics and culture. Thus far, they have focused attention on a series of formative events and processes: the precedent of British colonial treatment of the Irish (Allen, 1994); the early, multiracial resistance to indentured servitude and quasislavery, which culminated in the defeat of Bacon's Rebellion in late-seventeenth-century Virginia; the self-identification of "free" workers as white in the antebellum North (Roediger, 1991; Ignatiev, 1995); and the construction of a "white republic" in the late nineteenth century (Saxton, 1990).

These studies, in some cases quite prodigious intellectual efforts, have had a significant impact on how we understand not only racial formation, but also class formation and the developing forms of popular culture in U.S. history. What they reveal above all is how crucial the construction of whiteness was, and remains, for the development and maintenance of capitalist class rule in the United States. Furthermore, these analyses also show how the meaning of whiteness, like that of race in general, has time and again proved flexible enough to adapt to shifts in the capitalist division of labor, to reform initiatives which extended democratic rights, and to changes in ideology and cultural representation.

The core message of the new abolitionist project is the imperative of repudiation of white identity and white privilege. But how is this rejection of whiteness to be accomplished? Both analytical and practical measures are envisioned. On the intellectual level, the new abolitionist project invites us to contemplate the emptiness, indeed vacuity, of the white category:

It is not merely that whiteness is oppressive and false; it is that whiteness is *nothing but* oppressive and false. . . . It is the empty and terrifying attempt to build an identity based on what one isn't and on whom one can hold back. (Roediger, 1994, 13; emphasis in original)

On the practical level, the argument goes, whites can become "race traitors" by rejecting their privilege, by refusing to collude with white supremacy. When you hear that racist joke, confront its teller. When you see the police harassing a nonwhite youth, try to intervene or at least bear witness.

It is easy to sympathize with this analysis, at least up to a point. The postwar black movement, which in the U.S. context at least served as the point of origin for all the "new social movements" and the much-reviled "politics of identity," taught the valuable lesson that politics went "all the way down." That is, meaningful efforts to achieve greater social justice could not tolerate a public/private or a collective/individual distinction. Trying to change society meant trying to change one's own life. The formula "the personal is political," commonly associated with feminism, had its early origins among the militants of the civil rights movement (Evans, 1980).

The problems come when deeper theoretical and practical problems are raised. Despite their explicit adherence to a "social construction" model of race (one which bears a significant resemblance to my own work with Michael Omi), theorists of the new abolitionist project do not take that insight as seriously as they should. They employ it chiefly to argue against biologistic conceptions of race, which is fine; but they fail to consider the complexities and rootedness of social construction, or as I would term it, racial formation. Is the social construction of whiteness so flimsy that it can be repudiated by a mere act of political will, or even by widespread and repeated acts aimed at rejecting white privilege? I think not; whiteness may not be a legitimate cultural identity in the sense of having a discrete, "positive" content, but it is certainly an overdetermined political and cultural identity nevertheless, having to do with socioeconomic status, religious affiliation, ideologies of individualism, opportunity, and citizenship, nationalism, etc. Like any other complex of beliefs and practices, "whiteness" is imbedded in a highly articulated social structure and system of significations; rather than trying to repudiate it, we shall have to rearticulate it.

That sounds like a daunting task, and of course it is, but it is not nearly as impossible as erasing whiteness altogether, as the new abolitionist project seeks to do. Furthermore, because whiteness is a relational concept, unintelligible without reference to nonwhiteness—note how this is true even of Roediger's formulation about "build[ing] an identity based on what one isn't"—that rearticulation (or reinterpretation, or deconstruction) of whiteness can begin relatively easily, in the messy present, with the recognition that whiteness *already* contains substantial nonwhite elements. Of course, that recognition is only the beginning of a large and arduous process of political labor, to which I return in the concluding section of this paper.

Notwithstanding these criticisms of the new abolitionist project, many of its insights remain vital to the process of reformulating, or synthesizing, a progressive approach to whiteness. Its attention is directed toward precisely the place where the neoliberal racial project is weak: the point at which white identity constitutes a crucial support to white supremacy, and a central obstacle to the achievement of substantive social equality and racial justice.

CONCLUDING NOTES: WHITENESS AND CONTEMPORARY U.S. POLITICS

In a situation of racial dualism, as Du Bois observed more than ninety years ago, race operates both to assign us and to deny us our identity. It both makes the social world intelligible, and simultaneously renders it opaque and mysterious. Not only does it allocate resources, power, and privilege; it also provides means for challenging that allocation. The contradictory character of race provides the context in which racial dualism—or the "color-line," as Du Bois designated it, has developed as "the problem of the twentieth century."

So what's new? Only that, as a result of incalculable human effort, suffering, and sacrifice, we now realize that these truths apply across the board. *Whites and whiteness can no longer be exempted* from the comprehensive racialization process that is the hallmark of U.S. history and social structure.

This is the present-day context for racial conflict and thus for U.S. politics in general, since race continues to play its designated role of crystallizing all the fundamental issues in U.S. society. As always, we articulate our anxieties in racial terms: wealth and poverty, crime and punishment, gender and sexuality, nationality and citizenship, culture and power, are all articulated in the United States primarily through race.

So, once again, what's new? It's the problematic of *whiteness* that has emerged as the principal source of anxiety and conflict in the postwar United States. Although this situation was anticipated or prefigured at earlier moments in the nation's past—for example, in the "hour of eugenics" (Barkan, 1992; Kevles, 1985; Gould, 1981)—it is far more complicated now than ever before, largely due to the present unavailability of biologistic forms of racism as a convenient rationale for white supremacy.[5]

Whiteness—visible whiteness, resurgent whiteness, whiteness as a color, whiteness as *difference*—this is what's new, and newly problematic, in contemporary U.S. politics. The reasons for this have already emerged in my discussion of the spectrum of racial projects and the particular representations these projects assign to whiteness. Most centrally, the problem of the meaning of whiteness appears as a direct consequence of the movement challenge posed in the 1960s to white supremacy. The battles of that period have not been resolved; they have not been won or lost; however battered and bruised, the demand for substantive racial equality and general social justice still lives. And while it lives, the strength of white supremacy is in doubt.

The racial projects of the right are clear efforts to resist the challenge to white supremacy posed by the movements of the 1960s and their contemporary inheritors. Each of these projects has a particular relationship to the white supremacist legacy, ranging from the far right's efforts to justify and solidify white entitlements, through the new right's attempts to utilize the white supremacist tradition for more immediate and expedient political ends, to the neoconservative project's quixotic quest to surgically separate the liberal democratic tradition from the racism that traditionally underwrote it. The biologistic racism of the far right, the expedient and subtextual racism of the new right, and the bad-faith antiracism of the neoconservatives have many differences from each other, but they have at least one thing in common. They all seek to maintain the long-standing associations between whiteness and U.S. political traditions, between whiteness and U.S. nationalism, between whiteness and universalism. They all seek in different ways to preserve white identity from the particularity, the difference, which the 1960s movement challenge assigned to it.

The racial projects of the left are the movements' successors (as is neoconservatism, in a somewhat perverse sense). Both the neoliberal racial project and the new abolitionist project seek to fulfill the movement's thwarted dreams of a genuinely (i.e., substantively) egalitarian society, one in which significant redistribution of wealth and power has taken place, and race no longer serves as the most significant marker between winners and losers, haves and have nots, powerful and powerless. Although they diverge significantly—since the neoliberals seek to accomplish their ends through a conscious diminution of the significance of race, and the new abolitionists hope to achieve similar ends through a conscious reemphasizing of the importance of race—they also have one very important thing in common. They both seek to rupture the barrier between whites and racially defined minorities, the obstacle which prevents joint political action. They both seek to associate whites and nonwhites, to reinterpret the meaning of whiteness in such a way that it no longer has the power to impede class alliances.

Although the differences and indeed the hostility—between the neoliberal and new abolitionist projects, between the reform-oriented and radical conceptions of whiteness—are quite severe, it is vital that adherents of these two progressive racial projects recognize that they each hold part of the key to challenging white supremacy in the contemporary United States, and that their counterpart project holds the other part of the key. Neoliberals rightfully argue that a pragmatic approach to transracial politics is vital if the momentum of racial reaction is to be halted or reversed. New abolitionists properly emphasize challenging the ongoing commitment to white supremacy on the part of many whites.

Both of these positions need to draw on each other, not only in strategic terms, but in theoretical ones as well. The recognition that racial identities—*all* racial identities, including whiteness—have become implacably dualistic, could be far more liberating on the left than it has thus far been. For neoliberals, it could permit and indeed justify an acceptance of race-consciousness and even nationalism among racially defined minorities as a necessary but partial response to disenfranchisement, disempowerment, and superexploitation. There is no inherent reason why such a political position could not coexist with a strategic awareness of the need for strong, class-conscious, transracial coalitions. We have seen many such examples in the past: in the antislavery movement, the communist movement of the 1930s (Kelley, 1994), and in the 1988 presidential bid of Jesse Jackson, to name but a few. This is not to say that all would be peace and harmony if such alliances could come more permanently into being. But there is no excuse for not attempting to find the pragmatic "common ground" necessary to create them.

New abolitionists could also benefit from a recognition that on a pragmatic basis, whites can ally with racially defined minorities without renouncing their whiteness. If they truly agree that race is a socially constructed concept, as they claim, new abolitionists should also be able to recognize that racial identities are not either-or matters, not closed concepts that must be upheld in a reactionary fashion or disavowed in a comprehensive act of renunciation. To use a postmodern language I dislike: racial identities are deeply "hybridized"; they are not "sutured," but remain open to rearticulation. "To be white in America is to be very black. If you don't know how black you are, you don't know how American you are" (Thompson, 1995, 429).

REFERENCES

Allen, Theodore W., *The Invention of the White Race: Racial Oppression and Social Control*, Vol. 1 (New York: Verso, 1994).

Barkan, Elazar, *The Retreat of Scientific Racism: Changing Concepts of Race in Britain and the U.S. Between the World Wars* (New York: Cambridge University Press, 1992).

Butler, John S., *Inequality in the Military: The Black Experience* (Saratoga, CA: Century Twenty One, 1980).

Butterfield, Fox, "More Blacks in Their 20's Have Trouble With the Law," *New York Times* (Oct. 5, 1995).

Chalmers, David A. *Hooded Americanism: The History of the Ku Klux Klan* (New York: Franklin Watts, 1981).

D'Souza, Dinesh, *The End of Racism* (New York: Free Press, 1995).

Diamond, Sara, *Roads to Dominion: Right-Wing Movements and Political Power in the United States* (New York: Guilford, 1995).

Du Bois, W. E. B., *Black Reconstruction in America: An Essay Toward a History of the Part Which Black Folk Played in the Attempt to Reconstruct Democracy in America, 1860–1880* (New York: Atheneum, 1977 [1935]).

Duster, Troy, *Backdoor to Eugenics* (New York: Routledge, 1990).

Edsall, Thomas Byrne, with Mary Edsall, *Chain Reaction: The Impact of Race, Rights, and Taxes on American Politics*, rev. ed. (New York: Norton, 1992).

Evans, Sara, *Personal Politics* (New York: Random House, 1980).

Gallagher, Charles, "White Reconstruction in the University," *Socialist Review* 94, 1–2 (1995).

Glazer, Nathan, *Affirmative Discrimination: Ethnic Inequality and Public Policy* (New York: Basic, 1975).

Glazer, Nathan, and Daniel P. Moynihan, *Beyond the Melting Pot*, 2nd ed. (Cambridge: MIT Press, 1970 [1963]).

Gordon, David, "6% Unemployment Ain't Natural," in *Social Research* vol. 54, no. 2 (Summer 1987).

Gould, Stephen J., *The Mismeasure of Man* (New York: W. W. Norton, 1981).

Greenberg, Stanley B., *Report on Democratic Defection, Report Prepared for the Michigan House Democratic Campaign Committee* (Washington, D.C.: The Analysis Group, 1985).

Harding, Sandra, *The Science Question in Feminism* (Ithaca: Cornell University Press, 1987).

Harris, Cheryl, "Whiteness as Property," *Harvard Law Review* 106 (1993).

Herrnstein, Richard, and Charles Murray, *The Bell Curve: Intelligence and Class Structure in American Life* (New York: Free Press, 1994).

Ignatiev, Noel, *How the Irish Became White: Irish-Americans and African-Americans in Nineteenth Century Philadelphia* (New York: Verso, 1995).

Jaynes, Gerald D., and Robin M. Williams Jr., *A Common Destiny: Blacks and American Society* (Washington, D.C.: National Academy Press, 1989).

Johnson, Lyndon B., "To Secure These Rights," in Lee Rainwater and William Yancey, eds., *The Moynihan Report and the Politics of Controversy* (Cambridge: MIT Press, 1967).

Kelley, Robin D. G., *Race Rebels: Culture, Politics, and the Black Working Class* (New York: Free Press, 1994).

Kevles, Daniel J., *In the Name of Eugenics: Genetics and the Uses of Human Heredity* (New York: Knopf, 1985).

Langer, Elinor, "The American Neo-Nazi Movement Today," *The Nation* (July 16/23, 1990).

Lind, Michael, "To Have and Have Not: Notes on the Progress of the American Class War," *Harper's* (June 1995a).

Lind, Michael, *The Next American Nation: The New Nationalism and the Fourth American Revolution* (New York: Free Press, 1995b).

Lipsitz, George, "The Possessive Investment in Whiteness," *American Quarterly* vol. 47, no. 3 (September 1995).

Massey, Douglas S., and Nancy A. Denton, *American Apartheid* (Cambridge: Harvard University Press, 1993).

Moskos, Charles, *Soldiers and Sociology* (Alexandria: U.S. Army Research Institute for the Behavioral and Social Sciences, 1988).

Myrdal, Gunnar, *An American Dilemma: The Negro Problem and Modern Democracy*, Twentieth Anniversary Edition (New York, Harper and Row, 1962).

Neckerman, Katherine, and Joleen Kirschenman, "Hiring Strategies, Racial Bias, and Inner-City Workers," *Social Problems* vol. 38, no. 4 (November 1991).

Novick, Michael, *White Lies, White Power: The Fight Against White Supremacy and Reactionary Violence* (Monroe, ME: Common Courage, 1995).

Omi, Michael, and Howard Winant, "On the Theoretical Concept of Race," in Cameron McCarthy and Warren Critchlow, eds., *Race, Identity, and Representation in Education* (New York: Routledge, 1993).

Omi, Michael, and Howard Winant, *Racial Formation in the United States: From the 1960s to the 1990s*, 2nd ed. (New York: Routledge, 1994).

Quadagno, Jill, *The Color of Welfare: How Racism Undermined the War on Poverty* (New York: Oxford University Press, 1994).

Ridgeway, James, *Blood in the Face: The Ku Klux Klan, Aryan Nations, Skinheads, and the Rise of a New White Culture* (New York: Thunder's Mouth, 1990).

Roediger, David R., *The Wages of Whiteness: Race and the Making of the American Working Class* (New York: Verso, 1991).

Saxton, Alexander, *The Rise and Fall of the White Republic: Class Politics and Mass Culture in Nineteenth-Century America* (New York: Verso, 1990).

Southern Poverty Law Center, "Aryan World Congress Focuses on Militias and an Expected Revolution," *Klanwatch Intelligence Report* 79 (August 1995); available from Klanwatch Project, PO Box 548, Montgomery, AL 36101–0548.

Steinberg, Stephen, *Turning Back: The Retreat from Racial Justice in American Thought and Policy* (Boston: Beacon, 1995).

Thompson, Robert Farris, "The Kongo Atlantic Tradition," cited in Shelley Fisher Fishkin, "Interrogating 'Whiteness,' Complicating 'Blackness,' Remapping American Culture," in *American Quarterly* vol. 47, no. 3 (September 1995).

Walters, Ronald, "White Racial Nationalism in the United States," *Without Prejudice* I, 1 (Fall 1987).

Williams, Walter, *The State Against Blacks* (New York: McGraw-Hill, 1982).

Wilson, William Julius, *The Truly Disadvantaged: The Inner City, the Underclass, and Public Policy* (Chicago: University of Chicago Press, 1987).

Winant, Howard, *Racial Conditions: Politics, Theory, Comparisons* (Minneapolis: University of Minnesota Press, 1994).

NOTES

*Michael Omi and I conceived this paper together. Thanks, brother, as always. Comments from Chip Gallagher, Magali Larson, David Roediger, and Mun Wong are also gratefully acknowledged.

1. The obvious reference in these remarks is to Myrdal's framework (Myrdal, 1962 [1944]). Without endorsing his entire perspective, which I think proceeds in an idealistic fashion, it is possible to affirm the vitality of Myrdal's central premise: that democratic principles remain incompatible with racial subordination.
2. A thoughtful discussion of Duke may be found in Langer, 1990, 94–98. Already in the 1970s Duke had begun the renovation of his Klan ideology:

> We see [the Ku Klux Klan] as a social movement in the traditional sense. The same way that the Sons of Liberty were. The same way the Communist Party was. . . . In other words, a movement for social change and not just a fraternity for people to get together and have fun or salute the past. (quoted in Chalmers, 1981, 10)

3. Even in the later *Affirmative Discrimination*, Glazer affirms as one of the three formative principles of "the American ethnic pattern" the idea that ". . . no group . . . would be required to give up its group character and distinctiveness as the price of full entry into the American society and polity" (Glazer 1978, 5). Yet it is questionable how much this pluralism can be sustained without a recognition of racial difference, since race is at a minimum an important dimension of political mobilization and cultural distinctiveness.
4. Without entering too far into the question of what constitutes "objective" racial inequality it must be recognized that on such issues as housing (Massey and Denton, 1993), employment discrimination (Kirschenman and Neckerman, 1991), criminal justice (Butterfield, 1995), welfare (Quadagno, 1994), or unemployment, the evidence is rather unambiguous. If anything the data minimize inequality. Take unemployment: here official statistics neglect the informal economy, which is a primary source of employment and locus of discrimination against racially defined minority workers. Unemployment data measure only "active" job seekers, not those who have been without (formal) jobs for a long time or those who have become discouraged in their job search. These constructions of the data on unemployment have a political subtext: the reduction of the numerator on the monthly BLS report obviously improves the image of the party in

power (Gordon, 1987). There are also ample grounds on which to question the racial logic of unemployment figures, which rely on census categories (Omi and Winant, 1994, 3–4, 82).

5. Professor Troy Duster has raised important questions about my argument (with Michael Omi) that biologistic racism has been discredited, or at least relegated to a secondary status in contemporary debates about race. In his *Backdoor to Eugenics* (Duster, 1990) he suggests that biologism is as susceptible to rearticulation as any other ideological dimension of racism. Additional evidence for this argument is provided by the appearance of *The Bell Curve* (Herrnstein and Murray, 1994). Omi and I take the view that, while scientific grounds for racism are no more dead than religious ones, the biologistic argument cannot regain the cachet it possessed in the nineteenth and early twentieth centuries; the political dimensions of race will persevere as its predominant determinants (Omi and Winant, 1994; Omi and Winant, 1993).

White Performances: Academic Life

Witnessing Whiteness

Michelle Fine

Michelle Fine is Professor of Psychology at the City University of New York Graduate Center and the Senior Consultant at the Philadelphia Schools Collaborative. Her recent publications include *Chartering Urban School Reform: Reflections on Public High Schools in the Midst of Change* (1994), *Beyond Silenced Voices: Class, Race and Gender in American Schools* (with Lois Weis, 1992), *Disruptive Voices: The Transgressive Possibilities of Feminist Research* (1992), and *Framing Dropouts: Notes on the Politics of an Urban High School* (1991). She has provided courtroom expert testimony for cases including the Anthony T. Lee, et al. and the United States of America vs Macon County Board of Education; Shannon Richey Faulkner and the United States of America vs James E. Jones, et al. for The Citadel, The Military College of South Carolina; Ulcena vs Babylon School District, High School and Babylon School Board; and the Board of Education of the Borough of Englewood Cliffs vs Board of Education of the City of Englewood vs Board of Education of the Borough of Tenafly. In addition, she works nationally as a consultant to parents' groups, community groups, and teacher unions on issues of school reform. She was recently awarded the Janet Helms Distinguished Scholar Award 1994.

What if we took the position that racial inequities were not primarily attributable to individual acts of discrimination targeted against persons of color, but increasingly to acts of cumulative privileging quietly loaded up on whites? That is, what if by keeping our eyes on those who gather disadvantage, we have not noticed white folks, varied by class and gender, nevertheless stuffing their academic and social pickup trucks with goodies otherwise not as readily available to people of color?

It is to this question of "witnessing whiteness" that I chose to turn in this essay. With the raw nerve of reflection and the need for better racial thinking, I avert my gaze from the "inequities" produced through "colors" (where my work has lingered for so long) and turn, instead, to the "merit" that accumulates within the hue of "whiteness." While Toni Morrison (1992), Ruth Frankenburg (1993), Christine Sleeter (1993), Michael Novick (1995), and many others have argued that whiteness and "other colors" must be recognized in their rainbowed interdependence, if not in their parasitic webbing, I find myself trying to understand how whiteness accrues privilege and status; gets itself surrounded by protective pillows of resources and/or benefits of the doubt; how whiteness repels gossip and voyeurism and instead demands dignity.[1]

This essay focuses on three sites of research in which I have had the opportunity to witness not only the ways in which "people of color" accumulate "deficits," but the ways in which white adolescents and adults accumulate "benefits." My work has moved toward institutional analyses because I worry that those of us interested in qualitative inquiry and critical "race" theory have focused fetishistically on those who endure discrimination. By so doing we have been unable/

58

unwilling to analyze how those who inherit privilege do so. As such, we have camouflaged the intricate institutional webbing that connects "whiteness" and "other colors."

So, this essay tries to chart a theoretical argument about the institutional processes by which "whiteness" is today produced as advantage through schools and the economy. Historically, in both psychology and education, whiteness has remained both unmarked and unstudied. More recently, by some scholars, it has been elevated to the status of "independent variable," one that scientists use to predict other outcomes. In this essay I want to reverse conceptually this notion by asserting that institutions work by producing "whiteness" as merit/advantage within elites and, more elusively, within the working class/poor. Four theoretical assumptions arrange my thinking.

First, as I've said, whiteness, like all "colors," is being manufactured, in part, through institutional arrangements. This is particularly the case in institutions designed "as if" hierarchy, stratification, and scarcity were inevitable. Schools and work, for example, do not merely *manage* race; they *create* and *enforce* racial meanings. Second, in such institutions, whiteness is actually *coproduced* with other colors, usually alongside blackness, in symbiotic relation. Where whiteness grows as a seemingly "natural" proxy for quality, merit, and advantage, "color" disintegrates to embody deficit or "lack." Third, whiteness and "color" are therefore not merely created in parallel, but are fundamentally relational and need to be studied as a system; they might, in statistical terms, be considered "nested" rather than coherent or independent variables. Fourth, the institutional design of whiteness, like the production of all colors, creates an organizational *discourse* of race and a personal *embodiment* of race, affecting perceptions of Self and Others, producing both individuals' sense of racial "identities" and collective experiences of racial "tensions," even coalitions. Once this process is sufficiently institutionalized and embodied, the observer, that is, the scholar, can easily miss the institutional choreography which has produced a stratified rainbow of colors. What remains visible are the miraculous ways in which quality seems to rise to the glistening white top.

To understand this production, I import Pierre Bourdieu's (1991) writings, in which he invokes the word *institution*:

> The act of institution is an act of magic (p. 119). . . . An act of communication, but of a particular kind: it signifies to someone what his identity is, but in a way that both expresses it to him and imposes it on him by expressing it in front of everyone and thus informing him in an authoritative manner of what he is and what he must be (p. 121). This is also one of the functions of the act of institution: to discourage permanently any attempt to cross the line, to transgress, desert, or quit. (p. 336)

This essay is a plea to re-search institutions: to notice, to remove the white glaucoma that has ruined scholarly vision, as we lift up the school and work-related dynamics that make whites and other racial groups seem so separable, and so relentlessly rank ordered.

SCENE ONE, "WHITE LIES"

The scene is Wedowee, Alabama, the site where the principal, Hulond Humphries, was charged in 1994 with racial harassment. My involvement emerges because I am among those representing the United States Justice Department; I am meeting with students at Randolph County High School (RCHS). Callie is a young white woman. She's a junior at RCHS: "My mother asked for someone, you know, the principal, to watch me and find out if I'm dating a black boy. So Mr. Humphries called me in and he told me if I kept on dating John I wouldn't be able to get any white boys. No one else would go out with me. We could have a child who's not very smart. And if I go to a family reunion, I may be the only white woman there and no one's going to even talk to me. Then I'd be an outcast." Trina, an African American eleventh grader jumps in. "He called us all into the auditorium after their talk and asked how many of us are going to the prom with someone of the other race. Lots of us raised our hands. Then he asked Rovanda [a biracial student at the school], 'Rovanda, who you taking to the prom?' And Rovanda said, 'I'm taking Chris,' her white boyfriend. And he just looked up in the bleachers, and he said, 'I won't have it. No interracial dating in my school.' And Rovanda said, 'Who would you like me to take to the prom?' He said, 'You were a mistake, and we don't want other mistakes like you.'" Tasha joined in, "He said he was canceling the prom." King said, "When he called Rovanda a mistake, it was like he took an axe and cut through the heart of a tree. The heart of our school."

I opened with questions about tracking at the high school. This high school has an "advanced" and a "standard" track. Knowing something about the (unfortunately predictable) racial splitting by track, I asked the students in the group—white students and African American students—what track are you in? The white kids raised their hand when I said "advanced"; then the African American kids raised their hands when I said "standard." I later learned how profoundly the aggregate numbers, over time, bore out that simple hand-raising exercise.

It's important to know that at this school, like at many schools, students have what is considered a race-neutral "choice" about which track they opt into. And they "chose" by race. White racism here—and elsewhere—is so thoroughly institutionalized and embodied that young people, when given an opportunity, "choose" their "place," and seemingly with little protest. I asked "Why did you choose the standard track? The standard track doesn't allow you to attend a four-year college like University of Alabama. You don't take enough math or science to make it into a four-year college." African American students offered a litany of painful, if predictable, responses. "Because I was scared." "Because we thought it [advanced] was too hard." "Because my friends were in the standard track." When Tigray mumbled, "Because maybe they are smarter than we are," Callie, the young white woman who opened the scene, responded, "That's the scam they pull on you. There are plenty of dumb white kids in my classes, but they would never go to the standard track." I pressed Callie, "What would happen if you told your guidance counselor you wanted to be in a standard track?" She laughed, "She'd say, 'Callie, what are you talking about? You're not going into the standard track, you're going to college.'" Indeed in this "integrated" school the advanced track is almost all white; no varsity cheerleader has ever been Black; an African American boy who ran for President of the Student Council talks of harassment from the principal; almost all the faculty were white. Every strata of school life—academics, social relations, postsecondary opportunities, and sexuality—layered by race. Visually apparent, and vigilantly enforced (see Oakes, 1980; Rosenbaum, 1976).

Wanting to understand the principal's motive for his public performance of racializing, I met with Hulond Humphries. We met in the basement of the school district building. Clear that I represented the team for the Justice Department, I probed with pen in hand, "Why did you say what you said about the prom? You must have known it would cause the kind of hysteria that it did." To which he said, "It's not that I have anything against interracial dating. . . . It's just that those black boys really want our white girls." He continued, "Now with that feminism, Black girls are wanting our white boys." Clear lines. Blacks as sexual predators. Whites as prey. Bourdieu's verb spreads to sexuality.

The night before I went to the school, I had the privilege of visiting the African Zion Church just outside of town. I sat, stood, sang for hours, ecstatic and anxious to be part of chanting, singing, praying, preaching, and testifying about what it was like to be a student, a parent, a community member, Black, within reach of those schools. Then the most elder Reverend booms, "Every ten years or so God tests the racial waters of the United States. We are privileged that this year He chose Wedowee for His test. And what is our job? To *love* those people to death."

That was the racial tapestry of schooling in Wedowee, Alabama; the fabric in which young whites and African American children's lives were intimately interwoven. What is striking is how much the students, white and black, knew their place and rarely dared to protest aloud. White students' place was just "north" of black students'. Black students' place was just below white students'. In this small working-class town, southern affect and congeniality allowed little anger to seep explicitly into cross-racial interactions. The Black church was the "safe space," the emotional safety valve, the place to put and contain anger, the "sanity check" on Sunday evening which would allow all to return to the perverse, hostile, if sometimes congenial stratification that many explained constitutes community life Monday through Friday.

Discursively and materially whiteness is here produced and maintained through the withholding of opportunity from, and the denigration of that which is Black. The prom was simply a metaphor for all the attempts to separate and sanitize white from black, to insure privilege. But being *white*, in and of itself, in troubled economic times, today guarantees little in Alabama. At least for these poor and working-class families. Unemployment and poverty rates run high across racial groups. Therefore—and this is my major point—this racial formation was filled with parasitic interdependence such that *whites needed Blacks in order to become privileged*. African American students *were* getting less than white students. However, as true, *nobody* was getting a very rigorous academic education. No one was taking math courses more difficult than Advanced Algebra, and still none of the African American students had been enrolled even at this level. One might cynically argue that the white students were "lucky" to have the Black students so they could imagine themselves enjoying any "privilege." The cleansing of whiteness—in class tracks, dating, cheerleading, and college opportunities—was the job of the institution.

Two theoretical insights warrant attention. One is that these poor and working-class racial identities and concomitant "racial tensions," perhaps even "desires," were invented and sustained through privilege and power defined and insured by withholding. Whiteness was produced *through* the exclusion and denial of opportunity of people to color. In other words, giving Blacks access to white opportunities would threaten to stain, indeed blacken, that which is white. Access is a threat to whiteness when whiteness requires the exportation (and denigration) of color.

Second, this case points up evidence of how institutional leadership and seemingly race-neutral policies/practices work to insure white privilege. The leader of this institution, Hulond Humphries, articulated publicly what he fundamentally believed about race, capacity, sexuality, and who deserves to be educated. In a racially hostile environment, it's not only very hard for biracial and African Americans to participate with full heart and mind. As devastating, in such environments, *white students* develop a profoundly false sense of superiority premised almost entirely on denigration which requires opposition to sustain the racial hierarchy. Opposition and denigration became a fix, a steroid to white identity. This public school, in its leadership, policies, and daily practices, did little to interrupt—and much to produce—this steroid. All in the name of creating and maintaining merit and "quality." As the work of Sam Gaertner et al. (1995) reveals, we may be witnessing today a reassertion of prowhite policies and practices rather than (or in addition to) actively hostile discrimination targeted at people of color. If this is the case, that whiteness is "catching" privilege, then where we look for evidence of discrimination and prejudice will have to move to the cumulative benefits of being white, rather than the (exclusive) tracking of blatant racism against, in this case, Blacks. Documenting racism *against*, as if separable from racism *for*, may be a diversionary strategy by which our eyes have been averted from the real prize.

SCENE TWO: WHITING OUT SOCIAL CRITIQUE

In Wedowee, denigration by race among the poor and working class was publicly institutional-ized and personally internalized. And critique was hard to find. For Scene Two we head North to track an institution in which race and gender critique was once voiced vociferously, among the privileged, but it "disappeared" over time. This is a story of the University of Pennsylvania's Law School in which we (Lani Guinier, Michelle Fine, Jane Balin, Ann Bartow, and Deborah Satchel, 1994) studied the gender and race dynamics percolating within an elite law school. Again we wit-ness how white rises to the top through seemingly neutral policies and practices.

A first-year black woman law student offers: "I think it is still that people don't understand why African Americans are still struggling, or why we're struggling. To me it's incredible! It's like a blindness! And I listen to some of the comments in class, and I realize that I'm just coming from an entirely different world. From the perspective of most people, I'm just more aware of my his-tory and law and things as it relates to black people. And I think that part of it has to do to with the fact that white students think they're going to be a lawyer. They don't have to think about who they're going to represent, or that they have to represent all black people."

This is a study in which we surveyed first, second, and third year law students' attitudes, be-liefs, and experiences, and then we examined three cohorts of academic performance in a school in which dropouts are remarkably rare. We conducted individual and group interviews with stu-dents across the law school, men and women, and students of all colors. In the condensed version of the findings, the attitudinal data reveal vast initial differences in political perspective, levels of alienation, and visions for the future both by race and gender. But as bold as they were, these sta-tistically significant initial differences disappeared over time. They were barely discernable by graduation year. By year three, most law students saw the school, social justice, and the world as white males did in year one.

The sad tale is that social critique by race/gender doesn't age very well within educational in-stitutions. It gets snuffed out so that over time such concerns either turn inward or they get muf-fled. Through the process of what might be called "professional socialization," the young adults we studied grew anesthetized to things that they once, in the beginnings of their school career, considered outrageous (e.g., generic "he," adversarial method, differential participation by gen-der, inaccessible faculty, sexist jokes). Among first-year women, for instance, 25 percent were in-terested in Public Interest Law compared to 7 percent of the men. Yet by year three only 8 percent of women and 7 percent of men expressed an interest in Public Interest law. First-year women re-ported concerns with the issues of social justice and social problems, and even dismay at the use of the generic "he." By year three their political attitudes were akin to the white men's. Not that the men got more progressive. The women had "become gentlemen," as one professor encour-aged them to do.

Unlike Wedowee, where critique was ghettoized on Sunday and stratification embodied Mon-day through Friday, here critique saw light of day for year one of law school and then it turned inward, against self, obvious in lowered grades, worsened mental health, and conservatized poli-tics for white women, and women and men of color.

First-year black female: "I don't know, maybe I'm just paranoid or something. And I wonder how people are perceiving that, [they must be] thinking about it all the time. I get the sense that maybe people won't listen to me as much as if I were a white person saying it. And then people, when they do listen to me, they say, 'well of course she's going to say that, because she's thinking of her own self-interest.' " White people speak for the common good, and people of color speak for self-interest.

First-year Latino male: "It's one of the pressures, the initial pressures of being in a very social environment, like in law school. Feeling that what you contribute is not being weighed as much as everybody else's contribution because someone is attaching something else to what you're saying. It's very disconcerting for me, and it makes me kind of zone out of the whole process." Remember that, zoning out when you feel like no one's paying attention to what you're saying.

First-year black male: "Whenever a minority issue comes up I feel like I'm expected to say something. If I don't say something I'm shunning my race, and if I do say something nobody listens. So you're battling with both sides of the coin. And then if you come forth and you say something, people think they're complimenting you and they say, 'Wow! That's really a . . . statement!' 'That was really awesome!' 'That was really intelligent!' [laughter] As if I was the first person to have ever spoken in the place. And they had no idea that I had an education. I find it very disturbing, and you have to deal with it and get along with the rest of the class."

At Penn, like in Wedowee, institution-based racial/gendered sedimentation grew into "merit" over time. What began in year one as prominent race/gender differences in critical perspective grew silenced, converted into an institutional story of gendered/racial success and failure. By year three, these differences just looked like "merit" and its absence, not gender or race. Thus, when we study school-based "success" and "failure" as though they were *inherently individualistic* and therefore only *coincidentally* white (or not) and male (or not), we *deinstitutionalize* pathways toward success and failure, and we deny the racial and gendered scaffolding of academic hierarchies.

By the end of the law school experience, year three students of color and white women at Penn feel and look inadequate (see Guinier et al. for detailed analysis of the data). With their critique whited out and their progressive politics forced underground, their mental health falters and their achievement torpedoes. Over time, it seemed as though race and gender were simply (naturally?) the best "predictors" of performance. Few wanted to talk about this. It was considered heretic (if obvious) to conclude, as we did, that race and gender stratifications were instead products of institutional hierarchy, alienation, and stratification.

Liberal notions of *legal access* to historically white male institutions grow suspect under the scrutiny of these data. Institutional transformation is as necessary as it is feared. Without it, institutions (and equity advocates) may be inviting white women and men and women of color into institutions that are ultimately damaging (if credentialing), while these institutions remain unchanged.

SCENE THREE: "THOSE ANGRY WHITE MEN"

With the generosity of a Spencer Foundation grant, Lois Weis and I, with our graduate students, have been conducting interviews in Jersey City and Buffalo with white, African American, Latino, and Asian young adults—age twenty-one to twenty-nine—poor and working class. In one slice of this project we have collected oral histories from white working-class men, narrating, in part, their current economic plight. By listening to these "angry white men" one can hear how global flight of capital and the consequential labor-market scarcity has sharpened and prolonged racial identities, tensions, and sedimentation. While relative to their fathers these white working-class men have taken a disproportional hit under the macroeconomic policies of Reagan and Bush, the flight of capital out of the Northeast and out of the country, and the dismantling of blue collar unions, these men, when interviewed, lay blame for their economic woes squarely at the feet of African American males. Not Republicans, not global capitalists, not elites. African American men—as in Wedowee— are discursively imported to buffer the pain, protest the loss, and still secure the artificial privilege of whiteness (see Aronowitz and DeFazio, 1993; Harrison, 1982; Reich, 1991). Occluded are the macrostructures that have forced white working-class men out of the labor market and into an obsession with Black men, affirmative action, and welfare. The fetish of Wedowee returns.

"What's your experience been like here as a white male?" Jim reports: "For the most part I haven't noticed. I think more or less the white male has become the new minority. At this point blacks, Hispanics, or women, it's just that with all these quotas, instead of hiring who's best for the job, you have to hire according to your quota system. Which is very wrong." "Do you have any sense of, like, social movements, like civil rights?" "Civil rights, as far as I'm concerned, is way out of proportion." "Talk to me more about that." "Well, granted, the African Americans were slaves. But that was over two hundred years ago. They were given their freedom. And as a country, I guess you could say, you know, we tried. Well, I think that all of us try. But most of us really tried to make things a little more equal. We tried to smooth over the rough spots. And you get some of those other ones, some of those militants who are now claiming that after all this time they're still not treated equal.

"This takes me to another subject where," states Paul, "where blacks, I don't have anything against blacks, whether you're white or black or yellow, whatever. I mean I have black friends. I talk to them and they agree, you know. They consider themselves, well, let me give you an example. Like there's white trash and there's good white people. Right? And so there's black trash and there's good black people. And it's the same way with any race. But then, as soon as they don't get the job, right away they yell, 'discrimination.' "

Mark is a white fireman who paints the Jersey City firehouse as a historically reliable site for civil service work. A noninvaded space, once secure for, and exclusive to, working-class white males. "It's just right now with these minority quotas . . . Affirmative Action is about to blow us all apart." This Fire Department, as is true for many fire departments, has been a significant venue for not-very-well-educated, working-class white males to secure job security and benefits. Mark is as certain that minorities have gained access to the fire department unfairly as he is sure that white men have gained access through merit.

What we hear from these young white males across Buffalo and Jersey City are innocent identities carved in opposition to people of color. In our interviews, you can't go for more than fifteen, twenty minutes with a white man before affirmative action put-downs or quotes about "welfare cheats" are inserted into the conversation. We hear whiteness, again, being produced and narrated in contrast to Blackness and in response to an alleged "scarcity of opportunities." This rhetoric relies upon fetishistic opposition and denigration. These men, indeed powerfully assaulted by economic shifts, systematically refuse to examine the large structural conditions that have betrayed them. Instead of looking critically up and out, and organizing along class lines, they focus narrowly and virulently on men (and women) of color. Despite the evidence of class-based politics, they adhere to whiteness as their badge of deservingness.

CONCLUSIONS

Psychologists and educators have contributed mightily to the resurrection and reification of racial stratification. I want to suggest that we turn a corner and move ourselves into the role of what Gramsci (1971) has called public intellectuals; engaged in raising up a set of questions about racial formation that haven't been raised, certainly not within these two fields. In times and sites of constructed "scarcity" such as schools and labor in current times, whiteness is being reconstituted as quality, deservingness, and merit. We have a social science that colludes in this fantasy when we need one that dismantles.

All of these scenes raise up important questions about the theories, methods, and ethics by which we study what Winant and Omi call racial formation; the relation of whiteness and other racial/ethnic groups. If we—that is, psychologists and educators—persist in our analyses "as if" races/ethnicities were distinct, separable, and independent rather than produced, coupled, and ranked, then we will continue to "discover" that white kids (or adults) "have it" (whatever it is) and students/workers of color don't. Or we will continue to agitate for everyone to have access to inhospitable institutions—when in fact many forms of institutional life are fundamentally constituted through racial, class, and gender sedimentation and exclusion.

I don't mean to be cynical at the end of this essay, only to agitate for social scientists to understand that *we* collude in the seeming mystery of (non) "mobility" and (un) "equal opportunity" when we presume that we can disaggregate quantitatively and qualitatively in our studies what "whites" have and what "people of color" don't, and then—as liberals— "pump into those students/workers of color" the characteristics we think that white students/workers have, and others need. If institutions refuse to dismantle the filters which limit opportunities for intellectual and economic work, such analyses (and interventions) may ultimately boomerang and punish victims.

Those of us engaged in qualitative work in schooling and the economy have important decisions to make. We have documented well inequities in academic outcomes, and the disparate treatment of students by race (Banks and Banks, 1989; Delpit, 1993; Schofield, 1989), class (Fine, 1991; Weis, 1990) and gender (Bilkin and Pollard, 1993). We have advocated interventions "for" those historically at the short end of the proverbial stick. We have argued for access to historically hostile institutions for students and workers long denied such promising opportunities.

The work reported in this chapter cautions, however, that we may have reached a moment in which theoretically, empirically, and strategically it's time to shift gears (or multiply). If institutions are organized such that being white (or male, or elite) buys protection and if this protection necessitates the institutional subversion of opportunities for persons of color in policies/practices that appear race-neutral, then liberal strategies for access are limited. By that I mean that those who have been historically excluded may disproportionately "fail" to perform "to standard." Some will drop out. A few will go nuts. A handful will survive as "the good ones." The institutional mantra of deficit and merit will triumph.

Today the cultural gaze of surveillance—whether it be a gaze of pity, blame, or liberal hope—falls on persons of color. Whether we consider the school in Wedowee or the students at Penn or listen to white working-class men angry about affirmative action, social surveillance, as Foucault foretold, falls squarely on those who are marked: Colored. In this paper I have argued that social scientists too have colluded in this myopia, legitimizing the fetish, turning away from opportunities to surveil "white," refusing, therefore, to notice the institutional choreography that renders whiteness meritocratic and other colors deficient.

With this paper I invite colleagues to consider not only the unfair disadvantages that accrue institutionally to darker hues, but the institutionalized pillows and profit that surround and grow embodied, by "white." Social scientists need interrupt the cultural gaze, not make a science of it.

REFERENCES

Aronowitz, S., and Difazio, W. (1995). *The Jobless Future*. Minneapolis: University of Minnesota Press.

Banks, J. A., and Banks, C. M. (1989). *Multicultural Education: Issues and Perspectives*. Boston: Allyn.

Biklin, S. K., and Pollard, D. (1993). *Gender and Education*. Chicago, IL: National Society for the Study of Education.

Bluestone, B., and Harrison, B. (1982). *The Deindustrialization of America*. New York, NY: Basic Books.

Bourdieu, P. (1991). *Language and Symbolic Power*. Cambridge, MA: Howard.

Delpit, L. (1993). "The Silenced Dialogue." In L. Weis and M. Fine (eds.) *Beyond Silenced Voices*. Albany, NY: SUNY Press.

Fine, M. (1991). *Framing Dropouts*. Albany, NY: SUNY Press.

Foucault, M. (1978). *Discipline and Punish*. New York, NY: Vintage.

Frankenberg, R. (1993). *White Women, Race Matters*. Minneapolis: University of Minnesota Press.

Gaertner, S. L., Davidio, J. F., Banker, B. S., Rust, M. C., Nier, J. A., Mottola, G. R., and Ward, C. M. (in press). "Does White Racism Necessarily Mean Anti-Blackness? Aversive Racism and Pro-Whiteness." In this volume.

Gramsci, A. (1971). *Selections from Prison Notebooks*. New York, NY: International.

Guinier, L., Fine, M., Balin, J., with Bartow, A., and Stachel, L. "Becoming Gentlemen: Women's Experiences at One Ivy League Law School." *University of Pennsylvania Law Review*, 143(4), 1–110.

Morrison, T. (1992). *Playing in the Dark*. New York, NY: Harvard.

Novick, M. (1995). *White Lies, White Power*. Monroe, ME: Common Courage Press.

Oakes, J. (1988, January). "Tracking: Can Schools Take a Different Route?" *National Education Association*, 41–47.

Reich, R. (1991). *The Work of Nations: Preparing Ourselves for 21st-Century Capitalism*. New York, NY: Alfred Knopf.

Rosenbaum, J. (1976). *Making Inequality*. New York, NY: John Wiley and Sons.

Schofield, J. W. (1989). *Black and White in School*. New York, NY: Teachers College Press.

Sleeter, C. E. (1993). "How White Teachers Construct Race." In C. McCarthy and W. Crichlow (eds.) *Race, Identity and Representation in Education*. New York, NY: Routledge.

Weis, L., Proweller, A., and Contri, C. (in press). "Re-examining a 'Moment in History': Loss of Privilege inside White, Working Class Masculinity in the 1990s." In this volume.

Weis, L. (1990). *Working Class without Work*. New York, NY: Routledge.

NOTE

1. We need only note who among so many prominent adult males recently accused of violence against women have drawn and fixated our (whose "our" white woman) attention—and who appear too pudgy or dull or sleepy to watch. Need I note that we have not been obsessed with Senator Packwood's (non)hearings, the Joel Rifkin serial killings of prostitutes, esteemed Judge Sol Wachtler's masquerading as a cowboy and posing death threats to his former lover and her daughter anywhere near as passionately as "we" (there she goes again) have been obsessed by the O.J. hearings (which eventually wore off—but are still being telecast), Senator Mel Reynold's telephone sex, Colin Ferguson's masquerade as a lawyer, or Clarence Thomas.

This is not an invitation to "not look" at men of color who have committed, or been accused of committing, horrendous acts of violence against women, it is simply to notice that when white men do the same our cultural instinct is to resist voyeurism. Elite white men at least enjoy the dignity of "privacy." Not quite as vulnerable to gossip, they are rejected culturally as the site for social surveillance.

White Out:
Multicultural Performances in a Progressive School

SIX

Virginia Chalmers

Virginia Chalmers has been an antiracist worker, teacher, administrator, and curriculum developer over the past twenty-five years in alternative public schools and private laboratory schools in Cambridge, Massachusetts and New York City. The focus of her recent work has been the transformation of schools into multicultural democracies such that all children can learn, all teachers can enable that learning, and all parents have a meaningful voice. She is currently the Educational Director of the Beginning with Children School in Brooklyn, New York and a consultant to several alternative schools in Cambridge, Massachusetts.

I, like many white middle-class educators who came of age within a liberal progressive context in the early 1970s, embraced John Dewey as visionary for my work with children. I embraced his challenge that schools be structured to promote democratic values through scientific problem solving and social interdependence. I wanted to help develop new schools in which all children could experience respectful and meaningful education which could engage the evolving person, a social individual. Riding the second wave of the civil rights movement, we moved into schools, hoping to rid them of their previous failure with poor children and children of color. Alternative public schools were the context of this work for many of us. In these schools, politically active and vocal communities of teachers, parents, and students worked to revitalize both the vision and practice of teaching and learning. Our goal was to create schools that could strengthen the multiracial/multicultural democracy of America's future. We, like Dewey and his cohort of social reconstructionists in the early part of the century, believed that through a particular kind of pedagogy we could empower students to transform the world.

At this historical moment, however, conditions internal to the culture of schools as well as larger, macro, political, economic processes impinge upon this promise. Within communities of progressive educators we have had to confront the ways in which a progressive agenda has been co-opted and the differential impacts on curriculum, staffing, and the very children who are to be educated. How precisely are schools to become a laboratory for a true democracy under these conditions? Perhaps, as Cornell West has pointed out, not only was Dewey's scientific method ill suited to the messy interactions within schools, but its framing within a narrow white, middle class domain has helped to circumscribe a broader vision of social change:

> Dewey's central concern [was] to extend the experimental method in the natural sciences to the social, political, cultural, and economic spheres rather than to discern the social forces and historical agents capable of acting on and actualizing (i.e., approximating) his creative democracy. His relative confinement to the professional and reformist elements of the middle class makes such discernment unlikely. And his distrust of resolute ideological positioning as in political parties and social movements from below, leads him to elevate the dissemination of critical intelligence at the expense of collective insurgency.[1]

Messiness, however is precisely what needs to be analyzed; Dewey may not have confronted the current challenges of multicultural education nor the diffusion of multicultural ideology in what is essentially a racially segregated, inequitable educational system, but at this particular historical moment we can ill afford not to. Central to this paper is the analysis of real people ("historical agents") and interactions ("social forces") in a particular school in order to excavate the ways in which specific institutional and personal interests get played out and threaded together in the dailiness of school politics. I argue that these interests have different, yet nonetheless real, effects on various constituencies within the school community, oftentimes consolidating inequities and ideological dominance by the white community of parents and teachers. This paper, then, works to expose the effects of institutionalized racism. Schools work hard to explain away these effects with individual, often highly psychological, explanations. But, with analysis patterns emerge: patterns of withdrawal by dissatisfied families of color who are quickly replaced by new families; patterns of underachievement for a disproportionate percentage of children of color; and patterns of silencing of faculty of color. In order to understand these patterns, this paper does not focus on the individual; rather, it focuses on the institution and the actors who work for its interests. My aim is to uncover the ways in which whiteness operates within institutional contexts such that we can craft new strategies for effective school transformation.

Why, with such virulence, do those who claim an interest in building a diverse school community move so strategically to ensure that the influence of people of color is minimized? What contributes to these all-too-familiar responses? How can we better understand the origins and sustaining energy of these defensive reactions? This paper provides a response to these questions through a detailed analysis of one specific incident that occurred at the Bank Street School for Children, a progressive private elementary school and a division of the Bank Street College of Education in New York City during the two years I was its director. I had a catalytic role in the experience I will describe, thus my perspective is neither objective nor disinterested. My intent is to be self-reflexive about the contradictory relations of power, both having power as a white dean and losing it when I was positioned as a race traitor (Segrest, 1994). There are several theoretical threads woven together in this analysis. One focuses on the nature of progressive education, both its origins and current practice. Clearly one of the questions being considered here is whether an educational movement, conceived in whiteness and led by white people of privilege, can democratize itself (Delpit, 1986, 1988; MacIntosh, 1988; Noblit, 1993). Further, can the epistemological frame of education, which relies so heavily upon an individualized developmental psychology also conceived in whiteness explain childrens' failure, and in this instance the disproportionate failure of children of color in particular, as a failure of our curriculum and pedagogy rather than a failure of an individual's achievement (Alexander, 1994; Silin, 1995).

I want to use this paper to clarify the ways in which ideology and discourse are mobilized to protect both institutional and individual interests. The incident analyzed is a potluck supper for parents of children of color, and it put these mobilizations in stark relief.

At stake at each axis of conflict is a contest over which, and whose, narrative structure will prevail in the interpretation of events in the social world. We believe that the realm of interpretation, ideology, and narrative is a critical site in the production of American racial domination.[2]

Similar to the discourse surrounding the beating of Rodney King referred to by Kimberle Crenshaw above, the potluck supper and its aftermath makes explicit the ways in which "interpretation, ideology, and narrative" are used to influence whose meaning of "multicultural education" and "difference" will prevail in the educational policies and practices of this school.

This analysis is strengthened by the specificity of institution and actors: the particular events, voices, and political strategies which occurred in this real school from 1991 to 1993. Although I focus upon the genealogy of a particular institution, its founding leadership, and ongoing policies, this narrative is folded into a larger analytic framework in order that it can be used to understand the general through the particular: that it can enable us to draw the links between Bank Street's specific institutional codification of multicultural ideologies and the racial politics embedded in the everyday life of all schools. Not only is a very specific multicultural discourse deployed here, one which reduces difference to pluralism and attempts to erase racial power while simultaneously holding onto inherited privilege, but also a very particular set of multicultural practices is implemented in order to protect certain institutional and individual interests. Throughout this analysis, I work to identify and make explicit the particular political strategies, not unique to schools, but nonetheless pervasive, that are employed to secure the dominance of this particular multicultural discourse, one that I argue is maintained to insulate the institution from any meaningful change in racialized power relations.

So, my objective is to better understand the failure to transform the racial politics and inequities within institutions for the benefit of all students. My hope is that this process will generate components of a new vision of school communities committed to equity, engagement with difference, and redistribution of power, and as such help the large coalition of educators, parents, and researchers make more effective decisions about political and educational strategies that will move forward a reconstructionist agenda. Perhaps, however, this analysis will be most useful to those white progressive educators, who, like myself, are relative newcomers to positions of formal institutional power. In misjudging our positions as actors within the matrix of power, we render ourselves ineffective in critically utilizing our positions of power and privilege to further the agenda of educational justice for all children. Demystifying the operations of the institutions upon which we rely for jobs and financial security (West, 1993) requires that we recognize our own contradictory positions, and the contradictory nature of the very communities we have worked to change. Lulled into a sense of comfort and belonging in these informal institutions which privilege "home-like" behaviors (everyone on a first-name basis, greeting each other with hugs, food at meetings), comfortable to the predominant community of white, professional women, we sometimes act casually in the battlefield, losing significant skirmishes before we are even aware that we are in a war. So it is to us, mostly white female players, who would be given real power if we would just behave, that this paper is particularly addressed.

PROGRESSIVE LEGACIES

Bank Street College, with its laboratory setting in the School for Children, seemed to me to be ideally situated to explore what it takes to create an equitable school. With a distinguished history dating back to its beginnings in 1916, the School for Children has worked to translate the vision of progressive pedagogy envisioned by its founder, Lucy Sprague Mitchell, and her University of Chicago colleague John Dewey into two distinct yet closely related laboratory schools and teacher training institutions. These progressive educators' vision was to transform the nation's schools through study, experimentation and research [about] the complex development of children and to create the environments that support and promote their development (*Self Study*, Bank Street College of Education, January 1992, p. 1).

As I prepared to assume leadership of this school, I was particularly excited about the possibility of revitalizing the mission of the school as an experimental school. I hoped that this time the experiment would transform the racial and power inequities embedded in the school into a multiracial, multiethnic democracy. The demonstration site conceived of by Mitchell and her colleagues was not something static and safe, rather a site where theory was constantly held up against the messy and unpredictable practice of teaching children and adults. Their idea, and the idea I hoped to build on in the 1990s, was to develop a site that would allow for simultaneous experimentation by children, parents, professionals, and teachers in training, unfettered from the constraints of public school bureaucracies.

As I began my work, I quickly came to understand the ways in which fiscal constraints inhibit change in this private school, a significant change from the early years when it was a nursery school, supported in large part by the private wealth of Lucy Sprague Mitchell. The school as a laboratory for experimentation and participatory research long ago succumbed to the economic realities within which it functions. At risk of stating the obvious, private schools everywhere must ensure a healthy enrollment and thus the concern of those in charge when parents who provide significant financial support express displeasure over changes in the school. There are many inhibitors to change that operate in much more subtle ways than money, however, and these became clear as I came to understand the multiple ways in which change, problem solving, and difference would threaten this institution and the most powerful actors within it.[3]

I want to describe in more detail the experiences of children, families, and staff of color within this school in order to clarify the reasons for our initial efforts at change. The school had a chronic problem increasing the number of experienced faculty of color. Over recent years they have successfully recruited a few highly respected teachers of color who stayed for a few years and then moved on. Since 1989, with the introduction of a graduate student internship specifically designed for students of color, graduate students and beginning teachers have added a few other staff members of color to the faculty. There was never, however, a critical mass of experienced, respected faculty of color who could hold their own with the established and mature white faculty who held long-standing administrative and teaching positions at the school. The effect of this disparity is chronic silencing of the experiences and opinions of faculty of color, limiting their impact on the core educational experience provided by the school (Delpit, 1986).

In 1991 when I began, the racial composition of the school was 70 percent white and 30 percent of color, with 20 percent African American students and 10 percent Latino. Even with these respectable results of successful recruitment during recent years, parents of color described a condition of participation within the school that I came to call a *permanent guest status*. Although welcomed warmly, they felt that they were outsiders, expendable and never really able to influence the core of the institution. Guests come and go without much consequence. Although superficially they were treated perfectly politely, real interactions and relationships tended to be avoided. African American families in particular shared their initial experiences of isolation, fed by familiar racialized stereotypes (Black fathers were frequently mistaken for dangerous intruders and mothers "nannies"). Finally, although there was significant lip service given to the desire for families of color to have a more active role in the parent committee work of the school, the schedule and participation requirements of the Parents' Association precluded the possibility of meaningful participation by full-time working parents, thus excluding most parents of color.

According to teacher assessment and informal observations, many teachers and parents had noticed that a disproportionate percentage of children of color presented "problematic behavior" and "less mature" intellectual and social behaviors in both the classroom and playground. Faculty of color shared their observation that it was boys, especially African American boys, who were asked to leave the room most frequently for inappropriate behavior, usually identified as lack of compliance with teacher expectations and routines. In class placement discussions at the end of the year, the recommendation for placement in a developmentally "younger" classroom came more frequently for boys of color than any other group of children.

EXCLUSION BY AND FOR WHOM?

I move now to an analysis of a potluck supper for parents of children of color hosted by the staff of color and myself on Friday evening, November 15, 1991. This event had a catalytic effect on the community, and came, more than any other event, to represent the struggle within the school over whose assessment of the school's multicultural identity would prevail. The impetus for the potluck came from a discussion between the staff of color and myself. The faculty of color had been meeting as a group for a year (informally called the POC—People of Color) and had agreed to develop a more active working relationship with parents and families of children of color during this their second year. The parents, however, had not been involved in this process and were not informed of the separate faculty meetings. Early in the fall it became apparent that I needed to create a vehicle to meet and understand the needs and interests of parents of children of color in the school and I asked the POC to help me. We mailed invitations to the parents we had identified and posted invitations for those who would choose to self-identify and participate in the supper. For the first time in the school's recent history, virtually all the families of color joined the staff of color and myself to share a meal and then discuss the future of the school. As I wrote after the supper, in the first of a number of public relations efforts:

> [A]s I moved between meetings with faculty, parents and teachers, I felt most acutely the absence of parents of children of color. Some of these families did not feel that it was necessary to approach me because they felt their needs and interests were adequately addressed by the PA and the Multicultural Committee. Others, however, expressed an urgent need for a context in which they could feel "safe" to get to know each other and identify areas of common concern that would help create a sense of belonging for them at Bank Street. As a result of these conversations . . . I set up the meeting of last Friday night.

The dinner was an enthusiastic and fun-filled affair, with children and families buoyed by the sheer numbers of people of color in an environment where they are numerically in the minority in most group settings. The discussion was a very moving one in which people cried, laughed, yelled, and talked with varied voices. Parents described the lived discomfort of being new at the school; daily experiences of racism; rejection of their invitations to children to come to their homes in Harlem to play. They shared their priorities for more faculty of color and of the need for a curriculum which taught children more about the histories and experiences of their own ethnic and racial groups, as well as the history and experiences of the dominant culture. They also wondered aloud if their children could possibly be learning anything while "playing" all day. Those of us at the meeting were energized by the discussion, excited by the concern and commitment of the parents, and hopeful that this enthusiasm could be carried into future work together in the service of their children.

By the time school opened on Monday, the telephone and neighborhood conversations had constructed a pervasive and dominant ideology of exclusion in response to the potluck supper. The interpretation of this particular community-building event focused on who was not there, rather than who was, and over the next few weeks was fanned into a furious frenzy. The violation experienced by some of those not invited to the potluck supper was expressed in terms of threats to identity, community, and pedagogy, the very foundation upon which this school rests. During the next few weeks, clusters of parents could be seen (and felt) in the school cafeteria and surrounding cafes intensely discussing their responses to the potluck. I received six letters, one from a white and one from a black parent of a child of color plus four from white parents of white children. These letters and the concerns they express form the basis of the analysis which follows.

Many of the parents' statements worked to erase the complex set of racialized negotiations and historic relationships embedded in power and privilege that have contributed to contemporary race relations in America. They claim race as color only, trying to minimize its importance in understanding the nature of peoples' lived experience. Parent No. 1 states this position very clearly:

On Friday, November 15, 1991 other people decided for me who I am—a person of *no* color. I was denied access to a meeting in Bank Street because of the color of my skin. Why does it ring some historic bells for me?

This position of "white defensiveness" makes the "assertion that whites, like people of color, are history's oppressed subjects to racism."[4] One Jewish mother shared the pain she felt when confronted with the reality that the invitation list had been constructed based on race. Her historical experience of anti-Semitism made the construction of a race-based list exceedingly threatening. Others expressed resentment at being categorized as white, for it marked them as participants and beneficiaries of a racist structure. Coupled with the construction of race as color alone (and therefore not a significant difference) is the assertion that excluding white people from a discussion among people of color is unjustified. Parent No. 1 again:

I strongly resent the person who does not even give me the benefit of the doubt and who doesn't feel "safe" talking in my presence.

For whiteness to carry the benefit of the doubt would require that it be removed from its embedded position within a history of domination, an impossible feat in these contemporary times. The origin of resentment perhaps lies in our collective unwillingness to acknowledge the unearned but often exercised privilege that whiteness bestows upon us. The Potluck Supper made explicit several important aspects of white privilege at the school: the privilege to "belong," be understood, and have our concerns taken seriously, and perhaps most profoundly the privilege to assume that the public sphere would feel like home. Who we are, how we interact, what makes us comfortable becomes naturalized in this process of privileging. Parents of children of color felt some of those same advantages in the environment created at the potluck supper, however fleetingly. The white community resisted acknowledging their own unearned privilege and by extension any responsibility for the exclusions people of color experienced. This denial can cause discomfort within a community, because as Peggy MacIntosh describes in her analysis of differential privilege in gender relationships, "obliviousness of one's privileged state can [at the very least] make a person or group irritating to be with."[5] The potluck supper was an attempt to begin to even the playing field, to actively solicit the feedback from parents who in other contexts did not participate. And it worked! Parents came, they talked, they disagreed, they supported each other, and they began to build a relationship with me. Moving away from the more characteristic alliances formed out of race loyalty, these parents began to build solidarity across race with formal power, a threatening alliance to this school community.

In many ways, private education in urban areas evokes a heightened vested interest from parents as the enormous economic investment and in some cases hardship is staggering (most independent elementary schools cost $8,000–13,000 annually, increasing in cost as a child advances in grades). There are also parents for whom the selection and enrollment in a particular school comes to represent not only an essential self-image, but also an identity for their children. The violation, then, when one asks questions about institutional practice with diversity, is not principally a disagreement about ideas, but is experienced in a much deeper place as a violation of one's self-image. If the excavation is uncovering instances of institutional racism, then the parents in positions of power within the institution are co-implicated and the strength of the defensive response becomes understandable. Here I quote from other letters:

. . . I am very upset by what it (pot luck supper) means to me. I feel that the meetings I attend at Bank Street are open meetings. There is no exclusion. There is no list of who qualifies and who doesn't. As someone who is very involved in the school with 3 children here, who devotes a lot of energy to events that foster community building, and meetings that welcome all voices, I am left feeling isolated and at a loss. (Parent No. 2)

This parent, and others who agreed with her articulated concerns, misperceive that a harmonious community existed prior to the potluck, not reading the absences and silences of parents of color as a collective response to these very same meetings which were only functionally open to insiders. The parent quoted above felt the inclusive community she experienced had been violated and those who should belong (one "who devotes a lot of energy to events that foster community building and meetings that welcome all voices") are left out, feeling alone. This parent is identified with the objective of building a particular kind of harmonious, inclusive, and presumably race-neutral community, a community not engaged with difference, but rather sameness in different color.

Chandra Talpade Mohanty identifies the limitations of the discourse of "harmony in diversity," which cannot accommodate conflict or struggle and bypasses power:

[T]he most difficult question concerns the kind of difference that is acknowledged and *engaged*. Difference seen as benign variation (diversity), for instance, rather than as conflict, struggle, or the threat of disruption, bypasses power as well as history to suggest a harmonious, empty pluralism. On the other hand, difference defined as asymmetrical and incommensurate cultural spheres situated within hierarchies of domination and resistance cannot be accommodated within a discourse of "harmony in diversity."[6]

The supper exposed pervasive exclusion which had become naturalized into the social fabric of the school. Just as the not-guilty verdict of the abusive police officers in the Rodney King beating made clear how wrong we were to assume consensus about the meaning of the videotaped beatings, so too did the unprecedented turnout of parents of color for a potluck supper and the explosive response of the predominantly white community clarify that the concern here is not really about participation of all members of the school community.

One effect of the increased threat and conflict felt by our meeting was a heightened sense of belonging for those members of the community who were similarly committed to a "harmonious vision" of the multicultural community at the school, ostensibly the school community that was
there before I came. The following excerpt reflects this position:

> We are a community here and we talk about things and that is how it begins in the class-
> room and goes throughout the parent body. I feel this approach of defining who someone
> is and then putting them in categories and picking them out for meetings is very destructive
> in its divisiveness. I feel we have not done things here that way and that is our strength—the
> openness, the inclusion, the wish to talk and share. (Parent No. 2)

White parents were not the exclusive participants of this "outraged" community. Parents of
color and white parents of children of color who were invested in a similar picture of benign diversity were also opposed to the meeting. They constructed the opportunity for families of color
to meet and talk among themselves as "divisive" and antithetical to the moral code of the school.
They accused those of us who disagreed of "exploiting" children in the service of a politically correct, separatist agenda, thereby violating one of the central tenets of a good school: children
should be protected from politics and the power struggles that contaminate the world in order to
guard against unhealthy (read developmentally inappropriate) development. The aim is to
"grow" children for whom race (and presumably power) is not an issue. Jonathan Silin (1995)
tracks the ideology identified above to the Progressive Era's commitment to "keeping politics out
of the school," and the "emphasis on developmentally adequate curricula [which] allowed teachers to think they were noncoercive, unprejudiced practitioners. Because children were viewed as
vulnerable and fragile, teachers did not want to see themselves as influencing them in any way
that had ideological or political ramifications."[7]
Parents who wrote affirmed a color and power-evasive vision of Bank Street and its role in the
life of a child and family.

> I have no doubt we share the same goal, but we don't necessarily agree on the means to
> reach it. I do not believe in working for inclusion by creating exclusion. I believe in a pro-
> ductive dialogue and not in a monologue. I do not believe in artificially empowering a group
> whose only common denominator is that they are not white (negative definition is the com-
> mon cause of racism). (Parent No. 1)

This parent links race and power, naturalizing whiteness conjoined with power in her accusation
that the supper (and by implication my presence there) "artificially empowered a group whose
only common denominator is that they are not white." Power can be artificial only against an authentic or real power, which this parent accurately does not locate with the group of parents of
children of color. Real power in this school is found in the white power structure, to which this
parent belongs and to which some parents of color and white parents of children of color aspire.
The parents (and by extension their children) attending the potluck supper were empowered,
however fleetingly. By attending, people claimed a common identity and through their participation unearthed common experiences, feelings, and perspectives. However brief the meeting, the
effect of such a minor redistribution of power was profound.
Central to the multicultural discourse of these outraged parents was an evasion of race and
power. Ruth Frankenberg (1993) defines this position as one which selectively engages with only
the good and comfortable components of difference. In the "thinking through of race" that

Frankenberg analyzes, the ideology of "universal sameness overlaid with individual difference" and an evasion of race and power are echoed in these parents' statements.[8]

> When my husband and I started looking for a school for_____, there was only one school that appealed to us—Bank Street. Bank Street was the only school that projected a strong sense of community and at the same time, seemed to enable individuals to be who they are, so self-definition and self-respect grew up from within and were not artificially imposed by the outside world. (Parent No. 1)

In this description, children construct an identity separate from outside contamination and presumably, if the school is good enough, race and class are neutral in this process. This father speaks to the desire for the school to remain neutral on the question of race, leaving his mixed-race family with the task of helping his daughter develop a racial identity.

> Bank Street school, to me, has always stood for success based upon individual achievement, not culture and/or race. . . . The labels that now make me a "Caucasian, Euro-centric, Parent of a Child of Color" is offensive to me and my family. It also makes my daughter start to try to explain herself to herself and categorize her life by race and culture from outside sources. She is fighting it because she already knows who she is. Race and cultural awareness, in a child, is the job of the family. Now her school is trying to politically correctly define her. (Parent No. 3)

Ironically, this desire for a color-blind school is perhaps most clearly expressed by this African American parent. In arguing against the potluck supper that invited participation based on race, she articulates her assimilationist vision of an ideal, integrated school community.

> ____has been attending Bank Street since age five. As you well know, Bank Street has taught and supported the rights of all individuals while acknowledging diversity. This was the primary reason why I selected Bank Street to participate in ____ education. Our race has never been an issue for me or my son. . . . In twenty years, I still believe in the premise that through participation, assimilation is possible and viable. But it must be mutual and inclusive.

In the words of these parents one finds the desire for protection for their children in the race- and power-evasive stance which they propose. The school has and in their view should continue to provide such a protected context, a place where children can develop without imposition from the social/political realities of the larger world.

I think it is important at this juncture to analyze the discourse which has enabled the race- and power-evasive stance to come to dominate this school and its educational practice. The relevant discourse is organized around the questions of how children develop and the role of difference and power in that process. A particular form of developmentally appropriate practice has been institutionalized at Bank Street for over its almost century-long history. The progressive pedagogy operationalized at this school can be traced to its founders who were colleagues and theoretical partners of John Dewey. Jonathan Silin reminds us that:

> the progressive movement was not only about individual growth and social efficiency but also about the power residing within the group and possibilities of societal transformation.[9]

He clarifies that those founders who engaged in the project of developing Bank Street were among those most committed to societal transformation as an outcome of the educational experiments they were leading. This initial commitment continues to be articulated in recent publications, but has in practice been overwhelmed by the influence of psychologized child development which was just moving into ascendancy as Dewey and his colleagues were creating their laboratory schools. Their emerging emphasis on scientific, hence observable and measurable development of individual children came to dominate the theoretical as well as material reality of early childhood education and the particular laboratory settings they were creating. Stage theory of development became the lens through which all children could be understood and this particular form of developmental determinism became the framework for all of early childhood education. In this context, particular histories, social embeddedness, ethnicities, experiences, cultures, and prior knowledges are not actively engaged in the construction of ideal classrooms. The responsibility of teachers, and by extension the classrooms they create, is to nurture and protect children. The "ideal" classroom, instructional strategies, and teacher/child interaction patterns become comfortably rationalized as "developmentally appropriate practice." Silin describes the "often unbridgeable" distances between child and adult and between child and "the material realities in which they live" that are the result of an adherence to this theoretical framework (1995, p. 104). One can prefigure the distances that Silin identifies in current early childhood classrooms in the words of Lucy Sprague Mitchell as she defines the "developmentally appropriate" practice she envisions in schools in the 1950s:

> In brief, this means the schools are moving toward the conception that their job is to give children a good, a full, a rich all-round life at whatever stage of development they have reached, and full opportunities to keep growing at their own rate and in their own way in bodies, minds, emotions and social standards. . . . the school's aim is to be a place for children to grow in all-around healthy ways.[10]

Paradoxically, this particular progressive legacy and developmentally appropriate practice produced fertile ground within which the dominant multicultural discourse, devoid of engagement with difference and power, not only emerges but flourishes. It is the very notion of the individual as the center of development that has led educators, with the support of parents, to create protective school environments for young children, presumably apolitical and color and power blind. Schools have become places in which the complex realities of children's lived experience are often excluded.[11] Power is a particular facet of lived reality that dominant parents and faculty at Bank Street wanted left at the door. Lisa Delpit underscores this critical point in her observation that those with power are frequently least aware of—or the least willing to acknowledge—its existence and those with less power are often *most* aware of its existence.[12] A preference for a race- and power-evasive experience for children did not, of course, mean that these parents and staff withdrew from using the power they had to influence and in some instances control the direction of the school. Parents and staff with less power recognized and exposed these moves.

George Noblit explores in more depth the relationship between power and pedagogy in his piece "Power and Caring." Analyzing his own discomfort with the teacher's style and her unambivalent use of power, he returns to John Dewey and the theoretical roots that charge that:

> . . . schools should be structured to promote democratic values. Indeed, Dewey's faith in a scientific method of problem solving was coupled with his belief that this process allowed for more democratic decision making and the development of an interdependence in social

life and society. . . . critical theorists have joined in this refrain proposing that teachers need to use their authority judiciously so as not to repress youth.[13]

Noblit goes on to explore his assumptions about power ("saw power linked to oppression in everything") and caring ("somehow beyond issues of power") in a way that completes the picture of the progressive ideology, both in terms of individual development and power, that support the color- and power-evasive discourse so prevalent in these schools today.

The insistence on a uniform set of experiences to enhance each and every child's development would be seen as theoretically inconsistent if difference, not just individual characteristics, was engaged. I agree with Silin that an over-reliance on the biological determinism of child development and denial of the social has led to the creation of schools which

> leave the educator an observer of the child's growth through largely predetermined stages. The goal is not the transfer of information to groups of children or the promotion of social transformation but the fostering of individual change. Knowledge has become development, development the aim of education.[14]

Of central importance to this analysis is to understand the ways in which both institutional and individual identities are structured around an individualistic and psychological definition of multiculturalism that embraces not difference and engagement, but uniformity and autonomy. Current progressive discourses of multiculturalism assume a consensus of values and perspective. In fact, the School for Children goes so far as to invent a consensus on how children develop, how to teach them, and what an ideal classroom environment ought to look like. There is a correct way to teach everything from painting to social studies and a requirement for conformity based on the theoretically "incontestable" ground of developmentally appropriate practice. Child development is the guiding principal of this school and child development is individualistic, psychological, and "color and power blind." The social construction of identity becomes marginalized by the language of universal needs, and the necessity for powerful interactions between differences is avoided.

The struggle for interpretation of the potluck supper for families of children of color specifically, and the struggle for justice generally, persisted throughout my two-year tenure at the school. In many meetings, written documents, and informal conversations, my label as an "excluder" in the context of the potluck supper would reemerge. Resonating with the contemporary debate about affirmative action, my initiative to create a more even playing field for all members of the school community was blocked and in its place the ideology of exclusion was substituted; ironically, the very condition I was working to correct. In the dominant narrative, the exclusion that mattered was the exclusion of white parents and faculty who had historically defined what multiculturalism should be at this school. The exclusion we made visible by our meeting, the historical exclusion of underrepresented voices from meaningful engagement with each other, and the leadership of the school, was insignificant compared to this. Having a conversation with parents of children of color without white parents threatened their self-definition as progressive multiculturalists and evoked a defensive and aggressive reaction that reverberated throughout the following two years. Moving directly to exclude me as an "outsider," those at the center of the struggle succeeded within the contested terrain of interpretation and narration to define my position and actions as preferential and divisive, even "more understandable" as the entire community became aware of the particular composition of my family. It has always been the central prerogative of privilege to define the narrative, and once the battlefield was defined, parents and staff moved quickly to ensure that this prerogative was not usurped.

The aftermath of the potluck supper exploded the myth of "multicultural harmony" within the school and unearthed the contested meanings of multicultural education and commitment to diversity of parents and faculty at the school. The dominant ideology of power evasion, rooted in a belief in power as resource, led to the battle over whose definition of social justice and equity would win out. The potluck supper became a symbol for powerful parents and staff of the possibility of empowerment of "outsiders" and the resulting disempowerment of the "majority." As the conflict escalated so too did the sanctioned aggression against those of us who disagreed. In my case, the particular form of exclusion was positioned at the intersection of identity, race, and privilege. If I were to occupy this status position, I had to meet its conditions, which I had clearly violated by my "excluding and divisive" behavior. Race and status loyalty is a requirement of a private school head, and I was disloyal to white people, exposing them and the school of their choice to the possible influence of disorderly people of color.[15]

CONCLUDING CHALLENGES

So, what can those of us committed to creating democratic multicultural schools learn from this critical examination of an institution protecting itself? The struggle at Bank Street was located right at the heart of the contested terrain of difference, racial difference operating as white power. The challenge for private schools, which compete for an acceptable pool of students of color, is how to reconceptualize their mission beyond the constraints of whiteness. Drawn to the liberal ideal of pluralistic communities, schools become ensnared in complex, messy interactions that inevitably emerge in heterogeneous communities unwilling to pay attention to race and power.

Unfortunately similar narratives and multicultural performances have become all too familiar in our schools. Admittedly, explanations are frequently cited to explain the self-protective actions of the institution and the actors within it. The closing of other progressive institutions over this past decade, concerns about financing, and an increasingly conservative private school market all challenge school administrators to determine whether these conditions will exacerbate the patrolling of borders as witnessed at Bank Street. Not just border patrolling, but expelling those disgruntled, "different" outsiders were a very real consequence of these conflicts. Many families of color who became members of a Concerned Parent Group have withdrawn from the school during the following years. Their withdrawal is explained away with different "acceptable" reasons, but the fact is that these families were expendable, quickly replaced with other families of color wanting their children to have the "advantages" of a private education. The doors have closed securely behind us all.

Perry and Frazier challenge us to proceed with the project of building school communities that can realize social justice, even though the promise of multiracial democratic schools seems very dim.

Can we, as it were, step over the present, project ourselves and our schools into the future, into our vision of what a school would be like if power were shared among all races, ethnic groups and social classes, as if the new community (the new multiracial, multiethnic democracy) had actually come into being? Could we as an educational community begin to operate, make hiring and curricular decisions, conduct business, as if the new time were at hand? . . . How would we talk about its [the school's] meaning? What criteria would be used to determine what knowledge was worth passing on? . . . Who would we want to be our teachers? Who would hold positions of authority and how would authority be exercised? These are the fundamental questions which must be asked if schools, and the nation's society, are to be restructured to meet the promise and possibilities of a truly multicultural future.[16]

This process of envisioning might stimulate a new sense of possibility, but only if it is nourished by a critical analysis of our work to date. It is my hope that this analysis contributes to these critical reflections. I have focused on the contradiction between the promise and the practice of our progressive schools and attempted to bring into clearer view the institutional policies and practices and ideologies that keep these contradictions alive. I continue to struggle with the complex particularities of this situation and my professional, personal, and political history within it. As Evans and Boyte (1984) remind us, the hope of our future and the future of our children requires that we take the time and create the "free spaces" for engagement in this dialogue. We must call into question our most fundamental educational inheritances, ensuring that we not participate in the construction of additional deceptive discourse, masking the reality of the lives of children, teachers, and parents in schools. For it may in fact be the case that progressivism, conceived and constructed as it was in whiteness, may never work equitably for children of color. It is up to us to work with staff, parents, and children to imagine new postprogressive possibilities beyond the domination of whiteness.

NOTES

1. Frank Pignatelli, "Toward a Postprogressive Theory of Education," in *Educational Foundation* (Summer 1993).
2. Kimberle Crenshaw and Gary Peller, *Reading Rodney King, Reading Urban Uprising* (New York: Routledge, 1993) p. 57.
3. Resisting the inappropriate influence of white parents who donated large amounts of money was one of the initial, and perhaps most important areas of tension between myself and the president of the college. It seemed important to me that an equitable reorganization of the institution required that people's donations (either in money or time) not increase the influence of their opinions. As I tried to resist what I saw as inappropriate influence of money and access to power, tension mounted within the parent body, who used the president to censure me.
4. L. G. Roman, *Race, Identity and Representation in Education* (New York: Routledge, 1993), p. 71.
5. P. McIntosh, *White Privilege and Male Privilege: A Personal Account of Coming to See Correspondences Through Work in Women's Studies* (Wellesley College: Center for Research on Women, 1988), p. 4.
6. C. T. Mohanty, *Beyond a Dream: Deferred Multicultural Education and the Politics of Excellence* (Minneapolis, Minnesota: University of Minnesota Press, 1993), p. 42.
7. J. Silin, *Sex, Death and the Education of Children: Our Passion for Ignorance in the Age of AIDS* (New York: Teachers College Press, 1995), p. 95.
8. R. Frankenberg, *White Women, Race Matters: The Social Construction of Whiteness* (Minneapolis, Minnesota: University of Minnesota Press, 1993), p. 148.
9. J. G. Silin, *Celebrating Diverse Voices* (Newbury Park, California: Corwin Press, Inc., 1993), p. 222.
10. L. S. Mitchell, *Our Children and Our Schools*, (New York: Simon and Schuster, Inc., 1950), p. 23.
11. J. Silin, *Sex, Death and the Education of Children*, p. 105.
12. Lisa Delpit, *Other People's Children* (New York: The New Press, 1995), pp. 21–47.
13. G. W. Noblit, "Power and Caring," in *American Educational Research Journal*, (30) 1 (Spring 1993), pp. 25–26.
14. J. G. Silin, *Celebrating Diverse Voices*, p. 235.
15. Although the processes that we have identified in this analysis can not be traced to a single person or group of people and the work of institutional transformation generates inevitable struggles, the person in charge of an institution can have a profound impact on the nature and tenacity of an institution's resistance to change.
16. T. Perry and J. Frazier, *Beyond Freedom's Plow* (New York: Routledge, 1993), p. 19.

Underground Discourses:
Exploring Whiteness in Teacher Education

Pearl M. Rosenberg

Pearl M. Rosenberg is Assistant Professor of Education at the University of New Hampshire, where she teaches courses in Human Learning and Development and Ethnographic Research Methodology. She received her Ph.D. in Interdisciplinary Studies in Human Development from the University of Pennsylvania. Her research interests include issues pertaining to women and education, and the social and psychological development of teachers.

In her book, *Teaching to Transgress/Education as the Practice of Freedom*, bell hooks beckons us teachers to enter our classrooms "whole" and not as "disembodied spirits." Joining a conversation already begun by Madeleine Grumet (1987; 1988), Paula Salvio (1990; 1994a; 1994b), and others, hooks reiterates the need for autobiographical disclosure in academic work and teaching, asking us to participate in what she calls an "engaged pedagogy."

hooks writes:

> When education is in the practice of freedom, students are not the only ones who are asked to share, to confess. Engaged pedagogy does not seek simply to empower students. Professors who expect students to share confessional narratives but who are themselves unwilling to share are exercising power in a manner that could be coercive. It is often productive if professors take the first risk, linking confessional narratives to academic discussions so as to show how experience can illuminate and enhance our understanding of academic material. But most professors must practice being vulnerable in the classroom, being wholly present in mind, body, and spirit (1995, p. 21).

I am speaking as a white teacher educator in this discussion about what it means to raise issues of race and racism in teaching and learning with preservice teachers in a predominantly white teacher education program. This work is part of my ongoing efforts to help my students in the educational psychology class I teach each term to construct questions about race, racism, and teaching through the use of educational autobiography and other forms of writing and speaking as part of their teacher socialization process. These snapshots of life in my classroom illustrate the incomplete attempts at social change that I have engaged in with my students over the past four years.

I am concerned about how student discourses about race are more often than not of central concern to many participants in the class, even though these conversations take place only in private writings or in secret meetings with the teacher. Many of these students seem to think of their self-disclosures to the teacher as forms of sinful confession; they speak in hushed, shameful tones of stories about racist families or their own ignorance or wonderings about others.

Even though "self-disclosure" implies a range of discourses from confessional to revelatory, I would like to use David Bleich's (1995) definition of "disclosure" in this discussion of student disclosure. For he suggests that self-disclosure should be distinguished from "confession" and "revelation." He claims that to confess implies "sin" and to reveal implies "secrets," which may not be appropriate for the classroom. Disclosure in the classroom refers more to telling things in more intermediate contexts like groups or classes where estimations need to be made about appropriateness and helpfulness to others as well as the self. This definition asks us as teachers to think in terms of the student's needs, and our attention to their growth and development. This of course raises further questions about the teacher's own need to self-disclose in an "engaged" pedagogical relationship, as well as the unwitting disclosure that goes on between people all the time.[1] To the extent to which we believe that we are responsible for our students' growth, we must consider how much, what, and when it is appropriate for us as educators to share with our students our own process around understanding ourselves as white. This, of course, is made more problematic by the challenge of having these conversations in what I have called "the presence of an absence" (Rosenberg, 1996), which places teachers and students for the most part in the position of having to imagine other voices and circumstances that many of the students can only know from what they read or see on television or film, or infer from the news media, in regard to other people's lives.

THE PRESENCE OF AN ABSENCE

The "presence of an absence" as I am defining it here has to do with the figurative presence of race and racism, even in the virtual absence of people of color.[2] As of this writing, out of a student population of 12,500 students at this university (including both undergraduate and graduate students), there are 183 persons identified as Asian-American; 117 persons identified as Hispanic; 90 persons identified as African-American; and, 12 students identified as Native American. The presence of students of color in the education department in particular is limited to four African-Americans and two Asian-American students out of a group of 405 masters' degree students in education.

There are examples of both overt forms of racism and general discomfort and tension around issues of race in the college community, as evidenced by visual artifacts and public conversations. Most of the examples of this discomfort that I have observed in the community over the past few years are aimed at the African-American population in particular. I have found pamphlets on the wall in a local post office from the Grand Wizard of the Klu Klux Klan asking for membership. Students scrawl racial slurs on walls of dorms, especially after programs on campus celebrating black experience. And conversations wrought with racist undertones take place periodically (especially in January) about why Martin Luther King's birthday should not be a legal holiday in New Hampshire, the only state in the union not to so recognize it. Here in this often chilly cultural climate, I teach educational psychology to a predominantly white and female preservice teaching force.

Students may begin to feel lost in conversations of race and racism, especially when they begin to explore what it means to be white. Many of them come to see whiteness as an empty cultural space. For some, their identity as white people only takes shape *in relation* to others.[3] They see themselves as "not Japanese" or "not black." Or, they find a personality characteristic to use for self-definition like "I'm a generous person," or depend on categories like gender to announce, "I'm a woman." Some express envy in regard to groups whose histories they know are strong, where family or group identity seems to be a source of pride, like the Irish-, Italian- or African-

American populations. However, because of a general discomfort with the topic of difference, these admissions are not so easily made in the presence of others, and often are written in private messages to the teacher or spoken in confidence in the privacy of my office.

Moreover, even though the teacher education faculty are encouraged and often celebrated informally for including these issues in the curriculum, there is no system of support in place for those of us who raise these issues with students. Thus, discussions about our pedagogies and curriculum often take the form of subversive or "underground" conversations that take place in the stairwells, in parking lots, or in social meetings often held outside of the department.

The "underground" is sounding like a pretty interesting place, full of teachers and students engaging in the kind of pedagogy that bell hooks is advocating, but so hard to do given the realities of institutional life. As I tell the following stories, I will ask you the reader to consider the kind of space we need in order to do this work within the institution, in addition to the habits of mind and heart that make it possible to have these conversations in the first place.

SNAPSHOTS FROM THE UNDERGROUND

Jody: A Student's Self-Disclosure in the Classroom

As part of a unit on moral development, students were given a worksheet with six moral dilemmas for teachers and were asked to explore them in their small groups. The dilemmas include examples of various forms of student resistance to teacher authority, and student cruelty around issues of lying, cheating, teasing, and taunting. I have adapted these dilemmas from real-life events that occurred in various public school settings for these New Hampshire preservice teachers. Each scenario includes a situation that is framed by both developmental and contextual concerns, so that the class would need to consider a variety of factors in their understanding and generation of ideas for approaching the situation as a classroom teacher.

Students were asked to brainstorm responses and ideas for solutions to the dilemmas before they came to class. They were then asked to spend one entire 80-minute period working together with their peers in small groups, and another period presenting as a group their individual and collective exploration of the issues involved in their dilemma. Each group was asked to (1) *describe* how they understood the situation; (2) *list* what they thought the issues were; (3) *explore* what feelings were evoked for them as present students and future teachers; (4) *consider* what actions they would take as teachers in response to the situation; and (5) *imagine* what long-range planning at the beginning of the year might prepare students for the appearance of a situation like this that could arise during the school year.

One member of the all-white group read aloud the following scenario for the class and then proceeded to offer all of their suggestions for how to deal with this dilemma in bullet form:

> A large sign advertising the appearance of visiting poet Sonia Sanchez has been posted in the lobby of a predominantly white high school. The sign has a large photograph of Ms. Sanchez (a woman of color) which takes up most of the sign. Some person or persons have scrawled across the woman's face with a thick black marker: "WHO CARES WHAT SOME NIGGER SPIC BITCH HAS TO SAY?!"

The students offer the following responses to the class after their small group discussion:
  (1) "Ignore it. Don't give the person who did this the satisfaction of responding."

(2) "Post large sheets of white paper next to the desecrated sign and invite comments from the school community about what they think about the incident."

(3) "Ferret out the culprits and bring Sonia Sanchez in and have them have to be confronted by her." Another student adds "so that she could show them that those words don't hurt her."

(4) "Try and find out what was going on in their homes to try and understand why they would do such a thing." Another student adds: "Maybe they were unhappy about something else so they got angry."

The class is uncharacteristically silent after the group invites their comments. I experience a range of thoughts and feelings at the same time. I feel a sick feeling in my stomach like I am in a plummeting elevator. I feel disappointed by the group's apparent lack of awareness about human behavior in general and racism in particular. As I take a breath to begin the conversation, Jody, a 27-year-old white woman who has shared with the class anecdotes about her brother-in-law who teaches Native Americans in New Mexico in the past, speaks up firmly, yet clearly upset:

"If you think this is about anything else besides racism, you're wrong." The class is frozen.

Jody continues, seeming to fill the awkward silence with her tale about her brother who has been dating an African-American woman for a few years and her experience of being out with this woman in public and witnessing her experience of racism. She ends, "We always seem to find excuses for what people do."

I am proud of Jody for speaking out, and relieved that I do not have to do all of the work here. Yet, as I read the faces of my students looking scolded and ashamed, I realize the work continues. I began this course in educational psychology with framing conversations about power differentials among groups positioned by a variety of categorizations and inequalities. At this point, I decide that my goal for the class is that we deal with these issues collectively, without chastisement, even though I am getting the idea that students may be forgetting some of their earlier learning.

I attempt to repair this moment by thanking Jody for her self-disclosure. I make a comment about how some of us as white people are luckier than others to have opportunities to learn such lessons in relation to "persons of color," while many of us are dependent on each other as white people to teach us.

With only a few minutes remaining in the class before we say goodbye until a week later, I decide quickly to resurrect the third group solution for how to deal with the presence of the desecrated sign in the school, since that is the one that is bothering me the most. ("Ferret out the culprits and bring Sonia Sanchez in and have them have to be confronted by her so that she could show them that those words don't hurt her.") I am eager to hear more about how the group has reasoned that an appropriate solution is to have the wronged person be the administer of punishment to the "culprits," and how they are so sure that their "words [and actions] do not hurt her." Barely audible over the sound of shuffling books and jackets and chairs a student admits quietly: "Well, I *hope* she wouldn't be hurt by it." I curse the clock and return to my office.

Jody came to my office right after class, her usual calm and gentle manner clearly disrupted. She appears ready to burst. She speaks quietly yet quickly as she tells me how she regrets saying what she did even though she believed in what she did. "It just felt hard." Jody also told me that her brother's girlfriend Tashia (pronounced Tashey) and she have talked a great deal about racism, particularly after they have all been out as a group in a restaurant, for example. Here, Jody has witnessed Tashia as the recipient of stares and comments apparently because of her race. Jody's experience of witnessing Tashia in these situations makes Jody want to tell people off. Jody explains, "Tashia always says: 'Don't do it for me. If you're doin' it, make sure it's something you want to say for yourself.'"

Ideally, this is the conversation that should have been the central text of the class. But Jody was not willing to go public with her discomfort about her self-disclosure to the class or offer up for public consumption any more of her private life in the classroom.

What is so important about Jody's tale and the moral therein, is that so many white students see empathy for others as the ultimate act of generosity while missing the point that Tashia so pointedly makes clear.

The "Politics of Empathy." Those of us who teach in conservative environments may view students who express "true empathy" for other people as noteworthy and admirable. However, even though empathy is an admirable trait and a needed first step in the education of our students around issues of racism, teaching for empathy is not enough. Empathy has its own dangers. It can, I think, create a false sense of involvement. We can be misled. We can think that we have achieved something significant with our students, but we are actually just getting started, or diverted.

I am defining "empathy" as identification with and understanding of another's situation, feelings, motives. It is the aspect of "identification" and how it is used by my students that concerns me the most, especially if we consider how the process of identification may be used to assuage one's own sadness, or guilt. I think this is what is going on with the student response. How quickly the students seem to want to move all of us beyond the bad feelings and into action. Look at all of the action verbs in their solution: "ferret out," "bring [her] in," "have them be confronted," "show them." If we kick up enough dust and move around a lot maybe no one will notice that we are in the presence of cruelty, hatred, pain.

Preservice teachers in my educational psychology class appear eager to explore their own biographies around issues of growth and development while appearing to have a great desire for identification with diverse others who they read about. Unfortunately, these students often use other people's oppression in the identification and interpretation of their own lives. In my class we read classic articles by Rist (1970) on teacher expectations and the self-fulfilling prophecy in ghetto education; Gilmore (1985) on inner city girls creating their own expressions of literacy using jump rope rhymes in response to the rules of the school; and Fine (1985) on why students stay in and drop out of school in the urban ghetto. Many students respond to these readings in class by exclaiming, "Oh, I know exactly what s/he means! The same thing happened to me [in the mountains of New Hampshire]." They often see these narratives, theirs and the young people's in these inner city ghettos, as the same. It is crucial for these students not to weave their narratives together with their inner city counterparts in a blanket of shared victimization, which obcures the ways that racist domination impacts on the lives of marginalized groups in our society.

Megan Boler (1994) warns us of the "risks of empathy" and claims that using the model of "social imagination" to help our white students imagine themselves in the "others'" shoes can allow the [student] to indulge in nothing more than a "harmonious experience of reversibility and the pleasure of identification," but at whose expense?

No matter how genuine and heartfelt our feelings of brotherhood and sisterhood may be, our caring is made problematic by what Ron Scaap (hooks, 1992) describes as the "politics of empathy." Scaap claims that those who care (liberals) may think they have a vision of diversity and plurality while clinging to notions of denial and white privilege. He notes:

Liberals may pride themselves in their ability to tolerate others but it is only after the other has been redescribed as oneself that the liberal is able to be "sensitive" to the question of cruelty and humiliation. This act of redescription is still an attempt to appropriate others, only here it is made to sound as if it were a generous act. It is an attempt to make an act of consumption appear to be an act of acknowledgement. (hooks, 1992, p. 13)

In the case of many of my white students it is not that there has been no recognition of the pain and anger of the "other"; rather, the pain and anger of the other has been reduced to what they know. Unfortunately, what they know is limited and does not reflect back on themselves or their privilege.

The hardest task I have in raising issues of race with these students is to help them see that they are actually gaining privilege in some of their early attempts at addressing difference, which reinforces racism. The pedagogical question remains: how to build on this emotional recognition of sameness to an intellectual understanding of critique of differences.

Kristin: Identification with the Aggressor

The following student, whom I will call Kristin, contrasts with many of the students who write purposefully about race. This particular term I did a dialogue journal activity with students where teacher and student would write back and forth to each other, usually in discussion about a topic the student has chosen to write about. The first suggested journal entry was to write about a favorite and least favorite teacher. The least favorite teacher entries were usually obviously terrible. But what surprised me were the "most favorite teacher" entries. Often students' retrospective accounts of their best teachers seemed to have what I considered to be some of the worst possible teacher characteristics I could imagine, involving different forms of teasing, shaming, sexism, racism, homophobia, and all-around insensitivity.

Kristin writes about a memorable teacher as part of her educational autobiography:

My favorite teacher was my honors English teacher my sophomore year in high school. Mr. Gardner is short, stout and very crude. He nicknamed me the 'Redheaded Stepchild.' He is an extremely intelligent man with very definite ideas about life as well as about education. Mr. Gardner had a distinct, almost obscene sense of humor. We read *To Kill a Mockingbird* that year and also watched the movie. There is a scene in which someone spits in Atticus's face. He played the scene over and over and over again. It was so funny. I remember that book a lot better than many others that I read. I can't find words to do him justice.

This is an extremely emotional part of the story when Atticus (the white lawyer) visits the family of Tom Robinson (the black man who has been wrongly accused of raping a white woman) to tell them the latest news about Tom's trial. Atticus's young son watches from the car as Atticus leaves the Robinson's family front porch only to be met by Bob Ewell (the father of the violated Mayella) who spits in the lawyer's face for defending a black man. In actuality, Ewell has raped his own daughter and is attempting to frame Tom Robinson.

I am disturbed by her seeming to herald this teacher. I can not imagine one good reason to use that part of the film to make a joke. I restrain myself from losing my cool with Kristin and make a conscious effort to pose questions to her so that she will engage in a dialogue with me about her teacher's behavior. I am hoping she will be able to see his behavior in another light.

Not until a number of repeated attempts on my part does Kristin respond to my questions in writing about Mr. Gardner and what she claims to have learned from him. First, "What did you love about *To Kill a Mockingbird*?" Kristin responds in her journal:

I'm not sure what I learned from the book *To Kill a Mockingbird*, but I loved the story. There were racial elements in the book, also discrimination in general. I remember the book so well because I liked it so much I have since read it over more than once.

And then, regarding Mr. Gardner's pedagogy she writes:

> You asked me about the role his humor played in his appeal. I've never really thought about it in those terms before. I think part of it might have been just that he was different than most teachers. He communicated with us on a different level than most others. It always seemed that he was on our side (vs. the administration). He is a very confident teacher—not easily swayed by others.

I am frustrated that Kristin sounds as though she sees nothing wrong with her teacher's behavior in regard to the showing of *Mockingbird*. I push it a little further in our writing: "I find Mr. Gardner's choice to play a very moving and powerful part of the film *To Kill a Mockingbird* over and over, for what appears to be the sole purpose of getting the class to laugh, upsetting. What do you think?" Kristin's last entry of the term begins:

> In response to your comment about Mr. Gardner—His choice to play it over and over wasn't in order to get a laugh out of us. That was just one of the side effects. If I remember correctly, we had a big discussion about the significance of the scene and it was implanted in my mind forever.

Kristin repeats generalities over and over again about how *To Kill a Mockingbird* was really great but cannot offer any specifics. She adds a final defense of her teacher:

> He taught us about survival of the fittest. He made us feel special and was always promoting us as "gifted." I am not sure that he would be a good teacher for everyone, but I do know that I learned more from him than any other teacher I have ever had. I learned to write in his class. I learned to speak in front of a class and to believe in myself from him.

As I see it, here is an English teacher who presents the film *To Kill a Mockingbird* to a group of high school students in a New Hampshire class and in his choice of emphasis directs the students' attention to a moment of silliness by distracting them at the moment of high dramatic tension in the film.

Kristin does not question her high school teacher's choice to bypass a meaningful moment of the film *To Kill a Mockingbird* to teach an all-white New Hampshire class about racism. This student not only does not remember the "important lesson" she insists she got from that class, but wrongly remembers the man who spits in the lawyer's face as "the black man."

She insists that her teacher was a good guy, and pleads with me not to say anything bad about him in my writing. She adds, sensing my disapproval of her teacher's behavior from my questions during a conversation with her about him, "You don't understand. He taught me how to write." She may very well also be sensing my disapproval of her as she appears to feel caught by my probing questions.

I am impatient with her and angry at who I imagine Mr. Gardner to be based on her description of him. I am unable to help Kristin move forward because of my emotional involvement.

Pearl: "Double Autobiography"

My inability to do this, I believe, is because of my biography around race which intersects with Kristin's story in an ironic way. For when I was 11 years old in the early 60s I went to see *To Kill a Mockingbird* with a friend against my mother's wishes. It turned out to be the most important thing I could have done to help me understand what was to happen in the city of Philadephia in the summer of 1963. My father and his brothers owned a store that was destroyed during the rioting that resulted from increased racial tensions in the city.

Long before that summer, I would often experience feelings of jealousy, confusion, and hurt that my father would give free popsicles to neighborhood kids where his store was in North Philadelphia, a primarily African-American and Hispanic community. I would have to pay for my summer ice cream treats when I went to the corner store in my primarily white neighborhood across town. My father had explained over and over again about how some children were not as fortunate as I was and that meant I had to be more understanding. Sometimes I would see photographs that my father and his brothers would display in the store of themselves with the neighborhood kids smiling and laughing. My favorite photograph that always made me laugh was of one little boy carrying a loaf of "Wonder" bread and a quart of milk giggling as he clutched the remaining coins of the exchange in his little fist as he waved goodbye to my father and my uncles as he left the store. His two front teeth were missing and he was crossing his eyes on purpose to make a funny face for the picture taker. I thought he would be a fun friend. I longed to hang around my father's store and be part of the fun.

After I saw *To Kill a Mockingbird*, I would lay in bed at night and think about how my father was like Atticus, and even though that was frightening to me, perhaps that was a good thing. And I would think about the little kids who came into my father's store who were my age but didn't go to my school and didn't look like me. I fell asleep many a night wondering how they spent their evenings and who in their families might have disappeared. And I tried to make sense of how some people in my family's neighborhood hated my father for having to park an enormous truck filled with what they called "Nigger Food," which was spray-painted on the side of the truck. This food was salvaged from the burnt store after the rioting and sat on our street until my father and his two brothers could rebuild their business some months later. The feeling in my stomach from that summer memory returned as I sat at age eleven and watched Atticus's son on a wide screen watch as Mayella Ewell's father spit in his father's face for trying to help black people. The feeling in my stomach returns as I read Kristin's narrative.

My own memory now has become mingled with Kristin's experience, in what Gelya Frank (1979) would call "Double Autobiography," a process that blends together the consciousness of the investigator (teacher) and subject (student). I chose not to self-disclose my experience to her because I am caught up in my own memory work, worried that I may be attempting to meet my own needs by showing her how our experiences resonate. But, more than that, I worry that Kristin may personalize my tale and bypass the moral of the story, moving right into feeling guilty for not having the same experience, the same analysis, the benefit of experience. I need to ask as the teacher, "What are my goals? punishment? growth? peace?"

At the same time, I am annoyed with her teacher's insensitivity and want Kristin to have some insight into her own identification of her teacher as a model as well as her own prejudicial impulses. Two streams of psychological theorizing illuminate Kristin's situation and highlight the need for awareness.

Identification with the Aggressor. Kristin's defense of her teacher in response to my apparent criticism of him echoes various descriptions of motives for parental identification that children may adopt when they are beginning to incorporate the values and beliefs of another. Of all of them, "Identification with the Aggressor," as defined by Anna Freud (1936), seems to characterize Kristin's resistance to looking at Mr. Gardner critically. According to Anna Freud, a child behaves like a parent in order to protect him/herself from the parent's anger. As a form of projection, "identification with the aggressor" locates responsibility for one's behavior outside oneself and removes the guilt and conflict that the behavior would otherwise cause (Kelman and Hamilton, 1989). When we find denial, we know that it is a reaction to what is perceived as an external danger. My accusing Kristin's beloved teacher of being insensitive and irresponsible, and perhaps even a racist, may be too much for her to bear, for we learn racism from people we love.[4]

In this case, Kristin's sense of her own educational biography is being called into question by me. Moreover, the flow of recognition that she experiences in the retelling of her memory of her favorite teacher, a cherished authority person from her past and a role model for her future life as a teacher, is being interrupted. Kristin needs to bypass her teacher's irresponsiblity about race, as well as her own, in order to have a comfortable picture of herself as a past student and a future teacher.

Memory Errors. The social psychology literature abounds with evidence that people's prejudice mediates memory. When we see people through eyes clouded by stereotypes, we misperceive and misremember people and events. Yet only rarely do we notice these errors, for our stereotypes are protected by confirmatory biases that serve to affirm their validity. Stereotypes resist disconfirmation because we reinterpret the evidence until we see what we expect. Preexisting associations between pairs of facts or events can lead people falsely to perceive a correlation between those events (Hamilton and Rose, 1980). The person who believes that accountants are timid and waitresses are loud will not remember the extraverted accountant but will remember the boisterous waitress (Hamilton and Rose, 1980). People even forget the negative behaviors that members of their own group performed but recall with great acumen the objectionable actions undertaken by people in other groups (Howard and Rothbart, 1980). These stereotype-based memory biases have been implicated as one of the key causes of illusory correlations: overestimations of the strength of the relationship between unrelated characteristics (Hamilton and Sherman, 1989; Hamilton, Sherman, and Ruvulo, 1990).

Kristin's mistake in remembering Tom Robinson as the violent abuser of Mayella Ewell as well as her identification of "the black man" as the one who spits in the lawyer's face is a testimony to not just inevitable error in human memory, but as this case proves, our tendencies toward racism as well.

From "Underground" to "Dwelling Place"

bell hooks's invitation to us as teachers to participate in an "engaged pedagogy" presents us with an enormous challenge, especially around issues of race and racism. Since there is no prescription for engaged pedagogy, we all must negotiate our own knowledge, authority, and experience around these issues with ourselves as well as our students, taking care to recognize the contextual nature of this work.

The experience of becoming a teacher is seen too often as an individual experience and not a collective one, thereby leading many of us who are attempting to be engaged pedagogues to strive for classrooms where all participants may engage in conversations with each other. This work is not meant to be done in isolation. Nevertheless, given the realities of institutional life that we find ourselves in it is not surprising if conversations about whiteness in teacher education go underground. For these conversations about race and racism call into question what for many with power is already settled. We clearly need a new way of thinking about the *place* within which this type of work can happen, and the *process* we engage in with our students and ourselves. We are naive to think that exploring race and racism with white students will be a teaching perfomance like any other.

As a way of looking at the site for this work to take place in, I would like to resuscitate the notion of the "underground" as not just subversive, but as a site of unity, of control, of freedom—

a fertile place, only shameful under patriarchy.[5] The "underground" discourses that I hear from my students tell me that the most meaningful moments may be the most fleeting—a glimmer of light, a ray of hope, a raw nerve. But they are openings,[6] nevertheless.

But what kind of studio do we require for an educational experience that is at the same time cognitive, emotional, and spiritual? I assert that it is the process of creating these spaces that is as important as the spaces themselves. We need to think about what it means for us to "dwell"[7] in the institution. To ask our students and ourselves to "dwell" is to ask ourselves to exist in a given place, to fasten our attention, to tarry, to look again. We take root, day after day. If we are to be honest about this process, we must confront the institution on both emotional and intellectual grounds.

Maxine Greene (1995) is quick to remind us that the dialectical struggle is "never quite resolved," and we have to keep arousing ourselves to begin again. It is worth ending with her words of possibility.

I think of how much beginnings have to do with consciousness and the awareness of possibility that has so much to do with teaching other human beings. And I think that if I and other teachers truly want to provoke our students to break through the limits of the conventional and the taken for granted, we ourselves have to experience breaks with what has been established in our own lives. (p. 109)

REFERENCES

Beck, E. (1983). Self-disclosure and the commitment to social change. In C. Bunch and S. Pollack (eds.), *Learning our way: Essays in feminist education*. Trumansburg, NY: Crossing Press, 285–291.

Bleich, D. (1995). Collaboration and the pedagogy of disclosure. *College English*, 57 (1), 43–61.

Fine, M. (1987). Silencing in the public schools. *Language Arts*, 64, 157–174.

Frank, G. (1979). Finding the common denominator: A phenomenological critique of life history method. *Ethos 7* (1), 68–94.

Frankenberg, R. (1993). *White women, race matters: The social construction of whiteness*. Minneapolis, MN: University of Minnesota Press.

Freud, A. (1936). *The ego and mechanisms of defense*. NY: International Universities Press.

Gilmore, P. (1985). "Gimme Room": School resistance, attitude, and access to literacy. *Journal of Education*, 16, (1), 111–128.

Greene, M. (1995). *Releasing the imagination: Essays on education, the arts, and social change*. San Francisco: Jossey-Bass Publishers.

Grumet, M. R. (1987). The politics of personal knowledge. *Curriculum Inquiry*, 17, 319–329.

Grumet, M. R. (1988). *Bitter milk: Women and teaching*. Amherst, MA: University of Massachusetts Press.

Hamilton, D. L., and Rose, T. L. (1980). Illusory correlation and the maintenance of stereotypic beliefs. *Journal of Personality and Social Psychology*, 39, 832–845.

Hamilton, D. L., and Sherman, S. J. (1989). Illusory correlations: Implications for stereotype theory and research. In D. Bar-Tal, C. F. Gaumann, A. W. Kruglanski, and W. Stroebe (eds.), *Stereotyping and prejudice: Changing conceptions*. NY: Springer-Verlag, 56–82.

Hamilton, D. L., Sherman, S. J., and Ruvolo, C. M. (1990). Stereotype-based expectancies: Effects on information processing and social behavior. *Journal of Social Issues*, 46 (2), 35–60.

Heidegger, M. (1971). Building dwelling thinking. In A. Hofstadter (trans.), *Poetry, language, thought*. NY: Harper and Row.

hooks, b. (1994). *Teaching to transgress: Education as the practice of freedom*. New York: Routledge.

Howard, J., and Rothbart, M. (1980). Social categorization and memory for in-group and out-group behavior. *Journal of Personality and Social Psychology*, 38, 301–310.

Jourard, S. M. (1966). *The transparent self.* New York: Macmillan.

Kelman, H. C., and Hamilton, V. L. (1989). *Crimes of obedience: Toward a social psychology of authority and responsibility.* New Haven, CT: Yale University Press.

Rist, R. C. (1970). Student social class and teachers' expectations: The self-fulfilling prophecy in ghetto education. *Harvard Educational Review*, 40, 411–450.

Roman, L. G. (1993). White is a color! White defensiveness, postmodernism, and anti-racist pedagogy. In C. McCarthy and W. Crichlow (eds.), *Race, identity, and representation in education.* New York: Routledge.

Rosenberg, P. M. (1996). The presence of an absence: Issues of race in teacher education at a predominatly white college campus. In M. E. Dilworth and M. M. Bandele (eds.), *Considerations of culture in teacher education: An anthology in practice.* Washington, D.C.: AACTE.

Salvio, P. (1990). Transgressive daughters: Student autobiography and the project of self-creation. *Cambridge Journal of Education*, 20 (3), 283–289.

Salvio, P. (1994a). What can a body know? Re-figuring pedagogic intention into teacher education. *Journal of Teacher Education*, 45 (1), 53–61.

Salvio, P. (1994b). Writing the body: A composition in voice and movement. Paper presented at the National Reading Conference, San Diego.

Sleeter, C. E. (1994). Multicultural education, social positionality, and whiteness. Paper presented at the American Educational Research Association, New Orleans, April.

Spitz, E. H. (1990). Mothers and daughters: Ancient and modern myths. *The Journal of Aesthetics and Art Criticism*, 48, (4), 411–420.

Tatum, B. D. (1992). Talking about race, learning about racism: An application of racial identity development theory in the classroom. *Harvard Educational Review*, 62 (1), 1–24.

NOTES

1. See the work of Jourard (1966) and Beck (1983) for discussions of unwitting and willful disclosure.

2. I use this term in this paper with a certain amount of ambivalence. Leslie Roman (1993) reminds us that the phrase "people of color" implies that white culture is the "hidden norm" against which all other racially subordiante groups' so-called differences are measured. She points out that because the term can imply that whites are "colorless," thereby lacking any "racial subjectivities, interests or privileges," it may therefore exonerate whites from any responsibility to challenge racism.

3. Ruth Frankenberg (1993) found in her study of white women and race that they have a difficult time articulating a sense of cultural belonging. Only by shifting the discourse to ethnicity or regionalism could any coherence evolve regarding identity.

4. Christine Sleeter (1994) has documented her concern and experience with students regarding white silence on white racism. Her main argument is that white people generally frame racial issues in ways that are congruent with our own positions, experiences, and vested interests.

5. I am thinking here of the "underground railway," where opponents of slavery before the Civil War helped fugitive slaves escape to the free states or Canada; and the ancient myth of Demeter and Persephone, where Demeter is in search of her daughter, Persephone, who was captured by Hades (the god of the underworld) to be his wife. In relating a mother's search for her lost daughter, the story gives priority to the role of the mother over the daughter. Yet, its fabric importantly suggests that daughter and mother are one and that their experiences both reciprocate and replicate each other (Spitz, 1990). While the ancient myth associates youthful innocence in an enclosed space with playfulness and freedom from care, marriage on the other hand, is equated with brutality and death (Hades).

6. Maxine Greene (1995) inspires us to "teach for openings." She recalls Martin Buber speaking about teaching and the importance of what he calls "keeping the pain awake." She illuminates his notion when she says: "I suggest that the pain he had in mind must be lived through by teacher as well as student, even as the life stories of both must be kept alive. This, it seems to me, is when real encounters occur" (p. 113).

7. I have found the work of Martin Heidegger (1971) to be useful for my understanding of "dwelling thinking."

Resisting Diversity:
An Alaskan Case of Institutional Struggle

Perry Gilmore, David M. Smith, and Apacuar Larry Kairaiuak

Perry Gilmore is Associate Professor of Educational Anthropology at the University of Alaska, Fairbanks, where she teaches in the linguistics and education programs. She has conducted ethnographic research in the area of language and literacy in a variety or urban and rural settings in the United States and Africa. She has edited two books and published numerous articles on ethnography and education.

David M. Smith is Professor of Anthropology and Linguistics at the University of Alaska, Fairbanks. He has done extensive ethnographic research in educational settings both in Alaska and in Philadelphia, where he directed the University of Pennsylvania Center for Urban Ethnography.

Apacuar Larry Kairaiuak is a Yup'ik and a fluent speaker, reader, and writer of the Yup'ik language. He earned his B.A. in history from the University of Alaska, Fairbanks in 1991. He and his two siblings were the first generation of college graduates from their small village, Chefornak, on the Bering Sea coast. Kairaiuak has worked as a program developer and counselor for the Native Student Services program at the University of Alaska. Currently he is Assistant Project Director for the Circle of Strength Project Healthy Nations Initiative in San Francisco.

INTRODUCTION

In the following discussion an incident provoked by alleged comments regarding the preferential grading of Alaskan Native students at the University of Alaska Fairbanks is described and analyzed as a case study in the cultural-racial politics of education. As such it provides a vivid, even chilling, example of the techniques a white institution will marshal to resist cultural diversity and maintain its whiteness by completely missing, misunderstanding, and ultimately ignoring the responses, concerns, and actions of an aggrieved minority population in imposing its own institutional perceptions and interpretations of events. A deeply problematic and painful aspect of this resistance is that it is primarily accomplished through actions that the institution actually believes support minority success but in fact negate it. It is therefore necessary to illustrate and describe examples of the complexities and subtle machinations of white institutional privilege in order to begin to combat its devastating effects.

We present this case in order to raise the level of the discourse from one about individuals, specific programs, and groups to one which focuses on a critical self-examinination of institutional practices that consciously and unconsciously undermine diversity and nurture white privilege. (For a fuller discussion of this case and its historical context see Gilmore, Smith, and Kairaiuak, forthcoming; Gilmore, 1987; Gilmore, Kairaiuak, Kashatok, and Chase, forthcoming; and Smith, in press). This, then, is not a discussion about individuals, villains, or heroes, but about institutional postures, policies, and practices that on the surface may seem to be about race-neutral issues but, in fact, carry significant and damaging racial-political consequences.

In the summer of 1993 Michelle Fine visited the University of Alaska Fairbanks. In a colloquia address, drawing on examples from her data, she explored questions of both silencing and of speaking, commenting that neither was a "pretty picture." She reminded the audience that there was "plenty of evidence" to suggest that when people do speak "institutions from whom we expect better, surround elite interests." Fine's concluding analysis addressed the "responsibility" we as university scholars, practitioners, and activists have to both "speak the unspeakable" and to "support those who are gutsy enough to say some things out loud." Fine urged us (1) to rethink and document hidden transcripts of resistance; (2) to track consequences of institutional policies that may look neutral but are organized around hierarchical race/gender politics; (3) to document the costs of silencing and exclusion; (4) to rethink public discourse examining moments where comments which are said all the time suddenly fracture the discourse; and finally, (5) to nurture, create, and document free spaces through critique and creativity where silences can be interrupted and passion and outrage can be transformed into professionalism, scholarship, activism, and leadership (Fine, 1993).

The three authors of this chapter were all in the audience that afternoon. All resonated with the points that were being made. Each of us, two white professors and an Alaska Native graduate student, had shared experiences of silencing and speaking and witnessed the costs. We each knew well that the "grading controversy" on campus the year before had been our own poignant and powerful example of institutional silencing and resistance. We had each, along with many others in the university community, felt passion, rage, and confusion during the months of turmoil surrounding the fractured public discourse. Each of us had entered that discourse both on campus and in the media. Each of us could vividly recall our sense of exclusion as the institution "from whom we expected better" seemed to surround elite interests. We offer the following description and discussion of this controversial incident to interrupt an oppressive silence and to create a public place for critique and repair.

It is imperative that we take individual and institutional responsibility for critically examining the practices of our own institutions, and for initiating and maintaining an open dialogue that will ultimately nurture the possibilities for growth and change within our institutions. This dialogue is a difficult one to initiate. For example, after a limited circulation of an earlier draft of this essay, we had two very different sets of reactions. Members of the Alaska Native community (and the editors of this volume) felt we were extremely generous and diplomatic with regard to the institution and its actions while white administration and faculty tended to see our position regarding the institution as particularly harsh. We have tried to find a platform from which to speak that neither diminishes our critique nor inhibits our potential for repair.

In the first section of the chapter, we will present a description of the incident. In order to highlight the nature of the community's shared experience of the public discourse, the incident will be presented primarily through its depiction in the dominant culture narrative created and portrayed by the local media. Gates (1995), in a recent *New Yorker* essay which examines the national racial discourse surrounding the O.J. Simpson case and Million Man March, points out that "People arrive at an understanding of themselves and the world through narratives—narratives purveyed by schoolteachers, newscasters, 'authorities,' and the other authors of our common sense" (p. 57). In this essay, the local Alaska media headlines, through which we document the incident, capture a sense of the dominant culture reality in this particular community.

In the final sections of the paper we will argue that the incident itself functioned to maintain hegemonic practices at the university and to obscure the demonstrated and increasing successes of the Alaska Native student population there. We argue that the University, by almost exclusively focusing their responses to the incident on issues of academic freedom, standards, and grading practices, abdicated their responsibility to resist racial slurs and stereotypes and to provide a safe learning environment for the growing minority population. While issues of academic freedom, standards and grading practices are worthy concerns, they are not the focus of this essay. What is of concern to the authors is the fact that despite an official university investigation finding (reported early in the chronology of the incident) that there was *no* evidence to suggest any differences in grading practices for Native and non-Native students, the public discourse continued to almost exclusively concentrate on standards and grades. This dominant narrative managed to effectively squelch any analysis of the damaging racial politics at the core of the incident.

THE INCIDENT

The event that set off the incident occurred on September 5, 1991. It was described by the Chancellor in a report to the Board of Regents (January 8, 1992) four months later, in the following way:

> At a meeting off-campus, [a professor] was invited to present views on alternative methods of teacher certification. During a lively discussion that followed the presentation [the professor] apparently stated that UAF was under equity pressure to pass (graduate) Native students. No tapes of the meeting exist and accounts differ, but her remarks were interpreted as an attack on the integrity of grades and degrees awarded to Native students at UAF. [The professor] was not speaking as a representative of UAF at the meeting.

The comments made at that "lively discussion" and the reactions to them became the focus of a heated and intense discourse that was spotlighted and stirred by the local media and lasted for an entire academic year. Though rumors of the event were circulating, it was a month before the first article which made reference to the event was actually published. This was a letter to the editor in the student newspaper which was run with the headline, "Concerned with speaker" (*Sun Star*, October 4, 1991). The professor and a colleague replied in the following issue. Their letters to the editor were headlined, "Inaccurate rumor rectified" and "Let's all work together," respectively (October 11).

While the tone of these early student newspaper captions appears mild and almost understated, the drama was building across the campus and the community in private discussions, meetings, phone calls, letters, memos, and undocumented dialogues. In a letter to the chancellor, the executive director of the local Native Association wrote, "It is incredulous that statements like this can be made by one of the University's professors, and no reaction by anyone so far" (letter to the Chancellor, October 4, 1991). No official or public response from the administration was forthcoming.

Weeks later, on the first of November, the story broke in an Anchorage paper (a city located approximately 400 miles away from Fairbanks). The headline was big, bold, and almost unforgettable. It read, "Professor alleges UAF graduating unqualified Native students" (*Anchorage Times*, November 1, 1991). The article characterized the turmoil, reporting that "A professor's comments about grading standards for Native students at the University of Alaska Fairbanks has sharply split the community, pitting academic freedom against what some say is the devaluation of a degree in education." The director of the Native association mentioned above was quoted as being "concerned about the effect the statement has on Native students at the university. It has caused them great anxiety and concern—they don't want to have any doubt passed on their education, which the statement did."

The torrent of statewide headlines and media attention that followed for the next five months must have surprised even the media. The headlines below capture some of the focus of the controversy: "Professor's remarks raise ruckus: educators, students hit comments about Native performance at UA" (*Fairbanks Daily News-Miner*, November 3, 1991); "UAF Students want investigation" (*FDNM*, November 5); "Charge of favoritism riles Natives at UAF" (*FDNM*, November 5); "Students demand probe of lenient grading claim" (*Anchorage Daily News*, November 6); "UAF grading policies face close examination" and "Debate centers on preparation" (*FDNM*, November 7); "Native teacher shortage worries educators" (*FDNM*, November 7); "Natives express anger, hurt at forum" (*Sun Star*, November 8); "Controversy Reaches Fever Pitch" (*Sun Star*, November 8); "Regents seek report on UAF grading" (*FDNM*, November 10); "Racial animosity" (*FDNM*, November 29/30); and "Savage attack" (*FDNM*, December 2).

The headlines continued through December and final exams with articles, letters to the editor, and guest editorials each taking some position for or against the professor, the faculty, the education department, the Native students, the administration, etc. Accusations of racism, stereotyping, and cultural insensitivity, and defenses of academic freedom, university standards, and program quality were dominant themes. Residents in the immediate community as well as those across the state followed the daily headlines. In remote Native rural communities, residents are reported to have waited over fax machines for friends and relatives to send the most recent news reports. Even at a distance the incident carried an "electric" quality.

In January, after the holidays and at the start of a new semester, a report from the chancellor stirred the intensity of the headlines again. "Grading dispute continues: UAF chancellor's report finds no overall pattern" (*FDNM*, January 9, 1992). The *Anchorage Times* headline on the same day read, "Professor slams study: says UAF failed in analysis of grading Natives." Debate continued and accusations were made anew. "Professor bolsters favoritism charge: Inquiry does little to quell controversy" (*Anchorage Daily News*, January 10); "UAF grading charges fly" (*FDNM*, January 10).

The incident persisted and continued to create controversy and stir emotion and argument, and appeared to be not only irrepressible but also unresolvable. Most everyone felt wounded in some way. Law suits, threats of litigation, and legal action surrounded every interaction, further silencing a substantive or meaningful discourse.

In April a headline read, "Natives voice complaints on [the professor]" (*FDNM*, April 1). The newly appointed Native advisory committee in meetings with the chancellor were reported to have said that "the controversy over Native student academic abilities has not been resolved and they want to see action." Comments about the professor's "racial remark" were quoted. In response to much of the focus on academic freedom one committee member raised issues of academic responsibility, saying, "Academic freedom does not permit infringing on the rights of others. We have academic freedom of speech but we can also be judged by what we say." After almost a full academic year, despite committee reports, University plans and investigations, nothing seemed resolved; no one was satisfied.

In May of 1992, in response to the Native advisory committee's concerns, the chancellor issued a statement in which she acknowledged "that many Native students do not believe that the matter has been brought to satisfactory closure." With regard to grading practices she stated, "We believe without any doubt that, as a standard practice, UAF students, specifically including Native students, earn the grades and credentials they receive. We believe that there is no reason to question the efforts of faculty in general to grade all students fairly. The controversy was unfortunate, and on behalf of the University of Alaska, I apologize to Native students for any discomfort they may have felt."

These words and the public apology however, came too late. The semester was over. Many students were gone. In the *Fairbanks Daily News-Miner* on June 28, 1992 (nine months after the alleged remarks about preferential grades were made, and when most students were not on campus), a large ad was placed by the Alaska Native Education Student Association in order to have the chancellor's announcement made public. No articles, letters, or editorials accompanied or were forthcoming in response to the ad. Though the announcement carried large letters declaring "FAIR GRADING OF NATIVE STUDENTS AFFIRMED," the damage had already been done. One might only speculate about what might have been if such a statement had been forthcoming early in the controversy.

To the Alaska Native students the year's headlines had read like a catechism of hegemony; a litany of shame; a pedagogy for the oppressed (Freire, 1973). Questioning minority credentials and standards is unfortunately not a new or unfamiliar response to minority achievement. Nor are these discussions new to academia. (Unfortunately these are the common responses to interrupting any "gatekeeping" practices where race, class, and gender lines are crossed.) Remarks such as these must have been uttered many other times. But the intensity and persistence of this controversy and its continuous media frenzy with its unending stream of headlines seemed to surprise (and eventually exhaust) everyone.

OVERCOMING CLASHES OF EPISTEMOLOGY, EXPECTATION, AND STYLE

The seriousness of the controversy as measured by the pain and disruption it caused to Native students and their community of supporters demonstrated the separateness of the conflicting worlds they inhabit as subordinate participants in a white institution. This conflict resulted in clashes on several fronts.

In any conflict situation, the parties act according to their perceptions of the meaning of issues raised. Their reactions to the other's actions are colored by a complex set of expectations each has developed of the other. The mutual set of expectations that has evolved between Alaska Native students and the institution is far from simple, involving issues of academic expectations, silencing, and standards for assessment.

To the professor who had made the remark, and to most of the university community, the intense reaction seemed to come as a complete surprise. Comments about the abilities or inabilities of students and opinions about grading policy are the stock-in-trade of academic discourse. Many faculty members had often expressed similar concerns without serious consequence.

For most Alaska Native students the academic experience is loaded with import of a different sort. A pervasive expectation of failure confronts Native students and to a large extent governs how they are viewed and treated by the institution. But in many cases the institutional view is internalized by the students themselves. Many of the students on campus during the standards' controversy represented the first generation of those who attended high schools in their own villages, itself too often, as the narratives collected in another study by the authors (Gilmore, Smith, and Kairaiuak, forthcoming) illustrate, an experience with an alien white institution.[1]

Often in the small rural schools, where resources are limited, advanced math and science courses and various literature or language classes were not available to students. Therefore, many of the Native students, in order to fully matriculate into University degree programs, have to endure several semesters of "developmental" classes that do not count toward their degrees. These students have much to prove, to themselves and to their families, by their academic success. In their eyes and those of their families that they are earning good grades and graduating means that they have reached a major water mark in striving for success.

This is more the case because for many of them the approbation of professors, in the awarding of successful grades, bespeaks a deep cultural affinity they have experienced with elders or respected relatives in the village. In these contexts when a younger person is told to accept a responsibility by an older relative or elder, he or she accepts the assignment with pride, knowing that he or she would not be asked until they had proven themselves capable. Being told that they didn't deserve their successes, not only by the professor in question, but, through its reactions, by the institution itself, created not only palpable pain but a serious betrayal.

The institution treated the matter as purely academic, part of an ongoing debate about grading. It appeared taken back by the strong reaction of the Native community. One professor commented on the "hysteria" in the Native community. The institution didn't seem to know how to read the cues of, respond to, or acknowledge the Native community response. At least part of this reaction can be attributed to a serious and deep-seated clash of expectations. The institution expected that the university community would see the issue as academic and not personal, that it would welcome the proposed, impassionate, and rational attempts to sort out the "facts" as a positive contribution to resolving an ongoing debate.

Native students who had labored under a pervasive expectation of failure and who had, against all odds, registered impressive academic successes, expected the institution to celebrate these successes with them and to censure the faculty who had betrayed them. At the very least they expected the institution to hear their pain, understand the shame they risked bringing upon their families and their communities, and take steps to address these concerns. The institution views students as individuals; the students, in contrast, view themselves as part of a connected web of family and community. For the students their educations were not separable from their place in their families. This concept was expressed clearly in the following student narrative:

> The Native family infrastructure is fairly extensive when compared to a non-Native family; aunts, uncles and grandparents play a vital role almost equal to that of parents.
>
> I think, you know, within Native families, when you finish school they value it very highly. Because it's seen as part of the family, an accomplishment of the family. It's not just the individual. And so, in a sense, it's very highly valued.

However, the institution's response to the conflict surfaced another underlying conflict, a clash of conceptions of the nature of the University. One of the tenets of the positivism that characterizes western institutions is the need to separate facts from values or feelings and to make decision on the basic of facts alone. Universities celebrate their abilities to make academic distinctions, to look at issues "objectively" and dispassionately. The very bedrock of scientific inquiry is the ability to separate the investigator from the object of study—the need for objectification taken as unproblematic—and to eschew any emotional involvement.

This epistemology seriously clashes with that of Alaskan aboriginal society.[2] It is at the root of a number of other issues facing Alaska today, including the continuing debate of Native subsistence rights, which are seen as simple economic matters by the dominant majority, not matters of ideology and personal identity as they are perceived by Alaska Natives.

To the administration, and to much of the rest of the University community, the standards controversy was simply a matter of getting the facts and then finding a technistic resolution of the matter. For example, the chancellor repeatedly stated that this was an academic issue and would be addressed through academic channels. This impassionate, rationalistic, and technistic approach, in a Habermasian (1962) sense, clashed with Native students' views of reality as shaped both by their early experiences in traditional villages and by learning to succeed in an oppressive, often condescending and hostile educational environment. In the following discussion several dimensions of these views of reality are illustrated.

First, to these students grades, diplomas, and academic successes are not simply objective and depersonalized facts but valued personal accomplishments owned and celebrated not only by them but by their extended families and communities as well, and important to demonstrating self-worth. Many of the students came from traditional communities which allow for a pedagogy that provides room for error but goes to great pains to arrange for success. Noncompetitive and cooperative learning opportunities characterize the traditional pedagogy which holds the students in high esteem and maintains high expectations for them.

Second, contrary to the institutional assumption, the grading incident could not be seen as isolated and aberrant but was connected to other events serving as a whole to define the nature of their university experience. Their experiences of racism in the village schools, the stigma of being treated as potential failures, and their marginalization at the University form a connected web. Often Native people would recount several other seemingly (to many non-Natives) unrelated events of violence along with the grading controversy as a related cluster. There had been a drive-by shooting of a Native man in the town and the accused had been acquitted. A yet unsolved murder of a young Alaska Native woman student in the University dormitory had shocked, saddened, and traumatized the population on campus. These events along with the departure of several Native professors, the restructuring of the Rural College, and the grading controversy were all talked about in the Native community as part of the same problem.

The grading controversy could not be "taken care of" simply by ferreting out the facts, remediating the immediate breech, and proceeding with business as usual. To address it meant addressing the entire pattern of behaviors that constituted their experiencing of university existence. Virtually no one in the administration and few of the faculty or white students ever grasped, or acknowledged, the legitimacy of this reality.

Third, the roles some of the students were thrust into, as spokespersons and leaders, was inappropriate given their ages and kinship statuses. During the grading controversy the students went to the administration and to the faculty asking for explanations as to what was happening and for assurance that the issue was being addressed. Given their perception of the problem and appropriate action to be taken, they got little satisfaction. One student was told by his professor that he had deserved the grades he received but that he was different from other Native students. Even many of the professors to whom they looked for direction appeared weak and helpless in the turmoil. The faculty were unable to vindicate themselves or the students. As a result the students found themselves having to serve as their own spokespersons. They organized meetings, wrote letters to the media and the University committees, drafted position papers, and most difficult of all, were called upon to explain what was happening to their families.

While these were stressful and time-consuming roles, causing several students to drop classes and even drop out of programs, the net results were not all negative. Several students found a voice to surface what for them had been subjugated knowledge (Foucault, 1980). Some were able to challenge what had been a long-standing matter of conflict for them, that is, the way "white people" fragment reality and look at pieces of the whole. These examples illustrate Lather's (1991) contention that situations of this sort can result in the "historical 'others' mov[ing] to the foreground, challenging and reshaping what we know of knowledge." Many of the students assumed leading roles in newly organized student organizations and on advisory committees.

Finally, the confrontational style of the institution and the involved faculty was at first shockingly inappropriate and intimidating. In large part, the student response to the accusation was first to consult with faculty to see if it were true. On hearing it was not they asked the administration to deal with the professor who had made the accusation. As the institution failed to respond and the concern escalated both within the University and the larger community, the students began to participate in meetings and discussions with the media, in student organizations, and with student support service programs, faculty, and administration. The main topic of these meetings was the expression of their hurt, bewilderment, and feelings of betrayal.

The response to their initially expressed grievances, even though the administration repeatedly claimed that there was no evidence to support the accusation, was neither apology or retraction. Rather statements of policy were forthcoming from the institution and real or implied threats of legal action from the professor having made the accusation.

CONCLUSION: COUNTERING INSTITUTIONAL HEGEMONY WITH CULTURAL RESILIENCE AND COLLECTIVE RESPONSIBILITY

The data and discussion we have presented in this essay suggest that the unusual length and intensity of the incident described in this chapter can best be understood as an institution's resistance to the increasing successes of a visibly growing minority population on campus. The incident itself functioned to maintain hegemonic practices at the University and to obscure the demonstrated and increasing accomplishments of the Alaska Native population. The University, by almost exclusively focusing its responses to the incident on issues of academic freedom, standards, and grading practices, abdicated its responsibility to resist racial slurs and stereotypes (especially as depicted in news headlines), and to provide a safe learning environment for the growing minority population.

Consistent with theories of resistance and reproduction in education (e.g., see Bourdieu and Passeron, 1977; Giroux, 1983; Freire,1985), when it could no longer be predicted that Native students would "flunk out" or "get homesick" in their first year at the University, and when graduation statistics included growing percentages of Native students, the discourse shifted to questions of grading and unearned degrees.

Claude Steele (see Watters, 1995) has proposed the notion of "stereotype vulnerability" to explain poor black and minority academic performance. Steele states that,

> whenever [minority] students concentrate on an explicitly scholastic task, they risk confirming their group's negative stereotype. This extra burden . . . can be enough to drag down their performance (p. 45).

Steele argues that students have to "contend with this whisper of inferiority at the moment when their mental abilities are most taxed . . ." (Watters, 1995, pp. 45–46). In the case of the Native students on the Fairbanks campus this was not a whisper to contend with but a loud chorus that lasted through the midterms and finals of two semesters. Steele's research demonstrates that the cues that spark the vulnerability can be subtle. For example, stereotype vulnerability can negatively affect women's performance on a given math test if they believe the test shows gender differences or can similarly negatively affect white men's performance when told Asians tend to do better on the particular exam. What then might the effects of stereotype vulnerability be when the cues are bold, public, and clearly humiliating as they were throughout the incident described?

By not interrupting the damaging public discourse, the University failed to protect the educational lives and reputations of its Native student population. Many speculated about the damaging impact of the dominant public narrative on the students' potential for professional employment. Given these circumstances, the students demonstrated an unusual and inspiring amount of resilience throughout and after the incident. They displayed a remarkable ability to resist the public discourse.[3] The students seemed to draw their strength and direction primarily from their traditional values, families, and communities.

Many Alaska Native families want their children to be educated but are cautious about the potential vulnerability of their children in the white man's world, often far from home at the University. A poignant and illustrative example of this was shared in one of the open forums organized at the University during the grading controversy. A young Yup'ik woman came to the podium wearing a full length traditional fur parka. She stood proudly and explained that when she was leaving her village to come to the University to continue her education, her grandfather spoke to her. He said that she was Yup'ik and that she was beautiful. Because of that, he told her, the white people might try to harm her. (One might argue that this grandfather predicted the incident.) He continued, saying that the parka her grandmother made for her would protect her from harm. At the podium, she turned to model the full beauty of the parka she was wearing and told the audience that she always wears her parka and thinks of her grandparents' and their protection.

Though the University had not created a free or safe space, the students were able to maintain their traditional ties and seize a context for themselves. They learned the value of situated freedom which was not granted, but seized and created it in the context of many obstacles. For the most part students appeared to be able to transform anger, hurt, and confusion into professionalism and academic effort. That they could so strongly resist the stigma and vulnerability in such a hostile and assaulting environment is a remarkable story of resistance and resilience.

Almost one year after the incident occurred, a colleague, when asked how things stood with the controversy, responded that things were fine and that it was best to "go on and leave that all behind us now." The authors disagree. We have much to learn from these events and from the surrounding stories that were never told. If the incident and our reflections on it don't transform us, teach us, warn us, then we have not learned anything. Peggy McIntosh (1988) in a discussion of white privilege asserts that "[t]o redesign social systems we need to first acknowledge their colossal unseen dimensions. The silences and denials are the key political tool here."

BIBLIOGRAPHY

Bourdieu, P., and J. Passeron. *Reproduction in Education, Society and Culture*. Beverly Hills, California: Sage, 1977.

Fine, M. "Gender, Race, Class and Culture: The Politics of Exclusion in Schooling." Lecture. University of Alaska Fairbanks, August 1993.

Foucault, M. *Power/Knowledge: Selected Interviews and Other Writings, 1972–77*. New York: Pantheon 1980.

Freire, P. *The Politics of Education*. South Hadley, Mass.: Bergin and Garvey 1985.

Freire, P. *Pedagogy of the Oppressed*. New York: Seabury Press, 1973.

Gates, H. L. "Thirteen Ways of Looking at a Black Man," *New Yorker Magazine*. November 1995.

Gilmore, P. "Academic Literacy in Cultural Context: Issues for Higher Education in Alaska." Paper presented at The American Anthropological Association Meetings, Chicago 1987.

Gilmore, P., D. Smith, and L. Kairaiuak. "Resistance, Resilience, and Hegemony: An Alaskan Case of Institutional Struggle with Diversity," forthcoming.

Gilmore, P., L. Kairaiauk, G. Kashatok, and M. Chase. "Our Stories, Our Voices: Collaborative Analysis of Native Narrative Texts," in preparation.

Giroux, H. *Theory and Resistance in Education*. South Hadley, Mass.: Bergin and Garvey, 1983.

Habermas, J. *Strukterwandel der Offenlichkeit*. Neuwied: Luchterhand, 1962.

Kawageley, O. *Yup'ik World View: A Pathway to Ecology and Spirit*. Prospect Heights, Illinois: Waveland Press, 1995.

Lather, P. *Getting Smart: Feminist Research and Pedagogy With/In the Postmodern*. New York: Routledge, 1991.

McIntosh, P. "White Privilege and Male Privilege: A Personal Account of Coming to See Correspondences Through Work in Women's Studies." Working Paper Number 189, Wellesley College Center for Research on Women, Wellesley, MA, 1988.

Smith, D. M. "Aspects of the Cultural Politics of Alaskan Education," in *Ethnic Identity and Power: Cultural Contexts of Political Action in School and Society*. Henry Trueba and Yali Zou, eds., forthcoming.

Watters, Ethan. "Claude Steele Has Scores to Settle." *New York Times Magazine*, September 17, 1995.

NOTES

1. Village high schools are administered by regional school districts with virtually all superintendents being non-Native and the majority having been imported from other states. Furthermore less than 5 percent of the principals are Native and the great majority of teachers are non-Native from outside the village. There are local school boards comprised of village residents but with very few exceptions these are virtually powerless to seriously affect policy.

2. A provocative treatment of this issue is found in Kwageley, 1995.

3. Although it is difficult to capture accurately, it appears that neither the grades nor dropout rates of the Alaska Native students were significantly affected by the incident. One can only speculate how much better grades might have been in the absence of such negative stereotyping and attention.

The Art of Survival in White Academia:
Black Women Faculty Finding Where They Belong

NINE

Donelda Cook

Donelda Cook, Ph.D., is Assistant Vice President for Student Development and Director of the Counseling Center at Loyola College in Maryland. She is also an adjunct faculty member of the Pastoral Counseling Department and the Psychology Department at Loyola. She is published in the area of cross-cultural psychology, with an emphasis on counseling and supervision and training. She is coauthor, along with Janet E. Helms, of an upcoming book published by Harcourt Brace College Publishers, entitled: *Using Race and Culture in Counseling and Psychotherapy: Theory and Process.*

I AM AN ENDANGERED SPECIES
BUT I SING NO VICTIM'S SONG
I AM A WOMAN I AM AN ARTIST [SCHOLAR]
AND I KNOW WHERE MY VOICE BELONGS
I KNOW WHERE MY SOUL BELONGS
I KNOW WHERE I BELONG
                                                    —Jeanne Pisano

When the ideas expressed in this chapter initially occurred to me, they were not the subject of scholarship. Indeed, they were the confused feelings of a lone Black female faculty member in a prominent academic program in a predominantly White university. For some time, I was not even confident enough to admit my experiences to myself; let alone consider my experiences to be of worth to academic readers. However, I came to learn that the isolation that many Black women in White academia experience contributes to their self-doubt, confusion, anger, and oftentimes shame, as they attempt to sort out the emotional toll that they bear in being Black, female, competent, and alone in White academia.

Fortunately, Black scholars and authors in various disciplines and professions have published books which expose the racially discriminating conditions in which Black professionals thrive on a daily basis while working in White institutions. While many Black professionals feel alone and alienated in their White work environments, the recent authors remind us that we are not alone in our experiences with institutionalized Whiteness. Ellis Cose (1994), author of *The Rage of a Privileged Class: Why Are Middle-Class Blacks Angry? Why Should America Care?*, concluded from his interviews of a variety of successful Black professionals, that "many well-educated, affluent blacks . . . have not escaped America's myriad racial demons. Consequently, they remain either estranged or in a state of emotional turmoil" (p. 12).

Personally, journalist Jill Nelson's (1993) autobiographical bestseller, *Volunteer Slavery: My Authentic Negro Experience*, served as an awakening for me from the fugue-like state that I escaped to in coping with my experiences in White academia. The title of Nelson's book, *Volunteer*

Slavery, reflects her abandonment of personal and professional freedom for a commitment to "a life of slavery" in a powerful White corporate instititution.

Whereas Jill Nelson's story validated my experiences, it was not until I attended the first Black Women in the Academy Conference, held at MIT in January 1994, that I realized that someday I would have to write an academic version of the alienation that many African American faculty have endured at prestigious, and not so prestigious, White higher education institutions. During the conference of some two thousand participants, I had never observed so much competence, yet so much pain, as Black women from all corners of the nation, as well as internationally, presented in their disciplines of expertise and shared their stories (and literally their tears) of the institutionalized White racism that pervades the academy. Similarly, Derrick Bell (1994) brought to light the discriminatory practices that he endured as a law professor in White academia in his latest book, *Confronting Authority*.

This chapter is actually a work in progress. Using interviews of five Black female academians as a pilot study, I will apply the thematic experiences of Black professionals in White institutions as articulated by the aforementioned authors (Bell, 1994; Cose, 1994; Nelson, 1993) to the experiences of the interviewees. Given how vulnerable the Black women are in telling their stories, to protect their anonymity I can only describe the sample of five women as varied in academic disciplines and academic rank, from both public and private institutions. The narratives presented in this chapter suggest that the Black women faculty are oppressed in White academia; however, while victimized by White racism, they do not identify as victims! Once aware of the intricacies and realities of institutionalized Whiteness in academia, each woman developed personal survival techniques and carved out the places where she belongs. The primary aim of this chapter is to view, through the eyes of Black women faculty, expressions of institutional Whiteness in the academy.

INSTITUTIONALIZED WHITENESS IN ACADEMIA

I use the term "White academia" for several reasons. This chapter discusses the experiences of Black female faculty in predominantly White colleges and universities. One obvious reason for identifying academia as "White" is that in many instances in predominantly White colleges and universities, the academic departments consist of a resounding majority of White faculty members. Thus, the demographics create an environment of "Whiteness."

Perhaps less obvious is that the value systems upon which academic departments routinely function reflect the values of Western European, or White American cultural values. Furthermore, cultural racism within White academia is such that the White cultural values are strictly enforced and built into the power structure of academic departments.

I recently sat in on a presentation at a faculty teaching workshop conducted by Eugene Rice (1995), of the American Association of Higher Education. The timing of his presentation was perfect, as I was in the midst of conceptualizing "White culture" in academia for this chapter. Rice articulated a model, based on the ideas of Ernest Boyer (1991) and others, which contrasts traditional scholarship and academic culture to a proposed redefinition of scholarship and academic culture. Basically, the model represents a transformation of traditional faculty values of prestige and research toward a valuing of access and inclusion in learning. He described the traditional university setting as a place where faculty go to "hustle private advantage" rather than being responsible for the common good and shared values. One interviewee reported that she struggled in trying not to lead a "meaningless existence," which was tempting as she observed her colleagues teaching only one or two courses, seeing as few students as possible, coming into the department two or three days a week, and making money, privately, on the side.

The traditional setting Rice described above is consistent with the individualistic value orientation of White cultures. That is, for individualistic cultures, satisfaction of personal needs, goals, and desires are primary (Helms and Cook, in press). Through cultural racism within academia, White value orientations are institutionalized as the basis for hiring, promotion, and tenure decisions. Black women faculty, however, generally achieve from a collectivistic value orientation. Collectivistic cultures tend to be other-focused; concerns about the needs, expectations, and evaluations of others are central to one's own sense of well being (Helms and Cook, in press).

As Helms and Cook explain, in individualistic cultures, it is not unusual "for a person to forsake significant others (e.g., family, friends) in one's life in order to achieve great things for one self." This sentiment was relayed to one of the women interviewed, when early in her academic career her White department chair explained to her that the nature of academia is such that if a professor has a grant proposal due the next day and someone is bleeding at his or her doorstep, the professor must ignore the person and continue working on the grant proposal. The interviewee's reply was that she would probably opt to take the person *and* her work to the hospital and continue working at the hospital.

Black women faculty generally tend to contribute greatly to the social and moral redemption of academic scholarship. Due to their collectivistic and collaborative values, Black women may spend excess hours providing service to students, conducting action-oriented research programs, and using experiential-learning teaching methods. However, institutional racism is such that the reward structure of traditional academia is based on the individualistic values of White culture. Rice (1995) does make reference to the influence of gender and ethnic studies in the transformation of scholarship and the academic profession. Nevertheless, it appears that the ideas and strategies of women and men of color and White women may be co-opted for use by tenured faculty (who are primarily White men), while nontenured faculty will continue to be evaluated for tenure based on the traditional criteria. There has been a pattern in American society, as exemplified in the popular music industry, of Whites initially devaluing aspects of Black culture only to rename it and claim it as their own at a later date.

While the cultural values of White academia and those of many Black women may conflict, all of the women interviewed understood that they would be evaluated based on the criteria of White academic standards. To reach the levels of their achievements, such bicultural behavior was second nature to them. Their resentment, however, had to do with the flagrant insults and demoralizing assaults that they withstood from White colleagues, as their colleagues expressed Whiteness as the exclusive culture of academia.

Expressions of Institutional Whiteness

Expressions of institutional Whiteness are portrayed consistently in the interviews of the Black professionals conducted by Cose (1994), the personal accounts of Nelson (1993) and Bell (1994), and my interviews of Black women faculty. Themes have emerged related to Black professionals' perceptions of the hiring practices Whites use in hiring Blacks, day-to-day interactions of White colleagues with Blacks, Whites' expectations of Blacks' job performance, and subjective criteria Whites use to evaluate the performance of Blacks.

Each of the authors mentioned external pressures which urged their employers to establish affirmative action positions or to recruit Black employees. For Jill Nelson (1993), it was the Equal Employment Opportunity Commission. Bell (1994) described the influence of the urban insurrections following Martin Luther King's death in 1968 on the hiring practices of major institutions across the country:

> By early 1968, many of the nation's leading law schools, responding to both the national crisis and student pressures, were beginning to consider hiring one or two blacks for their faculties. Prior to that time, no more than a dozen blacks had ever held full-time faculty positions at white law schools.
>
> The changes that followed were neither voluntary nor significant. . . . Yet, to almost everyone, these surface changes seemed sufficient. (Bell, 1994, pp. 32–33)

The Black women faculty interviewed in this pilot study were recruited for set-aside positions. The motives for set-aside positions may have changed slightly since the sixties. That is, in addition to recognizing the inequities in hiring practices in higher education, more recent calls for action in diversifying universities appeal to the collective self-interest of responding to the changing demographics in the United States and the world (*Achieving Faculty Diversity*, 1988). Nevertheless, regardless of the motivations, the Black women faculty clearly perceived that they were perceived by their White colleagues as "tokens."

One woman told the story of a faculty retreat in which one of her White female colleagues literally cried out that she resented the external pressure to hire Blacks. The White colleague indicated that she was so outraged by affirmative action that she was actually sickened to the point of her stomach aching because she had worked her way through the academic ranks by following the same criteria as the White men who dominated academia.

Since the hiring process is typically different for set-aside lines, many Whites equate the calibre of the candidate as substandard to White candidates, even when the credentials reveal otherwise (Bell, 1994; Cose, 1994). One interviewee described a recent search for a new faculty member in her department:

> Oh, their [White colleagues] paranoia on the committee when qualified minority African Americans applied. . . . They didn't describe characteristics other than to say that they didn't see what this person had to offer and they didn't know why anybody on the committee really liked this candidate.

Cose (1994) uncovered evidence of subjective criteria being used to exclude Black candidates also. As one of his interviewee's disclosed:

> Someone will say, "Tom Jones is a wonderful lawyer. He really has a lot to offer. However . . ." One has to look out for the "however." I've seen them destroy people with the "however." Too often, he says, the "however" is followed by criticisms like "he cannot perform *on a day to day basis*, or *at a certain level*," phrases that seem to say something but in reality say nothing at all. (p. 17)

Alternatively, one of the interviewees indicated that her department appeared to view the set-aside lines as "free labor"; consequently, her department chair was willing to hire unqualified Blacks. When the interviewee served on one search committee in which the committee discerned that the *one* candidate under consideration was clearly unprepared to assume a faculty position, the department chair indicated that she would "find something for [the candidate] to do around the department."

Too often, Blacks are *only* hired on affirmative action lines. The interviewees cited examples of Blacks applying and qualifying for "mainstream" advertised faculty positions, and somehow during the negotiation process, the advertised position goes to a White candidate while the Black candidate ends up on an affirmative action line. In essence, the White candidate can only be hired if the Black candidate is hired on an affirmative action line. One interviewee referred to this type of arrangement as a "two for one deal."

As another interviewee reported,

> The year before I was hired, my department was reviewed for re-accreditation by an external professional body. The accrediting organization strongly recommended that the department recruit "minority" representation on the faculty. So, all of the candidates interviewed for the faculty position were Black, with the exception of one White candidate. However, when I was hired for the faculty position, I was informed that the department now had two positions, and the White candidate was also hired. Then, when we started the first semester, I discovered that the White candidate was appointed to the teaching assignments that were identified with the advertised position. I was assigned to teach practica courses during the fall semester and when I asked the department chair what I would be teaching during the spring semester, he said, "I don't know, what do you want to teach, Racism in _____ [the academic discipline]?" It was not until two months into the fall semester that my program chair, who was also chair of the search committee, explained the circumstances of the hiring situation to me. [The program chair] explained that I was the top candidate for the advertised position; however, [the program chair] requested that I be hired on a set-aside line so that the White candidate could also be hired. [The program chair] went on to explain to me, "I obtained the set-aside line so that I could *have my cake and eat it too*."

During our interview, the interviewee began telling this story with a good deal of composure; by the time she reached the end of the story, her voice and facial expressions were filled with indignation.

The White program chair targeted the interviewee as an object for the program chair's own consumption and use. This was further exemplified when later in that semester, the program chair asked the interviewee how she was getting along, and the interviewee answered quite honestly, "You know, I found myself thinking this morning that I wish my office was in another building." At which point the program chair began to cry and told the interviewee how it had been a dream that the department would become racially integrated before the program chair retired, and since the interviewee was unhappy there, the program chair's dream might not be realized.

Similar to Bell (1994) and Nelson (1993), the interviewees and authors perceived that they were solicited for their positions because they were Black; however, they did not perceive that their White colleagues acknowledged or even expected them to be competent.

> I knew they wanted to hire a minority person, it was very clear to me that that was one of their goals. I had not realized that all I needed to do was to be a minority so that annoyed me. . . . And I was in some respects kind of laughing to myself thinking, "oh this is going to be good"; good in the sense that I would have my chance to turn it around. I wouldn't fit the mold necessarily or the slot that they had set up.

Another Black woman recalled her interview for her faculty position.

[T]hey wanted to interview me on the same day that another candidtate was going to be there. When I questioned that, they said well, it was convenient for them to do it that way and to me, I just felt like . . . it was demeaning to subject us to running into each other. Eventually, I just marveled at the continuous insults that occurred during this interview. The first morning, I had breakfast with the search committee. While we were waiting to be seated, a very prominent member of the faculty turned to me and said, "At seven o'clock in the morning, you better be good." By then, I felt so detached that I just turned to the faculty member and replied, "So had you." I later found out from a colleague that the faculty member was actually impressed by my response. Go figure!

The woman accepted the faculty position, despite her perception from the interview that the environment was hostile and racially alienating. She accepted the position without expecting much support from her colleagues. In fact, when she applied for a major grant at the end of her first year, she felt that the acting department chair and college administrators were discouraging of her efforts, if not sabotaging.

When I met with the acting department chair to get the appropriate signatures for the grant application, he asked if I was sure that I wanted to go through all of the trouble of applying for grants. He said, "You know, research alone won't get you tenure," and then went on to suggest that the funding foundation might be rigged. . . . There was also . . . a tenured member of the College faculty, who . . . misinformed me about the appropriate signatures needed for the application. I accidentially, if not through the grace of God, encountered a Black man . . . who provided me with the correct information and assisted me through the grant application process.

Whites' comfort level with Black candidates also appeared as a common theme. One interviewee endured numerous incidents of social alienation and blatantly racially discriminating interactions with the majority of the faculty in her department.

They didn't know how to interact with me so they would look away . . . so I really felt invisibile and . . . the only times that I was visible was when I was absent. . . . I recall once telling that to the president and provost of the university in a meeting with Black faculty and administrators, and they both laughed. . . .

Jill Nelson (1993) described well Black professionals' invisibility:

Wherever we work, when we go to NABJ [National Association of Black Journalists] conventions every August it is as much to see each other and acknowledge our visibility as anything else. The other fifty-one weeks of the year we spend trying to make the white folks see us without being too scary, too black.

The woman who described her invisibility talked about her social withdrawal within her department as a way of protecting herself from the imposed isolation and the racially insensitive interactions that she had to endure with many of her colleagues. Eventually, she confided in one of the full professors about her unhappiness in the department. The interviewee explained that during the spring semester of her fourth year in the department, the department chair took me out to dinner and said to me, "Some of the faculty were talking and it occurred to us that you may not realize that the faculty like you." And I sat there and I looked at her and I said, "Well, you are absolutely right, I don't know that." So I said, "Well, why do you suppose it is that after four years I don't know that?" And she said, "Well it is because they don't know how to approach you, because you seem so distant. They think that you don't like them." And so I am thinking, now you are going to blame me for this! I said, "Why do you think it is that I am so distant? They are right, I don't like them! I had to become distant to protect myself from them. I have explained to you that there are clearly things that have happened that have made me need to protect myself from these people." But it had never occurred to her how insulting it was that someone would have to tell you, after four years, that people like you. That should have been something that I just experienced from them and came to know.

The interviewee reported that she had to abruptly excuse herself from the dinner table and proceeded to the restroom to vomit. She eventually resigned from her position, and during her exit interview the department chair told the interviewee that her problems centered around her having too much dignity.

Another interviewee explained that

people would tell me that I was hard to read and for whatever reason, they felt it was very important to be able to read me, to gauge what my reaction to stuff would be and so, I think I frustrated them in ways that they hadn't anticipated and they sort of frustrated the hell out of me because I couldn't just be a colleague, I had to deal with some barriers that I didn't set up. . . .

She continued to describe the "barriers":

Not being expected to do the job, so to speak, and the barriers were just the frustrations of having them believe that they could tell me how I should be. . . . So speaking out to disagree with something was not one of the areas that they prescribed. Speaking out in support in whatever they were suggesting of course was okay.

When asked how her White colleagues respond to her accomplishments, her reply was,

With surprise. Even though they consistently, but not daily, compliment me on what I have accomplished, it is always done with surprise. . . . I have to live internally because the external environment does not provide any of the rewards and supports that I would expect in a healthier environment for me.

As I write this woman's words, I can still feel the vibration of suppressed hurt and anger with which she recounted this portion of the interview.

Cose (1994) has devoted almost a complete chapter of his book to the suppressed anger that Black professionals experience in White work environments. He recounts that a trailblazing Black New York City politician concluded

that "whites don't want you to be angry." So black politicians in order to get along, often conceal their true feelings. "We're selective in our terminology. We waste a lot of time that ought to be devoted to candor." (p. 31)

Black professionals may use surpressed anger as a technique for their professional survival; however, to what expense of their personal survival? Some become interpersonally cold and detached, others withdraw altogether, still others' internalized anger leads to depression. One interviewee indicated that she took antidepressant medication for a period of time. Jill Nelson (1994) experienced a major depressive episode which she attributes to her work conditions at the Washington Post, and some of Cose's interviewees described both emotional and physical wakeup calls to the stress that they encountered in their positions.

To acknowledge the intensity of the anger and rage one feels in one's daily work environment, one would eventually have to ask the question, "Why do I stay here and tolerate this?" In fact, I did pose the question to the interviewees. Sentiments ranged from it being their right, and proving to White people that they could succeed; to making a better way for those who would come behind them, and especially to be there for Black students. One interviewee said that she made a decision not to apply for tenure because she realized that she was equally depressed at the thought of getting tenure and being denied tenure. She feared that if she put herself through the ordeal of the tenure process, that through cognitive dissonance alone, if she obtained tenure, she would feel obligated to stay. She realized that tenured or untenured, staying in such a hostile environment was not healthy.

Another interview ended with my asking the interviewee if she could think of anything else that was noteworthy. She responded,

Not really. I wonder, this is just wondering, I wonder how long I will be here . . . Because . . . I love my students but we have got so much work to do in our own communities. . . . I don't know where I will be next year. . . . This institution doesn't need me to go on. And that is being a token. . . . You know, I can say very good things. I could say I am glad I am here but I don't know how long I will be here.

CONCLUSION

The chapter began with a song verse which relates to the experiences of the Black women faculty interviewed. If anyone questions the status of Black women in White academia as an endangered species, all they have to do is call the personnel offices of predominantly White institutions and ask them for the number of Black women faculty employed, then ask how many are in tenure-track positions, how many are tenured, how many are full professors, and how many worked their way through the ranks of assistant professor to full professor there at the institution.

The women interviewed shared account after account of victimization within the academy, and still they are not victims. They are consumed by the Whiteness, and for some, finding their way within academia has meant finding a way out. For others, finding their way has meant finding ways to express their cultural values and selves within the dominance of White culture. They know who they are as Black women, as teachers, as scholars. Although they have not always been heard, they have consistently spoken up for themselves and for their students amid the oppression of their academic departments. They know that their souls do not belong to the ones who would hold tenure over their heads, they know where they belong, with their students and their communities.

The interviews of the Black women faculty members may have generated many emotions within the readers of this chapter. Some may empathize with the experiences and feelings of the interviewees, as they too have lived similar experiences. Some may harbor guilt feelings, as they reflect upon their conversations and interactions with colleagues who have objectified Black faculty, such as the "two for one" scenarios. Some may be infuriated by the feelings expressed by these Black women, rationalizing that the women just could not handle the rigor of academia. Still others may relegate the chapter to the emotional babblings of disgruntled Blacks looking for handouts, such as affirmative action. The readers' emotional reactions are significant data toward understanding individual roles in the survival or extinction of Black women in the academy. Whatever the emotional responses, whether those of the interviewees or the readers, important truths are being told.

For Blacks who identify with the experiences of the interviewees, it is important to acknowledge the existence of discriminatory and oppressive conditions in their environment so they do not internalize the messages communicated "about them" by some of their White colleagues. It is also important to seek out a support system which understands their experiences, so they can be emotionally replenished and intellectually rejuvenated by those who share their worldviews. Finally, they must always keep in mind that there are other options; that their fate and self-worth do not reside in the minds of their colleagues, whether they be tenured or untenured. For those contemplating the tenure process, the decision is not just whether the faculty will grant tenure to the Black tenure applicant, but also Black tenure applicants can decide whether they want to be tenured by a particular faculty. If the granting of tenure signifies, to some degree, a faculty saying to a tenure applicant that "you are one of us," the tenure applicant can decide if that is truly the faculty with whom he or she wants to be associated. Both tenured and untenured Black faculty can weigh whether or not it is important to have "colleagues" with whom they share common values and goals, or merely "coworkers" who share a common work setting.

White colleagues who are guilt-ridden must move beyond their guilt feelings and serve as advocates against the injustices they encounter in their departments. The system of institutionalized Whiteness will not change until White faculty recognize the ways in which they impose their cultural values on Black faculty, and value what Black faculty can offer their departments. Inclusivity is not just about "being nice" to Blacks by giving them positions in White departments; rather, it is about respecting the intellect of Blacks and including their frame of reference to enhance the offerings of the department and advancement in the discipline. The perspectives of White academia will not be broadened and redefined until Whites confront Whites on their White supremacist attitudes and behaviors.

Regarding the Whites who scoff at the emotionality of these interviewees and fight vehemently to maintain the White standards of academia, I wish that I could say that they will soon retire. However, I have been involved in enough meetings with faculty of various ages to know that there are still many who either genuinely believe that the White way is the only way that academia should be structured, or they believe that since they were tenured by these standards that others must also endure it. One must also wonder how much of this is about White privilege. Academia is a very elite profession, signifying intellectual prowess and selectivity; it may be difficult for many Whites to perceive Blacks as worthy of such designations and privileged lifestyles.

Ultimately, students and society suffer if Black women continue to be denied entry into academia or are "run out" of academia due to maltreatment. As stated early in this chapter and in the interviews, Black women faculty have a strong commitment to service to students and to their community. The privileged lifestyle that academia affords some does not have to be jeopardized by others' dedication to working toward the common good. There is room for multiple standards of excellence in academia, for individualistic and collectivistic pursuits of scholarship and teaching, for Black as well as White ways of being. Just as Black women academicians have much to pass on to their students, if their White colleagues would listen and welcome them into the academy as equal partners, there is much they too would learn.

REFERENCES

Bell, D. (1994). *Confronting Authority: Reflections of an Ardent Protester*. Boston: Beacon Press.

Boyer, E. L. (1991). *Scholarship Reconsidered: Priorities of the Professorate*. Princeton: Carnegie Foundation for the Advancement of Teaching.

Cose, E. (1994). *The Rage of a Privileged Class: Why Are Middle-Class Blacks Angry? Why Should America Care?* New York: HarperCollins Publishers.

Helms, J. E., and Cook, D. A. (in press). *Using Race and Culture in Counseling and Psychotherapy: Theory and Process*. Fort Worth, TX: Harcourt Brace.

Nelson, J. (1993). *Volunteer Slavery: My Authentic Negro Experience*. New York: Penguin Books.

Rice, E. (August, 1995). "Redefining Scholarship." Keynote presentation, Loyola College in Maryland Faculty Teaching Workshop, Baltimore.

fcBorder Guards: Ethnographic Fiction and Social Science

TEN

William G. Tierney

William G. Tierney is Professor and Director of the Center for Higher Education Policy Analysis at the University of Southern California. His most recent book is *Academic Outlaws: Cultural Studies and Queer Theory in the Academy* (Sage Press).

PREFACE

In what follows I offer a piece of ethnographic fiction. Writing of this kind is a relatively recent experiment in the social sciences, but it is also driven by questions that have bedeviled qualitative methodologists for much of the twentieth century. In particular, authors of ethnographic fiction offer a different response to what the best means may be to present "reality" to our readers (Tierney and Lincoln, forthcoming; Denzin and Lincoln, 1994; Richardson, 1994). Rather than a researcher-cum-narrator who collected data and unproblematically presents it, the following short story has an absent narrator much like we might see in fictional narratives.

Social science texts often attempt to telegraph to the reader one specific interpretation. A story of the kind presented here, however, rejects one reading and instead invites the reader to develop his or her own interpretations and narrative nuances. Fiction demands that we do not overdetermine the story's meaning, whereas science necessitates one reading. That is, the goal of a social science text is to lead the reader toward one singular interpretation of "reality" whereas in fiction the author hopes to engage the reader and provoke multiple interpretations. The story, then, is not told from merely the author's point of view. Instead, one reader may disagree, for example, with this story's protagonist, Scott, or another reader may think about how issues of gender are made invisible in the text. Thus, rather than a qualitative chapter that presents a particular interpretation, I offer a story that intends to engage the reader in multiple readings of a text dealing with oppression, race, gender, and sexual orientation.

I also am not suggesting that all stories must be presented in one way; if anything, I am saying the opposite. Different problems demand different methodological strategies—sometimes a survey is important and at other times a case study is warranted. Similarly, sometimes data presentation of a standard kind is necessary, and at other times, I am suggesting that issues should be presented in the manner attempted here.

As we approach the twenty-first century a culture of doubt permeates academic work in the social sciences. Words such as "reliability," "validity," and "trustworthiness" have become contested terms in a postmodern world, and researchers have sought to reinscribe them with meanings that would have been unheard of two generations ago (Tierney, 1993). Rather than the cool, stripped-down logic that authors of social science texts often strive for, as the author here, I do not want to give the readers all of the answers. I hope to raise issues and provoke commentary.

We do know, for example, that in cities such as New York, Los Angeles, and Philadelphia, events such as those described in "Border Guards" have happened. School districts, colleges, and universities have backed off on issues of sexual orientation, and quite often multicultural alliances are difficult to build around gay, lesbian and bisexual issues. This story, then, attempts to focus on the multiple levels of marginalization that exist in society, and brings to life the challenges that we face as participants in a multicultural society to deal with the manifold identities we all have.

* * *

The meeting room was down a long hallway cluttered with reams of computer print outs and office supplies. As Scott made his way to the room he smelled a mixture of patchouli and stale coffee. Frances, whose office station was immediately outside the room, often had patchouli at her desk in a small marble bowl. "It keeps me awake," she'd say, when one of the other secretaries complained about the sweet smell. Most people seemed oblivious to the odor. It reminded Scott of his days in the Peace Corps; he always commented on how much he liked the thick scent of incense. But the mixture of burnt coffee with the patchouli made a decidedly uncomfortable combination. He wrinkled up his nose as he entered the meeting room.

"Phwew, what a stink," he said, "it smells like a version of purgatory." Morgan and Felicia had already arrived for the faculty meeting. They were talking to one another, and they ignored Scott's comment.

Scott took a seat at the opposite end of the rectangular table from them and looked casually around the room. One long fluorescent light lit the windowless space. The white walls were completely blank except for a small blackboard that had scratchings on it from a previous meeting. "Looks like an interrogation room," Scott muttered. A handful of used styrofoam cups, plastic spoons and crumpled paper napkins littered the table. The glass sugar bowl had tilted onto the table so that sugar cubes had rolled haphazardly onto the floor. The waste paper basket overflowed with a pink and white Dunkin Donuts box that looked like it was suspended in air and about to fall.

Scott absent-mindedly began cleaning up the room as Morgan and Felicia continued talking. He hated messes and disliked even more that no one would clean up after themselves. He silently laughed for a moment as he thought about his daily battles with his nine year old son, Miguel, to clean up his room and get ready for school. "What's the big deal, Miguelito," he'd invariably say, "all I'm asking is that you make the bed and don't use the floor as your closet. Jeez." Miguel, a small boy with deep brown eyes and long dark hair, most often found the space beneath his bed as an adequate resting place for his clothes. Scott's partner, Bruce, usually absented himself from the morning argument Scott had with Miguel about making his bed and hanging up his clothes. Bruce did the morning dishes as Scott got Miguel ready for school.

Inevitably the three of them would get to the lab school just as the bell rang. Miguel would kiss Scott and Bruce good-bye, and Bruce would give the boy the once over to make sure he was presentable. "Tuck in your shirt, Miguelito," he'd yell as the olive skinned boy ran into the building waving good-bye to his fathers.

Scott and Bruce would drive the rest of the way to the university checking off who was to pick up Miguel after school, who was going to get the dry-cleaning, who would make dinner, and who would go to the post office to pick up the package that the mail carrier said he couldn't leave in the mailbox, or some other task that set and reset the rhythm for their lives. Felicia often teased Scott that he and Bruce seemed like a portrait out of a gay Norman Rockwell painting. "You even drive a Volvo, for chrissakes," she'd said one day. "And Bruce looks like he's out of a J. Crew ad with those turtlenecks of his. You guys are so normal it drives me crazy."

After he'd cleaned the table and put the wastepaper basket in the hall, Scott took the coffee pot to Frances, pointed to the layer of black crust on the bottom, and said, "Miguel would say there's lots of yuck here. Where can I find a sponge?"

Frances laughed and said, "I'll get it. It's in the women's room. You go to your meeting." He handed the pot over to her saying, "Do I have to? I've been to boring meetings all day. Can't I stay out here with you and make the coffee?"

She smiled and disappeared into the washroom.

When Scott reentered the room he brought new coffee cups, spoons, and napkins. Morgan looked up and said, "Oh, good, do we have fresh coffee?"

Morgan and Scott were in some respects opposite ends of the professorial spectrum. Where Scott never wore a tie, Morgan was always the best-dressed man in the room. Morgan today wore a three-piece suit with a scarlet silk foulard tie that looked as though it were designed and made in Italy. His gray hair and goatee looked as if it had been freshly manicured that morning. Scott imagined ruefully how he must look: sandy hair, thinning, and desperately in need of a good salon styling and cut; his jeans were clean and washed, but never "done" at the laundry with a sharp crease. The denim work shirt was faded at the collar and his loafers were in need of re-soling. Bruce often kidded Scott that he was an insult to the gay fashion world with the way he dressed. Scott would shrug his shoulders and say he didn't have time for flashy appearances.

The students called Morgan "Professor Hansen" and Scott by his first name. Scott seemed to enjoy ruffling feathers and Morgan did not. Nevertheless, they were often allies and frequently placed on similar committees such as this one. As an African American who was a full professor, Morgan was selected for twice as many committees as his white peers, but he did not complain. Now that he was a full professor, Morgan felt that people finally had to listen to him, that he had earned the right to be heard. Scott enjoyed being involved and thought he could make a difference on issues that he cared about, even though other faculty told him committee work was a waste of time.

"I should hire you to come to my house and clean for me, Scott," said Felicia. "You do such a good job."

"I've seen your office, and I've seen your home, Felicia. I wouldn't touch your house with the proverbial ten foot pole."

Anyone who knew Scott and Felicia was familiar with their banter. They teased one another unmercifully and sometimes an outsider was unsure if they actually were teasing or fighting. "An academic marriage," someone had once said, and they did not disagree. Felicia was a tall, thin woman with red hair that hung on her shoulders. She was recently tenured and frequently controversial. An older professor privately commented that it was not her feminism that "turns me off" but the manner in which she presented issues. She had an "agenda," other professors said, and they did not appreciate being labeled sexist or racist simply because they disagreed with her about one or another issue. Other faculty would quietly make fun of her heavy Puerto Rican accent, or make veiled comments complaining that they couldn't demand their students to speak perfect English if the faculty didn't.

Felicia was to chair the committee on multiculturalism. The dean had put the committee together and although he had chosen faculty with differing viewpoints, his choice of Felicia had sent a signal to the school that he wanted change. She sent a memo to everyone prior to this first meeting requesting that they bring "ideas, energy, and commitment," about how they might create a broad-based undergraduate course that dealt with multicultural issues. As was typical, she had no hidden agenda and hoped to develop ideas from the group, but senior faculty felt the opposite was the case. "She'll have us all teaching her stuff," one professor complained to Michael, another committee member.

Michael assured the professor that would not be the case: "I'm sure Felicia won't railroad anything or anyone. And she sure won't railroad me!"

In the ensuing weeks, other faculty spoke to Michael in his Spartan basement office about their own particular concerns. Some said they were worried about standards, and others bemoaned how the college was becoming politically correct. Michael liked the attention, and he also felt that he could play the role of conciliator. He always had gotten along well with Felicia, and Morgan was in his department. Scott was a bit of a smart aleck, Michael thought, but he wasn't really a bad guy.

Michael also was the only faculty member who had his graduate student on the committee. He had worked quite closely with Fatima, an Iranian woman, and they liked one another. Once a week for the past semester she had made an appointment and had him go over different parts of her dissertation proposal. He didn't know much about Iran, but he always was forthright and serious with her, and it was clear she respected him.

His ideas about multiculturalism reflected how he acted with Fatima. If people just treated one another fairly, then the world would be a better place. Everyone deserved the same treatment, and you had to just take one case at a time. He didn't read too much about all the debates about political correctness, but he felt that in general the problems were misunderstandings between individuals that could be worked out on a one-to-one basis. Michael had grown up in North Dakota, and he prided himself on his prairie sensibility. When the dean appointed Fatima to the committee as the student representative, Michael thought it was a good stroke; rather than a rabble-rouser, the faculty had someone who would work very hard.

Michael arrived with Fatima as Frances brought in the fresh pot of coffee. He was a tall man who seemed to wear a cardigan sweater over a short sleeve shirt and tie whether it was hot or cold, or the meeting was formal or informal. "I feel like I'm talking to Father Knows Best," Felicia had once joked to Scott about Michael. As Morgan grabbed his cup, Michael introduced Fatima. She wore a light gray chador and had a dark-colored polka-dot neckerchief draped over her head. She shook hands with Felicia, Scott, and Morgan as Frances filled people's cups. Felicia said, "Let's see, who's still not here? Has anyone seen Aaron? Kim told me she would be late, but I wonder where Aaron is."

Scott snorted, "Aaron's never on time. Why would you think he'd be different for this group? He's undoubtedly locked himself out of his office again." Aaron had a reputation for losing things. His wife had once said she'd like to have children's snap-on mittens for him given the number of gloves he'd lost. Michael settled into his chair and took a sip from the chipped white coffee cup that he'd brought that said "World's Best Golfer—Not!" Fatima moved her chair away from the table and silently watched Felicia. Just as Felicia said they should begin, Aaron entered. "Were your ears burning, Aaron?" she joked. "I won't say who, but someone here doubted your ability to arrive on time."

Aaron was a thin man who rivaled Morgan for the quality of his clothes. His suits were Armani and his shoes were Bally. Today he wore a light brown suit with a cobalt blue tie and a soft blue shirt. Scott thought he looked dazzling, "academe's answer to Denzel Washington," he laughed to himself. Aaron kept his hair short. He had the appearance of a body-builder—shoulder muscles, a tight chest, flat stomach. He was one of the most popular faculty members on campus. Although he had been at the university for only four years, he had made a name for himself as an outspoken professor who did not hesitate to speak up for students. When the African Amer-

114

ican students had taken over the Du Bois Center the year before they requested Aaron be their intermediary. Morgan initially had tried to counsel him about how to "make it" in the academy, but Aaron made it clear he knew what it meant to be an assistant professor who was Black. Although Morgan and Aaron had a civil relationship, they were not friends.

Aaron and Scott's relationship was more complex. Scott was outgoing and friendly to Aaron, and Scott was equally outspoken on issues. They frequently saw eye to eye. But Aaron was unsure how to deal with Scott's homosexuality; he had never thought much about people being gay, but when confronted with it he just thought it was weird, slightly disgusting. Men doing things to other men. Scott sensed Aaron's discomfort, but so many individuals were uncomfortable with someone who was not only gay, but open about it, that Scott had just learned to live with it. He respected Aaron's voice and thought of him as an ally. They never spoke directly about sexuality, but that too did not surprise Scott.

Aaron took an empty chair and said, "I would never want to be late for this committee, Felicia. I know I would never hear the end of it." They all laughed and looked toward Felicia. Scott folded his hands on his chest and slumped in his chair. He noticed that the grease stain on his left pants leg from last week's dinner had not come out in the wash. Frances closed the door on her way out and Felicia began to outline her plans.

"Our agenda is pretty open-ended. We're supposed to develop a position about how we intend to include multiculturalism in the undergraduate curriculum. It can be anything—a series of courses, one big course, something that includes all the faculty or just some of us."

Scott tried to wipe up a coffee stain in front of him as he listened. Aaron moved imperceptibly away from Scott as the cleaning strokes drew closer. Morgan had crossed his arms and sat impassive, Buddha-like, while Fatima stared intently at Felicia. Michael did not seem to be listening at all and instead was engaged in finding some spare napkins for Scott's campaign to clean up the table.

"What we're doing today is figuring out what we want, where we want to go with all of this. You know the rules. Even though it's early in the semester, if we're going to have this in the schedule for next year we need to present a plan to the curriculum committee by November. I propose we meet every other week, which only gives us about six meetings. What do you think?"

There was a moment of silence and then began what Scott called "faculty talk." One person spoke right after another and the dialogue had no basis in what the previous speaker said or, as Scott often said, "any basis in reality. It's blue sky talk."

"I think we should offer a year-long course sequence," said Aaron.

"I can't make every other week, Felicia," counseled Morgan.

"Things never move this fast. I wonder if it's even possible," asked Scott.

"Can we get released time for this?" queried Michael.

"This should involve fieldwork. Send them into the field so they get their hands dirty," continued Aaron.

"Are we the ones who plan the course or teach it?" asked Michael.

"We should involve faculty from other colleges, too," said Morgan, "and the multicultural resource center in Student Affairs should send over a person."

"I like the idea of fieldwork," said Scott. "We could have them work in the Women's Resource Center in town, the AIDS clinic, the homeless shelter, the lesbian and gay community center, even the churches. This could be really broad-based."

Fatima spoke for the first time. "What is the curriculum to be for?"

The group stopped for a moment as the door opened and Kim entered, dressed in black jeans and a black turtleneck. She was a short woman with bleached blond hair and eyeglasses that invariably hung around a cord on her neck. Scott loved the eyeglasses: they were black butterfly glasses that he hadn't seen anyone wear since the fifties. He was never sure if Kim wore them to be kitsch or because she had no idea how out of style they were, but either way, he liked that she wore them.

Kim taught in the philosophy program. She was good friends with Felicia and was one of the few tenured women full professors of color on the university's faculty. As an Asian American she also found herself on numerous committees, but unlike Morgan she resented being chosen simply because she was a "twofer"—a woman and a person of color. When the dean asked her to be on this committee she had consented only because Felicia was to be chair.

Felicia nodded to Kim and said, "We've just begun and already I'm confused! Perhaps we need more direction. Let's think about Fatima's question? What's the curriculum to be for?"

"Well, it's to advance their understanding of multiculturalism," said Morgan. "Students need more of a grounding in what America's heritage is—that it's not just the work of white people that made this country what it is."

Aaron quickly cautioned, "I'd hope this is not just a cultural literacy type thing that students read a little of this and a little of that. They need to understand theories behind things, what structural racism means, for example."

"I like Morgan's idea," said Michael. "I could see us offering a year-long course sequence that would be cotaught where we offer sections relating to different people's contributions."

Kim looked up to the ceiling and asked aloud, "Do we have a faculty who can do any of this—or want to?"

Scott paused before speaking. Kim always had a way of asking practical questions and he appreciated her for it. He crossed his legs, unfolded his hands, and began picking at a cut on his right thumb. Scott nodded his head in concurrence with what Kim said. "I was thinking the same thing. We don't even know one another very well. Doesn't multiculturalism demand some kind of investment in one another? Don't we have to have some sense of what it means to be African American or Hispanic or gay or a woman before we teach this stuff? For whatever it is we decide to teach? I hope I'm not here just as the queer delegate to multiculturalism. That I do my thing, and then Aaron does his thing, and on down the line. That all we do is sort of a 'culture on parade.' I think what we need to do today is figure out a plan for how we will cross our own borders, rather than start speaking about what borders students need to cross."

An uncomfortable silence followed that Fatima finally broke. "Are we saying that we have a particular point of view in these classes? I am Iranian. Are we saying that these classes will endorse an American point of view about women, for example?"

"Oh, no, of course not," said Michael.

"We won't take a stand that offends anyone, I wouldn't think," said Morgan. "Multiculturalism is about openness. It's not ideological, doctrinaire."

Felicia caught Scott's eye and she knew what he was thinking. This was not about feminism, about an "American point of view"; this was about gay issues in the curriculum. When Scott had walked in Morgan was speaking to Felicia about his definition of multiculturalism and he had made clear his discomfort about equating homosexuality with race. "It's just not the same thing," he'd said. "It's almost insulting."

Aaron didn't say anything and Scott looked directly at him as he spoke. "I disagree. We should take stands even if we offend people. This is a course that should be up front about what we believe. Right now the administration is questioning affirmative action and this is a place where I would see a fruitful debate taking place. The president just rejected domestic partners for the university without any murmur of protest. We have fewer incoming students of color this year than last. All of these things are areas of investigation and ultimately where we should take a stand. A multicultural course implies multicultural action."

Morgan asked, "Domestic partners. Does that have something to do with NAFTA?"

Michael chimed in: "I don't think we want a class that indoctrinates students to a way of life, a lifestyle, one way or another. We should be more open. At least that's my opinion."

Morgan agreed as Fatima commented, "In the Koran, there are specific rules about how we guide our life, about how to live. I could not sit in a course that went against my religion."

Felicia quickly pointed out that the university was a public institution where there was a separation between church and state, but Morgan said to no one in particular, "There are still state laws that we must adhere to."

Aaron quietly said, "And the state is quite clear about antidiscrimination, about supporting affirmative action, about increasing the number of students of color. There's nothing that should stop us in speaking about these things."

"And there you have it," thought Scott. "The queers get left by the roadside as this group marches to its own liberal tune." He remained quiet, reddening a little across the forehead. Felicia made one last effort at bringing people together. "What do people think about Scott's suggestion that we need to understand our own issues, our own problems, before moving on?"

"That's good, a good idea," offered Kim.

"Sort of like a faculty reading group," added Morgan. "We could do that."

"It might take us longer, but we could read things, yes," said Michael, "as long as we all agreed about the reading list. I mean we don't want to read Mao's red book."

"Of course we would agree on the reading list," laughed Morgan. "No one's suggesting that we have to do anything; after all, this is all volunteer. We're faculty. We're inviting people to join, not making them join."

Kim continued, "I don't know if I can do too much reading. I'm overloaded as it is."

"I'm not sure how the dean will look on this if I tell him we've decided to read books for a year," said Felicia. "Especially if the money comes from his budget."

The group turned its head to Scott who kept his eyes focused on the faded coffee spot on the table. Aaron glanced at his watch and motioned to Felicia with his forefinger that time was running out. Morgan drained his coffee cup. Fatima sat motionless. Quiet settled on the room so that for the first time the buzz of the fluorescent light became obvious. Scott again noticed the smell of Frances's patchouli. He offered a summary:

"I think this is what you probably want to do. Felicia's right about the dean. He wants an answer, not simply a comment that you want to read more books. What you might do is develop a course along the lines of what Morgan suggested. A semester- or year-long course that offers different readings that you all agree on. That seems do-able."

Felicia knew what Scott was doing, but she suspected no one else did. Scott always used language precisely, and by his comment he had taken himself out of the group. She felt let down, but she also felt the need to conclude. "All right, then, let's say that in two weeks we'll meet again. Why not come prepared with an example, a temporary kind of thing, a list or a syllabus of what you'd like to see in such a course, and we'll go from there. Is that ok?"

"Very good. Let's try to pass it around to one another ahead of time," said Morgan.

"We could put it on e-mail," said Aaron.

"I don't have e-mail," responded Kim.

"Well, then, just get it to me, and I'll see everyone get's a copy," concluded Felicia.

Aaron stood up, buttoned his suit coat, opened the door and left the room. Michael and Fatima left together. Morgan asked Kim if he could speak with her for a minute about a student whose oral exam they both had to attend that afternoon. Felicia and Scott gathered up their papers and left in silence.

"See you Frances," said Scott as he pushed open the office door. "Hang in there."

Felicia and he walked for a moment in silence. He did not need to explain to Felicia how he felt and what he had decided; she knew him better than anyone except Bruce. "I don't know what I could have done," she confessed. "I wasn't prepared for it. I should have thought. I'm surprised at Aaron, I guess."

"I'm not," said Scott. "I hadn't thought about it either, but I can't say I'm surprised. You know I won't be on it. I can't."

"I know. I think they'll be relieved."

"And that's the problem," said Scott. "They're the ones who need the course on multiculturalism. People shouldn't be relieved. Multiculturalism shouldn't be about making people feel comfy. We're saying we're going to educate students and we're the ones who need to be educated. I hope I'm not acting like a typical white boy—like if I don't get my way, I'm not gonna play. But how can I participate in a group that wants to shut me up simply because I'm queer? I've spent too much goddam time being invisible and silent to accept it anymore, especially in groups like that. You know, Felicia, sometimes I really hate liberals."

"That's why I'm surprised at Aaron. He's not liberal. Had you ever met Fatima before?"

Scott nodded his head no. "Aaron's body language says the whole thing. We were once joking around and I playfully hit his shoulder and you should have seen his eyes. You'd think I'd French-kissed him. I also ran into him in the locker room once and he probably set the world's record for getting dressed. He's got a cute body, too, by the way! Such a drag he's homophobic. How can someone who's Jewish and Black just sit there and let people pass judgment like that?"

Felicia laughed but also felt sad. She had wanted this group to be fun and now all that she saw was a round of boring, and probably counterproductive, meetings that would lead to nothing. "Don't forget to come over early Saturday afternoon," said Scott. "Miguelito wants you to get there before everybody arrives."

"Bruce is one step ahead of you. I called you last night and you were at the gym. Bruce filled me in and gave me some ideas about what I could bring for Miguel's birthday. Bruce seems to have the whole thing under control. I can't imagine a birthday party for forty kids. You'd be lost without Bruce, kiddo. You had better hang onto that man. And Miguel told me he's not a baby anymore so you also had better drop the 'ito' or someday soon he'll slug you."

Scott didn't make a big deal about his resigning, and in the coming weeks no one asked him or Felicia about it. Kim had dinner one night with Felicia and they discussed the committee a bit, but Kim was too busy to put much energy into the group. "It's too bad Scott feels that way," said Kim, but Felicia was sure that Kim wouldn't give it any more thought.

The next time the group had a meeting Aaron was absent and Kim came late again. Morgan and Michael and Fatima all had prepared their syllabi with exacting precision and they spent most of the meeting talking about readings. They had to cancel the following meeting because there was a professional conference that most of them attended. At the next meeting Fatima's child was ill so she was not in attendance and Michael simply did not show up. A week before the entire group was finally able to get together again no more progress had been made. When Felicia called the individuals Kim said guiltily, "I'm sorry Felicia. I shouldn't have ever said yes. I just can't do it. I've got two other things I'm supposed to do at that time. I'll sign whatever you like as long as you think it's OK, but don't count on me for the rest of the semester." Aaron said he was still interested, but couldn't make the next meeting. Felicia sent a memo to the dean saying that they were unable to meet the deadline and that perhaps a new group should be formed the following semester. The dean formed a reconstituted group with Michael as chairperson.

When Scott told Bruce about the meeting it was sandwiched in between Miguel's announcement that he had gotten into a fight at school and Bruce's discovery that the dry cleaners had lost one of his favorite plaid shirts. "I feel really bad for Felicia," concluded Scott. "I know she was counting on me, and I feel like I just checked out. But—"

He never finished his thought, as Miguel came into the kitchen with math homework that he needed help on. "That's not my area, kiddo," said Scott. "Daddy Bruce takes over here." Bruce gathered up the boy in his long arms and carried him into the dining room where they set out yet again to conquer long division. Scott finished the dishes and listened to their banter. Scott's impatience was balanced by the infinite patience of Bruce. Miguel would invariably get frustrated by a mistake and want to give up. "We're almost there, Miguelito," said Bruce. "C'mon, one more time. If you take the 6 and shove it into the 84—"

Scott placed the dish towel down and looked in on them. Miguel had his legs drawn up underneath him, and Bruce had his left arm thrown over Miguel's shoulders. Miguel looked so small sitting there as the sun set in the dining room window, but he also looked safe with his father. Bruce kept nodding his head yes as the boy worked on his numbers. Scott admired the way Bruce could get Miguel to keep working. He was so positive. "Numero uno otra vez," clapped Bruce when the boy had finished. "Go on and show your handiwork to Scott." The boy turned around and saw Scott standing in the doorway. Miguel raced to him and showed him the completed homework. Scott knelt down, and hugging his son, said, "How about if I take us for ice cream. My treat since you guys have been working so hard."

In the ensuing weeks what surprised Scott was how normal everything remained. He ran into Morgan at other meetings and they talked as if nothing had happened. At the dean's Octoberfest reception he talked with Michael about the football team's winning ways. It turned out that Fatima's daughter attended the same school as Miguel so they occasionally met one another coming or going, and offered quick, polite greetings. Kim acted as if nothing had happened, and Scott felt that to Kim, actually nothing had happened.

Aaron was the opposite. No one other than Felicia noticed how Scott and Aaron avoided one another. At the dean's reception Aaron almost physically ran into Scott at one point and they both deftly turned away from one another. Another faculty member and Scott went to Sam's Diner for lunch and when the waitress pointed to a booth near the window Scott said he had a cold and asked to be seated in another area, when actually he'd seen that Aaron was in the booth next to the one offered him.

Scott felt a mixture of anger, sadness, silliness, and ultimately, fatigue. He wouldn't be silenced by anyone, he thought, and if people couldn't deal with who he was, then fuck them. But he also felt lonely. If someone like Aaron, a product of civil rights and a victim of oppression, couldn't figure out where he was coming from, then what hope was there? Scott also didn't like the way he was acting. Typical man. Typical professor. Typical jerk. All the things he and Bruce tried to teach Miguel about seemed to be lost lessons. Making people invisible as a way of avoiding feelings was ultimately a mistake. But, then, why did he always have to be the one to reach out and justify who he was and how he felt? That he wasn't some monster who was going to molest children or harass frightened men in shower stalls?

All semester his mind went back and forth about the issue. He occasionally brought up his feelings to Bruce and Felicia, but he didn't know what his feelings were so he usually didn't talk to anyone. He walked through his daily activities, and that meeting would pop into his head for a moment and then disappear.

Toward the end of the semester he left his office on the run in order to get to his Volvo to pick up Miguel. The lab school had a policy that they charged five dollars for every five minutes a parent was late in picking up their child after four o'clock, and it was already four. Scott got to the car, threw his briefcase in the trunk, and jumped into the driver's seat. As he pulled the car out of the parking lot he saw Aaron standing at the side of his own car. Scott wasn't sure what made him stop, but he pulled up to him and rolled down the window.

"I lost my goddam keys."

"I can give you a ride somewhere, but I've got to pick up my boy at the lab first. I'm late."

Aaron got in the car and said, "I live near the lab school, thanks. I didn't know you had a kid. How old is he?"

"He's nine. From Bruce's—" Scott stopped, and then went on. "He's from my partner's, from Bruce's, first marriage."

There was yet another uneasy silence. Aaron tried to act nonchalant, relaxed, and asked, "Didn't the mother want the kid?"

"She has visitation rights. She lives in town. She's a good mother and we're good fathers. We all just thought it would be better this way." Scott's anger was visible; he gripped the steering wheel as if he wanted to break it, and he stared ahead as if he was in rush-hour traffic in a city rather than driving down a quiet village street. But more than appearances, or physical proximity, the tinge to Scott's voice made Aaron's heart beat faster. They hadn't been in the car a minute and Aaron felt as if he'd like to jump out.

"Hey, I didn't mean anything. I just thought—"

"Right, you don't need to tell me. You just thought it was odd, queer. Right? How could this be normal, right? You didn't mean anything, just that it's something you didn't expect and didn't want to think about and won't think about again as soon as I get you to where you're going."

Now it was Scott's turn to feel his heartbeat. He hadn't meant to sound so angry. Or had he? He didn't know what he felt, what he wanted to feel.

"Look Scott, I didn't—I don't know. I know you're angry for the meeting and I know we should have talked, but this is not something I know how to talk about. It's not something I've even thought about. Being Black and being Jewish I'm always forced, always forced into having to think, to be self-conscious, and sometimes I don't want to think. I just want to click off and rest awhile. I've had to navigate all my life about what it means to be something, to be somebody, and sometimes I just get weary.

"Then at the meeting it just seemed like I not only had to think, but to think, to feel, in a bigtime way, and I just wasn't ready. You don't know what it's like to be here, to be the only Black guy in a room, in a store, at the movies. Or to have the only other guy like yourself be someone like Morgan who thinks I'm too radical, or too Jewish, or too whatever. Or to have these students search you out as if you're a role model. The only gay guy I knew growing up was somebody in my neighborhood who was really effeminate and used to get beat up in school. I never bothered him, but I never helped him either. And I just don't think it makes me into a bad guy simply because—"

He paused and looked out his window. "I don't know."

"You just don't get it Aaron. You don't realize the pain out there and in here. I know kids in your classes who are gay, who are lesbian, and they're afraid. This is liberal bullshit, but these kids just want to be able to see you at those movies with their boyfriend or girlfriend and not have you go bug-eyed if you see them holding hands. Can't you see how much what queers go through is just like the racist crap, the anti-Semitic shit you have to put up with?"

Aaron cringed when Scott used the word "queer." He felt like Scott was spitting in his face and that Scott was making him out to be a bigot.

"You have no right," Aaron exploded, "no right to think I'm some Nazi storm trooper. I don't care what you do in your bedroom, I don't care—"

"Thanks so much for allowing me to use floral sheets in my bedroom if I like. You just don't want me to be gay anyplace other than the bedroom, huh? That's where we're different. Oppression comes in lots of shapes and sizes, amigo, and to get rid of one you've got to take on 'em all. I'm not gay simply because I fuck a man. I'm gay because I love another man and we love our kid. Can't you get that straight?"

They had arrived at the school and Miguel was kicking a soccer ball with his friends as he waited for his father. His book bag and coat lay in a pile on the driveway, and his white shirt looked like he'd been climbing trees all day. Scott honked the horn. When Miguel saw his father, he waved and smiled, picked up his things, and ran to the car. He went to the passenger side, saw Aaron, and got in the back seat.

"Miguel, this is Aaron. Aaron, this is my son."

Aaron turned around, winked at Miguel, and shook his hand.

Miguel said, "Is Aaron your friend, dad?"

As he backed the car into the street Scott first made believe he was concentrating too much to speak and then that he had forgotten the question.

"Are ya friends, dad?" Miguel yawned.

As they started down the street Scott said, "Well I don't know, Miguelito. We work together, that's all."

"That's too bad. It's nice to have friends. Can't you work and have friends, too? Like Felicia?"

Aaron said, "It's hard work to be friends, Miguel. Your dad and I don't know one another very well."

"What's the big deal? Why don't you get to know one another then," asked Miguel.

They stopped and waited at a red light.

BIBLIOGRAPHY

Tierney, William G., and Yvonna S. Lincoln, (1997). *Representation and the Text: Reframing the Narrative Voice*. New York: SUNY.

NOTE

The author appreciates the feedback of Yvonna Lincoln, Julie Neurerer, Roger Platizky, and Greg Tanaka.

Consuming the Other:
Whiteness, Education, and Cheap French Fries

Michael W. Apple

ELEVEN

Michael W. Apple is John Bascom Professor of Education at the University of Wisconsin, Madison. He has worked with dissident groups, unions, and activist groups nationally and internationally to democratize educational policy and practice. He has written extensively on the relationship between knowledge and power in education. Among his recent books are *Official Knowledge* (1993), *Education and Power* (1995), and *Cultural Politics and Education* (1996).

EATING CHEAP FRENCH FRIES

The sun glared off of the hood of the small car as we made our way along the two-lane road. The heat and humidity made me wonder if I'd have any liquid left in my body at the end of the trip and led me to appreciate Wisconsin winters a bit more than one might expect. The idea of winter seemed more than a little remote in this Asian country for which I have a good deal of fondness. But the topic at hand was not the weather; rather, it was the struggles of educators and social activists to build an education that was considerably more democratic than what was in place in that country now. This was a dangerous topic. Discussing it in philosophical and formalistically academic terms was tolerated there. Openly calling for it and situating it within a serious analysis of the economic, political, and military power structures that now exerted control over so much of this nation's daily life was another matter.

As we traveled along that rural road in the midst of one of the best conversations I had engaged in about the possibilities of educational transformations and the realities of the oppressive conditions so many people were facing in that land, my gaze somehow was drawn to the side of the road. In one of those nearly accidental happenings that clarify and crystallize what reality is *really* like, my gaze fell upon a seemingly inconsequential object. At regular intervals, there were small signs planted in the dirt a few yards from where the road met the fields. The sign was more than a little familiar. It bore the insignia of one of the most famous fast food restaurants in the United States. We drove for miles past seemingly deserted fields along a flat hot plain, passing sign after sign, each a replica of the previous one, each less than a foot high. These were not billboards. Such things hardly existed in this poor rural region. Rather, they looked exactly—exactly—like the small signs one finds next to farms in the American Midwest that signify the kinds of seed corn that each farmer had planted in her or his fields. This was a good guess, it turned out.

I asked the driver—a close friend and former student of mine who had returned to this country to work for the social and educational reforms that were so necessary—what turned out to be a naive but ultimately crucial question in my own education. "Why are those signs for _____ there? Is there a _____ restaurant nearby?" My friend looked at me in amazement. "Michael, don't you know what these signs signify? There's no western restaurants within fifty miles of where we are. These signs represent exactly what is wrong with education in this nation. Listen to this." And I listened.

The story is one that has left an indelible mark on me, for it condenses in one powerful set of historical experiences the connections between our struggles as educators and activists in so many countries and the ways differential power works in ordinary life. I cannot match the tensions and passions in my friend's voice as this story was told; nor can I convey exactly the almost eerie feelings one gets when looking at that vast, sometimes beautiful, sometimes scarred, and increasingly depopulated plain. Yet the story is crucial to hear. Listen to this.

The government of the nation has decided that the importation of foreign capital is critical to its own survival.[1] Bringing in American, German, British, Japanese, and other investors and factories will ostensibly create jobs, will create capital for investment, and will enable the nation to speed into the twenty-first century. (This is of course elite group talk, but let us assume that all of this is indeed truly believed by dominant groups.) One of the ways the military-dominated government has planned to do this is to focus part of its recruitment efforts on agribusiness. In pursuit of this aim, it has offered vast tracts of land to international agribusiness concerns at very low cost. Of particular importance to the plain we are driving through is the fact that much of this land has been given over to a supplier for a large American fast food restaurant corporation for the growing of potatoes for the restaurant's french fries, one of the trademarks of its extensive success throughout the world.

The corporation was eager to jump at the opportunity to shift a good deal of its potato production from the United States to Asia. Since many of the farm workers in the United States were now unionized and were (correctly) asking for a liveable wage, and since the government of that Asian nation officially frowned on unions of any kind, the cost of growing potatoes would be lower. Further, the land on that plain was perfect for the use of newly developed technology to plant and harvest the crop with considerably fewer workers. Machines would replace living human beings. Finally, the government was much less concerned about environmental regulations. All in all, this was a fine bargain for capital.

Of course, *people* lived on some of this land and farmed it for their own food and to sell what might be left over after their own—relatively minimal—needs were met. This deterred neither agribusiness nor the government. After all, people could be moved to make way for "progress." And after all, the villagers along that plain did not actually have deeds to the land. (They had lived there for perhaps hundreds of years, well before the invention of banks, and mortgages, and deeds—no paper, no ownership). It would not be too hard to move the people off of the plain to other areas to "free" it for intensive potato production and to "create jobs" by taking away the livelihood of thousands upon thousands of small-scale farmers in the region.

I listened with rapt attention as the rest of the story unfolded and as we passed by the fields with their miniature corporate signs and the abandoned villages. The people whose land had been taken for so little moved, of course. As in so many other similar places throughout what dominant groups call the Third World, they trekked to the city. They took their meager possessions and moved into the ever-expanding slums within and surrounding the one place that held out some hope of finding enough paid work (if *everyone*—including children—labored) so that they could survive.

The government and major segments of the business elite officially discouraged this, sometimes by hiring thugs to burn the shanty towns, other times by keeping conditions so horrible that no one would "want" to live there. But still the dispossessed came, by the tens of thousands. Poor people are not irrational, after all. The loss of arable land had to be compensated for somehow and if it took cramming into places that were deadly at times, well what were the other choices? There *were* factories being built in and around the cities which paid incredibly low wages—sometimes less than enough money to buy sufficient food to replace the calories expended by workers in the production process—but at least there might be paid work if one was lucky.

So the giant machines harvested the potatoes and the people poured into the cities and international capital was happy. It's not a nice story, but what does it have to do with *education*? My friend continued my education.

The military-dominated government had given all of these large international businesses twenty years of tax breaks to sweeten the conditions for their coming to that country. Thus, there was now very little money to supply the health care facilities, housing, running water, electricity, sewage disposal, and schools for the thousands upon thousands of people who had sought their future in or had literally been driven into the city. The mechanism for *not* building these necessities was quite clever. Take the lack of any formal educational institutions as a case in point. In order for the government to build schools it had to be shown that there was a "legitimate" need for such expenditure. Statistics had to be produced in a form that was *officially* accepted. This could only be done through the official determination of numbers of registered births. Yet, the very process of official registration made it impossible for thousands of children to be recognized as actually existing.

In order to register for school, a parent had to register the birth of the child at the local hospital or government office—none of which existed in these slum areas. And even if you could somehow find such an office, the government officially discouraged people who had originally come from outside the region of the city from moving there. It often refused to recognize the legitimacy of the move as a way of keeping displaced farmers from coming into the urban areas and thereby increasing the population. Births from people who had no "legitimate" right to be there did not count as births at all. It is a brilliant strategy in which the state creates categories of legitimacy that define social problems in quite interesting ways (see, e.g., Curtis, 1992; Fraser, 1989). Foucault would have been proud, I am certain.

Thus, there are no schools, no teachers, no hospitals, no infrastructure. The root causes of this situation rest not in the immediate situation. They can only be illuminated if we focus on the chain of capital formation internationally and nationally, on the contradictory needs of the state, on the class relations and the relations between country and city that organize and disorganize that country.

My friend and I had been driving for quite a while now. I had forgotten about the heat. The ending sentence of the story pulled no punches. It was said slowly and quietly, said in a way that made it even more compelling. "Michael, these fields are the reason there's no schools in my city. There's no schools because so many folks like cheap french fries."

I tell this story about the story told to me for a number of reasons. First, it is simply one of the most powerful ways I know of reminding myself and all of us of the utter importance of seeing schooling relationally, of seeing it as connected—fundamentally—to the relations of domination and exploitation of the larger society. Second, and equally as important, I tell this story to make a crucial theoretical and political point. Relations of power are indeed complex and we do need to take very seriously the postmodern focus on the local and on the multiplicity of the forms of struggle that need to be engaged. It *is* important as well to recognize the changes that are occurring in many societies and to see the complexity of the "power/knowledge" nexus. Yet in our attempts to avoid the dangers that accompanied some aspects of previous "grand narratives," let us *not* act as if capitalism has somehow disappeared. Let us not act as if class relations don't count. Let us not act as if all of the things we learned about how the world might be understood politically have been somehow overthrown because our theories are now more complex.

The denial of basic human rights, the destruction of the environment, the deadly conditions under which people (barely) survive, the lack of a meaningful future for the thousands of children I noted in my story—all of this is not only or even primarily a "text" to be deciphered in our academic volumes as we pursue our postmodern themes. It is a reality that millions of people experience in their very bodies every day. Educational work that is not connected deeply to a powerful understanding of these realities (and this understanding cannot evacuate a serious analysis of political economy and class relations without losing much of its power) is in danger of losing its soul. The lives of our children demand no less.

ON WHITENESS

It would not have been wrong to end this chapter with the last sentence of the previous paragraph. But, I want to engage in a few more reflections about what the story I told means, for I think that the issue of cheap french fries provides an extremely important example both of the politics of commonsense and of the politics of "whiteness."

In the story I have told, race and class intersect with colonial and neocolonial relations, both nationally and internationally. I have focused on the connections between consumption practices in the United States and the immiseration of identifiable people in one Asian nation. The emerging class relations that are created here are clear I think. The destructiveness of the relations of production and the accompanying impoverishment of thousands upon thousands of people in one nation go hand in hand with the ability of people in the other nation to consume.

Yet this is also a story of racial dynamics and their institutionalization in colonial and neocolonial forms (see McCarthy and Crichlow, 1995). Relations of "whiteness" are structurally recreated here. It is not a historical accident that such international relations are created and tolerated between an arrogant "center" and a "periphery" that—when it is seen at all—is seen by those in that "center" as populated by "disposable" people who to imperial eyes are somehow "different" and "less than." Why isn't this obvious?[2]

As educators, we are involved in the struggle over meaning. Yet, in this society as in all others, only certain meanings are considered "legitimate," only certain ways of understanding the world get to be called "official knowledge" (Apple, 1993; Apple, 1990). This doesn't just happen. Our society is structured in such a way that dominant meanings are more likely to circulate. These meanings, of course, *will* be contested, will be resisted and sometimes transformed (Willis, 1990); but, this does not lessen the fact that hegemonic cultures have greater power to make themselves known and acceptable.

John Fiske articulates the point that our ordinary meanings are implicated in power relations well.

> Culture making (and culture is always in process, never achieved) is a social process: all meanings of self, of social relations, all the discourses and texts that play such important cultural roles can circulate only in relationship to the social system, in our case of white, patriarchal capitalism. Any social system needs a cultural system of meanings that serves either to hold it in place or destabilize it, to make it more amenable to change. Culture . . . and meanings . . . [are] therefore inherently political. [They are] centrally involved in the distribution and possible redistribution of various forms of social power. (Fiske, 1989, p. 1)

As he goes on to say,

> Knowledge is never neutral, it never exists in an empiricist, objective relationship to the real. Knowledge is power, and the circulation of knowledge is part of the social distribution of power. The discursive power to construct a commonsense reality that can be inserted into cultural and political life is central in the social relationship of power. (Fiske, 1989, pp. 149–150)

These are general claims, but when they are applied to the specifics of the situation I related earlier they become even more cogent. They place my need to be taught about the conditions on that verdant plain into its wider sociocultural context. They crystallize in one story differences in meaning making that separate what in the "West" might be seen as simply eating potatoes and in that Asian nation is seen by many activists as destroying any possibilities for a better future for thousands of children. The story documents the importance of asking "Whose understandings circulate? Why did I not know about this? What is my own structural location in an international system of economic relations that produces these conditions?"

The story speaks to the continued circulation of colonial forms of understanding, associated in complex and everchanging ways to the modes of economic production, distribution, and consumption we inhabit. In many ways, most of us are caught up in the universalizing discourses of our own world, a world that assumes that we somehow already "know" how to understand the daily events in which we engage. Yet, the story I was told on that car ride and what I saw speak to the issue of whose reality, whose knowledge, is made public. Edward Said's apposite words come to mind here.

> Without significant exception the universalizing discourses of modern Europe and the United States assume the silence, willing or otherwise, of the non-European world. There is incorporation; there is inclusion; there is direct rule; there is coercion. But there is only infrequently an acknowledgement that the colonized people should be heard from, their ideas known. (Said, 1993, p. 50)

Said's points speak to the relationship between the forms of understanding that dominate "our" society and the silencing of the voices of the "non-European," "non-Western" world. Yet it is not only the voices that are silenced (and I consciously employ the word silenc*ed* rather than silent to signify that this is an active process in which dominant groups have to *work* to maintain the power of their hegemonic meanings) (see Apple, 1996), so that it is nearly by accident that I am in a position to be taught to see the world differently. It is the determinate connections between lives in what unfortunately and arrogantly has been called "center" and "periphery" that are made invisible at the very same time.

This invisibility is crucial. There is a social geography of whiteness. Whiteness is a spatial concept in many ways. In this case, it implies living a life that is intimately connected—in identifiable ways—to the international dynamics that are so radically altering the economic, political, and cultural relations in many nations throughout the world. It is not necessarily based on a conscious choice. Rather, it is deeply cemented into our commonsense understandings of daily life. We buy our clothes, eat our food, and do the things we do in a manner that naturalizes the social and economic relations that actually created the conditions for the production and consumption of those clothes and that food. Whiteness, then, is a metaphor for privilege, for the ability to eat cheap french fries.

Of course, this is neither a very new nor original point. There is quite a long tradition within political economy of reminding us that any manufactured object is not merely a thing that one can, say, hold in one's hand. Such a view is more than a little reifying in fact. Rather, a manufactured or processed object—from cars to sneakers to shirts and even to the food we place in our mouths—is the concrete embodiment of the human labor and the productive and destructive social relations that resulted in or were the result of its making. Thus, eating cheap french fries is putting food in one's mouth, chewing, and swallowing. Yet, at the very same time, it is also and profoundly a fully social act. It is engaging in the end point of a long chain of relations that drove people off the land, caused their flight to the slums, and denied their children health care and schools. Even more immediately, it is to be in a relationship with the workers who cooked the fries and served them at that fast food restaurant, workers who usually have extremely low pay, no benefits, no unions, and must try to cobble together two or three part-time jobs to try to put food on their own tables. I am tempted to say here that eating cheap french fries is one of the ultimate expressions of whiteness.

In much the same way, nearly all of the economic benefits enjoyed today by the affluent—and even by the not so affluent—in this country rest on the historical development of an economic infrastructure that was dependent on cheap and/or unpaid labor, labor that often had race as a constitutive dynamic underpinning it. Thus, it would not be an overstatement to say that the North's industrial base of textile mills was fed by the unpaid labor of slaves who grew the raw material in the South (as, of course, the entire economy was dependent on the unpaid labor of women in the home and on the farm). For hundreds of years, capitalism and slavery were bound together in a tense relationship. In this way, whiteness as privilege is not only a spatial metaphor, but a temporal one as well. The conditions of existence out of which our current economy grew have their roots in the soil of the hundreds of years of such labor. "We" *currently* live the benefits of that labor. (It is unfortunately the case that a serious discussion of the fact that these current and so unequally controlled and distributed "benefits" *are* fully dependent on these historical relations hardly ever surfaces in the official knowledge of the school curriculum. This speaks volumes about the importance of what is *not* taught in schools, as well as what is part of the corpus of "legitimate" knowledge).

Take the chapter you are reading. This morning, Michael Apple came into his office, opened the door, turned on the lights, and began to type. We can interpret this as a simple physical act. Apple puts his hand on the light switch, flips the switch up, and the light comes on. Yet this simple act is not so simple, for it too must be understood relationally. Michael also just had an anonymous—but no less real—relationship with the men and women miners who dug the coal, in often dangerous and increasingly exploitative conditions, that was burned to produce the electricity. The act of typing this paper is utterly dependent on that labor.

My aim here is to make a serious point about the nature of commonsense. "Our" (here read largely white, economically advantaged group(s) ordinary ways of understanding our daily activity inside and outside of education can make it extremely difficult for us to fully appreciate the nexus of social relations in which we participate. In Fiske's words, I want to "destabilize" our ordinary understandings of education and of our own places in the larger society. As Antonio Gramsci reminded us, racial, gender, and class dominance is legitimated through the creation of commonsense, through consent. This point is especially important now given the conservative restoration that is so powerful in the economic, political, and cultural spheres of society, since an understanding of the structural nature of these connections is being evacuated from our daily lives (Apple, 1993; Apple, 1996).

My basic wish is to have us think the social, recognize that we live lives involved in domination and subordination in very hidden ways. Comprehending this may require that we wrench ourselves out of commonsense, for we are deeply connected whether we like it or not. This requires that we see whiteness as itself a relational term. White is defined not as a state, but as a relation to black, or brown, or yellow, or red. Center is defined as a relation to periphery.

In our usual ways of thinking about this, whiteness is something you don't have to think about. It is just *there*. It is a naturalized state of being. It is "normal." Anything else is "other." It is the there that is never there.[3] But, it is there, for in repositioning ourselves to see the world as constituted out of relations of power and privilege, whiteness as privilege plays a crucial role.

This very sense of connectedness, of relationality, in its international context is made clear in the stammering words of Mr. "Whiskey" Sisodia in Salman Rushdie's *The Satanic Verses*. "The trouble with the Engenglish is that their hiss hiss history happened overseas, so they dodo don't know what it means" (quoted in Bhabha, 1994, p. 6). Substituting the word "American" for "Engenglish" does little damage to Rushdie's insight about the nature of our understanding—and lack of it—of international relations and the differential benefits that come from the ways these relations are structured today.

AFTERTHOUGHTS BY WAY OF A CONCLUSION

Now I often find autobiographical accounts and narrative renderings compelling and insightful. And, clearly, since I have used that form in this chapter, I do not want to dismiss their power. However—and let me be blunt about my worry here—just as often such writing runs the risk of lapsing into possessive individualism (Apple, 1995). Even when an author does the "correct thing" and discusses her or his social location in a world dominated by oppressive conditions, such writing can serve the chilling function of basically saying, "But enough about you, let me tell you about me," if we are not more reflexive about this than often has been the case. I am still committed enough to raising questions about class and race dynamics to worry about perspectives that supposedly acknowledge the missing voices of many people in our thinking about education, but still wind up privileging the white, middle-class woman's or man's seemingly infinite need for self-display.

Do not misconstrue what I am saying here. As so much feminist and postcolonial work has documented, the personal is often the absent presence behind even the most eviscerated writing (see, e.g., McCarthy and Crichlow, 1993). But, at the same time, it is equally crucial that we interrogate our own "hidden" motives in those instances when we employ such modes of presentation. Is the insistence on the personal, an insistence that underpins much of the turn to literary and autobiographical forms, partly a class discourse as well? We should grant their power in uncovering how the world is constructed along multiple axes of power and in uncovering our personal participation in these axes. However, while "the personal may be the political," does the political end at the personal? Furthermore, why should we assume that the personal is any less difficult to understand than the "external" world?

I raise these questions, but I cannot answer them for all situations. What I can say is that these questions need to be asked of all of us who are committed to the multiple projects involved in struggling for a more emancipatory education. For this very reason, I have told a story of my own education—as a white, foreign visitor—that is consciously connected to a clear sense of the realities of structurally generated relations of exploitation and domination that play such a large part in whether education is even there. It was an education about "being white" internationally, an education that clarified for me how privilege works its way out even in our most basic human acts such as eating. As you might expect, as I am certain many of you would have done if you had a similar experience, I am now much more consciously involved in supporting the actions of democratic movements in that Asian nation both here in the United States and there. As you also might expect, I don't eat cheap french fries.

REFERENCES

Apple, Michael W. (1990). *Ideology and Curriculum*, 2nd edition. New York: Routledge.
Apple, Michael W. (1993). *Official Knowledge*. New York: Routledge.
Apple, Michael W. (1995). *Education and Power*, 2nd edition. New York: Routledge.
Apple, Michael W. (1996). *Cultural Politics and Education*. New York: Teachers College Press.
Bhabha, Homi. (1994). *The Location of Culture*. New York: Routledge.
Curtis, Bruce. (1992). *True Government by Choice Men?* Toronto: University of Toronto Press.
Eagleton, Terry (1983). *Literary Theory*. Minneapolis: University of Minnesota Press.
Fiske, John. (1989). *Reading the Popular*. Boston: Unwin and Hyman.
Fraser, Nancy. (1989). *Unruly Practices*. Minneapolis: University of Minnesota Press.
Herrnstein, Richard, and Murray, Charles (1994). *The Bell Curve*. New York: Free Press.
McCarthy, Cameron, and Crichlow, Warren, eds. (1993). *Race, Identity, and Representation in Education*. New York: Routledge.
Said, Edward. (1993). *Culture and Imperialism*. New York: Vintage Books.
Willis, Paul, with Jones, Simon, Canaan, Joyce, and Hurd, Geoff. (1990). *Common Culture*. Boulder: Westview Press.

NOTES

1. I realize that not naming the country runs the risk of essentializing "Asia." It can make it seem as if all "Asian" countries can be merged into one undifferentiated representation. This ideological risk is real. However, given the volatility of the political situation there and the possible threat to colleagues who have been challenging government policies such as the one I describe here, I think that it is better to err on the side of caution and to allow for anonymity of both nation and people in this case.

2. *Internal* class and ethnic dynamics of power need to be considered here as well. It is also not an accident that these ideological forms so long associated with the growth of colonialism and neocolonialism and with the internationalization of capital are appropriated by elites within nations that are seen as "peripheral." Thus, this focus on international dynamics in which class and race intersect and influence each other needs to be complemented by an internal analysis. Specific people buy the hamburgers and french fries—products that have made this restaurant so famous the world over—*within* this Asian nation as well. And the price is well above what the average worker can afford. Eating these french fries is an option only for the affluent. They too reap the benefits of these relations. They eat; and they pay no taxes to support the building of schools, the salaries of teachers, the cost of textbooks, the availability of even minimal health care—and the list seems endless—that the state has declared is "unnecessary" for the "invisible" children whose very absence speaks even more eloquently to their social presence on the landscape of exploitative relations.

On an even more general level, obviously much more needs to be said about the distinct yet overlapping dynamics of race, colonialism, and class here. These are *overdetermined* situations, both nationally and internationally, in which multiple relations of power work off of, mediate, transform, and even contradict each other in extremely complex ways. This issue is discussed in more detail in Apple (1993) and Apple (1995).

3. There is evidence that the reactionary politics of the current conservative restoration is changing this, however. A consciousness of "being white" is growing, but in dangerous ways. This can be seen in the organized attacks on affirmative action policies, in the increasing acceptance once again of pseudoscientific explanations of racial and gender "inferiority" (see, e.g., Herrnstein and Murray, 1994), and in the militant and racist Christian Identity movements that are gaining more power in a number of nations.

Racing in America

William C. Ayers is a school reform activist and Professor of Education at the University of Illinois at Chicago, where he teaches courses in elementary education, curriculum, interpretive research, urban school change, and the cultural contexts of teaching. He is codirector of the Small Schools Workshop, cofounder of the Annenberg Challenge in Chicago, and cochair of the Chicago School Reform Collaborative. A graduate of Bank Street College of Education and Teachers College, Columbia University, he has written extensively about the importance of creating progressive educational opportunities in urban public schools. His interests focus on the political and social contexts of schooling, and the meaning and ethical purposes of teachers, students, and families. His articles have appeared in many journals including the *Harvard Educational Review*, the *Journal of Teacher Education*, *Teachers College Record*, *The Nation*, and *The Cambridge Journal of Education*. His books include *The Good Preschool Teacher* (Teachers College Press, 1989) and *To Teach: The Journey of a Teacher* (Teachers College Press, 1993), which was named Book of the Year in 1993 by Kappa Delta Pi and won the Witten Award for Distinguished Work in Biography and Autobiography in 1995. His latest books are edited volumes: *To Become a Teacher: Making a Difference in Children's Lives* (Teachers College Press, 1995), and (with Pat Ford) *City Kids/City Teachers: Reports from the Front Row* (The New Press, 1996).

When our child Malik was three years old and attending the day-care center where I then taught, we had a troubling exchange about Indians. The center was well-known throughout New York for its advocacy of multicultural and antibias perspectives, as well as for the activism of parents and staff on issues of racism, equity, and social justice. Part of the normal experience of youngsters in this community was active involvement in neighborhood events and activities. And so it seemed quite ordinary and natural that we attend a pow-wow at a nearby junior high school sponsored by the American Indian Movement.

When we told the kids about the pow-wow there was general excitement and eagerness: there would be drums; there would be food to eat. But Malik wanted none of it. He whispered to me anxiously: "Will the Indians be wild? Will they be scary?" No, I assured him. It would be engaging and interesting and we would have a good time. And we did. But Malik insisted that I hold him for the first hour, just to be sure.

Where did he get the idea that the Indians would be wild or scary? He was only three, after all, and we had no television at home. His middle name is Cochise; he had pictures of Cochise in his room and had read many positive books about Cochise and other Native Americans. How did this stereotype get into his head?

Of course he had seen Richard Scarry's books filled with headdresses and hatchets; he knew Maurice Sendak's *Alligators All Around* with "I" for "Imitating Indians," and the accompanying illustration of alligators whooping around and acting crazy—why didn't Sendak use, I wonder, "J" for "Jumping Jews" or "N" for "Nice Negroes?" In any case, Malik was part of the culture of disappearing Indians (ten little, nine little, eight little Indians—a particularly appalling popular poem filled with suggestions of holocaust), wooden Indians, cowboys and Indians, sitting Indian-style, and all the rest. It would be a few years before he would encounter *Little House on the Prairie* and Laura's shivery description of the wild, stinking, animal-like Indians of her imagination, but he was already set up to accept the crass justifications for social piracy and mass murder. He already knew Indians were the enemy. Where did he get these ideas? They were, of course, knit deeply into the fabric of his culture; they were a toxic substance in the air he breathed, they came without asking, they were available without effort. They got put in his head, as they get put into all of our heads, early and often.

* * *

Look at the dictionary, a seemingly authoritative source. Under "white" we find "free from spot or blemish," "free from moral impurity," "not intended to cause harm," "innocent," "marked by upright fairness"; and then phrases like "white knight," "white horse," and "white hope." "Black" doesn't fare so well: "dirty," "soiled," "thoroughly sinister or evil," "wicked," "sad, gloomy, or calamitous," "grim, distorted, or grotesque." Associated terms include black art (sorcery), black and blue (discolored from bruising), blackball (to exclude from membership), blackmail (to extort by threats), black market (illicit trade), black out (to envelop in darkness), black heat (evil), black day (characterized by disaster), and on and on. Under Jew ("a member of the tribe of Judah") we find a fourth meaning: "a name of opprobrium or reprobation, specifically applied to a grasping usurer, or a trader who drives hard bargains or deals craftily." To "Jew" is to "cheat or over-reach," like "to gyp." An "Indian-giver" is someone who welches (from Welsh—well-known swindlers), a dramatic instance of "the pot calling the kettle. . . ." In our society, divided racially and culturally, stratified along racial and cultural lines, language is encoded with privilege, oppression, bias, bigotry, and power. Modern American English tells us something of who we are, where we have been, and where we are going.

* * *

Around the same time I was on a crowded bus in New York with Zayd, then five. "What's a kike?" he asked in a loud, curious voice. I froze as two hundred eyes riveted on me.

"Where did you hear that word?" I stalled for time.

"Right there on that seat: 'I hate kikes.' "

Sure enough.

"Well," I swallowed. "That's a racist, hateful thing people call Jews. Some people would call you that to hurt your feelings."

"Oh," he said neutrally, and watched as I pulled out my magic marker and obliterated the filthy phrase. There was a palpable sigh of satisfaction from the crowd, and for me a sense of small pride, colored by the knowledge that I might well have ignored the thing—as I do a blizzard of ugliness each day—had Zayd not pointed out and, in his innocence, expected action.

* * *

Each of us, as Andrew Hacker notes, could write a book about race. Mine begins with a child's question: "Why is Celeste brown?" Celeste cleaned our house and I had just noticed something interesting. A difference. "Shush," my mother scolded. "We don't talk that way." Growing up in an entirely racialized surround, and one in which, as Cornell West reminds us, almost no one acknowledges its existence, means that we draw race into ourselves with our every breath, that we drink it in, beginning with our mother's milk. A society founded on genocide, built on the labor of African slaves, developed by Latino serfs and Asian indentured servants, made fabulously wealthy through exploitation and masterful manipulation and mystification—a society like this is a society built on race.

But race is unspeakable. "We don't talk that way." I'll say. We don't talk at all. And in silence a lens of distorted images, fears, misunderstandings, and cool calculatedness slips neatly into place. We are born into race and place, and all the early lessons are about knowing something of each. Reading Derrick Bell, several white students in my graduate school class enthusiastically supported his notion of "the permanence of racism," and were then taken to task by African American students who insisted that Bell's purpose was to analyze concrete conditions realistically in the service of resistance, not to offer a simple, resigned, passive alternative to white people.

* * *

Just a few months ago the student chapter of Amnesty International in our kids' high school was permitted to organize a special day to recognize political prisoners. One of the planned events was to be an assembly at which a former political prisoner would speak. A week before the event the national office told the students that the former political prisoner would be a Palestinian from the occupied territories. Pandemonium in the administration: "some families will be offended"; "this is controversial"; "now it's become political." The principal wrote the students that they would have to find an "appropriate" political prisoner, even though he "had nothing against Palestinians." All of this is linked in my mind to a recent spate of political cartoons depicting fat, greedy sheiks with huge noses sitting atop oil fields, and the traveling rodeo that played at the pavilion at my university, and featured a horse dressed up as a camel led by "A-hab the A-rab."

One afternoon I asked my students to write down three stereotypes other people have of their own cultural or social groups. Then we filled the chalk-board with them: Italians are mobsters; blonds are stupid; P.E. majors are lesbians; fat people are lazy; Blacks are oversexed. Elysse wrote, "Jews are stingy," "Jewish women are JAPS," "All Jews are smart." She explained later that her parents were both professors, and in every class in school she was expected to excel. "I'm an average student, but I do other things well; I always feel the burden of the stereotype of smart Jews."

Later, when we brought in cultural artifacts for a museum of culture, Elysse brought a prayer shawl. Dima brought an olive-pit necklace that belonged to her cousin who was killed in the *intifada*.

* * *

Painting others with a broad brush is a commonplace; when the tables turn and we are objects of someone else's casual stroke, we shrink. I'm *more* than that, I want to insist; I'm always more. I cannot be easily summed up, fixed like a bug to a board, reduced to a simple definition or a single strand. There are dynamic dimensions about me, things unseen, unrealized, unexplored. Just the thought of being numbered and labelled makes each of us, I think, want to rebel; the poisonous impact of casual categorization (at least when applied to ourselves) causes us to recoil. And yet schools are built on labelling, categorizing, sifting, and sorting. When we look out onto our classrooms we are shaped to see in shorthand: B.D., E.M.H., T.A.G., L.D. These caricatures become the commonsense of schooling, even though each label is a stereotype that conceals more than it reveals. And each diminishes teaching, constrains learning, and causes at least some youngsters to carom this way or that.

* * *

While racism is indeed a bad idea, it is an idea brought forth and sustained by an unjust reality. The bad idea is not its own source or self-reference. Fighting racism in the realm of ideas alone without undermining the structures that give birth to those ideas is a hopeless mission. Remember, for example, the relationship between two characters in the film version of Alex Haley's *Roots*. The captain of the slave ship considers himself a Christian and a liberal, and he finds the transporting of slaves odious work. He is particularly appalled by the behavior of his first mate, a crude unpolished fellow who regularly abuses the human cargo and taunts the captain for his squeamishness. In one particularly revealing encounter the captain, all worry and hand-wringing, implores the brute to treat the slaves a bit better, insisting that they are also human beings and God's children. The first mate looks him squarely in the eye and responds with astounding lucidity: Of course they're human beings, he sneers, and if we're to profit from this enterprise we'd best convince them and everyone else that they're dogs or mules, anything *but* human beings. With that the captain retreats into his ineffectual anguish.

The point here, of course, is that prejudice and the idea of inferiority based on race grows from and is fed by the need to justify and perpetuate inequality, domination, control, and exploitation. While discrimination and slavery go back to antiquity, chattel slavery based on race—that is the enslavement of an entire people and their transformation into commodities without any family, property, or rights whatsoever, bound for life and for generations to come—was the "peculiar institution" born in America of the African slave trade. Racism as a primary social and cultural dividing line is the legacy of that institution. The ideology of racism developed from a greed for profit and was achieved by deception and a monopoly of firearms, not by biological superiority, real or imagined.

This understanding of the centrality of the social structures of racial oppression providing the wellspring of racist ideas is not something recently discovered. In 1903, the great historian, educator, activist, and social commentator W. E. B. Du Bois predicted that the problem of the twentieth century would be "the problem of the color line." As we approach the twenty-first century the problem of racism is more acute and entangled than over. Leon Litwick, in his 1987 presidential address to the Organization of American Historians, notes:

> The significance of race in the American past can scarcely be exaggerated. Those who seek to diminish its critical role invariably dismiss too much history—the depth, the persistence, the pervasiveness, the centrality of race in American society, the countless ways in which racism has embedded itself in the culture, how it adapts to changes in laws and public attitudes, assuming different guises as the occasion demands.

Dr. Du Bois dealt brilliantly with the question of privilege by revealing how sections of the laboring class were historically bought off and corrupted. But he also showed time and again that "the plight of the white working class throughout the world today is directly traceable to Negro slavery in America, on which modern commerce and industry was founded. . . ." Du Bois made a concrete historical analysis of white labor being unable to compete with free labor (slavery), and often joining with their bosses to keep Blacks in chains; when they opposed slavery, it was from a position of destitution, economic need, and a developing sense of common cause. During slavery poor whites were completely degraded and rendered desperate and hungry by the system. While free labor replaced them, they were largely unable to link with their fellow Black laborers. This was the result of white supremacist ideology being rained down upon them—no matter how bad things were for them, they were still white. It was this racist "education" that induced many to become slave catchers and guards rather than allies and coproducers. The existence of an oppressed nation of people, wrote Du Bois, also kept white labor from emancipating itself, while white labor's privileged position—its access to land, its relative class mobility—dimmed its class consciousness.

Racism, again, is more than bias or prejudice, more than a few bad ideas floating around aimlessly—it includes the structures of privilege and oppression linked to race and backed up by force, powerful structures that are the roots of prejudice. The endurance and strength of prejudiced ideas and values lies in their renewable life-source: the edifice of inequality based on color. In Illinois, for example, we have created what amounts to two parallel school systems—one privileged, stable, well-financed, and largely white; the other ineffective, chaotic, disadvantaged in countless ways, and largely African American, Latino, and poor. Racism is expressed through this duality, through inadequate resources for those in need, through isolation, through unresponsiveness. When Governor James Thompson called Chicago schools "a black hole" while refusing to release more funds, he excited all the racist justifications that flow and are fed from that unjust reality. Politicians continue to call schools "a rat hole," and "a sink hole"—rotten language propping up a rotten structure.

Changing ideas and changing reality are distinct although potentially interactive enterprises. The lifeblood of racism is the concrete situation it supports, but, it is also true that when an idea is the accepted currency of a large enough number of people, it becomes a force of its own, a material reality with a real, palpable power on people's lives. For example, when virtually all of Europe believed the world was flat, that belief became itself a barrier beyond which exploration proved impossible. To break through the barrier required an assault on the old ideas, but it was the actual going beyond the edge of the earth that proved decisive in discrediting and eventually destroying the incorrect idea.

In the realm of social interaction this dynamic is even more problematic and more difficult to disentangle. I taught for several years in a school where we worked diligently to create a liberating and empowering environment for young children. One thing we struggled with was our own language. We wanted to free our language from the artificial constraints of a racist and sexist society, and so it became natural and not jarring in our school to hear conversation laced with terms like "mail carrier," "police officer," "cowhand," and, my personal favorite, "waitron." Not only did "firefighter" replace "fireman" but our dramatic play area had a poster of a Black firefighter in action, and our block area had a unique collection of little figures and wedgies including a white male nurse and a Black woman firefighter. "Firefighter, firefighter, firefighter."

Now, here's the problem: our school was across the street from a firehouse and the firehouse was staffed exclusively with white, male firefighters. We visited the firefighters, tried on their hats, rang the bell, and got to know a few of them. Children are, of course, careful observers, diligent classifiers, and concrete learners. Reality is their most powerful teacher. And so our nonsexist language and our nonracist materials were in combat with some hard facts, and for the children, fireman became a perfectly reasonable word for many situations. Changing language does not in itself change worlds. Nor is changing minds identical to changing structures or institutions.

The world of children is not neatly bounded from other worlds and larger realities, and the explorations of children are neither logical nor discrete. They are, rather, organic and unlimited. Those inquiries become the fertile ground for further inquiries and reconstructions. They know no bounds.

One of the most challenging and refreshing things about living with children is that they go on exploring, asking whatever enters their fields without regard to what is controversial or what is in bad taste or what is off limits. Children's comments are often dazzling in their insightfulness and their questions are as often confounding in their illumination of human mystery. Why is mom angry? Why didn't dad come home last night? Riding a city bus with a group of kids can be a constant challenge: Why is he talking loud? Why is she in a wheelchair? Why is that man sleeping on the sidewalk?

Because racism is rooted in real (not imagined) oppression, and because that oppression is reflected in actual (not fantasy) inequality and injustice, it is not surprising that children discover the hard lessons about race and social value early. Kenneth and Mamie Clark showed with poignant clarity that Black preschool children understood not only that they were Black, but they knew that to be white was an advantage and to be Black a disadvantage. These studies have been repeated again and again, and the general findings have consistently been confirmed. By the age of four, children of all races in our society tend to know who has cultural power and who has not, who to befriend and who to fear, who to choose and who to refuse.

This confronts us as teachers and educators with an enormous teaching problem. Because education is essentially a process that opens doors, opens spaces, and open minds, anything that constrains or limits or closes is the enemy of education. Racism, sexism, and other forms of organized oppression are anti-education. For this reason alone teachers and educators must struggle for ways to understand, engage with, and resist racism (the reality and the ideology) in their classrooms and in the larger world.

* * *

Thinking of race and racism as objective, immutable, individual, and existing in the world of ideas alone leads to paralysis and inaction. This conclusion is shared from right to left. Chester Finn, for example, analyzes the problems in Chicago's schools and concludes that the "financial problems . . . seem virtually unsolvable," and "no one sees a way out of the morass." Paralysis. No struggle, no strategy, no action. Resignation. Further, he repeats a number of cliches: "By mid-afternoon, many children are turned out onto the mean streets . . . unsupervised, poorly nourished, not given adequate health care, and hardly encouraged to supplement the school's educational activities"; "when children spend much . . . time trying to survive in dangerous neighborhoods, watching television, eating poorly, or failing to do homework . . . even the best schools find it difficult, perhaps impossible, to boost student achievement." This recitation of received wisdom is Finn's idea of research. And note: schools can do nothing, the goal of boosting achievement is impossible.

Describing youngsters by their putative circumstances, careful to avoid the obvious fact that he is referring to African American and Latino youngsters and families, he manages to simultaneously lower our expectations for school success. This old story is in sharp contrast with much of the exciting work of reform which is premised on the idea that all youngsters can learn, that they have a right to a decent education, and that they bring important assets with them to school. When Finn is challenged for defending a racist status quo, he takes cover in the time-worn tradition of seeing racism as only an idea: he claims personally to expect a lot from "kids of every hue." This is almost sweet in its naivete but it is entirely beside the point. He also insists on silence: raising the issue of race "may play well in Chicago" (read: any discussion of race panders to African Americans), but that it is "counter productive."

Perhaps more troubling because it is more tortured is the liberal James Joseph Scheurich's "Toward a White Discourse on White Racism" (*Educational Researcher*, 22 (8), 5–10). Scheurich creates a bizarre hierarchy: "middle-class Cuban-Americans," "upper-class Whites," "lower-class Hispanics," "White lower-class females," "Asian middle-class males." None is explained and so each must be assumed to have obvious explanatory power. But what does it mean to say, for example, "Asian middle-class male" in terms of income, relation to production, outlook, attitude, politics, experience, language, occupation, status, and on and on? Absolutely nothing. It is vague and unhelpful, mystifying and harmful both to those who are labeled and to those who wield the pens. It is part of the banal racist discourse that masks as meaningful.

Scheurich accepts wholesale the popularized mythology about race and class in America. The "fact" of an American middle class is left unexamined, and the "fact" of a lower class is glibly asserted again and again. There's a virtual industry cranking out the lower-class/underclass myth—a blame-the-victim story that both "explains" poverty based on the putative behaviors of the poor (behaviors that in anyone else are isolated events rather than group signifiers) and justifies the existence of an elaborate "helping" industry. Scheurich simply nods and glibly pins his specimens to the wall.

If you can understand the rather simple and naive notion of "social positionality"—that membership in a social group impacts one's experience of events and encounters—you've got his whole argument. There is no attempt to uncover or examine the material base of racism, the complex interplay of culture, class, and individual experience, the structures of privilege and oppression based on race, or possible courses of action that could challenge that bulwark. The answer to his central question—"how can we determine whether a person or group is racist or not?"—is this: find out what color they are and enter them onto his hierarchy.

The hollowness, the paucity of his argument is most glaring when he offers his two-paragraph program to fight racism. He proposes that we 1) "understand and make conscious, especially in our intellectual work, the fact that . . . all people are socially influenced in significant ways by their membership in a racial group," and 2) "undertake this effort in a way that does not attempt to separate 'good' Whites, willing to confront White racism, from 'bad' Whites, unwilling to fight White racism." His is a program of study, inquiry, thought, and reflection, carefully emphasizing that we tend our gardens inside our own walls, and that we stick together as "Whites." He does not, for example, call for common cause with poor parents fighting for a decent education for their youngsters in urban schools. He does not call for building partnerships with African American communities resisting the effects of environmental racism. He does not urge an action research agenda that could be constructed of, by, and for victims of oppression and exploitation. No. Let's clink tea cups and chat.

Paulo Freire reminds us of the importance of grounding our work in the actual and the real: "The starting point for organizing the program content of education or political action must be the present, existential, concrete situation, reflecting the aspirations of the people. Utilizing certain basic contradictions, we must pose this existential, concrete, present situation to the people as a problem which challenges them and requires a response—not just at the intellectual level, but at the level of action."

* * *

Schools, of course, are not neutral and teaching is never value-free. In *Beloved*, Toni Morrison's dazzling novel of slavery, freedom, and the complexities of a mother's love, Schoolteacher, the character with no other name, comes to Sweet Home with his efficient, scientific interest in slaves and makes life unbearable for the people there. He is a disturbing, jarring character. We want to think of school teachers as caring and compassionate people; this cold, sadistic school teacher challenges that. When Paul D, Sethe's link to the past and tie to the present, thinks to himself: "Watch out! Watch out! Nothing in the world is more dangerous than a white school teacher," we cringe.

While sometimes difficult to discern in our own familiar context, it is plain when we look outside ourselves that schools are institutions embedded in societies and that teachers must choose their teaching in problematic situations. We need only to look at the schools in Korea, say, or Chile or Poland. We know, for example, that South African schools were until recently organized to perpetuate a particular social order, to initiate children into the horror and brutality of apartheid. We observed a school system relentlessly sorting children for lives of privilege and power on the one hand, or for lives of narrow exploitation and unrelieved toil on the other, masking their true intentions with the most outrageous claims of genetic superiority and the natural order of things. While white children were then educated for wealth and leisure, Black children were channelled into the mines, the factories, the plantations, and the townships. While a few children experienced opportunities and openings to possibility and choice, the great mass of children were coerced toward constrained and scripted lives. Importantly, all of this was attempted behind the polished appearance of a commonsense world.

Of course, the authoritarian and unjust social and political system requires an authoritarian and unjust school system. When we see that the struggle against the South African system was led by Black students and youth who built a pedagogy of liberation in the whirlwind of militant opposition, and when we note that the schools themselves became a major battleground of the resistance, we realize the absurdity of neutral schooling in the South African context. We reflect on the lives of those children and think again of teachers and some of the old questions resonate with a new urgency: What is taken to be valuable in teaching? What knowledge is of most worth? What are reasonable goals for children in unreasonable situations?

We return home with a view of education that is more troubling. For if education is conceived as an initiation of the young into the world, we need to somehow account for and justify that world. If education is thought of as preparation for life in society or as the effort of a community to reproduce and replenish itself, then we need to be able to recommend that society and warrant that community in some way. Justifying our teaching and our schools requires that we also understand our multiple contexts. Are we, as teachers, cops, or comrades, armed guards or allies? We must take responsibility for our connections and affiliations, even those that are not of our own choosing or making. It is not simply that schools are porous institutions, and that historical, economic, political, social, and cultural aspects touch school life fairly freely, it is, rather, that those dimensions become the essential ground for education. Having access to those critical but often hidden aspects encourages teachers to engage children at the deepest levels of their beings, and helps them to find ways to join hands in a fundamental quest—to make and remake society.

Stories of Colonial and Postcolonial Education

THIRTEEN

Dennis Carlson

Dennis Carlson is Associate Professor in the Department of Educational Leadership and Director of the Center for Education and Cultural Studies at Miami University. He is the author of *Teachers and Crisis: Urban School Reform and Teachers' Work Culture* (1992) and *Making Progress: Education and Culture in New Times* (1997). He also has published widely in scholarly education journals, including the *Harvard Educational Review*, *Educational Theory*, and *Curriculum Inquiry*.

In what follows I want to argue that we cannot understand the particular character of education for racial "Others" in the United States without appreciating the extent to which it has been influenced by colonial beliefs and power relations. In the twentieth century, white hegemony has been maintained less through the legal denial of rights and military force and more through control of popular culture and education. Specifically, I want to view colonial forms of education as involving *deculturation* (the erasure of non-European culture and language), *assimilation* (bringing the racial Other into the dominant or hegemonic culture, and more particularly into the lower rungs of the labor force), and *policing* (the surveillance, disciplining, and control of racialized bodies).[1] Colonial education, then, is education that is organized around these three themes. While colonial education originally and most typically involves the education of nonwhite and native peoples by white educators, this is not necessarily the case.[2]

I want to approach this discussion through the telling of two "stories" about colonial education in schools that, at least on the surface, appear to be quite different. The first story describes a U.S. Bureau of Indian Affairs (BIA) boarding school on the Navajo Indian Reservation in the late 1960s, based on my observations and experiences living and teaching in the school for five weeks as part of Peace Corps training. My observations and reflections were recorded in a journal at that time; and over several decades of telling the story of the school in various classes I have taught at the university, it has been condensed or crystallized down into its basic elements. To me, it has become a case study of colonial education in an almost classic form, since the BIA is the formal agent of the colonial control of Native American peoples in the United States. The second story I relate is based on my recent work in an inner-city middle school in Ohio serving poor African American and Appalachian students. Over the course of two years (1992–1994) I spent approximately one-half day each week observing and working in the school as part of a school-university "partnership" in school renewal.[3] This is a story of a less formal and overt form of colonial education; yet I mean to suggest that many of the discourses and practices found in an inner-city school are deeply implicated in colonial projects. In both stories I also point to the existence of oppositional discourses and practices as well which seem to me consistent with postcolonial perspectives.

COLONIALISM AT A NAVAJO BOARDING SCHOOL

Fresh out of college in that tumultuous year, 1968, I was accepted into the Peace Corps and assigned to become a teacher of English in Libya, North Africa. In this case, I and other Peace Corps trainees bound for Libya were placed for five weeks in various boarding schools on the Navajo reservation where we were to "practice teach" on Navajo children. I and several other trainees were assigned to a middle school (grades five through eight) in the New Mexico "badlands," tucked up against the side of a massive and (to the Navajo) sacred mesa. The nearest small trading post was five miles, and the nearest town of any size was over fifty miles away. The administrators and teachers, I soon learned, were primarily Anglo and in their twenties and thirties. There were several Navajo teachers who taught bicultural education classes; but most adult Navajos in the school served as custodians, dormitory supervisors, cooks, and security staff. Maintenance staff jobs in particular appeared to be reserved for Navajos.

In my conversations with the principal and teachers in the school, they often invoked an "immersion" metaphor to make sense of the school's mission and how it was accomplished. They used this metaphor to refer to a number of related things. First, they viewed the boarding school itself as a tool or mechanism for immersing Navajo children in American culture, since it effectively isolated Navajo children from their native culture except for vacations and weekend visits by parents and family. Boarding schools thus were not just "efficient" in a desert region where the population was very spread out. More importantly, they were efficient as apparatuses of immersion. According to the principal, research had shown this was the best way to help Native Americans learn "correct" English and learn to deal with the "modern world." Second, the immersion metaphor was used to legitimate the fact that most teachers were Anglo, since they could most effectively teach Navajo children "correct" English and prepare them to enter the modern world. Students were not allowed to speak Navajo in their classes with Anglo teachers. A third element of immersion in white culture enacted at the boarding school was exposure to Christianity. The BIA invited representatives of major Christian denominations (Catholic, Episcopal, Mormon, Methodist, and Baptist) to hold after-school religious classes which (at the strong urging of teachers and administrators) all Navajo children "chose" to attend. Mormonism was by far the most popular of these Christian denominations among Navajos since it was associated with the belief that Christ visited America and that Native Americans are one of the lost tribes of Israel. Students were not offered the choice of attending an after-school class on Navajo religion.

A final element of immersion was exposure to a westernized curriculum. Teachers relied heavily on early elementary school basal readers since most of the students were reading two to five years below the Anglo "norm" for their grade level, and none of these basals were specially written for Navajo children.[4] They depicted Anglo children in Anglo homes and communities. In all classes teachers placed a strong emphasis on "basic skills" using individualized instructional workbooks and drill sheets—this in spite of the fact that Navajo culture values cooperative more than individualized work. The curriculum also placed a strong emphasis on career education, and in many cases lessons and units interwove basic skills and career education objectives. Most classrooms had displays of supplemental materials designed to help students explore various trades—particularly in the maintenance and service industries. Students also got "on the job" training around the school. All students worked at least several hours each day as helpers assigned to maintenance crews. In this capacity they helped wash dishes and clean tables, polish floors, and wash laundry. Although this was clearly a way of keeping youngsters busy and thus out of trouble, it was always legitimated as educational and as "good experience." There was one relatively small crack in this apparatus of immersion. Students had one or two bicultural education classes each day, taught by Navajo teachers. In these classes, students were allowed to speak mixed English and Navajo and study the myths and rituals of Navajo culture. These classes, I was told, were a relatively new idea and were added in response to pressure from the tribal council.

For the most part, students did not resist this immersion in white culture in violent or overtly aggressive ways, but rather through a withdrawal into self and a refusal to actively participate in class that were just as effective in challenging the power of the institution and of white culture to define them. In the journal I kept of my teaching experiences in the school, I observed that "the students are well-behaved but distant and hard to reach. They appear to pay attention to the lesson, but it soon becomes obvious they haven't understood anything." Other teachers warned me that this was a "game" students tried to get away with, of pretending to not understand or being too dumb to understand. The other major form of resistance I observed among students was that many continued to respond to questions in Navajo or mixed Navajo and English, even when it was clear they knew the English words. Other students resisted in more self-destructive ways. One of the ongoing responsibilities of the staff, including teachers, was to jump in the pickup truck and try to round up children who had run away back to their "hogan" homes. The year before I arrived, I learned, three brothers had run away together on a cold January night. They had been found huddled together in the open desert, the two on the outside dead while the brother on the inside, warmed by his brothers' bodies, was still alive. There were other stories I heard from teachers of children who committed suicide in the dormitories by putting their belts around their necks and hanging themselves in their closets. As a result, boys were no longer allowed to wear belts. One frail young boy at the school had stopped talking entirely to any white staff and was slowly withdrawing into a world of his own. During recess, he often was to be found sitting alone in the sand with his legs crossed, sometimes slowly rocking himself.

In the dormitories a staff of primarily Navajo workers struggled to care for the children; but there were far too few staff to meet the needs of so many children. As a result, the staff relied heavily upon regimentation, routine, and militaristic discipline—at least in the boys' dormitory that I observed. Every school morning, the boys and girls were marched out of their dormitories and into the school in single file, with watchful teachers and security guards continually counting student bodies and calling out names to make sure everyone was in line. At the end of the school day, the ritual was repeated in reverse. The counting and naming of bodies, as in prisons, was one of the most pervasive rituals of power in the school and very closely related to the fear that these bodies might escape surveillance or even "make a run for it."

If student resistances to this form of colonial education appeared to be contained, there was evidence of a more politicized resistance forming among the Navajo people. My visit to the boarding school occurred at a particularly unsettling time in relations between Whites and Native Americans. BIA officials and school administrators, I learned, were facing resistance from a small but vocal group of parents and some young Navaho leaders outside the tribal council who wanted all boarding schools closed and replaced with day schools. This dispute had begun to gain attention in Congress, and in 1967, Senator Robert Kennedy had visited the Navajo reservation and joined in a call for an end to boarding schools as quickly as possible.[6]

Things *have* changed significantly—and for the better—since then, although I suspect much remains the same as well. Since the early 1970s a whole series of federal laws have shifted a historic policy of attempting to destroy the language and culture of Native Americans and Christianize them to a policy that recognizes the rights of Native American peoples to be educated bilingually and biculturally, in day schools rather than boarding schools when feasible, and in schools operated by tribal councils (with BIA oversight). Furthermore, the number of Native American teachers in reservation schools has continued to rise.[7] Joel Spring, in his history of the education of

Native American peoples, notes that it is ironic that the "federal legislation of the 1970s and 1980s, . . . required many tribes to discover and resurrect languages and traditions that the federal government had already partially destroyed."[8] Still, the transition from a colonial to a postcolonial form of education is full of dilemmas and unresolved questions. For example, if Native Americans, and other native peoples, withdraw too much into a localized tribal culture and language, they risk further exploitation. South Africa provides a good case in point here. In the 1950s, in an effort to maintain political and cultural hegemony in South Africa, the apartheid regime passed the Bantu Education Act, which required that all Native (i.e., black) South Africans living on tribal lands were to be educated in their own tribal languages, customs, and history.[9] In this case, the celebration of native African tribal culture by the white government was tied to a colonial project of keeping Africans divided tribally and marginalized politically and culturally. Within a multiculturally American society, Native Americans will need to preserve their unique cultural identity at the same time that they learn to live and exercise power within the modern world.

LIFE IN A NONEXEMPLARY MIDDLE SCHOOL

In most big cities around the United States in the 1990s, there are some exciting things going on educationally. The trouble is that while the media and professional educators have focused their gaze on the "magnet schools" and exemplary programs that are cropping up in big city school districts, they have tended to forget that most schools for inner-city young people are still very non-exemplary. One of these is a school I will call Jefferson Middle School (grades seven and eight), located near the center of a large Ohio metropolitan area. Sixty percent of the students are African American and 40 percent are Appalachian whites. Over 90 percent of all students are AFDC welfare recipients. One-fourth of the teaching and administrative staff is black and the rest white, including the principal. Over the course of two academic years (1992–94), I visited Jefferson Middle School regularly. My formal purpose was to support projects in educational renewal involving collaboration between the school and the university; but I also spent considerable time in the school just observing, walking the halls, sitting in on classrooms (at least those that teachers made me feel welcome in), and talking to teachers and administrators to get their impressions of life in the school. My initial impressions of the school building were negative. Architecturally, it represented an early-1950s industrial plant, complete with towering smoke stack. Throughout its four floors there were visible signs of disrepair. Medal gratings covered windows on the street level. Surrounding the school was a buckling asphalt lot and behind it an area surrounded by a high wire fence for staff parking. The school was bounded on three sides by housing projects where most of the students lived. On the other side was the beginning of a "gentrification" project—condominiums for professional people without children. Perhaps partially in response to this gentrification, the school district allocated some funds for a school beautification project, and the asphalt in front of the school was finally replaced with bricks and grass. From the top floor of the school, looking out the windows (as so many students did so much of the time), it was possible to survey the housing projects, and even watch drug deals going down. The halls were dark and drab except for a few posters made by teachers, such as: "I pledge to be drug free," with space for students to sign, or "Our mission: pass the IAT (Instructional Assessment Test) and the CAT (California Achievement Test)." Rarely was children's own art work or writing displayed in the halls.

Disempowerment—a sense of being at the bottom of a long pecking-order and thus too often overlooked, abused, and not given one's fair share—was a pervasive theme embedded in staff discourse in the school. A number of teachers, both white and black, complained that the school was a "dumping ground" for welfare kids who could not get into any "good" schools (i.e., magnet schools) and that the "powers that be" downtown did not care about the kids or the school. Part of the reason teachers felt powerless was that the composition of the student body was changing—in their mind for the worse. As magnet schools continued to cream off academically oriented and middle class students, the city's neighborhood schools had become institutions that served poor minority youth almost exclusively. In the early 1990s, the school district divided the city into a number of minidistricts as part of a decentralization initiative, and Jefferson Middle School was assigned to a minidistrict consisting of six elementary schools, two middle schools, and a "comprehensive" high school—all of them serving poor black and Appalachian students. The minidistrict's "partner" in restructuring was a local agency called Urban Youth Collaborative (UYC), organized by elite elements of the business community and committed to improving the education of inner-city youth. The UYC, in collaboration with the superintendent and his staff, had decided to reorient the high school curriculum in the minidistrict around "tech prep," an increasingly influential model of secondary education that emphasizes work skills, occupational exploration and specialization, and linkages between high school programs and technical and paraprofessional programs in local community colleges. As tech prep was being instituted, the remaining small college preparatory "track" at the high school was eliminated.

Because of the changes in the high school curriculum in the minidistrict, the central office decided to discontinue the small "accelerated" program at Jefferson Middle School that was designed to be college-preparatory. Central office officials argued that to continue the accelerated program was to promote ability grouping practices that the school district was officially opposed to. Ironically, while eliminating ability groups is typically presented as a progressive reform, and can be, it is not necessarily so. In this case, homogeneous grouping resulted in the lowering of expectations for all students to "basic skills" mastery. Such an orientation to the curriculum did not prepare students for college, in either the kinds of courses they took or the kinds of intellectual skills they were learning. In an early conversation with the director of UYC, I once suggested that one of the effects of these changes might be to strengthen the school's role in reproducing class and race inequalities from generation to generation. His response was that I was being idealistic and that "it doesn't serve their [students'] needs to raise their expectations for college." They needed, he said, "marketable job skills." But the job market and wages were not good for high school graduates from the local high school; and only about 50 percent of those who currently left Jefferson Middle School and went on to the high school could expect to graduate.

Within this context, the mission of Jefferson Middle School, at least as the central office and the UYC saw it, was to make sure that students passed the necessary standardized tests and courses and so that they could move up to the high school on schedule and not have to be retained a year or more in the eighth grade. The principal had been hand-picked by the leader of the UYC to achieve this mission and was businesslike in his approach. In intercom messages to students and teachers each day, he used almost identical words to hit again and again on the importance of doing well on tests. "Remember students, you're here for only one purpose. You're not here to have a good time. You're not here to visit with your friends. You're here to pass the IAT test and do well on your CATs. That's our mission, so I want you all to give it 100 percent, and give somebody a smile." He pointed with pride to the fact that of all the middle schools in the city, Jefferson was the only one that had consistently raised test scores over the past two years. It was almost as if by focusing narrowly on rising test scores, it was possible not to see the bigger picture or acknowledge one's part in a system that was heavily implicated in the education and policing of the new American underclass. Of course, the principal had few perceived options. As he frequently reminded me, he and other principals in the district were now being evaluated on a yearly basis, and test scores were a major consideration in their evaluations. In order to raise test scores, teachers were encouraged to drill students in the specific skills to be tested, and this meant most teachers relied heavily upon drill sheets and textbooks to structure their lessons.

The basic skills students were tested on had nothing to do with multicultural education, so as one might expect multicultural perspectives in the curriculum were few and far between. During African American and Appalachian history months—which were officially recognized months in the school district—guest speakers were usually invited to talk to students. I observed two speakers one year for African American history month as they addressed students in the school's auditorium. One of the speakers was a black television reporter for a local television station, and the other a black minister. Both focused their remarks on the importance of avoiding drugs, sexual relations, and bad influences. They told similar stories of how they came from the inner city and made it, "and you can too." While these are important messages, nowhere did the speakers acknowledge the continuing need to confront racism or advance civil rights agendas. For Appalachian history month, a speaker from the local Appalachian council came around to each class to display some Appalachian folk art and tell some folk stories from the mountains. While this representation of Appalachian folk art and stories helped reveal, among other things, that Appalachian people have a rich craft and oral tradition of which to be proud, it tended to connect Appalachian identity with a rural, idealized past rather than the inner-city life these students knew. Furthermore, since the rural, idealized past invoked by the speaker was one in which a college education was simply unheard of and viewed as unnecessary, the presentation may also have encouraged some Appalachian-identified youth in the audience to believe that they did not need a college education either. In fact, in my conversations with students, I consistently found that Appalachian students were less likely than African American students to think of themselves as "college material."

The curriculum at Jefferson Middle School, as I have described it, took for granted a colonial worldview in a number of interrelated ways. However, it was not the curriculum which first struck the outsider as he or she entered the school. When I occasionally brought graduate students or other professors with me on my visits to the school, their initial reactions were very similar. What struck them right off was the ethos of the school, a sense that this was an institution dedicated to policing and disciplining bodies as much or more than it was about teaching the formal curriculum. Despite efforts to reduce conflicts and disruptions in the school, there were many arguments and fights, and most of the principal's time each day was spent managing one conflict after another. The most common and ritualistic cause of student conflict was "capping," in which one student would make derogatory comments about the family members of a fellow student as they passed each other in a hall or in leaving a class. For students used to being looked down upon by "respectable" society, fights over capping enacted a ritualistic defense of one's family honor and respectability.

Jefferson Middle School staff placed a heavy emphasis upon punitive forms of student control. The in-school detention room often was packed to overflowing, and students assigned to detention were not allowed to work on their assignments. To allow them to work on assignments in detention, the principal argued, would encourage some students to "be bad" so they could be sent to detention and get a free study hall. So students spent their time in detention copying their "student rights" over and over again—often one hundred times or more. These "rights" were actually classroom rules of conduct, such as "I have the right to listen to the teacher without being disrupted by others," and "I have the right to speak without being interrupted," etc. This disciplinary environment in the school, however, did not seem to be very effective in reducing conflict. By increasing tensions between students and staff, it may even have contributed to discipline problems. I remember watching one day in the office as a black male student was about to be taken downtown to juvenile detention for starting several fights that day. As the police and security guards began to move him towards the door, he suddenly assumed a defensive physical posture and began yelling, "don't touch me," over and over again like a litany, as the policy and security guards circled in. This young man had come to expect abuse from adult authority figures in both the home and in the school. "Don't touch me" is thus the cry of the oppressed; but it is a cry of defiance that ends up being self-defeating.

If Jefferson Middle School was a colonial institution, that is, an institution of white, upper-middle-class culture and power where colonial subjects were being constructed, it was also a place where some teachers struggled hard to empower their students. These were, for the most part, teachers who had grown up in similar or slightly better circumstances than their students. Yet, after two years, I began to feel, like many of the teachers, pessimistic about the prospects for dramatic change at Jefferson Middle School—at least outside of some very major shifts in power in the school district and the broader culture.

TOWARD POSTCOLONIALISM IN EDUCATION

These two stories—one about life in a Navaho boarding school in the late 1960s, and one about life in an inner-city middle school in the 1990s—provide concrete examples of the continuing discourse and practice of colonial education in the United States in the late twentieth century. Among other things, they suggest that democratic educational renewal will not be easy in schools serving racial groups historically marginalized and oppressed in the United States so long as the colonial worldview, and the power relations it constructs, continue to play a powerful role in shaping educational practice. Nevertheless, as I have also indicated, some elements of postcolonial education may be found in even the most colonial of schools. These experiences, along with the theoretical framework provided by postcolonial scholarship in the academy, provide a grounding for building a dialogue on postcolonial education and democratic educational renewal. Let me then point to some of the implications of this postcolonial discourse and practice for educational policy and curriculum reform.

First, postcolonialism may be associated with the reconstruction of public schools as "embryonic" multicultural communities, sites where diverse individuals and identity groups are brought together to engage in dialogue across difference, build common interests, and construct a hybrid culture.[9] As Cameron McCarthy suggests, in literature classes students might read a text from a European literary canon alongside texts from African and Asian literary canons to explore similar and dissimilar cultural themes; and they might also read that growing body of hybrid literature produced by the intersection of African, Asian, and European cultures.[10] In this way, no cultural tradition gets represented as "the" significant tradition, and each is understood in relation to the others. Cultural hegemony is dependent upon the presentation of a "selective tradition" that excludes and silences marginalized groups, so a postcolonial curriculum must be associated with a multicultural and polyvocal tradition that finds room for all.[11]

Second, I think that a postcolonial educational policy would work to shift control of public schools serving racial minorities and the poor to the communities they represent, and also dramatically increase the proportion of minority administrators and teachers in these schools. Native American schools continue to be under the ultimate authority of the federal BIA in Washington, D.C., which has always been an agency that represents Eurocentric cultural values and interests;

and most of the teachers in BIA schools continue to be "Anglos" who have little long-term investment in Native American culture. As I indicated, this has begun to change over the past several decades; but much more needs to be done to turn control of Native American schools over to Native American peoples. Similarly, Jefferson Middle School was a captive of the white corporate power structure in the city in which it was located, and its professional staff too was overwhelmingly white. As I argued earlier, one's class and race do not determine how one thinks and acts towards others; and there are highly qualified, dedicated, and effective white, middle-class teachers and administrators working in BIA and inner-city schools. Conversely, racial minority teachers and administrators may adopt many of the beliefs and practices of colonial education. Nevertheless, race and class do matter. Since colonial education involves the active construction of power relations of domination and subordination, it also always involves control of the schooling process by the dominating culture, in this case a white dominating culture. This domination is represented visually to students and the community in the fact that teachers and administrators are primarily white. It is also the case that many white teachers, like many whites in the United States more generally, view black, Hispanic, and Native American students in terms of cultural deficits and fail to set high expectations for them.

Of course, turning control of schools serving racial minorities over to the communities they serve or increasing the number of black, Hispanic, and Native American teachers are not panaceas. Each is full of dilemmas that will have to be cautiously negotiated. For example, conservatives have often supported greater local control of schools because it allows for the perpetuation of greater inequality between schools. Rich suburban and middle-class communities can spend a great deal on the education of their children and at the same time withdraw money from the state and let inner-city schools serving the racial and class Other face fiscal crisis. Similarly, increasing the proportion of minority teachers in schools serving racial minorities could be consistent with a rightist policy of resegregating the schools, in which white teachers are shifted to all-white schools and black teachers are transferred to all-black schools. During the segregationist era in the South, there were many more black teachers than there are now since black teachers were hired to teach in all-black schools. It is estimated that approximately 32,000 African American teachers lost jobs in the seventeen southern and border states between 1954 and 1979 as a direct result of desegregation (Ethridge, 1979). In Kentucky alone, the number of black teachers plummeted by 41 percent between 1955 and 1965 (Stewart, Meier, and England, 1989). While these teachers provided important role models for black youth and pushed children to excel, they did not change the overall colonial and inferior nature of education in segregated schools. At the same time, then, that a democratic progressive policy seeks to increase local control of schools and increase the proportion of nonwhite teachers in schools serving primarily nonwhite students, it must also be about the business of building more multiculturally diverse communities and schools. This is the real challenge of the coming decades.

Finally, as colonialism has always been closely linked to economic exploitation of lands and peoples, so a postcolonial policy discourse must seek to reverse two simultaneous tendencies: an increase in the disparity between the rich and poor in the United States, and an increase in the proportion of lower-tier workers who are racial minorities.[12] As the U.S. economy has been more closely integrated into the postmodern global economy, the workforce is being restructured around two major tiers, separated by a widening gap in income and lifestyle.[13] So far, many white Americans have been able to cushion themselves from the full effects of economic restructuring because the labor force is racialized. This economic cushioning results from both continuing white advantages in the labor market and from historic privilege that has been passed down to the current generation. For example, the white working poor is often better off financially than the black working poor because the former's parents owned homes and amassed capital during the days of heavy industry, whereas the latter have no such cushion to enable them to lessen housing costs.[14] Conservative and rightist politics in the years ahead are thus likely to be based on a tacit appeal to maintaining white economic privilege in the face of massive economic shifts. However, if economic disparities continue to increase and more white Americans slip into the expanding lower-tier work force and feel culturally and politically marginalized, they may begin to see they have some common interests with black and Latino workers that cross racial boundaries. The challenge for progressives in the years ahead is to begin forging these overlapping interests and agendas.

NOTES

1. In developing notions of deculturation and assimilation I have been influenced by Joel Spring (1994), *Deculturation and the Struggle for Equality: A Brief History of the Education of Dominated Cultures in the United States.* New York: McGraw-Hill. Notions of the policing, surveillance, and disciplining of bodies are central in the work of Michel Foucault (1979), *Discipline and Punish: The Birth of the Prison* (A. Sheridan, trans.). New York: Vintage.
2. For an introduction to postcolonial discourse and its applications in education see Cameron McCarthy and Warren Crichlow, eds. (1993), *Race, Identity, and Representation in Education.* New York: Routledge.
3. The Miami University Institute for Educational Renewal, which sponsored my work in the school, is affiliated with the National Network for Educational Renewal led by John Goodlad at the University of Washington.
4. The overreliance on basal readers in BIA schools has been a pervasive phenomenon. See Daniel McLaughlin (1993), "Personal Narratives for School Change in Navajo Settings," in McLaughlin and Tierney, eds., *Naming Silenced Lives*, 95–118.
5. Kennedy was a member of the U.S. Department of the Interior, which oversaw the BIA, and head of a Special Subcommittee on Indian Education, which began its work in 1967. In 1969, under the leadership of Senator Edward Kennedy, the subcommittee issued its report—a stinging indictment of a system that "has had disastrous effects on the education of Indian children." See Margaret Szasz (1974), *Education and the American Indian: The Road to Self-Determination since 1928.* Albuquerque, NM: University of New Mexico Press, 149–150.
6. See Szasz, *Education and the American Indian*; and Guy Senese (1991), *Self-Determination and the Social Education of Native Americans.* New York: Praeger.
7. Joel Spring, *Deculturation and the Struggle for Equality*, 91.
8. See E. F. Dube (1985), "The Relationship between Racism and Education in South Africa." *Harvard Educational Review*, 55 (1), 86–100.
9. See Nicholas Burbules and Suzanne Rice (1991), "Dialogue across Differences: Continuing the Conversation." *Harvard Educational Review*, 61 (4), 393–416. For a discussion of the notion of "hybridity," see Cornel West (1990), "The New Cultural Politics of Difference." In Russell Ferguson, et al. *Out There: Marginalization and Contemporary Cultures* (Cambridge, Mass.: MIT Press), 19–36.
10. Cameron McCarthy (1993), "After the Canon: Knowledge and Ideological Representation in the Multicultural Discourse on Curriculum Reform." In McCarthy and Crichlow, eds., *Race, Identity, and Representation in Education*, 289–305.
11. See Raymond Williams (1989), "Hegemony and the Selective Tradition." In Suzanne De Castell, Allan Luke, and Carmen Luke, eds., *Language, Authority, and Criticism: Readings on the School Textbook* (New York: Falmer, 1989).
12. Howard Winant (1990), "Postmodern Racial Politics in the United States: Difference and Inequality." *Socialist Review*, 20 (1), 121–147.
13. Between 1978 and 1987, the poorest fifth of Americans saw their real incomes decline by eight percent;

while the richest fifth saw their incomes grow by 13 percent. See Robert Reich (1989), "Why the Rich Are Getting Richer and the Poor Poorer." *The New Republic* (March 1).

14. Ethridge, S. (1979), "Impact of the 1954 Brown v. Topeka Board of Education Decision on Black Educators." *Negro Educational Review*, 30, (3–4), 217–232.

Stewart J., K. Meier, and R. England (1989), "In Quest of Role Models: Change in Black Teacher Representation in Urban School Districts, 1968–86." *Journal of Negro Education*, 58, (2), 140–152.

Living Whiteness:
Nations, Colonialism, and Identities

Keeping the White Queen in Play

Michael Billig

Michael Billig is currently Professor of Social Sciences at Loughborough University. He trained as an experimental social psychologist at Bristol University. He has written a number of books investigating ideological issues and, along with other colleagues at Loughborough, he is concerned to develop discursive and rhetorical approaches to social psychology. Among his recent books are *Talking of the Royal Family*, *Banal Nationalism*, and a new edition of *Arguing and Thinking*.

Younger Son: I don't think he would have married a black girl either
Mother: Oh no
Younger Son: Or a Chinese girl
Mother: No {*laughs*}
Older Son: Or a Greek {*Father and Mother laugh*}
Mother: Or an I-tie {*general laughter*}
Father: Would you
Younger Son: So, I mean in that, in that sense, he's dictated to, as to who he can fall in love
    and get married

It is an English family, sitting in their own home, talking about the British Royal Family. The older son, a thirty-year-old photographer, is the only one arguing an antiroyalist position. The conversation is relaxed, with much friendly banter between the older son and the other three members. The talk had got round to the question whether Prince Charles, as heir to the throne, would have been free to marry anyone of his choice. They were agreeing that palace authorities would have inspected the background of any prospective wife, checking in particular for her capacity to produce royal offspring. The younger son, much more traditional than his older brother, then raised the issue of race. Prince Charles would not have been free to marry a black girl. In the exchange, which followed, there was the joking and the laughter, outlined above.

Why should laughter accompany the turn toward race? In the exchanges about checking a prospective royal princess, there was little humour. The older son had mentioned that any prospective queen by marriage would have been required to undergo a gynecological examination to see whether she could have children. No jokes were made. The mother had said that, should the tests prove unsatisfactory, Charles would have been required to find another partner. Still no joking. Then the hypothetical black girl is suggested. And the joking begins. Perhaps, the timing was fortuitous. Yet, jokes can often be revealing. They can indicate a breaking of social and discursive codes, as the impermissible is briefly permitted to be uttered in a changed, safely humorous, form (Mulkay, 1988). The codes and taboos are not directly challenged by the jokes, which can protect the codes, which they appear to infract.

Although jokes appear to permit the unsayable to be uttered, some things still remain unsaid.

As will be suggested, the jokes of the family touch upon deep issues of identity and nationhood—issues which are too hedged with social taboos to be spoken directly. Even in the jokes, there is much to be left unsaid, especially in relation to the unsayable assumptions of race and whiteness. In this instance, the unsayable themes indicate how the assumptions of race can deeply permeate conventional talk about British national identity.

The family had been taking part in a research project about the ways in which English families talk about the Royal Family. An interviewer had contacted over sixty families; all but one was white. The resulting discussions were recorded in the families' own homes (for details, see Billig, 1992). Speakers would typically talk at length about the desirability of royalty representing the nation, or setting standards for ordinary people. In the majority of cases the issue of race was not a topic which was raised. But when it was, the discursive turns were revealing, both in terms of what was said and, also, most importantly, what was not said.

In the extract just quoted, the laughter did not start with the mention of a black girl. That was to be considered as a serious possibility. Britain has an estimated population of over two and a half million nonwhites, of whom over a half a million could be identified as "African" or "Afro-Caribbean" (Skellington and Morris, 1992). There is evidence of an increase of inter-ethnic couples, so that there are now more people described as "mixed origin" than "West Indian"; almost 40 percent of those described as "mixed origin" are under ten years of age (Skellington and Morris, pp. 39–40). Also, British people, especially whites, consistently overestimate the number of nonwhites in the country (see, for example, the results of the NOP poll, reported in Skellington and Morris, p. 153). If the idea of white and black falling in love in contemporary Britain is not considered a fanciful prospect, then it is not beyond the bounds of imagination to entertain the possibility that the Royal Family might be faced with the prospect of nonwhite in-laws.

However, the possibility was not seriously discussed in that particular conversation. Jokes turn the conversation away from the topic, after the idea of a black queen is mooted. The mother raises the possibility of Charles falling in love with a Chinese girl. There is laughter. Why is it funny? Certainly, there is a much smaller British Chinese population than black or "Asian" (in Britain, "Asian" generally refers to people from the Indian subcontinent). The idea of a Chinese Queen of England is itself a mixing of codes: a sense of incongruity is invoked by the very idea. The idea is beyond the conventionally possible idea that the heir, in common with increasing numbers of his white subjects, might fall in love with a black Briton. The joke is taken up and pushed further by the older son: "or a Greek," he says. Slyly, it is back to reality: the Queen's husband was originally Prince Philip of Greece. But the reality is itself a source of jokes: this man, who looks and sounds so aristocratically British, is *really* Greek ("just a Greek").

The mother, far from rebutting the implication (and far from seeing her son's comment as a criticism against the biased customs of royal matrimony) joins in the fun: "Or an I-tie." It's all become a joke. If Greeks are not inappropriate (so long as they appear English), then nor are Italians. But the mother uses the derogatory slang, to reverse the reversal: an "I-tie" is inappropriate, for an "I-tie" would be a most Italian Italian. And the word itself is inappropriate: a breaking of codes is indicated by the socially impolite slang, which can only be uttered in jest. To have used "I-tie" in earnest would be coarse, especially in front of a stranger—the interviewer. It would hardly have conformed to codes of middle-class, English politeness.

The matter is not left as a joke, for these jokes, like most jokes, are not "merely" jokes. The younger son sums up the position, to which the comments, jesting and serious, are leading. "So," he says, using a little word, which conventionally indicates that a point is to be drawn from the preceding remarks (Schiffrin, 1985). So, the prince is dictated to: he cannot choose who to fall in love with. The point is to sympathise with the prince—not to sympathise with any black, Chinese, or "I-tie" who might be rejected as inappropriate for royal position.

But, something is being left unsaid. The jokes allude to, but skirt around, a crucial issue. There is no articulation of the principle, according to which prospective brides might be accepted or rejected. But the principle is understood—and is understood beyond humour. It is, of course, the principle of presumed "whiteness." There can be jokes about Chinese or Italian royal spouses—but not about "blacks." "I-tie" can be uttered, but not the equivalent for blackness. The word "white" is absent in the exchanges. And the jokes move the conversation on from "colour" (black and, perhaps "yellow"), so the concluding principle (itself based on an unarticulated principle) can be drawn. The jokes, about the white (or possibly "whitish") foreigners leave the unsayable unsaid, but in place: the future Queen must be white.

According to Pajaczkowska and Young (1994), white identity possesses an "absent centre" (p. 202). If identity is discursively constructed (Shotter and Gergen, 1989; Shotter, 1993; Wetherell and Potter, 1992), then this absent centre will be supported by codes of utterance, rather than inner psychic structures. Just as conversations can jointly produce collective memories (Edwards and Middleton, 1988; Middleton and Edwards, 1990; Billig and Edwards, 1994), so, too, they can accomplish denials and projections, as speakers combine to move talk away from tabooed topics, jointly protecting what cannot be uttered. In this way, the unsayable will be present, even if marked by its absence.

In the case of British royalty there is a taboo of race and identity. The Royal Family, as many British speakers claim, is to be seen as a symbol of the nation. If nations are, to quote Anderson (1983) "imagined communities," then monarchy occupies a central place in the imagination of contemporary Britain. Often respondents said that Britain would not be Britain without a monarchy: it would be like other countries (for details, see Billig, 1992). As the mother of the family, quoted above, said in another part of the conversation, "it's part of our background, you know, as English people." The equation between the nation and the Royal Family is also an equation of identity: it's part of "us," "our" background, "our" selves. If Britain is not Britain without the Royal Family, then "we, the British" would not be British: "we" would not be "us." Imagining "us" as "not-us" was something to be avoided.

In this way, the Royal Family is defended as an object of national identification; people would say that they wanted a Royal Family in whom they could see themselves. Royalty should, in many ways, be ordinary—like "you" and "me." But, they should not be too ordinary: they should also be figures of respect. In Nairn's (1988) phrase, royalty should be super-ordinary (see also Edley, 1993). How, as English (or British) people, could "we" recognize "ourselves" in a foreigner? More than this, how could "we" see "ourselves" *as British* in the image of a foreigner—for "we" look to royalty to reflect "our" own sense of national self? The objects of "our" national identification must be objects of national identity. A Greek who looks and talks British is possible. But a Chinese person . . . an "I-tie' . . . a black . . .

Something, here, cannot be uttered directly because of the conventional dilemmas of race. According to Etienne Balibar, contemporary racism is a "racism without races" (1991, p. 21). Racism itself must be denied, for its cultural undesirability, and more generally that of "prejudice," is firmly established. Denials can be heard as white persons talk about nonwhites. The utterance of complaint has its own etiquette. "I'm not prejudiced but . . ." is a common preface, uttered as speakers, especially in European countries, begin their rhetoric of criticism directed against "immigrants" (Billig, 1991; van Dijk, 1991, 1992, and 1993; Potter and Wetherell, 1988; Wetherell and Potter, 1992). The phrase itself draws attention to the social undesirability of

152

"prejudice." Speakers claim the credentials of being "unprejudiced." In so doing, they recognize that their words might well be heard as being "prejudiced." In this way, the prefix seeks to disarm criticism in advance. In the United States, it is claimed that whites likewise disavow the open racism of two generations ago (Gaertner and Dovidio, 1986; Kinder and Sears, 1981; Kinder, 1986; McConahay et al., 1981; McConahay, 1986). Criticisms of blacks are seldom outwardly made on the ground of race in this new racism. Always some other reason—some deracialized justification—is found (Barker, 1981; Reeves, 1983; van Dijk, 1993).

The phrase "I'm not prejudiced but . . ." also indicates that there is a "prejudice" (*the* "proper" prejudice) existing beyond speakers' complaints. Speakers are implicitly distancing their own remarks, and their own selves, from the category of "prejudice." Thus, the implied image of some further extreme is justifying their own claims to nonprejudice. In Europe, the *real* prejudices are often presumed to be those of the fascist far-right (Billig, 1991). In the United States, it is the "rednecked" racism of segregation. The image of *real* prejudice, through which white speakers deny their own racism, is an image of racialised racism, with racial epithets and theories of race. There is more. A racism with races is not merely a racism against "them." It is a racism about "us." The fascist groups proclaim a theory of race, openly claiming to defend the racial purity of the white race (Billig, 1991). In this, they go beyond the bounds of politeness and social acceptability of the "normal" discourse of deracialized racism, which denies its own racism. In this denial, whiteness becomes invisible.

When race is talked about by whites in conventional ways, it must be socially managed to prevent the discursive intrusion of "whiteness," while, all the same, permitting the distinction between "whiteness" and "blackness" to be maintained, just out of argumentative reach. In the case of conventional talk about royalty, it is assumed that the nation should be represented by the image of a British, white family. But if the figures of identification are to be white, then this cannot be justified directly. Discursive projections and denials are necessary.

Traces of such denials are visible in the conversations about Royalty. Although over sixty family discussions were recorded with white families, only on five occasions was the issue of royalty marrying outside their race raised. This, in itself, might be considered as a sign of avoidance. But when the issue was raised, the conversational delicacies became evident. Here was an "ideological dilemma," especially for the majority who were royalists (Billig et al., 1988). The whiteness of royalty was to be protected, but it could not be defended directly. Not only must "we" deny "our" own racism, but so must the racism of royalty be denied. To support a racist royal family—to identify openly with those who practice racial purity—would be to condemn "ourselves," both personally and nationally. Some other code of talking, together with a means of discursive avoidance, must be found.

A denial of choice was sometimes asserted, as if no one was making racial decisions. The older son in the family, already quoted, sums up his family's view: Prince Charles is "dictated to" in his choice of partner. Who is dictating this and why they are doing so are left unsaid. It is as if a hidden hand of necessity is operating in a vacuum. A sixty-eight-year-old, retired tool-maker is talking with his daughter and son-in-law. What would have happened if Prince Edward had "wanted to marry somebody from Asia or Africa?" asked the interviewer. "Well, I don't think he would have been allowed to," answered the father. Daughter and son-in-law agreed. Then, the father dismissed the question:

> I don't think the question would ever come up anyway because if they found out that he was involved with a coloured person, then, err, he, think, she would, she would, err, slowly go out of the limelight.

Hesitations and pauses, evident in his remarks, are conventional signs of discursive difficulty. Who was doing the allowing again is unspecified, as the passive tense is used. But one thing could be stated. The father said that "I don't think the Queen would be prejudiced, but I'm sure the old royalty would have been."

In another discussion, the mother, a sixty-eight-year-old former cleaner, agreed that royalty would not "be allowed to marry someone coloured." Her son, a forty-three-year-old school caretaker, agreed: "It would all be hushed up . . . before it even got to holding hands . . . they'd be shipped abroad or somewhere, you know, out of the way." Who would be doing the shipping abroad, or the hushing up, of the nonwhite illicit lover is not specified. Somehow, magically, the black figure would be eliminated, with no questions asked.

Even so there is the problem of racism, conceived not as an injury to nonwhites, but as an accusation against whites, including the speakers themselves. The caretaker continued, straight after his remarks about the hushing up and shipping away, to mention the possibility of racism:

> I don't think it would happen, not because they're racist, I'm not saying they're racist, you know, 'cause they mix with the [*pause*] um, I can't see it myself, I don't know why.

Not even "blackness" was mentionable here, let alone "whiteness": royals are not racist because they mix with the "um." No suitable description was at hand. None of the listeners needed to ask for clarification. The speaker's denial of royal racism was, also, a denial of his own racism: he was not supporting a racist figurehead. It wasn't racism; it just wouldn't happen. But why, he couldn't say: "I don't know why."

Neither his mother nor wife pushed him to specify. They were agreeing with him, supporting his point. "I mean it's what's expected of royalty," added his wife. "Yeah, that's it, it's imagery, yeah," added her husband taking up the point: "It wouldn't look right in the public eye." His mother agreed: "Well, it isn't right in the public eye, is it really." A double projection had been achieved. The wish for white royals was projected onto the royals themselves. And, then, to escape the possible charge of racism, which the speakers were themselves raising, the royals were claimed to be acting in accordance with public opinion. The speakers did not associate themselves with "the public eye." It was as if this eye were something existing objectively outside of themselves—as an objective necessity beyond criticism. The royal whiteness, which this eye is presumed to need to gaze upon, is left unidentified. It is merely something whose absence would not look right. A discursive collusion enables "us" not to gaze upon (or mention) what is the nature of the right look.

A mother, who works as a cleaner is talking with her seventeen-year-old daughter, a factory worker. They had been talking about the way that the young royals have to ask permission to marry. The interviewer asked the mother whether she expected her children to ask her for permission to get married. The mother replied: "As long as the bloke can keep them and look after them, I mean, I don't care if he's black, white, with pink spots or what he is." But what if "they"—royalty—wanted to marry a black person? Now it was a matter for joking—and hesitation:

> Oh dear, I doubt it [*pause*], they'd have to scrub the poor devil to get it clean [*laughs*], no I doubt it, I mean, I know sort of [*pause*], well you know, they'll marry *different* nationalities, but [*pause*] coloured *no*.

"I don't think the Queen would like it," said her daughter in agreement. "I think she'd put a stop to it." They would "bleach them," joked the mother again.

The components of avoidance are there. "They," not "us," would forbid it; jokes about scrubbing and bleaching draw attention away from the details of forbidding; the mother mocks the irrationality of the prohibition; but the jokes leave it in place. The two women are not criticising royalty on this issue. The issue is spoken of as a matter of blackness, of colour, but not of whiteness. The term "white" is avoided. Royalty would not marry "coloured," but they would different "nationalities": an opposition between "colour" and nationality is assumed. Listeners are to understand "nationalities" as "white foreigners": Greeks, French, Germans, even Italians or, perhaps, "I-ties." The meaning of race—and particularly of "whiteness"—is conveyed without the word "white."

Significantly, the mother does use "white" in her previous statement, when she is talking of permission rather than prohibition. When she talks about her own daughters, she expresses a tolerance which she does not attribute to royalty. Colour, she said, was irrelevant. Her daughters can marry whom they want: black or white or pink spots. She was speaking in front of her own unmarried daughter, and so her words can be understood as a message of permission. Whiteness is mentioned when it is specified as irrelevant: this message carried no danger of accusation. But when whiteness becomes relevant, as the object of a prohibition, then it must be semantically camouflaged.

In this way, "whiteness" is kept in place as an unnamed standard, representing the national self: "colour" is the deviation. The retired tool-maker, his daughter, and son-in-law have already been mentioned. After mentioning that "a coloured person" who might get romantically entangled with a royal would be removed from the limelight, the tool-maker switched the conversation to religion. "They wouldn't be allowed to marry a Roman Catholic," said the old man. After a few exchanges on this theme, the son-in-law said:

I think the whole issue between different sects, religion and colours and races is to try and keep things as neutral as possible politically, that's how I personally see it.

The interviewer asked him what he meant. He replied: "Generally as a nation if you introduce something like a Catholic, a Jewish person, a black person or an Asian, you're immediately putting a bias on the situation." What is neutral is unnamed: it is the normal terrain, the unmarked, national ground against which the biased figures stand out. And the biases, as compared with the pale background, can be identified by name. This identification itself can be claimed as an example of "neutrality," for the speaker, too, is laying claim to a position of neutrality. In this neutrality, race is treated alongside other categories, such as religion, and, thus, the particularities of race are absorbed into an outwardly deracialized general principle. Negative terms are avoided: there is no semantic hint of an "I-tie" here, nothing to attract the accusation of racism, antisemitism or whatever. It is a defence of neutrality, which leaves the background in the background, its proclaimed neutrality—"our" neutrality—as the standard, untouched and pure.

In all these defences of the whiteness of the Royal Family (and, thus, the white personification of the nation), the word "white" is avoided. As John Heritage (1988) has argued, the conventions of discourse are often revealed in the exceptional case. Thus, the mother revealed the discursive conventions of "whiteness" by including the word in her permissions but not in her prohibitions. There was one discussion, in which the topic of royalty marrying a nonwhite was mentioned, and a speaker specifically used the word "white" in this connection. The utterance indicated the assumptions behind the absences on other occasions.

A middle-class mother and father—secretary and salesperson—were talking with their sixteen-year-old daughter and her school friend, also sixteen. They had been discussing the religious restrictions on royal marriages: "They don't allow them to marry into different religions," said the mother, using the impersonal mode, which ascribes power and responsibility to a mysterious "them." The daughter, then, raised the issue of race, the white race:

> Daughter: It makes me wonder, right, 'cause, you know, all of the Royal Family are white, it makes me wonder whether they'd allow if they wanted to marry a coloured person; I just thought of that 'cause I don't think they would
> Daughter's Friend: I don't see why not
> Daughter: Yeah, I don't see why not, but I don't think they would
> Father: I don't think it would ever happen
> Daughter's Friend: No

As soon as the daughter introduces the topic and uses the term "white," her friend distances herself from the assumed royal position. She makes it plain that she sees no reason why royals should marry white. And the daughter agrees, distinguishing herself from the position attributed to royalty. The interviewer then asked the question, "how coloured would you have to be?" The daughter replied: "I think you've got to be pure white, I think that's how they'd take it." Again, an expression of distancing accompanies the outward expression of whiteness: that's how *they* would take it, emphasising that it is not the way she takes the issue. "Pure whiteness" is the sort of phrase to be used in earnest by the open racist: here, the phrase is turned around as critique. If royalty wish to remain "pure white," then they are being exposed: and she, the exposer, distances herself from the exposed racism.

Her mother and father utter no phrases, which either criticise royalty or distance themselves from the presumed royal policy of racial purity. Their words can be heard as evasions. And significantly, the word "white" is absent. The father agrees that royalty would not allow such intermarriage to happen. But he offers no words to criticise the presumed royal stance. Having stated the royal position, he, together with the mother, talk about whether the situation is ever likely to occur. The mother says the possibility hasn't ever cropped up. But it could in the future, says the father, " 'cause there's more colours and everything coming into England and now it's a possibility." He did not think that there was "anything stated that they can't do that." The Queen would have the final say, said the mother.

As mother and father talked thus, they only described the Queen's stance, not their own. When their daughter and her friend had made their stance, there had been a parental silence. Words of criticism had not been uttered. Nor had words of "whiteness." Instead, their words were moving the point of conversation to the discussable topic of whether the situation might arise, and who would have the final say. And, finally, there was escape. They settled into discussing whether the royals could marry divorcees. This was a safer topic for the business of giving opinions. The mother now offered her stance: all those years ago, it had been wrong to prevent Princess Margaret from marrying the person of her choice. A divorcee. And, in fact, a white man. But the latter was not said. It was not her point.

In this sort of context, the discursive avoidances of whiteness leave the assumptions of whiteness in place. However, as the statements of the sixteen-year-old girl and her school friend indicate, the assumptions can be challenged. The issues at stake are not trivial. In Britain, the topic of royalty is centrally bound up with the imagining of the nation. As such, it is a form of banal nationalism and a key theme of national identity (Billig, 1995). As the conversational extracts suggest, this imagining of national identity has its racial aspect. However, the assumption of whiteness is not to be directly expressed, and certainly not directly justified. Hence, there is the projection of the wish for a white Royal Family onto the Queen, onto unspecified "them," or onto "public opinion." It is anywhere but here in "us."

The Royal Family was commonly justified as the personalized representation of national identity (see Billig, 1992). The mother, quoted above, said that it's part of "our" background as "English" people; royalty is part of the national "us." To reflect "our" national selves, this object of identification must offer the possibility that "we" can recognize "our" national selves in their reflection. Too Greek—too "I-tie"—too swarthy: and such recognition is not possible. Blackness, Jewishness, Chineseness absorb the light of British self-reflection—at least for the majority of "us." Here the tones of hegemony are to be heard. The "others" are to recognize themselves in the projected image of the majority, but "we" cannot recognize "our" national selves in "them." There is no equality in this exchange. The exotic peripheries must not be allowed to move towards the centre of Narcissus's nationalist mirror. But, hush. This is "our" background, "our" nation, "our" tolerance. Polite silences are required to keep it thus.

REFERENCES

Anderson, B. (1983). *Imagined Communities*. London: Verso.

Balibar, E. (1991). Is there a "neo-racism"? In E. Balibar and I. Wallerstein, *Race, Nation, Class*. London: Verso.

Barker, M. (1981) *The New Racism*. London: Junction Books.

Billig, M. (1991). *Ideology and Opinions*. London: Sage Press.

Billig, M. (1992). *Talking of the Royal Family*. London: Routledge.

Billig, M. (1995). *Banal Nationalism*. London: Sage.

Billig, M., Condor, S., Edwards, D., Gane, M., Middleton, D., and Radley, A. R. (1988). *Ideological Dilemmas: A Social Psychology of Everyday Thinking*. London: Sage Press.

Billig, M., and Edwards, D. (1994). La construction sociale de la mémoire. *La Recherche*, 25, 742–745.

Edley, N. (1993). Prince Charles—our flexible friend: accounting for variations in constructions of identity. *Text*, 13, 397–422.

Edwards, D. and Middleton, D. (1988). Conversational remembering and family relationships: how children learn to remember. *Journal of Social and Personal Relationships*, 5, 3–25.

Gaertner, S. L., and Dovidio, J. F. (1986). The aversive form of racism. In J. F. Dovidio and S. L. Gaertner (eds.), *Prejudice, Discrimination and Racism*. Orlando: Academic Press.

Heritage, J. (1984). Explanations as accounts: a conversation analytic perspective. In C. Antaki (ed.) *Analysing Everyday Explanation*. London: Sage.

Kinder, D. R. (1986). The continuing American dilemma: white resistance to racial change 40 years after Myrdal. *Journal of Social Issues*, 42, 151–171.

Kinder, D. R., and Sears, D. O. (1981). Prejudice and politics: symbolic racism versus racial threats to the good life. *Journal of Personality and Social Psychology*, 40, 414–431.

McConahay, J. B. (1986). Modern racism, ambivalence and the Modern Racism Scale. In J. F. Dovidio and S. L. Gaertner (eds.), *Prejudice, Discrimination and Racism*. Orlando: Academic Press.

McConahay, J. B., Hardee, B. B., and Batts, V. (1981). Has racism declined in America? *Journal of Conflict Resolution*, 25, 563–579.

Middleton, D., and Edwards, D. (1990). *Collective Remembering*. London: Sage.

Mulkay, M. (1988). *On Humour*. Cambridge: Polity.

Nairn, T. (1988). *The Enchanted Glass*. London: Radius.

Pajaczkowska, C., and Young, L. (1994). Racism, representation, psychoanalysis. In J. Donald and A. Rattansi (eds.), *"Race," Culture and Difference*. London: Sage.

Potter, J., and Wetherell, M. 1987 *Discourse and Social Psychology*. London: Sage.

Potter, J., and Wetherell, M. (1988). Accomplishing attitudes: fact and evaluation in racist discourse. *Text*, 8, 51–68.

Reeves, F. (1983). *British Racial Discourse*. Cambridge: Cambridge University Press.

Schiffrin, D. (1985). Everyday argument: the organization of diversity in talk. In T. A. van Dijk (ed.), *Handbook of Discourse Analysis, Volume 3*. London: Academic Press.

Shotter, J., and Gergen, K. J. (1989). *Texts of Identity*. London: Sage.

Shotter, J. (1993a). *The Cultural Politics of Everyday Life*. Milton Keynes: Open University.

Skellington, R., and Morris, P. (1992). *"Race" in Britain Today*. London: Sage.

van Dijk, T. A. (1991). *Racism and the Press*. London: Routledge.

van Dijk, T. A. (1992). Discourse and the denial of racism. *Discourse and Society*, 3, 87–118.

van Dijk, T. A. (1993). *Elite Discourse and Racism*. Newbury Park: Sage.

Wetherell, M., and Potter, J. (1992). *Mapping the Language of Racism*. Hemel Hempstead: Harvester/Wheatsheaf.

The research reported in this chapter was supported by the Economic and Social Research Council on the project "Socio-psychological analysis of family discourse" (Grant Number R000231228). The author would like to thank, once again, Marie Kennedy for her interviewing skills.

Colonial Remnants: Assumptions of Privilege

Louise H. Kidder

FIFTEEN

Colonial Remnants: Assumptions of Privilege

Louise H. Kidder

FIFTEEN

Louise H. Kidder is Associate Dean and Professor of Psychology and Women's Studies at Temple University. She has also taught in India and Japan and her research interests in social justice include cross-cultural studies. She is coauthor of *Research Methods in Social Relations* and has contributed articles to the *Journal of Social Issues, American Psychologist,* and *International Journal of Intercultural Relations.*

Becoming a "master" or "madam" happened overnight. It required only a day's flight from North America or Western Europe to India, and even people who went with no desire to rule over servants or service workers slipped into positions that had been prepared by colonial rulers. Those roles persist long after colonial rule ended and one need not be British to be a "master." One need only be western and white.

I lived in India twice: in 1964 to teach in one South Indian city and in 1970 to conduct research in another city. What I learned the first time informed how I lived the second time. My first sojourn made me want to return and study how western sojourners fit in or altered their roles. What I have written here is foreshadowed by my earlier writings (1971, 1977). It goes further, however, and breaks the boundaries of prudent analysis and pleasant memories to examine the back stage and backside of western sojourns, the making of "masters" in the "servant's" land.

The people I studied were all nationals of other countries living in a South Indian metropolis for periods ranging from one month to 29 years. I too lived in that city for a year to study the lives of expatriates. Soon after arriving I obtained membership lists from the European and North American cultural and social clubs. Those lists provided several points of entry into the foreign communities. Once I began interviewing people they also included me in the social life of expatriates. Some became my friends and others were primarily respondents who agreed to be interviewed and to tell me their stories. I talked with more than one hundred expatriates; most were North Americans, the second largest group were Europeans, and two expatriates were from North East and South East Asia. All the Americans and Europeans were white; this chapter is about them, and being one of them I am inevitably writing also about myself.

Like the people I studied, I was noticeably wealthy and white. My dollar income was small but its purchasing power was magnified by currency exchange rates that made me relatively rich. Even Peace Corps Volunteers, perhaps the lowest-paid expatriates, were poor only by comparison with more highly paid expatriates, and theirs was a temporary vow of poverty for the duration of their stay. Despite some expatriates' attempts to plead poverty, we were visibly well off in India, by virtue of being western.

Being western and wealthy does not necessarily mean being white, but in India being white automatically meant being western and therefore wealthy. During my first stay in India, as a fresh college graduate in 1964, I naively thought I could disguise my whiteness, westerness and relative wealth if I wore sarees and Indian hair-pieces. Indian friends in America had said I could "pass" as a fair-skinned light-eyed Indian, perhaps from the North. And in North India people sometimes said they had a relative who looked like me. The possibility that I might "pass" seemed like a bit of reciprocal flattery—many Indians place a premium on fair skin color, and I placed a premium on not being too white. But my efforts to blend in fell flat. I could not pass at all as I bicycled by the police colony where children ran to the road and called *"vellakaracheee"* [white woman] every day. They never stopped for two years, and I never ceased being white.

During my first term in India I thought I could assume a neutral social class or caste but lost that naivete when for $100 a month my husband and I could rent a comfortable home and employ the help of a man and woman to shop, cook, carry water, launder, clean, and sweep. They and we were age-mates, in our twenties, but Bob and I were "master" and "ma'm" and they were "Jodi" and "Sylvi." They were newly married and Sylvi was pregnant. One day neither Jodi nor Sylvi came to work. I cleaned our outdoor toilet despite warnings from Indian friends about jobs that were dirty, low caste, for servants. When Jodi came the next day he might have sensed my irritation and explained why he had missed work. He said simply, "Ma'm, my baby died."

I recall this incident to place myself within the frame of what I say about other expatriates. Tempting as it is to distance myself from the less than flattering portrayals that follow, it is useless to pretend that I did not benefit from "white privilege" (cf. Mannnoni, 1964). In some expatriates' stories they sound guilty of arrogance and abuse of privilege while they tacitly claim innocence. By their accounts it is the "other" who is guilty—for overcharging, stealing, or threatening the expatriate's well-being. Like the subjects of social psychology experiments who do not see their own self-serving attribution errors, these expatriates do not point the finger at themselves (cf. Jones and Nisbett, 1971; Jones, et al., 1971). They do, however, point their fingers at *other* expatriates who seem more privileged than themselves.

NEOCOLONIAL PRIVILEGES AND PRIVATIONS

From the perspective of shopkeepers, vendors, school teachers, taxi drivers, civil servants, hotel operators, and the average person on the street, white people were wealthy (Kidder, 1971; 1977). From the perspective of the white westerners themselves there were great disparities within their group in the extent of their privileges and privations. They had come to India under various auspices, for varying purposes, with different "perks" and benefits. These comparisons were frequent topics of conversation among foreigners. They knew who had a refrigerator or not, who drove what type of car or none at all, and how much money someone was able to accumulate by being in India.

> JK: then there are some others, the [agency] people who live like kings and still try to make more money on it. Most of them just hate it here, and whenever they talk about another couple leaving they say they're so happy for them. Yet they want to stay long enough to save a big pile. They'll usually say something like "I'll stay another 2 years to finish my work," but what they really want to do is save another $25,000 for their kid's college. It's really pathetic. You'll see an example tonight. They're staying another two years just to save that money, yet she's absolutely miserable here . . . she hates it. I think it's awful to lure people out here by offering them that kind of money. But one thing I must say, they do their jobs. They do good work, to satisfy themselves too.

Goods and services that North Americans and Europeans took for granted they sometimes shared liberally with their compatriots; modern conveniences were necessities for people like themselves. These transfers seemed smooth, lateral, sometimes charitable but not demeaning. Other expatriates like themselves were deserving of goods and services they all took for granted back home. Sometimes they loaned each other equipment or those who were better off made outright gifts of appliances to their poorer compatriots. They seemed to draw the line, however, if an Indian family was in the market for foreign goods. When expatriates left to go home, they did not automatically bequeath their goods to Indian acquaintances. They frequently sold their "necessities" at high prices to Indians who bought them as "luxuries." The expatriates behaved like subjects in social psychological studies of justice who extended protection and generosity mainly to people like themselves. Susan Opotow describes how people "draw the line." The less similar the other, the less likely people are to include them in their moral community (Opotow, 1990; 1995). Indians were the "others" and had to pay dearly for the privilege of purchasing used foreign goods.

I was a beneficiary of goods and services from other westerners as well as from Indian colleagues. For the first few months I had no phone and this posed a serious barrier; almost everyone I wanted to interview had a phone through the influence of a foreign government or industry. I relied on the generosity of neighboring Americans who gave me free access to their phone. They recognized my need and were glad to provide what we all considered a "necessity." My chief benefactor, however, was an Indian whom I had a met a month earlier. Without his help I would have spent a year waiting for service because phone lines and equipment were in short supply and the city had a long waiting list of applicants. Within two months I had a phone because my Indian colleague asked his friend to move my name to the front of the list. I owed my colleague a favor in return so when we left India he inherited our motorized bike, another item in short supply. This was not a gift but a bargain, a fair trade in the complex calculus of privileges and privations. Because I could afford a motorized bike, I was able to offer a luxury to "another" who used his influence to provide me with a necessity, a phone.

The disparate privileges among foreigners that may have seemed unimportant to Indians were noted by expatriates themselves. As Thibaut and Kelley's theory predicts, when weighing their own benefits expatriates were quick to compare themselves with other expatriates who had more (Kelley and Thibaut, 1978; Thibaut and Kelley, 1959). They made comparisons "upward" rather than downward so instead of counting their blessings "poor" westerners described with envy the privileges of the "rich" (cf. Brickman and Bulman, 1977; Brickman and Campbell, 1971). But they were also quick to add they did not want to be like "them." A missionary expressed her ambivalence this way:

Sometimes I think it would be nice to come on a government program . . . they do take good care of their people, providing all the furniture, a house, and all. They just have to go over to the [government] warehouse and pick out the things they want. And they have cars and drivers provided . . . some even bring their own personal cars with them. But of course, we're not out here to make money.

An expatriate who wanted the convenience of a car without the guilt or "stigma" of being a rich foreigner created his own middle ground. He was a young North American who worked in an Indian research institute without the benefits conferred by foreign governments or companies.

DE: I used to feel so guilty about our car. But now I've gotten over it and I just drive around like nothing was wrong. When we came I decided I would get the oldest most beat-up looking car around. And as it is the [wealthy] people would catch a cold before they'd ride in our car! But you know that I'm the only person in my department with a car!? I used to feel terribly guilty. But I got over it.

Perhaps he "got over it" because he was leading a life of relative privation. He did not enjoy all the comforts of "home" and he compared his material comfort with the level of other Americans who had much more. Most expatriates did not see their privileges as remarkable. Their refrigerators, phones, and cars served not as the figure but the ground; what stood out for them was how vulnerable they were. They faced daily threats to their well-being by being "cheated" or falling ill. Instead of remarking on their privileges they focused on their vulnerability.

NOT PRIVILEGED BUT VULNERABLE

By telling and re-telling stories of being "cheated," expatriates kept alive the image of themselves as the innocent background against which shopkeepers, servants, and rickshaw drivers enacted immorality plays. The following conversation was told at a dinner party:

AB: Well, you know they really learn how to cheat you. Like we have this little paper boy who bills us for three months at a time. So the first time he brought the bill it was for June, July, and August and I paid it around the end of June. Then he came about a month later with a bill for August, September, and October, and I was outside in the garden and didn't want to go in and look up the receipts so I paid it, but I thought there was something funny. Then the next month he came with a bill for September, October and November. So I told him to leave the bill with me and come back in an hour or so because I didn't have any change on me. So I went up and checked on those receipts and saw what was happening. And when he came back I told him, "Look, I've paid for August twice and you're about to charge me for September three times." So I said, "You go away and don't come back until sometime after Christmas, then I'll pay you." Well, he started to give me some story about how he was being honest and wasn't cheatin' me, so I said, "Do you want me to go down to the head office and explain this, or do you want to go?" Well, I'm tellin' you, he lit out of there so fast, and he hasn't showed up since. So they'll try to cheat you as far as they can, but if you get smart and threaten 'em they'll stop.

Stories like these did not portray expatriates as wealthy beneficiaries and Indians as victims of colonialism or economic imperialism (cf. Lerner and Simmons, 1966; Ryan, 1971). On the contrary, in these stories Indians were the wily merchants and expatriates were innocent patrons who soon became "wise" to scams and caught the offender. This plot line also appeared to have entertainment value, and like any good story some of these were told repeatedly, sometimes with sequels. A second story at this dinner party illustrates this; it was a sequel to a prior telling of this incident:

[DF had heard about KL's loss of 100 rupees and asked whether she had recovered her money.]
DF: K, did you ever get your 100 rupees back?
KL: Oh yes. But that was really something. We had the chief of police in on that one.
Me: [not knowing the beginning of the story I asked] What happened?
KL: Oh, this was a long time ago. I went out to the airport with two other people who were leaving on the plane and I stopped at the magazine stand to buy *Time Magazine*. Well, I paid

for it, and got my change and didn't think anything of it until I got home and G [her husband] asked me for that 100 rupee note I had in my purse, and I discovered that I didn't have it anymore. Well, I went back out there and told the fellow that I had given him a 100 rupee note by mistake, and he had only given me change for a 10, and I said he should give me the other 90 back. Well, he insisted that I had given him only 10, and he wouldn't give in. He pulled out all his money, and he had one 100 rupee note, but he said that a man had given that to him early in the morning and that I had only given him a 10. Well, I went back to the car, and he followed me all the way, and he even said, "Madam, you will never miss that 100 rupees." . . . Finally we had the chief of police out there asking the guy all sorts of questions. And they found out that he had sent a 100 rupee money order home that afternoon. So the police made him give me the 90 back. He did—he gave me a money order for 90, but he wrote on it, so that everybody could see, "To be returned to me when you realize your mistake."

So he still hasn't given in. I said to G [her husband] "Do you think it was worth it?" I wonder what we might be missing one of these days—you know, the revenge that these people seek, we might wish we had never gotten the 90 back from him.

DF: Yes, I know. It's really frightening.

Listening to her story, I cannot be sure of the "truth." Conceivably both sides were right. It is plausible that she gave him a 100 rupee note and he gave her change as though she had paid only 10. The presumed deceit is revealing, however, for the reason the merchant gave: "Madam, you will never miss that 100 rupees." One hundred rupees could have been a merchant's weekly income or a servant's monthly pay. For the American it was $13. The disparities between the expatriate's income and the merchant's were so large that had her husband not asked for the 100 rupee note she might never have known it was gone. The merchant could have been right when he said she would never miss it.

These tales of being "cheated" led to more tales. The dinner guests who told the stories about merchants changed the topic to servants and told about household items that "disappeared." They all suspected their cooks.

WHO IS IN WHOSE KITCHEN?

As the dinner guests told stories about being "cheated" by servants there were cooks and butlers serving them dinner. The guests were dining in the master's house on foods prepared by a servant's hands. Occasionally the irony was noted by some expatriate women commenting that they no longer felt comfortable or competent in the kitchen. It was not clear whose kitchen it was.

GH: L and I were talking about this the other day. And we both said how we love to cook interesting things and do things in the kitchen at home. But here we haven't done a single thing—we don't even walk into our kitchens! And we really miss that. Our kitchen here is such a mess that I just let [the cook] run the whole thing.

When women gathered at monthly meetings of the American Women's Club they often exchanged information about who had recently fired a servant or who was looking for one. A woman sitting beside me said she was looking for a new cook again, then turned to me to explain: "I've gone through six cooks already. This is my seventh now." Later in the meeting several women described their situations as follows:

SX: I'm looking for an ayah who can help me with the cooking and do other work after the baby is born.

MN: Do you have a cook now?

SX: No, I just have two women who help with the housework and cooking. Two ayahs. But I'll want more help after the baby. Because now I help with the work too. But that's an awfully difficult house to keep clean.

N: Well, I might be able to find you one. I think I'm going into the employment business! I've found cooks for so many people lately, and here I don't have one myself.

MN: You don't? Do you do the cooking?

N: Yes, I have a woman to help but I do much more of it. And I'm so much happier ever since I got rid of my cook. I mean, I smile now!

Talking about servants was both commonly engaged in and frowned on. A woman who had told "servant stories" herself promptly criticized others who did it to excess. She said she tried to

stay away from the American ladies, except to meet them at the American Women's Club meetings . . . They spend most of their time together talking about their servants and other gossip, and I'm just not interested in that. Really, that's their main topic of conversation. And it's funny, because almost every cook is named "Anthony" and his wife "Theresa," so they have to say "My Anthony . . ." or "Whose Anthony are we talking about?"

DEPENDENCE ON DEPENDENTS

The symbiosis of masters and servants makes each dependent on the other (Memmi, 1984). Servants working without written contracts would seem to be the more dependent party because they could be dismissed without notice. They could also quit without notice, however, and if they did not cook, shop, provide water, and perform the myriad other tasks expatriates counted on, the expatriates appeared helpless. The expatriate woman who said she did not want to spend time with "the American ladies" talking about servants provided her own account of servants:

MI: Sometimes I think we should have let [servant] go . . . I mean, every morning I have to tell him to turn the water pump on for my shower. You know it would just be much simpler if I did it myself. Because he never remembers. Every morning I have to tell him again.

When expatriates lamented that they "have to explain everything" they implied that they could have done the work themselves. They knew enough to explain the particulars to a servant. They chose to hire help, however, and felt entitled to have the services performed in a safe, reliable, and trustworthy manner. When the hired hands failed to provide the right food, water, and services the expatriates sometimes felt threatened. In turn they threatened their servants. An American said she had "gone through" several cooks because she could not "trust" anyone to keep the kitchen clean. She also felt she had been "cheated" and accused a series of cooks of taking money and household items. She was doing her own cooking when I interviewed her and she wondered aloud whether anyone would work for her:

N: Maybe they've put me on their black list, because I had a fellow who said he'd come work for me and he was supposed to come yesterday morning but he never showed up. . . .

Expatriates who fired Indian workers still tried to hire others. To recreate western ways of living they were dependent on servants' skills and knowledge. In a country where beef was rarely eaten and cakes were rarely baked it was servants accustomed to working for westerners who knew where to find tender beef or how to make a sponge cake over a kerosene burner.

Cooks more than other servants symbolized the power of hired hands to control the life and health of people they served. An American who said she was grateful to have a cook who furnished her entire kitchen with his vessels and implements that he brought from previous jobs also reported that he nearly "poisoned" her husband:

> JK: We discovered that we were poisoning [my husband] right in our own kitchen. I wasn't getting sick at all, but he had something all the time. And we weren't eating out. Finally we realized that he was eating sandwiches and I wasn't—and it must have been the mayonnaise that [the cook] was making—I don't know if it was a batch of bad eggs or what, but that was doing it—he was getting poisoned in our own house!

To say he was being "poisoned" sounds extreme but reflects her sense that this could have been fatal. Most westerners who travel to India are likely to fall ill with various forms of dysentery. They (like Indians who have lived in North America or Europe for many years) lack the immunity of long-term India residents.

WHO RECEIVES THE CREDIT OR BLAME

The self-serving biases that social psychologists have observed when people make attributions about responsibility were woven throughout expatriates' accounts of their life with servants (cf. Weary, et al., 1982). If they fell ill while eating in their homes they were quick to blame their cooks. When they enjoyed good health and fine meals, however, they were likely to credit their personal precautions and good judgment. Cooks, butlers, and other hired hands who helped at western dinner parties occasionally took a bow as they served the food, but the hosts were likely to accept most of the credit because they were in charge. Servants' names were invoked when they caused problems or "did not work out" more so than when they succeeded.

A woman organizing the finishing touches for the American Women's Club Charity Bazaar implored members to bring works they could be proud of, to bring credit to American women:

> KK: Be generous in your cookies. We sometimes say that with the rich ingredients we put into our cookies, we can't be making much money. But let's be generous. And if anyone of you feels particularly ambitious, I would love to have a gingerbread house to put on our cookie table. Maybe if one of your cooks knows how to make it, you could let me know. Let's have nice things like that so that we can show the Indian community how clever the American women are. . . .
> [laughter, and several women noted with irony] You mean, show them how clever the American women's cooks are!

When expatriates gave credit to servants for knowledge and skill, they could also credit themselves as good employers who knew how to "manage" servants and made good decisions. These self-serving attributions are a human frailty so their appearance is not so much an indictment of expatriates as an illustration of the pervasiveness of the bias.

Many of the foreigners I interviewed said they wished they had close Indian friends and envied people who did because Indian friends could teach them about the culture. Without Indian friends as peers many respondents said they learned a lot from their cooks. One woman who learned from a servant captured the ambivalence of having enough money to buy all the things she wanted but not knowing their cultural meaning:

> Whenever I go to the little junk brass shops and buy these things . . . [gestures to pots and vessels] I ask Raj [a servant] what they use these things for and he explains it all to me . . . and whenever they have their festivals he tells me about them. . . .

CONCLUSIONS

As postcolonial "masters" and "madams" expatriates experience privileges and enjoy services far in excess of what they would enjoy back home. The expatriates I interviewed adjusted to their sudden rise in status as social psychology's theories predict they would. They compared their privileges with people who had more, not less, than themselves. They attributed successes to their own efforts even if the final products were made by the hands of an Indian servant. And none said their own privilege was unjustified (cf. Lerner and Lerner, 1981). These expatriates living in privilege presumed themselves to be innocent and would have disavowed imperialist motives (cf. Rafael, 1995). Their words and actions are colonial remnants, the result of assuming privileges overnight.

REFERENCES

Brickman, P., and Bulman, R. J. (1977). Pleasure and pain in social comparison. In J. Suls and R. Miller (eds.) *Social comparison processes*. Washington: Hemisphere.

Brickman, P., and Campbell, D. T. (1971). Hedonic relativism and planning the good society. In M. Appley (ed.), *Adaptation-level theory: A symposium*. NY: Academic Press.

Jones, E. E., Kanouse, D. E., Kelley, H. H., Nisbett, R. E., Valins, S., and Weiner, B. (eds.) (1971). *Attribution: Perceiving the causes of behavior*. Morristown, NJ: General Learning Press.

Jones, E., and Nisbett, R. (1971). *The actor and the observer: Divergent perceptions of the causes of behavior*. NY: General Learning Press.

Kelley, H. H., and Thibaut, J. W. (1978). *Interpersonal relations: A theory of interdependence*. NY: Wiley-Interscience.

Kidder, L. H. (1971). Foreign visitors: A study of the changes in selves, skills and attitudes of westerners in India. Unpublished doctoral dissertation. Northwestern University, Evanston, Illinois.

Kidder, L. H. (1977). The inadvertent creation of a neocolonial culture: A study of Western sojourners in India. *International Journal of Intercultural Relations*, 1, (1), 48–60.

Lerner, M. J., and Lerner, S. C. (eds.) (1981). *The Justice Motive in Social Behavior: Adapting to times of scarcity and change*. New York: Plenum

Lerner, M. S., and Simmons, C. H. (1966). Observer's reaction to the innocent victim: Compassion or rejection? *Journal of Personality and Social Psychology*, 4, 203–210.

Mannoni, O. (1956). *Prospero and Caliban: The psychology of colonization*. NY: Praeger.

Memmi, A. (1967). *The Colonizer and the Colonized*. Boston: Beacon Press.

Memmi, A. (1984). *Dependence: A sketch for a portrait of the dependent*. Boston: Beacon Press.

Opotow, S. (ed.) (1990). Moral Exclusion and Injustice: An Introduction. *Journal of Social Issues*, 46 (1), 1–20.

Opotow, S. (1995). Drawing the Line: Social categorization, moral exclusion, and the scope of justice. Chapter 11 in B. B. Bunker and J. Z. Rubin (eds.), *Cooperation, conflict and justice: Essays inspired by Morton Deutsch*. San Francisco: Jossey-Bass.

Rafael, V. L. (1995). Mimetic subjects: Engendering race at the edge of empire. *Differences: A Journal of Feminist Cultural Studies*, 7 (2) 127–149.

Ryan, W. (1971). *Blaming the victim*. NY: Vintage Books.

Thibaut, J. W., and Kelley, H. H. (1959). *The social psychology of groups*. NY: Wiley.

Weary, G., Harvey, J. H., Schweiger, P., Olson, C. T., Perloff, E., and Pritchard, S. (1982). Self-presentation and the moderation of self-serving biases. *Social Cognition*, 1, 140–159.

Thanks to friends and colleagues for helpful readings of early drafts: Susan Opotow and Niama Williams for long letters of response; Katie Day, Judy Goode, Terry Kershaw, Bob Kidder, Annette Lareau, and David Watt for an hour-long discussion in our ethnography study group. They each helped improve my vision. The remaining stubborn errors are still mine.

Does White Racism Necessarily Mean Antiblackness?
Aversive Racism and Prowhiteness

Samuel L. Gaertner, John F. Dovidio, Brenda S. Banker, Mary C. Rust, Jason A. Nier, Gary R. Mottola, and Christine M. Ward

SIXTEEN

Samuel L. Gaertner received his Ph.D. in 1970 from the City University of New York Graduate Center. His current research interests focus on identifying strategies that reduce racial prejudice and other intergroup biases. He is currently Professor of Psychology at the University of Delaware. Together with John F. Dovidio, he won the 1985 Gordon Allport Intergroup Prize for work on aversive racism. Currently their research focuses on reducing intergroup basis and is supported by NIMH. Professor Gaertner is currently on the editorial boards of the *Journal of Personality and Social Psychology* and the *Personality and Social Psychology Bulletin*.

John F. Dovidio received his Ph.D. in 1977 from the University of Delaware. He is a social psychologist whose major research focuses on racism, intergroup relations, prosocial behavior, and interpersonal dominance. Together with Samuel L. Gaertner, he won the 1985 Gordon Allport Intergroup Prize for their chapter on aversive racism. Currently, their work on reducing intergroup bias is supported by NIMH. Professor Dovidio is currently Professor of Psychology at Colgate University. In addition, he is currently Editor of the *Personality and Social Psychology Bulletin* and also on the editorial boards of the *Journal of Personality and Social Psychology* and the *British Journal of Social Psychology*.

Brenda S. Banker is currently a graduate student in the social psychology program at the University of Delaware, where she is pursuing her interests in intergroup relations. Her current research examines the utility of an intergroup perspective for understanding the development of family harmony within stepfamily units in which both adults arrived with children from previous relationships.

Mary C. Rust received her Ph.D. in Psychology from the University of Delaware. Currently she is Assistant Professor of Psychology at American International College. As a social psychologist, her current research focuses on processes that promote the generalization of the benefits of intergroup contact to outgroup members who were not present in the contact situation.

Jason A. Nier is currently a graduate student in the social psychology program at the University of Delaware. His current research involves implicit and explicit measures of intergroup attitudes with a special focus on how the dimension of activity determines how people think about, feel about, and behave toward outgroup members.

Gary R. Mottola received his Ph.D. in Psychology from the University of Delaware. As a social psychologist with applied interests, his research examines the effects of status differences between merging companies on the degree to which employees identify with the merged organization.

Christine M. Ward is currently a graduate student in the social psychology program at the University of Delaware. Her current research involves studying attributions of culpability for a rape incident as a technique for detecting interracial biases.

This chapter is about white Americans who possess genuinely egalitarian values, who identify with a politically liberal agenda, who believe that they are not prejudiced against blacks or other minorities, and who do, in fact, discriminate in subtle but consequential ways. How do we explain the persistence of discrimination among "liberal" whites who claim no prejudice against blacks? If, indeed, these whites are not prejudiced *against* blacks, is it possible that they discriminate due to *prowhite* attitudes? And, what difference does it make *why* whites discriminate?

Prejudice has traditionally been considered to be an unfavorable attitude toward another group, involving both negative feelings and beliefs. For example, Allport (1954) defined prejudice as "an antipathy based on faulty and inflexible generalization. Ashmore (1970, p. 253) described it as "a negative attitude toward a socially defined group and any person perceived to be a member of that group." Perhaps as a consequence of this perspective, the prejudice of whites toward blacks has typically been measured using attitude scales reflecting whites' degree of endorsement of a range of statements about negative attributes of blacks (such as inferiority), negative feelings toward the group (e.g., hostility or fear), and support for policies that restrict opportunities for blacks (e.g., in housing or in intimate relations) (Brigham, 1993; McConahay, 1986; Sears, 1988; Woodmansee and Cook, 1967).

In our earlier work on aversive racism, however, we challenged the assumption that whites who *appear* nonprejudiced on these types of questionnaire instruments, and who may truly believe that they possess egalitarian principles, are nonracist. Specifically, our research on *aversive racism* (see Dovidio, Mann, and Gaertner, 1989; Gaertner and Dovidio, 1986; Kovel, 1970) revealed that many of these presumably nonprejudiced whites have not entirely escaped cultural and cognitive forces that promote racial bias. Rather, those who appear nonracist on these measures do discriminate in subtle, rationalizable ways that insulate them from awareness of their own prejudice (see Crosby, Bromley, and Saxe, 1980; Devine, 1989). Ironically, these people believe that if everybody's racial attitude was like theirs, racism would not be a problem in this country.

In this chapter, we review our work on aversive racism and examine the potential motivational dynamics underlying this type of racism. Specifically, we explore the "flip side" of the conventional assumption that the racial bias of whites primarily reflects antiblack (or anti-outgroup) attitudes. We consider the possibility that modern, subtle forms of bias—such as aversive racism—may be characterized by a significant component of prowhite (i.e., pro-ingroup) attitudes which do not seem racist to the individual him/herself (Brewer, in press).

AVERSIVE RACISM

Whereas traditional forms of prejudice are direct and overt, contemporary forms seem to be indirect and subtle. Aversive racism (see Gaertner and Dovidio, 1986; Kovel, 1970; Murrell, Betz, Dovidio, Gaertner, and Drout, 1994) has been identified as a form of modern prejudice that characterizes the racial attitudes of many whites with egalitarian values who regard themselves as nonprejudiced, and who nevertheless discriminate in subtle, rationalizable ways. Aversive racism represents a particular enactment of *ambivalence* when a white person's egalitarian value system is brought into conflict with unacknowledged negative racial beliefs and feelings that resulted from (1) historical and contemporary culturally racist contexts, and (2) the informational processing biases that result when people are categorized into ingroups and outgroups (see Hamilton and Troiler, 1986). Relative to symbolic (see Sears, 1988) or modern racism (see McConahay, 1986) that are forms of contemporary racism that seem to exist among political conservatives, aversive racists are more strongly liberal and egalitarian. Aversive racists are more strongly motivated by the desire to not see themselves as bigoted or harboring negative feelings about blacks. To the contrary, awareness of such beliefs and feelings would seriously threaten their non-prejudiced, non-discriminatory self-images. Without being hypocritical, when the task is clear, aversive racists actively avoid behaving in ways that could be attributable, by themselves or by others, to bigoted intent. Indeed, they may over-compensate in social contexts where norms for appropriate behavior are clear by responding more favorably to blacks than to whites. When the context is normatively impoverished, however, with the distinction between appropriate and inappropriate behavior more ambiguous, or when the context permits unfavorable behavior to be attributed to non-race related factors, aversive racists reveal their intergroup biases.

AN ATTRIBUTIONAL ANALYSIS OF ANTI-BLACK VS. PRO-WHITE ATTITUDES

In many circumstances, behavior that favors members of one's own group or family is regarded as appropriate but does not necessarily denote negative feelings toward others. Inviting only members of one's immediate family to a holiday dinner, for example, would not be interpreted as expressing ill will toward people outside of family. Given the normative appropriateness of inviting only family to such an event, the failure to invite others, at best, may only inform us about attitudes toward family. Of course, if invitations were issued to some non-family members, or if invitations were withheld from some family members, the attitudinal implications would be clear. These events would inform us about the positive feelings toward invited non-family members and the likely negative feelings toward the uninvited family members.

As we review our earlier experiments, which usually involved the delivery of pro-social behavior to blacks or to whites, we use an attributional strategy that considers the normative structure and social forces within the situation to determine whether the racial discrimination that we observed among our white subjects most likely resulted from either anti-black or pro-white feelings. We argue that when the social pressure to intervene and help is very weak or perhaps even strongly inhibiting (e.g., the fire department has already arrived), a bystander's *not helping* would not be particularly revealing of his or her feelings toward the victim (see also Campbell, 1963). However, taking action by *helping* the victim under these circumstances may inform us about the bystander's positive attitude toward the victim. Only when social forces strongly promote intervention would *not helping* be revealing of the bystanders' possibly negative feelings toward the victim.

In general, the pattern we observed in our research is that whites treated blacks and whites differently only when the normative forces to help were weak (i.e., the fire department already arrived)—when helping, but not the failure to help, could inform us about the bystander's attitude toward the victim. In the next section, we describe some of our earlier studies in view of their potential to possibly reflect pro-white sentiments among people with liberal, egalitarian values—but who do discriminate on the basis of race.

The Wrong-Number Study

The first study, which initiated our interest in aversive racism, was a field experiment that examined the likelihood of black and white persons obtaining non-emergency assistance from caucasian Liberal Party and Conservative Party members residing in Brooklyn, New York (Gaertner, 1973). Members of these political parties received apparent wrong-number telephone calls from black and white members of the research staff whose race was clearly identifiable from their dialects. Each caller explained that his or her car was disabled and that he or she was trying to reach a service station from a parkway telephone. Just about all subjects explained that our caller had reached the wrong number. Then our "motorist" explained that he or she did not have more coins to make another call and asked if the subject would telephone the garage to report the problem.

Conservative Party members who learned of the motorist's entire dilemma discriminated on the basis of race, supportive of the authoritarian personality framework (Adorno et al., 1949). Conservatives telephoned the garage significantly less frequently for black than for white motorists (65 percent vs. 92 percent). Liberal Party members, in contrast, helped black and white motorists equivalently (75 percent vs. 85 percent). Not every subject though, stayed on the line long enough to learn of the full dilemma; indeed, many subjects hung up "prematurely" immediately after the opening greeting, "Hello, Ralph's Garage this is George Williams. I'm stuck out here on the highway. . . ." Hanging up prematurely was particularly characteristic of Liberal Party members—and we soon discovered that they *did not* ignore the "motorist's" race in this regard. Rather, Liberal Party members hung up prematurely much more frequently on blacks (19 percent of the time) than on whites (3 percent of the time), while the premature hang-up rate for Conservative Party members was very low (about 5 percent).

Initially, we assumed that both Liberal and Conservative Party members discriminated against blacks, but in different ways. We believed that learning of the motorist's full dilemma would arouse the a sense of social responsibility—a norm suggesting that a person usually should help others in need of assistance. In the presence of this norm, Conservatives, but not Liberals, were more likely to refuse help to blacks than whites.

But why did Liberals discriminate by hanging up prematurely more frequently on blacks than on whites? Initially, we believed that Liberals unwittingly expressed antiblack affect in this way. At the stage of the encounter when premature hang-ups occurred there was no clear norm for appropriate behavior. Indeed, the appropriateness of staying on the line or hanging up quickly has no clearly prescribed answer. Thus, Liberals could hang up prematurely on blacks because it would be difficult to self-attribute this decision to negative racial attitudes. It would not be clear that they did anything wrong. We believed that hanging up prematurely permitted Liberals to express antiblack feelings and also protected their nonprejudiced self-images.

The attributional reanalysis of this behavior that we are proposing in this chapter, however, suggests that because the normative structure to stay on the phone beyond this point was so weak, hanging up would not necessarily be informative about a person's attitude toward the caller. Instead, staying in the interaction and not hanging up prematurely can be regarded as behavior beyond the call of duty or normative obligation. It is this type of behavior that our analysis suggests would be informative about the person's attitude toward the caller. From this perspective, white Liberals remaining in the encounter more frequently with other whites than with blacks could be reflective of their positive attitudes toward whites rather than reflective of antiblack attitudes. Just as the failure to invite nonfamily members to holiday dinner does not inform us of the host's attitude toward them, Liberals hanging up prematurely more frequently on blacks than on whites may not indicate their attitudes toward blacks. Liberals just did not treat blacks as *positively* as they treated family.

If the responses of aversive racists reflect primarily ingroup favoritism, and not necessarily negative behavior toward the outgroup, these actions should be most apparent when they have the opportunity to benefit the person even when there is ample reason *not* to help. The premature hang-ups in the telephone study suggested that in the absence of clear norms for helping, Liberals were more responsive to the need of whites than of blacks. In effect, however, blacks end up not being helped by white liberals at anywhere near the rate they could have been.

Diffusion of Responsibility

Gaertner and Dovidio (1977) engaged white students in a laboratory experiment in which a simulated emergency involving a black or a white student was overheard. A stack of heavy chairs ostensibly fell on another participant, who was located in a different room than the subject. This experiment systematically varied the victim's race (using picture ID cards) and also the presence or absence of two other white bystanders, each located in separate rooms. In their classic study, Darley and Latane (1968) discovered that when a person is alone at the time of an emergency all of the responsibility for helping is focused on this one bystander, but as the number of additional bystanders is increased the responsibility for helping becomes diffused. In the multiple bystander condition, the forces propelling intervention on any one bystander become weaker.

Gaertner and Dovidio introduced the presence of other bystanders in their study to provide subjects with a non-race-related justification that "others can help" and thus would allow them to rationalize their failure to intervene. It was predicted that the belief that other bystanders are present would have a greater inhibiting effect on subjects' helping a black victim than a white victim. We suspected that subjects' negative affect for blacks would sharply increase their susceptibility to diffuse responsibility for helping black victims. The presence of other bystanders, not bigoted intent, could be used by subjects to explain their failure to help. Thus, there should be hardly any awareness that the victim's race influenced the subjects' behavior. When subjects were the only bystander however, the situation was quite different and it was expected that they would help readily, regardless of the victim's race. In view of the clarity of the emergency, failure of the single bystander to help a black victim could very easily be self-attributed to bigoted intent. Therefore, the forces propelling action were expected to be especially strong and effective on behalf of black victims when the bystander was alone.

The results were supportive of these predictions. White subjects believing themselves to be the only bystander helped black victims somewhat more than white victims (94 percent vs. 81 percent). White bystanders who believed that two other bystanders could also intervene, however, helped white victims more frequently than they helped black victims (75 percent vs. 38 percent). As we expected, subjects with other bystanders succumbed to the opportunity to diffuse responsibility more readily for black than for white victims. But, again we ask, does this reflect subjects' antiblack sentiment as we initially believed?

The tendency to diffuse responsibility more readily for black victims than for white victims in the Gaertner and Dovidio experiment most likely informs us only about subjects' positive attitudes toward fellow whites and does not necessarily suggest that subjects were antiblack. But again, blacks are less likely to be helped by white bystanders.

In summary, the empirical studies reviewed in this section of the chapter illustrate that evidence originally interpreted as indicating subtle antiblack prejudice may instead represent prowhite bias. This attributional analysis may similarly account for the results of other studies, examined in the next section, that have revealed asymmetries in the attributions and associations of positive and negative characteristics to blacks and whites.

POSITIVE AND NEGATIVE ATTRIBUTIONS, ASSOCIATIONS, AND ACTIONS

The assumption that the expression of aversive racism may be more subtle than traditional forms led us to explore alternatives to the conventional ways of assessing prejudice. Evidence has demonstrated that aversive racists do not express their bias openly on self-report scales in which the assessment of negative racial attitudes is obvious. For example, when we asked college students to evaluate black and white people on bipolar scales (e.g., good _ _ _ _ _ _ bad) we found no differences in the evaluative ratings of blacks and whites (Dovidio and Gaertner, 1991). When a biased response ("bad") is obvious, aversive racists would avoid the negative end of the scales and evaluate blacks as favorably as whites. Thus, we explored more indirect measures of assessing bias in an attempt to capture the more subtle manifestations of contemporary forms of racism.

ATTRIBUTIONS AND ASSOCIATIONS

To assess ingroup favoritism and outgroup favoritism independently, we modified the rating-scale instrument by creating separate scales for positive characteristics (e.g., good) and negative characteristics (e.g., bad). No racial bias appeared on the negative scales. However, on the positive scales, whites were evaluated more favorably than blacks. This pattern of bias is entirely consistent with the thesis that contemporary bias may primarily reflect prowhite attitudes than antiblack sentiments.

Because self-reports are susceptible to impression management motivations, we followed up these studies with a series of response latency experiments (see Dovidio and Gaertner, 1993). For example, in one study (Gaertner and McLaughlin, 1983) participants were asked to decide whether two strings of letters presented simultaneously were both words. Faster response times reflect greater association between the words. The results were consistent with the self-report study. Participants did not respond differently to negative words paired with the racial categories "blacks" and "whites," but they did respond faster to positive words appearing with "whites" than with "blacks." This prowhite bias, which is spontaneously activated, may systematically bias decisions of serious consequence, such as juridic judgments.

Juridic Decisions

This experiment by Faranda and Gaertner (1979) investigated the hypothesis that, whereas the racial biases of those who are likely to have traditionally racist attitudes (high authoritarians) will reflect primarily antiblack biases, the racial biases of those who are likely to exhibit aversive racism (low authoritarianism) will mainly represent prowhite biases. Specifically, the experiment examined the extent to which high- and low-authoritarian scoring white college students playing the role of jurors would follow a judge's instruction to ignore inadmissable prosecution testimony that was damaging to a black or white defendant.

Participants in this study were presented with a court transcript of a fictitious criminal case in which the defendant was accused of murdering a storekeeper and the storekeeper's child while committing a robbery. White subjects receiving a description of the trial in one condition were presented with the prosecution evidence which was weak. Subjects in a second condition were presented with the same weak prosecution case plus an extremely damaging statement which indicated that the defendant confessed about the crimes to a third party. The defense attorney objected to this statement as hearsay because the prosecution was not able to produce the third party in court. The judge instructed the jurors to ignore this inadmissible evidence.

Both high- and low-authoritarian subjects showed racial biases in their reactions to the inadmissible evidence, but they did so in different ways. In their ratings of certainty of guilt, high authoritarians did *not* ignore the inadmissible testimony when the victim was black. They were more certain of the black defendant's guilt when they were exposed to the inadmissible evidence than when they were not presented with this testimony. For the white defendant, however, high authoritarian subjects followed the judge's instructions perfectly: Ratings of certainty of the white defendant's guilt were equal across the two conditions. High authoritarians thus showed an anti-outgroup bias. Low-authoritarian subjects, in contrast, followed the judge's instructions about ignoring the inadmissible testimony when the defendant was black. However, they were biased *in favor* of the white defendant when the inadmissible evidence was presented. That is, low-authoritarian subjects were *less* certain of the white defendant's guilt when the inadmissible evidence was presented than when it was omitted. These subjects later reported that they were angry with the prosecution for trying unfairly to introduce hearsay testimony. They did not express this anger, however, when the defendant was black. Thus low-authoritarian subjects demonstrated a pro-ingroup bias. It is important to note that the anti-outgroup bias of high-authoritarian subjects and the pro-ingroup bias of low authoritarians both disadvantage blacks profoundly relative to whites—if in fundamentally different ways.

This distinction may have relevance for theories that propose how interracial biases can be reduced. If mere social categorization results largely in pro-ingroup biases and if aversive racism reflects primarily prowhite rather than antiblack orientations, then the process of social categorization may play a central role in contemporary forms of racism and perhaps should be the process that is targeted for change. Factors that induce an ingroup social identity that is inclusive of both blacks and whites should prime more positive feelings, beliefs, and behaviors toward people who would otherwise be regarded as outgroup members. This, essentially, is our objective as we review the potential of the Common Ingroup Identity Model to change intergroup behavior and then consider its potential to modify the patterns of interracial behavior similar to those we observed in our earlier research on aversive racism.

REDUCING SUBTLE BIAS: THE COMMON INGROUP IDENTITY MODEL

Although there has been some agreement about the utility of undoing the rigidity of social categories to reduce intergroup bias, different strategies have been developed to accomplish this goal. The decategorization strategy attempts to erase members' perceptions of the intergroup boundary by inducing members to conceive of one another primarily as individuals, in more personalized terms, rather than as group members (see Brewer and Miller, 1984; Wilder, 1989). Alternatively, the Common Ingroup Identity Model (Gaertner, Dovidio, Anastasio, Bachman, and Rust, 1993; Anastasio, Bachman, Gaertner, and Dovidio, 1996) proposes a strategy of re-categorization to reduce intergroup bias by restructuring a definition of who is in the ingroup. Specifically, the Common Ingroup Identity Model proposes that if members of different groups come to see themselves as a single group rather than as separate ones, attitudes toward former outgroup members will become more positive through processes involving pro-ingroup bias (see Social Identity Theory, Tajfel and Turner, 1979; and Self-Categorization Theory, Turner et al., 1987).

In application, recategorization from two groups to one group can be achieved by increasing

174

the salience of existing common superordinate group memberships or by introducing new factors (e.g., common goals or fate) that are perceived to be shared by the memberships.

Social Categorization and Bias

Research has been generally supportive of the Common Ingroup Identity model across a variety of laboratory and natural intergroup settings. An initial laboratory experiment (Gaertner, Mann, Murrell, and Dovidio, 1989) examined the benefits of both recategorization and decategorization strategies. It was found that intergroup bias could be decreased by inducing members of two separate laboratory-formed groups either to recategorize themselves as one more inclusive entity or to decategorize themselves and return to separate individuals. These representations were manipulated by varying the seating arrangements of the members, using group or individual nicknames as well as varying the nature of the interdependence between the participants. In both cases, relative to a control condition in which groups maintained their separate two-group categorized identities, intergroup bias in evaluative ratings was reduced but in different ways. Decategorization of the two groups to separate individuals reduced bias by decreasing liking of one's former ingroup members. In contrast, recategorization to a common group identity facilitated a reduction in bias by increasing the liking of former outgroup members almost to the level of the original ingroup members. As specified by Turner et al., (1987), "the attractiveness of an individual is not constant but varies with ingroup membership" (p.60).

Two field studies involved surveys administered to (1) students attending a multi-ethnic/racial high school (Gaertner, Rust, Dovidio, Bachman, and Anastasio, 1994; 1996), and (2) banking executives experiencing a corporate merger (Bachman, Gaertner, Anastasio, and Rust, 1993). The results of each of these correlational studies suggest that the relationship between perceptions of favorable contact conditions between the different groups (of students and banking executives) and reduced intergroup bias was mediated, in part, by members' conceptual representations of the aggregate as one inclusive group. The more favorable the students' and executives' perceptions of the degree of cooperative interaction, equal status, supportive norms, and opportunities for interaction between the groups (in their respective contexts), the lower the degrees of intergroup bias they reported and the more they perceived the total aggregate of students or employees to be one group. Additional analyses revealed that the common, one-group identity, in part, mediated the relations between these perceptions of the contact conditions and intergroup bias, as proposed by the model.

Combining the advantages of laboratory experiments and field surveys, the next study attempted to examine the effects of experimentally manipulating a common ingroup identity on interracial prosocial behavior in a natural context. Thus, this study represents our first attempt to experimentally integrate the types of behaviors we used to study Aversive Racism and the implementation of a strategy derived from the Common Ingroup Identity Model to influence interracial behavior.

A Game They Came to Watch

The major proposition of the Common Ingroup Identity Model is that outgroup members will be treated more favorably in the context of a common ingroup identity than they would be if they were regarded only as outgroup members. To test this idea experimentally in a natural context our research team was composed of eight black and white, male and female students who visited the University of Delaware football stadium approximately one hour and fifteen minutes prior to a football game between the University of Delaware (UD) and West Chester State University (WSU). Claiming to be surveyors of fans' food preferences, our student researchers systematically varied whether they wore UD or WSU signature hats to systematically vary their apparent university affiliation. [Only white fans whose own clothing revealed their university (UD or WSU) affiliation were approached by our black or white student surveyors (of the same sex as the fan) just before they were about to enter the stadium.]

When the surveyors and fans did not share common university identity, black and white surveyors, contrary to our prediction, received equivalent levels of compliance (37.8 percent vs. 40 percent). Nevertheless, the findings pertaining to the effect of a common university ingroup identity received some support. Although the presence or absence of common university identity did not affect compliance with a white surveyor (43 percent vs. 40 percent), fans who shared common university identity with black surveyors complied reliably more frequently (59.6 percent) than when they had a different university identity with the black surveyor (37.8 percent). Thus, consistent with the major proposition of the Common Ingroup Identity Model, white fans treated blacks *more* favorably when they shared common ingroup identity with these surveyors than when they did not.

Just why the black surveyors who shared common university identity with the fans elicited somewhat more compliance than comparable white surveyors is difficult to specify. We suspect, however, that although many of these fans regard themselves as unprejudiced, they rarely felt a sense of connection or common identity with blacks and thus, they felt especially positive when they had the opportunity to share a such a contextually important ingroup identity with them. In our future research to extend these findings we will include measures of mood to examine this amplified positivity explanation. In any event, this study offers further support for the idea that outgroup members will be treated more favorably in the context of a common ingroup identity than they would be if they were regarded only as outgroup members. Apparently, ingroup forces that usually foster intergroup discrimination and bias can be used to increase positive behaviors toward outgroup members, as proposed by the Common Ingroup Identity model. Clearly, these findings did not reveal that whites are antiblack; rather, whites did reveal a pro-ingroup bias toward blacks with whom they shared common ingroup identity.

CONCLUSION

This chapter has examined the possibility that racial bias, particularly in its contemporary manifestations, may reflect a prowhite, not simply antiblack sentiment that many traditional theories and measures have implied. Specifically, the studies reviewed pertaining to aversive racism seem amenable to this prowhite rather than antiblack interpretation. Prowhiteness does not necessarily imply antiblackness. This does not mean, however, that antiblack intentions do not drive interracial behavior among many whites. Not all racists are aversive types.

Considering prowhiteness as an important element in intergroup relations has both theoretical and applied value for understanding, assessing, and addressing issues of racism in our society. With respect to enhancing an understanding of contemporary racism, this perspective helps to identify when and how whites' bias will be expressed. By and large, within the studies reviewed here, blacks were treated differently than whites only when the forces to act favorably were weak. With regard to assessing prejudice, our analysis suggests that traditional prejudice scales that measure primarily antiblack attitudes, either directly or indirectly, are limited in the extent to which they can capture whites' racial attitudes. They may provide relatively accurate assessments of the intergroup attitudes of traditional racists, whose attitudes are composed mainly of antiblack sentiments, but they offer relatively poor estimates of the attitudes of aversive racists, whose interracial attitudes apparently have a significant prowhite emphasis. Indeed, we have found across a range of studies that responses on traditional prejudice scales do not predict behavioral expressions of aversive racism (Gaertner and Dovidio, 1986). The development of self-report and response latency measures that separately assess prowhite and antiblack sentiments (see Dovidio and Fazio, 1992) may provide more valid representations of racial attitudes.

Appreciating the impact of prowhite attitudes in contemporary racism also offers important insight into legal, social, and personal actions that can eliminate racial bias. Current antidiscrimination laws are based largely on the premise that racial discrimination by whites is primarily the result of antiblack attitudes and actions. For example, the second author of this chapter served as an expert witness for the plaintiff in an employment discrimination case. The plaintiff, a black man, was placed on probationary status by his employer because of some deficiencies in his performance. After review of his performance during the probationary period, the employer terminated his appointment with the company and had him physically escorted off the premises by security. The plaintiff's claim was not that his treatment violated the company's procedure but that another person—a white man—who was also on probation and whose performance during this time was comparable to that of the plaintiff's was retained and given reassignment with the company. The argument was that this represents different and unfair treatment for equivalent performance. The defense argued successfully that although the plaintiff was indeed treated differently for equivalent performance, he was not treated unfairly. His case was handled in accordance with the procedures of the company. It was acknowledged that, perhaps because of a closer personal relationship between the other worker and the supervisor, that the white employee was given an *extra* opportunity within the company. However, this special and favorable treatment toward the white (ingroup) worker, the defense claimed, is not valid *legal* grounds for demonstrating unfair and discriminatory treatment toward the black (outgroup) employee. The defense's arguments were persuasive, and the plaintiff's case was dismissed. Thus, laws designed to protect disadvantaged individuals and groups from one type of discrimination based on anti-outgroup actions may today be ineffective or outdated for addressing biased treatment based on *ingroup favoritism*. Awareness of the changing nature of contemporary racism may require a reconceptualization of policies and laws to address the consequences of persistent, if changing racism.

Ironically, however, motivations toward ingroup favoritism may also provide a mechanism for combatting this subtle form of intergroup bias. As we have demonstrated within the context of the Common Ingroup Identity model, redirecting this pro-ingroup orientation to produce more favorable attitudes toward former outgroup members can have positive effects on intergroup, including interracial, behavior when the situational context can induce people to increase the inclusiveness of their ingroup identities. When recategorization changes "Us and Them" to "We," outgroup members are treated more favorably. Also, we can envision multi-racial and ethnic coalitions within educational, church, military, or government settings, particularly in times of crises, work together with a vision of benefiting their larger common constituency. The benefits of this strategy for inducing more positive intergroup attitudes is further suggested by studies that find that in integrated school settings the students with the most positive interracial attitudes are those who have participated on sports teams or on cooperative learning teams composed of students from different racial groups (Slavin and Madden, 1979). More recently, Smith and Tyler (in press) reported that middle-class, white San Francisco Bay residents who identified themselves more strongly as Americans—a more inclusive group identity—than as caucasians had more positive attitudes toward policies intended to benefit disadvantaged black citizens. Thus, although prowhiteness can form a basis for contemporary forms of racism, understanding its dynamics, restructuring the definition of the ingroup, and redirecting the forces of ingroup favoritism offers a powerful strategy for addressing, socially and personally, the unintentional but insidious racial biases of aversive racists.

ACKNOWLEDGMENTS

Preparation of this manuscript was facilitated by an NIMH Grant (MH 48721) to Samuel Gaertner and John Dovidio.

REFERENCES

Allport, G. W. (1954). *The Nature of Prejudice*. Cambridge, MA: Addison-Wesley.

Ashmore, R. D. (1970). Prejudice: Causes and Cures. In B. E. Collins (ed.), *Social Psychology: Social Influence, Attitude Change, Group Processes and Prejudice* (pp. 245–339). Reading, MA: Addison-Wesley.

Anastasio, P. A., Bachman, B. A., Gaertner, S. L., and Dovidio, J. F. (1996). In R. Spears, P. J. Oakes, N. Ellemers, and S. A. Haslam (eds.). Categorization, Recategorization and common Ingroup Identity. *The Social Psychology of Stereotyping and Group Life*. Oxford: Blackwell.

Bachman, B., Gaertner, S., Anastasio, P., and Rust, M. (April 1993). When Corporations Merge: Organizational Identification Among Employees of Acquiring and Acquired Organizations. Paper Presented at the 64th Eastern Psychological Association Convention, Crystal City, VA.

Brewer, M. B. (in press). In-group Favoritism: The Subtle Side of Intergroup Discrimination. In D. Messick and A. Tenbrunsel (eds.), *Behavioral research and business ethics*.

Brigham, J. C. (1993). College Students' Racial Attitudes. *Journal of Applied Social Psychology*, 23, 1933–1967.

Campbell, D. T. (1963). Social Attitudes and Other Acquired Behavioral Dispositions. In S. Koch (ed.), *Psychology: A study of science* (vol. 6). New York: McGraw-Hill.

Crocker, J., and Schwartz, I. (1985). Prejudice and Ingroup Favoritism in a Minimal Intergroup Situation: Effects of Self-esteem. *Personality and Social Psychology Bulletin*, 11, 379–386.

Crosby, F., Bromley, S., and Saxe, L. (1980). Recent Unobtrusive Studies of Black and White Discrimination and Prejudice: A Literature Review. *Psychological Bulletin*, 87, 546–563.

Devine, P. (1989). Stereotypes and Prejudice: Their Automatic and Controlled Components. *Journal of Personality and Social Psychology*, 56, 5–18.

Dovidio, J. F., and Gaertner, S. L. (1991). Changes in the Expression and Assessment of Racial Prejudice. In H. J. Knopke, R. J. Norrell, and R. W. Rogers (eds.), *Opening Doors: Perspectives of Race Relations in Contemporary America*. Tuscaloosa, AL: University of Alabama Press.

Dovidio, J. F., and Gaertner, S. L. (1993). Stereotypes and Evaluative Intergroup Bias. In D. M. Mackie and D. L. Hamilton (eds.), *Affect, Cognition and Stereotyping*. Orlando, FL: Academic Press.

Dovidio, J. F., Mann, J., and Gaertner, S. L. (1989). Resistance to Affirmative Action: The Implications of Aversive Racism. In F. A. Blanchard and F. J. Crosby (eds.), *Affirmative Action in Perspective* (pp. 83–102). New York: Springer-Verlag.

Faranda, J., and Gaertner, S. L. (1979, April). The Effects of Inadmissible Evidence Introduced by the Prosecution and the Defense, and the Defendant's Race on the Verdicts of High and Low Authoritarians. Paper Presented at Eastern Psychological Association Meetings, New York City.

Gaertner, S. L. (1973). Helping Behavior and Racial Discrimination Among Liberals and Conservatives. *Journal of Personality and Social Psychology*, 25, 335–341.

Gaertner, S. L., and Dovidio, John F. (1977). The Subtlety of White Racism, Arousal and Helping Behavior. *Journal of Personality and Social Psychology, 35*(10), 691–707.

Gaertner, S. L., and Dovidio, J. F. (1986). The Aversive Form of Racism. In J. F. Dovidio and S. L. Gaertner (eds.), *Prejudice, Discrimination, and Racism* (pp. 61–89). Orlando, FL: Academic Press.

Gaertner, S. L., Dovidio, J. F., Anastasio, P. A., Bachman, B. A., and Rust, M. C. (1993). The Common Ingroup Identity Model: Recategorization and the Reduction of Intergroup Bias. In W. Stroebe and M. Hewstone (eds.), *The European Review of Social Psychology* (Vol. 4, pp. 1–25). London: Wiley.

Gaertner, S. L., and McLaughlin, J. (1983). Racial Stereotypes: Associations and Ascriptions of Positive and Negative Characteristics. *Social Psychology Quarterly, 46*, 23–30.

Gaertner, S. L., Rust, M. C., Dovidio, J. F., Bachman, B. A., and Anastasio, P. A. (1994). The Contact Hypothesis: The Role of a Common Ingroup Identity on Reducing Intergroup Bias. *Small Groups Research, 25*(2), 224–249.

Gaertner, S. L., Rust, M. C., Dovidio, J. F., Bachman, B. A., and Anastasio, P. A. (in press). The Contact Hypothesis: The Role of a Common Ingroup Identity on Reducing Intergroup Bias Among Majority and Minority Group Members. To appear in J. L. Nye and A. M. Brower (eds.), *What's Social About Social Cognition?* Newbury Park, CA: Sage Publications.

Green, C. W., Adams, A. M., and Turner, C. W. (1988). Development and Validation of the School Interracial Climate Scale. *American Journal of Community Psychology, 16*, 241–259.

Hamilton, D. L., and Trolier, T. K. (1986). Stereotypes and Stereotyping: An Overview of the Cognitive Approach. In J. F. Dovidio and S. L. Gaertner (eds.), *Prejudice, Discrimination, and Racism* (pp. 127–163). Orlando, FL: Academic Press.

Kovel, J (1970). *White Racism: A Psychohistory*. New York: Pantheon.

McConahay, J. B. (1986). Modern Racism, Ambivalence, and the Modern Racism Scale. In J. F. Dovidio and S. L. Gaertner (eds.), *Prejudice, Discrimination, and Racism* (pp. 91–125). Orlando, FL: Academic Press.

Murrell, A. J., Betz, B. L., Dovidio, J. F., Gaertner, S. L., and Drout, C. E. (1993). Aversive Racism and Resistance to Affirmative Action: Perceptions of Justice are Not Necessarily Color Blind. *Basic and Applied Social Psychology, 5*, 71–86.

Sears, D. O. (1988). Symbolic racism. In P. Katz and D. Taylor (eds.), *Towards the Elimination of Racism: Profiles in Controversy* (pp. 53–84). New York: Plenum.

Slavin, R. E., and Madden, N. A. (1979). School Practices that Improve Social Relations. *American education Research Journal, 16*, 169–180.

Smith, J. H., and Tyler, T. R. (in press). Justice and Power: When Will Justice Concerns Encourage the Advantaged to Support Policies which Redistribute Economic Resources and the Disadvantaged to Willingly Obey the Law? *European Journal of Social Psychology*.

Tajfel, H. (1969). Cognitive Aspects of Prejudice. *Journal of Social Issues, 25*, 79–97.

Tajfel, H., and Turner, J. C. (1979). An Integrative Theory of Intergroup Conflict. In W. G. Austin and S. Worchel (eds.), *The social psychology of intergroup relations* (pp. 33–47). Monterey, CA: Brooks/Cole.

Turner, J. C. (1985). Social categorization and the Self-Concept: A Social Cognitive Theory of Group Behavior. In E. J. Lawler (ed.), *Advances in group processes* (Vol. 2, pp. 77–122). Greenwich, CT: JAI Press.

Turner, J. C. (1981). The Experimental Social Psychology of Intergroup Behavior. In J. C. Turner and H. Giles (eds.), *Intergroup behavior* (pp. 66–101). Chicago, IL: The University of Chicago Press.

Turner, J. C., Hogg, M. A., Oakes, P. J., Reicher, S. D., and Wetherell, M. S. (1987). *Rediscovering the Social Group: A Self-Categorization Theory*. Oxford: Blackwell.

Wills, T. A. (1981). Downward Comparison Principles in Social Psychology. *Psychological Bulletin, 90*, 245–271.

Woodmansee, J. J., and Cook, S. W. (1967). Dimensions of Verbal Racial Attitudes: Their Identification and Measurement. *Journal of Personality and Social Psychology, 7*, 240–250.

Confessions of an Affirmative Action Mama

Faye J. Crosby

Faye J. Crosby is a social psychologist. She teaches at Smith College and is the COO of the Nag's Heart Conferences. Faye has conducted research on socially relevant topics since obtaining her Ph.D. twenty years ago. Her 1996 book on affirmative action, *Affirmative Action: The Pros and Cons of Policy and Practice,* is published by American University Press and is coauthored with Sharon Herzberger and Dick Tomasson.

Here I sit in a hotel room in Iseltwalt; I face the Alps and know that whatever I write will be inadequate to the task at hand. Mine is a well-traveled thought. I have carried it in my head and heart around New England and New York, to the Caribbean, and now to Switzerland. And the voyage isn't over yet.

The job, as I understand it, is to describe with some coherence the associations between my professional work, on the one hand, and my awareness—faltering in its intensity—of myself as a White person. Coherence poses the problem. The questions are vast, the issues pervasive, and the connections entangled. I feel like a hiker intoxicated on thin air, disoriented by a vastness of snow and sky. To chart a course in the vastness, I first outline my work on social justice and then linger over the connections between my work and my ethnic self-awareness.

MY ACADEMIC WORK

As a theorist and empirical researcher, I have obsessed for twenty years over the connections between subjective and objective reality. While the obsession has remained fixed, the form of working through it has changed. I have been evolving away from being an abstract theorist whose work has practical application to being a practitioner whose work has theoretical implications.

My earliest work centered on the theory of relative deprivation. The theory states that people's feelings of discontent or deprivation cannot be predicted from an outside assessment of their "objective situations" but rather vary as a function of how closely their situations match some psychological standards which are themselves inferred from such factors as the situation of one's peers (Crosby, 1976).

In 1978 and 1979 I conducted a survey in Newton, Massachusetts. Included in the study were three samples: employed women, employed men, and housewives. Half of the employed samples had high-status jobs and half had low-status jobs. Half of the housewives had husbands in high-status jobs and half in low-status jobs. All of the housewives were married mothers. One third of the employed samples were single; one third married and childless; one third married parents. All respondents were White and were between the ages of 25 and 40.

Assembling the sets of attitudes, we saw that employed women in our sample were much more upset about the situation of their membership group (women) than about their own personal situations. They seemed to recognize their own good fortune relative to other employed women. The vast majority of the women in the sample saw themselves as the exception to the general rule of discrimination.

The question naturally arose: were they?

The answer, gleaned from hard numeric data was: no. We had gone to great pains to equate the samples of employed women and employed men in Newton, and in all the "input characteristics" we measured, characteristics such as years of education, years of on-the-job service, hours worked per week, workforce attachment, and job prestige ratings, we succeeded. Yet, in both the high- and low-status samples, the employed men earned reliably more money than the employed women. The self-congratulations of the employed women was, it turned out, unwarranted: Although they seemed to imagine themselves to be more privileged, the women in Newton suffered the same discrimination as other American working women. This phenomenon we labeled the denial of personal disadvantage (Crosby, 1982).

As soon as other studies, some by independent researchers, confirmed the robustness of the phenomenon (Branscombe, 1995), my colleagues and I set about to understand why the denial existed. We conceptually distinguished between cognitive and emotional factors. Emotionally, it is hard to countenance that harm does or can come to the self. To the extent that emotional factors account for the phenomenon of denial, we should find that people process information about discrimination against the self differently than they process information about other individuals. Cognitively, it is difficult to detect patterns of discrimination with insufficient data. To the extent that cognitive or information-processing factors account for the phenomenon of denial, we will find that people's judgments of unfairness are influenced by the form in which information is presented.

For both practical and theoretical reasons, my associates and I decided to look first at the cognitive underpinnings of the phenomenon we had found in Newton. In a series of experiments we presented subjects with materials about the "inputs" and "outcomes" of contrasting groups (e.g., women and men; people from Plant A and Plant B) and would then ask our subjects to make determinations about the extent of discrimination. We always built unfairness into the system so that, for example, averaging across ten departments, men received more "outcomes" (e.g., money) on average than women who, on average, had identical "inputs" (e.g., education).

We found that subjects could readily perceive unfairness when they were presented with the relevant information assembled on one page. The same subjects were typically incapable of perceiving discrimination when they encountered the information piecemeal. If the individual comparison contained a gross violation of ordinal equity (e.g., she had more education and more motivation, and he got a higher salary), subjects could detect unfairness in the piecemeal condition, but even sophisticated subjects could not make accurate estimates of magnitude (e.g., she had more education and more motivation, and she received a higher salary; but her salary was only a little higher than his even though she had much more education and motivation).

Our laboratory findings provided compelling proof of the cognitive bases of the phenomenon first encountered in Newton. When people make judgments about individuals (even when one of the individuals is the self), they cannot usually perceive patterns of unfairness. The ability to detect discrimination, furthermore, is unrelated to someone's political attitudes. Feminists, for example, are no better able than nonfeminists to detect sex discrimination in individual comparisons.

That imperfect information processing can cause even the best-intentioned to deny that the existence of discrimination is a finding with extraordinary ramifications. As anyone who works in organizations knows, organizations function better when the people who make up the organization feel that it operates in a fair way. As most organizational specialists also know, when perceptions of fairness are based, in part at least, on denial, repression, or suppression, rapid—even revolutionary—changes can occur in people's points of view. An extremely unstable situation is one in which the impression of justice is illusory. Thus, for the sake of organizational stability as well as for simple social justice, any organization needs to have a way to monitor aggregated data about the inputs and outcomes of groups. Relying on more passive techniques, such as waiting for the victims of unfairness to step forward on their own behalf, is not sufficient.

In the United States, there is only one legally mandated policy that requires organizations to monitor their treatment of designated groups through the systematic collection and aggregation of data. That policy is called affirmative action. No other policy requires that organizations proactively take steps to assure fairness; all other policies, including so-called equal opportunity, are reactive rather than proactive.

As a researcher I could not walk away from the findings or the implications of my own surveys and experiments. If my findings were valid, then organizations needed affirmative action. By affirmative action I meant any program in which resources were expended to assure that discrimination did not exist.

The words "affirmative action" evoke strong reactions; they are not very well understood. I have had to explain to audiences (even very well-educated audiences) that the majority of affirmative action programs involve employment and not education and that they are both voluntary and relatively nonintrusive.

Classical affirmative action has been the law since 1965. Any organization in the United States that has more than fifty employees and that is a federal contractor is required by law to have an affirmative action plan. The plan needs to show that members of designated categories (e.g., women or workers of color) are being utilized in proportion to their availability. If an organization does not currently utilize people in the designated groups in the same proportion as their availability, the organization must articulate reasonable plans for remedy. As long as reasonable efforts are being made, there is no penalty for a continued gap between utilization and availability. (Clayton and Crosby, 1992).

Given how innocuous the policy is, I have been searching for some reasons for resistance to affirmative action. Raw self-interest accounts for some, but not very much of people's support for or opposition to affirmative action (Ozawa, Crosby, and Crosby, 1996). Racism and sexism—including internalized racism and sexism—are more potent explanations for resistance than is self-interest (Tougas, Crosby, Joly, and Pelchat, 1995). Most of the resistance to affirmative action springs, I believe, from both a deep commitment to the individualistic meritocratic ideal and from an insufficient understanding of what affirmative action entails (Crosby, in press).

A WHITE PERSON

I can and do, without any hesitation, speak of People of Color and of White People. It is only within the last ten years or so, however, that I have attempted to apply the tincture descriptor with equal frequency to the numeric majority as to the numeric minority. Bernardo Ferdman has written some very interesting work about how asymmetric and insulting it is to differentiate between "people of color" on the one hand and "people" on the other (Ferdman, 1989).

For individuals, too, the asymmetries bear scrutiny. I speak of the individual person of color and, sometimes, of the individual White person. Am I more likely to apply the pigmentation adjectives to a non-White person than to a White person? The truth, which I regret, is that perhaps

I am. I also wonder if I am readier to speak of, say, an African American or an Asian American without reference to her or his social class, religious affiliation, marital status, parental status, or family background than I am ready to speak of a White American without reference to her or his social class, religious affiliation, marital status, parental status, or family background. I wonder, in other words, if I am more attuned to (expectant and tolerant of) individual variation among the numerically dominant group, which is also my group, than among people of color. If so, I am the kind of person Milton Rokeach (Rokeach, 1960) described as close-minded, which may be to say I am a racist. Maybe not a raging racist, but a racist nonetheless.

Whether or not I am a raging racist, I am certainly an enormous egoist. Whenever I enlist the demographic marker of skin pigmentation as a descriptor of myself, I can barely repress the awareness of other demographic markers. I feel that I am not a White person so much as a White woman. To be sure, I am a particular White woman with my own somewhat distinguishing parcel of demographic markers. I am, for example, a middle-aged, middle-class divorced mother of two boy-men, and I am daughter of a Protestant midwesterner (father) and a Jewish French colonialist (mother).

To notice my resistance at the clause "I am a White" is to ignite a number of other awarenesses. First, there is the imbalance between ethnicity and gender. While the particular descriptors of family status, social class, and so on often seem important, the gender distinction always does. It is the thought of myself as a *White woman* that immediately shoves off stage any consciousness of myself as a *White person*. I ask myself: Does the same rush toward complexity exist when I say "I am a woman?" No, it does not. I can say "ah, yes, I am a woman" without instantly bringing into the discourse my parents and children, my job, and my bank account. What I cannot do for color, I can do for sex.

Why?

I think the answer has to do in large measure with unfair treatment. As I grew up, I experienced situations that should have taught me that it was not only women and men of color in America who suffered from stereotyping and discrimination. As a college applicant, for example, my test scores—and a clerical error—made me eligible for an ROTC scholarship. Thinking I was a young man, the Army offered to pay a good portion of my tuition. Of course, as a young woman, I was ineligible in 1965 for an ROTC scholarship, and once the Army found out that I was not in fact a male, they withdrew the offer of a scholarship.

The problems did not stop when I was twenty. Surprise, surprise. Like every other professional woman whom I know over the age of thirty, I have a storehouse of accumulated insults and injustices. It took me a very long time to recognize that I was not the one woman in America to have escaped sex discrimination; but I finally did understand. And that is perhaps one reason why I can say with ease "I am a woman" but find myself choking on the words "I am a White."

Perhaps one reason I am at relative peace with the self-description of "White woman," furthermore, is that I am intrigued by the implicit status inconsistency of the condition. To be a White woman in America is simultaneously to enjoy high and low statuses. All White people in America, as Peggy MacIntosh puts it so beautifully, wear the invisible backpack of privilege in America (McIntosh, 1988). And yet all women—including, of course, all white women—are more likely to face discrimination on and off the job in America than are comparable men.

Although I have savored the status inconsistency of being a White woman for at least two decades, there was a time in life when the inconsistency caused me puzzlement and embarrassment. When I was a child, the only people of color whom I had met were domestic workers in the homes of friends and acquaintances and in my own home. I would have been unable then to identify the source of my discomfort, but I now see that I was bothered by the asymmetrical use of first and last names. It perturbed my sense of an orderly universe to have within it grown people (with a dark pigmentation) who were treated with the same puny respect accorded the other children and me.

I have not come to feel at peace with disrespectful treatment of people of color. Please do not misunderstand. It is just that complexity, absurdity even, I now tolerate in others better than I could in my youth.

The tolerance is fostered by and, in turn fosters, a forgiveness of some limitations. Privilege, like bright sunlight, can blind us. I have been blinded. And so have those whom I love, including my relatives who were French colonists, known as *pieds noirs*. Once, a friend described her family's butler in French Algeria during the 1940s. The butler had been a handsome and elegant man, and an Arab. The storyteller commented on the butler's memory. "Although he was highly intelligent," she said, "he was illiterate. And so he committed to memory long telephone messages and recounted them verbatim." Much later in the day, I asked the storyteller if the handsome Arab butler could read and/or write Arabic. "Oh," she waved, "I have no idea."

How many times have I called someone illiterate because they did not read my language? How many times have I called myself illiterate because I have not read theirs? How often have I thought about standard English and presumed that people of color are speaking ungrammatically when their rules don't match my own?

Not all blindnesses concern color. In 1990 I was working on a book. The topic was gender and multiple roles. I came to feel that the practice of pretending that people's lives contained wholly separate spheres of work and home was a subtle but effective way of perpetuating an androcentric bias. So, self-consciously crusading, I decided to add a line to the personal section of the Curriculum Vita that stated "married, two children." The decision was not an easy one: To include the line meant risking the opprobrium of my male colleagues and possibly undermining my own sometimes shaky "scientific" credibility. But ethics won out over careerism.

Or so I thought. One day as I was proudly recounting my position to some colleagues, a woman in the group took me to task. She pointed out the difficulties that would arise for lesbians if everyone adopted my policy in this still homophobic world. As I was campaigning away for my just cause, I was—it turned out—potentially making life harder for lesbians than it had been. It was simple insensitivity that undermined my efforts at being a good ally.

Throughout my life I have been sheltered and protected by vast amounts of good fortune. Challenges have—of course—abounded, but the resources to meet the challenges have always been at hand. Privilege bred in me the overestimation of my own capabilities that is the hallmark of the nondepressed person.

In my more mature days it has occurred to me to question whether the daughters and granddaughters of Dad's secretaries have passed through life with the same optimism and confidence that became mine. I believe their circumstances were less likely than mine to make them think they could and should run the world. But even as I am aware of the differences of social class, I remember the similarities of skin coloring. My father's staff was White, and their offspring were too. At whatever "level" one's family is in the American social hierarchy, it is surely easier to feel in possession of this country when your skin is White than when it is more darkly colored.

SELF-CONSCIOUSNESS THROUGH WORK

In 1980 *Psychological Bulletin* published an article on racism in which I was the lead author. The article pointed out that the White avowal of racial equality, increasingly audible in every passing study of verbally measured attitudes, was not matched by changes in behavior when the behavior was assessed through unobtrusive measures. Thus while White people in 1980 said they liked Black people as much as White people, they did not, for example, pick up the grocery bags of a Black person but did help a hapless White shopper (Crosby, Bromley, and Saxe, 1980).

The 1980 piece, coauthored with Stephanie Bromley and Len Saxe, resulted in more than a few invitations to present colloquia. One time I waited a very long time at the airport for the graduate students to pick me up. It turned out that they—having read the *Psychological Bulletin* article—were waiting for a Black woman to emerge. The White woman with the suit and briefcase (me) did not fit their expectations.

I was delighted at the confusion of the graduate students. Fundamentally, I was deeply flattered to imagine that my analysis of racism had been so trenchant that even those most directly harmed by discrimination felt I had understood its dynamics. I was happy, furthermore, that the Black graduate students seemed to feel validated by the discovery that a White professor took racism seriously. We felt like mutually admiring allies.

But a similar confusion, occurring in reverse, did not delight me. The incident in question involved a speaker who was invited to give a talk at Smith College. The College dispatched a driver to pick up the speaker at the airport. I asked the Grounds Service if they would like a photo or a description of the speaker. "Oh no," I was informed "that would not be necessary." I assumed that the driver, having more experience in such matters than graduate students, would know to take a placard with him. A telephone call from the speaker left at the airport proved that confidence unjustified. Later, when the chauffeur told me that he had in fact driven to the airport and that no speaker had alighted, I discovered that it had never occurred to him that a Black woman might be coming to speak to the Psychology Department of Smith College about mental health issues. The man had not even held up a sign with the speaker's name because he saw in the group no one who, in his mind, could even potentially be a speaker.

These twin incidents in my work life made me conscious of my White skin and also of society's racist assumptions. I could not help but notice the asymmetry of a world which confers legitimacy on a topic if a White person is involved while the involvement of a person of color offers less of an automatic stamp of approval. Bernardo Ferdman would have a lot to say on this subject.

It is a sensitivity to the asymmetry that impels me to self-identify as a White researcher and citizen when I enter into public debates about affirmative action. The same sensitivity obliges me to make reference to my two White sons virtually every time I give a public speech on the topic of affirmative action. Given the current conservative climate in the country and the continuing misunderstanding of what affirmative action is in principle and in practice, I am always at pains to declare that my fervent support of affirmative action comes ultimately from being the mother of White boy-men. It is because I want a better world for my children that I bother to fight for affirmative action.

Work-induced consciousness of my Whiteness comes not only from the research I do but also from my teaching. In my work as a professor I have come to realize that the contours of my life and of my studies are bounded by my White skin color. Sometimes the realization has arrived like a thunderbolt.

Donna Nagata hurled one thunderbolt. As she hurled, she acted with grace and courage. But I was dumb-struck by my own stupidity.

Several years ago Donna and I were on the team to teach Introduction to Psychology at Smith College. Donna, a clinical psychologist, is Japanese-American, and had conducted a massive survey on the intergenerational effects of the internment of Japanese-Americans during World War II (Nagata, 1993). At the time of the incident Donna was the only untenured professor on the team.

I was lecturing the class about Milgram's studies of obedience. As was my wont, I was seeking to engage the students in the material by having them physically move about the lecture hall. I wished to instruct one group of students to come up on stage and then to entice another group to follow the first group, to surround them, to point a finger, and then to say bang. Then, in my plan, we would discuss how great evils can be accomplished through the progression of tiny incremental steps in which small, rather than large, acts of obedience were required. I had done the exercise in previous classes to good effect.

Standing on the stage as I reached the point in my lecture where the demonstration was to begin, I looked out at the students to see what markers I could use as quick-and-easy selection criteria. The first group had to number about ten and the second about fifteen or twenty. I noticed that about fifteen or twenty students had on red sweaters, but there were no other aspects of clothing or accessories that applied to only ten or twelve women. I did notice that there were about ten Asian American or Asian women in the class.

With a stunning display of insensitivity, in the heat of orchestrating my lecture, I ended up instructing the Asian American women to come to the stage and then enticed women in red sweaters to surround the first group on the stage, point their fingers and pretend to shoot. I then thanked the participants, ushered them offstage, and initiated the class discussion. After a very few minutes, Donna Nagata asked for the class to pause and reflect on what had happened. With all the best intentions in the world, I had created a dreadful situation for the Asian American students whom I had, in effect, asked to play the part of the "stereotypic passive" Asian female. Worse, I had treated ethnic features as though they could be put on or taken off just like a sweater.

Fortunately for the students, the other faculty, and me, Donna was a skilled clinical psychologist and a woman with the courage of her convictions. Also fortunate was our close personal friendship. We could assure the students that our friendship would continue. I endured my shame and apologized to one and all, and Donna accepted the apology and helped me to see how to make my behavior conform to my nonstereotypic and egalitarian attitudes.

SAFEGUARDING MY WORK

If it is through my work that I have developed an awareness (however imperfect) of my Whiteness, it is in part because of my work that I refuse to ignore my Whiteness and all the privileges that pertain to my skin pigmentation. Most of my current research centers on issues of affirmative action. For those who study affirmative action, the attitudes of angry and frightened White males can provoke some impatience. But to end the impatience and become sympathetic with aspects of the resistance to affirmative action, I need only remember how privilege has blinded me too.

Why is the sympathy necessary? Why not simply consider that the opponents of affirmative action are to be neutralized and forgotten? What is gained by taking them seriously and by engaging in reasoned debate with them?

What is gained is the ability to resist a restricted or exclusive moral world (Opotow, 1990). And so, ultimately, from an acknowledgment of my own privilege—including but not limited to my White skin—comes a hope of doing studies *with* people rather than *on* people. My epistemological stance seems appropriate to research that looks less at the causes of behavior than at the reasons for behavior. There is no one "true" view of the mountain, just many different perspectives.

REFERENCES

Branscombe, N. (June 1995). Denial and More. Paper presented at thirteenth Nag's Heart Conference. Amherst, MA.

Carson, C. G., and Crosby, F. (Winter 1989). Rx: Affirmative Action. *Smith Alumnae Quarterly*.

Clayton, S., and Crosby, F. (1992). *Justice, Gender and Affirmative Action*. Ann Arbor, MI: University of Michigan Press.

Crosby, F. (In press). A Rose By Any Other Name. In K. Arioli (ed.), *Affirmative Action: Quotas and Equality*. Zurich, Switzerland: (Swiss) National Science Foundation.

Crosby, F. (1982). *Relative Deprivation and Working Women*. New York: Oxford University Press.

Crosby, F. (1976). A Model of Egoistical Relative Deprivation. *Psychological Review, 83*, 85–113.

Crosby, F., Bromley, S., and Saxe, L. (1980). Recent Unobtrusive Studies of Black and White Discrimination and Prejudice: A Literature Review. *Psychological Bulletin, 87*, 546–563.

Ferdman, B. M. (1989). Affirmative Action and the Challenge of the Color-Blind Perspective. In F. A. Blanchard and F. J. Crosby (eds.), *Affirmative Action in Perspective* (pp. 169–176). New York: Springer-Verlag.

McIntosh, P. (July/August 1989). White Privilege: Unpacking the Invisible Knapsack. *Peace and Freedom*, 10–12.

Nagata, D. K. (1993). *Legacy of Injustice*. New York: Plenum Press.

Opotow, S. (1990). Moral Exclusion and Injustice. *Journal of Social Issues, 46*(1), 1–20.

Ozawa, K., Crosby, M., and Crosby, F. (1996). Individualism and Resistance to Affirmative Action: A Comparison of Japanese and American Samples. *Journal of Applied Social Psychology, 26*, 1138–1152.

Rokeach, M. (1960). *The Open and Closed Mind*. New York: Basic Books.

Tougas, F., Crosby, F., Joly, S., and Pelchat, D. (1995). Men's Attitudes Toward Affirmative Action: Justice and Intergroup Relations at the Crossroads. *Social Justice Research, 8*, 57–71.

EIGHTEEN

"I'm White! So What?"
The Construction of Whiteness for Young Londoners

Ann Phoenix

Ann Phoenix is with the Department of Psychology, Birkbeck College, University of London, United Kingdom. Her publications include *Young Mothers?* (Polity Press: Cambridge 1991); (with B. Tizard) *Black, White or Mixed Race? Race and Racism in the Lives of Young People of Mixed Parentage* (Routledge: London 1993); *Shifting Identitities, Shifting Racisms*, edited with Kum-Kum Bhavnani (Sage: London, 1994); and *Crossfires: Nationalism, Racism and Gender in Europe*, edited with Helma Lutz and Nira Yuval-Davis (Pluto: London, 1995).

Studies of "race", racism, ethnicity, and identities have, historically, tended to focus on black people and those from other minority ethnic groups. Over the last decade, however, there has been increasing recognition (much of it inspired by debates within feminist scholarship) that "whiteness" is as much a social construction as is blackness. As such, it has always constituted a central part of the context within which black and other minority peoples are racialized (Hall, 1992; Ware, 1992). The absence of focus on "whiteness" coupled with implicit constructions of white people as "the norm" (Phoenix, 1987) serves to maintain the privileged position of whiteness, but to obscure the ways in which it is implicated in power relations (Mun Wong, 1994; Trepagnier, 1994).

Those who have contributed to the burgeoning literature on whiteness generally agree that "race," racism, and ethnicity are part of the lives of white people (Frankenberg, 1993). In other words, white people's lives are racialized. Attempts to understand racism thus require a focus on the white majority as well as on black or other minority experiences (Back, 1993; hooks, 1992; Troyna and Hatcher, 1992; Wetherell and Potter, 1992; van Dijk, 1987). However, the relative absence of focus on "whiteness" in comparison with the numerous pieces of research which focus on "blackness" may well contribute to making whiteness as an identity position silent and, hence, less tangible than "black identity."

At one level, it is not surprising that being asked to think about "being white" leads to consideration of what it means *not* to be white. Just as what it means to be black is lived out in relation to white people, so "being white" only has meaning in relation to what it means to be black. Identity, after all, requires consideration of difference. Yet, black people, on the whole, are able to speak about blackness because in western societies black people encounter racism and racialized discourses in such a way that they are likely to have thought about "being black." Since these discourses are also available to white people, it is perhaps not surprising that white people can talk readily about blackness (Dyer, 1993).

The difficulty of talking about being white, however, does require explanation. Reasons proposed in the literature for this absence include denial of power (Pajaczkowska and Young, 1992; Young, 1995), the general failure of the dominant to reflect on dominance (Ware, 1992), and the lack of recognition of historical power relations between black and white people (Hall, 1992; Ware, 1992).

This chapter presents examples from a study of the social identities of 248 young Londoners (aged 14–18 years of age) in order to examine whiteness as a social identity.

This chapter argues that many white young people found it difficult to talk about what being white meant to them and few presented themselves as having white identities. Those white young people who had ancestry other than white English generally had more to say about ethnicity and being white than those who were white and English. Thus, Irish, Jewish, or Scottish white young people were more likely to say that they had thought about issues related to ethnicity and to being white. Generally, however, the white young people consistently played down the significance of colour while frequently producing accounts which indicated that their lives are racialized. Such accounts demonstrate the complexity of essentialism. Many of the young people appeared to be refuting essentialist thinking by insisting on the individualism of "people just being people, whatever colour they are." At the same time, they gave essentialist accounts of black people as Other.

Racialized Identities: An Issue in Black and White

While it is often believed that racialized identities are relevant only to black people, they are increasingly being recognised as relevant to white people (Frankenberg, 1993). Growing up as they were in what has been called "multiracist Britain" (Cohen, 1988), "race" and racism featured in white young people's lives in various ways, albeit often in different ways from those reported by black and mixed-parentage young people. However, because they occupy different social positionings from black people, white people's racialized identities are experienced and expressed differently. In looking at some of the young people's answers, it becomes evident that young white people are uncertain about how to answer questions about "race" and racism because they have given less thought to such issues. At the same time, they are more likely to report that they are never conscious of their colour and less likely to report that they have ever wanted to change their colour.

So, for example, young white people spontaneously expressed more uncertainty about which colour terms to use than did black or mixed-parentage young people. Twenty-nine percent of the white sample expressed such uncertainty, compared with 15 percent of each of the other two colour groups. They were also more likely to use the term "coloured" than were black or mixed-parentage young people (62 percent, 30 percent, and 43 percent respectively) and to confine use of the term "black" to people of African and African Caribbean descent rather than, for example, to include people of South Asian descent (72 percent of white young people compared with 52 percent and 53 percent of black and mixed-parentage young people respectively). Relatively few of the sample of all colours included people of mixed-parentage as black (24 percent of black young people spontaneously said this compared with 5 percent of the other two groups). This probably reflected two factors. First, that they had given less thought to "race" and racism and, second, that many were more concerned than their black and mixed-parentage peers that their accounts should not be construed as racist.

It was because white young people had much less experience of racism that they were the colour group least likely to have wished to be another colour in the past. Thus, while 12 percent (ten) black young people and 23 percent (thirteen) young people of mixed-parentage said that they had often wished to be a different colour in the past, only two white young people reported this. There was a less marked difference between the colour groups for occasional desire to be a different colour.

Since much literature on racial identity suggests that some young black children wish to be white, we asked all the young people if they had ever wished to be another colour. A minority of the sample overall said that they had ever wanted to change their colour. This was also colour differentiated. Twenty-eight percent of black young people, 14 percent of white young people, and 51 percent of mixed-parentage young people said that they had, at some time, wished to be a different colour. The high percentage of young people of mixed-parentage saying this generally felt that they would prefer to be either black or white rather than of mixed-parentage.

More of the young people, whatever their colour, reported that they had wanted to be a different colour in the past than currently. The most marked reduction, however, was for black young people (none of whom said that, currently, they often wanted to be a different colour and only two of whom said that they currently sometimes wished that they were not black) than for mixed-parentage and for white young people. Although the numbers involved are small, they demonstrate racialized differences between young people. Young black people who had wanted to be white tended to say that they had wanted to be white earlier in life in order to avoid racial discrimination or name calling; in order not to "be different" or to have the same hair as their white peers. The 14 percent of young white people tended to want to change colour later in life for reasons of style or youth culture or to look like many people of mixed-parentage do.

We asked the young people whether they were ever conscious of their colour. Black and mixed-parentage young people were most likely to say that they were sometimes conscious of their colour (68 percent black, 63 percent mixed-parentage, and 45 percent white young people). Only one white young person said that they were always conscious of their colour in comparison with twelve black young people and five of mixed-parentage.

One of the arguments often made against transracial adoption is that black young people growing up in white households will not be proud and pleased to be black. Presumably, those who advance these arguments assume that white young people will necessarily be proud to be white since they are not subject to the racial discrimination and devaluation that black young people are subject to. However, since issues of "race" and racism are generally not assumed to be relevant to white young people, they are generally not investigated, but left implicit. We asked the sample whether they were pleased and proud to be the colours they were. Fewer young white people said that they were pleased or proud to be their colour. Ninety-five percent of black young people said that they were pleased to be their own colour. Eighty-one percent of mixed-parentage and 60 percent of white young people also said this. With regard to pride in their colour, the percentages were 92 percent, 77 percent, and 34 percent respectively. Black young people were much more likely to have been told to be proud by their parents than the other groups (66 percent black, 40 percent mixed parentage, and 6 percent white young people).

The Salience of Whiteness

The overall differences between white, black, and mixed-parentage young people in their experiences of "race" and racism, in the terms they use and in whether or not they have ever wanted to change their colour, might well be expected given previous research and the pervasiveness of racism in Britain. Are such differences reproduced when young people are asked to reflect on being their own colour? Does whiteness constitute an absent discourse for white young people?

It is hardly surprising that white young people were the least likely ever to be aware of their own colour, with over half of them (55 percent) saying that it almost never impinged on their consciousness (with approximately one third of black and mixed-parentage young people). More of the white young people said that they never thought about their colour than that they did, while the mixed-parentage and black young people were most likely to report themselves to be aware of colour.

Q. Is the fact that you are white nearly always in your mind or do you never think about it or only at certain times?
A. I don't think about it, unless I am talking about it. [white young man]

Pleased and Proud to Be White?

Comparatively few young white people said that they were unequivocally pleased to be white (60 percent cf 81 percent mixed-parentage and 95 percent black young people) or that they were proud to be white (34 percent cf 77 percent of mixed-parentage and 92 percent of black young people). White young people were much more likely than young people from the other two groups to suggest that they considered colour to be irrelevant and were proud of themselves as individuals. Thus, although most of the young people reported themselves to be happy to be their colour (78 percent) and almost two thirds (65 percent) said that they were proud to be their colour, this was colour-differentiated, with only one third of white young people expressing pride in their colour (cf 92 percent of black and 77 percent mixed-parentage young people). While being pleased to be their own colour was less colour-differentiated, with the majority of young people saying that they were pleased to be their colour, young white people were the least likely to say that they were pleased.

Most of those white young people who eschewed pleasure or pride in their colour gave accounts which indicated that it was unwarranted to take pleasure in, or be proud of, a characteristic that they had no influence over. Their accounts mainly indicated that they were pleased to be themselves and consistently played down the significance of colour. At first sight, the pattern of the young white people's responses appear to fit into the egalitarian ideology commonly advocated by most of the young people in the study. They presented individualistic arguments when asked to talk about their racialized identities:

Q. Right, on balance, are you pleased to be white?
A. Not pleased. I wouldn't say pleased. I'm happy being white, but um, I don't think I'd be unpleased if I was black or white [laughs] yes.
Q. Right, are you proud of being white?
A. No. I don't think it's something to be proud about, because it's your colour. [white young woman]

The notion that colour is largely irrelevant and that all colours are basically the same was sometimes expressed even by those who said that they felt proud to be white.

Q. On balance, are you pleased to be white?
A. I shouldn't really mind what colour I am but, yes, I am quite pleased with my colour.
Q. Are you proud of being white?
A. Yes.
Q. Did your parents ever tell you should be proud of being white?
A. No, I don't really think they had to tell me. I realise whatever colour you are, you should be proud to be yourself and it doesn't really matter what colour you are. [white young man]

Recognition of Difference

It would appear from these accounts that whiteness does not constitute part of young white people's identities. Asked directly the questions that black young people and those of mixed-parentage are frequently asked in studies of racialized identities, most indicate that if they are pleased to be white, it is because they are pleased to be themselves. Colour, they argue, does not matter to them and, hence, they give it little thought. Yet, although whiteness was a silent/absent discourse for the young Londoners we interviewed, they were positioned, and did position themselves, as white. It was an implicit part of their identities in as much as many positioned themselves in contradistinction to black people. This emerged not when they were asked about their individual feelings about being white, but when they were asked about the circumstances in which they became conscious of their colour (if they ever did); their feelings about black people collectively; whether or not they considered that their lives would be different if they were not white; and about racism. The accounts many gave in response to such questions contradicted both the egalitarian ideologies and the individualism of their earlier accounts. For, in talking of black people as a collectivity, they gave largely essentialist accounts, treating all black people as if they are the same and necessarily behave in particular ways *because* they are black. This view was partly because out of school, few white young people mixed with black people, and informal segregation allowed the perpetuation of stereotypic views.

The social construction of black people is such that many of the stereotypes attached to young blacks of African Caribbean origin are gender specific. The content of these stereotypes is mainly related to violence and lawlessness and is associated with young black *men* rather than young black women. These stereotypes were reproduced in many young people's (of all colours) spontaneous discourses about black people. In the accounts which follow, young people talked about black people or "coloured" people in general either really being, or erroneously being seen to be violent and threatening. However, they were actually usually referring to young black men.

> There's a lot of black people that don't like white people and because they have been picked on or whatever because they're black . . . they go out robbing and beating up white people and mugging white women . . . just because they're white . . . [white young man].

From the accounts young black people (women and men) gave, it is possible to see that, for black young men, there are deleterious consequences of this pervasive social construction of black male youth. Young black men were generally upset about the ways in which they were stereotyped and many young black men and women (as well as some of their white friends) told stories about being stopped by the police for no apparent reason.

> There was an old white lady. . . . She walked past me and she goes 'oh don't mug me! I haven't got nothing in my bag". . . [black young man].
> Well me and my friend, we were just out on a school day and we just get picked up (by the police) because they say things like you should be at school and everything, but I don't think it was that really, because it was late at night [black young man].

Some young black men's accounts also suggested that they accrued benefits from this negative social construction, which pleased them. These benefits were directly related to the ways in which young white people often talked of black people as objects of fear, particularly on the streets.

Whiteness as Social Relation

While saying that colour was largely irrelevant, then, many of the young white people experienced whiteness as social relation through fear of black people on the street. In their perpetuation of the racist stereotype of back people as dangerous and frightening, their discourses were suggestive of racialized differences between black and white people. Thus, while they did not necessarily consciously experience themselves as white, they did experience racialized social relations, predicated on the differences between their whiteness and the blackness of Others.

One of the reasons that some white young people to be pleased to be white was because they recognised that whiteness conferred some advantages. They thus understood whiteness in social relationship to blackness.

Q. On balance, are you pleased to be white?
A. I think so, yes. It probably makes life easier. [white girl]

This also explained why two thirds of the white young people said that they were not proud to be white, but some were equivocal and others negative about taking pride in whiteness. This was largely to do with their recognition that being white signifies a social location and, as such, has a history and interconnections with other colours. The reticence about claiming whiteness as something about which to be proud was related to their awareness that, around the world, white people have often oppressed black people. There were thus contradictions, for some young white people, inherent in being proud of whiteness. These contradictions differentiated them from black and mixed-parentage young people who expressed no such qualms about being proud to be black or of mixed-parentage.

Q. Would you say you are pleased to be white?
A. Yes.
Q. Would you say you are proud to be white?
A. Sometimes not, no.
Q. Did your parents ever say you should be proud of being white?
A. No, never. They would say be proud of what you have got, not anything like white.
Q. Would you say you feel proud sometimes?
A. When I see this stuff on telly about what white people do like in South Africa and things like that, that doesn't make me proud to be white, no.
Q. But sometimes you are proud?
A. Yes.

Q. Do you think that your life so far would have been different if you had not been white, if you had been black?
A. Yeah, it would have been different.
Q. How do you think it would have been different?
A. The way people feel about me.
Q. So what difference do you think it would have made to you?
A. What do you mean, the difference in life?
Q. Yes, I mean if you had been black, do you think it would have made a big difference to where you are at now?
A. Yeah.
Q. And can you think of how, what sort of things would have been different?
A. No.
Q. You can't imagine it?
A. I know things would have been different, but I can't think what would have been different. People like towards me would have been different.

Q. How?
A. Like I wouldn't get called whatever a white person gets called, but if I was different, coloured I would be called a name. [white young man]

The above respondent was clearly groping towards an answer. For whatever reason, emotional or to do with articulateness, he did not have a clear, available discourse of the difference being black would have made to his life. This may well go hand-in-hand with discourses of egalitarian ideology that render it illegitimate to acknowledge differences between people of different colours. However, the respondent clearly did have notions that he would have been treated differently by other people if he were black. The following respondent is clearer about what the difference would have been, but only about the present, during which he presumably has experience of seeing what happens with black and white people of his age group.

Q. Do you think that your life so far would have been different if you had not been white?
A. Yeah probably would have, probably would have experienced a lot more racism towards me.
Q. And how about the future if you were black now, do you think your future would be very different?
A. Don't know. [white young man]

Two types of reasons were advanced for ambivalence about being proud to be white. One, that white people were responsible for many atrocities against black people, and the other that claiming pride in whiteness was tantamount to being racist and having far-right sympathies.

Q. Would you say you are proud of being white?
A. No, definitely not, not with the kind of things that go on in the world. [white young woman]
Q. And would you say you are proud of being white?
A. I wouldn't say that, because if you think you are proud of being white, if everybody thinks they are proud of being white, then—problems.
Q. Like what kind of things.
A. Go round and beating up all the coloured people, try and get them out of the country, because I know some people who are really racist, just telling people to go back to their own country, I just walk away from them.

Positioned Differently: Differentiated by Nation

A further way in which the young people's responses were differentiated related to how they perceived membership of the English nation and the British state. Michael Billig (1995) has coined the term "banal nationalism" to indicate that everyday nationalism and the processes by which it is reproduced are not innocent and insignificant. The findings of the Social Identities study indicated that "banal nationalism," expressed through national identities, was racialized.

There were significant differences (by respondents' colour) in the answers given to questions about whether the English are white or merely people who live in England. In both cases, young white people were more likely than young mixed-parentage or black young people to give answers which were less exclusionary. Thus, fewer said that the English were white (38 percent cf

61 percent of black young people and mixed-parentage young people) and more (although still a minority) said that residence was sufficient for inclusion as English. Rather more young people considered that being born in England would confer Englishness than that residence would, but this answer was not significantly differentiated by colour of respondent. Few mentioned that parents would have to have been born in England and white for their children to be English, although that factor emerged in answer to other questions. With regard to most of these answers, young people of mixed-parentage were more similar to black than to white young people. Those who gave answers in the "born there" category were also likely to say "white."

Overall, the young people's accounts thus partly reproduced pervasive, "little England" discourses, which construct the English as white, upper-class males, superior to all others. Few (4 percent) mentioned social class in response to questions about whom they considered English. However, some produced discourses that combined colour, descent, and upbringing. They thus produced elements of a "primordial" view of ethnicity, predicating the symbolic boundaries of "Englishness" on fixed (rather than flexible) notions of colour and descent (Smith, 1984). "Race" was thus intertwined with nation in the young people's constructions of national identities.

In this context, it seems surprising that young white people produced responses which were less exclusionist than those of black or mixed-parentage young people. How can this be explained? It seems most likely that the complex concept of Englishness is constructed and interpreted through everyday experiences. The social identities study included many more areas than those reported here. It was evident from their accounts that many black and mixed-parentage young people had experienced racism. White young people were better able to maintain their egalitarian ideology in response to these questions because they are not constructed as outsiders or subject to racism in the same way. This is apparent from some of the answers given in response to whether they considered themselves English or British. Their answers were thus probably ideal and theoretical, while the black and mixed-parentage young people's answers were more practical, arising from racialized experience. It is for these same reasons that many young white people said that being white was irrelevant to their lives.

Being asked about national identities was not necessarily easier for white than for black young people. There sometimes seemed to be some embarrassment for white young people about too readily defining themselves as English in case this appeared "racist" or jingoistic. The following example illustrates Billig et al.'s (1988) "dilemmatic" notion of ideology. The dilemma is to do with expressing their views while not appearing racist.

Q. And what sort of people do you think of as being English?
A. Um [pause].
Q. . . . Do you think of English people as being white?
A. Yes, probably yes I do . . . I know I shouldn't but I probably do.
Q. Why do you think you shouldn't?
A. Because I think that's probably racist.
Q. Why . . . ?
A. Um, because I think it's discriminating. It's saying that people who are not white are not like fully a part of this country . . . which is wrong. It's kind of a subconscious thing . . . like the stereotyped English man. [white young man]

The equation of "race," nation, and culture poses dilemmas for some young white people and, consequently, leads them to use rhetorical devices that are "two-sided," in which "two contrary themes are expressed simultaneously" (Billig et al., 1988: 109). In the above instance, the young man suggests that he recognises that it is racist and exclusionary to equate Englishness and white-ness. He thus expresses reluctance to espouse the idea and, indeed, does not do so until expressly asked. It may be, of course, that other young people refused to give answers they thought would be considered racist. In their response to questions about how they found the interview, some white young people expressed anxieties about putting forward their views without appearing racist.

The term British was also occasionally considered to be imbued with a sense of national pride.

British seems to have some sense of nostalgia about it you know—sort of British pride and things. But er—English is more factual, the country you come from. [white young woman]

Discomfort on the part of white young people could be warded off by viewing ethnicity and nationality as optional and voluntary rather than as related to subject positions.

They *can* call themselves English, but some of them choose to call themselves West Indian. They can still do that. [white young man]

From this perspective young white people perceived black people as having more choice than white people about opting into or out of Englishness. They thus saw black people as benefiting from in-strumental aspects of nationality in a way white people could not. They may, perhaps, be envious of black people's (assumed) wider horizons in having knowledge of at least two countries and cultures. Ethnic and national differences could thus provide a focus of resentment in a similar way to that de-scribed in the Burnage report of the inquiry into the murder of a young Asian boy by a white boy in their school playground (Macdonald et al., 1989). They found that many of the white working-class boys considered that they did not have a culture and that whites were disadvantaged by the presence of black people and other minority ethnic groups, who they perceived to have cultures and identities. This is a finding echoed by Cohen (1987), who argued that his taped interview with ten- and eleven-year-old boys "illustrates the main normative elements to be found in working class racism . . . its constant refrain of relative deprivation 'the blacks are doing better than us' " (Cohen, 1987: 31).

It is, of course, not being suggested that all young people are positioned in the same way with regard to whiteness. Young white people of Irish descent and young Jewish people in Britain often themselves had experienced racism and so were differentiated from the white majority. In addition, young white people had differentiated narratives about black people and racism. All were, how-ever, positioned in relation to black and other minority people and to racism in complex ways (Bur-man, 1994; Hickman and Walter, 1995). The fact that fewer white than black or mixed-parentage young people said that they were ever conscious of their colour; that they had given less thought to issues of terminology; and that they were less likely to report ever having wanted to change their colour is related to the fact that they had little or no experience of being subjected to racism but are positioned, often unwillingly, as potential agents of racism. For many white young people, this re-alisation sits uncomfortably with their fear of black people as violent criminals.

CONCLUDING THOUGHTS

One of the striking features of the study reported here was the reluctance of many white young people to think of themselves as white or to view whiteness as having any social meaning. Their accounts were of whiteness as natural and involuntary rather than constructed, socially signifi-cant, and open to question. Their constructions of themselves might be called "raceless."

Disavowal of whiteness often went hand-in-hand with disavowal of the symbols of nation. Many white young people considered it unacceptable to be proud of the British flag on the grounds that, as a symbol, it had been appropriated by the racist far right. In consequence, some felt ashamed to claim Britishness or Englishness and vacated national identity. As with "blackness," whiteness was dynamic and differentiated, for example, by social class and gender.

These findings complement other work which indicates that some white, working-class young people have come to feel themselves to be disadvantaged in comparison with young people from minority ethnic groups, who they construct as having their ethnicity buttressed at the expense of the white majority (McDonald et al., 1989).

This chapter has argued that such findings can only be understood in the context of the young people's lives. On the one hand their lives are racialized in such a way that whiteness in itself accrues some privileges. On the other hand, in late twentieth-century Britain, multiculturalist and antiracist educational strategies have made racism unacceptable and, to some extent, have encouraged "colour-blind" approaches which, paradoxically, do not take sufficient account of racialized power differences between young people. These policies have not necessarily made any difference to the ways in which young people from different racialized groups construct each other. As a result, some young people have stereotypic and static notions of people racialized as Other and many white young Londoners feel particularly tentative and uncertain when asked to discuss issues of "race." Not surprisingly then, processes of racialisation continue to be part of a contested terrain where blackness is constructed as a signifier of identity but where many white young people deny that whiteness has any meanings and do not consider it to confer any identity.

Paradoxically, the necessity for whiteness to be an overt identity position is obviated by the fact that many black and mixed-parentage young people overtly position themselves as having racialized identities. Young white people can thus consider themselves "raceless" while continuing to accrue the privileges associated with whiteness. It is thus possible to see how silence about "whiteness" implicitly serves to maintain the status quo of power relations between black people and white people, minorities and majorities.

While general patterns emerged from the white young people's answers, there were differences between young white people with regard to their racialized identities. Just as "blackness" is increasingly being demonstrated to be multiple rather than unitary, "whiteness" is itself complex and plural. Writing on whiteness over the last decade makes it clear that, just as "blackness" is not a unitary or essential category, so "whiteness" is differentiated by, for example, age, gender, and social class (Hickman and Walter, 1995). For example, Billig (1991) has studied white young people who are members of racist organisations while Hewitt (1986) and Jones (1988) have found groups of young people who were highly attracted to the expressive cultures of black youth. While this syncretism does not necessarily signify opposition to racism (Back, 1993) and while racism itself is often theorized in a reductionist and oversimplistic way, those young people who spend their spare time with black people are likely to differ from those who have no contact with black people (whether through lack of opportunity or avoidance). A great deal of further work is required if young white people's racialized identities are adequately to be theorized.

REFERENCES

Back, Les. (1993). "Youth, race and nation within a predominantly white working-class neighbourhood in south London." *New Community*, 217–233.
Billig, Michael. (1995). *Banal Nationalism*. London: Sage.

Billig, Michael. (1991). *Ideology and Opinions*. London: Sage.

Billig, M., Condor, S., Edwards, D., Gane, M., Middleton, D., and Radley, A. (1988). *Ideological Dilemmas: A Social Psychology of Everyday Thinking*. London: Sage.

Burman, Erica. (1994). "Experience, identities and alliances: Jewish feminism and feminist psychology." *Feminism and Psychology*, 4(1): 155–178.

Cohen, Phil. (1988). "The perversions of inheritance." In Philip Cohen and Harwant S. Bains. (eds), *Multiracist Britain*. Basingstoke: Macmillan.

Cohen, Phil. (1987). *Reducing Prejudice in Classroom and Community: Report on the First Year*. London: PSEC/CME Cultural Studies Project.

van Dijk, Teun. (1987). *Communicating Racism: Ethnic Prejudice in Thought and Talk*. London: Sage.

Dyer, Richard. (1993). *The Matter of Images: Essays on Representations*. London: Routledge.

Frankenberg, Ruth. (1993). *White Women, Race Matters: The Social Construction of Whiteness*. London: Routledge.

Hall, Catherine. (1992). *White, Male and Middle Class*. Cambridge: Polity.

Hewitt, Roger. (1986). *White Talk, Black Talk*. Cambridge: Cambridge University Press.

Hickman, Mary, and Walter Bronwen. (1995). "Deconstructing Whiteness: Irish women in Britain." *Feminist Review*, 50, 5–19.

hooks, bell. (1992). *Black Looks: Race and Representation*. Boston, MA; South End Press.

Jones, Simon. (1988). *Black Culture, White Youth: The Reggae Tradition from JA to UK*. Basingstoke: Macmillan Education.

Macdonald, I., Bhavnani, R., Khan, L., and John, G.. (1989). *Murder in the Playground*. London: Longsight Press.

Pajaczkowska, Claire, and Young, Lola. (1992). "Racism, representation, psychoanalysis." In James Donald and Ali Rattansi (eds.), *"Race," Culture and Difference*. London: Sage.

Parker, David. (1995). *Through Different Eyes: The Cultural Identities of Young Chinese People in Britain*. Aldershot: Avebury.

Phoenix, Ann. (1987). "Theories of gender and Black families." In Gaby Weiner and Madeleine Arnot (eds.), *Gender under Scrutiny*. London: Hutchinson.

Smith, A.. (1984). "Ethnic myths and ethnic revivals." *Archives Europeenes de Sociologie*, 24(3): 283–303.

Trepagnier, Barbara. (1994). "The politics of white and black bodies." *Feminism and Psychology*, 4(1): 199–205.

Troyna, Barry, and Hatcher, Richard. (1992). *Racism in Children's Lives: A Study of Mainly White Primary Schools*. London: Routledge.

Ware, Vron. (1992). *Beyond the Pale: White Women, Racism and History*. London: Verso.

Wetherell, Margaret, and Potter, Jonathan. (1992). *Mapping the Language of Racism: Discourse and the Legitimation of Exploitation*. London: Harvester Wheatsheaf.

Wong, L. Mun. (1994). "Di(s)-secting and dis(s)-closing 'whiteness': two tales about psychology." In Kum-Kum Bhavnani and Ann Phoenix (eds.), *Shifting Identities, Shifting Racisms: A Feminism and Psychology Reader*. London: Sage.

Young, Lola. (1995). *Fear of the Dark: "Race," Gender and Sexuality in the Cinema*. London: Routledge.

Is White a Race? Expressions of White Racial Identity

Robert T. Carter

NINETEEN

Dr. Robert T. Carter received his BA and M.Ed from Columbia University and his Ph.D. in counseling psychology from the University of Maryland (1987). He is currently an Associate Professor at Teachers College, Columbia University in the Department of Counseling and Clinical Psychology, and before that in the Department of Social, Organizational and Counseling Psychology. He was formerly a member of the Psychology faculty at Southern Illinois University. He is a consultant and private practitioner in New York City as well. He teaches research methods, racism, racial identity and mental health, and cross-cultural psychology and education. He has published research in the areas of psychotherapy process and outcome, career development, cultural values, racial identity issues, educational achievement, and equity in education through the lens of racial identity. He has been retained to consult on legal and educational issues associated with race and diversity such as teacher training, desegregation, cross-racial adoption, and biracial custody. He has been or is on the Editorial Boards of the *Journal of Counseling and Development*, the *Journal of Multicultural Counseling and Development*, *The Journal of Counseling Psychology* and *The Counseling Psychologist*. Recent publications include *The Influence of Race and Racial Identity in Psychotherapy: Toward a Racially Inclusive Model* (1995) and "Racial Identity and Education" in *Review of Research in Education* (1994).

INTRODUCTION

In my role as an educator and psychologist, I have provided clinical treatment and training to a racially diverse group of people. In my classes and clinical practice and during consulting about issues of race, ethnicity, social class, and other cultural elements, it is apparent that people of color, for the most part, know that they have been classified according to their race and that this racial grouping has meaning and significance for their personal identity. Whites, on the other hand, seem to be unaware of race as a group and personal characteristic. This lack of conscious awareness is expressed in various ways. For instance, White women and men, many in their mid-twenties and thirties, when asked to reflect on their race say things like:

> I have always thought of race as something belonging to persons of color, defined by the difference between us. The first memory I have of interacting with someone non-white involved my grandmother's maid Sally who was a Black American.

The predominant comment of Whites is that they are not aware of themselves as White. This is interesting when one considers the fact that Whites, specifically Europeans and Americans, essentially created racial classification and the ideological and sociopolitical meanings associated with race (Allen, 1994; Smedley, 1993). Moreover, Whites, through various mechanisms, continue to this day to maintain racial divisions in the society. Much of this effort is not conscious or direct. But it has the unintended or intended effect of racial exclusion and the maintenance of white dominance or privilege.

The emphasis and focus of racial classification systems have mostly been to display both the superiority of White European-American cultural patterns and values (i.e., view of existence, thought patterns, language, temporal focus, social relationships) and how people of color are different from the White norm, where difference is and was thought to be inferior. Until recently, Whites have not had a way to understand the psychological meaning of their race.

The purpose of this chapter is to discuss and explain White racial identity as an aspect of personality development (Carter, 1995; Frankenberg, 1993). I will describe White racial identity theory and illustrate various expressions of racial identity ego statuses taken from interviews, vignettes, and case descriptions. The illustrations of White racial identity will be used to highlight how the various forms of White racial identity reflect unexamined, subconscious, or conscious forms of racial knowledge and in many cases embody individual, institutional, and cultural racism.

White Racial Identity Theory

More often than not reference to racial identity in the minds of most people refers to how one thinks about issues of race. The idea usually is applied to people of color. When Whites' racial identity is discussed it is done in terms of their political views or in terms of how they view people in other racial groups. Whites, while socialized in a racially constructed world, are taught not to be aware of themselves in racial terms. More importantly, in everyday language there is little recognition of the fact that race has personal psychological significance for Whites and, as such, is an aspect of each person's personality and developmental processes.

Whites' racial identity is a psychological orientation towards their racial group membership. From that orientation grows one's view of other racial group(s). Current theory (Helms, 1994, 1995; Carter, 1995) contends that White racial identity is a psychological template which operates as a "world view" and serves as a filter for race-based information.

Most people are familiar with the idea set forth by Sigmund Freud that the personality is divided into three parts: the id, ego, and superego. The ego negotiates between the need for gratification and constraints of reality. For instance, we may be hungry and want to eat immediately, but our reality scanner—the ego—tells us that the food we need and desire must be prepared before we can eat.

While contemporary theorists have modified some of Freud's ideas about the components of the personality, the notion of the ego being a primary aspect of the personality has endured. The idea of the ego becoming an increasingly large part of our personality is called differentiation. When we are born we are not psychologically differentiated from our mother and father. We are dependent upon them. Only slowly do we begin to learn that we are separate and unique. We also learn that we are members of specific racial groups.

The ego is the psychological structure that holds and transforms race-based information through one's racial identity ego status. Helms (1994) has recently proposed the use of the term ego "status" to refer to the various differentiations of ego that mark more mature and complex forms of development. I have referred to the notion of "status" by using the term "level" (Carter, 1995; Carter and Goodwin, 1994). So in this chapter, the terms racial identity "status" and "level" will be used interchangeably.

White racial identity levels are composed of attitudes, thoughts, feelings, and behaviors toward both self as a member of the White racial group and members of nondominant racial groups (i.e., people of color). Helms and Piper (1994) explain it this way:

> The maturation process potentially involves increasingly sophisticated differentiations of the ego, called "ego statuses." Although it is possible for each of the racial-group appropriate statuses to develop in a person and govern her or his race-related behavior, whether or not they do depends on a combination of life experiences, especially intrapsychic dissonance and race-related environmental pressures, as well as cognitive readiness. The statuses are hypothesized to develop or mature sequentially. That is, statuses share space within a multilayered circle (symbolizing the ego) and the status(es) which occupies the greatest percentage of the ego has the most wide-ranging influence over the person's manner of functioning. (pp. 126–128)

White racial identity theory was initially introduced by Helms in 1984. At that time she proposed a five-stage developmental model (Contact, Disintegration, Reintegration, Pseudo-Independence, and Autonomy) in which one moved from a low level of White racial identity development to a higher level. Most research on White racial identity has been conducted with the scale developed to measure the five-stage model (Helms and Carter, 1990). More recently (Helms, 1990; 1995), her revised and expanded model incorporates the relationship between White racial identity, ego functioning, and racism.

Helms's revised theory of White racial identity development (1994) proposes a six-level status process. Three levels—Contact, Disintegration, and Reintegration—represent the movements away from racism, and three latter levels—Pseudo-Independence, Immersion-Emersion, and Autonomy—represent more complex and sophisticated ego identity statuses characterized by the eventual formation of a nonracist White racial identity.

It is important to emphasize that each level of White racial identity, excepting perhaps the last (Autonomy), are intimately intertwined with individual, institutional, and cultural racism. Each person has elements of the three types of racism as part of his or her ego identity status. The individual racist is one who has come to accept without question consciously or subconsciously the societal and in some cases family messages that Black people and people of color as a group are inferior to Whites because of physical (genotypical and phenotypical) traits.

Institutional racism consists of established laws, customs, and practices which systematically reflect and produce intentionally and unintentionally racial inequalities in American society. Individuals and institutions apply and create rules, guidelines, standards, procedures, and practices that create racist effects. Institutional racism exists when gross and identifiable disparities occur on the basis of racial group membership. Thus, in education, criminal justice, housing, health care, economics, and labor force participation, if it can be shown that distinct racial differences exist, then what is observed is institutional racism. Marger (1994) describes modern institutional racism this way:

> The structural form of [racism] is difficult to perceive easily, because it does not use [race] as the subordinating mechanism, but uses other devices only indirectly related to [race] . . . most new industrial jobs have been created . . . in outlying and suburban areas, . . . where highways are more accessible . . . the outlying location of these jobs handicaps nonwhites who qualify for them but who reside mainly in central cities. (p. 90)

Cultural racism is the conscious or subconscious conviction that White Euro-American cultural patterns and practices, as reflected in values, language, belief systems, interpersonal interaction styles, behavioral patterns, political, social roles, economics, music, art, religious tenets, and so forth, are superior to those of other visible racial/ethnic groups (Asian, Black, Hispanic, Indian Americans).

WHITE RACIAL IDENTITY EGO LEVELS

Contact

The first level of White racial identity development, Contact is an immature, externally defined, and personally unexamined racial identity. The person is not aware of herself as a racial being, is oblivious to any acts of individual racism, and yet benefits from institutional and cultural racism. The person has adopted an essentially "color-blind" [read: White] view of race and racial issues. The person may acknowledge past acts of racism in the society but will contend that he did not personally discriminate or erect racial barriers so it is not appropriate to characterize his behavior as racist. Such an individual is minimally aware of race and racial issues as they shape his or her life and lacks awareness or direct experience with people of color.

People whose identity statuses are predominantly Contact usually have what I call situational, interracial, social, or occupational interactions with People of Color (i.e., they will interact when they cannot avoid such situations, such as in work settings). Their "color blind" racial perspective, in their view, allows them to interact with people presumably without regard to color. However, this type of color blindness is quite distinct from the physical type where one can not perceive color. In the social situation where color blindness is advocated, one first recognizes a person's color and then claims to ignore it. In reality it is not possible to be color blind where race is concerned. The very claim illustrates that a person can see but then denies race.

For most Whites, a conscious sense of their whiteness does not emerge until adolescence or adulthood, depending on their gender, social class, and where they grew up. This does not mean they were not aware of their Whiteness during childhood. The majority of Whites know and understand fully issues of race from age three or four. They know in retrospect that they lived in racially homogenous communities.

Racial socialization is a powerful process that communicates to Whites, through a variety of mechanisms, that they are different than Latinos, Asians, Blacks, and American Indians. Even in the absence of direct contact messages about each group, the White person comes to form a view of himself or herself in contrast to these "others." This racial socialization process is central to the formation of White racial identity ego statuses. The process is described by a 44-year-old White middle-class male who grew up in upstate New York. In his representation one hears the inherent contradiction in his awareness of racial identity. He expresses his Contact attitudes in an interview about race. He is asked:

I: What kind of messages did you think you got about being White?
R: What kind of messages I got about being White? There was no one to compare ourselves to. As you would drive through other neighborhoods, I think there was a clear message of difference or even superiority. The neighborhoods were poorer, and it was probably subtle, I don't remember my parents being bigoted, although by today's standards they clearly were. I think there was probably a message of superiority. The underlying messages were subtle. No one ever came out and said, White people are this and Black people are this. I think the underlying message is that White people are generally good and they're like us, us and them.

Here we see how one might come to believe that race is not salient, given that no explicit messages about race were communicated. Nevertheless, the social and psychological reality of racial comparisons seemed to shape the man's life as it does for most Whites. Again race belongs to someone else.

Frankenberg (1993) describes an interview with Clare, a 36-year-old White woman who grew up in California and seems to describe a Contact-level racial identity. She describes the town as conservative socially, withdrawn from general social issues and racially as "redneck." However, Native Americans, Mexicans, and a few Blacks were around. Her first cross-race contact came as she started school. She describes feeling afraid of the Mexican boys. Frankenberg (1993) summarizes Clare's world this way:

> The composition of Clare's friendship group in high school further supports this picture of a daily life that was in effect patterned by race: structured around the student council and a church youth group, it was all White. What shaped Clare's description of all three groups—Whites, Mexican Americans, and Native Americans—was on the one hand the absence of a conscious conceptualization of cultural and racial deference per se, but on the other hand, the *experience* of a racially structured environment, not understood as such at the time. In sum, Clare saw individuals in her immediate community through a racial lens, but did not consciously see race . . . or racism. (Frankenberg, 1993, p. 58)

DISINTEGRATION

The awakening recognition of racial differences leads the White person to Disintegration. At this level, the person has some experiences that involve race, whether in a class, with a friend, some social event which receives media attention, or through personal growth. One comes to realize that the humanistic or "color blind" racial perspective is not accurate. The individual learns that race does matter, that racism does exist, and that they are White. The experience shatters the person's ego structure at its core and he or she often feels like falling apart. Thus the term disintegration. The discovery process associated with this status is wrought with emotional turmoil. For the first time one's race is consciously acknowledged. This may be minimal and fleeting but denial of race usually gives way to some feelings of conflict and confusion because of the discontinuity racial self-awareness creates.

Racial self-awareness, no matter how dimly experienced, reveals previously hidden personal and social dilemmas. What is of particular difficulty is learning the social price Whites pay for violating the rules associated with cross-racial interactions. As a result, the person comes to realize that his or her world is constructed systematically along racial lines. And that to maintain a certain position among Whites depends on following racially determined rules even when the person may not personally endorse such practices. Encountering the rules of racial interaction often is associated with emotional turmoil and cognitive confusion. One's stable and ordered world is disrupted. To reduce the emotional and cognitive confusion and conflict, one may retreat back into a Whites-only world and ignore or avoid the new information. Or one may conclude that racism really does not exist in the present, or, that if it does, it is reflected in a few aberrant individuals. One can decide to act and "help" people of color by trying to convince other Whites that people of color are not inferior. Or one can join with oppressed peoples by identifying with their plight and movements.

One woman describes growing up this way:

> I grew up in a White homogeneous upper-middle-class community. There were some Hispanic and African-American students with whom I attended school, but the majority and minority students rarely mixed. All of my friends were White. I was aware of the fact that I did not know any of the students from other races, but was not bothered by it. I did not try

to socially mix across-races because I was afraid. I was intimidated by the unknown (the cultures and traditions of people of color), afraid of being rejected by them because I am different and White. Perhaps my strongest fear was being rejected by my White peers. My White friends did not have any friends of color so if I did I would stand out.

This woman opts to avoid and retreat. She was aware that to interact across race meant that she would violate White's rules of racial engagement, jeopardizing her standing as White. So she chooses to remain in a White-only world. She states that Blacks and Hispanics went to school with her yet she has constructed a White-only world by claiming that she grew up in a White homogenous community.

People who were characterized by high levels of Disintegration racial identity ego statuses were reported by Westbrook (cited in Helms, 1990) to endorse the statement, "Blacks need help to graduate," and yet they had a hard time understanding the anger some Blacks expressed. Pope-Davis and Ottavi (1994) found that White men at this level of racial identity endorsed racist practices. Helms and Carter (1991) found that these attitudes were associated with preferences for White male and female counselors. A person at this level of White racial identity may be capable of empathy when Blacks experience racial discrimination but may be unable to understand feelings of anger of Blacks.

The power of wanting to belong and be accepted by one's group coupled with the sociocultural depth of the beliefs in White superiority and Black and people of color inferiority, make it more likely that one would come to believe that racism doesn't exist or that if it does it is a remnant of the past. Thus, one with these ideas has more ego space devoted to the externally derived and somewhat more differentiated identity status, Reintegration.

REINTEGRATION

Reintegration rests on the conscious or subconscious belief that Whites are better than people of color. These views may be held explicitly, as is the case with White supremacists, or implicitly, as is typical of large numbers of White Americans.

He or she comes to believe that White cultural and institutional racism is the White person's due because he or she has earned such privilege and preferences. Race-related negative conditions are assumed to result from Black [and other visible racial-ethnic group] people's inferior social, moral, and intellectual qualities. Thus, people at this [point] tend to selectively attend and reinterpret information to conform to stereotypes common to the society. Effectively, people at this stage may feel fear and anger; however, these feelings usually are not that conscious and are seldom overtly expressed. (Helms, 1990, p. 61)

People who hold these views may just stay far away from Blacks and people of color, or such a person may even work with people of color, fighting various forms of oppression. Yet they do so with the belief that people of color should learn how to adopt White American or European ways of being and lifestyles.

The 44-year-old male above who expressed Contact status beliefs also, at different points in his life, expressed Reintegration attitudes. In high school he pointed out that he was aware of only two Black girls and that one left the school. He could not recall whether she stayed for the full four years. He was asked:

I: Do you know what that was about?

R: Oh yeah. She found it very difficult. There was no one there for her to associate with. One of the issues was the dating. There was nobody there for her to date, which meant of course that no one expected that any of the White boys were going to date her.

I: What does this convey to you about being White?

R: I don't know if it was superiority or just difference, a segregated difference. I'm not sure that people thought, and I certainly didn't think, that you shouldn't date them because you're better. I think there was a separation, clear separation.

It may take some powerful event either with Blacks or Whites for a person to question and begin to abandon this type of racial identity. The multicultural movement may be the type of event that for many White Americans triggers an examination of long-held beliefs about race and Whiteness in particular. It is also possible that one's own commitment to personal growth could bring about a process of exploration or allow one to choose a path that brings one into contact with people of color whom they come to admire. Such people may stimulate exploration and self-examination. This type of questioning may begin the process of developing a nonracist White identity.

PSEUDO-INDEPENDENCE

Once the decision to abandon racism is made, a person may begin the intellectual process of learning about and fighting against racial oppression. This process involves questioning prevailing notions about people of color that suggest they are innately inferior or deprived. What is revealed in this cognitive search is an understanding that Whites as a group and as individuals have responsibility for maintaining and/or undoing racism. Individuals become uncomfortable with the status quo role for White people, and they start to alter their outlook and role. Initially, these changes are primarily intellectual. Missing at this level of racial identity ego status development is a grasp of how one responds emotionally and behaviorally to the lessons of racial socialization. For instance, left unexamined are a person's standards for evaluating people and behavior. Such a person is likely to perceive himself or herself as capable of "assisting" and "teaching" people of color how to succeed in the society. The best example of this level lies in the behavior of individuals who "discover" and accept the wrongs of racism and decide to work against them. They immediately turn to the victims of racism for solutions. They may seek out a person or community of people of color and ask for explanations and descriptions of racism and race in their lives. These processes avoid self-examination. The person stays with this activity only as long as the person of color will participate. If the people of color do not oblige or reject his initiatives, they may come to be seen as less than deserving. White people operating from this racial identity ego status maintain and promulgate their own values, derived from a White cultural framework.

The Pseudo-Independent level of White racial identity is characterized by a sense of marginality. One is distanced a bit from Whites and typical White behavior; however, he or she is emotionally distant from racial issues.

Consider the views of Jim and Kathy Kish, a couple interviewed by Terkel (1992). They are blue-collar Whites who were both born and raised in Chicago and they live in an integrated suburb near the city. Both Kathy and Jim describe how they have learned from Black people. But, they also revealed strong personal fears associated with race. These fears suggest that their acceptance of racial differences and similarities was not integrated into their personalities. Within Pseudo-Independence, Jim asks,

Want to know my personal fear? I don't want to live in an all-black neighborhood. My next-door neighbor wants to live in an area that would be 70 percent white and 30 percent black. That way he knows his kids will get a proper education.

Pseudo-Independence is a level of racial identity in which one has begun to consider race but at this point the expression of the understanding of self and others is limited to cognitive issues and one has not let go of his or her own unique experience as the primary mechanism for understanding other racial groups and people.

IMMERSION-EMERSION

Emotional and intellectual integration takes place when one begins to understand that victims of oppression cannot stop their victimization. They can fight against it, protect themselves from its effects, learn to achieve in spite of it, but they can not stop something they are not creating. Whites invented race and maintain racial oppression in all its forms: individual, institutional, and cultural. The White person who comes to feel this reality and is able to communicate it no longer looks to the victims for solutions to their oppression. Instead they turn to Whites to help them challenge racism. They seek out other like-minded Whites. The process of internalizing a positive definition of Whiteness begins as the individual pursues an Immersion-Emersion racial identity ego status. Whites at the Immersion-Emersion level exchange myths and misinformation about Blacks, people of color, and Whites for accurate information about racial group memberships.

Karp (1981) describes the emotional process in terms of coming to accept one's inhumaneness, which she contends characterizes all Whites who have internalized racist messages and ideas. She states that subconsciously one may begin to experience feelings of guilt and shame accompanying the realization that one has operated on the basis of racist ideas. She points out that:

> Guilt and shame are painful to feel. Some people try to escape feeling them by being defiantly racist (Reintegration), while others act in a "do-gooder" fashion (Pseudo-Independence), condescendingly being supportive of non-Whites. People trying to uncover the origins of their own racist attitudes have to contend with these emotions first. (p. 93)

When the emotions are expressed and accepted it is possible to learn that one can be White and nonracist and to actively reject oppression of all people. Once this realization is accomplished it becomes possible to understand race and racism as described by Katz (1978):

> Racism is a White problem in that its development and perpetuation rests with White people. . . . The racial prejudice of White people coupled with economic, political, and social power to enforce discriminatory practices on every level of life—cultural, institutional, and individual— is the gestalt of White racism.

AUTONOMY

Autonomy is a racial identity status in which the person has freed self from racism and White racial denial. One has, through a process of self and group discovery, learned to value one's self in a noncomparative and nonoppressive way. Because race, one's own or that of others, is no longer a psychological threat, he or she is able to have a more flexible view of the world, one's own racial group, and that of others. The more differentiated ego identity status makes it possible to abandon cultural, institutional, and personal racism. Denial and distortion about one's race no longer is present. Therefore, he or she is better able to benefit from racial-cultural exchanges and sharing between members of various races. The White person at this level of racial identity also values and seeks out cross-racial/cultural experiences.

At this level of racial identity, one has evolved a complex and differentiated understanding of Whiteness and racism. In an essay on male and White privilege, McIntosh (1995) provides an example of such a comprehension of Whiteness. In her essay she points out that Whites are taught about racism as something which puts others at a disadvantage, not as something that harms Whites. She goes on to say that:

> I've come to see white privilege as an invisible package of unearned assets that I can count on cashing in each day, but about which I was meant to remain oblivious. White privilege is like an invisible weightless knapsack of special provisions, assurances, tools, maps, guides, code books, passports, visas, clothes, compass, emergency gear, and blank checks. (p. 77)

She goes on to note that writing about White privilege has been difficult in part because

> My schooling gave me no training in seeing myself as an oppressor, as an unfairly advantaged person, or as a participant in a damaged culture. I was taught to see myself as an individual whose moral state depended on her individual moral will. At school we were not taught about slavery in any depth; we were not taught to see slave holders as damaged people; slaves were seen as the only group at risk for being dehumanized. . . . whites are taught to think of their lives as morally neutral, normative and average, and also ideal, so that when we work to benefit others, this is seen as work which will allow them to be more like us. (p. 78)

Autonomy attitudes were related to support of racial integration and the belief that there were no differences in Blacks and Whites in committing crimes on campus (Westbrook, cited in Helms, 1990). Helms and Carter (1991) found no preference for White counselors among those with high Autonomy attitudes. Tokar and Swanson (1991) found that "a secure appreciation and acceptance of oneself and others (Autonomy) appears to be associated with a liberation from rigid adherence to social pressures and with a strong inner reliance (inner directedness)" (p. 299). High levels of Autonomy attitudes clearly show a qualitative difference in one's perception of race and race relations. There is less emphasis on only White relationships and the person is secure in his/her relationships. The individual also has developed a stronger self-concept.

SUMMARY AND CONCLUSIONS

Is White a race? The answer is *yes* it is. Race is not primarily determined by biology, although skin color is a marker for race. Race in the United States is a social and political reality. Decisions about whom to marry and date, where to live, where to go to school, what is taught, how to move about in one's community and surrounding area, where to shop, for whom to vote, and what occupation to pursue are all consciously or unconsciously influenced by racial considerations. If race were an accepted and valued part of personality (Carter, 1995) and social life, it would not have the powerful, usually inhibiting effect it currently has on Whites' lives and psychological functioning. Racial identity offers a way to understand the multiple ways in which race is expressed as well as the various types of internal and external factors that influence its expression. The expressions of White racial identity presented in this chapter reveal that race and racial identity status constitute a complex psychological orientation influenced by and interacting with other reference groups such as gender, age, social class, religion, ethnicity, political views, geography, and social-political circumstances.

So, why should a White person strive and struggle to develop a positive nonracist White racial identity ego status? Why should he or she accept race as a positive aspect of self and other? There is no easy or right answer to this question. Most reasons pertain to how one views himself or herself as a person. The outcome of such a process can help Whites be less fragmented in their self-appraisal. They can come to value and respect themselves without reservation or doubt. They can rid themselves of feelings of guilt, fear, anger, and hopelessness. They can be proud of personal accomplishments without concern that their benefits come as a result of skin color privileges. He or she can benefit from a greater mental freedom in that he or she no longer has to distort, deny, or avoid everyday realities. The result of this process is an integrated and complete human being. As Alderfer (1994) points out, drawing on his twenty years of personal and professional experience in working on racial issues, about why Whites should bother:

> We have a more complete awareness of ourselves and of others to the degree that we neither negate the uniqueness of each person, regardless of that person's group memberships, nor deny the ever-present effects of group memberships for each individual . . . I am one of-a-kind as a person—as is everyone . . . I am also a member of the White racial group—. . . I am male . . . [e]ven if I were to try to escape my racial or gender-group memberships, members of my own and other racial and gender groups would treat me as if I were a member of my groups. (p. 202)

The benefit in addressing race as an aspect of identity is beyond calculation.

REFERENCES

Alderfer, C. P. (1994). A White man's perspective on the unconscious process within Black-White relations in the United States. (pp. 201–229). In E. J. Trickett, R. Watts, and D. Birman (eds.), *Human diversity*. San Francisco: Jossey-Bass.

Allen, T. W. (1994). *The invention of the white race: racial oppression and social control*. London, England: Verso.

Betancourt, H., and Lopez, S. R. (1993). The study of culture, ethnicity, and race in American psychology. *American Psychologist, 48*(6), 629–637.

Carter, R. T. (in press). Exploring the complexity of racial identity measures. In G. R. Sodowsky and J. Impara (eds.). *Multicultural assessment*. Lincoln, Nebraska: Buros Institute of Mental Measurement.

Carter, R. T. (1995). *The influence of race and racial identity in psychotherapy: Toward a racially inclusive model*. New York, N.Y.: John Wiley and Sons.

Carter, R. T. (1990). Cultural value differences between African-American and White Americans. *Journal of College Student Development, 31*, 71-79.

Carter, R. T. (1990a). Does race or racial identity attitudes influence the counseling process in Black/White dyads? In J. E. Helms (ed.), *Black and White racial identity attitudes: Theory, research, and practice* (pp. 145–164). Westport, CT: Greenwood Press.

Carter, R. T. (1990b). The relationship between racism and racial identity among White Americans: An exploratory investigation. *Journal of Counseling and Development, 69*, 46–50.

Carter, R. T. (1991). Racial identity attitudes and psychological functioning. *Journal of Multicultural Counseling and Development, 19*, 105–115.

Carter, R. T., and Cook, D. A. (1992). A culturally relevant perspective for understanding the career paths of visible racial/ethnic group people. In Z. Liebowitz and D. Lea (eds.), *Adult career development* (2nd Ed.) (pp. 192–217). Washington, DC: National Career Development Association.

Carter, R. T., and Goodwin, A. L. (1994). Racial identity and Education. *Review of Research in Education, 20*, 291–336.

Carter, R. T., Gushue, G. V., and Weitzman, L. M. (1994). White racial identity development and work values. *Journal of Vocational Behavior, 44*, 185–197.

Carter, R. T., and Helms, J. E. (1987). The relationship of Black value-orientation to racial identity attitudes. *Measurement and Evaluation in Counseling and Development, 19*, 185–195.

Carter, R. T., and Helms, J. E. (1988). The relationship between racial identity attitudes and social class. *Journal of Negro Education, 57*(1), 22–30.

Carter, R. T., and Helms, J. E. (1990). White racial identity attitudes and cultural values. In J. E. Helms (ed.), *Black and White racial identity: Theory, research, and practice* (pp. 105–118). Westport, CT: Greenwood Press.

Carter, R. T., and Helms, J. E. (1992). The counseling process as defined by relationship types: A test of Helms' interactional model. *Journal of Multicultural Counseling and Development, 20*, 181–201.

Carter, R. T., and Parks, E. E. (1994). White racial identity and psychological functioning. Submitted for publication.

Claney, D., and Parker, W. M. (1988). Assessing White racial consciousness and perceived comfort with Black individuals: A preliminary study. *Journal of Counseling and Development, 67*, 449–451.

Frankenberg, R. (1993). *White women race matters: The social construction of Whiteness*. Minneapolis, Minnesota: University of Minnesota Press.

Gotanda, N. (1991). A critique of "Our Constitution is color-blind." *Stanford Law Review, 44*(1), 1–73.

Marger, M. N. (1994). *Race and Ethnic relations* (3 rd Edition): Belmont, CA: Wadsworth.

Helms, J. E. (in press). Towards an approach for assessing racial identity. In G. R. Sodowsky and J. Impara (eds.) *Multicultural assessment*. Lincoln, Nebraska: Buros Institute of Mental Measurement.

Helms, J. E. (1990). *Black and White racial identity: Theory, research, and practice*. Westport, CT: Greenwood Press.

Helms, J. E. (1990). Three perspectives on counseling and psychotherapy with visible racial/ethnic group clients. In F. C. Serafica, A. I. Schwebel, R. K. Russell, P. D. Isaac, and L. B. Myers (eds.), *Mental health of ethnic minorities* (pp. 171–201). New York: Praeger.

Helms, J. E. (1992). *Race is a nice thing to have*. Topeka, KS: Content Communications.

Helms, J. E. (1994). Racial identity and "racial" constructs. In E. J. Trickett, R. Watts, and D. Birman (eds.), *Human diversity* (pp. 285–311). San Francisco: Jossey-Bass.

Helms, J. E., and Carter, R. T. (1986). Manual for the Visible Racial/Ethnic Identity Attitude Scale. In R. T. Carter (1995). *The influence of race and racial identity in psychotherapy: Toward a racially inclusive model*. New York, N.Y.: John Wiley and Sons.

Helms, J. E., and Carter, R. T. (1990). The development of the White Racial Identity Inventory. In J. E. Helms (ed.), *Black and White racial identity attitudes: Theory, research, and practice* (pp. 145–164). Westport, CT: Greenwood Press.

Helms, J. E., and Carter, R. T. (1991). Relationships of White and Black racial identity attitudes and demographic similarity to counselor preferences. *Journal of Counseling Psychology, 38*(4), 446–457.

Helms, J. E., and Parham, T. A. (in press). The development of the Racial Identity Attitude Scale. In R. L. Jones (ed.), *Handbook of tests and measurements for Black populations* (vols. 1–2). Berkeley, CA: Cobb and Henry.

Helms, J. E., and Piper, R. E. (1994). Implications of racial identity theory for vocational psychology. *Journal of Vocational Behavior, 44*, 124–138.

Johnson, S. D. (1990). Toward clarifying culture, race, and ethnicity in the context of multicultural counseling. *Journal of Multicultural Counseling and Development, 18*(1), 41–50.

Jones, J. M. and Carter, R. T. (in press). Racism and White racial identity: Merging realities. In B. P. Bowser and R. G. Hunt (eds.), *Impacts of racism on White Americans*. Beverly Hills, CA: Sage.

Katz, J. H. (1978). *White awareness*. Norman, Oklahoma: University of Oklahoma Press.

Martin, J. K., and Nagayama-Hall, G. C. (1992). Thinking Black, thinking internal, thinking feminist. *Journal of Counseling Psychology*, 39, 509–514.

McCaine, J. (1986). *The relationships of conceptual systems to racial and gender identity, and the impact of reference group identity development on interpersonal styles of behavior and levels of anxiety.* Unpublished doctoral dissertation, University of Maryland, College Park.

McIntosh, P. (1995). White privilege and male privilege: A personal account of coming to see correspondences through work in women studies In M. L. Andersen and P. H. Collins (eds.), *Race, Class, and Gender: An Anthology*. (2nd ed). Belmont, CA: Wadsworth Publishing Co.

Mitchell, S. L., and Dell, D. M. (1992). The relationship between black students' racial identity attitudes and participation in campus organizations. *Journal of College Student Development*, 33, 39–43.

Ottavi, T. M., Pope-Davis, D. P., and Dings, J. G. (1994). The relationship between White racial identity attitudes and self-reported multicultural competencies. *Journal of Counseling Psychology*, 41, 149–154.

Parham, T. A., and Helms, J. E. (1981). The influence of Black students' racial identity attitudes on preference for counselor's race. *Journal of Counseling Psychology*, 28, 250–257.

Parham, T. A., and Helms, J. E. (1985a). Attitudes of racial identity and self-esteem in Black students: An exploratory investigation. *Journal of College Student Personnel*, 26(2), 143–147.

Parham, T. A., and Helms, J. E. (1985b). Relation of racial identity attitudes to self-actualization and affective states of Black students. *Journal of Counseling Psychology*, 32, 431–440.

Parham, T. A., and Williams, P. T. (1993). The relationship of demographic and background factors to racial identity attitudes. *Journal of Black Psychology*, 19(1), 7–24.

Pinderhughes, E. (1989). *Understanding race, ethnicity, and power: The key to efficacy in clinical practice.* New York: Free Press.

Pomales, J., Clairborn, C. D., and Lafromboise, T. D. (1987). Effects of Black students' racial identity on perceptions of White counselors varying in cultural sensitivity. *Journal of Counseling Psychology*, 33, 57–61.

Ponterotto, J. C., and Casas, J. M. (1991). *Handbook of racial/ethnic minority counseling research.* Springfield, IL: Charles C. Thomas.

Pope-Davis, D. B., and Ottavi, T. M. (1992). The influence of White racial identity attitudes on racism among faculty members: A preliminary examination. *Journal of College Student Development*, 33(5), 389–394.

Pope-Davis, D. B., and Ottavi, T. M. (1994). The relationship between racism and racial identity among White Americans: A replication and extension. *Journal of Counseling and Development*, 72, 293–297.

Pyant, C. T., and Yanico, B. J. (1991). Relationships of racial identity and gender role attitudes to Black women's psychological well-being. *Journal of Counseling Psychology*, 38, 315–322.

Rothenberg, P. S. (1995). *Race, class, and gender in the United States* (3rd ed.), New York, N.Y.: St. Martin's Press.

Smedley, A. (1993). *Race in North America: Origin and evolution of a world view.* Boulder, CO: Westview Press.

Stewart, E. C., and Bennett, M. J. (1991) *American cultural patterns: A cross-cultural perspective.* Yarmouth, Maine: Intercultural Press.

Taub, D. J., and McEwen, M. K. (1992). The relationship of racial identity attitudes to autonomy and mature interpersonal relationships in Black and White undergraduate women. *Journal of College Student Development*, 33(5), 439–446.

Terkel, S. (1992). *Race.* New York: Free Press.

Tokar, D. M., and Swanson, J. L. (1991). An investigation of the validity of Helms' (1984) model of White racial identity development. *Journal of Counseling Psychology*, 38, 296–301.

Watts, R. J., and Carter, R. T. (1991). Psychological aspects of racism in organizations. *Group and Organizational Studies*, 16(3), 328–344.

Re-examining "A Moment in History": Loss of Privilege Inside White Working-Class Masculinity in the 1990s

Lois Weis, Amira Proweller, and Craig Centrie

TWENTY

Lois Weis is Professor of Sociology of Education at SUNY Buffalo. She is the author or editor of numerous books and articles which deal with social class, race, and/or gender. Her most recent publications include *Working Class Without Work: High School Students in a De-Industrializing Economy* (Routledge, 1990) and *Beyond Silenced Voices* (with Michelle Fine, SUNY Press, 1993).

Amira Proweller is Assistant Professor of Foundations of Education at DePaul University in Chicago. She is the author of a forthcoming book, *Constructing Female Identities: Meaning Making in an Upper Middle Class Youth Culture*, to be published by SUNY Press.

Craig Centrie is Executive Director of El Museo Francisco Oller y Diego Rivera, a Latino art gallery in Buffalo, New York. He is an adjunct faculty member in the Department of American Studies, SUNY Buffalo at and is completing his Ph.D. in Social Foundations at SUNY Buffalo.

In the past ten years, we have come a long way toward unraveling the identity production processes of various groups within American society. Feminist work, in particular, has helped us understand the ways in which girls and women fashion their own identities in relation to what Dorothy Smith calls textually mediated discourses. Drawing from Foucault, Smith argues that

> social forms of consciousness, "femininity" included, can be examined as actual practices, actual activities, taking place in real time, in real places, using definite material means and under definite material conditions. Among other matters, this means that we do not neglect the "textual" dimensions of social consciousness. By texts, I mean the more or less permanent and above all replaceable forms of meaning, of writing, painting, television, film, etc. The production, distribution and uses of texts are a pervasive and highly significant dimension of contemporary social organization. "Femininity," I'm going to argue, is a distinctively textual phenomenon. But texts must not be isolated from the practices in which they are embedded and which they organize. (39)

Smith's observations are helpful as we work toward understanding the production of femininity, and work by Leslie Roman, Linda Valli, Nancy Lesko, Claire Wallace, Amira Proweller, and others enhances our knowledge of the production of womens' identities. Here we want to shift our gaze to the production of masculinity, and particularly the production of white masculinity. While feminists have undertaken work on the production of femininity and theorized it as such, scholars who have focused on the production of boys' and men's identities have rarely theorized their work specifically along gender lines. Well-known work by Paul Willis, for example, although wholly centered on the production of male culture, does not theorize it as such. Rather he employs a class-based paradigm through which he understands the lads' culture as working class, and develops an analysis through class-based terms. He fails, however, to employ theoretical work on gender to begin to decode these processes as specifically gender-based practices. Where Willis does focus on gender, he employs a classic Marxist notion of gender (and race) that speaks to the divide-and-rule tactics associated with the capitalist class. We want here to place the production of masculinity and, in particular, the production of white masculinity, at the center of our analysis, naming our focus as the culture of working-class men. Along these lines, we will highlight the production of white masculinity in this particular class fraction as it takes shape at the intersectionalities of social class, race, and gender. Theoretically this represents a departure from previous work and relies on Kimberle Crenshaw's important discussion of intersectionality as being key in the production of identity across variegated sites of meaning-making.

ON BEING WHITE

Theorists and researchers including Dorothy Smith, Carol Cohn, Peggy McIntosh, Leslie Roman, Stanley Aronowitz, Joel Kovel, Judith Rollins, bell hooks, Toni Morrison, and others have argued for the study of privileged standpoints, for "studying up." Few, however, have taken up this challenge. White standpoints, privileged standpoints, are generally taken as an unstated norm, rather than offering a site for theoretical excavation. Certainly the work of Peggy Sanday in her analysis of fraternity men at an elite university stands out as an exception (1990). Dorothy Smith's analysis of corporate workplaces excavates privileged standpoint as does Judith Rollins's (1985) study of domestic workers and their white employers. Roslyn Arlin Michelson, Melvin Oliver, and Stephen Smith similarly focus on privilege when they study the ways in which universities, in spite of affirmative action policies, work to exclude the voices of people of color.

In this discussion, we take up this challenge as we begin to unravel white male identity inside working-class culture in a time of economic restructuring and deindustrialization. Gone are the jobs in heavy industry that sustained white mens' fathers and grandfathers, that allowed them to earn the "family wage" which bought them the privilege of dominating their wives and children in the home. Most of the truly "masculine" jobs, those that demand hard physical labor, are gone, replaced by jobs in the service sector, jobs that not only pay less but do not offer the "hard" real confrontation with physicality that was embedded in jobs of former years, jobs that encouraged the production of a certain type of masculinity (Connell, 1995). We wonder, then, not only how white males in the 1980s and 1990s, in the midst of feminism, affirmative action, and gay/lesbian rights manage to sustain a sense of self, individually and collectively, but also how they sustain a belief in a system that has, at least for working-class and middle-class white males, begun to crumble, eroding their once-certain advantage over white women and women and men of color (Newman, 1993).[1] As scholars begin to recognize that "white is a color" (Roman, 1993; Wong, 1994), we write in order to make visible the borders, strategies, and fragilities of white, working-class male culture in insecure times, at, in Dorothy Smith's words, "a moment in history."[2]

This renders the study of privilege more complex than standpoint theorists generally recognize. While white working-class men are privileged via their color, they are relatively less privileged than their economically advantaged white male counterparts. Too, they are currently losing the edge they had in the economy over men of color. White working-class men represent a position of privilege at the same time they represent the loss of such privilege. It is this simultaneous moment of privilege and loss that we excavate when we turn our attention to the production of white masculinity. It is their whiteness and maleness which privileges them. But it is also in this space of historical privilege that they begin to confront the realities of loss.

Through an analysis of data collected with poor and working-class white, Latino, and African-American men and women, ages 23–35, as to their concrete experiences in family, job, community, religion, political activism, and schooling, we unearth the territory mapped by white men inside indepth interviews. Interviews were normally done in two segments, each approximately 1–1.5 hours in length, and were conducted with low-income people in Jersey City and Buffalo. Respondents were drawn from meaningful urban communities, to use William Julius Wilson's term, such as schools, Headstart, literacy centers, churches, and social agencies directly involved with local ethnic and racial communities.

We argue that white working-class men feel themselves to be under siege—in their jobs, in their neighborhoods, in their homes, and in their schools. Whether true or not in material terms, they feel themselves to be decentered, to no longer hold the position of privilege that they sense is rightfully theirs. This is, of course, stated in much more coded language, and no individual alleges that whites deserve more in the society simply by virtue of their skin color. That, unfortunately, may be one of the real outcomes of the civil rights struggle—that whites have to justify privilege in ways other than simply skin color. The expectation of privilege due to whiteness and maleness must be coded differently so that the demand for privilege does not rest on skin color alone, or skin color as related to intelligence. (We do, however, see a resurgence of this latter argument as well currently; see Herrnstein, *The Bell Curve*). Rather, these men are involved in the production of elaborate justifications of privilege, justifications which serve, in their minds, to recenter what they argue is the decentered white male. Much of their identity production swirls around the creation and maintenance of the dark "other" against which their own whiteness and goodness is necessarily understood. The social construction of this goodness, then, provides moral justification for privileged standpoints. We do not mean to argue here that this type of discursive work has not been done historically. Clearly that is not the case, as Toni Morrison and David Roediger make clear. However, what is important in the late twentieth century is that these productions co-exist with a dismantled apartheid legal system. Discursive productions swirling around race therefore undermine ostensible equality under the law. These discursive productions are, as Dorothy Smith reminds us, textually mediated. They do not arise out of the thin air of class culture, "on the ground," so to speak, but are dialectically linked to the media, popular culture, and other forms of consumerist culture that directly articulate with economic arrangements structuring daily experience.

On Whiteness

Recent work by Ruth Frankenberg (1993) is extremely provocative. As she argues, "to speak of the social construction of whiteness" reveals locations, discourses, and material relations to which the term "whiteness" applies. She further asserts that "whiteness refers to a set of locations that are historically, socially, politically, and culturally produced and moreover are intrinsically linked to unfolding relations of domination. Naming 'whiteness' displaces it from the unmarked, unnamed status that is itself an effect of its dominance. Among the effects on white people both of race privilege and of the dominance of whiteness are their seeming normativity, their structured invisibility"(6). As Frankenberg asserts, to analyze whiteness is to focus squarely on a site of constructed dominance.

In the United States, the hierarchies of race, gender, and class are embodied in the contemporary "struggle" of white maleness. As you will hear, these men work to sustain both an identity within dominance and the very hierarchies which assure their ongoing domination. Among the varied demographic categories that spill out of this race/gender hierarchy, white males are the only ones who have a vested interest in maintaining both their position and their web of power. The irony here, of course, is that white working-class males, themselves, are not the biggest beneficiaries of privilege itself. In sustaining the hierarchy, they are reproducing the very conditions that render them relatively expendable in the current economy. The assertion of dominance in one arena (race) implies the lack of such dominance in another (class). To accomplish the myth of race privilege, white males have had to sustain the notion of egalitarianism or at least the potential for equality. White male power necessitates a commitment on the part of white working-class males to engage the struggle for cultural dominance. Yet the location of struggle is far removed from the actual center of power and privilege residing inside the elite community. Lower income and working-class white males form a necessary buffer that, if eliminated or realigned along class rather than race lines, would destabilize elite domination.

Scholars of colonial discourse have highlighted the ways in which discourse about nonwestern "others" are produced simultaneously with the production of discourse about the western white "self," and this work becomes relevant to our analyses of race/gender domination. Scholarship on West European expansion documents the cultural disruptions that took place alongside economic appropriation, as well as the importance of the production of knowledge about groups of people that rendered colonization successful. As Frankenberg states, "The notion of 'epistemic violence' captures the idea that associated with West European colonial expansion is the production of modes of knowing that enabled and rationalized colonial domination from the standpoint of the West, and produced ways of conceiving other societies and cultures whose legacies endure into the present" (16). As she argues:

> Colonial discourse (like racist discourse) is in many ways heterogeneous rather than univocal, not surprising given the extent and geographical dispersion of European colonizing projects. However, if a common thread runs through the whole range of instances of colonial discourse, it is the construction of alterity along social and/or cultural lines—the construction of others conceived as fundamentally different from, and inferior to, white, European metropolitan selves (Said, 1979). It must also be noted—and this is a point perhaps more difficult to grasp upon first encounter with it—that it is precisely by means of the construction of a range of others that the self or dominant center constitutes itself. White/European self-constitution is, in other words, fundamentally tied to the process of discursive production of others, rather than preexisting that process (63).

It is precisely this point that gives rise to the voices inside Afrocentric scholarship, particularly the work of Asante (1990, 1991), which assert that the colonial European has no identity other than that which has been constructed vis-a-vis "others." In the United States, Mohanty (1988) and Roediger (1992) talk carefully about the production of white racial identity and the ways in which this identity is intimately tied to the production of black identity. What is important here is that the legacy of colonialism, more specifically the legacy of colonial discourse, rendered the category "white" a simultaneously *empty* but *normative* space—in other words, "white" could only be defined in relation to the constructed other. It is by these very processes of othering that "white" becomes the norm against which all other communities (of color) are judged (usually to be deviant). Colonialism and neocolonialism have sanctioned the normativity and structured invisibility of the West, partially through the production of knowledge but mainly by positioning an "other" as knowledge consumer. This has served to bolster the inscrutability of whiteness through naming and labeling the "other." Internal colonialization in the United States has achieved this same dynamic through the marginalization of people of color and the resulting normativity of whiteness. It is, therefore, possible to name cultures precisely because they are excluded from the normative, thus enabling the dominant "white" to engage in a process of establishing what Trin Min-ha (1989) calls boundedness. Thus much of white identity formation, stemming from colonial times to the present, involves drawing boundaries, engaging in boundedness, configuring rings around the substantively empty category "white," while at the same time discursively constructing "others." The dominant white self can, therefore, only be understood in relation to the constructed other. Without it, the white self pales into nonexistence.[3]

Central, then, to the colonial discourse and the construction of whiteness in America is the idea of the "other" being wholly and hierarchically different from the "white" self. Discursively inventing the colonial "other," for example, whites were parasitically producing an apparently stable Western, white self out of a previously nonexistent self. As Gayatri Chakravorty Spivak (1985) argues: "Europe . . . consolidated itself as sovereign subject by defining its colonies as 'others,' even as it constituted them for purposes of administration and the expansion of markets" (as cited in Frankenberg, p. 17). Thus the Western (read white) self and the colonial "other" are products of this discursive construction.

One continuing effect of colonial discourse is the production of an unnamed, unmarked, white, Western self against which all others can be named and judged. It is the unnamed, unmarked, white self which must be deconstructed, named, and marked. This paper takes up this challenge. As we will argue, white male identity is indeed parasitically coproduced as white men name and mark others, thereby naming and marking themselves. At a moment of economic crisis when white working-class males are being squeezed, the construction of others proliferates.[4]

Centered inside these constructions is the white male self—the male "under siege" in the economy, the community, and the family. We now turn to each of these sectors at their complex intersections as we explore the assault on historical privilege as white working-class men forge lives that increasingly appear to hang in the balance.

UNDER SIEGE IN THE ECONOMY

While it is indeed the case that massive restructuring has taken place in the American economy and white working-class male jobs have been substantially reduced and/or pay less than they did before, the changes in the economy are due almost entirely to the concrete decisions made by elites in order to compete more profitably in the global market economy. It is the case that there has been some preferential hiring of people of color and that this accounts for some loss of white male jobs, but the loss of jobs associated with affirmative action policies pales in comparison with job loss associated with massive restructuring and deindustrialization (Perry, Bluestone, and Harrison; Harrison and Bluestone, 1988). It is most interesting, therefore, that not one of the white men we interviewed held elites accountable for the relocation of industry, closing of industries, and so forth. Rather the finger was always pointed at affirmative action policies which allegedly accorded preferential treatment to minorities, positioned differently as undeserving. This is why, according to white males, they are not working, or not working in jobs for which they feel entitled.

Because of the economy, many working-class white males have had, at times, to seek and obtain welfare benefits. What they do discursively with welfare is very important here. Welfare becomes a site wherein people of color are defined as lazy and undeserving, while at the same time, white men define themselves as hard working and only going on welfare when absolutely necessary. This set of discursive constructions serves to draw their own boundaries of what constitutes acceptable conditions for "not working," welfare receipts, and government-sponsored programs, thus establishing a state of "boundedness." Having created an "other" who holds a set of unpleasant personal characteristics, white men can, then, at the same time, deny their own participation in the welfare state, their own experiences with unemployment, their own moments on the dole. Race affords them the opportunity to project and deny, defining themselves as the men who know how to take care of the family, and not "live off the government." The subordination of women in these families is absolutely essential to the propping up of white men vis a vis men of color. This set of discursively drawn distinctions, however, keeps white men from looking carefully at the real source of their difficulties—elites. It encourages them to trade on their whiteness, offers them a way of being white, and therefore dominant, at the expense of seriously analyzing the system and what it has, in fact, done to working-class white men. The white male critique is grounded fundamentally in the notion that people of color do not want to work.

LW: Are there tensions?
Larry: Probably not so much between them [blacks and Hispanics], but like for us, they think, I mean, it gets me angry sometimes. I don't say I'm better than anybody else. But I work for the things that I have, and they [blacks and Hispanics] figure just because you're ahead, or you know more and you do more, [that it's] because you're white. And that's not really it. We're all equal, and I feel that what I've done, I've worked for myself to get to where I'm at. . . . If they would just really try instead of just kind of hanging out on the street corners. That's something that really aggravates me, to see while I'm rushing to get to work, and everybody is just kind of milling around doing nothing.

At the heart of the white male critique is the notion that people of color, blacks, in particular, simply do not wish to work, that they are lazy. We can hear the victory of psychology over economics in this explanation. Personal, moral attributions of blame thrive despite rampant evidence of private-sector and public-sector abandonment. This is juxtaposed to notions of self which assert that although white men may be out of a job, they always want to work. From this flows an overt racial critique of affirmative action programs, as well as a somewhat more racially coded critique of welfare abusers and cheats. We, actually they, take up the issue of affirmative action first.

Pete: For the most part, it hasn't been bad. It's just that right now with these minority quotas, I think more or less, the white male has become the new minority. And that's not to point a finger at the blacks, Hispanics or the women. It's just that with all these quotas, instead of hiring the best for the job, you have to hire according to your quota system, which is still wrong.
LW: Do you have any sense of social movements? Like the Civil Rights Movement?
Pete: Civil rights, as far as I'm concerned, is being way out of proportion.
LW: Talk to me more about that.
Pete: Well, um, granted, um, the Afro-Americans were slaves over two hundred years ago. They were given their freedom. We as a country, I guess you could say, has tried to, well, I can't say all of us, but most of us, have tried to, like, make things a little more equal. Try to smooth over some of the rough spots. You have some of these other, you have some of these militants who are now claiming that after all these years, we still owe them. I think the owing time is over for everybody. Because if we go into that, then the Poles are still owed [he is Polish]. The

Germans are still owed. Jesus—the Jews are definitely still owed. I mean, you're, you're getting cremated, everybody wants to owe somebody. I think it's time to wipe that slate clean.

The critique of affirmative action (often referred to as "quotas") is that it is not "fair," that it privileges blacks, Hispanics, and at times white women above the white male, and that this contradicts notions of equal opportunity and a flat playing field. It is noteworthy that nowhere in these narratives is there any recognition of the fact that white men as a group have been historically privileged, irrespective of individual merit.

Where men give credence to affirmative action, it takes highly essentialist forms. John, for example, feels that affirmative action programs "have their place," that they "shouldn't be completely out of the question." For example, he feels that "women can speak with women or children a lot better than men can"; and that, "in the areas of crime, you have to have blacks and Hispanics working in community programs, so you have to have certain jobs and responsibilities where they can deal with people, like say, with people of their own race or background." In other words, women should be privileged for *certain* jobs dealing with women and children, and blacks and Hispanics should be privileged in jobs dealing with crime. That is where, he suggests, affirmative action is useful. In general, though, white men concur with Tom when he states, "as soon as they [blacks] don't get a job, they yell discrimination. . . . But the ones who are really lazy, don't want it [to become educated and work one's way up], they start yelling discrimination so they can just get the job and they're not even qualified for it. And they might take it away from, whether it's a, you know, a woman or a guy [white]."

The assertions about affirmative action offer white men a way of "othering" African Americans, in particular. "We" whites, even though we might be unemployed, want to work. "They," blacks, just want a free ride—they just want to get the job without having to really work for it. This encourages the discursive coconstruction of blacks as lazy, as wanting a handout, unlike hard-working whites. This theme is further elaborated in discussions of welfare abusers and cheats.

AP: Have you ever applied for welfare?

Ron: No.

AP: Or, have you ever had to?

Ron: Never had to. I, probably very early in our marriage, um, when the first company I worked for, and they closed up. And um, we, we went through a period where we probably could have, had we applied, I think we would have been eligible. I mean, our income was really low enough that we probably should have.

AP: But you didn't. How come?

Ron: I guess both of us pretty much feel the same way. You know, we look at welfare as being something, um, less than admirable.

AP: And that's what it would have amounted to for you? Sort of less than admirable?

Ron: Yeah, I think, had we been any lower, as far as income and gotten to the point where we absolutely couldn't even afford to eat. Um, I mean, I'm not opposed to doing what I have to do. . . . But, um, to me, it should be a strictly a last resort. I think the welfare system is very much abused.

AP: Can you talk to me a little about that?

Ron: Well, um, . . . I think for the most part, I think most people get out of life what they put into it. You know, because some people have more obstacles than others, there's no doubt about it. But I think a lot of people just expect things to come to them, and when it doesn't, you know, they've got the government to fall back on. . . . You know, I think it [falling back on the government] is more common for black people. . . . I mean social services, in general, I think, is certainly necessary, and Sheila [wife] and I have taken advantage of them. We've got food stamps several times. . . . But, you know, as soon as I was able to get off it, I did. And not for any noble reasons, but just, you know, I think I'd rather be able to support myself than have things handed to me.

* * *

CC: What do you think of welfare?
Tom: I think it's good for people who deserve it. And I think there's a lot of people that don't deserve it. The system stinks. If you're on welfare, I think if you're willing to work, I think the . . . you know, I think the State should, I mean look out here, there's a lot of things that need to be cleaned up. Let 'em clean the streets; let 'em do something. Just don't let 'em sit at home and just collect their check. There's some that can't [work]. There's some who deserve it and they have to . . . for the most part, yeah. I mean, if you deserved it, fine. But if you don't, don't play the system.

Katherine Newman's (1993) insights are particularly helpful here. She suggests that:

American culture is allergic to the idea that impersonal forces control individual destiny. Rather we prefer to think of our lives as products of our own efforts. Through hard work, innate ability and competition, the good prosper and the weak drop by the wayside. Accordingly, the end results in peoples' lives—their occupations, material possessions, and the recognition accorded by friends and associates—are proof of the underlying stuff of which they are made. Of course, when the fairy tale comes true, the flip side of meritocratic individualism emerges with full force. Those who prosper—the morally superior—deserve every bit of their material comfort. (p. 89)

White men, then, script poor blacks as deserving of their plight and unwilling to work, while they [white men] "sincerely" strive for the American Dream. They, that is, white men are coconstructed as highly deserving, willing to work, and eager to participate in the American economy.

Although there are some exceptions to this, the primary function of discussions about welfare abusers is to draw the boundaries of acceptable welfare receipt *at themselves*—the hard-working white man who is trying to support his family. Pete, for example, states, "There's definitely some people who abuse the system, I can see that. But then there are people who, when you need it, you know, it's like they have something to fall back on. And they're [the case workers] basically shoving everybody into one category. They're [all welfare recipients] all users. But these [the case workers] are the same people that if the county closes them off, they won't have a job, and they're going to be there next too." Since most of the case workers are white, Pete is discursively aligning himself with the hard-working people who have just fallen on hard times, unlike the abusers, largely black, who exploit the system. His criticism of the case workers is that they treat all welfare recipients as cheats, as like African-Americans, thus denying differential positionality vis a vis welfare.

The discussions of affirmative action and welfare abuse enable white men to draw distinctions between themselves and a largely black "other," whom they discursively construct as lazy, unwilling to do what is necessary to get a job, and more than happy to take advantage of government handouts, including affirmative action programs, which they script as a "handout," as going to those undeserving. In discursively constructing a black "other," white men simultaneously construct themselves as hard working and only going on welfare and accepting government help when absolutely necessary.

This splitting of Self and Other is reminiscent of Weis's working-class white high school boys. Boys in Freeway High constructed the black "other" as highly sexualized and drug prone. This construction at one and the same time served to authorize white boys as clean, respectful of women, and definitely heterosexual. Beyond high school, into young adulthood, these discursive constructions layer on top of one another, so that black men, in particular, are now discursively constructed as lazy, unwilling to work, and so forth. This weaves through the high school constructions revolving around drugs and sexuality, ultimately leaving young white men highly resentful of blacks in general, whom they see as drug prone, oversexualized, and lazy, but also of affirmative action programs, in particular, which they feel privileges inferior human beings. This, then, is social critique to white men. Interestingly enough, it leaves totally unexamined and even unrecognized the role of whites who self-consciously closed industries and/or enabled legislation which moved capital across state and international borders, thus interrupting far more white male jobs than affirmative action ever could (or has). (Perry, 1987; Bluestone and Harrison, 1982).

UNDER SIEGE IN THE NEIGHBORHOOD

A felt assault invades the perceptions of many white men in talk about their neighborhoods as they begin to express a sense of no longer belonging, or that their neighborhood is "deteriorating," further evidence that it is no longer a space that belongs to them in both physical and psychological terms. Most often this encroaching instability is attributed to an influx of blacks or Hispanics who they clearly position as the Other. As Larry says;

I really feel—I'm not going to say out of place. I do. I've grown up in the neighborhood [the Italian west side], but I don't really feel as though I belong here anymore. I don't know, not strictly because I'm a white male, and there's not many of us. I mean, there's not really that many in my neighborhood that I can say, "Well, I have a neighbor, the guy who lives next door to me or the somebody across the street." There is, I'm kind of like the minority. I'm, I don't really, there's not a lot of people I associate with. There's some people I'll say hello to, or, you know, you talk with your neighbors to associate.

A focus group discussion with three men in a west-side church uncovers similar sentiments:

CC: What was it like when you guys were little?
Ron: I think it was different—ten times different.
Craig: What did happen? What did you see happen?
Ron: I just seen more kids on the streets, more of them starting to dress up like the rappers on TV, white kids, black kids, Hispanic, it didn't matter. I just seen, you know, more hanging out.
Pete: The west side has always been like a low income type of area, and it's always been a tough neighborhood. But what I think is, more or less, it's getting more violent. We both went to Grover [high school], so we know what it's like to grow up in kind of like a tough atmosphere, but nothing like it is now. There's a lot of drug dealing, a lot of guns.
Ron: The thing is, they're getting younger.

Pete: Thirteen, fourteen-year-old kids are carrying guns. It's really not that out in the open, but you hear about it. You hear about the shootings. . . . There was a rape at School 18 [elementary school], maybe about a month ago. I heard it on the news.
Ron: . . . I did see a drug bust. As a matter of fact, right on my street. The cop more or less blocked me in my driveway, because they just pull up, and they park unmarked cars, and they just rushed into a couple of houses down.

Ron, in an individual interview, elaborates as follows:

A: Just look at the school. It's just . . . you know . . . and you hear the loud music all over the place now. I mean, it's not as bad as I might be making it sound . . . but . . . my car got broken into, stuff like that . . . that never happened back then.
Q: It didn't?
A: Uh uh. I'd say up to four-five years ago, it didn't happen.
Q: Interesting. What proportion of the people are still Italian?
A: There's a lot of older ones still there. Um, oh, my God, I'd say 30 to 40 percent.
Q: Still? Well that's quite high then.
A: . . . See, you have the lower west side and the upper west side, say . . . you know what I'm talking about . . . that's predominantly Puerto Rican. The upper west side still has got a lot of Italians through there.
Q: But you said a lot of the Puerto Ricans and blacks are moving into the upper west side?
A: Oh yeah, they're coming. I mean, which is . . . which is fine. I have no problem with that. A lot of Italians are moving to the North side, so that's starting to be Italian Heaven over there. But there's been a definite change, no doubt about it.

Ron is interesting since he, himself, is a border crosser in the sense that his girlfriend (who he later became engaged to) is Puerto Rican. However this presents no conceptual difficulty for him since she is among those Puerto Rican families that have been there for a while and who also object to the new Puerto Ricans and blacks moving in. As he notes, "Yeh, she'll talk to me. Coming from her mouth herself, she would say the same thing I did. It's really sad I can't walk through my old neighborhood, you know, it's really sick. It's ignorant, you know. They, her family, feels the same way. Her mother, because her mother doesn't have a car, so she has to walk a lot of places, and she knows what's going on."
Dave, who during the course of our interview let us know that he was Native American, said the following:

A: It was a real friendly neighborhood. I lived on Connecticut and Normal Avenue, and at the time, it was a predominantly Italian neighborhood. It was very close knit. I mean, you could leave your doors open and bikes unchained, and all that kind of stuff, and now it's not like that anymore.
Q: How is it different?
A: Well, now it's a Hispanic and black neighborhood, and you practically have to . . . you know . . . chain things up, nail them down, put bolts on them, and it's something that shouldn't be . . . we should all be able to live together and respect each other's personal artifacts, whatever they are.

Many of the white men interviewed hope to exit the areas they define as "under siege" as soon as they they can. In Larry's case, he has bought some land in a suburb where his two brothers live, because he can't imagine raising children where he currently resides. Several others plan to move to the suburbs, or to North Buffalo, when they are married, and especially when they have children. This will not necessarily be easy to accomplish, since many are living in properties owned by their parents, properties bought with monies that white privilege was able to amass in the parental generation, when white men were easily able to secure full-time work in industry. Those that foresee staying in the city are working to establish block clubs, neighborhood watches, and small-scale organizations designed to patrol the borders of their communities. Tom, for example, is very active in the block club in his community.

Q: What is the purpose of the block club?
A: To watch the neighborhood. You know, if you see trouble happening, to call 911. Or if one of the neighbors is having a problem, you know, it's better to come out in groups, you know, don't cause any violence. . . . And you know, if we see somebody else, like the lady across the street is an older elderly lady. And we watch for her. You know, we see somebody strange up that driveway or at her house, you know, we'll confront them. We'll ask them [who they are]. And I think that shows too. I think people see that.

While he narrates this as very supportive, and indeed it is in many ways, the borders they are patrolling are those basically encasing the white community against encroaching "others." It is whiteness that people are attempting to protect in these neighborhoods. This does not deny the fact that some blacks live in white neighborhoods as well, but rather points out that in these white neighborhoods bordered by the "other," it is the other against whom white communities are attempting to protect themselves. This is also not to ignore the fact that several families of color live in these white neighborhoods, but rather to note that these families are considered settled—as "just like us" in the case of the "Spanish" family who lived in the Italian neighborhood. It is the racial "other"—the "other" constructed as lazy, violent, dangerous, as not working, as hanging around, that is at issue here. And it is this group to whom block clubs are formed in response. As Tom says, "If I move, it's going to be because I want to move, not because the kids are going to force me out. You know, I'm not afraid of the kids. I'm not afraid of, you know, people moving in. You know, I'm not afraid of the colored coming in. They don't bother me. If I'm going to move, it will be because [I want to]." In the meantime, he is organizing with other white men and white women to patrol the borders of his neighborhood, a relatively "safe space," from the onslaught of the "other."

Some, like Bill below, recognize that the block clubs can engage in seemingly racist practices:

Q: Do you belong to any groups of any kind?
A: No, none.
Q: Um, any groups that, like anything that tries to change the community? Like, do you belong to a block club?
A: Um, the block club I won't join . . . I totally hate their views. I mean, they're like, "Get them out, kick their ass," just . . .
Q: Who is saying "Get them out, kick their ass"?
A: Oh, people who live a few doors from me. And they're very prejudiced.
Q: So, they're whites?
A: Yeah.
Q: Whites want to kick out the blacks.
A: Exactly. It doesn't matter to them if they're good or bad. You know if they're renters or

owners. They just want them out. And talking to them, I mean their views on good white people is ridiculous, because there's a few streets over, um, off William, and he, well, the guy who,
whose main view, he loves that area because it's mostly white.
Q: Is that a place called Kaisertown?
A: No. It's off of William by the Dolsky Center. About half way to the Dolsky Center. And,
um, I mean, it's equivalency, it's the equivalency of black people, black kids running around in
their underwear, where, here's white kids running around in their underwear. It's like, he thinks
it's a much better area. Why, because you can buy your crack there? Which, um, he does.

White men then take up a protectionist stance in an effort to secure their "turf" from assault
in a time of increasing racial diversification and with that, the fracturing of working-class neighborhoods. Block clubs emerge as freely organized and co-opted spaces for group meeting and exchange designed to bolster the community, but they also exist as site for the deployment of tactical
strategies meant to arm the neighborhood against the other. A "good" community initiative in the
interests of engagement across difference thus doubles as a legitimate form of border patrolling.
Initiatives on the part of white working-class men need, then, to be seen as counter-strategies for
reclaiming lost power and privilege in their communities which they perceive as being under immediate threat of dislocation.

Under Siege in the Home: Contesting Gender Roles

White working-class men express strong sentiment about the family and, specifically, about male
roles and responsibilities within the family. The family is idealized and even valorized, at least in
theory, if not altogether in practice. For men, who have lost real material space inside shopfloor
culture, they turn to the family and attempt to assert or re-assert dominance in that realm. While
this may have always been the case, as Lillian Rubin (1976) and others have argued about the
working-class family, the move to sustain dominance in the white working-class home is particularly key at this moment in time where there are genuine material losses in other spheres of working-class life. Men no longer have a clear-cut material sphere in which they can assert lived power.
Working-class men are forced, in a sense, into a symbolic realm, the realm of family, which is not
their material space, in order to assert a form of symbolic dominance. Turning to the family as the
symbolic domain of male power, they insist or re-insist on reclaiming gender privilege. Much of
the patrolling of the borders of community must be seen in these terms as well. The borders of
community as patrolled by white men are drawn in the name of the family—men are protecting
their wives and children (all of whom are constructed as absolutely less than men) from what they
construct as an encroaching assault. Thus they envelop the family sphere within their own symbolic dominance, a dominance which they substitute, although not wholly consciously or completely, for their former authority in the material realm.
   The next set of conversations was conducted in a focus group in an Italian church located in
one of the borderlands of Buffalo. The family is absolutely essential to the construction of manhood in these narratives and, indeed, to the propping up of the discourse of masculinity inside
working-class culture:

CC: What do you think the role of the family is right now?
Pete: I think there is definitely a fall in the American family right now.
Ron: That's the major contributor to any of the problems, I think.

Pete: What I see it is, is it used to be a man could work, make a paycheck, and the woman could stay home and be a housewife, but now you need either two incomes or a man cannot support the family, he cannot get a job to support the family, so he bolts, he leaves, and goes on his own, and that's what I see. . . . He takes the easy way out. All the other pressures of the world. . . .

CC: What other pressures?

Pete: The age itself. Men are tempted away from their wives; wives are tempted away from their husbands because of sex.

CC: Is that new, though?

Ron: No. It's not new, but it's more frequent now because of everything—it's just thrown at you no matter what. You could watch TV and you could just turn it—I mean even regular cable—and you could see some gross stuff, even for kids, you know. It's the temptation of bad. It's the temptation of money and it's just, you know, it's the temptation of well, I've got to please myself first.

CC: What do you think is going to happen to the family in the future? Is it going to get better or worse?

Ron: I hate to say it, I don't think it's going to get better.

Pete and Ron attribute what they see as the fall in the American family to a variety of factors. In fact, we hear them searching for explanations as they scan Reagonomics, popular culture (cable TV), commodified sex, and the lack of jobs. However, it is clear in these narratives that the lynchpin of the family is the man as breadwinner and protector of wife and children. The economy and popular culture have made that difficult since two people now need to work, and sex tempts both men and women away from family commitments. Thus there is a moral component to the breakdown of the American family as well. But the male as provider must, they argue, be restored if the family is to regain its strength. There is a clear valorization of traditional gender-based roles, without which the family is undermined.

CC: Do you think that the roles of men and women are now changing to some extent because of the changes in the family and the changes in society?

Pete: Definitely. There is more of a leadership role for women.

Ron: There is nothing wrong—I mean I agree with women being able to be independent and stuff like that, but the women's lib, when that started, it really threw things into a little bit of chaos too because, like you said, the family. For one thing, it took the mother out of the family.

Pete: Right. The role of the woman has definitely changed because the woman has to work now.

Ron: Now there are babysitters or the baby is at day care all day long.

Pete: I think for one thing, the roles have changed because again, of the single parent households. There is a lot of that, and the mother has to be the father and the mother at the same time.

Ron: Yeah that's true.

Pete: And it's very hard for a mother to discipline a teenage boy.

Ron: You need two parents.

CC: Given everything that you just said right now, what is the meaning of maleness?

Pete: First of all, I think the meaning of maleness is more than, you know, helping to produce a child. I still think that the meaning of maleness is to go out, earn a living, support a family, I still feel that should be the meaning of maleness. I don't know if it is, I really don't think it is.

Ron: . . . Just like pretty much what he said. Just to keep—a real man will keep what he be-

lieves in and not stray from it to please everybody. He'll get a wife. He'll love her uncondi-
tionally and she, in return, will respect him and want to do things for him, and vice versa, and
just to follow the example of maybe the church or of Christ. That's pretty much it. Just an un-
selfish provider willing to sacrifice for his family, or sacrifice for whoever, and not take everyone else's values, to please the other person.

Pete: . . . I think they should be responsible. The male should be more responsible for the family.

Ron: Right, exactly. That's what he is in society. Like it was back in the days—like the *Leave
It to Beaver* times, when the man went out, and the woman stayed home.

Pete: I think that's when there were really no problems in America. I don't know, I wasn't
there, but from what I see, it seemed like everything was better.

Men reclaim their waning dominance in the material sector by centering the family in their collective memory of the past as youth coming of age, from which point they move toward its valorization as the main resource for financial, but, even more to the point, emotional support.
These same men continue to draw on their memories and present experiences as they pin their
hopes for the future on family as well, projecting their own marriages, their own families, and
building lives in neighborhoods and communities in proximity to family and kin.

Conversation that captures the importance of the intact family sets the stage for discussion of
the central role played by men in the household as they argue their significance to the home space
despite the fact that they understand themselves as only symbolically dominant therein. In other
words, these men are left to reclaim the waning privileges of male dominance through a traditional vocabulary of gender roles and relationships

Q: What's the most important thing in terms of life?

Pete: Family.

Q: Why?

Pete: Because that's your flesh and blood. That's who you grew up with. That's who loves you
the most. That's your most trusted, prize possession, your family. That is the most important
thing in my life.

Q: Anything else?

Pete: Belief in God and sticking together as a family, and that's basically it.

The centrality of family to the provision of emotional support inside working-class culture is best
captured in Pete's admission of family as "your most trusted, prize possession." Attaching material value to the family unit allows white working-class men to position the family as the fulcrum
point on which masculine domination hinges. This line of argument is sustained inside Tom's attention to the family and the provisor of emotional support whose example makes the future possible.

Q: Could you have predicted that your family would have been so important to you? Do you
come from a family where your family is . . .

Tom: Yes, Yes. Even though my sisters—like I said, the one sister—I mean, we . . . I'm still close.
I mean, if she calls me to do something, I'll still do it for her. Ahm, my parents were close . . .

Q: So you're not surprised to see this in yourself?

Tom: No. Ahm, my father's brothers and sisters, my mother, on her side, the cousins and that,
we're just close. . . . I mean, it just goes from brother and sister, from wife and kids to brother
and the whole family.

224

Establishing the foundational aspects of the family unit, these white working-class men are able to build an argument that validates male authority, albeit symbolic, inside the home. Normalization of working-class cultural forms mandates a vocabulary that subscribes to the traditional sexual division of labor inside the home. Out of these terms, white working-class men position themselves as bordered by white women who they see as not being in their correct place. Men are trying hard to re-assert male dominance in the home, attempting to make certain that they maintain dominance in this symbolic realm. In other words, although the space materially belongs, in large measure, to women, and the men wish it to stay that way, they want to make it absolutely clear that they are dominant symbolically. They are the head of the household even though they do not materially inhabit and/or take care of this household in ways they expect of their women. While this has always gone on, the depth to which this is being asserted, we would argue, is due to the erosion of dominance in their own material space, shop floors and so forth in the wage labor sector.

REFERENCES

Aronowitz, Stanley. 1992. *The Politics of Identity*. New York: Routledge.

Asante, Molefi K., and Mark T. Mattson. 1991. *Historical and Cultural Atlas of Africans*. New York: Maxwell Macmillan International.

Asante, Molefi K. 1990. *Kemet Afrocentricity and Knowledge*. Trenton, New Jersey: Africa World Press.

Bluestone, Barry, and Bennett Harison. 1982. *The Deindustrialization of America: Plant Closing, Community Abandonment, and the Dismantling of Basic Industry*. New York: Basic Books.

Cesaire, Aime. 1969. *Return to My Native Land*. Baltimore: Penguin Books.

Cesaire, Aime. 1955, 1962. *Discourse sur colonialisme*. Paris: Presence Africaine.

Cesaire, Aime. 1947. *Cahier d'un retour au pays natal*. New York: Brentano's.

Connell, R. W. 1995. *Masculinities*. Cambridge: Polity Press.

Fanon, Franz. 1967. *Black Skin, White Masks*. New York: Grove Weidenfeld.

Fanon, Franz. 1967. *Pour la revolution*. New York: Africaine Monthly Review Press.

Fanon, Franz. 1963. *The Wreched of the Earth*. New York: Grove Press.

Fine, Michelle. 1993. "Sexuality, Schooling, and Adolescent Females: The Missing Discourse of Desire." In Weis, Lois, and Michelle Fine (eds.), *Beyond Silenced Voices: Class, Race, and Gender in United States Schools*. Albany: State University of New York Press.

Foucault, Michel. 1980. *The History of Sexuality*, Vol. 1. New York: Vintage Press.

Frankenberg, Ruth. 1993. *White Women, Race Matters: The Social Construction of Whiteness*. Minneapolis: University of Minnesota Press.

Harrison, Bennett, and Barry Bluestone. 1988. *The Great U-Turn: Corporate Restructuring and Polarizing of America*. New York: Basic Books.

Herrnstein, Richard J. 1994. *The Bell Curve: Intelligence and Class Structure in American Life*. New York: Free Press.

hooks, bell. 1989. *Talking Back, Thinking Feminist, Thinking Black*. Boston: South End Press.

Lesko, Nancy. 1988. *Symbolizing Society: Stories, Rites and Structure in a Catholic High School*. New York: Falmer.

Memmi, Albert. 1965. *The Colonizer and the Colonized*. Boston: Beacon Press.

Michelson, Roslyn Arlin, Stephen Samuel Smith, and Melvin L. Oliver. 1993. "Breaking through the Barriers: African American Job Candidates and the Academic Hiring Process." In Lois Weis and Michelle Fine (eds.), *Beyond Silenced Voices*. Albany: State University of New York Press.

Mohanty, C. T. 1988. "Under Western Eyes: Feminist Scholarship and Colonial Discourses." *Feminist Review* 30, 61–88.

Morrison, Toni. 1992. *Playing in the Dark: Whiteness and the Literary Imagination*. Cambridge, Massachusetts: Harvard University Press.

Newman, Katherine S. 1993. *Declining Fortunes: The Withering of American Dream*. New York: Basic Books.

Perry, David. 1987. "The Politics of Dependency in Deindustrializing America: The Case of Buffalo, New York." In Michael Smith and Joe Feagin (eds.), *The Capitalist City: Global Restructuring and Community Politics*. Oxford (Oxfordshire) and New York: Basil Blackwell.

Price-Marce, Jean. 1928. *Ainsi parla l'oncle*. Port Au Prince: Imprinerie du Comparegne.

Proweller, Amira. 1995. "Inside Absence: An Ethnography of Female Identity Construction in an Upper Middle Class Youth Culture." Unpublished Ph.D. dissertation, SUNY Buffalo.

Roediger, David R. 1991. *The Wages of Whiteness: Race and the Making of the American Working Class*. New York: Verso.

Rollins, Judith. 1985. *Between Women: Domestics and Their Employers*. Philadelphia: Temple University Press.

Roman, Leslie G. 1993. "White Is a Color! White Defensiveness, Postmodernism, and Anti-Racist Pedagogy." In Cameron McCarthy and Warren Crichlow (eds.) *Race, Identity, and Representation in Education*. New York: Routlege.

Roman, Leslie, and Linda K. Christian-Smith (eds.). 1988. *Becoming Feminine: The Politics of Popular Culture*. Philadelphia: Falmer Press.

Rubin, Lillian. 1976. *Worlds of Pain*. New York: Basic Books.

Sanday, Peggy. 1990. *Fraternity Gang Rape: Sex, Brotherhood, and Privilege on Campus*. New York: New York University Press.

Senghor, Leopold. 1961. *Nation et voi Africaine du Socialisme*. Paris: Presence Africaine.

Smith, Dorothy E. 1988. "Femininity as Discourse." In Leslie G. Roman and Linda K. Christian-Smith (eds.), *Becoming Feminine: The Politics of Popular Culture*. Philadelphia: Falmer Press.

Spivak, Gayatri Chakravorty. 1990. "Can the Subaltern Speak?" In S. Harasym (ed.), *The Post-Colonial Critic: Issues, Strategies, Dialogues*. New York: Routledge, pp. 271–313.

Trinh, Min-ha. 1989. *Woman, Native, Other*. Bloomington: The University of Indiana Press.

Valli, Linda. 1986. *Becoming Clerical Workers*. Boston: Routledge and Kegan Paul.

Wallace Claire. 1987. *For Richer, for Poorer: Growing Up In and Out of Work*. London, New York: Tavistock.

Whatley, Marianne. 1985, 1987. "Raging Hormones and Powerful Cars: The Construction of Men's Sexuality in School Sex Education and Popular Adolescent Films." In Henry Giroux, *Postmodernism, Feminism, and Cultural Politics: Redrawing Educational Boundaries*. Albany: State University of New York Press, 1991.

Willis, Paul. 1977. *Learning to Labour: How Working Class Kids Get Working Class Jobs*. Farnborough, England: Saxon House

Wilson, William J. 1980. *The Declining Significance of Race: Blacks and Changing American Institutions*. Chicago: University of Chicago Press.

Wong, Mun. 1994. "Di(s)-secting and di(s)-closing Whiteness, 'Two Tales From Psychology.' " *Feminism and Psychology* 4, 133–153.

NOTES

This study is supported through generous funds from the Spencer Foundation. Michelle Fine and Lois Weis are co-investigators on the grant.

1. A similar erosion of privilege existed for white males in the Southern United States after the Civil War. This era found white men "retaliating" for their felt loss of privilege through the organization of hate groups like the Ku Klux Klan.

2. The now classic works of Franz Fanon, *Black Skin, White Masks* and *The Wretched of the Earth* and Albert Memmi's *The Colonizer and the Colonized* have undertaken the delicate task of providing a psychological analysis of the colonial identity complex of both the colonizer and the colonized. These authors have

laid the foundation for African-American and White scholars to examine the complex nature of racial identity as it intersects with class and gender in the current discourse on the loss of privilege inside the culture of white working-class males.

3. The European construction of the colonized identity has given voice to scholars of color who earlier in the twentieth century began to question its validity. Authors of negritude, among them Aime Cesaire, Leopold Senghor, and Jean Price-Mars, have asked the question—are we French or are we Black—in protest of the French Metropolitan practice of linguistic and cultural imperialism. This movement has given rise to an impressive body of work which deconstructs the identity construction of Caribbean as well as North and West Africans under French colonial or neocolonial domination, legislating French colonialist identification as the "superior white."

4. One might speculate as to the extent to which these proliferations are linked to social change. One might speculate, for example, that the intensification of such coproductions is strongly linked historically to economic crisis and/or colonial expansion. One could empirically examine this claim.

White Screens:
Media and Cultural Studies

Race, Suburban Resentment, and the Representation of the Inner City in Contemporary Film and Television

Cameron McCarthy, Alicia Rodriquez, Shuaib Meecham, Stephen David,
Carrie Wilson-Brown, Heriberto Godina, K. E. Supryia, and Ed Buendia

Cameron McCarthy teaches cultural studies and curriculum theory at the University of Illinois at Urbana-Champaign. He is Associate Professor of Communications in the Institute of Communications Research. He is also jointly appointed in the departments of Curriculum and Instruction and Educational Policy Studies. He has published widely on the topics of problems with neomarxist writings on race and education, institutional support for teaching, and school ritual and adolescent identities, in journals such as *Harvard Educational Review, Oxford Review of Education, Educational Theory, Curriculum Studies,* the *Journal of Curriculum Theorizing, Urban Education, Education and Society, Contemporary Sociology, Interchange,* the *Journal of Education,* and the *European Journal of Intercultural Studies.* Cameron is the author of *Race and Curriculum* (1990) published by Falmer Press. With Chris Richards of the Institute of Education at the University of London and Glenn Hudak of Columbia University, he is currently working on a book on popular music and adolescent identities entitled *Sound Identities,* to be published by Garland Press. Along with Warren Crichlow of the University of Rochester he is the coeditor of *Race, Identity and Representation in Education* published by Routledge last fall. Cameron is the editor of a special issue of the journal *Discourse* on the topic "Popular Music and Adolescent Identity." He is also a coeditor of a special issue of *Cultural Studies* on Toni Morrison and Pedagogy. In 1994, a translation (*Racismo Curriculum*) of his *Racism and Curriculum* book was published in the Critical Pedagogy Series of Morata Press in Madrid, Spain. He is currently under contract with Routledge for his latest book, *The Uses of Culture.*

INTRODUCTION

Much contemporary mainstream and radical theorizing on race and popular culture places television, film, and advertising outside the circuits of social meanings, as though these practices were pre-existing, self-constituting technologies that then exert effects on an undifferentiated mass public (Parenti, 1992; Postman, 1986). This essay counters that tendency. We see television and film as fulfilling a certain bardic function, singing back to society lullabies about what a large hegemonic part of it "already knows." Like Richard Campbell (1987), we reject the vertical model of communication that insists on encoding/decoding. We are more inclined to theorize the operation of communicative power in horizontal or rhizomatic terms. Television and film, then, address and position viewers at the "center" of a cultural map in which suburban, middle-class values "triumph" over practices that drift away from mainstream social norms. In this arrangement, the suburb, in the language of Christopher Lasch (1991), becomes "The True and Only Heaven": the great incubator and harbinger of neo-evolutionary development, progress, and modernity in an erstwhile unstable and unreliable world.

Suburban dweller here refers to all those agents travelling in the covered wagons of post-sixties white flight from America's increasingly black, increasingly immigrant urban centers. White flight created settlements and catchment areas that fanned out farther and farther away from the city's inner radius, thereby establishing the racial character of the suburban-urban divide (Wilson, 1994). As tax-based revenues, resources, and services followed America's fleeing middle classes out of the city, a great gulf opened up between the suburban dweller and America's inner-city resident. Into this void contemporary television, film, and popular culture entered creating the most poignantly sordid fantasies of inner-city degeneracy and moral decrepitude. These representations of urban life would serve as markers of the distance the suburban dweller had travelled away from perdition. Televisual and filmic fantasies would also underscore the extent to which the inner-city dweller was irredeemably lost in the dystopic urban core. Within the broad vocabulary of representational techniques at its disposal, the preference for the medium shot in television tells the suburban viewer, "We are one with you," as the body of the television subject seems to correspond one-for-one with the viewer.

As Raymond Williams (1974) argues in *Television: Technology and Cultural Form*, television, film, advertising, textbooks, and so forth are powerful forces situated in cultural circuits themselves—not outside as some pure technological or elemental force or some fourth estate, as the professional ideology of mainstream journalism tends to suggest. These are circuits that consist of a proliferation of capacities, interests, needs, desires, priorities, and commitments—fields of affiliation and fields of association.

One such circuit is the discourse of resentment, or the practice of defining one's identity through the negation of the other. This essay will call attention to this discourse in contemporary race relations and point to the critical coordinating role of news magazines, television, the Hollywood film industry, and the common sense of black filmmakers themselves in the reproduction and maintenance of the discourse of resentment—particularly its supporting themes of crime, violence, and suburban security.

Drawing on the theories of identity formation in the writings of C. L. R. James (1978, 1993) and Friedrich Nietzsche (1967), we argue that the filmic and electronic media play a critical role in the production and channelling of suburban anxieties and retributive morality onto its central target: the depressed inner city. These developments deeply inform race relations in late-twentieth-century society. These race relations are conducted in the field of simulation as before a putative public court of appeal (Baudrillard, 1983).

STANDING ON THE PYRES OF RESENTMENT

I feel deadly faint, bowed and humped, as though I were Adam, staggering beneath the piled centuries since Paradise. (Ahab in Herman Melville's *Moby Dick* [1851, p. 535])

These words uttered in a moment of crisis in the nineteenth-century canonical text of Herman Melville's *Moby Dick* (1851) might well have been uttered by Michael Douglas as D-fens in the contemporary popular cultural text of *Falling Down* (1993), or by Douglas as Tom Sanders in the antifeminist, proto-resentment film, *Disclosure* (1995). Douglas is the great twentieth-century suburban middle-class male victim, flattened and spread out against the surface of a narcotic screen "like a patient etherized upon a table" (Eliot, 1964, p. 11).

In two extraordinary texts written in the late forties, *Mariners, Renegades, and Castaways: The Story of Herman Melville and the World We Live in* (1978) and *American Civilization* (1993), C. L. R. James made the provocative observation that American popular cultural texts—

popular film, popular music, soap operas, comic strips, and detective novels—offered sharper intellectual lines of insight into the contradictions and tensions of modern life in postindustrial society than the entire corpus of academic work in the social sciences. For James, comic strips such as *Dick Tracy* (first published in 1931) and popular films such as Charlie Chaplin's *Modern Times* (1936) and John Huston's *The Maltese Falcon* (1941, based on the novel by Dashiell Hammett) were direct aesthetic descendants of Melville's *Moby Dick*. These popular texts removed the veil that covered twentieth-century social relations "too terrible to relate," except in the realm of fantasy and imagination (Morrison, 1990, p. 302).

For James, these popular texts foregrounded the rise of a new historical subject on the national and world stage: the resentment-type personality. This subject was a projection of the overrationalization and sedimented overdeterminations of the modern industrial age ("the fearful mechanical power of an industrial civilization which is now advancing by incredible leaps and bounds and bringing at the same time mechanization and destruction of the human personality," [1978, p. 8]). James's new subject articulated an authoritarian populism: the mutant, acerbic and emotionally charged common sense of the professional middle class (Douglas with a satchel of hand grenades in *Falling Down*, Harry and Louise of the anti–health care reform ads). This authoritarian personality was, in James's view, willing to wreck all in the hell-bent prosecution of his own moral agenda and personal ambition. According to James, what was unusual and egregious about the resentment personality type in *Moby Dick* and the nineteenth-century world of Melville had become pseudonormative by the time of *The Maltese Falcon* in the 1940s—a period marked by the rise of what James (1993) called "nonchalant cynicism" (p. 125).

Thus in *The Maltese Falcon* (1941), detective Sam Spade (Humphrey Bogart) puts the woman he loves in jail for the murder of his corrupt partner, Miles Archer. Their love is overridden by the ideology of professionalism and the socionormative priority of making wrongdoers pay. As the paranoid Spade says plaintively to his lover, "I don't even like the idea of thinking there might be one chance in a hundred that you'd played me for a sucker" (Spade quoted in James, 1993, p. 125). In Sam Spade's world, lovers do not have any special privileges beyond the domestic sphere. Spade is playing by his own ethics and chucking human relations and feelings as encumbering eruptions of irrationality. This is a tart dish of public common sense. As the eternal proxy for middle-American values, Spade holds the line against the threat of invasion by the morally corrupt other, the socially different and the culturally deviant and deprived.

Contemporary popular discussion of crime and violence also follows this logic of closed narrative where the greatest fear is that the enemy will be let into our neighborhoods. And the greatest stress on public policy may be how to keep the unwanted off the tax payer–dependent welfare rolls and out of our town, safely in prisons, and so forth. Sam Spade's worries have had a melt down in our time, at late century. And they have become a potent paranoid resentment brew that spills over from the fantasy land of television and film into the social world in which we live.

What James's astute comments point us toward is the fact that the filmic and televisual discourse of crime and violence is not simply about crime or violence. Art is not here simply imitating life in some unthinking process of mimesis. Art is productive and generative. Televisual and filmic discourses about crime and violence, as Gerbner (1970) and others argue, are fundamentally urban fables about the operation of power and the production of meaning and values in society. They are about moral re-evaluation, about our collective tensions, crises, and fears. They are about how we as a society deal with the social troubles that afflict us: sexism, racism, and the like. In this sense, popular culture—the world of film noir and the grade B movie, of the tabloids, and of the mainstream press—constitutes a relentless pulp mill of social fictions of transmuted and transposed power. At late century, Sam Spade has been replaced by the towering popular and preternatural intelligence of Sweeney Erectus, our guide into the moral inferno. James wrote almost prophetically about resentment mutations and the time lag in the modern world in the late forties (Bhabha, 1994). The aim of this essay is to describe the operation of resentment a half century later in our time—a time in which racial antagonism has been the host of a parasitic resentment stoked in the media and circulating in popular culture.

DANGER IN THE SAFETY ZONE

> The crisis of the middle class is of commanding gravity. . . . The crisis is hardening the attitude of the middle class toward the dependent poor, and to the extent that the poor are urban and black and Latino and the middle class suburban and white, race relations are under a new exogenous strain . . . (Jack Beatty, 1994, p. 70)

Within the past year or so, *Time* magazine published two articles that together document the contemporary rise of suburban middle-class resentment. In these articles, crime and violence are fetishized, transmuted in the language of the coming invasion of the abstract racial other. According to the first article, "Danger in the Safety Zone," murder and mayhem are everywhere outside the suburban home: in the McDonald's restaurant, in the shopping mall, in the health club, in the courtroom (Smolowe, 1993, p. 29). The article also quoted and displayed statistics indicating that crime in the major cities had been declining somewhat while residents of the suburbs—the place where the middle classes thought they were safest—were now increasingly engulfed in random violence.

The second article is entitled "Patriot Games." It is about the mushrooming of heavily armed white militias in training, preparing for the war of wars against the federal government and nameless invading immigrants and foreign political forces that the Clinton administration has somehow, unwittingly, encouraged to think that America is weak and lacking in resolve to police its borders. About these armed militias we are told:

> In dozens of states, loosely organized paramilitary groups composed primarily of white men are signing up new members, stockpiling weapons and preparing for the worst. The groups, all privately run, tend to classify themselves as "citizen militias." . . . On a home video promoting patriot ideas, a man who gives his name only as Mark from Michigan says he fears that America will be subsumed into "one big, fuzzy, warm planet where nobody has any borders." Samuel Sherwood, head of the United States Militia Association in Blackfoot, Idaho, tells followers, absurdly, that the Clinton Administration is planning to import 100,000 Chinese policemen to take guns away from Americans. (Farley, *Time*, December 19, 1994, p. 48–49)

What does all of this mean? These articles announce a new mood in political and social life in the United States: a mood articulated in suburban fear of encirclement by difference, and increasingly formulated in a language and politics of what James and Nietzsche called "resentment." The dangerous inner city and the world "outside" are brought into the suburban home through television and film releasing new energies of desire mixed with fear. As we approach the end of the century, conflicts in education and popular culture are increasingly taking the form of grand panethnic battles over language, signs, and the occupation and territorialization of urban and suburban space. These conflicts intensify as the dual model of the rich-versus-poor city splinters into fragmentary communities signified by images of the roaming homeless on network television. For our late twentieth-century Sweeney Erectus, standing on the pyres of resentment in the culturally beleaguered suburbs, the signs and wonders are everywhere in the television evening news. Sweeney's cultural decline is registered in radically changing technologies and new sensibilities, in spatial and territorial destabilization and re-coordination, in the fear of falling, and in new, evermore incorrigible patterns of segregation and resegregation (Grossberg, 1992). Before his jaundiced eyes, immigrant labor and immigrant petty bourgeoisie now course through suburban and urban streets—the black and Latino underclasses after the Los Angeles riots, announces one irrepressibly gleeful news anchor, are restless. The fortunes of the white middle classes are, in many cases, declining. And the homeless are everywhere.

This new world order of mobile marginal communities is deeply registered in popular culture and in social institutions such as schools. The terrain to be mapped here is what Hal Foster (1983) in the *Anti-Aesthetic* calls postmodernism's "other side"—the new centers of the simulation of difference that loop back and forth through the news media to the classroom, from the film culture and popular music to the organization and deployment of affect in urban and suburban communities—Sweeney's homeground.

THE POLITICS OF AFFECT

The America of the diverging middle class is rapidly developing a new populist anti-politics. (Beatty, 1994, p. 70)

You will recall that Fredric Jameson (1984), in his now famous essay "Postmodernism, or, the Cultural Logic of Late Capitalism," maintained that a whole new emotional ground tone separated life in contemporary postindustrial society from previous epochs. He described this ground tone as "the waning of affect," the loss of feeling. While we agree with Jameson that emotions, like music, art, film, literature, and architecture, are historically determined and culturally bound, we disagree with his diagnosis that contemporary life is overwhelmingly marked by a certain exhaustion or waning of affect. We maintain that a very different logic is at work in contemporary life, particularly in the area of race relations. Postmodernism's other side of race relations—of the manipulation of difference—is marked by a powerful concentration of affect, or the strategic use of emotion and moral re-evaluation.

Like James, Nietzsche regarded the deployment of retributive morality as central to the organization and mobilization of power in modern industrial society. He also called this use of retributive morality resentment. In his *Genealogy of Morals* (1967), Nietzsche defined resentment as the specific practice of defining one's identity through the negation of the other. Some commentators on Nietzsche associate resentment only with "slave morality." We are here taken genealogically back to "literal slaves" in Greek society, who being the most downtrodden had only one sure implement of defense: the acerbic use of emotion and moral manipulation. But we want to argue along with Robert Solomon (1990) that contemporary cultural politics are "virtually defined by bourgeois resentment" (p. 278). As Solomon maintains: "Resentment elaborates an ideology of combative complacency—a 'levelling' effect that declares society to be 'classless' even while maintaining powerful class structures and differences" (p. 278). The middle class declares there are no classes except itself, no ideology except its ideology, no party, no politics, except the politics of the center, the politics of the middle, with a vengeance.

A critical feature of discourses of resentment is their dependence on processes of simulation

234

(Baudrillard, 1983). For instance, the suburban middle-class subject knows its inner-city other through an imposed system of infinitely repeatable substitutions and proxies: census tracts, crime statistics, tabloid newspapers, and television programs. Lastly, the inner-city other is known through the very ground of the displaced aggressions projected from suburban moral panic itself: it is held to embody what the center cannot acknowledge as its own (Beatty, 1994; Reed, 1992). Indeed, a central project of professional middle-class suburban agents of resentment is their aggressive attempt to hold down the moral center, to occupy the center of public discourse, to stack the public court of appeal. The needs of the suburbs therefore become "the national interests." By contrast, the needs of the inner city are dismissed as a wasteful "social agenda." Resentment is therefore an emotion "distinguished, first of all, by its concern and involvement with *power*" (Solomon, p. 278). And it is a power with its own material and discursive logic. In this sense it is to be distinguished from self-pity. If resentment has any desire at all, it is the "total annihilation. . . . of its target" (p. 279). Sweeney offers his own homemade version of the final solution: take the homeless and the welfare moms off general assistance. Above all, build more prisons!

A new moral universe now rides the underbelly of the beast—late capital's global permutations, displacements, relocations, and reaccumulations. The effect has meant a material displacement of minority and other dispossessed groups from the landscape of contemporary political and cultural life. That is to say, that increasingly the underclass or working-class subject is contemporaneously being placed on the outside of the arena of the public sphere as the middle-class subject-object of history moves in to occupy and to appropriate the identity of the oppressed, the radical space of difference. The center becomes the margin. It is as if Primus Rex had decided to wear Touchstone's fool's cap; Caliban exiled from the cave as Prospero digs in. Resentment operates through the processes of simulation that usurp contemporary experiences of the real, where the real is proven by its negation or its inverse. Resentment has infected the very structure of social values.

This battle over signs is being fought in cultural institutions across the length and breadth of this society. We are indeed in a culture war. We know this, of course, because avatars of the right like Patrick Buchanan (1992) and William Bennett (1994) constantly remind us of their books of values. As Buchanan put it bluntly, sometime ago, "The GOP vote search should bypass the ghetto" (quoted in Omi and Winant, 1986, p. 124). From the cultural spiel of the 1992 and 1994 election campaigns—from family values to Murphy Brown, to the new Corporate multicultural advertizing—from rap music to the struggle over urban and suburban space—from the Rodney King beating, to Charles Stuart, to Susan Smith, to O.J. Simpson—a turf battle over symbolic and material territory is under way. The politics of resentment is on the way as the suburbs continue to draw resources and moral empathy away from the urban centers.

Of course, a fundamental issue posed by the theories of resentment of James and Nietzsche is the challenge of defining identity in ways other than through the strategy of negation of the other. This, we wish to suggest, is the fundamental challenge of multiculturalism, the challenge of "living in a world of difference" (Mercer, 1992). Education is a critical site over which struggles over the organization and concentration of emotional and political investment and moral affiliation are taking place. The battle over signs that is resentment involves the articulation and rearticulation of symbols in the popular culture and in the media. These signs and symbols are used in the making of identity and the definition of social and political projects. Within this framework the traditional poles of left versus right, liberal versus conservative, democrat versus republican, and so forth are increasingly being displaced by a more dynamic and destabilizing model of mutation of affiliation and association. A further dimension of this dynamic is that the central issues that made these binary oppositions of race and class conflict intelligible and coherent in the past have now collapsed or have been recoded. The central issues of social and economic inequality that defined the line of social conflict between left and right during the civil rights period are now, in the post–civil rights era, inhabited by the new adversarial discourses of resentment. Oppositional discourses of identity, history and popular memory, nation, family, the deficit, and crime have displaced issues concerning equality and social justice. New Right publisher William Rusher articulates this displacement by pointing to a new model of material and ideological distinctions coming into being since the 80s:

> A new economic division pits the producers—businessmen, manufacturers, hard-hats, blue-collar workers, and farmers [middle America]—against a new and powerful class of non-producers comprised of the liberal verbalist elite (the dominant media, the major foundations and research institutions, the educational establishment, the federal and state bureaucracies) and a semipermanent welfare constituency, all coexisting happily in a state of mutually sustaining symbiosis. (Rusher quoted in Omi and Winant, 1986, p. 124)

Let us examine some manifestations of one of the principal articulations of resentment: the discourse of crime, violence, and suburban security. In the next section of this essay, we will discuss examples from television evening news, film, and popular magazine and newspaper features that show the variability, ambiguity, and contradiction in this discourse of conflict. We will see that signifiers of the inner city as the harbinger of violence, danger, and chaos loop into the mass media and the suburbs and Hollywood and back again in the constructions of black male directors of the reality of the "hood."

"REFLECTING REALITY" AND FEEDING RESENTMENT

> Too often, Black artists focus on death and destruction arguing that it is what's out there so we got to show it! Please!! What needs to be shown is the diversity and complexity of African-American life. (*The Syracuse Constitution* August 2, 1993, p. 5)

The logic of resentment discourse does not proceed along a straight line in a communication system of encoding/decoding. It does not work one-way from text to audience. Its reach is more diffuse, more rhizomatic, deeply intertextual. Resentment processes work from white to black and black to white, from white to Asian and Asian to white, and so on, looping in and out and back again as second nature across the bodies of the inhabitants of the inner city—the black world available to the black director who delivers the black audience to Hollywood. The inner city is thereby reduced to an endless chain of recyclable signifiers that both allure and repel the suburban classes.

But there is also the shared ground of discourses of the authentic inner city in which the languages of resentment and the reality of "the" hood commingle in films of black realism of black directors such as John Singleton and the Hughes brothers. This is a point that Joe Wood (1993) makes somewhat obliquely in his discussion of the film *Boyz 'N in the Hood* (1992) which is set, incidentally, in South Central, Los Angeles. In a recent article published in *Esquire* magazine entitled "John Singleton and the Impossible Greenback Bind of the Assimilated Black Artist," Wood notes the following:

> *Boyz's* simplified quality is okay with much of America. It is certain that many whites,

including Sony executives and those white critics who lauded the film deliriously, imagine black life in narrow ways. They don't want to wrestle with the true witness; it might be scarier than "hell." Sony Pictures' initial reaction to *Boyz* is instructive: John confides that the studio wanted him to cut out the scene in which the cops harass the protagonist and his father. "Why do we have to be so hard on the police?" they asked. An answer came when Rodney King was beaten; the scene stayed in—it was suddenly "real." (Wood, August 1993, p. 64)

Here we see the elements of repeatability, the simulation of the familiar, and the prioritization of public common sense that evening television helps to both activate and stabilize. Hollywood drew intertextually on the reality code of television. Television commodified and beautified the images of violence captured on a street-wise camera. Singleton's claim to authenticity, ironically, relied not on endogenous inner-city perceptions but, exogenously, on the overdetermined mirror of dominant televisual news. *Boyz 'N the Hood* could safely skim off the images of the inner city corroborated in television common sense. For these Hollywood executives, police brutality became real when the Rodney King beating became evening news. As Wood argues:

What Sony desired in *Boyz* was a film more akin to pornography. . . . a safely voyeuristic film that delivered nothing that they did not already believe. . . . But how strenuously will they resist his showing how Beverley Hills residents profit from South Central gangbanging, how big a role TV plays in the South Central culture. (p. 65)

Of course, what even Joe Wood's critical article ignores about a film like *Boyz 'N the Hood* is its own errant nostalgia for a world in which blacks are centered and stand together against the forces of oppression; a world in which black men hold and practice a fully elaborated and undisputed paternity with respect to their children; a world that radically erases the fact that the location of the new realist black drama, Los Angeles, South Central, the memories of Watts, etc., are now supplanted by an immigrant and migrant presence in which, in many instances, black people are outnumbered by Latinos and Asian Americans (Davis, 1992; Fregoso, 1993; Lieberman, 1992).

Like the Hollywood film industry, the mainstream news media's address to black and brown America directs its gaze toward the suburban white middle class. It is the gaze of resentment in which aspect is separated from matter and substance undermined by the raid of the harsh surfaces and neon lights of inner-city life. In the sensation-dripping evening news programs of the networks—CBS, NBC, and ABC, and CNN—as they pant to keep up with the inflamed journalism of the tabloids—black and Latino youth appear metonymically in the discourse of problems: "kids of violence," "kids of welfare moms," "car jackers," the "kids without fathers," "kids of illegal aliens," "kids who don't speak 'American.'" The skins of black and brown youth are hunted down like so many furs in the grand old days of the fur trade. The inner city is sold as a commodity and as a fetish—a signifier of danger and the unknown that at the same time narrows the complexity of urban working-class life. You watch network evening news and you can predict when black and brown bodies will enter and when they will exit. The overwhelming metaphor of crime and violence saturates the dominant gaze on the inner city. News coverage of the cocaine trade between the United States and Columbia routinely suggests that only poor and black inner-city residents use cocaine, not rich suburban whites who are actually the largest consumers of the illegal drug.

The mass media's story of inner-city black and Latino people pays short shrift to the stunning decline of opportunity and social services in the urban centers within the last fifteen years: poor public schools, chronic unemployment, isolation, the hacking to death of the public transportation system, the radical financial disinvestment in the cities, and the flight of jobs and resources to the suburbs. All of these developments can ultimately be linked to government deprioritization of the poor as middle-class issues of law and order, more jail space, and capital punishment usurp the Clinton administration's gaze on the inner city. Instead, the inner city exists as a problem in itself, and a problem to the world. The reality of the inner city is therefore not an endogenous discourse. It is an exogenous one. It is a discourse of resentment refracted back onto the inner city itself.

It is deeply ironic, then, that the images of the inner city presented by the current new wave of black cinema corroborate rather than critique mainstream mass media. Insisting on a kind of documentary accuracy and privileged access to the inner city, these directors construct a reality code of "being there" after the manner of the gangster rappers. But black film directors have no *a priori* purchase on the inner city. These vendors of chic realism recycle a reality code already in the mass media. This reality code operates as a system of repeatability, the elimination of traces, the elaboration of a hierarchy of discourses—the fabrication and consolidation of specular common sense.

Menace II Society (1993), created by Allen and Albert Hughes, is the capstone on a genre that mythologizes and beautifies the violent elements of urban life while jettisoning complexities of gender, ethnicity, sexuality, age, and economy. Instead of being didactic, like *Boyz 'N the Hood*, the film is nihilistic. The reality of the hood is built on a trestle of obviousnesses. Its central character, Caine Lawson (Tyrin Turner), is doomed to the life of drug running, car stealing, and meaningless violence that claims young men like himself (and before him, his father) from the time they can walk and talk. It is a world in which a trip to the neighborhood grocery can end in death and destruction, and gangbangers demand and enforce respect at the point of a gun. This point is made at the very beginning of the movie when Caine and his trigger-happy buddy, O-Dog (Larenz Tate), feel disrespected by a Korean store owner. The young men had come to the grocery to get a beer but are provoked into a stand-off when the store owner hovers too close to them. The young men feel insulted because the Korean grocer makes it too obvious that he views them with suspicion. In the blink of an eye, O-Dog settles the score with a bout of unforgettable violence. When Caine and O-Dog leave, the store owner and his wife are dead. And one act of violence simply precipitates another: by the end of the film, Caine too dies in a hail of bullets—a payback by the gang of a young man that Caine had beaten up mercilessly earlier in the film.

This film sizzles with a special kind of surface realism. There is a lot of blood and gore in the 'hood in *Menace II Society*. Shot sequences are dominated by long takes of beatings or shootings, almost always shot in extreme close-ups. Caine's life is supposed to be a character sketch of the inevitability of early death for inner-city male youth reared in a culture of violence. We have already seen it on television evening news before it hits the big screen. Black film-makers therefore become pseudo-normative bards to a mass audience, who, like the Greek chorus, already knows the refrain. These are not problem-solving films. They are films of confirmation. The reality code, the code of the 'hood, the code of blackness, of Africanness, of hardness, has a normative social basis. It combines and recombines with suburban middle-class discourses such as the deficit and balancing the federal budget; taxes; overbearing, overreaching, squandering government programs; welfare and quota queens; and the need for more prisons. It is a code drenched in public common sense. The gangster film has become paradigmatic for black filmic production out of Hollywood. And it is fascinating to see current films like Singleton's *Higher Learning* (1995) glibly redraw the spatial lines of demarcation of the inner city and the suburbs onto other sites such as a university town: *Higher Learning* is *Boyz 'N the Hood* on campus.

It is to be remembered that early in his career, before *Jungle Fever* (1991), Spike Lee was berated by mainstream white critics for not presenting the inner city realistically enough—for not showing the drug use and violence. Lee obliged with a vengeance in *Jungle Fever* in the harrowing scenes of the drug addict Vivian (Halle Berry) shooting it up at the "Taj Mahal" crack joint and the Good Doctor Reverend Purify (Ossie Davis) pumping a bullet into his son (Samuel Jackson) at point-blank range (Kroll, 1991).

By the time we get around to white-produced films like *Grand Canyon* (1991) or *Falling Down* (1993), the discourse of crime, violence, and suburban security has come full circle to justify suburban revenge and resentment. In *Falling Down*, directed by Joel Schumaker, we now have a white suburban male victim who enters the 'hood to settle moral scores. Michael Douglas as the angst-ridden protagonist, D-fens, is completely agnostic to the differences within and among indigenous and immigrant inner-city groups. They all should be exterminated as far he is concerned—along, of course, with his ex-wife who won't let him see his infant daughter. D-fens is the prosecuting agent of resentment. His reality code embraces Latinos, who are supposedly all gangbangers, and Asian store owners, who are portrayed as compulsively unscrupulous. In a bizarre parody of gang culture, he becomes a one-man gang—a menace to society. In a calculated cinematic twist, the world of D-fens is characterized by a wider range of difference than the world of the films of black realism. However, ironically, blacks are for the most part mysteriously absent from this Los Angeles (Douglas apparently, feels more confident beating up on other racial groups). On this matter of the representation of the "real" inner city the question is, as Aretha Franklin puts it, "Who's zooming who?"

What is fascinating about a film like *Falling Down* is that it too is centered around a kind of hyper-normative, anomic individual, who is "out there." He is the purveyor of what Jacques Lacan calls "paranoiac alienation" (Lacan, 1977, p. 5). Singlehandedly armed with more socionormative fire power than any gangbanger could ever muster, D-fens is ready to explode as everyday provocations make him seethe to the boiling point. We learn for instance that he is a disgruntled laid-off white-collar employee—a former technician who worked for many years at a military plant. Displaced as a result of the changing economy in the new world order—displaced by the proliferation of different peoples who are now flooding Los Angeles in pursuit of the increasingly elusive American dream—D-fens is part of the growing anxiety class that blames government, immigrants, and welfare moms for its problems. He is the kind of individual we are encouraged to believe a displaced middle-class person might become. As Joel Schumaker, the film director, explains:

> It's the kind of story you see on the six o'clock news, about the nice guy who has worked at the post office for twenty years and then one day guns down his co-workers and kills his family. It's terrifying because there's the sense that someone in the human tribe went over the wall. It could happen to us. (Morgan, 1993)

D-fens is a kind of Rambo nerd, a Perot disciple gone berserk. *Newsweek* magazine, that preternatural barometer of suburban intelligence, tells us that D-fens is the agent of suburban resentment. D-fens's actions while not always defensible are "understandable":

> *Falling Down*, whether it's really a message movie or just a cop film with trendy trimmings, pushes white men's buttons. The annoyances and menaces that drive D-fens bonkers—whining panhandlers, immigrant shopkeepers who don't trouble themselves to speak good English, gun-toting gangbangers—are a cross section of white-guy grievances. From the get-go, the film pits Douglas—the picture of obsolescent rectitude with his white shirt, tie, specs and astronaut haircut—against a rainbow coalition of Angelenos. It's a cartoon vision of the

beleaguered white male in multicultural America. This is a weird moment to be a white man. (David Gates, March 29, 1993, p. 48)

D-fens's reactions are based on his own misfortunes and anger over the anticipated disempowerment of the white middle class. Despite his similarities with the neo-Nazi, homophobic army surplus store owner in the movie, they are not the same type of social subject. Unlike the neo-Nazi, D-fens reacts to the injustices he perceives have been perpetrated against him. Like his alter ego Tom Sanders in *Disclosure* (1995), he is the post–civil rights scourge of affirmative action and reverse discrimination.

With *Falling Down*, Hollywood places the final punctuation marks on a discursive system that is refracted from the mainstream electronic media and the press onto the everyday life of the urban centers. Unlike D-fens in *Falling Down*, the central protagonist in *Menace II Society*, Caine, has nothing to live for, no redeeming values to vindicate. He is pre-existentialist—a man cut adrift in and by nature. What *Menace II Society* and many other black new wave films share with *Falling Down* are a general subordination of the interests and desires of women and a pervasive sense that life in the urban centers is self-made hell. Resentment has now traveled the whole way along a fully reversible signifying chain as black film-makers make their long march along the royal road to a dubious Aristotelian mimesis in the declaration of a final truth. The reality of being black and inner-city in America is sutured up in the popular culture. The inner city has no interior. It is a holy shrine to dead black and brown bodies—hyperreal carcasses on arbitrary display.

CONCLUSION

There is a country-western song popular, we are told, among the rural suburban dwellers of the Southwest. Its refrain is an urgent plea to God to keep the penitent middle American on the straight and narrow. "Drop kick me Jesus through the goal posts of life," the song goes. Here, the importunate penitent draws down lines of social location in an edict of moral specificity and separateness from the contagion of all that dwells outside the security of the home and the neighborhood. The fictive goal posts morally keep the unwanted out. The trope of resentment exists in the empty space of the center, between the homoerotic legs of the goal posts, so to speak.

In many respects, then, the resentment discourse of crime, violence, and suburban security that now saturates American popular cultural forms, such as the country-western song quoted above, indicates the inflated presence of suburban priorities and anxieties in the popular imagination and in political life. It also indicates a corresponding circumscription of the control that blacks and Latinos (particularly black and Latino youth) and other people of color have over the production of images about themselves in society—even in an era of the resurgence of the black Hollywood film and the embryonic Latino cinema. The discourse of crime, violence, and suburban security also points to deeper realities of abandonment, neglect, and social contempt for the dwellers in America's urban centers registered in social policies that continue to see the inner city as the inflammable territory of "the enemy within" and the police as the mercenary force of the suburban middle classes. Those who articulate the anxieties repressed in and by their own privileged access to society's cornucopia of rewards—dwellers of the suburban city and the parvenu masters of the fictive hyperrealisms of the 'hood—bear some responsibility to the urban city which their practices of cultural production and overconsumption both create and displace. In these matters, to use the language of the Guyanese poet Martin Carter, "All of us are involved, all of us are consumed" (1979, p. 44).

REFERENCES

Baudrillard, J. (1983). *Simulations*. New York: Semiotext(e).

Beatty, J. (1994, May). Who speaks for the middle class. *The Atlantic Monthly*, pp. 65–78.

Bennett, W. (1994) *The Book of Virtues*. New York: Simon and Schuster.

Bhabha, H. (1994). *The Location of Culture*. New York: Routledge.

Buchanan, P. (1992). We stand with President Bush. C-Span Transcripts (eds.), *1992 Republican National Convention* (pp. 6–9). Lincolnshire, Illinois: Tape Writer.

Campbell, R. (1987). Securing the middle ground: Reporter Formulas in 60 Minutes. *Critical Studies in Mass Communication*, 4(4), pp. 325–350.

Carter, M. (1979). You are involved. *Poems of Resistance* (p. 44). George Town, Guyana: Guyana Printers Limited.

Davis, M. (June 1, 1992). Urban America sees its future: In L. A. burning all illusions. *Nation*, 254(21), pp. 743–746.

Dunn, T. (1993). The new enclosures: Racism in the normalized community. In R. Gooding-Williams (ed.), *Reading Rodney King* (pp. 178–195). New York: Routledge.

Eliot, T. S. (1964) The love song of J. Alfred Prufrock. In T. S. Eliot, *Selected Poems* (pp. 11–16). New York: Harcourt Brace Jovanovich.

Farley, C. J. (December 19, 1994). Patriot games. *Time*, pp. 48–49.

Fedarko, K. (August 23, 1993). Holidays in hell. *Time*, pp. 50–51.

Foster, H. (1983). *The Anti-Aesthetic*. Seattle: Bay Press.

Fregoso, R. L. (1993). *The Bronze Screen. Chicana and Chicano Film Culture*. Minneapolis: University of Minnesota Press.

Gates, D. (March 29, 1993). White-male paranoia. *Newsweek*, pp. 48–53.

Gerbner, G. (1970). Cultural indicators: The case of violence in television drama. *Annals of the American Association of Political and Social Science*, 338, pp. 69–81.

Grossberg, L. (1992). *We Got to Get out of this Place*. New York: Routledge.

James, C. L. R. (1978). *Mariners, Renegades, and Castaways: The Story of Herman Melville and the World We Live In*. Detroit: Bewick/ed.

James, C. L. R. (1993). *American Civilization*. Oxford: Blackwell.

Jameson, F. (July–August 1984). Postmodernism, or, the cultural logic of late capitalism. *New Left Review*, no. 146, pp. 59–82.

Kroll, J. (June 10, 1991). Spiking a fever. *Newsweek*, pp. 44–47.

Lacan, J. (1977). The mirror stage as formative of the function of the I. *Ecrits* (pp. 1–7). Trans. A. Sheridan. New York: Norton.

Lasch, C. (1991). *The True and Only Heaven: Progress and Its Critics*. New York: Norton.

Lieberman, P. (June 18, 1992). 52% of riot arrests were Latino, study says. *L.A. Times*, p. B3.

Melville, H. (1851). *Moby Dick: Or the White Whale*. New York: Harper.

Mercer, K. (1992). "1968": Periodizing postmodern politics and identity. In L. Grossberg, C. Nelson, and P. Treichler (eds.), *Cultural Studies* (pp. 424–449). New York: Routledge.

Morgan, S. (March 1993). Coastal disturbances. *Mirabella*, p. 46.

Morrison, T. (1990). The site of memory. In R. Fergusson, M. Gever, T. T. Minh-ha, and C. West. *Out There: Marginalization and Contemporary Cultures*. New York: The Museum of Contemporary Art.

Nietzsche, F. (1967). *On the Genealogy of Morals*. Trans. W. Kaufman. New York: Vintage.

Omi, M., and Winant, H. (1986). *Racial Formation in the United States*. New York : Routledge.

Parenti, M. (1992). *Make Believe Media: The Politics of Entertainment*. New York: St. Martin's Press.

Postman, N. (1986). *Amusing Ourselves to Death*. New York: Penguin.

Reed, A. (1992). The urban underclass as myth and symbol: The poverty of the discourse about the discourse on poverty. *Radical America* 24(1), pp. 21–40.

Smolowe, J. (August 23, 1993). Danger in the safety zone. *Time*, pp. 29–32.

Solomon, R. (1990). Nietzsche, postmodernism, and resentment: A genealogical hypothesis. In C. Koelb (ed.), *Nietzsche as Postmodernist: Essays Pro and Con* (pp. 267–294). New York: SUNY.

The Syracuse Constitution (August 2, 1993). A menace to society, p. 5.

Williams, R. (1974). *Television, Technology and Cultural Form*. New York: Schocken Books.

Williams, D. (1994). Society, spatiality, and innercity disinvestment in a large U.S. city. *International Journal of Urban and Regional Research*, 17, pp. 578–594.

Wood, J. (August 1993). John Singleton and the impossible greenback of the assimilated black artist. *Esquire*, pp. 59–108.

Who's White?
Television Talk Shows and Representations of Whiteness

Corinne Squire

Corinne Squire teaches at the University of East London and is researching HIV's relation to "identity" and "community." She is coauthor with Ellen Friedman of *Morality USA: Representations of Morality in Contemporary Culture* (University of Minnesota Press, 1997). She edited *Women and AIDS: Psychological Perspectives* (Sage, 1993) and wrote *Significant Differences: Feminism in Psychology* (Routledge, 1989). She has also worked in a video company and as an HIV antibody test counselor.

. . . a lot of you all white people in the country is black and didn't know it. And it's shaking some people up, let me tell you.

—Oprah Winfrey

(Reaction shot of white audience members, laughing)

July 18, 1994 was not a special day in the history of daytime talk shows. A certain convergence around "bad girls" was noticeable, and on *Geraldo* a confrontation occurred of which the host said, "I can't . . . remember seeing that level of animosity and naked hatred between a mother and a daughter" (*Geraldo*, 1994: 13). But the day did not fall in a period when networks screen the most spectacular shows to maximise points in the quarterly ratings battles. Since that time, some shows like *Bertice Berry*, *Jane Whitney*, and *Vicki Lawrence* have come off air; new shows—*Charles Perez*, hosted by an ex-*Ricki* producer, and the *Oprah*-like *Rolonda*—have appeared; and the shows have become more diverse, incorporating elements from game shows, lifestyle magazine shows, and Court TV. Nevertheless the original format of dealing with personal and social issues through exchanges between audience, guests, experts, and host, remains dominant. This chapter focuses mainly on the July 18, 1994 talk shows that stayed within that format. Channel-hopping, the chapter tries to elucidate the shows' representations of whiteness.

Television talk shows are derided, but much-watched. The shows' perceived insignificance permits a relatively laissez-faire approach to their structures and topics. It may be this disregard for the genre that allows white and black women, and black men, to host the shows. While no nighttime talk shows currently have black or Latino presenters (*New York Times*, 1995b), daytime shows presented by blacks or Latinos number at least five. Moreover, while you are very often when watching television part of a more ethnically diverse community than the one you live in, daytime talk shows consistently impose that diversity upon you through their studio audiences and guests. The shows also represent "race" more frequently than most prime-time television (Squire, 1994). They may approach the subject implicitly, when for instance a show on "women who pay for their men" diverts into an exchange between black women about the advisability of finding a black professional man (*Ricki Lake*, 1995). They may encounter "race" incidentally, as in the July 18 *Donahue* go-go dancers' accusations of white bar owners' racism. Or they may intentionally "do" the topic, as in *Sally Jesse Raphael*'s "racism update" (1995) or the *Charles*

Who's White? Television Talk Shows and Representations of Whiteness

243

Perez show on discrimination against dark-and light-skinned black women (1995a). The host sustains the talk show, and black and Latino hosts like those now common on daytime television seem to raise "race" issues more (*New York Times*, 1995b).[1]

However, the daytime talk show genre derives from *Donahue*, a show in which a white host, paternal and liberal, roams around the studio with a microphone, encouraging confession and catharsis, introducing experts who offer solutions or programs for growth, and providing entertainment that ranges from mild fun to prurient fascination, for an audience that is assumed to be all part of the same human and television family (Carbaugh, 1986).[2] This white model for the genre might be argued even now to coopt the representations of African Americans and Hispanics on offer in talk shows, either whiting them out or reducing them to stereotypes of oversexed Latinas, loud black women, and infantile black men (hooks, 1992). Given the diverse nature of the genre's hosts, audiences, topics, and structures, though, how white can it be?

WHITE AS UNIVERSAL, WHITE AS NOT-BLACK

[T]he habit of ignoring race is understood to be a graceful, even generous, liberal gesture. . . . To enforce [race's] invisibility through silence is to allow the black body a shadowless participation in the dominant cultural body. (Morrison,1992: 9–10)

Academic interest in the representation of whiteness is growing. This concern has had little effect on popular notions of whiteness, which remain so unformulated that "white" seems only transparency and nothingness: Not a color, not an identity (Dyer, 1988; Frankenberg, 1993; Ware, 1992). This white absence shows up all over television, including talk shows. Its effect is to assimilate gracefully, as Morrison says, black to white.

How does this assimilation happen? Most often talk shows deal with "race" indirectly, through the racial diversity of their protagonists. The shows' failure to be explicit about such differences can make them seem unraced—implicitly, white. On the July 18 *Bertice Berry Show*, a photograph of a young white woman's black child was shown twice, when her responsibilities as a mother were being discussed. The issue of "race" only arose later, in an argument over the family's responses to her pregnancy, and even in this discussion "race" became subsumed by other concerns: her young age, a narrow-minded smalltown environment: "that's why we were upset, not the black—," said her stepmother, and then, "we love Arianna, that's our baby" (*Bertice Berry*, 1994, 13). Here, family feeling turned a black baby white.

Though black as well as white experts appear on the shows, the difference again is verbally unmarked, even when it is visually obvious and might well be salient. On the July 18 *Maury Povich* "Drug Deals Gone Wrong" show, the customs official interviewed to provide an authoritative account of drug smuggling is an African American woman, the women who say they were duped into carrying drugs are Latina and white, and "race" goes unmentioned. African American and Latino hosts are also sometimes said by critics to act white—Winfrey for instance, who often says her show transcends "race," by hugging whites too much or losing weight. Finally, every American becomes honorarily white on the shows when the absolute Otherness of the un-American looms. The *Maury Povich* show presented the women who carried drugs as dupes of foreigners; even the Latinas were all-American. They "went down" to Peru and experienced "barbaric" conditions in Bahamaian prisons; Povich signed off, "until next time, America." These women had been lured, Povich said into "glamorous trips to exotic places with strange-sounding names"; as Morrison (1992) points out, the Other is even linguistically alien, incomprehensible and unpronounceable.

Network television audiences, like other general media audiences, are assumed to watch "white" even if they are black, that is, to be concerned about representation of minorities and clearly marked race issues but not to be worried about race in other contexts or about the dominant raced style of the medium (Gaines,1988). The glossing-over of "race" on television talk shows has a more medium-specific rationale too. Television viewers may listen when they are not watching; they may not be listening or watching continuously (Ellis, 1982);[3] and daytime audiences are especially likely to treat television casually. If the audience is so little involved, television-makers believe, diversions or expansions of argument will lose it. A show titled "My Daughter's Sleeping with a Jerk" cannot suddenly take on "Interracial relationships." But when a medium relies thus heavily on sound, silences, like the talk shows' silences around "race," are especially noticeable.

The *Donahue* ethic specifies racial indifference by decreeing that talk shows present themselves and their audiences as giant families, united by love and understanding. Family issues dominate the shows; on the July 18 *Oprah Winfrey* show two-thirds of the moral dilemmas considered concerned relationships and children. Rolonda declares her show to be "about" family. This talk-show-as-family trope prescribes the personal, psychological solutions that are everywhere in daytime talk shows, a psychologizing that in turn helps whiteness survive as the dominant and unmarked term. Hosts, guests, and audience members repeatedly say it's what's inside that counts, there's good and bad in every race, you have to consider the individual: mantras that by obscuring the significance of "race" categories revalorize whiteness, that color which is not one. The "Family Secrets" show from which the quote at the beginning of this chapter comes had as its major guest a woman who believed herself white until her mother, in the middle of a divorce, told her her real father was black. Talk around these events shifted from "race," towards the emotions of betrayal, trust, and protection. After the woman met her father for the first time onscreen, "race" was abandoned entirely for the topic of "birth secrets."

At times, some figures of black operate in talk shows, unspoken, representing what white is not. Most notable among these figures are the black women who like Winfrey are loud and strong, talk straight about sex, and offer spiritual uplift. The July 18 *Donahue* provided another example, Leta, an African American woman who described the racism of bar owners; emphasized the hard work of go-go dancing; argued for an informal union and proper pay—"we are the power. We are those bars"—and declared herself "born to boogie" and "a little bit of a show-off, . . . wanting to . . . be that thing" (*Donahue* 1994: 7, 2). Black men have less frequent and individualized presences on the shows, either as epitomes of sleaze who only care about sex, cheat on their women, do not provide for their children, and may be violent; or, occasionally, as ideals, perfectly athletic or socially responsible.

These figures' representational status as inimitable heroes or villains is distanced from whiteness. The viewer, who is assumed to be watching "white" even if black, can only look at them and say, "I am not like that"—not as good, not as bad. A similar racialized representational distance is described in *Black Like Me*, the story, once read by millions of U.S. schoolchildren, of John Howard Griffin, a white journalist who darkened his skin and travelled through the South in 1959. Faced with his black image for the first time, Griffin saw not himself but "a fierce, bald, very dark Negro" who "glared" at him (1960: 15), frightening him unutterably. Griffin also represented blackness as distanced from whiteness by its virtue. Of a poor Alabama family he stayed with, he wrote, "the bravery of these people attempting to bring up a family decently . . . their willingness to share their food and shelter with a stranger—the whole thing overwhelmed me" (1960: 110). Black, the marked color, here displays a plethora of contradictory meanings, "evil and protective, rebellious *and* forgiving, fearful *and* desirable" (Morrison, 1992: 59). These

Who's White? Television Talk Shows and Representations of Whiteness

245

meanings are separated absolutely from whiteness, the absence of color. White is everything they are not—moderate, everyday, and unremarkable.

WHITE LIKE WHO? WHITENESS AS A TRAILER PARK

(G)et yourself a mobil home. . . . Do whatever you have to do. (Older sister to Melanie and her boyfriend Ricky, *Jane Whitney*, 1994: 6)

Talk shows' representations of whiteness do not function only by colonising blackness and distancing themselves from it. At times they also have their own highly specific meaning. Though "white" alone often seems to mean nothing, being white working class, white Irish American, or white Italian American has definite content (Frankenberg, 1993). On the talk shows, though, the most clearly formulated representation of whiteness is "trailer park" white, a low-class, deviant "color" analogous to "project black."

Often class seems to cut across "race" on the shows. On the July 18 *Montel Williams*, for example, a Latina who used to be in a gang told a white 15-year-old gang girl called Snoopy, "when you're six feet under all they're gonna do is write on a wall, 'Snoopy, rest in peace,' " and predicted a future for her like her own: in jail, or on welfare with a child (*Montel Williams*, 1994). But economics does not obliterate "race." Snoopy's whiteness went along with relative affluence and a concerned, present mother. Television could not represent her as just another gangbanger; Williams, who is black, ironically asked why she didn't just join the Girl Scouts. Moreover, the shows provide dramatic and frequent instances of the representation I am calling "trailer park" white.

When white guests tell their stories, the shows often detail economic struggle to an extent that produces a picture of abject and longlasting poverty—not, as is the case with black guests, a relatively restrained picture of "getting by." On the June 18 *Jane Whitney*, for instance, devoted to families who thought that their daughters were dating deadbeats, a woman asked Ricky, the boyfriend of her young sister Melanie, "(D)o you have any money in the bank? . . . Do you have any money right now to support my sister?" and later broadened the critique: "He doesn't have his high school diploma. . . . He doesn't have a driver's license right now" (*Jane Whitney*, 1994: 8, 16). Ricky defended his work committment: "This is wintertime. We work 40 hours a week. Tha—if—I can't go to work when there ain't nobody to work with" (*Jane Whitney*, 1994: 9). When Melanie's sister suggested he made $6 an hour, Melanie quickly corrected her: "He's making $7 and he's going up for $8. Thank you." Talk shows' ethic is to value everyone for themselves, and such judgments of worth by wage get questioned. One man in the audience said, "I think that [Melanie's mother and stepmother] are—want—the aspirations of your daughter to live up to someone else. I don't think you respect him (Ricky) as a person . . ." (*Jane Whitney* 1994: 17).[4] Despite such qualifications, the exposed, piled-up details of financial suffering and impossibility remain.

In such representations, the trailer park is the metaphorical margin of economic viability, screening off destitution yet allowing glimpses of it. It is, audiences see, the potential destination of any white American living in hard times. Melanie's sister asks her and Ricky at least to get themselves a mobile home. Here the trailer park is presented as the minimal requirement for family life, allowing borderline participation, albeit as "white trash," in the "family" of the talk show audience and the nation.

Talk shows link the economics of "trailer park" whiteness to family dysfunctionality. Guests disgorge tales of unplanned pregnancies, doomed early marriages, and other failed and byzantine relationships; neglected and out-of-control children; men verbally, physically, and sexually abusing other men, children, and women; and men, women, and children hitting and knifing them back.[5] On *Jane Whitney*, Ricky, who was 18, was living in Melanie's family's house because his own was crowded with eight people. He was previously engaged to a friend of Melanie's, Brandy, who "gave up a baby for a car" and was now going out with his uncle. Melanie, 17, had had another boy living with her at the house before. Melanie's mother and sister had their own stories of marrying early and unsuccessfully.

One guest on *Geraldo* was a young woman whose family thought she was off the rails. "The majority" of her friends did drugs, she said. When her sister worried about her walking around the local trailer park at night, she said dismissively she was not about to get lost wandering in such an inconsiderable, known space, "like I was going to go somewhere." Her sister responded, "No, but . . . somebody can take you . . . out in the woods and rape you" (*Geraldo*, 1994: 29). In the trailer park of whiteness, something dreadful hovers on the edge.

The shows' representation of "trailer-park" whiteness both presents a cautionary tale of what life as a poor white means, and metaphorically represents whiteness in general, suggesting that it always borders abjection. Here, whiteness displays some of the larger-than-life, fantastic properties that characterize the shows' stereotypic renderings of blackness. "Trailer park" whiteness thus seems close to the white horror that, Toni Morrison suggests, coexists with images of blackness in the U.S. literary canon. Alongside its abundances of black meanings, Morrison says, white American literature offers up an image of a paralysing, silent whiteness like that of the whale in *Moby Dick*, "mute, meaningless, unfathomable, pointless, frozen, veiled, curtained, dreaded, senseless, implacable" (1992: 59).[6] Talk shows' representations of "trailer park" whiteness render white abjection with particular frequency and insistence.

Whites may try to reserve themselves a place apart from talk shows' trailer trash—a place that lets them say, "these people are white, but not like us." However, the intense opprobrium and fascination with the "white trash" representations of talk TV suggests that links with these representations are half-perceived. It may be easier for blacks to perceive such representations as unconnected: as "white, not like us." hooks (1992) though has pointed out the powerful interest in the contents of whiteness that black audiences have. Whiteness's power is "terrorising" (hooks, 1992: 169). In relation to "trailer park" whiteness this fear seems circumspect.

The shows' inchoate representations of whiteness as degradation may be driven by the same nonspecific fears that fuel black stereotyping; certainly the representations take on black stereotypes' sexual and violent content. But "trailer park" whiteness does not replace this stereotyping. Its familial aggression and economic embattlement often seem, indeed, to have "blacks" as their implicit objects. The white men struggling to make more than $6 an hour and moving from unstable relationship to relationship are economically and culturally indistinguishable from those who appear on "race" episodes of the shows as "angry white men" (*Charles Perez*, 1995b), railing angrily about what black men have taken from them. In the realm of television's "trailer park" whiteness, too, live the drifting, weapons-hungry men whom news reports have recently shown, often literally in trailer parks, telling tall tales about the government and eager to call blacks "niggers."

VANILLA NIGHTMARE[7]

Some Whites will say . . . this is the white man's experience as a Negro in the South, not the Negro's. But this is picayunish, and we no longer have time for that. (Griffin, 1960: 5)

Who's White? Television Talk Shows and Representations of Whiteness

247

"Trailer park" white is both white and nonwhite. Miscegenation is the metaphor for its intimate, inextricable mixing of white with black meanings. This miscegenation is evident on the shows partly in explicit representations of interracial relations and children of mixed parentage. On *Bertice Berry*, the stepmother of Joy, the young white woman with a black child, said Joy was called "a nigger lover, white trash and shit" (1994: 13). More importantly white concerns are played out within images of blackness and representations of blackness are incorporated within white figurations. These exchanges disturb talk shows' whiteness, rendering it impure.

On the shows, the emotionality, assertiveness, and sexuality of African American women offer possibilities for white identification, as well as a racially secured distance. When black male athletes appear, they invoke the same reified yet deeply engaging dreams of bodily power they do elsewhere in the popular media. Televisual conflicts between black women and men, while they resonate with important gender issues in black politics, also gladitorially play out "white" gender conflicts, simultaneously providing the insurance of ethnographic detachment. Displays of black male misogyny towards black and white women ("project girls," "white meat") discharge misogyny for everyone. Shows on discrimination by black men against dark- or light-skinned black women have as their subtext slavery and white racism. The emotionality of this subtext is displaced safely into the insults black men hurl, and the anger and hurt of dark- and light-skinned black women.

Sometimes a reverse miscegenation occurs. White figures with black-identified failings or gifts "become" black, like "white trash" Joy with her black child. In discussions of girl gangs, welfare, young girls' sexuality and men who cheat, a metaphorical blackness is the problem the show and its viewers solve, independent of guests' visible or spoken "race." The success of white female hosts like Ricki Lake depends on a black-associated honesty and brashness whose most immediate referent is Oprah Winfrey. Citation does not stop here: the televisual performances of Montel Williams, Rolonda and Bertice Berry, themselves black, also quote Winfrey's emblematic black success.

hooks (1992) and Willis (1990) think the appropriativeness of popular media like talk shows outweighs the possibilities offered by their miscegenatory openness and flexibility—a more sophisticated version of the criticism Griffin (1960) cites at the beginning of this section. hooks nevertheless thinks whites should "identify with . . . difference" (1992: 13), a call that suggests the value of a close, miscegenating cultural relationship. Kobena Mercer gives a more precise description of this relationship. He discusses black esthetics as both dialogic, "talking back," and syncretic, appropriating, and adapting; and argues that these "creolising" (1987: 45) cultural forms are redeployed by the mainstream and cannot but have effects on it. For miscegenation is also about the power of the marked, discriminated-against group. It demonstrates, as Adrian Piper says, "the reality of successful infiltration that ridicules the ideal of assimilation" (1991: 26). Whiteness is always struggling to maintain itself against the Other that defines it, and thus is perpetually miscegenated, perpetually facing "the loathsome possibility that everyone is "tainted" by black ancestry" (Piper,1991: 26; see also Bhabha, 1988).

It is possible to discern in talk shows resistant, miscegenatory representations of the kind Mercer (1987) describes. For example, the unremarked presence of black and Latino hosts, guests, and experts; the visual but unspoken displays of interracial friendships, adoptions, and relationships; and the shows' casual talk across race though unmarked disrupt the genre's snow-white model. The shows' racial stereotyping of for instance welfare mothers and irresponsible fathers often seems uneasy; the stereotyping has to be repeated and is hard to maintain. The representations of "trailer trash" that are now recognized as defining talk shows (*New York Times*, 1995c) also continually blur the white-black boundary on the shows through their racial indistinctness. Finally, the shows' deployments of blackness as projections and metaphors also allow representations of blackness to "talk back' within the mainstream. Blacks on and watching talk shows participate in growth-psychological and new-ageist traditions that evolved in specifically white contexts, for instance, but their own use of these traditions miscegenates them. Maya Angelou's insistence on *Oprah* that black women's belief in themselves is integral to their spirituality occurs within a specific African American history of economic and gender oppression. When on *Sally Jesse Raphael* the *Essence* columnist Gwendolyn Goldsby Grant gets a white woman to repeat after her, "No one in this world is better than me" (*Sally Jesse Raphael*, 1994: 6), self-esteem, a concept that was appropriated for African American self-improvement in the 1980s, is translated back into a priority for all women in oppressive heterosexual relationships.

Since daytime talk shows are constructed as "about" family, the intermixtures described above have intimate effects within the genre that can aptly be described as miscegenation. While the shows' own representations of family often work to erase "race," sometimes they too pose an interesting challenge to color boundaries. Griffin (1960) used "family" to ground his text's anti-racism. Staying with a black family, he writes of "Negro children's lips soft against mine, so like the feel of my own children's goodnight kisses" (1960: 110). Talk shows' overflowing emotionality similarly encourages white viewers to identify, albeit briefly, with the suffering, efforts, and hopes of black mothers, fathers, and children. Simile separates Griffin's from the black children, "so *like* my own," but there is often no such space between whites and blacks in the talk show family. Whiteness may even be enrolled within representations of black "family." On the "Family Secrets" show Winfrey greeted the woman who thought she was white and recently discovered she had a black father, "Welcome to the family, sister" (1995: 6). Later she cited Maya Angelou to help a white woman understand why her mother concealed her adoption. The shows' representations of family can thus render "miscegenation," the compromise of whiteness by even the least trace of nonwhiteness, as a moment of resistant utopian possibility. It is as if talk shows have heard Adrian Piper's rhetorical injunction (in "Cornered," 1988) to declare yourself black if your ancestry is even slightly nonwhite, and are in their own way responding. Besides talk shows' ritual fights and strivings for psychological profundity, then, besides their faked-up racial democracies, gleeful stereotyping of "blackness," and melodramatic representational construction of "white trash," you can see in them an unnamed but significant color that is rarely visible elsewhere, a less than sparkling white.

References

Benson, J. (1995). Talk shows rate murder case an ethical dilemma. *Variety* March 20–26: 23, 61.

Bertice Berry. (1994). My daughter's sleeping with a jerk. July 14. Burrelles Information Service, Livingstone, NJ: c. Fox Center Productions.

Bhabha, H. (1989). Signs taken for wonders. In H. Gates (ed.), *Race Writing and Difference*. Evanston, Ill: Northwestern University Press.

Boehmer, M. (1987). Correlating lead-in show ratings with local television news ratings. *Journal of Broadcasting and Electronic Media* 31: 89–94.

Carbaugh, D. (1986). *Talking American: Cultural Discourse on Donahue*. Norwood, NJ: Ablex Publishing.

Charles, H. (1994). Whiteness. Shifting Identities, Shifting Racisms day conference, London.

Charles Perez. (1995a). Discrimination within the African American community. May 24.

Charles Perez. (1995b). White men who believe they are discriminated against. May 25.

Dempsey, J. (1995). "Jenny" incident raises specter of control. *Variety* March 13–19, 36.

Donahue. (1994). True confessions of a go-go dancer. July 18. c. Multimedia Entertainment.

Douglas, A. (1977). *The Feminization of American Culture*. New York: Knopf.

Doyle, L. (1994). Talk show host sells soul . . . today on Donahue. *New York* 27: 16, June 20.

Dyer, R. (1988). White. *Screen, Last Special Issue on Race* 29.

Ellis, J. (1982). *Visible Fictions*. London: Routledge and Kegan Paul.

Fogel, A. (1986). Talk shows: On reading television. In S. Donadio, S. Railton, and S. Ormond (eds.). *Emerson and his Legacy*. Carbondale, Ill: Southern Illinois University Press.

Frankenberg, R. (1993). *White Women, Race Matters*. Minneapolis, MN: University of Minnesota Press.

Gaines, J. (1988). White privilege and looking relations: race and gender in feminist film theory. *Screen. Last special issue on Race*, 29: 12–27.

Geraldo. (1994). I have a terrible secret: women confront their past. July 18. Livingstone, NJ: Burrelles Information Services.© Investigative News Group.

Goodman, F. (1991). Madonna and Oprah: the companies they keep. *Working Woman* 16: 52–55.

Gregory, S. (1994). Bertice Berry. *Essence* 24: 51. April.

hooks, bell. (1992). *Black Looks: Race and Representation*. Boston, MA: South End Press.

Jane Whitney. (1994). I'll do anything to stop their marriage. July 18. Livingstone, NJ: Burrelles Information Services. c. River Tower Productions.

Jenny Jones. (1994). Growing up too fast. July 18. Livingstone, NJ: Burrelles Information Services. © The Jenny Jones Show.

Livingstone, S., and Lunt, P. (1993). *Talk on Television*. London: Routledge.

Masciarotte, G-J. (1991). C'mon girl: Oprah Winfrey and the discourse of feminine talk. *Genders* 11: 81–110.

Mercer, K. (1987). Black hair/style politics. *New Formations* 3: 33–54.

Morrison, T. (1992). *Playing in the Dark: Whiteness and the Literary Imagination*. Cambridge, MA: Harvard University Press.

New York Times. (1995a). They'll risk life, face and ride for a little air time. *Week in Review* 7. May 14.

New York Times. (1995b). An emptiness in the late night laughter. *Arts and Leisure* 29. May 21.

New York Times. (1995c). Wages of deceit: Untrue Confessions. *Arts and Leisure* 1, 29. June 11.

Oprah Winfrey. (1994). What would you do? July 18. Livingstone, NJ: Burrelles Information Service © Harpo Productions

Oprah Winfrey. (1995). What's your family secret. April 25. Livingstone, NJ: Burrelles Information Service © Harpo Productions.

Piper, Adrian. (1991). "Flying" in *you/know*. Birmingham and Manchester: Icon Gallery and Corner House.

Ricki Lake. (1995). Women who think men should give them more money. May 22.

Sally Jesse Raphael. (1994). I'm sorry I did it. July 18. © Multimedia Entertainment.

Sally Jesse Raphael. Racism update. May 22. © Multimedia Entertainment.

Slonim, J. (1994). To the man who put the "tell" into television. *Interview* 24: 48ff. July.

Squire, C. (1994). Empowering women? The *Oprah Winfrey Show*. *Feminism and Psychology* 4(1): 63–79.

Ware, V. (1992). *Beyond The Pale*. London: Verso.

Willis, S. (1990). I want the black one. *New Formations* 10: 77–98.

NOTES

1. Such shows, particularly those of Winfrey and Geraldo Rivera, have been responsible for major change in the talk show format, in the first case toward an empathetic, emotive style with lots of touching; in the second, toward baroque problems and visceral confrontations. *Geraldo* is also said to have affected reality programming (Slonim, 1994). The press, especially the black press, covers black-hosted shows with interest (Gregory, 1994); occasionally, academic writers have also pointed out these shows' value (Livingstone and Lunt, 1993; Masciarotte, 1991; Squire, 1994).

2. Donahue's recent move in a trashier, "bad Phil" (Doyle, 1994) direction does not affect this paradigm.

3. It is for this reason that the chapter often cites what is said, not shown, and even when mentioning the latter tends to use general examples of image types.

4. The *Bertice Berry* show of the same day played out a very similar scenario of financial exposure and defence.

5. For contrast, consider the respectable representations appearing on the July 18 *Montel Williams* show, where the gang girls were both Latina and white. All had graduation as their goal and two were still in school. One young woman's history of incarceration and two single-parent families were politely ignored. A young Latina who blamed her situation on her family's poor communication said, "a lot of things happen in my house you guys don't know about," and no one pressed her for details.

6. A similar representation of whiteness as horror appears in *Black Like Me* when Griffin, dyed black but writing as a white, describes the unseen, chilling presence of racist whites when he rides into Mississippi on a bus packed with blacks: "We felt strongly the need to establish frienship against an invisible threat. Like shipwrecked people, we huddled together in a warmth and courtesy that was pure and pathetic" (1960: 63).

7. This subtitle comes from Adrian Piper's 1986 series *Vanilla Nightmares*, charcoal drawings of black faces and figures, in chains, naked, or juxtaposed with white women, superimposed on *New York Times* South Africa reportage and credit card and perfume ads.

Whites Are from Mars, O.J. Is from Planet Hollywood: Blacks Don't Support O.J. and Whites Just Don't Get It

James M. Jones

James M. Jones is Professor of Psychology at the University of Delaware and Director of the Minority Fellowship Program at the American Psychological Association. A second edition of his classic book *Prejudice and Racism* has just been published by McGraw-Hill.

We, the jury in the above entitled action, find the defendant, Orenthal James Simpson, not guilty of the crime of murder. . . .

In response to this simple declarative pronouncement of O.J.'s lack of guilt,[1] Black America cheered, raised their fists in victory. White America gasped in horror and pain. While Black America felt victory, I doubt that White America felt defeat. I suspect they felt more like betrayed. *Those* Blacks on the jury had perverted *our* justice system for group aggrandizement. There was little question, in the mind of White America, that O.J. was guilty (polls showed about 65 percent of them felt so). In a display of racial arrogance (read racism) they lambasted the jury for deliberating too little, for identifying with the defendant on the basis of race, and for letting that identification gain emotional leverage on their reason, and in the final analysis, for not seeing the evidence the way *they* did!

There were two elements to Black reactions: (1) Legal Retribution for past Injustice, and (2) Existential Reality of the Racism Evidence. For Whites, too, there were two reactions: (1) O.J. was dispositionally and physically capable of the crimes, ergo he was guilty; and (2) Blacks *had to ignore* the evidence to reach that verdict. For Blacks, institutional and cultural context provided reasonable doubt based on the idea that racism provided a plausible alternative explanation for both the evidence and O.J.'s culpability in the crime. For Whites, dispositional characteristics of jealousy, violent temperament, egocentrism, provided the strongest suspicion that DNA evidence confirmed beyond reasonable doubt—O.J. did it!

While Black America may have claimed victory, they did not embrace O.J. as a hero. In fact, the depth of Black reaction to the verdict is given precisely because O.J. was no hero to Black America. O.J. was a Planet Hollywood celebrity who had abandoned his Black wife, hung out at the Riviera country club with his rich white friends, and forgotten how to find the inner city. Why then did Black America cheer?

The LAPD beat Rodney King on video and walked. For many Blacks, the O.J. trial was about the LAPD, and whereas they walked when the venue was shifted to Simi Valley, they were convicted when it was brought back to downtown LA. Blacks cheered the conviction of the LAPD, Whites lamented the acquittal of O.J. Blacks cheered racism revealed. Whites jeered justice denied. Different worlds, different experiences, different emotions.

In the few pages that follow, I will advance the idea that 1) racial differences in reactions to the verdict stem from cultural differences in social perception; 2) racial differences in experience provide a different data base from which to extrapolate the interpretive meaning of evidence; and 3) White ethnocentrism and subtle racism lay behind their reaction to the verdict.

From Dispositions to Acts: Attributional Biases in Perceiving the Behavior of Others

Jones and Davis (1965) outlined the process by which people infer causes for the behavior of others under the title, "From Acts to Dispositions." The general idea is that we infer the causes of behavior by working backwards to figure out the correspondence between the behavior and a plausible set of underlying dispositions that could have caused it. We are satisfied most when the causes for behavior are located internal to the actor, imply dispositional stability, and correspond best to the act itself.

So important is it to us that we Americans find a dispositional explanation for behavior, that we err in the direction of seeing more disposition than is there. This tendency has been labeled the Fundamental Attribution Error (FAE) (cf. Ross, 1979). This "error" occurs because we see others' actions as dispositional, failing to perceive the possibility that circumstances in their environment may importantly affect their behavior. Behavior, in this view, is a mirror on the soul, a reflection of personal traits and qualities that define one's character and worth. Weiner (1994) suggests that when negative outcomes occur and a dispositional attribution is made, the actor is held accountable and consequently blamed for his *sin*.

Western cultures can be described as "independent"—hardening of boundaries between self and other; focus on internal attributes, preferences, traits, and abilities. In an independent culture, our judgments of others focus on internal or dispositional proprieties of the self and these are seen as defining of character and causal for behavior. It is this hardening of boundaries between self and other that gives rise to the FAE. By contrast, other cultures are less prone to this FAE tendency to the extent that they could be described as "interdependent"—blurring of boundaries between self and other; focus on the interdependent relationships among people where duty, obligation, and responsibility are paramount (Markus & Kitayama, 1991). In an interdependent culture, judgments of others are contextualized by interdependent relationships and expectancies, and these define the self in relation to others and offer contextualized causes for individual behavior.[2]

The point to be made here is that in a cultural-independent context, the biases all operate so as to focus attention on the individual culpability for behavior, and when negative outcomes can be linked to this internal cause evaluative judgments quickly follow. O.J. was guilty for Whites, in part, because over time, the horrendous outcome became attached to dispositional properties of O.J.—the 911 tapes established his violent temper, his self-absorbed egocentrism, his jealousy, and his public self-consciousness (cf. Scheier and Carver, 1980). This tendency to make a dispositional attribution made it all the easier to accept the blood evidence. It was the biological counterpart to the dispositional character evidence. This point only comes together if we assume, as I clearly do, that Whites as a group adopt the cultural-independence beliefs with all the cognitive and evaluative implications outlined above.

But, this is not a one-way street. Blacks, too, made a dispositional attribution—Fuhrman was a racist. His racism was shown just as clearly by his taped interviews with Laura Hart McKinny as O.J.'s violence was shown by the 911 tapes. But whereas O.J.'s dispositional culpability went directly to his murderous acts, Fuhrman's went directly to the context, the community of the LAPD. The evidence of a racist police department is revealed by a racist cop. O.J.'s dispositional character explained his individual act. Fuhrman's dispositional character explained the entire context of racism in the LAPD.

RACIAL DIFFERENCES IN EXPERIENCE—AFFECT CONTROL AND INJUSTICE—
WHITES 2,178, BLACKS 1!

The previous section argued that Blacks and Whites activated somewhat different perceptual and cognitive processes as they assessed the evidence and made the critical judgments of guilt. We now make the claim that because of fundamentally different experiences, Blacks and Whites developed different emotional sensitivities which influenced their interpretations of justice in the verdict.

One of the pivotal differences between Blacks and Whites was that Fuhrman's racism, which all could see and abhor, ultimately meant less to Whites than to Blacks. It had the capacity to explain more for Blacks than for Whites. Henry Louis Gates (1995) suggests that

> people arrive at an understanding of themselves and the world through narratives—narratives purveyed by schoolteachers, newscasters, "authorities," and all the other authors of our common sense. Counternarratives are, in turn, the means by which groups contest the dominant reality and the fretwork of assumptions that supports it . . . much of black history is simply counternarrative . . . fealty to counternarratives is an index to alienation, not to skin color . . . (p. 57).

Counternarratives tell the story of our dominant cultural reality-freedom, liberty equality—from the other side. That race had nothing to do with the O.J. trial is a narrative told from the dominant view point. In the counternarrative, race had everything to do with it. More important than the perspective, which is important, is the fact that these narratives and counternarratives define reality! They define not only our collective cultural realities, but our individual, personal realities as well. Counternarratives are not simply a reification of skin color as a dividing line, they reflect alienation from the White cultural narrative that marginalizes Blacks as a group, while ambivalently and ambiguously accepting individual Blacks. Black emotions attach to the narratives and specific events which exemplify them.

In the first instance, O.J. was famous, *not* Black. In the final analysis, O.J. was Every Black Man who, in the counternarrative, had been victimized by injustice. The emotional attachment we saw was to the counternarrative. Whites' emotional attachment was to the narrative in which race was not an issue. When the verdict came down, Whites saw what in their mind was an irrelevant feature define reality. Blacks saw an atypical situation where a perspective from their counter reality was given voice. This verdict now is added to the counternarrative which now reads Whites 2,178, Blacks 1.

To put this thinking into a conceptual framework, we offer Affect Control Theory (ACT) (Sher and Heise, 1993) as a plausible basis for differential emotions (see also, Izard, 1991; Smith, 1993). ACT proposes that a given situation may arouse justice-related emotions, which once triggered can affect the subsequent judgment of justice. By this reasoning, Whites's perception that the verdict was unjust, and Blacks judgment that it was just, can be derived from the justice-related emotion that accompanied the trial.

The fundamental ACT proposition is that:

> When people involved in transaction feel anger or guilt, and the emotions are not ameliorated, they may decide that the transaction is unfair or unjust.

Many people were angered by O.J.'s abusive treatment of Nicole. That anger, in their context of the trial for murder, aroused justice concerns. The verdict, then, was judged unfair because of the prior emotion-laden anger held toward O.J.

The same emotion-laden anger may have occurred for those upset by Fuhrman's racism. For them, though, the verdict vindicated their anger and reduced any feelings of justice incongruence (i.e., injustice).

Smith (1993) argues that the experiences of members of our group can evoke emotional feelings in us such that we feel as though we have had their experience. This group-identification basis of emotion may further explain the differential reaction of Whites and Blacks. Blacks have experienced Whites directly or vicariously over hundreds of years, the murder, torture, and abuse of their people at the hands of Whites. The disfigured face of Emmitt Till in *Jet* magazine in 1954 is one vivid example. The face of Rodney King rekindled that image and the failure to convict Till's attackers and to convict the LAPD officers who beat King resulted in emotional anger at justice-related scenarios. Adding fuel to the fire is the image that it is Black men who are violent and who are dangerous. Charles Hughes killed his wife in Boston, and by simply calling 911 and reporting a Black male attacker, he had the community up in arms searching for a Black man. Susan Smith, a copy cat accuser, did the same thing when she drowned her two sons in South Carolina. The fact that these stories were plausible and believable attests to the idea that in the counternarrative account, Injustice and Justice trade places. The cultural narrative that pronounces Black men guilty until proven innocent is rewritten innocent until proven guilty. And to this jury, the burden of proof was not met. It is possibly true that the burden of proof is heavier when the evidence is viewed through counternarrative scenario lenses, and the defendant is a Black man.

Whites, by contrast, may have cognitive understanding of these scenarios, but certainly not emotionally laden experiences of a personal nature. Did O.J.'s crime become emotional because his victims were White? Would the anger-mediated judgments have been as severe if his alleged victim had been his Black first wife? Such counterfactual thinking is a bit mushy here, but it does seem intuitively less likely that the media frenzy and the emotional fascination of the American people would have been so great if it were a within-group situation.

Justice indifference is an important concept in ACT. It refers to the extent that a given interaction or situation arouses justice concerns. The high-profile nature of the case certainly made it low (near zero) in justice indifference. Whites were angry at O.J., Blacks at Fuhrman. Had the verdict been reversed, it would have been Blacks who saw injustice and whose emotions would have been strong.

This ACT analysis suggests that Whites, already angered by O.J.'s behavior toward Nicole, found the verdict escalated the justice-incongruence in their minds. This escalation, mediated by emotional anger, found release and explanation in the perception of unfairness. ACT theory argues that emotion mediates judgments of unfairness, and are not simply reactions to what are perceived to be unfair outcomes. Thus it was their anger at his abusiveness and their prior belief in his guilt that triggered the reaction.

For Whites, then, a not guilty verdict was unjust but a guilty verdict would have been just. For Blacks the reverse was true. What we saw in the initial reactions, shown widely on network TV all over the country, was the emotional concomitant of affect control processes.

A second aspect of this case and one of the important principles of ACT is transient impression of actors. The Behavior-Object relationship suggests that behaviors are evaluated more negatively when they are out of character—powerful behaviors are evaluated more negatively when they are directed at weak objects; and behaviors are judged worse when performed by a bad than a good actor.

Put these things together and you have the context for strong, negative emotion associated with O.J. These strong negative emotions then mediate perceptions of unfairness in the verdict and intensify the emotional feelings already present.

One provocative implication of ACT is "that a sequence of negative events might push the transient impressions of participants (O.J.) down sufficiently that even a procedure decided by a 'benevolent judge' would evoke injustice-related emotions." This analysis suggests that perceptions of judicial bias may be triggered by the sequence of emotion-mediated judgments, not by a cognitively objective appraisal of the decision and the rationale's provided by jurors for it.

WHITE ETHNOCENTRISM AND SUBTLE RACISM—EVEN MY ERRORS ARE CORRECT!

The first two analyses above suggest that Whites differed from Blacks in the ways in which evidence was processed, and this difference revolved, in part, around different experiences Blacks and Whites have had in America. These analyses sought to explain, in part, differential perceptions of guilt and innocence as well as differences in the degree of justice perceived in the jury verdict. We now look at White's reactions to the verdict and to the Black reactions to it. I suggest here that the strong, negative judgments of Blacks and the Black influence on the jury verdict may be associated with White ethnocentrism and subtle racism.

As Gates (1995) put it, "for many Whites a sincere belief in Simpson's innocence looks less like a culture of protest than like a culture of *psychosis*" (p. 56, emphasis added). That is, you got to be crazy to think he is innocent. In fact, one person noted that as a result of this verdict, she would no longer be able or willing to vote for General Colin Powell, because "I don't want to give *them* any more power."

Ethnocentrism refers simply to the preference for aspects of one's own ethnicity or culture. There is a strong tendency for most groups in the world to maintain such ethnocentric attitudes and beliefs. Deviations from this pattern are usually associated with subjugation to hegemonic groups (e.g., Sidanius, 1993). In these instances, it is argued that reduced levels of ethnocentrism can be traced to acceptance of "legitimizing myths" which are stories (narratives) that endorse the structure and extol the virtue of the social hierarchy, embrace its inevitability, and even assert its inherent morality. *The Bell Curve* (Herrnstein and Murray, 1994) can be viewed as such a myth in this light.

The preferences for one's own group's ways of being have been shown to produce a preference for members of one's own group (Brewer, 1979) known as in-group bias. Social psychologists have become quite expert at demonstrating the subtle ways in which such ethnocentrism or in-group bias operates. For example, Dovidio, Evans, and Tyler (1986) showed subjects a slide with the words, white, black, or house, followed by a slide that contained adjective traits associated with positive or negative stereotypes of Blacks or Whites. Subjects had to determine whether the adjective words "could ever be true" of the group shown in the first slide. White subjects responded fastest when they judged whether a positive attribute associated with Whites was true of Whites.

More recently, Fazio et al. (1995) demonstrated a subtle unobtrusive measure of racial attitude. They define attitude as an affective reaction to a stimulus object. Therefore, a positive attitude toward Blacks could be reflected in a positive affective reaction to a photograph of a Black person. Conversely, a negative reaction would suggest a negative attitude. Fazio et al. primed subjects with both white and black photographs just prior to them making judgments about whether specific adjectives were predominately positive or predominately negative. If the picture evoked a positive attitude, they reasoned, this judgment should be facilitated when it was a positive word, and inhibited when it was a negative word. Thus, the speed with which these adjective judgments were made indicated the racial attitude of the subject.

Fazio et al. found that for white subjects, responses were facilitated most when a positive adjective judgment followed a white photo, and next most when a negative adjective judgment followed a black photo. This is precisely the pattern of in-group bias. Moreover, the more this pattern was true of a given subject, the more likely he or she was to rate a Black experimenter negatively. So this unobtrusive measure of racial attitude actually was manifested in differential race-relevant behavior.[3]

How does this relate to the jury verdict? Specifically, I suggest that the attributional processes, the salience and legitimacy of personal experience, or the emotion-mediated sense of fairness, which could reasonably be shown to differ between racial groups, was largely dismissed by Whites in their reaction to Black reactions to the verdict. From an ethnocentric perspective, the perceptions of Blacks had no merit because the basis on which their view could be correct had little legitimacy within a White ethnocentric context. If a narrative has no meaning within a sociocultural context, it is likely to be ignored or rejected or at best to be tolerated. Within this ethnocentric cultural matrix of reasoning and analysis, legitimate belief in innocence is simply not possible.

But the verdict did *not* confer innocence on O.J., it merely acknowledged an absence of guilt. But as a White female colleague said, "he was guilty of something" (namely domestic violence). But as a Black female juror noted emphatically, this was not a domestic violence case. So what is the legitimate perspective on the case? What determines the basis of guilt, innocence, and doubt when there are such divergent perspectives operating? How important are violent temperament and racism and how should they be judged? And finally, what about the brutally murdered victims? Someone certainly did it, and we have not legally determined who it is.

The next element of this analysis is the hated R word, racism. First, we must recognize that racism is a belief in the superiority of one's own group. Nikki Giovanni captured this spirit in her poem, ". . . I am so great even my errors are correct!" I have argued that racism as name-calling is not a very profitable enterprise (Jones, 1972; 1992). There are, to be sure, individuals who can by any account be considered a racist. Abraham Lincoln comes immediately to mind as the following quote suggests:

> I am not, nor ever have been, in favor of bringing about in any way the social and political equality of the white and black races; I am not, nor ever have been, in favor of making voters or jurors of Negroes, nor qualifying them to hold office. . . .
>
> I will say in addition to this that there is a physical difference between the white and black races which I believe will ever forbid the two races living together on terms of social and political equality. And in as much as they cannot so live, while they do remain together there must be the position of superior and inferior, and I as much as any other man am in favor of having the superior position assigned to the white race. (Abraham Lincoln, 1894, pp. 369–370, 457–458)

But what is most important is that racism operates across multiple levels from individual psyches to institutional practices to cultural values and meanings. It is within the fabric of this interlocking network of perceptions, beliefs and values, laws and institutional practices, and cultural expressions that racism lurks.

Racism operates at three levels; *individual* (beliefs in the superiority of one's own racial group), *institutional* (institutional practices that produce systematic advantages for one racial group over another, whether intended or not), and *cultural* (a race-based normative standard of value, merit and meaning that places one's own group at the apex of a value hierarchy and judges other racial groups deficient in comparison) (Jones, 1972). The levels are interlocking in that individual beliefs are partially derived from the outcomes of institutional racism, and the power to define racial difference as deficiency, and racial similarity as the exception that proves the rule (Jones, 1988).

One group's figure is another group's ground. As we saw with the ethnocentrism analysis, own-group standards are figure when concerned with something positive. Other groups become figure when a negative judgment is at hand. Racism is in the end about figure and ground. As one student at my university noted, "the defense brought race into the trial because they needed an issue to divert jurors away from the evidence in the trial." For this White student, the "evidence" was figure and the possibility of racism was ground. Linking blood to O.J. is evidence, but linking racism to the policemen who found and preserved the blood is a diversionary tactic. In the counternarrative that tells the story of injustice and oppression in Black America, racism is the figure and virtually all else is ground.

Conclusion

The dramatically different reactions of Black and White Americans to the verdict in the O.J. Simpson murder trial clearly focused our attention on the great racial divide in America. Did it deepen and widen it? I think not. But I think it did most definitely expose the depth and breadth of it. I have tried in the preceding pages to suggest ways in which we may understand this divide using the reactions to the jury verdict as text, and social psychological theory and research as hermeneutic analysis.

As the data from the Fazio et al. (1995) study suggests, Blacks and Whites have different foci of attention. Whites are most strongly biased toward their own experiences, values, beliefs, and the products of their culture. Blacks, who have so often been victimized by those very beliefs and cultural outcroppings, mistrust them and ultimately dislike them. The stories are different, the symbols that attach to them are different, and the experiences from which they are derived are different. The racial divide is deep, wide, and real.

Is this to say there is no hope? Alas, can't we all get along? It seems to me that the starting point is to recognize the profound differences in experiences and the perceptual, emotional consequences to which they give rise. In the jury verdict reaction, there is a profound sense that Whites as a group declared their perspective superior, denigrated the Black viewpoint and the jury itself as an extension of a Black perspective. Such a failure to escape cultural biases reflects the patterns of racism that cause the divide in the first place. Moreover, it suggests that, left unchecked and unexamined, differences will grow rather than recede, and lack of communication will exacerbate the already profound differences in experience and expectation between Black and White Americans.

But I believe that there is a strong positive sentiment in most Americans, Black and White, to make this society a kinder and gentler one. To tone down the race rhetoric, I believe, we must be willing to recognize variations in experience and perspective, and try to understand it. To examine our viewpoints and the *possibility* that other viewpoints not only exist but have merit.

References

Brewer, M. B. (1979). In group bias in the minimal intergroup situation: Cognitive-motivational analysis. *Psychological Bulletin, 86,* 307–332.

Fazio, R. H., Jackson, J. R., Dunton, B. C., and Williams, C. J. (1995). Variability in automatic activation as an unobtrusive measure of racial attitudes bona fide pipeline? *Journal of Personality and Social Psychology*, 69, 1013–1027.

Gates, H. L. (1995). Thirteen ways of looking at a Black man. *The New Yorker*, LXXI, October 23. 56–65.

Izard, C. E. (1991). *The Psychology of Emotions*. New York: Plenum.

Jones, E. E., and Davis, K. E. (1965). A theory of correspondent inferences: From acts to dispositions. In L. Berkowitz (ed.), *Advances in Experimental Social Psychology, Vol. 2*. New York: Academic Press.

Jones, J. M. (1972). *Prejudice and Racism*. Reading, MA: Addison Wesley.

Jones, J. M. (1988). Racism in Black and White: A bicultural model of reaction and evolution. In P. A. Katz and D. A. Taylor (eds.), *Eliminating Racism: Profiles in Controversy*. New York: Plenum. pp. 117–135.

Markus, H., and Kitayama, S. (1991). Culture and the self: Implications for cognition, emotion and motivation. *Psychological Review*, 98, 224–253.

Murray, C. A., and Herrnstein, R. E. (1994). *The Bell Curve*. New York: The Free Press.

Ross, L. (1977). The intuitive psychologist and his shortcomings: Distortions in the attribution process. In L. Berkowitz (ed.), *Advances in Experimental Social Psychology* (vol. 10, pp. 174–221). New York: Academic Press.

Scheier, M. F., and Carver, C. S. (1980). Private and public self-attention, resistance to change and dissonance reduction. *Journal of Personality and Social Psychology*, 39, 390–405.

Scher, S. J., and Heise, D. R. (1994). Affect and the perception of injustice. In E. Lawler, B. Makovsky, and J. O'Brien (eds.), *Advances in Group Processes, Vol. 10*. New York: JAI Press

Sidanius, J. (1993). The psychology of group conflict and the dynamics of oppression: A social dominance perspective. In S. Iyengar and W. J. McGuire (eds.), *Explorations in Political Psychology* (pp. 183–219) Durham, NC: Duke University Press.

Smith, E. R. (1993). Social identity and social emotions: Toward new conceptualizations of prejudice. In D. M. Mackie and D. L. Hamilton (eds.), *Affect, Cognition and Stereotyping: Interactive Processes in Group Perceptions* (pp. 297–315). San Diego, CA: Academic Press.

Weiner, B. (1993). On sin and sickness: A theory of perceived responsibility and social motivation. *American Psychologist*, 48, 957–965.

NOTES

1. I do not take a stand here on the issue of the *actual* guilt or innocence of O.J. Simpson. Rather, my purpose is to explore the basis of dramatically different reactions of Black and White Americans to the verdict.

2. It is curious though, that while the conventional analysis suggests that FAE is more prevalent in Western cultures such as the United States, Whites seem to lose this bias when it comes to themselves and race. That is, they often fail to see the contextual basis for their own situation relative to Blacks. Blacks are less well off because of their dispositional inadequacy as FAE would have it. But, Whites are relatively better off because of their superior character, contrary to FAE's claim that context is more salient in self-attributions. When it comes to race, the environmental context is undervalued in its explanatory power by Whites for the differential standing of *both* Blacks and Whites.

3. The opposite was true for Black subjects. Their responses were facilitated most when a negative judgment was made following a White photo, and next by a positive response to a Black photo. So, Whites are most affected by positive *in-group* feelings, and Blacks by negative *out-group* feelings. This may be the flip sides of racism—Whites feel superior and Blacks hate them for it!

Double Binds of Whiteness

Elizabeth Ellsworth is Professor of Curriculum and Instruction at the University of Wisconsin–Madison. She teaches courses in the Educational Communications Technology Program that focus on media and the politics of representation in pedagogy and curriculum. She is currently completing a book on difference and modes of address in pedagogy.

I was an adult before I ever saw the picture. But even as a girl I knew there'd been a lynching in Marion. That was my father's hometown. And on one of many trips to visit my grandparents, I heard the family story: The night it happened back in 1930 someone called the house and spoke to my grandfather, whose shift at the post office began at three in the morning. "Don't walk through the courthouse square tonight on your way to work," the caller said. "You might see something you don't want to see." There was laughter at the end of the story—which puzzled me. *Something you don't want to see.* Then laughter.
. . . We white people don't want to feel guilty, of course. And guilt isn't useful. But, too often, we compensate by feeling nothing. We can at least begin to tell the truth about the past. I decided to, hoping in some way to uplift my race.

—C. Carr

C. Carr is the author of "An American Tale: A Lynching and the Legacies Left Behind" (Carr, 1994). Her essay is haunted by the laughter of family members as they recounted to her the story of that night. She returns to that laughter over and over. It causes her shame, and she has often left out the part about the laughter when she has told other people this family story.

"We can at least begin to tell the truth about the past," Carr writes. Yet she does not seek, in this telling, some single, correct, complete account of the lynching and her family's and neighbors' relations to it. Rather, she strives to produce a telling that does not end in laughter. Nor in useless guilt. Instead, her story is one of seeing and of bearing witness to the legacy of this lynching in her life—not her life as autonomous and individual, but her life as one who is "from the lineage of those who laughed." What counts for her as "the truth about the past" is this bearing witness to historical, racial, familial, religious, geographical, and economic meanings and workings of "the lineage of those who laughed"—of particular repeated enactments of "whiteness."

Unlike her grandfather that night in 1930, Carr does walk through the Marion, Indiana, courthouse square. She walks there through newspaper photos and clippings; through a visit with James Cameron, the man who was nearly lynched that night and survived to write what is probably the only written record of a lynching survivor; through her memories of family stories and silences. And she sees something she does not want to see. And she tells what she sees, without laughing, through autobiography, journalism, personal essay, and cultural analysis.

Carr reworks paralyzing guilt and shame—and ignore-ance—from the space between laughter and silence. She is determined that the laughter that has traditionally punctuated her family's telling of this event will stop with her. At the same time, she refuses to continue telling her family's story without also questioning the laughter that surrounded it. Doing so, she works to change guilt, shame, and ignore-ance into something else that can be of use to her: a story about whiteness that, as she puts it ironically, she tells "hoping in some way to uplift my race" (1994, p. 36).

In this essay, I want to explore the ways that educators might in turn be educated by C. Carr's account of a 1930 lynching in her Indiana hometown—and by Carr's reworking and rewriting of the story her family tells about that lynching. "An American Tale: A Lynching and the Legacies Left Behind" is one white woman's attempt to use journalism, autobiography, personal essay, and cultural analysis to change guilt, shame, and ignore-ance into a story about whiteness that can be of use to her as she attempts to respond to her family's particular performance of whiteness.

Here, I will argue that one of the ways "white selves" are made intelligible and enacted in ways that extend and support racist dynamics and interests is through a power-inflected communication process called the double bind. I use the notion of the double bind (which I define and discuss below) as a heuristic tool—as a way of pointing to the performative and intersubjective demeanors of whiteness. And I use it to provoke interest in tracing the affiliations between the double bind that structured Carr's family story of whiteness and those structuring stories about whiteness currently being told among academics and educators.

I want to show here that the power of the social, cultural, and educational work that Carr performs in and through the rewriting of her family's version of the lynching is that it significantly and usefully reframes the question of whiteness. Instead of defining whiteness as a fixed, locatable identity, ethnicity, or even social positioning, Carr addresses whiteness as *a dynamic of cultural production and interrelation.* By telling the lynching story differently than the way she heard it told for years growing up, she breaks the rules of her family's relating to each other *as white* and understanding each other as white *through this story.* Carr demonstrates that enactments and relations of whiteness are learned social and cultural performances. I explore how Carr's story and her reframing of whiteness from identity to social relation might be used in teaching against racisms. And I end with a discussion of how particular academic research "about and from whiteness" may be too much like Carr's family's story, and may unintentionally reinscribe those very same (white) social relations that it is meant to challenge.

Carr's story about her family's relation to the lynching recognizes that whiteness is always more than one thing:

> When I first learned that [my grandfather had] been a member [of the Klan], I remembered that his was the only one of my relatives' homes in which I ever saw black people—women from my grandma's Sunday school class. And I remembered that my grandma herself was one-quarter Indian. But these are the paradoxes of American racism. (1994, p. 35)

Always more than one thing, in her grandfather's life whiteness "was" being a member of the Klan *and* the rare-for-Marion, Indiana host to black people in his home *and* husband to a woman who was "one-quarter Indian." And, Carr's story points to the ways that whiteness is never the same thing twice:

> Then, one day while Cameron [the survivor of the lynching] was out in the town of Anderson, he saw a man on a bicycle, riding with a little blond girl perched on the handlebars—both of them laughing. Suddenly Cameron realized that this was one of the raging men who had grabbed him in the Marion jail [the night of the lynching] and pulled him out into the

street. And he felt a flicker of intense anger, but mostly he felt confounded by the purely human mystery of it. How could it be that this "happy-go-lucky man with that equally happy child had been capable of doing the things I knew he had done"? (1994, p. 34)

Never the same thing twice, whiteness can be performed "as" a raging man pulling Cameron into the street to his death by lynching *and*, at another time and in another circumstance, a laughing, loving father giving his daughter a ride on bicycle handlebars through the same street, as Cameron looks on.

With images such as these—of multiple and shifting enactments of whiteness—Carr tries to reframe whiteness from identity to social relation. By framing whiteness(es) as performances that are never just one thing, and "never the same thing twice," Carr shows whiteness as historically framed and situated. Each use of the socially and historically produced meanings and consequences of whiteness takes place within a particular time period and place, and within particular relations of power. What whiteness can and will mean, how it can and will be performed, and with what consequences to relations of power and dynamics of social interrelation—cannot be specified before any particular performance, or projected to other times and places.

This doesn't mean, however, that generalizations about social dynamics, such as "racism," are impossible and no longer useful in constructing knowledge about events or in organizing political work. What it means is this: if whiteness is always more than one thing, and if it is never the same thing twice, then discourses and actions that refuse to perform the racist work associated with any one enactment of whiteness must be recognized and staged as historically situated and context specific.

For example, Carr's rewriting of the story that her family told enacts one person's learning-to-respond-in-context to one family's highly particular performance of whiteness. By "respond-in-context," I don't mean to suggest that contexts are self-evident or unitary, with neat and locatable boundaries between them. Nor do I mean to suggest that we're ever able to "know" a context fully and thereby "read off" what would constitute correct or most effective response within it. While the story her family tells of the lynching is its time-honored performance, unique in its particularities—*it is not unique in its history or consequences*. It may have been an especially seductive performance, because it served, in part, to define a family and Carr's "home" in it. But even as the contextual particularities of Carr's seduction into her family's whiteness were unique, the historical and social consequences of defining family in this way are not. As Patricia Williams puts it:

I also believe that the personal is not the same as "private": the personal is often merely the highly particular. I think the personal has fallen into disrepute as sloppy because we have lost the courage and the vocabulary to describe it in the face of the enormous social pressure to "keep it to ourselves"—but this is where our most idealistic and our deadliest politics are lodged, and are revealed. (1991, p. 93)

To my reading, Carr's achievement is a story that unsettles neither an essential, nor an idiosyncratic white identity—but a "highly particular" structure of "white" social relations. While this structure may be highly particular to her family, it also exceeds and complicates the boundaries of her family's specific context.

This structure was made up of certain rules of speaking and silence about the lynching. These rules, when obeyed by Carr and other members of her family, produced a particular performance of whiteness, shaped by the particularties of time, place, and audience. It was that performance that became intolerable to Carr and compelled her to fashion her retelling in the first place. Performing that story differently meant performing her white self differently in relation to the story. It also meant performing her white self differently in relation to her family.

Carr's rewriting of the lynching story breaks her out of the only two options for acting white offered to her each time her family told the story: if she's "white," she either laughs at this lynching story (whether or not she finds it funny), or she keeps silent and goes numb about what it does to her to hear it.

According to Carr, these had been the only two options thinkable, allowable, intelligible from within the (white family) context of this story's telling. Caught, immobilized, in a series of unresolvable relations to the lynching story, Carr found herself boxed in by a white family system not unlike the schizophrenic family systems studied by Bateson and Laing. Those systems are characterized, according to Bateson and Laing, by a communication process they called the "double bind."

> The double bind is not merely a "damned if you do, damned if you don't" situation. In and of itself, a no-win situation cannot drive someone crazy. The crucial element is not being able *to leave the field, or point out the contradiction*; and children often find themselves in just such a situation. Thus Laing sums up the double-bind predicament as: "Rule A: Don't. Rule A.1: Rule A does not exist. Rule A.2: Do not discuss the existence or nonexistence of Rules A, A.1, or A.2."

> . . . the entire family structure is implicated, along with the society that is made up of such neurotic (and psychotic) building blocks. (Berman, 1981, p. 228, my emphasis)

To break out of the white self that her family's repeated telling of its story constructed and fortified around her, Carr had to "leave the field" of the communication processes that made such a white self intelligible. She had to leave that self's family and community context—its "highly particular" structure of relations—through which the story of the lynching was taught and told:

> Somehow a survivor hadn't made it into the family story. But the clipping my brother sent said that this man, James Cameron [the survivor], had opened a museum devoted to the history of lynching. (1994, p.32)

> Last August I went to Milwaukee to meet James Cameron. (1994, p. 35)

Feeling, questioning, and letting the lynching survivor—the other—"into the family story" shatters an unspoken, perhaps even unconscious, agreement among her family members. It shatters the unspoken, power-inflected rules or conditions of telling this story. Carr had to fulfill those rules in order for a particular performance of whiteness to be repeated and renewed, and in order for a particular context of white social relations to be reestablished *through* the telling of this story. But she breaks these rules. Carr retells the story without laughing, and she feels and tells what it has meant for her to hear it not only from her family, but now, from Cameron.

Breaking out of a double bind and into metacommunication about the double bind means that some other way of making sense not only of the story, but of the rules of communicating about the story, is available and accessible. That Carr "found" Cameron's "other" story of the lynching, and was able to put it to use as leverage to move herself out of the double bind of her family's story of the lynching, is not a happy accident. It was the result, in part, of Cameron's years of struggle to make his story available and accessible—he wrote and self-published a book, and he fought for years to establish a lynching museum in Milwaukee. Just as double binds are historical and cultural achievements, implicating entire family and social structures in their neuroses and oppressive relations of power—breaking out of a double bind and into metacommunication about it also a social and historical achievement—the result of historically situated dynamics of cultural production and interrelation.

ACADEMIC DOUBLE BINDS OF WHITENESS

Stories about and from whiteness are proliferating in the academy right now. Told, for the most part, by academics to and for other academics, they are becoming part of the "family stories" of academe. Rarely read by those outside of the academy, these stories are places of intellectual and political struggle (and bonding) over what ways of conceptualizing white should and will become thinkable, allowable, intelligible within "families"—fields—of academics.

Most of these academic stories about whiteness differ from Carr's. Their differences go beyond the common distinctions between academic and popular language or social criticism and autobiography. Unlike Carr's story, most academic stories about whiteness are preoccupied with definition and analysis. They are determined, primarily, to define and name and understand what whiteness is or how it works.

At issue are the ways various stories about whiteness address their readers, and through their addresses, invite them into different sorts of relations to whiteness. When I use stories about whiteness in classrooms, one question I'm concerned about as a teacher is: What relations to and performances of whiteness do I hope to construct and enact through our engagements with these stories?

Carr, for example, struggles within and against history, language, and experience, to construct a way of representing the story of the lynching in language and narrative structure that positions her neither as guilty perpetrator nor as unimplicated bystander. One way she tries to "uplift her race" by retelling this story, then, is to come up with a way of addressing her white readers that does not require them to see themselves as either guilty perpetrators or unimplicated bystanders in order to make sense of her story. She needs an address capable of breaking a double bind that secures a particularly immobilizing performance of whiteness, namely: white as either guilty perpetrator (laughing at the lynching story) or as unimplicated bystander (remaining silent, unresponsive).

Teaching Carr's story in graduate classes in education, I am confronting how some antiracist scholarship unintentionally addresses us, as readers, in ways that catch us up in various double binds of whiteness. It does this, for example, at the times it addresses us as either perpetrators or as innocent bystanders of racism. But beyond this, antiracist scholarship is never only antiracist. It is also scholarship—governed by rules that, I want to argue, produce and insure its own particular performances of double binds of whiteness.

Current struggles over the meanings and uses of whiteness in academic writing and teaching are shaped not only by political commitments to end racism, but also by debates, anxieties, desires, and fantasies that are driving work in a variety of academic (inter)disciplines. They are further shaped by expectations for and vested interests in particular ways of writing—particular ways of addressing readers and the (racialized) academic social relations that such addresses enact.

For example, various disciplinary discourses are framing scholarship about whiteness through questions such as: Should we academics, of any color, be conceptualizing whiteness as an identity? What is gained and/or lost in attempts to "end racism" when whiteness is defined not as an identity, but as a practice; a form of property; a performance; a constantly shifting location upon complex maps of social, economic, and political power; a form of consciousness; a form of ignorance; a privilege; something those of us who "are" white must unlearn; something we whites fear, something that gives us pleasure, something we desire; something we must name and describe and understand; something we must change; an invisible something that we must make visible, finally, at this moment in history, to our white selves?

Depending on which of these defining characteristics of whiteness I take to be true or relevant, I am confronted in various academic literatures with a variety of related educational practices. For example, should we educators of any color teach whiteness in ways that interrupt racism; work to end white supremacy; avoid the debilitating effects of white guilt; make "us" white teachers allies to "them"—those who have been targets of white racism; and make us allies to each other—those other white people committed to working against racism? Should our talk to each other in academic contexts be about the ways racisms impoverish all of us, even those of us who "are" white? Can we who "are" white do all or any of this in ways that do not reinscribe our "white skin privilege," or produce too deft a conclusion about it, one that would suggest whites have the final word about whiteness?

These are some of the preoccupations of current academic writing on whiteness. Many academics are addressing whiteness for the purpose of naming, defining, ending, or at least contesting whiteness as it has been used in the service of racist interests. And yet, my experience as a reader of much academic writing about whiteness is of being caught up, with their authors, in what seem to be academic versions of double binds of whiteness similar to the ones that structured Carr's family story.

Explicit or implicit in many current academic analyses of whiteness are arguments and/or assumptions that (re)place writer and reader in no-win relations to whiteness. But as Bateson and Laing defined the double bind—a no-win relation to whiteness isn't in and of itself paralyzing. What can paralyze an academic's ability to respond to racist uses of whiteness is his or her inability or unwillingness *to leave the field, or point out the contradiction.* No-win relations to whiteness become double binds of whiteness when academics trying to produce antiracist scholarship fail to metacommunicate about how academic discourses and writing are themselves structured by racial relations.

In other words, no-win relations to whiteness become paralyzing double binds for academics when we fail to question the racialized paradoxes produced by certain academic practices. These include academic attempts to define whiteness in the name of antiracism without recognizing that the definitional process itself is part of the problem of racism.

THE DEFINITIONAL DOUBLE BIND

For example, much of the academic literature on whiteness contends that as a white person, I should be doing the definitional work of naming and analyzing what has secured and perpetuated my white skin privilege, including the "invisibility" of whiteness—its namelessness and unspoken taken-for-grantedness. Dyer, in his attempt to name and analyze whiteness in popular movies, concludes:

> In the realm of categories, black is always marked as a colour (as the term "coloured" egregiously acknowledges), and is always particularizing. Whereas white is not anything really, not an identity, not a particular quality, because it is everything—white is no colour because

it is all colours. This property of whiteness, to be everything and nothing, is the source of its representational power. (1993, p. 142)

Whiteness, Dyer argues, is all—in that it is the normalized center against which its others are delineated. At the same time, it is nothing—in that its power lies, in part, in its ability not to name or admit its particularity, and thus its limits.

But, if I, as a teacher or scholar, take up this academic work of naming—the work of becoming the one who "knows" whiteness—I assume yet again the position within knowledge that has been historically reserved for me given my white skin: the position of one who names, who knows, who defines. And yet, if I do not do this work, I assume (whether I intend it or not) a privileged position within whiteness which is (re)secured for me each time I do not do this work: the unmarked, unraced, unspoken norm.

DiPiero, in a recent article on the connections between whiteness and masculinity, finds himself caught up in this particular double bind. At the end of his analyses of the films *White Men Can't Jump* and *Grand Canyon*, and with the last words of his article, he writes:

> I cannot attempt too deft a conclusion, one that would suggest that I have the final truth about white men or how we work, yet I nevertheless cannot force the last word on someone else. It seems, then, that white masculinity's ideological strength and weakness, which might in fact coincide almost completely, inheres in the simultaneous privilege and responsibility it grants its others of defining what it is. (1992, p. 133)

This yokes the definitional double bind to the "having the last word" double bind.

THE "HAVING THE LAST WORD" DOUBLE BIND

Having the last word, giving away the last word, forcing the last word, granting the last word. The last word. DiPiero attempts to dismantle the white masculinist privilege of having the last word. But he makes that attempt through the academic practices of scholarly writing, analysis, authorship, establishment of expertise. All of these academic practices are masculinist prerogatives historically and politically inseparable from whiteness.

The problem is that these scholarly practices are predicated precisely on being able to formulate and assert the last word. And definitions make good last words. Asserting the last word usually demands a kind of authorship that drives toward definition, naming, and expertness. DiPiero, by writing within this context—by not leaving the field by metacommunicating about the rules that structure it—has the last word despite his intentions and desires. Giving away the power to speak the final truth and definition of whiteness, he concludes by claiming that white masculinity problematically grants its others the power and responsibility of defining it. Yet doing so, he reinscribes white masculinity as the position from which this responsibility and power are granted, in conclusion. At the same time, when he associates taking social and political responsibility and the using or giving away of racial power with the academic work of defining, he reinscribes a particular kind of scholarship. He leaves intact an academic family structure that requires the (white) one who defines, grants, and concludes. Unlike Carr, DiPiero does not question the nature of his academic family's conversation.

And so, the double bind: "in this academic family, we talk about racism (like most everything else) through definitional processes and having the last word, and we don't talk about how the definitional process and having the last word have themselves participated, historically and today, in constructing and securing racist relations of academic and other power."

Other double binds are generated when definition and identity drive educational research aimed at alleviating racism in classrooms. They often take this form: "Here is a definition of whiteness that can guide good educational practices against racism in classrooms. We're offering a definition because that's what's expected and rewarded in academic work. But we're also trying not to be definitional because we recognize that whiteness is multiple and shifting in its meanings and uses. But to count as academic work in education, we have to come up with an effective educational practice—that is, a last word. So don't talk about the ways that having to be definitional and effective leads to practices that actually reinscribe some of the very racist uses of whitenesss we're trying to work against."

THE "WHITENESS IS UNSTABLE" DOUBLE BIND

Implicit in many contemporary articles in the field of cultural studies is a double bind produced by the theoretical position that "my whiteness is unstable." According to this position, whiteness is a social construct, an impossible identity, a fiction, something never fully achieved or achievable. It is never pure or real. And yet, this position argues that despite such instability, individuals or groups cannot, at this present historical moment, destablize whiteness enough to escape it, make it collapse under the weight of its own paradoxes, or ever speak or act outside of it. And yet, at the same time, this fiction that is whiteness has real effects, and if I do not work against it . . .

THE "WHITENESS IS WHITENESS IS WHITENESS" DOUBLE BIND

Another position that structures some anti-oppression pedagogies is this: whiteness is a social construct used historically in the interest of racist agendas. One of the effects of this work over time has been to attach (unearned) privileges, opportunities, safety, and status to whiteness at the expense of people of color—whether or not I want those privileges.

A problem with this position is that I and other white people are never just white. We are also always positioned within gender, language, sexuality, class, ability, size, ethnicity, and age, for example. At some times and in some places, those privileges and that safety that come with white skin can be temporarily and problematically overridden or eclipsed by the oppressions and discriminations associated with queerness, Jewishness, femaleness, poverty, homelessness.

Yet these "additional" identities are themselves never just one thing, and never the same thing twice. For example, these additional identities never mean or operate in the same ways when "added on" to white skin, black skin, yellow skin, red skin, brown skin. And yet, white and queer may at some times and places have more "in common" with black and straight than with white and straight. But white and queer, at this moment in history, can never mean or perform the same as black and queer—no matter how multiple and shifting the meanings and uses of each of these categories. Just as black and queer[1] never perform the same way as black and queer.[2]

Whiteness, like racism, is always more than one thing, and it's never the same thing twice. I am never always, and never only, the carrier of white skin privilege. So most remedies for racism predicated upon working against some singular, unified notion of white skin privilege place me in a relation to whiteness that diminishes my abilities to respond effectively to racisms in context (Fuller, 1994).

THE "WHITENESS IS MADE AND MAINTAINED THROUGH ASSOCIATION" DOUBLE BIND

Current within cultural studies is the notion that whiteness as a social positioning is constituted through an unconsciousness of white skin privilege. If I then, a white woman, actively work against racism, how "am" I white? Or, if one of the conditions of whiteness as a social positioning is the exclusivity of association, then if my lover is a person of color, how "am" I white? If I am bashed for being queer by a straight black man or woman, what of my white skin privilege— at that particular historical moment?

At the same time however, while each of the above paradoxical attempts to construct anti-definitional definitions of whiteness recognize that whiteness may be more than one thing, "the tension may be that racism is repetitive," and its repetitions are aided by "discourses of visiblity and the insistence on stable meanings" (Britzman, 1994). No matter how multiple and shifting our academic "definitions" of the meanings and performances of whiteness, white skin has its effects within contexts governed by visibility and the insistence on stable meanings.

THE "WHITE ALLY" DOUBLE BIND

Here is one double bind that structures some discourses and practices of multicultural education that attempt to teach against racism by defining what it means to be a white ally. Educators, especially, write about the importance of teaching white students how to be allies to people of color and to other white people committed to working against racism. This teaching, according to some writers, can take the form of educating white students to take pride in the long and extensive history of white people who, in addition to people of color, have been champions of antiracist work. Ways of being allies include interrupting racist jokes, interrupting racial violence, interrupting misinformation and stereotypes about others, and becoming conscious of the histories of racisms and of how racisms work.

And yet, the notion of allies reinscribes the exclusive and fixed categories friend/enemy, oppressed/oppressor, knowledgeable/ignorant. Exclusive categories such as these ignore the complexities of social positionings and of the structures of social relations that come from the shiftings and multiplicities described above. They undermine abilities to grapple with the incompleteness of any ally's knowledge about the other *and* of any ally's knowledge of self. (I may pledge to be an ally/friend today, but what if my commitment, energy, vigilance, interest, ability to be an ally/friend wavers tomorrow?) Exclusive categories foreclose the possibilities of the context-specific responses made possible when whiteness is considered in relation to the other social positionings that people live out and live through.

Furthermore, white allies, by virtue of being allies, are positioned as helpers and legitimizers of the struggles and complaints of people of color. It's hard to avoid the paternalistic connotations of white ally as helper, especially given the argument that at this moment in history, white allies could never be "equal" to people of color because we're always more privileged, therefore more powerful, and therefore make good helpers.

Because racism never operates twice in the same way with the same meanings and effects, the specifics of when and how our help as white people is appropriate, wanted, or useful are crucial. Yet the complex situatedness of being an ally is seldom addressed in curricula focused on creating white allies. Rather than alleviating the oppressor/oppressed, white/nonwhite dichotomies, the practice of creating definitions of white allies reinscribes them, even as it tries to alleviate them.

And yet, not to take responsibility for interrupting racism on behalf of those it injures is untenable. And yet, to do so—*in these terms*—invites white allies to act primarily on the ways racism hurts its targets, with little attention to the ways racism normalizes and reinscribes the allies' own whitenesses. The reading that I offer here of Carr's educational and cultural work is, in part, an attempt to shift the terms of what might be counted and recognized as "a white ally." Carr acts not as a parternalistic helper of the oppressed. Rather, she acts back on the fabrications, normalizations, and reinscriptions of her own whitenesses and the ways they get played out to extend and support racist interests, knowledges, and dynamics.

The act of locating double binds of whiteness as they are played out in academic discourses such as these, then, is not about throwing my hands up and saying: "See, there's nothing I can do about being white. It's a double bind. You tell me to name my whiteness, and when I do, you tell me: 'Ha! There you go, being white again—the one who defines . . .' " and so on.

No, by locating situations such as these, I mean to suggest that part of the racist potential of whiteness as a dynamic of social production and interrelation, lies precisely in the ways that its academic performances can be made into double binds. Academic double binds can confuse and paralyze, insuring repetitious performances of whiteness that (unintentionally, unconsciously) reiterate its racist work in academe and other educational contexts.

At this moment in the histories of whitenesses, it seems imperative that academic attempts to critique and destablize whiteness must, at the same time, leave the contexts of cultural production and social relations that structure academic double binds of whiteness. The racialized frames that structure academic ways of knowing and of interrelating, such as defining, speaking from the position of the one who knows, having the last word—must be responded to not as frames, but as questions. They must not be allowed to remain part of the premise of academic conversations. Academe must be made to comment on itself directly.

LEAVING ACADEME

Carrying Carr's story across to a graduate classroom transforms both Carr's story and my academic contexts. And carrying it into this chapter, I try to negotiate the paradoxes raised in my own attempt to leave the academic field while writing to and from that field. The (leaving the field) academic writing of Patricia Williams (1991) and Kirin Narayan (1993), for example—writings that are not autobiography, or theory, or ethnographic study, or editorial, or allegory, but which partake of all of these—show me the power, pleasures, and possibilities of leaving academe while writing to and from it. They show me this even if I haven't yet accomplished such powerful and useful leave-taking in my own work.

Carrying Carr's story over into a graduate class in education, juxtaposing it in this chapter with academic stories about whiteness such as Dyer's and DiPiero's, I want to leave academe. The process of writing this article leaves me wanting to write myself into another story of being a professor, being a scholar, being white. I want it to be a story that responds to the particular double binds of whiteness constructed and enforced in and through academic family contexts, and the rules of speaking and silence that form them.

REFERENCES

Berman, M. (1981). *The Reenchantment of the World*. Ithaca: Cornell University Press.

Britzman, D. (1994). Personal communication.

Carr, C. (1994). "An American Tale: A Lynching and the Legacies Left Behind." *The Village Voice*, February 1, 31–36.

DiPiero, T. (1992). White Men Aren't. *Camera Obscura* 30, 113–137.

Dyer, R. (1993). *The Matter of Images: Essays on Representations*. New York: Routledge.

Fuller, L. (1994). "Hey, Where's My Body and What's On it? Whiteness and Twists on Gender, Race, and Education." Paper presented at the *Journal of Curriculum Theorizing* Conference on Curriculum and Teaching, Banff, October, 1994.

Levine, J. (1994). "The Heart of Whiteness: Dismantling the Master's House." *The Village Voice Literary Supplement*, September, 11–16.

Narayan, K. (1993). "How Native Is a 'Native' Anthropologist?" *American Anthropologist* 95, 671–686.

Schon, D. (1988). "Coaching Reflective Teaching." In P. Grimmett and G. Erickson (eds.), *Reflection in Teacher Education*, pp. 19–29. New York: Teachers College Press.

Williams, P. (1991). *The Alchemy of Race and Rights: Diary of a Law Professor*. New York: Routledge.

Thank you, Sousan Arafeh, Deborah Britzman, Pat Encisco, Laurie Fuller, Janet L. Miller, Mimi Orner, and Alberto J. Rodriguez for reading drafts of this chapter and giving me vital suggestions and critique.

Denying (White) Racial Privilege: Redemption Discourses and the Uses of Fantasy

Leslie G. Roman

Leslie G. Roman is Associate Professor of Educational Studies within the Faculty of Education at the University of British Columbia. Recently she has been a Scholar in Residence with the Centre for Research in Women's Studies and Gender Relations at UBC and is one of the 1996/97 Killam Memorial Fellows. She writes in the overlapping and sometimes disjunctive areas of feminist theory, antiracist pedagogy, neocolonialism, critical ethnography, and cultural studies. Her work has been published in such journals as *Educational Theory* and *Discourse: Studies in the Cultural Politics of Education*, and in edited collections on qualitative research and critical approaches to racism and sexism. She introduced and coedited with Dennis Dworkin *Views Beyond the Border Country: Raymond Williams and Cultural Politics* (New York: Routledge, 1993). She also introduced and coedited with Linda Christian-Smith and Elizabeth Ellsworth *Becoming Feminine: The Politics of Popular Culture* (Sussex: Falmer Press, 1988). Currently, she is coediting with Linda Eyre a book tentatively entitled *Dangerous Territories: Struggles for Equality and Difference in Education* (forthcoming with Routledge). Her forthcoming book (with Routledge), tentatively entitled *Transgressive Knowledge*, compares the contributions of recent developments in cultural and feminist theories for anti-oppression on coalition practice and pedagogies.

Precisely because orientalism has many guises—both decadent and progressive, in the form of sexual adventures and textual devotion, and also, in the form of political idealization, fascination with subaltern groups and disenfranchised classes, and so forth—what we need to examine even more urgently is fantasy, a problem which is generally recognized as central to orientalist perceptions and significations.

—Rey Chow, "The Dream of a Butterfly"

Investing in heroines and heroes involves myth-making and lived ideology, and it blurs the modernist disciplinary lines between history and fiction, sociology and literature, and education and mis-education. Such investments and the Western disciplinary knowledge they produce are rarely examined in relation to how forms of racial privilege and national supremacy are constructed and taught. Yet the significance of allegories which represent those who are the subjects/objects of colonial, neocolonial, and racial political idealization and fascination is more complicated than what they make visible about so-called "subalterness," "racial otherness," and so forth. If, as Walter Benjamin reminds us, "allegory . . . means precisely the non-existence of what it presents," then the process of creating nonpresence is both a function and an effect of historical amnesia/memory as realized through language (Benjamin 1977, 233). Never innocent, allegories of culture and national heritage at once realize and repress, stage and make invisible, the problematic location of the imperial observers themselves (Bhabha, 1990, 1992, 1994; Chow 1995; Pyle, 1993; Radhakrishnan, 1993; Viswanathan, 1993).

Since Edward Said's influential critique of orientalism, it has been commonplace for intellectuals, particularly those in subaltern and cultural studies, to point out both the role of the Western imperial gaze in constructing cultural "others" and the racist, sexist, nationalist conception of "culture" in cultural studies itself (Bhabha, 1994; Gilroy, 1993; Viswanathan, 1993). Yet, located as "we" are in such a reflexive state of postmodernity and postcolonial thought, it is difficult to discern the difference between ritual enactments of confession and genuine self-/social criticism. Reflexivity has often given way to uncritical narratives of redemption, for, even as the epistemological positions and self-locations of the observers are problematized, they are also contained within (and thus appropriated by) an imperialist milieux (e.g., the Western education system).[2] Imperial cultures forge the greatness of their subjects (whether in heroic or demonic terms) by sexualizing their "racial otherness" and racializing their "sexual" and "gender otherness" in the context of transglobal class inequalities.[3] In such a context, it is difficult to move away from one of two apparently polarized but nonetheless intimately linked discursive positions: (1) a righteous, smug progressivism—what I call the problematic elements of an "anti-ism critique" (whether of anti-orientalism, antiracism, antisexism, or antiheterosexism), and (2) the celebration of presumed essential "differences" between groups. So commonplace are these two positions that to attempt to speak more directly to the conditions and limits of postcolonial narrativity and representation is to raise seemingly impertinent questions regarding their methods, epistemologies, and politics.

Far less commonplace than the debunking efforts of "anti-ism critiques," as Rey Chow (1996a) so persuasively argues in relation to anti-orientalism and the "difference criticism" of certain versions of postmodernism and poststructuralism, is the acknowledgment of the work that needs to be accomplished in order to exceed the polemical limits of such frameworks. Such work would recognize that constructing particular historical subjects as free of contradictions, complex agency, and/or historical/political/material context (or, in other words, as heroic or demonic) is neither innocent nor unambivalent. If Said would have us vigorously problematize the dangerous presumption of stable racial and ethnic identities, it seems clear that, as Chow (1996a) indicates, we should also ask "what . . . there is to learn beyond destabilized identities themselves" (p. 62). The postcolonial limits of representation of "difference criticism" itself imbue the histories of imperial, racial, and sexual injustice—histories which, in turn, condition imagination, public memory, and narratives (Chow, 1996a; Pyle, 1993; Romero, 1993).

Following Chow's (1996a) logic, I wish to make clear that to critique the polemical limits of "anti-ism critiques" is neither to dismiss nor to diminish their crucial role in analyzing systemically oppressive practices (e.g., racism, sexism, heterosexism, classism, and so forth). Rather, it is to suggest that there are other pressing problems which are *incapable* of being comprehended through rigid binary oppositions. These problems deal with the complex interrelations between the reading/writing subjects of historical representations as well as between "our" desire to know "the other" and the ability of those who have been written about to make themselves known (whether through verbal texts such as oral history or visual images). They also deal not only with the limits of human vision as Chow (1996a) suggests, but more particularly with those of feminist and antiracist/imperialist vision and historical representation.

Reading, writing, and rewriting history and cultural politics are intertwined with people's complex stakes and feelings. These stakes are at once affectively ideological and material. They leave traces of the asymmetries of unequal power distribution between dominant and subordinate racial groups within all forms of representation. Yet, they also discountenance easy assumptions that "racial others," "subaltern," or otherwise disenfranchised groups are passive in either resisting and/or producing and reproducing the structures of imperial domination—whether or not they emanate from European and American contexts.

FANTASIES OF REDEMPTIVE IDENTIFICATION: MINEFIELDS OF POWER, SHAME, AND DENIAL

In order for historians or, for that matter, contemporary feminist and/or antiracist writers\schol-ars to consciously identify with their subjects, they must be able to fantasize their relation with an other or others. Here, what Chow (1996a) argues with regard to fantasy, after literary critic Cora Kaplan (1986), is relevant to the postcolonial limits of (historical) imagination and representa-tion.[4] Seen as a constituent part of the act of historical representation, fantasy is less a "matter of willful exploitation or distortion" than "an inherent part of consciousness" or "a wakeful state of mind" (Chow 1996a, 63).

What I like about this formulation is that it gives us a way *through* (rather than out of or around) the polemics of anti-ism pedagogies. It speaks to the polemics of these pedagogies, which often imagine themselves as (1) unwaveringly and unambivalently *identified* with the racially oppressed, and (2) as free of orientalizing tendencies which in turn may manifest them-selves in the classroom as gendered forms of "white defensiveness" (Roman 1993b; Kenway 1995) and, thus, as capable of offering an *automatically* reflexive and strictly rationalist basis for pedagogy. At the same time, it also calls into question what is imagined, for example, by the white (North American) Western subject who asserts so much "difference" these days (whether in terms of scholarly articulations or in everyday populist forms of antistatist indi-vidualism). Clearly, the discursive production of identification (or dis-identification) with an imagined or fantasized "other" involves crucial, complex, and contradictory relations of power. As Chow (1996a) argues, following Jean Laplanche and Jean-Bertrand Pontalis (1968), "fantasy is not merely the domination of an other"; rather, it involves the variable position of the subject, whose reality shifts between dominance and submission (Chow 1996a, 63). This disturbs the usual binary relations between, say, those who write and those who are written about insofar as it problematizes the notion of a one-way interaction between the subject and the purported object of the fantasy or gaze. It also problematizes various fantasies of white (feminist or non-feminist) avowed identification (and implicit dis-identification) with "racial" or "subaltern others."

I suggest that, in the present context of the spectacle of multiculturalism (which commodifies and appropriates "racial" and "national" otherness rather than redressing racial and imperialist inequalities),[5] white fantasies of identification with those rendered "racial" or "subaltern others" are to be read not merely as sentimental narratives of "identification with," or love for, an objec-tified "exotic" or "strong other," but as one likely provisional effect of "institutionally produced redemption discourses" (Roman 1993a, 1993b, 214; Roman and Stanley 1994). By this I mean the residual and emergent ways colonial and neocolonial power relations attempt to impose their own limits on everyday discursive practices through forms of consciousness and conventions of representation, signification, and pedagogy that more generally characterize liberal educational institutions and liberal humanism (Karamcheti, 1995; Mohanty, 1988; Mohanty, 1989/90).[6] Re-demption discourses mask the desire to know one's own systemic complicity (both individually and collectively) in racial inequality and exploitative nation-building and its concomitant de-struction of existing communities and nations. They may accomplish or be accompanied by coun-tervailing subversive or resistant discursive/political strategies, which is why I speak of their effects in provisional terms.

Fantasies of identifying with and, hence, knowing others through the dualism of "us and them" are an inevitable part of redemption discourses, and they represent both the worst and the best liberal humanism has to offer. Claims by racially privileged whites, for example, to know "racialized others," who are at once seen as a "them" *exposed* to an "us," reify purported differences while they simultaneously establish a normative (e.g., white) self against which "racial otherness" is brought to light.[7]

Sojourner Truth has been used to defend and valorize particular contemporary Western feminist theories (often in the name of a larger redemptive genealogy of Western feminism) from the normative place of their unspoken whiteness.[8] This point was driven home to me by Nell Irvin Painter's (1994) excellent article, "Sojourner Truth's Knowing and Becoming Known," which challenged me to rethink my own representations of Truth as a figure for feminist materialism (Roman, 1993c). Painter's work challenges the historicity and dematerialization of Sojourner Truth evident in so many commonplace past and present representations of her. She shows how such representations deny Sojourner Truth's own agency, material interests, and gender-specific struggles in the abolition movement by reducing her to a couple of famous speeches,[9] which were, in the first place, mediated by white suffragists, who recalled them from memory years after they were given. Given that, for complex material and political reasons, Sojourner Truth refused to become formally literate as an adult (when the first opportunities for formal education and tutoring emerged), the meanings, or, as I would argue, the public/official record of her persona "were much more subject to other people's interpretation than [is the case] when a [formally] literate person moves onto the stage" (Painter, 1994, 470). Painter is one of the few historians to show how Sojourner Truth, despite her illiteracy and consequent reliance upon others in white society to represent her in print, actively engaged in the creation of herself as a "racial icon" in order to support herself. Painter shows how Truth skillfully marketed herself by selling her photographic portraits. The medium of photography afforded her more control than did the medium of print because she could set the terms under which her photos were sold (p. 470).

Not surprisingly, given the primacy of written over spoken/oral communication in Western metropolitan culture, Sojourner Truth is known, even to this day, primarily through the least reliable of these sources—printed words mediated from memory by whites. Through Painter, we learn that what is known about Sojourner Truth in print primarily derives from the writings of four educated white women (Olive Gilbert, Harriet Beecher Stowe, Frances Dana Gage, and Frances Titus), "who were fascinated by her and sought to capture her in writing" (Painter, 1994, 471). For example, Painter shows how the most famous of Truth's alleged speeches, "Ar'n't I a Woman?" is an invention of the white suffragist Frances Dana Gage, who, twelve years after the speech was given in Akron, Ohio, in 1851, published her memory of it in a letter to a local newspaper, *The Independent*. As Painter points out, the famous phrase, "Ar'n't I a Woman?" is "sometimes rendered more authentically Negro" when it appears as "Ain't I a Woman?" (p. 464). This speech was subsequently republished and popularized in one of the primary texts of the women's suffrage movement, *History of Woman* [sic] *Suffrage* (1881–1886, vol. 1, 110–13) by Elizabeth Cady Stanton, Susan B. Anthony, and Matilda Joslyn Gage. White suffragists and writers of Truth's day, who, according to Painter, had access to, and materially benefited from, publishing slave narratives as well as those of abolitionists, did more than simply record and transcribe Sojourner Truth's words (as if naturalistic description were ever fully possible); they also embellished and constructed them in already racialized language and imagery—sometimes making "careless" or "contrived mistakes" about the important biographical moments of her life.[10]

Redemptive discursive claims may even go so far as to appropriate experiences of racial oppression.[11] More often, however, due to liberalism's appeal to universalism and its reliance upon putatively "color blind" or "neutral" social democratic reforms, redemption discourses may present themselves as witnesses to, or dreams of, racially unequal subjects merging or becoming one, communicating lovingly in spite (or because) of the great chasms of inequality. However, as Renate Salecl (1994a) puts it, love [itself] is an inherently historical phenomenon: its concrete configurations are so many (ultimately failed) attempts to gentrify, tame, symbolize, the unhistorical [sic] traumatic kernel of *jouissance* that makes the object bearable . . . love is never "just love," but always the screen, the field on which battles for power and domination are fought. (p. v)

Redemption discourses claim that loving identification with, and caring for, the "racial other" partially overcomes and appropriates what the racially privileged are *not* able to know (consciously) from their own *direct experiences*—that is, the concrete effects of racism. By considering such inequalities to be merely problems of translation/miscommunication across purported "cross-cultural" divides, a kind of *premature* and *undeserved absolution* is accomplished.[12] [Mis]read as problems of cross-cultural communication, such absolutions displace political responsibility for the systemic consequences of racism, colonialism, and neocolonialism onto the act of (gloriously) recovering "racial" and "subaltern" others. In other words, it displaces political responsibility onto those racial and colonial/neocolonial subjects who are recovered for the express purpose of participating, both textually and politically, in a redemptive discourse of "common struggle" and nation-building. As U.S. American studies scholar George Lipsitz (1994) points out, in historically specific contexts and ways, political coalitions among differentially located white European American ethnic groups in the United States have been brought together into an imaginary unified white community through the discourse of the "common man" and its appeals to white supremacy (as evidenced in Woodrow Wilson's "New Freedom" and Franklin D. Roosevelt's "New Deal," which were, in turn, prefigured and announced on stage and screen by D.W. Griffith's cinema and Al Jolson's racial imagery).[13]

Such fantasies are not abberations belonging exclusively to the Right, racist extremists, and the formally uneducated or to whites in the United States or Canada. Rather, they structure the outer limits of the terms for both the formally educated and uneducated as well as for the Left and the Right. Indeed, they often confuse Left and Right, educated and uneducated, blurring subjects, agendas, interests, and alliances in uneasy ways through a common discourse of white ambivalence about racial equality and national belongingness. They articulate languages used in defending as well as in attacking multiculturalism and antiracist pedagogy. It is the pedagogical and social contexts in which such fantasies are read, acted upon/out, and/or resisted which determine whether or not they have deleterious consequences for the racially oppressed as well as for the larger society.

One common discursive strategy evident in redemption fantasies is the staging of the way in which the white (normative) colonial self supposedly comes to know and be at one with the "racialized other," whose qualities and life struggles against racism and colonialism become the familiar self (rather than the estranged other) within "us." Such fantasies set the contemporary stage for seeing/representing those excluded from the rights and protections of the liberal state (à la classical liberalism) as human and, thus, like "us" whites, albeit in ways which prevent fundamental critical re-examination of the white privileges built into putatively race-neutral liberal social democratic reforms. Thus, such fantasies imply that the struggles of the racially oppressed are (in the appropriative sense) accessible to, and knowable by, a fictive homogenous community of whites. Despite differences in our own ethnic experiences of whiteness, redemptive discourses consolidate the terms for emergent formations of whiteness. Such formations are vested in claims of national belongingness, citizenship rights, anti-affirmative action, and property rights—in short, whites are constructed as the original and deserving citizens of the nation (Lipsitz, 1994).

My contention is not that such fantasies are always or necessarily at odds with counter-hegemonic political activism or pedagogy. Nor is it that they ultimately or necessarily will curtail the potential for pan-ethnic alliances across race, class, and gender. Much depends on the material/political contexts in which they are invoked, used, and/or refused and how they are made to signify pedagogically. My contention, following the work of George Lipsitz (1994), is that such fantasies are one means by which colonial and neocolonial institutional structures and regulatory practices enable European white (North Americans)[14] to create and to sustain their "possessive investment in whiteness" (p. 4). Yet the fact that such fantasies display a desire for a *benevolent white redeemer* who comes to know her/his estranged racialized self points to the intransigent appeal of their colonialist and dominating impulses within public political discourse itself (Cvetkovich, 1992). It also shows us how both official multiculturalism and antiracism (and even the more rarefied and hardly official postcolonial analyses of schooling and curricula) are imprisoned by the limits of liberal humanism and social democracy with regard to their ability to achieving any kind of formal equality.

What is not fantasized, and hence not exposed, is the *alterity* of benevolent redemption discourses or the ugly state of the "State of Whiteness" as "we" (McFarlane, 1995, 20).[15] With increasing legitimacy, the corporate management of "diversity" produces the spectacle of so-called "minor identities," historical figures, and textual subjects as vehicles through which privileged whites may come to know the purported "universal human condition" and thus lose (or fail to gain in the first place) historical memory of the consequences of racism and colonialism for different groups in the present as well as in the past.

Confronting this alterity means that white writers/authors of the fantasies of redemption must not flinch from recognizing and critiquing the various forms of patriarchal colonialism/neocolonialism that sustain them.[16] It raises questions about what it means to achieve formal equality when the fantasy structure of dreaming about multi- and pan-ethnic/racial coalitions still involves little discussion of how disinvestment in white racial privilege would look. How, for example, would it be articulated in classrooms beyond the introduction of the new texts of the "racial" or "subaltern others" as the "invented greats"? How would a postcolonial practice be an anti-imperialist and antiracist practice that might, say, challenge traditional colonial allegories of Western national identity? How would the cultural and discursive crisis of representation be linked to the general and widespread underrepresentation of "minority" teachers and staff (which at present is disproportionate to the multi-ethnic/racial, immigrant, and non-English-speaking populations of students) (Sleeter, 1993)? To get at these issues means to talk seriously about disinvestment in privilege as a redistribution of material and social resources, power, and so forth.

The problematic of fantasy as the performative crisis of representation between racial unequals is not reducible to reified notions of racial or cultural difference—as though racist cultures could be abstracted from asymmetries of power, political enfranchisement, and material conditions. Nor is it reducible to (psychological/psychoanalytical) matters between individuals who are abstracted from racist structural practices. Yet such dualisms are a common discursive strategy of redemption narratives, which attempt to do antiracist work from within racist systems of knowing and to separate the psychic from the material. Such separations are asymmetrically negotiated in the daily contexts of institutional and nonformal social life.

With regard to the political sphere, that which is repressed in some variants of psychoanalysis and neo-Marxism as well as in the question of white fantasy is the untold allegory of our (white) desire to know the "racialized other." In fact, the real appeal of such redemption fantasies and discourses may be that they express the desire *not to know* the stories of (white) complicity with various forms of colonial and neocolonial oppressions. In other words, while they participate in dehistoricizing those "racial" or "national others" effaced in history by valorizing (or demonizing) the few, they also erase from view the knowledge of the complex ways in which white racial privilege is constructed so as to benefit whites collectively (e.g., through ideologies of gender, sexuality, and nationality), thus consolidating and/or renewing expectations of entitlement on the parts of whites (albeit in unequal ways). While all whites do not benefit equally or, as Lipsitz (1994, 26) argues, in "precisely the same way[s]," it is wrong to suggest that possessive investment in whiteness does not positively advantage the economic and political power of whites across social classes and genders. The fantasy of a universal racial self also works to render institutionally irrelevant the gender, sexualized, class specificities of racial oppression. For example, African American women (like Latina, Native American, Pacific Island, and First Nations women) are often put into the position of forsaking discussion of gender issues such as sexual harassment and violence against women for the sake of advancing or, more accurately, protecting the perceived racial interests of their communities—which are often not acknowledged to center around men.[17] It is a strategy that barely masks, and which cannot always contain, its own semiotic excesses and mixed feelings; that is, its professed desires for, yet fears and anxieties over, "racial miscegenation" and hybridity as the loss of an illusory but finally dangerous (fictive) notion of "racial purity."

Such fantasies of identification (which are indeed part of wakeful political consciousness) and their ambivalences are not simply side effects of a cathartic disjunction from the alienated side of white desire; nor are they mere projections from the (white) selves we at once both disavow and avow. While they can be read in these strictly psychoanalytic terms, such terms often insist upon a priori deference to an individualistic analysis that ignores the social, political, and material determinants and historical contexts of self-formation. Making psychoanalysis useful with regard to *radical* democratic analyses of social and institutional structure means determining the connections between institutional and individual defensiveness.

At the same time, those who wish to further a genuinely sensitive account of the interrelated material and ideological bases of racism and neocolonialism cannot afford to ignore the deep psychic investments people and institutions make in particular notions of "race" and nation. This is because these two notions get articulated together and then presented as an inevitable and naturalized system of hierarchical differences. Institutional uses of fantasies of identification with "racial" and "national others" which prevent the radical redistribution of power, wealth, education, employment, and social services must become a feature of feminist materialist accounts of education. Part of the task of critically investigating sites of declared multicultural, antiracist, or postcolonial pedagogy would then be to show whether (and how) their discursive practices participate in redemption discourses and fantasies. If they do, it behooves us to show to what *extent* and, more important, to what *effect* and upon *whom*. Given that multicultural, antiracist, and postcolonial pedagogies may serve contradictory functions, audiences, and interests, closer attention to their symbolic and pedagogical language would enable more vigilant scrutiny of their political consequences. For example, while discourses of redemption may allow the racially privileged some insight (however partial and interested) into the dehumanizing effects of racism and imperialism on particular individuals and groups and, thus, have certain counterhegemonic or progressive effects, they also create/support notions of racial, national, and imperial normativity in which certain forms of white ethnicity and nationality (e.g., the United States as a nation in the larger Western empire) are rendered unquestionable.

If we take seriously the idea that the defensiveness of individuals is not unrelated to institutional defensiveness and its systemic effects, then the rich theoretical resources within postcolonialism, materialism, feminism, and psychoanalysis may need to form a new hybrid relationship.[18] Fantasies of identification (or disidentification) also function to construct those deemed to be either somehow outside of, or a subordinate class in relation to, formal equality and citizenship rights. Thus, the failure of, say, academic or corporate institutions to actively listen to subaltern voices, while nonetheless advertising diversity at every turn, is an undeniable effect of the spectacle of multiculturalism and its redemption discourses, both of which now strain under the weight of conservative calls for a return to monoculturalism.[19]

REDEMPTION DISCOURSES: MOVING AWAY FROM CONFESSION OR TOWARD A NEW ORIENTALISM?

In conclusion, it should be noted that redemption discourses do not function in isolation from other discourses of power and resistance; they are in dialogic play, much like Bakhtin's carnival (Volosinov, 1986),[20] with the social protests and activism of different community groups. In other words, voices of resistance (whether, for example, from the renewal of Civil Rights activism to fighting the nonenforcement of affirmative action legislation in the United States or First Nations land claims in Canada) may contest and subvert the univocality and authority of redemption discourses. Thus, redemption discourses do not wholly determine the agendas and actions taken by those deemed "other" in historical struggles or in struggles over historical representations. However, "racially" and "nationally othering" redemption discourses do articulate well with the present institutional spectacle of multiculturalism, which at once valorizes/demonizes and tokenizes those deemed its subjects.[21]

To deconstruct the terms of redemption discourses is not to suggest that the figures they teach about (e.g., Sojourner Truth) should be abandoned as pedagogical subjects/texts. It is, however, to suggest that the asymmetries of a colonial reading practice and a practice of the complex interrelation between historical amnesia and memory may embody a legacy into the present. They prefigure the limits within which they may be read, imagined, challenged, and rewritten. To romanticize those deemed "racial" or "subaltern others" as essential subjects who can tell "us" how to recover some fictive "originary" or "authentic/pure self" is not only to reinscribe those limits, it is also to take part in the creation of "racial" or "subaltern aliens" and "others." Like demonization, romanticization participates in the same binary logic of projective narcissism and historical amnesia. It forgets and sometimes actively denies that such representations are symptoms of colonialism that cannot be corrected by a naive faith in "native testimony." As Gayatri Spivak (1990) reminds us in a 1986 interview conducted by Sneja Gunew:

> if one looks at the history of post-Enlightenment theory, the major problem has been the problem of autobiography: how subjective structures can, in fact, give objective truth. During these same centuries, the Native Informant [was] treated as the objective evidence for the founding of the so-called sciences of ethnography, ethnolinguistics, comparative religion, and so on. So that, once again, the theoretical problems only relate to the person who knows. The person who *knows* has all of the problems of self-hood. The person who is *known*, somehow seems not to have a problematic self. (Spivak in Harasym, 1990, 86)

More frightening, such discourses may easily find comfortable niches (especially in the places academics and the formally educated often like to think are safest from authoritarian populist sentiment—the academy and progressive scholarly discourse itself). It behooves us to turn some of our critical attention to the ways in which progressive scholars and pedagogies articulate mixed feelings and the spectres of unacknowledged power and privilege. In the present context, actively voiced white supremacist ideologies may function less as guilt-ridden confessions serving to redeem the racially privileged and more as examples of nonapologetic and variously gendered white defensiveness.

White moral panic over what some have called "the specters of race" requires more than the usual binary frameworks of anti-ism pedagogies and critiques. Ideologies that naturalize racial dominance and Western imperialism are part of the liberal humanist principles upon which official multicultural/antiracist programs and policies are founded. Thus, challenging their terms means studying how official categories and spectacles of "race" (which after all are a reification of forms of racism), and "nation" are used, read, received, and transformed within and across a variety of contexts. Most important, it means understanding and showing how they are taken up or resisted within different contexts.[22]

Paradoxically, to get *off* white, as the title of this collection suggests, first requires that we get *on* it in critical and politically transformative ways. To analyze the many differential ways whiteness confers privilege through its apparent nonpresent and yet omnipresent allegories and institutional workings is the best way to begin disinvesting in its "possessiveness" (Lipsitz, 1994); at the very least, it opens up the possibility for a third term and offers space for rewriting and speaking culture from its different interested locations.

REFERENCES

Andrews, Lynn V. 1986. *Star Woman: We Are Made from Star and to the Star We Must Return.* Warner Books: New York.

Benjamin, Walter. 1977. *The Origin of German Tragic Drama.* Translated by John Osborne. London: New Left Books.

Bissoondath, Neil. 1994. "I Am Canadian." *Saturday Night,* October, pp. 14–22.

Bhabha, Homi K. 1990. *Nation and Narration.* London: Routledge.

———. 1992. "Postcolonial Authority and Postmodern Guilt." In *Cultural Studies*, edited by Larry Grossberg, Carey Nelson, and Paula Treichler, 55–66. New York/London: Routledge.

———. 1994. *The Location of Culture.* New York: Routledge.

Breines, Wini. 1992. *Young, White and Miserable: Growing Up Female in the Fifties.* Boston: Beacon Press.

Carby, Hazel (Fall 1992). "The Multicultural Wars." *Radical History Review.* 54:7–20.

———. 1993. "Encoding White Resentment." In *Race, Identity and Representation in Education,* edited by Cameron McCarthy and Warren Chrichlow, 236–247. New York: Routledge.

Chow, Rey. 1995c. *Primitive Passions: Visuality, Sexuality, Ethnography and Contemporary Cinema.* New York: Columbia University Press.

———. 1996a. "The Dream of a Butterfly." In *Human, All Too Human, Papers from the English Institute,* edited by Diana Fuss, 61–92. New York: Routledge.

———. (forthcoming, 1995b). "Women in the Holocene: Ethnicity, Fantasy and the Film, *The Joy Luck Club.*" In *Feminisms and the Pedagogies of Everyday Life,* edited by Carmen Luke, pp. 204–221. Albany: State University of New York Press.

Cowie, Elizabeth. 1986. "Fantasia." In *The Woman Question,* edited by Parveen Adams and Elizabeth Cowie, pp. 149–66. Cambridge: MA: MIT Press, 1990.

Cvetkovich, Ann. 1992. *Mixed Feelings: Feminism, Mass Culture and Victorian Sensationalism.* New Brunswick, New Jersey: Rutgers University Press.

Frankenburg, Julia. 1993. *White Women, Race Matters: The Social Construction of Whiteness.* Minneapolis, MN: University of Minnesota.

Gilroy, Paul. 1993. *The Black Atlantic: Modernity and Double Consciousness.* Cambridge, MA.: Harvard University Press.

Harasym, Sarah, ed. 1990. *The Post-Colonial Critic: Interviews, Strategies, Dialogues.* New York/London: Routledge.

Haraway, Donna. 1992. "Ecce Homo, Ain't (A'rn't) I a Woman, and Inappropriate/d Others: The Human in a Posthumanist Landscape." In *Feminists Theorize the Political,* edited by Judith Butler and Joan W. Scott, pp. 86–100. Routledge: New York.

Haig-Brown, Celia (June 1995). "Two Worlds Together: Contradiction and Curriculum in First Nations Adult Science Education." *Anthropology and Education Quarterly* 26 (2): 193–212.

Haig-Brown, Celia, and Jo-Ann Archibald (in press). "Transforming First Nations Research with Respect and Power." *International Journal of Qualitative Studies in Education.*

Hall, Stuart. 1994. "Cultural Identity and Diaspora." In *Colonial Discourse and Postcolonial Theory,* edited by Patrick Williams and Laura Chrisman, pp. 392–403. New York: Columbia University Press.

Harris, Cheryl I. 1993. "Whiteness as Property." *Harvard Law Review* 106 (8): 1707–91.

Kaplan, Cora. 1986. *Sea Changes: Culture and Feminism.* London: Verso.

Karamcheti, Indira. 1995. "Caliban in the Classroom." In *Pedagogy: The Question of Impersonation,* edited by Jane Gallop, pp. 138–146. Bloomington/Indianapolis: Indiana University Press.

Kenway, Jane. 1995. "Masculinities in Schools: Under Siege, On the Defensive and Under Reconstruction?" *Discourse: Studies in the Cultural Politics of Education* 16 (1): 59–80.

Kristeva, Julia. 1995. *New Maladies of the Soul.* Translated by Ross Guberman. New York: Columbia University Press.

Laplanche, Jean, and Pontalis, J.-B. 1968. "Fantasy and the Origins of Sexuality." *International Journal of Psychoanalysis* 49 (1): 1–17. Later published in *Formations of Fantasy*, edited by Victor Burgin, James Donald, and Cora Kaplan, 1986. London/New York: Methuen.

———. 1973. *The Language of Psycho-Analysis.* Translated by Donald Nicholson-Smith with an introduction by Daniel Lagache. New York/London: W. W. Norton.

Lipsitz, George. 1994. "The Possessive Investment in Whiteness: Racialized Social Democracy and the "White" Problem in American Studies." Unpublished manuscript, University of San Diego, Department of Ethnic Studies.

Massey, Douglas S., and Nancy Dentin. 1993. *American Apartheid: Segregation and the Making of the Underclass.* Cambridge, MA: Harvard University Press.

McFarlane, Scott. 1995. "The Haunt of Race: Canada's *Multiculturalism Act*, the Politics of Incorporation and Writing through Race." *Fuse* 18 (3): 18–31.

Modleski, Tania. 1991. *Feminism Without Women: Culture and Criticism in a "Postfeminist Age."* New York: Routledge.

———. (Autumn 1988). "Under Western Eyes: Feminist Scholarship and Colonial Discourses." *Feminist Review* 30: 61–88.

Mohanty, Chandra Talpade. 1989/90. "On Race and Voice: Challenges to Liberal Education in the 90's." *Cultural Critique* 18 (14): 179–208.

Mohanty, Chandra Talpade, and Alexander Jacqui, eds. 1995. *Feminist Genealogies, Colonial Legacies, Democratic Futures.* New York: Routledge.

Painter, Nell Irvin. 1994. "Sojourner Truth's Knowing and Becoming Known." *Journal of American History* 81 (September): 461–92.

Penley, Constance. 1989. *The Future of an Illusion: Film, Feminism and Psychoanalysis.* Minneapolis, MN: University of Minnesota Press.

Pyle, Forest. 1993. "Raymond Williams and the Inhuman Limits of Culture." In *Views Beyond the Border Country: Raymond Williams and Cultural Politics*, edited by Dennis Dworkin and Leslie G. Roman, pp. 260–74. New York: Routledge.

Radhakrishnan, R. 1993. "Cultural Theory and the Politics of Location." In *Views Beyond the Border Country: Raymond Williams and Cultural Politics*, edited by Dennis Dworkin and Leslie G. Roman, pp. 275–94. New York: Routledge.

Riley, Denise. 1988. *"Am I That Name?": Feminism and the Category of "Women" in History.* Minneapolis, MN: University of Minnesota Press.

Rogin, Michael. 1987. *Ronald Reagan, the Movie: And Other Episodes in Political Demonology*. Berkeley, CA: University of California Press.

———. 1992. "Blackface, White Noise: The Jewish Jazz Singer Finds His Voice." *Critical Inquiry* 18 (3): 417–44.

Roman, Leslie G. 1993a. " 'On the Ground' with Antiracist Pedagogy and Raymond Williams's Unfinished Project to Articulate a Socially Transformative Critical Realism." In *Views Beyond the Border Country: Raymond Williams and Cultural Politics,* edited by Dennis Dworkin and Leslie G. Roman, pp. 158–214. New York: Routledge.

———. 1993b. "White Is a Color!: White Defensiveness, Postmodernism, and Antiracist Pedagogy." In *Race, Identity and Representation in Education*. Edited by Cameron McCarthy and Warren Chrichlow, pp. 71–88. New York: Routledge.

———. (1993c). "Rethinking Cultural Studies in a 'Post-feminist' Age." Paper Presented at the annual American Educational Research Association Meeting in Atlanta, Georgia, April 16–18.

———. 1995. "(The Whiteness Within) The Many Likenesses of Sojourner Truth." Paper given at The International Conference on Psychoanalysis and Postcolonialism: Nation, Identity, Self at George Washington University, Washington, D.C., 12–14 October 1995. Also forthcoming in Leslie G. Roman, *Transgressive Knowledge*. Routledge: New York, 1996/7.

Roman, Leslie G., and Stanley, Timothy. 1994. "Empires, Emigrés, and Aliens: Young People's Negotiations with Official and Popular Racism in Canada." Paper Presented at the American Educational Research Association Meeting in New Orleans, LA, April 1994, and at the International Conference on Critical Multiculturalism, University of Victoria, Victoria, British Columbia, 27–28 January 1994.

Romero, Lora. 1993. "When Something Goes Queer: Familiarity, Formalism, and Minority Intellectuals in the 1980's." *Yale Journal of Criticism* 6 (1): 121–41.

Rushton, Phillippe. 1995. *Race, Evolution and Behavior: A Life History Perspective*. New Brunswick, NJ: Transaction

Salecl, Renata. 1994a. "Editorial." *New Formations* 23 (Summer): v.

———. 1994b, Summer. "Love: Providence or Despair[?]," *New Formations*. 23: 13–24.

———. 1994c. *The Spoils of Freedom: Psychoanalysis and Feminism After the Fall of Socialism*. New York: Routledge.

Saxton, Alexander. 1992. *The Rise and Fall of the White Republic*. London/New York: Verso.

Simon, Roger (1995). "Face to Face with Alterity: Postmodern Jewish Identity and the Eros of Pedagogy." In *Pedagogy: The Question of Impersonation,* edited by Jane Gallop, pp. 90–105. Bloomington/Indianapolis: Indiana University Press.

Sleeter, Christine. 1993. "How White Teachers Construct Race." In *Race, Identity and Representation in Education,* edited by Cameron McCarthy and Warren Chrichlow, pp. 151–71. New York: Routledge.

Smitherman, Geneva, ed. 1995. *African American Women Speak Out on Anita Hill/Clarence Thomas*. Detroit, MI: Wayne State University Press.

Snead, James. 1994. *White Screens/Black Images*. Edited posthumously and foreword by Colin MacCabe and Cornel West. New York: Routledge.

Spivak, Gayatri Chakravorty. 1990. "Questions of Multiculturalism." In *The Post-Colonial Critic: Interviews, Strategies, Dialogues,* edited by Sarah Harasym, pp. 59–66. New York/London: Routledge.

Stanton, Elizabeth Cady, Susan B. Anthony, and Matilda Josylyn Gage, eds. (1881–1886). (Three volumes). *History of Woman (sic) Suffrage*. New York: Fowler and Wells.

Viswanathan, Gauri (1993). Raymond Williams and British Colonialism: The Limits of Metropolitan Cultural Theory. In *Race, Identity and Representation in Education*, edited by Cameron McCarthy and Warren Chrichlow, pp. 217–230. New York: Routledge.

Volosinov, Valentin Nikolaivich (neé Bakhtin, Mikhail). (1986). *Marxism and the Philosophy of Language*. Translated by Ladislav Matejka and I. P. Titunik. Cambridge, MA: Harvard University Press.

Ware, Vron. 1991. *Beyond the Pale: White Women, Racism, and History*. London: Verso.

NOTES

1. This essay takes its leave from a longer essay of mine (Roman, 1995 and forthcoming) that analyzes contemporary white American feminists' investments in particular representations of Sojourner Truth and their unacknowledged complicity with the legacy of slavery and colonialism. In particular, I analyze the discourses of Donna Haraway (1992), Tania Modleski (1991), Constance Penley (1989), Denise Riley (1988) and myself (Roman, 1992).

2. For example, in relation to one of the paradoxes of higher education in the 1990s in the United States, demands for racial integration and agitation for civil rights may have been supplanted by the virtual reality of inclusive curricula and the appearance of texts about "racial others" on course syllabi, with few other structural changes in evidence. Such a paradox about Western education causes Hazel Carby (1992) to ask compellingly: "Have we, as a society, successfully eliminated the desire for achieving integration through political agitation for civil rights and opted instead for knowing each other through cultural texts?" (p. 17).

3. For an interesting discussion of political demonology in the United States context see Rogin (1987).

4. Rey Chow (1996a), who draws upon Cora Kaplan (1986) in order to discuss the social and "cross-cultural" implications of fantasy, avoids "finely tuning" her own definition of fantasy in terms of clinical psychoanalytic distinctions between unconscious and conscious fantasies. I, too, find this particular usage amenable to analyses of subjectivity that must consider the implications of asymmetric power. Following Kaplan's commonsense working definition, I use "fantasy" to mean those forms of wakeful consciousness, such as daydreaming, written narrative, and social imagination, inflected by the desires, pleasures, anxieties, and fears of socially determined interests (e.g., gender, race, class, sexuality, and nation). See Kaplan's discussion in her chapter, "The *Thorn Birds*: Fiction, Fantasy, Femininity," especially pages 117–146.

For other useful work on fantasy (which avoids the moralizing stigmata which adhere to distinctions between fantasy as unconscious fiction and daydreaming as conscious political agency), see Cvetkovich (1992) and Cowie (1990), especially pages 149–196. For a more clinical approach, see Laplanche and Pontalis (1973), especially pages 314–318, in which they discuss Freud's distinctions between different modes of fantasy. See also Kristeva's (1995) analysis of the relations between defensive speech and defensive idealization.

5. By "spectacle of multiculturalism" I mean the management of issues of racial inequality through a discourse of reified cultural differences which treats ethnicity and power differentials between, among, and within racial groups as token differences of culture. The management of diversity in education often appears as a spectacle parading "ethnic" and "racial differences" as commodifiable items of costume, folklore, and food. See Roman and Stanley (1994).

6. Mohanty (1989/90) also shows the connections between liberal education and neocolonialism.

7. In Roman (forthcoming) I analyze and critique the disquieting attempts by Haraway (1992), Modleski (1991), Penley (1989), Riley (1988), and other contemporary white feminists (myself included) to valorize Sojourner Truth as a projective metonymic figure and contradictory symbol of racialized and gendered heroism. I also address what gets lost and forgotten when white feminists deal with the issues which slavery raised for white suffragists at the time of Sojourner Truth's speech-making.

8. See Mohanty and Jacqui (1995) for an excellent example of how comparative feminist theory is able to show the connections between contemporary feminist theory and colonialism.

9. Painter (1994) shows how Sojourner Truth changed her name in June 1843 from Isabella Van Wagner, thus demarcating her Pentecostal imperative to begin an itinerant ministry that would, according to Painter, "teach people of all nations the wonderful works of God" (p. 461). This imperative, argues Painter, divided her life between slavery and freedom. According to Painter, like the names of many African Americans who were once were slaves, Isabella Van Wagner's changed several times. Her father, a slave, was known as James Bomfee, but she was known only by her first name, Isabella. According to Painter, her surname, "Van Wagner," came from the name of her last employers, the Van Wagener's of Ulster County, New York, where she was born into slavery in about 1797. Variations on that surname and on her first name ("Isabel," "Isabella") appear in the Northampton Association of Education and Industry Records, 1836–53 (Painter 1994, 461).

10. For example, among these mistakes, Painter (1994) shows how Stowe emphasized Truth's Africanness

and otherness by exaggerating the degree to which she spoke in Negro dialect and by praising her naivete in a discourse which is reminiscent of her representations of black characters in *Uncle Tom's Cabin*. Painter also traces how Stowe incorrectly wrote, in an article entitled "Sojourner Truth, the Libyan Sibyl" (published in the *Atlantic Monthly* in 1863), that Truth had come from Africa, though she was born into slavery in New York state. And, even though Truth was very much alive and politically active in Washington, D.C., at the time of Stowe's writing, Stowe erroneously wrote that Truth was dead. In fact, Truth did not die until 1883. In a similar vein, Painter makes clear that, in Frances Dana Gage's invention of the "A'rn't I a Woman?" speech, Sojourner Truth is erroneously quoted as saying that she had thirteen children, all of whom had been sold into slavery. In fact, Truth had five children. It was not until 1863, according to Painter, that these famous lines appeared for the first time: "And ar'n't I a woman? Look at me. Look at my arm . . . I have plowed and planted and gathered into barns, and no man could head me—and ar'n't I a woman?" (Frances Dana Gage quoted in Painter 1994, 489).

11. For classroom examples of white defensiveness, see Roman (1993a). For comparative feminist theorizing on white defensiveness, see Roman (1993b). I discuss how appropriative white supremacist discourse functioned in David Duke's successful bid for congressperson in Louisiana. His organization gained strength by referring to itself as the National Association for the Advancement of White People.

12. I am indebted to Celia Haig-Brown for pointing out one notable example of this discourse of white redemption by a white American writer, Lynn V. Andrews, who appropriates Manitoba Cree culture in *Star Woman: We Are Made from Stars and to the Stars We Must Return*. See Andrews (1986). For correctives to Andrews's appropriative politics, see Haig-Brown (1995) and Haig-Brown and Archibald (in press).

13. For related work critiquing the "race-neutral" premise, see Rogin (1992) and Saxton (1992).

14. Here, I have altered Lipsitz's reference to Americans so as to include white Canadians.

15. What I call the "spectacle of multiculturalism," Scott McFarlane (1995) identifies as the "spectre of race" in his article critiquing antiracist initiatives in the arts and writing in Canada.

16. I model the notion of "alterity" after Simon (1995), whose illuminating discussion of teaching through the differences of his Jewishness with doctoral students raises important questions about the political and ethical project of pedagogy from a position of articulated social differences. Of course, confronting the alterity of particular forms of white privilege confounds the questions of difference raised by Simon.

17. For an excellent analysis of this contradiction as experienced in the landmark Clarence Thomas confirmation hearings and Anita Hill's subsequent allegations of having been sexually harassed by Thomas, see the essays collected in Smitherman (1995).

18. Example of work in this vein can be found in Renate Salecl (1994b and 1994c).

19. See Roman and Stanley (1994) with regard to calls for a neoconservative return to monoculturalism. For example, Phillippe Rushton's (1995) biodeterminist research, which was echoed by some Canadian professors who founded a right-wing lobby group (the Society for Academic Freedom and Scholarship), which recently aimed to quash a racial harassment policy proposed at York University. One of the latest neoconservative attacks on multiculturalism in Canada comes from Neil Bisoondath (1994), who critiques the "needs-based" perspective of multiculturalism. His account appears to have incorporated many elements of white defensiveness, and it illustrates that racial minorities or people of color can become active (conservative) agents in attacks on racial equality. For other examples of contemporary popularized white resentment, see Carby's (1993) account of encoded white resentment in the Hollywood film, "Grand Canyon" by Lawrence Kasdan, as well as Roman (1993b).

20. I am indebted to a conversation with Richard Cavell for reminding me of Bakhtin's understanding of discourse.

21. For an analysis that conceptualizes a "third space" or "term" to the polarized spectacle and haunt of "race" (which is a reification of the effects of colonialism, neocolonialism, and racism), see Hall (1994).

22. For examples of studies of whiteness as enacted in historically and materially interested national and local contexts, see Frankenburg (1993), Breines (1992), Carby (1993), Snead (1994), Harris (1993), Massey and Denton (1993), Rogin (1992, 1987), Sleeter (1993), and Ware (1991).

The Revolution of Little Girls

Pat Macpherson

TWENTY-SIX

Pat Macpherson's publications include *Reflecting on Jane Eyre* and *Reflecting on The Bell Jar* for the Routledge series *Heroines?* With Michelle Fine she has coauthored three articles on adolescent girls, "Over Dinner," "Hungry for an Us," and "Insisting on Innocence." "The Revolution of Little Girls" is part of a work-in-progress on heterosexuality and film.

Ann-Margaret has more than a boyfriend by the end of *Bye, Bye, Birdie* (1963). She has a body that sings and dances with her own erotic energy. From the girdled, coiffed, and pinned-to-a-steady model of wifedom-in-training that was the highest attainment of 1950s femininity, Ann-Margaret throws herself off the white family pedestal and into the streets. She runs with a crowd of rocking and rolling teenyboppers and shrieks and faints in sexual ecstasy at a rebel hero sex object. She dramatizes the shift in heterosexuality itself in the early 1960s, from a (sexual) male protecting his (asexual) female loving object, to a permissive reciprocal current of desire and initiative between two interested parties.

In 1962 Helen Gurley Brown announced in *Sex and the Single Girl* that career girls were as entitled to sex as Hugh Hefner's playboys (Ehrenreich, 1986). In 1963 Betty Friedan announced in *The Feminine Mystique* that women were human underneath their aprons, and therefore entitled to work outside family (Bowlby, 1987). In 1948 and 1954, Albert Kinsey reported that heterosexual experiences were more similar than different for males and females, and that lots of sex was "natural" for all (Irvine, 1990). Progressives like these three were proposing a basic human nature underneath socially imposed gender roles. This radically challenged the 1950s consensus that gender was the most basic natural essence—mother's milk flowing from the ladies, sexual fluids spurting from the gents. Nobody was yet challenging the invisible assumptions that human nature was white, middle-class, and male.

Meanwhile teenage girls, taught to be both the virgin bait and the brakes on their premarital sexual experiences, were beginning to find the ways and means to define and act on their own (rather than their boyfriends') sexuality. The sexual revolution began, I am arguing, when young women effected this change in themselves from innocent little girls to sexually motivated people. I take my title from Blanche McCrary Boyd's novel, *The Revolution of Little Girls*, which explores the cross-class and cross-race roots of revolt in one young white girl whose family lost one protector and was abused by another.

Five films of the early 1960s show the sexually significant differences emerging in the nature and roles of single white females. Natalie Wood stars in *Splendor in the Grass* (1961), *Love with the Proper Stranger* (1964), and *Sex and the Single Girl* (1965). Audrey Hepburn stars in *Breakfast at Tiffany's* (1961), and Ann-Margaret stars in *Bye, Bye, Birdie* (1963). A sixth, *A Summer Place* (1959), shows this change coming when a forward-looking father "permits" his daughter her sexual desire. All are the girl's story of how she found and claimed a sexuality that then disrupts the traditional family and its rituals of reproduction. This revolution of little girls challenged two central postwar norms: the male dominance of heterosexuality and the invisible white racial dominance embodied in the safe family norm protected by the suggestive white picket fence.

The postwar expansion of the middle class and its move into the suburbs fed the "myth of affluence" and "the general sense that America had finally been homogenized into a level mass," Barbara Ehrenreich argues in *Fear of Falling* (1989: 18). Most suburbs were kept white by realtors and local interests; indeed, the suburbs were a whitening process for "young white families looking to shed ethnicity as a primary marker of social identity," Kathleen S. Newman argues in *Declining Fortunes* (1993: 71). Television sitcoms projected this whitening of the middle-class norm, Lynn Spigel argues in *Make Room for TV* (1992: 147, 154): "More generally, the erasure of ethnic urban roots became an industry prescription for success," for instance by "placing men such as Cuban Desi Arnaz and Lebanese Danny Thomas into safely middle-class settings where their ethnicity was just one more running gag." Embarrassingly ethnic relatives from the past pop up in three of these five films, with "easy" ethnic girls in a fourth. All act as "off-white" markers that show off the whiteness of the norm.

Young white women were the family jewels of middle-class gentility and racial purity (Breines, 1992). When a few disgraced themselves they were disappeared. But when enough of them dirty danced their sexuality in public and then insisted on a seat at the family dinner table—as Baby does in *Dirty Dancing* (1987)—a change *in* the family has occurred. The story of these films and later accounts, then, is the story of how little girls changed the white family's most basic signifier—white female purity as whiteness itself—and had "the time of their lives" doing it, as *Dirty Dancing* sings it. By refusing to take on sexual guilt, they redefined female innocence to include an active sexuality that was once considered off-white.

Splendor in the Grass was written by the gay playwright William Inge to star Warren Beatty in his first film. Natalie Wood plays Deanie, Bud's (Beatty's) girlfriend, and their teen heat was the extra-scandalous subject of the film when their affair during the filming was publicized. In turn, when parents forbade teens from seeing the film, illicit viewings reinforced rebellion and the importance of film and sex to identity.

Teen sex is mostly the girl's problem, and Deanie and her mother fight over its nature and limits. The daughter won't accept her mother's version of unwilling wifehood for the sake of motherhood:

> "Boys don't respect a girl they can go all the way with. Boys want a *nice* girl for a wife. Wilmadean, you and Bud haven't gone too far already, have you?"
> "No Mom. . . . Mom, is it so terrible to have these feelings about boys?"
> "No *nice* girl does."
> "Doesn't she?"
> "No nice girl."
> "But Mom, didn't you ever? I mean—feel that way about Dad?"
> "Your father never laid a hand on me until we were married. . . . I just gave in because a wife *has* to. A woman doesn't enjoy those things the way a man does. She just lets her husband—come near her—in order to have children."

The pair replay this scene after the daughter's sexual frustration mounts and she has abandoned all good girl behavior, eating, studying, fixing her hair. Again her mother asks, "Did he spoil you?" "Yes! No Mom, I'm just as fresh and virgin as the day I was born—naked." Since Deanie is in the bathtub, her bodily purity and its social truth about herself seems poignantly apparent. "I'm a good little girl—I've always done everything Daddy and Mommy told me—and I hate you!"

Rebellion erupts in her flailing body flung out from the tub and down the hallway. But censors wouldn't allow the full shot of her running nude, director Elia Kazan writes in his memoir (Kazan, 1988). White girls' bodies, especially in all-too-naked resistance, are not for public consumption in 1961. But the real rebellious point has already been made. The Victorian past, embodied in the sex-denying mother, is bad. The daughter's bold bodily rebellion is good—which means, crucially for femininity, still innocent, pure, white.

Bud's sister in the film is a bad rich girl who gets drunk at parties and does it indiscriminately. Deanie is a good middle-class girl who only wants to do it with her boyfriend—especially after he's done it with the local not-white-enough-to-count Juanita. Deanie's nervous breakdown is expressed as bad-girl party behavior like the sister's, only for Deanie it's unnatural, a sign of her desperation rather than her badness.

The film argues for Deanie, in the form of a waterfall, that it's natural and healthy for her to seek and find sexual release. The 1950s social proprieties of femininity look as Victorian as the furniture darkening and crowding her family house. Her mother's denial of female sexuality, and the father's enforcement of the double standard, drive the kids crazy. The mental hospital where Deanie spends the next two years is, lucky for her, a modern institution where a hip father figure guides her therapeutic self-reconstruction. She emerges in a stunning white hat and chic dress—autonomous, adult, beautiful. Upward mobility is her reward. She bids a fond farewell to the past and its punishing castrations, in the person of a rurally ground-down Bud, toiling the farm for the pregnant ex-waitress Italian wife he'd met in New Haven. Deanie hatches herself and emerges a poised white woman with an even brighter white future that includes paid-in-full sexual entitlement.

Audrey Hepburn's first outfit in *Breakfast at Tiffany's* resembles Natalie Wood's final outfit in *Splendor*, a broadbrimmed white hat and a slim dark sheath dress. Holly Golightly wears effortlessly the sexual self-possession that it takes most girls a long adolescence to compose. Actually Holly first appears without a dress: she's just answered her door in a tuxedo shirt when George Peppard rings in the middle of the afternoon. Talk about a kooky bohemian life in New York! "How do I look?" she asks when she's quickly and casually transformed herself into the sophisticated working girl. But (as Helen Gurley Brown warned) she's hardly been waiting for him—she's off to work, he's just a new tenant in the apartment building. Their similarities make them friends rather than lovers, each struggling to survive with integrity when patronage is how they support their bohemian lifestyles. (He's a rich woman's gigolo to support his writing; she's paid by a gangster to visit him in jail.) He's enchanted with her insouciance; he's captivated because she's a free spirit. She's trying to marry rich, but he knows she's really innocent of such cynicism or material appetite.

As with Natalie Wood and all the heroines, a pure—yet still sexual—innocence is essential to her character's sexually dubious position. She avoids the 1950s caricatures of single women, either frigidly afraid of sex or guiltily slutty in getting it. She is innocent of Helen Gurley Brown's *Cosmo* girl's ambition and appetites. Audrey Hepburn plays an androgynous pubescent virgin sprite with no virginity at stake, a new social possibility: a sexually active woman who's Teflon-coated inside and out so neither guilty regret nor sexual reputation stick to her.

Her (guilty) secret is revealed by the arrival of Fred:

"She was Lulumae Bonner. I'm her husband. . . . Them's her children: four. When I married Lulumae she was goin on 14. Never could understand why that woman run off."
"I love you—but I'm not Lulumae anymore," she tells him.

As a figure of Holly's hickest of pasts, he and his plot development are improbable at best. But its shock value measures the social change from a backwards rural past entrapping and impoverishing women, to a liberating present where fragile birds like Holly can find freedom in the city's pleasures and opportunities.

Holly's complex innocence might have to work overtime with this adult material, but the effort never shows in Audrey Hepburn. She seems impervious to charges that could be brought by a 1950s morality: adultery and abandonment of family, semisexual racketeering, and gold-digging. Her appetite itself is innocent and androgynous, seeking only experience, arty bites of life, like not naming your cat and wanting breakfast at Tiffany's. When they take off their Woolworth's masks after a day adventuring through the city being spontaneous, their kiss is fresh with the sincere wonder of it all, not groping for possession or broiling with lusty longings unleashed. They are like children who have not learned that sex is a gender business deal. They pioneer the promise of the sexual revolution that humans enjoy better sex when they take off their social masks and gender roles.

Credit the complex gay sensibility of Truman Capote, who like William Inge made the hero as beautiful and desirable a sexual object as the heroine, and the heroine even more hungry for experience outside conventional arrangements, and determined to pursue it, whatever the social costs, than the hero. The beautiful man plays more of the woman's traditional role: lovely to look at; interested in sex once romance has secured the partner's affections; and blooming like a flower into a having-and-holding nurturant center for future family procreation. And the woman plays more of the man's—and none of the mother's—role. Most radically, she's innocent of maternal instinct and emotional possessiveness, the sine qua non of 1950s femininity. So she turns down marriage when it's offered:

> "Holly, I love you. You belong to me."
> "I'll never let anyone put me in a cage. . . . I don't know *who* I am."
> "You're chicken. . . . People *do* fall in love. People do belong to each other. That's the only way they find happiness. . . ."

Finally in the rain, among the woman's tears and retrieval of her lost cat, they kiss, and—the camera pans back and the credits roll. Cohabitation more likely than marriage.

In both films the moral justification for "free sex" is "nature," the "human nature" of sexual appetite and fulfillment. Left behind are old-fashioned gender roles and prohibitions and hypocrisies and separate spheres for women and men. Sex is nature, love awakens sex in woman and man, and—if no archaic relatives stand in the way—fulfillment follows.

Love with a Proper Stranger has Natalie Wood again fighting her parents for a better life than their domestic death. Only this time *she's* the Italian (Angie) and already pregnant from a one-night stand with a stranger, Steve McQueen. Angie starts off off-off white, in other words. She asks him to help pay for an abortion, and he gets money from his parents, then rescues her from imminent butchery on the floor of an empty room. *Love with a Proper Stranger* was filmed in black and white for a gritty urban "ethnic" (off-white) realism: lots of crowded streets and buildings and cold winds of alienation, especially before the abortion.

Angie's revolt is to remain resolutely single. She refuses two marriage offers. Dominic, her suitor, says of McQueen, "When he told me my whole stomach turned over on me. He came to me like a man and he's willing to marry yah."

"Why?" Angie asks. "Do you want to get married?"

"I said I would," McQueen answers. But: "Who wants to get married? . . . I'm willing to take my medicine."

"And I'm the medicine?" Angie challenges him—his attitude, the "old" deal of unwilling husband, anxious entrapping wife. "It may come as a shock to you but underneath this hair and skin is a human girl." Essentially *human*, not female, the key innovation of permissive heterosexuality: the promise of sex without gender. "I don't want to be a warden all my life. As long as you feel that being married is being in jail then you're not happy."

The rest of the film follows McQueen's awkward fighting courtship of the independent (and still pregnant) Angie. She moves out of her Italian-speaking mother's apartment where boiling spaghetti and a steaming clothes iron fog the air. She serves McQueen a modern dinner in her working girl's modest apartment, wearing a scoopneck black dress. "Man you look wild. You look like a woman," he raves. "This is kind of a test run for me," she confesses shyly. "If you didn't try so hard to play against it you'd be a really nice person," he says as they kiss. As in the other films, *he* seems to offer the having and holding, complementing her "business girl" talents.

Earlier he had asked her, "Why did you go with me—up in the mountains?" (Their sex, like everyone's it seems, is in "nature.") She answers that it was "just a stupid experiment." He concurs in their mutual disappointment: "Boy, how they build things up in all the books and movies." Their attempt at the illusions of romance and glamor and independence landed them in more trouble than their marginal lives can support. For him, "bells and banjos playing" is "how they brainwash you" into marriage. The husband becomes "the prisoner of Zenda." For her, "the dead" are the people who live alone, without love to support them. How does real love grow from gritty working-class lives? Together they resist the separate spheres of gender in their parents' lives, the men playing bocci, the women silently waiting. Together they move into a partnership based on mutual needs, for "human" interdependence both emotionally and economically, and for more distance from the bondage of the past—their parents' ethnicity a symbol of both their deadend working class, and their premodern entrapped gender types. By moving them up and out, middle-class marriage promises to turn ethnic off-white to white.

Natalie Wood plays Helen Gurley Brown in *Sex and the Single Girl* and Tony Curtis plays Bob, a magazine writer intent on exposing her as a virgin marriage counselor. He'll do anything to get *his* (1950s) story: the lead career girl who advocates sex for single women is actually a frigid old maid terrified of sex and men. He disguises himself as an impotent married man and seeks treatment from her.

Her story is more modern (with a 1960s heroine): "Single women should stop being ashamed of sex and of being single." From that challenge, problems (like Bob) pursue her. Joseph Heller's screenplay (with David Schwartz) identifies the catch-22 for single working women: If she's sexually experienced, her suited career girl autonomy is splattered all over with her "sex." If she's a virgin, as rumored, she's not only suspect psychologically and socially as old-maid frigid, but her authority as a marriage counselor is completely shot. As his editor suggests, "Make your grab for her, let her tell you she's not that kind of a girl—and we'll sue to make her prove that she *is* that kind of a girl. . . . I'm going for a Pulitzer Prize." The gender stakes are explicit. If women "stop behaving like mice and start behaving like men," as Helen advocates, "Who's going to take care of all of us married men?" Bob wants to know.

Helen's dilemma in the film is resolved by marriage to Bob, in the tradition of 1950s sex comedies like *Pillow Talk*. She is relieved to discover she wants sex (because his cons succeed in turning her on), and he is relieved to discover he wants marriage (because her energetic and sincere struggles as a professional and a woman can be "solved" by his intervention). The fighting couple get tangled in the conflicts of a married couple with a similar issue: Does the wife's working make or break the marriage? While the comedy makes hay from its gender misunderstandings, disguises, and different interests, it moves the characters toward happy marriage as mutual recognition. In this "modern" tale, they recognize the human nature or sameness of desire and need and ability in each other, rather than the difference of gender.

The comedy explores the sexual politics that occur when single career women interrupt the old gendered arrangements of the working world. Helen Gurley Brown claims the privileges of men and an identity that dumps the deficits of old-fashioned femininity:

"I wouldn't give up my career for marriage."

"I have work I care about much more [than marriage]."

"When I marry it won't be for love or romance or sex—I can get those things outside of marriage—just like you."

"I'm not going to give up one iota of freedom or dignity for a man."

"I won't be dominated by any man."

Bob gradually acquires the sensitivities and values formerly associated only with femininity:

"For me it's only the beginning," he tells his boss when he's fired for refusing to run his original story on Helen Gurley Brown. "You may have the money and power and sex. But I've got *love*."

From the predator using the double standard to track down and expose his prey as "that kind of girl" (female object degraded by sexuality), he comes to the permissive conclusion that "Dr. Helen Brown is a decent human being. It would be indecent to malign her." He respects the doctor's (ungendered) professionalism and (ungendered) humanity.

When he gets Helen drunk on champagne and happily necking, he confesses his *love* for her, his dirty little secret as a bachelor supposedly only interested in scoring. As in the other films, the cynical bachelor finds his arms outstretched, chasing after the free-spirited working woman.

Bob dons Helen's frilly robe while she dries his wet clothes after a comic contrived splash in the river. As they drink and neck on her sofa in her robes, they joke that he looks like Jack Lemmon in *Some Like It Hot* (1959). But close as he got to the woman in impersonation and intimate contact, Jack Lemmon remained a man, which as he famously says is "a whole 'nother sex." Sex like gender was assumed to be a very different experience for men and women, as the difference between Monroe's "real woman" and Jack Lemmon's fake woman so comically illustrate. Monroe's fifties-style female "innocence" was that she played a desirable woman with no sexual desires of her own. Such a gender identity is archaic by 1963. The revolution of such little girls has already occurred.

The couple's modern moves on the sofa of the sexual single girl include her emerging erotic capacity (and disinterest in possession), and his emerging emotional capacity (and disinterest in scoring). Predator and sex object gender—clothes off, same-sex robes on, what comes out is hetero heat, a reciprocating current of sexual and emotional initiatives and hesitations. They are more alike than different.

A Summer Place (1959) reveals what goes missing by the early 1960s: the good father. In *A Summer Place* he remains central as moral arbiter and protector and point of view. Fathers are disappointing in *Splendor* and *Proper Stranger*, missing in *Tiffany's* and *Single Girl*. In *Bye, Bye, Birdie*, Paul Lynde is a fair fool schooled by his clever daughter in what's modern and fun.

A Summer Place was written by Sloan Wilson (whose *Man in the Gray Flannel Suit* was also made into a movie). The film's point of view makes for fascinating social history: the first divorced father coping with his angry teen kids. Two enlightened adults divorce archaic spouses (a drunk and a prude) and marry each other (as they should have when they had their affair as teens) and sponsor the affair of their teen children. Molly (Sandra Dee) gets pregnant, Johnny (Troy

Donohue) marries her and they take over running the summer place where their parents consummated their teenage lust. What's at stake here? Whiteness is actually made whiter by the two blond children reproducing.

The battle over sex is waged between Molly and her "frigid" mother, who makes her wear "an armor-plated bra and girdle" because "she says I bounce when I walk. Do I?" she asks her father. "In a pleasant and unobjectionable way," Mr. Natural assures her. Her mother's advice on premarital sex is meant to sound cold-blooded and prehistoric, but it merely exposes the economics of the maidenhead and the marriage deal:

> Don't you ever underestimate the value of a good reputation. . . . You could do worse [than Troy Donohue]. Play your cards right. You can't let him think your kisses come cheap. You're a good girl. You have to play a man like a fish. You have to make him want you and never betray that you want him—that's what's cheap—wanting a man. Love should be more than just animal attraction. Promise me you won't let him kiss you til I say it's time.

As in *Splendor*, the mother "denies" female desire before marriage, and there's no sign of her feeling it inside marriage either—perhaps from the strain of so much premarital inhibition and manipulation, a real psychic problem of real couples in the 1950s (Breines, 1992).

Molly tells her father what she thinks of her mother's point of view. (She does not tell her mother.) "She's antisex. She says it's all a boy wants out of a girl and when they marry it's something she has to endure. I don't want to think like that. She makes me ashamed of even having a body." Her mother is the "dismissed" archaic model of denied (or vindictively killed) female desire. She's excluded from the current of father-daughter conversation. The father represents the modern view that sex is part of love: "to love and be loved—that's our sole reason for existence." What Molly and Johnny are left to figure out on their own is whether sex can be safe outside marriage. The film's answer seems to be, as in *Proper Stranger*'s pregnancy, that it's not, unless "love" can assure that marriage will follow.

What's interesting about *A Summer Place* is its lecturing advocacy of women's entitlement to sex—provided the father approves and the boyfriend protects. With all the film's 60s-style permissive tolerance for rolling joyously among the waves, and living the modern (second marriage) way in a Frank Lloyd Wright house on the beach, Molly is still dated 1955. She parades and puckers and withholds like a doll, the clean and saintly boyfriend still wins possession through declaring love, and the father still hands over his daughter to the boyfriend: the prerevolutionary hetero contract of male protectorship in exchange for the woman's freely given body. Molly's stepmother accurately described the deal (to Molly's father) at the very moment of exchange (in the boathouse on the dock), "I'm perfectly willing to come when you want me." Molly says the same to Johnny before they do it in the beach shack: "If you need me then I need you—only twice as much." Desire: his. Security: hers.

Revealingly, *race*—in the form of racism—raises its ugly head right at the moment of their tender gender contract, right when they're about to break her virgin vessel. The extra-blond Molly reminds the fair Johnny that *King Kong* is the movie they're supposedly seeing, so she'll summarize the plot so they won't get caught. "Now about *King Kong*," she says as they kiss. "There's this giant ape . . . but they kill him." Scene dissolves in kisses, while we ponder *King Kong*'s implicit question: Doesn't every beast in the jungle want the whitest and squishiest of blonds, and doesn't her all-innocent heart bleed for the victims of her own desirability? (Snead, 1994). The crudest myth of white supremacy waves its giant arms in *King Kong*—showing what's at stake in the maidenhead even in the most liberally furnished of summer places.

What's radical about *Bye, Bye, Birdie* is the new source and the disrupting effects of desire in teen heterosexual culture. Conrad Birdie represents not just Elvis but the impact of several emerging "off-white" cultures in the protect-the-pedestal formation of the all-American family. As Barbara Ehrenreich, Elizabeth Hess, and Gloria Jacobs explained about Beatlemania in *Re-Making Love* (1986), Wini Breines explained about cross-class and cross-race relationships in *Young, White and Miserable* (1992), and Susan J. Douglas explained about cross-over music in *Where the Girls Are* (1994), white middle-class girls were exploring the possibilities in a newly desegregated teen culture for remaking their sexuality.

Some used a hood boyfriend, as in Alice McDermott's retrospective novel (1987) and then the film *That Night* (1994); John Sayles's film *Baby, It's You* (1983), from a story by Amy Grant; the film *Dirty Dancing* (1987); and Ann Imbrie's memoir *Spoken in Darkness* (1993). Some had a black friend or lover, as in Lyn Lauber's novel *White Girls* (1990), Hettie Jones's memoir *How I Became Hettie Jones* (1990), and Alice Walker's novel *Meridian* (1977). Some had abusive father figures: Sylvia Fraser's *My Father's House* (1988), Dorothy Allison's *Bastard Out of Carolina* (1992). Most had depressed mothers: Janet Vandenburgh's *Failure to Zigzag* (1989), Marilyn Robinson's *Housekeeping* (1982).

What such retrospective accounts explore is exactly what was so successfully denied in the common culture (like Hollywood movies) of the time that it was (almost) invisible. Supposedly, white girls needed white men's protection from King Kong—all those off-white muscle-packed predators drunk and delirious from the desirability of white femininity.

White girls who *seek* pleasure from off-white men take from the family the purity that is the justification for all protection of "innocent" privilege. They destroy denial, the illusion of (racial) innocence that covers racial discrimination and inequality. Crossing and recrossing the tracks, white girls unpinned their bodies from the boyfriend/father protector. In pursuing off-white men, in enjoying the mass female hysteria of lusting after writhing male performers, little girls renounced innocence and purity and gentility—but not necessarily goodness or membership in the family. And after their own desire and sexual experience, the passivity and purity of "desirability" are revealed as the secondhand experiences that they are. This radically rewrites the grammar of the hetero sentence: who's desiring subject and who's desirable object in sex.

Bye, Bye, Birdie celebrates the "mass jailbreak" of white girls using rock 'n' roll. In the "before" (rock 'n' roll) scene, Ann-Margaret's coy freshly pinned miss (Kim) is "happy to be a woman" in the best tradition of prerevolutionary consciousness. Kim's best friend does perky till it's bubbling out her swinging blond ponytail. "How do you absolutely feel in your deepest secret soul?" she asks Kim about being pinned. "Like I've been reborn. Like all my life until this very moment I was nothing—and now I'm alive. Now I know what it means to be a woman!"

What's revolutionary about *Bye, Bye, Birdie* is that it's ironic, even *camp* about teen rituals and desires, about parents' limited control, and about safe family norms and defenses—all the components of heterosexuality and whiteness. So all the singing celebrations are quite caricatured *and* gaily enjoyed—the phones buzzing with Kim and Hugo's playing-at-marriage "steady" contract, Kim's song of self-loveliness at now being a woman, which includes her wifely plan "to pick out a boy and *train* him . . . and then when you are through, you've made him the man you want him to be." As for *her* desires, "It gives you such a glow just to know you're wearing lipstick and heels," and "how marvelous to wait for a date in simply beautiful clothes." Even while she's singing about 1950s femininity she strips off her orange chiffon and slides into 60s casual—a bulky sweater and capris and fluffy slippers. She loosens her coiffed do and piles her masses of red hair aside for a baseball cap on sideways.

She goes downstairs and greets her parents the modern way by their names and tries to bum a cigarette. "Times are changing," she informs them of Bob Dylan's news. But unlike the beat and folk countercultures, her teen rebellion is offered and taken in the greatest of good humors by her "modern" parents, played by Jennifer Leigh and Paul Lynde. This sets the comic tone for all further family conflict. As one song goes, it's "Kids Today," but it's entirely benign, ritualistic, and even—once you get the archaic relatives out of the way—fun. A deep, bitter, thorough, and long-lasting cultural conflict is here made into dancing confrontations and singing resolutions rich and resonant in the details of white middle-class family politics. Enormous good fun, with backup singers and dancers multiplying the significance of the nuclear family's spats, fields and gyms and bars full of teens dancing through their dilemmas using full body language.

Conrad Birdie has been drafted and Kim has been selected to receive Birdie's "Last Kiss" and song on the Ed Sullivan Show. Kim's white purity is assured by her location, Sweet Apple, Ohio, and her all-American family portrait, and her blandest of blond boyfriends, Hugo. Hugo is already his father. He's all letter-man sweater and crooning about love as if it were only about loyalty. Even when he later joins the dance "I've got a lot of livin' to do" it's hard to spot even a twitch of sexual impulse. Hugo embodies the security premise of the safe family: trade sex for security. Purity is maintained by exclusive possession.

Birdie and his crowd ride motorcyles right into the crowd of milling—and willing—girls. He dismounts between two raised electric guitars and hardly waits for the official welcome before blasting into his song. "You've gotta be sincere—you've gotta feel it here," he gestures with a pointed pelvic thrust, and the girls start vibrating into ecstatic frenzies. His gold lame body suit and boots, song, and delivery are more Las Vegas than Memphis (certainly a sign of where Elvis and Ann-Margaret were actually headed the following year—*Viva Las Vegas!* (1964) and an affair during the filming).

Birdie refers to Elvis as Elvis referred to black music and culture with his brilloed pompadour and pelvic swivel-and-thrust dancing and sexually coded lyrics and erotic 4/4 rhythms. At the same time, Birdie caricatures the white clean-up act exploiting the black sexuality that was the heart of the whole white youth rebellion against white sexual purity. And he caricatures the way whites saw black music as real and honest, "sincere." "Yah gotta feel it here, honestly sincere. . . . In everything I do, my sincerity shows through. . . . When I sing about a girl, I really feel that girl. . . ." And he caricatures sincerity by looking bored with the scene even as he lays waste to the townfolk in a final swooning mass. The mayor's wife in particular keeps fainting with spread legs. Even the next day her knees seem to have been permanently disreputably separated.

The boredom was showing in Elvis by 1963, and the Beatles' fresh sincerity was imported the following year, with the same white-boy coverage of black beat/black heat. For girls who couldn't afford to cross the tracks, the culture of rock 'n' roll had transgressive opportunities that could be explored without leaving home.

Symbolically this is what happens to Kim. Her dance numbers become increasingly sexualized and farflinging and publicly broadcast. She manages her nervous boyfriend by singing that he's her "one special boy," between bouts of Birdie fever and fainting fits from Birdie's kisses. Her mother helps convert her father to the fun of Birdie fandom by arranging for him to join his daughter on the ultimate family hour, the Ed Sullivan show, after Birdie's rock 'n' roll number. As for Elvis and the Beatles, this show helped these boys "enter" the white family home.

Bye, Bye, Birdie is about the transformation of Kim by consuming the rock 'n' roll body language of Birdie. At the beginning when she sings "Bye, Bye, Birdie" she is the coyest of little girls. Each regret is about her lack when he's gone, the ultimate female dependency. "I'm gonna miss ya so." She promises to write every night, and guesses "I'll always care." At the end of the film, Birdie has left town and she is reunited with Hugo, back in the premarital virgin loyalty mode, her head on his shoulder. But when she sings "Bye, Bye, Birdie" by herself directly to the camera, windmachine blowing her orange chiffon, her body is now fully alive and offered as evidence of the difference Birdie made. Her goodbye is grateful for "Your swivel and your sway, your superduper Class. . . ." Her loyalty isn't about regret or waiting: "No more sighing each time you move those lips, No more dying [shimmying] each time you twitch those hips." Instead it's now "Time for me to—FLY!" As she sings "fly-ay-ay-ayee" she shakes her breasts like a pro. Continuously walking forward in an exhilarated self-arousal, Ann-Margaret throws her woman's body behind the revolution of little girls.

In the best and worst tradition of white middle-class feminism, these heroines' revolutionary act is to claim the (sexual) privileges of white middle-class men. By 1960, they can start from a position of relative economic and social equality—in the family as teens, or in the workforce as adults. The Pill came on the market in 1960, and though it's never mentioned in these films, it made possible women's equal access to permissive sex.

For those women living off-camera, outside the white picket fences of the affluent suburbs, the battles over their bodies and futures were very differently waged. Their stories and studies are just beginning to be written. Hollywood film, that most expensive of cultural products, did not often focus its camera on off-white girls.

West Side Story (1962) is the story of Puerto Rican and Anglo boys in gangs and the interethnic conflicts that keep them in their dog-eat-dog "culture of poverty and juvenile delinquency," as Barbara Ehrenreich (1989) describes the early 60s liberal view of those who can't get organized to pass into the ever-open doors of the vast middle class. Although the musical mocks this view of juvenile delinquency and explores dilemmas of immigration and family conflict over sex and prospects, the solution remains the suburbs. This is Tony and Maria's "place for us," where "peace and quiet and open air waits for us." Their primary loyalty to ethnic roots cuts off their escape route. The girls' sexuality remains tied to their boyfriends, their marriage chances, and future economic prospects. Their revolt or escape from such circumstances is yet to come.

REFERENCES

Allison, D. *Bastard Out of Carolina*. (New York: Penguin, 1992).
Bowlby, R. " 'The Problem with No Name': Rereading Friedan's 'The Feminine Mystique,' " in *Feminist Review* No. 27 (Autumn 1987).
Boyd, B. *The Revolution of Little Girls*. (New York: Random House, 1992).
Breines, W. *Young, White and Miserable: Growing Up Female in the Fifties*. (Boston: Beacon Press, 1992).
Douglas, S. *Where the Girls Are: Growing Up Female in the Mass Media*. (New York: Times Books, Random House, 1994).
Ehrenreich, B. et al. *Re-Making Love: The Feminization of Sex*. (New York: Anchor Press, 1986).
Ehrenreich, B. *Fear of Falling: The Inner Life of the Middle Class*. (New York: HarperPerennial, 1989).
Fraser, S. *My Father's House*. (New York: Ticknor and Fields, 1988).
Imbrie, A. *Spoken in Darkness: Small-Town Murder and a Friendship Beyond Death*. (New York: Hyperion, 1993).
Irvine, J. *Disorders of Desire: Sex and Gender in Modern American Sexology*. (Philadelphia: Temple University Press, 1990).
Jones, H. *How I Became Hettie Jones*. (New York: E. P. Dutton, 1990).
Kazan, E. *A Life*. (New York: Alfred A. Knopf, 1988).
Lauber, L. *White Girls*. (New York: Norton, 1990).
McDermott, A. *That Night*. (New York: Harper and Row, 1987).

Newman, K. *Declining Fortunes: The Withering of the American Dream*. (New York: Basic Books, 1993).

Robinson, M. *Housekeeping*. (New York: Bantam Books, 1982).

Snead, J. "Spectatorship and Capture in *King Kong*: The Guilty Look," in *White Screens, Black Images: Hollywood from the Dark Side*. (New York and London: Routledge, 1994).

Spigel, L. *Make Room for TV: Television and the Family Ideal in Postwar America*. (Chicago and London: University of Chicago Press, 1992).

Vandenburgh, J. *Failure to Zigzag*. (New York: Avon Books, 1989).

Walker, A. *Meridian*. (New York: Pocket Books, 1977).

White Politics: Coalitions and Borderlands

Through the Looking Glass: Implications of Studying Whiteness for Feminist Methods

Aída Hurtado and Abigail J. Stewart

Aída Hurtado is Professor of Psychology at the University of California, Santa Cruz. Dr. Hurtado's research focuses on the effects of subordination on social identity. She is especially interested in group memberships like ethnicity, race, class, and gender, which are used to legitimize unequal distribution of power between groups. Dr. Hurtado's expertise is in survey methods with bilingual/bicultural populations. She has published on issues of language and social identity for the Mexican-origin population in the United States. Her most recent publications include *The Educational Achievement of Latinos: Barriers and Successes* (coedited with Dr. Eugene García. Santa Cruz: University of California, Latino Eligibility Study, 1994). Dr. Hurtado received her B.A. in Psychology and Sociology from Pan American University in Edinburg, Texas, and her M.A. and Ph.D. in Social Psychology from the University of Michigan.

Abigail Stewart is a professor of psychology and women's studies at the University of Michigan and former director of the women's studies program. Since 1995, she has been director of the Institute for Research on Women and Gender. Ms. Stewart has published over 70 scholarly articles and several books, focusing on the psychology of women's lives, personality, and adaptation to change. Her current research focuses on comparative analyses of longitudinal studies of educated women's lives and personalities. She earned a Ph.D. in personality from Harvard University in 1975, an M.Sc. in social psychology from the London School of Economics in 1972, and an AB in psychology from Wesleyan University in 1971.

I'll tell you all my ideas about Looking-glass House. First, there's the room you can see through the glass—that's just the same as our drawing-room, only the things go the other way. I can see all of it when I get upon a chair—all but the bit just behind the fireplace. Oh! I do wish I could see *that* bit!

—Lewis Carroll

Feminist methods were developed to provide an accurate reflection of women—in fact, to bring women, usually absent, into the center of research. Feminist methods also emphasized the need to have women studying women to provide an accurate reflection of women's lives. However, in studying whiteness, feminist methods have to go beyond providing undistorted knowledge about women, to simultaneously look behind the privilege that whiteness provides—to try to see "that bit" which has not been central to the study of race. Like Alice in Wonderland, going through the looking-glass will be necessary to *see* how the study of whiteness is and is not the same as the study of "race."

Whiteness is suddenly interesting—to social scientists and politicians—in the 1990s. Implied, but concealed, in the concept of "race," whiteness has rarely before been interrogated. In *Play-*

ing in the Dark, Toni Morrison (1992) brilliantly exposed how whiteness operates in public and literary discourse; it remains for social scientists to build on her work by exploring how whiteness operates in individual psyches and social relations. As we try to do that, we must consider the possibility that analytic tools and research methods that helped us understand systems and experiences of oppression may not be as appropriate for understanding privilege.

When social scientists began to study "race" they first examined the operation of prejudice and stereotypes—that is, individuals' racist attitudes about Blacks or people of Color (see, e.g., Allport, 1958). The focus, then, was on attitudes about people of different (nonwhite) "races." This individual-focused approach eventually yielded to examination of how racism operated as an impersonal *system* of discrimination and institutionalized disadvantage (e.g., Feagin and Feagin, 1978). This important shift to a systemic analysis continued to obscure "whiteness," because social scientists explored the impact of institutional racism on those who "had" race in the sense that their race was marked, noted, taken as "other" in U.S. society (for example, Pettigrew, 1964; Wilson, 1987; Zweigenhaft and Domhoff, 1991). Whiteness, like maleness, was viewed as background; being of Color, like being female, was understood to shape and define one's personality, as one's life. To be white or male was simply to be, in fact to be subject to highly idiosyncratic, individualized shaping processes. As we move now to considering the significance of whiteness (and maleness) for individuals' lives and personalities, we may be tempted to rely on the analytic tools and research methods that have proven so useful both in identifying racist and sexist limitations in social science theory and research, and in studying the experience of women and people of Color.

Feminist social scientists made a case for the need for new methods and approaches by showing that the apparently, or supposedly, "neutral" studies of sex differences were riddled with bias and sexism (see, e.g., Sherif, 1979). As antiracist social scientists did for race, feminist social scientists showed that the scientific method alone did not guarantee gender neutrality; they demonstrated how distorted our understanding of "women" was, when men were taken as the human norm. In order to build an alternate account, feminist scholars developed and honed strategies for uncovering bias and identifying aspects of female experience that were devalued or ignored (Fonow and Cook, 1991). In particular, the value of adopting a female "standpoint" or position, or actually empowering women to articulate their own perspective, was developed as a methodological ideal (see, e.g., Harding, 1991). By bringing women "to voice," missing experiences—of groups of women, even of all women—could be articulated and understood. These methods have yielded enormous value in our understanding of rape, sexual harassment, women's work, and family roles.

They have been equally useful as feminist scholars increasingly recognized that women were not all alike, and that therefore it was important to study different groups of women's experience directly. Thus, the standpoint or voice of each group—lesbians, poor women, women of color, women with disabilities—must be identified and articulated (Hurtado, 1989; Landrine, Klonoff, and Brown-Collins, 1992; Reid, 1993). The processes of bringing these standpoints and voices into social science is far from complete. Nevertheless, defining them has inevitably made clear how the viewpoints previously seen as neutral are in fact inflected by class (upper), race (white), and gender (male). Therefore, feminist scholars have made efforts to shift their gaze to the privileged side of oppression (see especially Ostrander, 1984; Ostrove and Stewart, 1994; Sturgis, 1988). At the same time, some scholars' efforts to bring the experiences of understudied groups of women into social science research and theory have resulted in sophisticated reflections on the importantly different standpoints of the researcher and the researched (see, e.g., Belle, 1994; Fine, 1979; Lykes, 1989). As feminist social scientists begin to study whiteness (and other markers of privilege), we think they must continue to reflect on the different—and similar—standpoints of the researcher and the researched; even more important, we must think about the implications of sharing and not sharing a *privileged* standpoint for the use of methods that have been used to study people whose lack of privilege was our focus in the past.

Some of our most cherished "feminist research methods," and the implied or explicit "standpoint epistemology" associated with them, must be rethought as we approach the study of a culturally valued characteristic. Issues of voice, empowerment, and standpoint, as well as objectivity and distance, are particularly relevant here. Thinking about how best to study whiteness should also help us identify features of feminist methodological discussions that apply with equal, or greater, force to the study of whiteness. These will surely include tools for critical analysis, and attention to the perspective and social characteristics of the researcher as an integral part of the method. We will begin by reviewing what we know about how whiteness matters, turning after that to an analysis of methodological issues raised by this research.

CONTRIBUTIONS TO OUR UNDERSTANDING OF WHITENESS: PREVIOUS RESEARCH

No clear paradigm and method has emerged to study whiteness, although the few studies that address whiteness directly give us more than the expressed knowledge the mostly white authors purport. The unintended outcomes of these studies on whiteness are the revelations of the researchers themselves, thus making the results multilayered—that is, they tell us more than the authors intended and more than the respondents knew they were revealing. With this notion in mind, we address what we consider the best contributions these studies have made to how we study and conceptualize whiteness in the United States.

Denaturalizing Whiteness

A recurrent finding in the study of whiteness is the fact that white respondents do not consider their "whiteness" as an identity or a marker of group membership *per se*. That is, whiteness is a "natural" identity because it has not been problematic and therefore salient to most respondents in these studies. In fact, most white respondents are hard-pressed to define whiteness and the privileges that it brings to those who own it. Interestingly enough, whiteness becomes much more definable when the privilege it accords its owners is lost. For example, Fine and her colleagues (Fine et al., 1994) document white working-class men's frustrations as they see their jobs "being taken" over by people of Color. It is in the loss of their way of life, which includes their jobs, that they begin to articulate what it means to be white. Tatum (1992) and Gallagher (1995) describe how students in multicultural college classrooms similarly, and painfully "discover" their whiteness.

Ironically, although race is a central organizing component of U.S. society—whether someone is white, Black, Asian, or Brown—there has been a norm of explicitly ignoring race as a form of denying its importance in the subordination/domination process (Tatum, 1991). However, Toni Morrison (1994) appropriately points out that even in this nonmention, the racialization process continues. For example, Morrison observes, in analyzing the Africanist presence in American literature, that intellectuals are sometimes proud they have not read any African American texts, a feeling tied to the notion that not *noticing* race is polite and humanistic; that it indicates a certain political consciousness. So not "seeing" is turned on its head to mean "politeness" or generosity when in fact it only reinforces the existing racist power arrangements.

Morrison's (1994) point (made in reference to U.S. literature) is also well documented in Frankenberg's (1993) research on what their race means to white women from all walks of life. Almost all her respondents mention having been socialized *not* to "see" people of Color. However, not "seeing" is an integral part of their identity formation because the privilege of "whiteness" is based on the availability of "surrogate, serviceable Black bodies for her [their] own purposes of power without risk, so the author[s] employs them in behalf of her [their] own desire for a safe participation in loss, in love, in chaos, in justice" (Morrison, 1994, p. 28). People of Color are the serviceable others who are the blank slates on which white people can project all those fears, emotions, and attitudes that give whiteness purity because there are others to live out that which would taint whiteness. Roediger (1991) describes in detail how this process worked for different groups, at different times in U.S. history in the construction of white working-class men's selfhood. If whiteness is never articulated, then it is people of Color, *as a group*, who can be scrutinized and blamed to exalt the perfection of that which is "natural" and left unexamined. Precisely because of the "naturalness" of white identity and because of the cloaked secrecy of its manifestation, it is difficult to take the time and energy to listen to whiteness. It isn't viewed as problematic, given that it provides privilege (we are much more passionate about injustice; it makes us feel we are doing something worthwhile) and that it is "natural" and therefore difficult to describe. It also seems like useless "work," like pressing the already ironed dress or putting clean dishes in the dishwasher—since it isn't a problem and everybody knows what it is, why indulge in introspective angst that leads nowhere? There is the rub; privilege has the semblance of naturalness that in itself defends it from scrutiny. Much of the struggle in the twentieth century has been to problematize "the natural," and progressive scholarship has accomplished an admirable body of research problematizing many forms of oppression. But the challenge of the twenty-first century will be to continue the work of the enlightenment—when royalty was problematized and the privilege of lineage was dismantled to provide avenues for democracy to flourish. Race privilege has substituted for lineage of royalty in our time. It countervails class, at times, just like "royal blood" did in the past. We believe in its goodness as former subjects believed in the direct connection to God through their kings.

The Documentation of the Dynamics of Power

The power that whiteness holds for its owners (Harris, 1993b) has not been explicitly documented—it is a birthright that is socialized from generation to generation in the largely racially segregated living arrangements that exist in the United States (McIntosh, 1992, p. 77). Like the construction of manhood through lifetime socialization in sports (Kimmel, 1993), the process is largely hidden, unless you have been admitted to this exclusive club. The current research on whiteness begins the process necessary for understanding both the power of whiteness and the beginning of its deconstruction. It can draw from research on social class that has already identified some of the mechanisms used to pass on class privilege. This is not to suggest that race and class can or should be collapsed, but rather that the mechanisms used to conceal and perpetuate one kind of institutionalized privilege may have counterparts in the analysis of other kinds of institutionalized privilege. It is important to note, though, that the intersection of privilege and subordination will always complicate things. Thus, the mechanisms associated with race privilege will be affected by its co-occurrence with poverty or wealth; maleness or femaleness; etc. Nevertheless, we must begin to identify and define the mechanisms so we will be able to recognize them in the many forms in which they appear.

Distancing

Ostrander (1984), in her study of upper-class women, gives us an intimate portrait of how women in the upper crust of U.S. society make sense of their class privilege. In this particular instance, class privilege is inextricably tied to race privilege because Ostrander's definition of her sample required them to have had wealth in their families for generations as measured by their membership in registered clubs. However, it should be noted that many of her observations are echoed in Wellman's (1993) case studies of white racism in various social classes, as well as Roediger's (1991) analysis of the social construction of white identities in working-class men. The women Ostrander interviewed consistently distance themselves from the origins of their race/class privilege by claiming that it was based on an accident of birth that they had nothing to do with creating. Their class and race membership was not borne out of a conscious intention on their part; therefore, they do not take any responsibility for the costly consequences of their privilege for others. The respondents in Ostrander's (1984) study *distance* themselves from the phenomenon as if it were a natural disaster they had nothing to do with creating and resent having to clean up. Even though these women recognize their privilege, most feel it is the "natural" arrangement of things and they do their personal best to help those less fortunate through their charity work.

Denial

Many researchers have documented the psychological strain in "passing" from a subordinate group to a dominant group, say fair-skinned Blacks passing as whites (Harris, 1993b). The same strain has been documented for those individuals who become conscious of racism and perceive the omnipresence of its effects in all areas of social life. That's one of the reasons individuals resist acquiring a "double" consciousness, because becoming conscious of power and domination creates enormous psychological strain and pain (Harris, 1993b, p. 1711; Du Bois, 1961; Tatum, 1992). It is not surprising, then, that many of the white respondents in these studies claim that "whiteness" does not bring unearned privileges—that is, that whatever privileges are accorded to whiteness are earned through merit because whites, *as a group*, perform better than people of Color in all kinds of arenas. In fact, denial of white privilege is only fully documented when it is lost. It is in the process of being dislocated and making sense of that dislocation that white respondents begin to fully acknowledge the privileges they previously denied whiteness brought them (Fine, et al., 1994; Gallagher, 1995).

Superiority

The articulation of exactly what whiteness constitutes is difficult for most respondents in these studies. However, what is not as difficult for them to articulate is the superiority they feel in comparison to nonwhite people. For example, McIntosh (1992) tries to articulate precisely what white privilege provides for her, giving us insight into the superiority that most white people come to expect in almost all social contexts. Because white privilege is perceived as the "natural" state of affairs, then by definition it embodies an attitude of superiority: "whites are taught to think of their lives as morally neutral, normative, and average, and also ideal, so that when we work to benefit others, this is seen as work that will allow 'them' to be more like 'us'" (McIntosh, 1992, p. 73). In other words, even though McIntosh does not see herself as oppressing anybody, the list of privileges she was socialized to expect in almost all daily interactions have trained her to feel and act superior to nonwhite people.

Ostrander (1984) similarly finds in her sample of upper-class women a feeling of unquestioned superiority that is their birthright. Because they do not feel they had much to do with constructing the structure of inequality, these women feel that their superiority is "natural." Furthermore, these women are very conscious of the pleasures that their material privilege affords, which is intertwined with their feeling of superiority at the same time that they don't see how it is related to whiteness. The legitimacy of their superiority because of their birthright allows them not to question their class position. Many of these respondents proudly announced that "The door opens for position" and that access to every sphere is "just a phone call away" (Ostrander, 1984, p. 29). As Wellman (1993) argues, racism is not only a "system of exclusion and privilege" but *also* "a set of ultimately acceptable linguistic or ideological constructions that defend one's location in that system" (p. 25).

The pleasure upper-class women feel in their superiority prevents them from challenging the class and race legitimacy on which it is based. In Ostrander's study, these women do not challenge their husbands because they recognize that these men "... know how to rule and are masters of the exercise of power" (Ostrander, 1984, p. 151). The women understand that masters rarely recognize their dependency on slaves. Furthermore, if they are not likely to be shaken from their positions of power outside the home, how likely are they, really, to be successfully challenged as heads of their households? Ostrander (1984) astutely points out that in the unlikely event that these women successfully challenged their husbands on their gender superiority, they might be putting their own class status in peril. Therefore these women submit to their husbands: "They will do so perhaps in part because the gains of *gender* equality would not be enough to balance the losses of class equality" (Ostrander, 1984, pp. 151–52).

These women are not passive recipients of their class privilege but actively participate in maintaining it. First and foremost is the code of silence to hide imperfection (Ostrander, 1984, p. 30). The code of silence is intricately related to what these women refer to as "social graces" that define their class [race] status (see also Domhoff, 1983; Ryan and Sackrey, 1984). Ostrander observes that "These social graces are not just optional amenities of upper-class life; they are essential to the ways in which the upper-class persons are able to control—with great civility and charm—virtually any social situation in which they find themselves" (Ostrander, 1984, p. 89). Similarly, Wellman (1993) argues that "European Americans have advantages that come from their social location in the racial hierarchy, and . . . they explain, or ignore, their privileged position in socially acceptable terms."

Belongingness

One of the major advantages of privilege is the sense of absolute belonging and importance. Belongingness can be communicated in a variety of ways. Sturgis (1988), in her autobiographical essay, beautifully discusses how the unmarked history she was taught in school provided a direct measure of her importance as a descendant of "founding fathers," and of the importance of those who can make history. The historical lessons she learned about whites' (mostly male) accomplishments gave her a sense of their centrality and belonging to the mainstream of life. Not to belong, because of race and/or class, is a way to control and diminish those who are outside this well-defined mainstream. Again, when the sense of belonging is taken away, white respondents immediately "see" how belonging is an integral part of their whiteness and they openly complain about being robbed by the invasion of minorities tainting their neighborhood or demanding equal participation in the mainstream (Fine, et al., 1994, pp. 8–9). It is clear, then, how dependent this sense of belonging is on processes of exclusion. Gallagher (1995) quotes one white student as saying, "We can't have anything for ourselves anymore that says exclusively White or anything like that. But everyone else can" (p. 177).

Solidarity

Ultimately, white privilege depends on its members not betraying the unspoken, nonconscious power dynamics socialized in the intimacy of their families. White solidarity may on first sight appear to be an oxymoron. However, many of the respondents and essayists covered in our review reveal a tacit understanding of white solidarity (see especially Gallagher, 1995, and Roediger, 1991). Although whiteness is "natural" and although few can articulate the privileges that whiteness brings, most can detect when whiteness is being questioned and its privilege potentially dismantled. Therefore, solidarity on the basis of whiteness will have to be fully understood and dismantled for the deconstruction of race privilege to continue. In fact, it is precisely when that solidarity dissolves that differences *among* whites (class, sexuality, etc.) emerge—a process viewed as liberating by some and upsetting or frightening by others.

In summary, some of the mechanisms of power employed in the exercise of whiteness, like class privilege, are distancing, denial, superiority, belongingness, and solidarity, all of which are both daily practices and psychological processes that simultaneously support and reflect the position-justifying beliefs Wellman (1993) and others find whites hold about race. Thus these mechanisms are geared to the maintenance of structural power for white people as a whole. Whether individual whites use these mechanisms or not is irrelevant to the outcome of the white group's superiority and certainly the studies conducted so far suggest that most whites are socialized to employ, whether or not they actually do.

THE USE OF WHITENESS TO MAINTAIN STRUCTURAL PRIVILEGE AND TO PROMOTE RACISM

The objective of the mechanisms of power described in the research on whiteness is to maintain the very real structural privilege of whiteness. An integral part of maintaining structural privilege is racism—the belief that whites are superior to other nonwhite "races." The superiority of whiteness is codified into law as a form of property whose value has not been thoroughly articulated (Harris, 1993b). In fact, law professor Cheryl Harris claims that whiteness has been an exclusive club that has been protected by the courts more than any other kind of property (Harris, 1993b, p. 1736). Whiteness, codified in law, by definition coerced nonwhites into denial of their identity to insure survival (see also Williams, 1995); therefore, it makes no sense to study race as if the mechanism of construction were the same for all groups (Harris, 1993b, p. 1744).

But how exactly does the construction of whiteness form the basis for the maintenance of structural privilege for its owners? It is especially pressing to find answers when apparently its possessors are so oblivious to its effects and some of its nonpossessors seem to agree it is not whiteness *per se* that confers privilege as they strive to climb into the (white) mainstream wagon. The answer may lie in the different functions groups serve in the domination/subordination process as outlined by Apfelbaum (1979). In her theory of intergroup relations, the formation of groups in industrialized society is not independent of the process of enforcing power. The dominant group de-emphasizes its function as a group and instead portrays its existence as the "norm" or as "natural" to mystify how its members obtain power by their group membership. Apfelbaum (1979) names this as the "universal rule" where supposedly *anybody* that "acts" according to prescribed standards is meritorious and deserving of societal and economic rewards. The "universal rule," in theory, is open to everybody and, in fact, applies primarily to those who possess whiteness, and secondarily to those who "act" as white as possible. An unspoken double standard gets set up in which, as Harris (1993b) points out, democracy and rules are exclusively for whites (or those who act as white as possible), while tyranny is justified for Blacks. This double standard is not dictated by the democratic state, but by the "inherent" difference between Blacks and whites. The "inherent difference" is biological race which is codified into law through the one-drop rule—those individuals with at least one drop of Black blood are *legally* considered Black. Belief in a biological basis for whiteness insures that it will take many generations of intermarriage with "pure" whites before individuals can *legally* possess the privileges of whiteness; meanwhile, they are without its property (Harris, 1993b).

On the other hand, the subordinate group is *marked* or stigmatized. The value attached to being white and the devaluation of being nonwhite makes group membership in a nonwhite ethnic/racial group problematic for its members. In effect, the nonwhite ethnic/racial group is (de)grouped and cannot serve the usual positive functions that groups serve—providing a basis for positive social identity, group solidarity, a sense of belonging, and empowerment (Apfelbaum, 1979). At the same time, whiteness does serve those functions for its possessors (Sturgis, 1988; McIntosh, 1992). Degrouping as a basis for group subordination is also a very effective means of sabotaging resistance to domination. While ethnic/racial membership is not supposed to matter in the United States, all privilege and power is distributed according to race, class, and gender (Harris, 1993b, p. 1741, 1761): "In effect, the courts erected legal 'No trespassing signs'—passing, therefore, is largely a phenomenon from subordinate to dominant group rather than the other way around." This is reminiscent of the movie *La Cage Aux Folles* II, where a gay man passes as a woman in Italy and, having to do grueling woman's work, he looks up from the floor he is scrubbing and states, "I want to be a man!"

Apfelbaum (1979) argues that a critical stage in overthrowing domination is when the subordinate group, which has been degrouped, begins to use its own norms and standards for positive identity formation and political mobilization. When a previously degrouped group begins to fight back, the dominant group steps up its restrictive controls. Therefore, it is not surprising that when there are increasing numbers of people of Color in the United States, as well as increasing awareness of how "race" is socially constructed and therefore not about inherent merit—that is, at the very moment when race is on the verge of taking center stage in the analysis of oppression—all of a sudden, race doesn't matter and we should be colorblind (Harris, 1993b, p. 1768). In fact, the deconstruction of white privilege has brought a backlash of countercharges of reverse racism. The increasingly openly expressed response to charges of racism is the assertion that whiteness is a legitimate criterion of resource allocation because merit is color-blind and it is coincidence (or inherent superiority) that most meritorious persons happen to be white and male. Nowhere are the unmentioned assumptions of the "inherent" merit of whiteness more clear than in the legal battles on reverse discrimination. For example, in the now famous Bakke case, the defendant only claimed discrimination on one criterion—whiteness. Other selection criteria like applicants being the offspring of wealthy donors went unchallenged, largely because these hierarchies are perceived as legitimate. Whiteness as property is possessed by all members of the defined group and lends itself to race solidarity. Wealth is possessed in varying degrees and doesn't lend itself to being the criterion for solidarity—not universal enough. In fact, whiteness may be the only uniformly unifying characteristic of the dominant group (Harris, 1993b, p. 1773). In Professor Harris's (1993b) words: "Bakke expected that he would never be disfavored when competing with minority candidates, although he might be disfavored with respect to more privileged whites . . ." (p. 1773). That is, competition among whites is *fair* because they are his equals.

The inherent right for whiteness to serve as valuable property is based on biology; it is therefore property that groups of Color cannot possess immediately, and results in *a priori* structural privilege. To treat white identity as no different from any other group identity when, at its core, whiteness is based on racial subordination, ratifies existing white privilege by making it the referential base line (Harris, 1993b, 1775). This is not only done in the courts and throughout the legal system, but this is the same thing that has been done in the study of whiteness in the social sciences. When whiteness, because of its "natural" order and its elusive nature, remains unquestioned, we have *racial realism*, leaving no room to question whiteness/privilege (Harris, 1993a).

THE RELATIONSHIP BETWEEN PRIVILEGE AND SUBORDINATION IN DEFINING A WHITE IDENTITY

Because whiteness is the "natural" state of affairs, or mainstream nonwhites are the outsiders or the marginals. In the United States, national identity has been constructed as white (Harris, 1993b, p. 1790; Roediger, 1991). To be nonwhite is to be non-American. Congruently, "normal" to white people means "normal" as defined by their worldview (McIntosh, 1992, p. 73). The same is true about being a "good" person. However, this country's national identity, normality, and superiority are not independent of the existence of nonwhites. An integral part of defining free Americans is by contrast to those who are non-American and unfree. White identity is largely constructed through social comparison of those less fortunate (mostly nonwhites). White identity supersedes other identifications—poor white people at least have the consolation that they are not Black (see Roediger, 1991, for several detailed accounts of this process in U.S. history). A white woman at least has the consolation that her status is above nonwhites—at least she is not a woman of Color.

Many of the studies focusing on whiteness explicitly use social comparison between whites and nonwhites to delineate white identity. For example, McIntosh (1992), in her brutally honest essay on whiteness, lists the nonconscious "privileges" that whiteness brings her on an everyday basis. Perhaps, not surprisingly, the list is shaped by *comparisons* to people of Color rather than an introspective focus on herself and her group. (McIntosh is not alone in this practice.) As a result, the list is an account of privileges based on what people of Color do *not* have, rather than what whites possess in the absence of the presence of people of Color. The element of superiority comes through because people of Color in this paradigm have no subjectivity and the dominant assumes that what he/she wants and has is exactly what all people desire. The notion that people of Color may have a different "list" of what a good life is, or what a "good person" is, is not acknowledged in a paradigm where whiteness reigns supreme (McIntosh, 1992, pp. 73–74). McIntosh is fully aware of this contradiction and her essay is an attempt to deconstruct the privileges of whiteness. Again, her honesty, which may be perceived as betrayal by some whites and offensive to some people of Color, allows her to begin to rethink whiteness and by definition the inferiority assigned to nonwhites.

The use of people of Color for the exaltation of whiteness, although gendered, still is used by both men and women. Whiteness and maleness are defined in opposition to "color" and "femaleness"—the other has to exist to exalt the centeredness of the subject. If the other refuses to be the other, it creates chaos in the subject because they have to reconstitute themselves (Fine et al., 1994, p. 2). The presence of nonwhites creates a "humanity" scale in which white men are the pinnacle of human development—they are rational, logical, unemotional, industrious, adventurous, in control, creators (Harris, 1993a)—all of these characteristics would be difficult to judge if it were not for the presence of nonwhites. Even the gender relations between whites are more "human" because of the presence of people of Color. Morrison (1993) illustrates this when discussing Hemingway's *To Have and To Have Not*. In the novel Harry and his wife Marie are making love. Marie asks her husband:

"Listen, did you ever do it with a nigger wench?"
"Sure."
"What's it like?"
"Like a nurse shark."

Morrison (1993) goes on to remark that for Hemingway, the Black woman is

the furthest thing from human, so far away as to be not even mammal but fish. The figure evokes a predatory, devouring eroticism and signals the antithesis to femininity, to nurturing, to nursing, to replenishment. In short, Harry's words mark something so brutal, contrary, and alien in its figuration that it does not belong to its own species and cannot be spoken of in language, in metaphor or metonym, evocative of anything resembling the woman to whom Harry is speaking—his wife Marie. The kindness he has done Marie is palpable. His projection of black female sexuality has provided her with solace, for which she is properly grateful. She responds to the kindness and giggles, "You're funny." (pp. 84–85)

It is in the owning of people of Color, historically through slavery, not through their labor, that white men's manhood was transformed in the new world (Roediger, 1991). As Morrison (1993) points out, ". . . whatever his social status in London, in the New World he is a gentleman. More gentle, more man. The site of his transformation is within rawness: he is backgrounded by savagery" (p. 44). The presence of people of Color and the potential threat of their darkness and their concomitant "savagery" opens the gateways for white people to assume their color burden and protect the "civilized world" through the use of brutality which by definition is not uncivilized. This tautology leads to the most brutal acts, like the imprisonment and execution of more poor Black people in the United States than in any other country—all done in the name of civilization.

Morrison (1993) argues that the use of people of Color, historically, to give whiteness its identity is largely because there was no "royalty" in the United States as there was in Europe, from which to draw a counterdistinction:

. . . Americans did not have profligate, predatory nobility from which to wrest an identity of national virtue while continuing to covet aristocratic license and luxury. The American nation negotiated both its disdain and its envy in the same way Dunbar did: through the self-reflexive contemplation of fabricated, mythological Africanism. For the settlers and for American writers generally, this Africanist other became the means of thinking about body, mind, chaos, kindness, and love; provided the occasion for exercises in the absence of restraint, the presence of restraint, the contemplation of freedom and of aggression; permitted opportunities for the exploration of ethics and morality, for meeting the obligations of the social contract, for bearing the cross of religion and following out the ramifications of power. (p. 47)

Morrison (1993) quotes sociologist Orlando Patterson's observation that ". . . we should not be surprised that the Enlightenment could accommodate slavery; we should be surprised if it had not. The concept of freedom did not emerge in a vacuum. Nothing highlighted freedom—if it did not in fact create it—like slavery" (p. 38). The significance of white identity is still in reference to the presence of dark others—the definitions of social issues are as well. For many whites the passion that propels their lives stems from the need to "help" save, and by default indirectly control, the dark others. In Morrison's (1993) words: "Africanism is the vehicle by which the American self knows itself as not enslaved, but free; not repulsive but desirable; not helpless, but licensed and powerful; not history-less, but historical; not damned, but innocent; not a blind accident of evolution, but a progressive fulfillment of destiny" (p. 52).

In sum, people of Color are the experimentation ground where real lives get hurt, trashed out, dumped, and disposed of, while whites psyches remain intact—or do they? It is not their children who have been killed in disproportionate numbers by drugs, guns, or war, but will their children not inherit their consequences? Will the anger whites have been systematically cultivating for so long be unleashed on those they care about most because they represent their immortality—future generations of white children?

METHODOLOGICAL ISSUES

In reviewing both direct accounts of whites' experience of race, and more indirect accounts of other kinds of privilege, we have been struck by the challenge this research poses to our understanding of "feminist methods." Feminist methods have grown out of efforts by researchers to dismantle privilege—both gender and scientific privilege. An integral part of feminist epistemology and methods has been to create an activist scholarship at the root of which is the hope of changing existing power relations. Analytic and procedural techniques flowing from these goals have been used to great advantage in studying subordinate groups; they are, however, much more problematic in the study of "dominants." Recognition of this fact may help feminist social scientists articulate more precisely the conditions under which various research approaches are useful or appropriate.

Research as Empowerment

Many feminist scholars have thought hard about the intertwined ethical and methodological issues involved in conducting research with people who are disadvantaged in terms of gender, class, and/or race (see Bowles and Duelli Klein, 1983; Fonow and Cook, 1991; Nielsen, 1990; Reinharz, 1992; Roberts, 1981). Thus, for example, Oakley (1981), in an important early paper, described the importance of *not* withholding crucial information and knowledge from research participants who needed it. Generally increased openness with research participants about the purposes and goals of the research has been advocated (Cook and Fonow, 1990). Mies (1983) argued early on for the importance of research participants' role in shaping and defining the research questions. Many worried about how to encourage those who have been "shut up and shut out" to tell what they know (Belenky, et al., 1986; Reid, 1994). As a result, there has been considerable—and critical—development of methods that support and affirm participants' perspective and leave plenty of space for its articulation.

Parallel recommendations have been made about how we write up what we learn. Thus, feminist scholars have recommended that we avoid representing research participants' experience, but instead permit those participants—who often have not been heard directly before—to speak "in their own voice." This concern has been expressed in extensive quotation from participants, provision of richly detailed accounts of the context (or "ethnography"), as well as in inclusion of participants' own reflections on the researchers' claims (see Franz and Stewart, 1994; Stacey, 1990).

How do these suggestions, flowing as they do from a concern about the power imbalance between the researcher and the researched, fare when we turn to research on whiteness? Many of these studies have employed open-ended interview, or ethnographic, techniques of data collection *from people who are white* and therefore already "empowered" at least with respect to their location in the racial hierarchy; and they have included extensive quotations from the research participants. These techniques can leave researchers in the ethically complex situation of eliciting, recording—and not challenging—participants' racist views. On the one hand this approach seems consistent with feminist methodological preoccupations with supporting and encouraging participants' "voices" and with facilitating identification of multiple "standpoints." However, we doubt that recording, and repeating, racist views of whites in a racist society could ever have the same moral or ethical standing as recording and repeating the views of those whose opinions are not institutionalized and reified throughout the culture (and we note that feminist researchers have not been interested in documenting sexist views in rich detail). Moreover, for an antiracist researcher simply to record racist sentiments is certainly not open or honest. (Wellman (1993) discusses an interesting case in which a Black interviewer repeatedly presses a white respondent to explain her views on race more clearly. The interview sounds uncomfortable but "honest" in a way not quite envisioned in most writing on feminist methods.)

Quoting hate-filled sentiments puts scholars in the position of giving those sentiments more "air time" than they already have. This is not to say it is never justified; but here we must ask not for "thick" description or empowerment and giving voice, but for "thick" analysis (Wellman, 1993, provides a good model of this ratio of analysis to quotation). The repetition of certain opinions will, in itself, inflict pain on some who read them; that pain must be justified by a gain in understanding provided by explication and critique. An appropriate strategy for reporting may be to provide *minimal* documentation, when views are all-too-familiar and oppressive, while holding ourselves and others to a very high standard of analytic depth when work carries such a high risk of causing suffering in those already the objects of daily racism.

Who Are the Experts on Whiteness?

Research on whiteness carried out with people of Color has very different risks and benefits. We have seen that many whites are not able to articulate any clear meaning of whiteness in their lives. In contrast, we suspect that people of Color have a rather well-developed understanding of how "whiteness matters" (just as women tend to have a clearer sense of male privilege than men do). In fact, Dill (1988), Rollins (1985), and Romero (1992), in their studies of domestic workers have often provided perspectives on whiteness. Even more directly, Philomena Essed (1990) set out to study "racism" from the perspective of women of Color (in the Netherlands and the United States). She adopted a "feminist method": "I wanted the women to describe and illustrate their experiences at length. With this in mind, I tried to direct the interviews as little as possible" (p. 3). In her study of racism from the perspective of women of Color, she certainly identified many important features of whiteness. She identified three main forms of "everyday racism": inferiorization, social or spatial distancing, and social or physical aggression. Each of these tells us something important not only about the experiences of racism of women of Color, but also about the experience of whiteness of white women and men. In addition, Essed suggests that:

> Everyday racism implies that people of color can, potentially, experience racism every day. As a result, people of color learn to systematically observe the behavior of whites. They develop expertise in judging how whites behave toward them. They also gain insight into the white delusion of superiority and the ideology defining people of color as inferior. They have daily opportunities to test new insights, because they have contact with all sorts of whites every day. (p. 258)

In short, people of Color are experts about whiteness, which we have learned whites most emphatically are not. We suggest that feminist methods used to study whiteness from the perspective of people of Color are likely to produce substantial knowledge, without posing the same kinds of ethical dilemmas they pose when studying the perspective of whites.

Revisiting the Researchers' Perspective

Attention to the perspective of the researched must be matched by attention to the perspective of the researcher. It is critical for scholars exploring the meaning of whiteness to articulate the implications of their own relation to whiteness. Essed discussed what it meant for her research:

Doing research among one's own group has the advantage of making it easier to discuss negative views about an "out group," in this case whites. Thus I was in an advantageous position as a black researcher of experiences of racism. (p. 3)

In this case, then, she is able to encourage and support expression of negative views not normally sanctioned by the larger culture. In the reverse case—as a white person, facilitating the expression of negative views of people of Color by whites—the researcher is on much less defensible ground, both in terms of the likelihood of uncovering previously invisible features of the social landscape, and in terms of the ethics of the situation, given her own social position. Interestingly, Wellman (1993) experimented with having Black interviewers interview whites about race; at least some of these interviews were brilliantly successful (see, e.g., chapter 4).

One technique for addressing the limitations of one's own standpoint is actively to seek out literature written from other standpoints. Thus, for example, Caraway's (1991) analysis of "racism and the politics of American feminism" employs a brilliant strategy of combining thoughtful recognition of her own position as a white female feminist *and* the rich literature written by feminists of Color. She argues for a "crossover politics" in which

feminists try (but never truly succeed) to see and hear from "other" vantage points, perhaps sharing some of their experience and knowledge with someone else, some of whose own experience and knowledge might rub off. (p. 172)

The argument that precedes her case for a "multicultural feminist politics of solidarity" is powerful precisely because she presents—in respectful detail—the viewpoints of feminist theorists of Color and reacts to them from her own perspective. Studies of whiteness by white scholars would not be so likely to create a sense of eavesdropping on a particularly ugly conversation if they incorporated at least this academic form of "walking in others' shoes"—reading, taking seriously, citing, quoting—the scholarship by people of Color about race.

Reinventing Feminist Methods

It is, then, crucial for researchers to keep the power dimension of standpoints or perspectives in focus. Methods which serve constructive aims when used with subordinates may have very different implications when used with dominants. We do not advocate the use of different methods for different groups because they are "different" in an essentialist way but rather that social location gives access to power. In progressive scholarship where the goal is to dismantle oppression, social location is crucial in determining our research methods. In fact, this is one of the main cornerstones of feminist epistemology—that women's subordination, historically, did not permit the use of western positivist, male paradigms and methods without inevitably eclipsing women's experiences and therefore distorting their lives. One way to mitigate the impact of one's own social position may be to employ more complicating collaborative research practices. Methods in which whites are provided an opportunity to express views about race *while being held accountable for them* can be created, as Wellman (1993) has shown. Focus groups constructed to include individuals with different views could offer one such approach; interview techniques involving two (or more) interviewers from different social locations might be another. In any case data collected can always be analyzed—by focus groups, collaborators, other participants—from multiple perspectives. And written reports can include those multiple perspectives in a single "voice" or in several. When exploring hegemonic experiences like whiteness, the trick is to find ways to retain a critical, counterhegemonic presence in the research. Recognizing the complexity of that task will help us enrich "feminist methods" to include techniques that more fully acknowledge the complexity of the power relations among and between women and men.

REFERENCES

Allport, G. (1958). *The nature of prejudice*. Garden City, NJ: Doubleday.

Apfelbaum, E. (1979). Relations of domination and movements for liberation: An analysis of power between groups. In W. G. Austin and S. Worchel (eds.), *The social psychology of intergroup relations*. (pp. 188–204). Monterey, California: New York: Plenum.

Belenky, M. F., Clinchy, B. M., Goldberger, N. R., and Tarule, J. M. (1986). *Women's ways of knowing: The development of self, voice and mind*. New York: Basic.

Belle, D. (1994). Attempting to comprehend the lives of low-income women. In C. Franz and A. J. Stewart (eds.), *Women creating lives*. Boulder, CO: Westview.

Bowles, G., and Duelli Klein, K. (1983). *Theories of women's studies*. London: Routledge.

Caraway, N. (1991). *Segregated sisterhood: Racism and the politics of American feminism*. Knoxville, TN: University of Tennessee Press.

Carroll, L. C. (1946). *Through the looking glass*. New York: Random House.

Dill, B. T. (1988). "Making your job good yourself": Domestic Service and the construction of personal dignity. In A. Bookman and S. Morgen (eds.), *Women and the politics of empowerment* (pp. 33–52). Philadelphia, PA: Temple University Press.

Domhoff, G. W. (1983). *Who rules America now?* Englewood Cliffs, NJ: Prentice-Hall.

Du Bois, W. E. Burghardt. (1961). *The souls of black folk*. Greenwich, Connecticut: Fawcett Publications, Inc.

Essed, P. (1990). *Everyday racism: Reports from women of two cultures*. Alameda, CA: Hunter House.

Feagin, J., and Feagin, C. B. (1978). *Discrimination American style: Institutional racism and sexism*. Englewood Cliffs, NJ: Prentice-Hall.

Fine, M. (1989). Coping with rape: Critical perspectives on consciousness. In R. K. Unger (ed.), *Representations: Social constructions of gender* (pp. 167–185). Amityville, NY: Baywood.

Fine, M., Weis, L., Addelston, J., and Marusza, J. (forthcoming). White loss. In M. Zeller and L. Weis (eds.) *Beyond black and white*. Albany, NY: SUNY Press.

Fonow, M. M., and Cook, J. A. (1991). *Beyond methodology*. Bloomington: Indiana University Press.

Frankenberg, R. (1993). *White women, race matters: The social construction of whiteness*. Minneapolis, MN: University of Minnesota Press.

Franz, C. E., and Stewart, A. J. (1994). *Women creating lives*. Boulder, CO: Westview.

Gallagher, C. A. (1995). White reconstruction in the university. *Socialist Review*, 24(1–2), 165–185.

Harding, S. (1991). *Whose science? Whose knowledge? Thinking from women's lives*. Ithaca: Cornell University Press.

Harris, C. I. (1993a). Bell's blues. *The University of Chicago Law Review*, 60, 783–793.

Harris, C. I. (1993b). Whiteness as property. *Harvard Law Review*, 106, 1707–1791.

Hurtado, A. (1989). Relating to privilege: Seduction and rejection in the subordination of white women and women of color. *Signs*, 14, 833–855.

Kimmel, M. S. (1993). Invisible masculinity. *Society*, 30, 28–35.

Landrine, H., Klonoff, E., and Brown-Collins, A. (1992). Cultural diversity and methodology in feminist psychology: Critique, proposal, empirical example. *Psychology of Women Quarterly*, 16, 145–163.

Lykes, M. B. (1989). Dialogue with Guatemalan Indian women: Critical perspectives on constructing collaborative research. In R. K. Unger (ed.), *Representations: Social constructions of gender* (pp. 167–185). Amityville, NY: Baywood.

McIntosh, P. (1992). White privilege and male privilege: A personal account of coming to see correspondences through work in Women's Studies. In M. L. Andersen and P. Hill Collins (eds.), *Race, class, and gender* (pp. 70–81). Belmont, CA: Wadsworth.

Mies, M. (1983). Towards a methodology for feminist research. In G. Bowles and R. Duelli Klein (eds.), *Theories of women's studies* (pp. 117–139). London: Routledge.

Morrison, T. (1992). *Playing in the dark*. New York: Vintage.

Nielsen, J. M. (1990). *Feminist research methods*. Boulder, CO: Westview.

Oakley, A. (1981). Interviewing women. In H. Roberts (ed.), *Doing feminist research* (pp. 30–61). London: Routledge.

Ostrander, S. (1984). *Women of the upper class*. Philadelphia, PA: Temple University Press.

Ostrove, J. M., and Stewart, A. J. (1994). Meanings and uses of marginal identities: Social class at Radcliffe in the 1960s. In C. Franz and A. J. Stewart (eds.), *Women creating lives* (pp. 273–288). Boulder, CO: Westview.

Pettigrew, T. F. (1964). *Profile of the Negro American*. New York: Van Nostrand.

Reid, P. T. (1993). Poor women in psychological research: Shut up and shut out. *Psychology of Women Quarterly, 17*, 133–150.

Reinharz, S. (1992). *Feminist methods in social research*. New York: Oxford.

Roberts, H. (1981). *Doing feminist research*. London: Routledge.

Roediger, D. R. (1991). *The wages of whiteness*. New York: Verso.

Rollins, J. (1985). *Between women: Domestics and their employers*. Philadelphia, PA: Temple University Press.

Romero, M. (1992). *Maid in the U.S.A.* New York: Routledge.

Ryan, J., and Sackrey, C. (1984). *Strangers in paradise*. Boston: South End Press.

Sherif, C. W. (1979). Bias in psychology. In J. A. Sherman and E. T. Beck (eds.), *Prism of sex: Essays in the sociology of knowledge* (pp. 93–133). Madison: University of Wisconsin Press.

Stacey, J. (1990). *Brave new families*. NY: Basic.

Sturgis, S. J. (1988). Class/act: Beginning a translation from privilege. In C. McEwan and S. O'Sullivan (eds.), *Out the other side: Contemporary lesbian writing* (pp. 7–13). London: Virago.

Tatum, B. D. (1992). Talking about race, learning about racism: The application of racial identity development theory in the classroom. *Harvard Educational Review, 62*(1), 1–24.

Vanfossen, B. (1979). *The structure of social inequality*. Boston: Little Brown.

Wellman, D. T. (1993). *Portraits of white racism* (2nd ed.). New York: Cambridge University Press.

Williams, G. H. (1995). *Life on the color line*. Dutton.

Wilson, W. J. (1987). *The truly disadvantaged: The inner city, the underclass, and public policy*. Chicago: University of Chicago Press.

Zweigenhaft, R. L., and Domhoff, G. H. (1991). *Blacks in the white establishment*? New Haven, Yale University Press.

We would like to thank the following individuals for their throughtful comments: Linda Blum, Michelle Fine, Pat Gurin, Gerry Gurin, Rosario Ceballo, Lois Weis, Joan Ostrove, and Mun Wong.

Surfacing Our-selves:
¿Gringa, White—Mestiza, Brown?

M. Brinton Lykes and Amelia Mallona

M. Brinton Lykes is Associate Professor of Psychology at Boston College and has worked in Latin America since 1986 in the development of community-based psychological assistance programs in contexts of war and state-sponsored violence. Her writings explore the importance of culture and indigenous practices in the lives of women and child survivors and the dilemmas encountered in multicultural, engendered action research. She has also written about constructions of self and theorizing the self in cultural context. She is coeditor (with Ali Banuazizi, Ramsay Liem, and Michael Morris) of *Myths about the Powerless: Contesting Social Inequalities* (1996) and (with Abigail J. Stewart) *Gender and Personality* (1985).

Amelia Mallona is a Nicaraguan Ph.D. candidate in developmental and educational psychology at Boston College. She received her B.A. in psychology at Universidad Centroamericana in Nicaragua and her M.A. in sociology at the University of Missouri–Columbia. Before entering the program at Boston College Amelia was Regional Coordinator of Community and Socioeconomic Development at the Institute of Social Actioin: John XXIII/UCA, working in rural war zones of Nicaragua. Her dissertation research investigates the sense of self in low-income Central American immigrant women in the United States. She plans to teach and conduct participatory action research with low-income Latinas and university students.

The Culture Workshop is a group of faculty and doctoral students in Boston College who organize their work in psychology and education around issues of culture, both within and beyond the U.S. context. The group provides an interdisciplinary context where students and faculty present their ongoing research and dialogue about ways of thinking culturally about and developing research within diverse communities. Many of the group members also participate in more activist efforts to diversify the Boston College campus and curriculum and to fight institutional oppression on campus and beyond.

Amelia (Nicaraguan woman, international student, Ph.D. candidate, activist, researcher) and Brinton (white United Statesian[1], southern woman, professor, activist, researcher), are "joined by our commitment to justice and freedom" (hooks, in *Trend*, 1995, p. 121). However, this experience of commonality is neither static nor unitary. In this paper we surface our brown/mestiza, white/gringa selves through multiple conversations and multiparty talk that explores the multiple meanings of that commitment within the context of our work at Boston College.

SOCIAL IDENTITIES: KNOWING HOW WE CONSTRUCTED SELF-KNOWING

Through intentional conversation or what we call here a semistructured "co-interview" we discovered that our respective awarenesses of being "white" (Brinton) and "brown"/"mixed"/"mestiza"[2] (Amelia) have taken multiple and diverse forms at different historical moments and within different social contexts. Our method of discovery included a ninety-minute co-interview which was tape recorded and transcribed. We also took our dialogue to a group of colleagues at Boston College who describe their research within the rubric of "cultural psychology" and meet monthly in a Culture Workshop to discuss work-in-progress. We hoped to widen our lenses of reflexivity, particularly as the group is remarkably diverse. White middle- and upper-middle-class United Statesians are in the numerical minority and participants include, in addition to ourselves, African Americans, an Asian American, Iranians, a Palestinian, a Chinese, an Indian, and a Maya; women and men, with the former outnumbering the latter about three to one; slightly more students than faculty, and the full range of social classes, at least in terms of social class of origin.[3] This conversation of approximately two hours was also transcribed.

More than forty different codes that characterized the multiple and frequently divergent paths within this talk were developed and reduced to three categories around which we organized our analysis of our conversations and the group discussions (Charmaz, 1988; McIntyre, 1995; Strauss and Corbin, 1990). The categories are *shifting social identities*; *whiteness at home and abroad*; and *problematizing invisible privilege*.

We explain the constructed meanings of the three categories through displays of segments of texts coded from the co-interview and the workshop transcriptions. We conclude by deconstructing these categories, clarifying what we saw to be, on closer examination, strengths and weaknesses in the ways in which we spoke about race, color, nationality, and self. We also include some reservations about the implications of this "new and growing field, the study of 'whiteness'" (McMillen, 1995, p. A23).

At each step in the process we found ourselves reexamining personal experiences and returning to earlier books or articles that had shaped our previous understandings of our respective "origin stories" (see, e.g., Smith, 1949/1961, for Brinton; Melville, 1993, for Amelia). We also sought additional resources, struggling to understand dimensions of our stories that had remained hidden to us (see, e.g., Gould, 1993, on the history of the eradication of the indigenous of Nicaragua and the creation of the "myth of mestizo/a"; and Rodríguez, 1992, on race, class, and Latino/a "otherness" in the United States). These experiences and our ongoing dialogues as we analyzed our "talk" and wrote this paper confirm for us the partiality and the highly contextualized nature of knowledge about whiteness, including that which we have constructed here.

MAKING CONNECTIONS, NARRATING OUR STORIES

We began our *estudía* in Boston College in September of 1992. We had both recently arrived or returned to this Chestnut Hill campus. Despite differences in power and privilege associated with faculty and graduate student statuses within the university we forged a working relationship through a shared language (Spanish) and a shared ideology (progressive, Left, feminist/womanist and anti-imperialist). This relationship developed as Amelia immersed herself in U.S. culture and psychology while participating in the analysis of data from Brinton's participatory action research with Guatemalan Maya women and children. We shared an experience of "otherness" in relation to the Maya, while our nationalities as United Statesian and Nicaraguan differentially positioned us as we sought to make psychological and cultural meaning of the lived experiences Brinton had shared with the Maya.

Our dialogues were situated in the "land of opportunity," where we were both benefiting from the educational resources accorded to the privileged within the United States. We also recognized more and more the social and historical rootedness of our respective analyses of the causes of political terror in Guatemala. Brinton's sense of self as white and privileged is deeply rooted in her southern childhood. She has written about her "situated otherness" as a "white, female, educated United Statesian whose government sponsored the overthrow of the democratically elected government of Guatemala in 1954" (Lykes, 1994). She discussed how this position informed her meaning making of war and its effects in Guatemala.

Amelia resisted Brinton's focus on race, emphasizing the importance of economic relations and social class position, insisting that race was not a salient issue in Latin America. She was reading about Latinas, self, and identity, towards the development of her dissertation research. Ironically—and often painfully—she was also being forced into a new awareness of her "brownness" and its consequences for her within a U.S. context. Repeated experiences of being marginalized by whites in favor of "their own color" forced her to reconsider firmly held beliefs.

We challenged each other to "explain" ourselves and our "situated othernesses" in our teaching and research. Our co-interview began with our recalling our childhood experiences of being white and brown and included more recent experiences of "self as other," in Guatemala for Brinton, in the United States for Amelia.[4]

> Amelia: Well it is very interesting your question about how I came to think about myself as "white." I never thought about my skin color before—because "mixed" people like myself are the majority of the population in Nicaragua . . . (I, p. 1)
>
> Brinton: My understanding of whiteness is constructed and constrained by my understanding of blackness and my understanding of the experiences of African Americans in the United States, and of the differences between the immigrant experience in the United States and the experience of slavery. My grandparents on both sides of my family immigrated to the United States from Northern and Southern Europe so I have a kind of mix. . . .
>
> For me the meaning of being white has something to do with that story of my ethnic roots but much more to do with the history of race relations in this country and with having grown up in the South in the 1950s and 1960s. (I, p. 8)

SIMILARITIES AND DIFFERENCES IN THE WAYS IN WHICH WE HAVE APPROPRIATED CATEGORIES OF WHITE/BROWN — GRINGA/MESTIZA

Our longer narratives, excerpted here, suggest that color cannot be described "out of context." The multiple contexts in which we have come to understand and to make meaning of our color include our gender, social class, culture, language, nationality, religion, and political identifications. In reflecting upon the "text" coconstructed in our interview we identified several dimensions along which our understandings converge, and others along which we diverge. We found, for example, that although our particular experiences of gender, class, religion, and ideology were not identical there were many similarities. Each of us has come to identify herself as a feminist/womanist and for both of us religion and gender politics were formative of our early and young adult experiences and our ideology, although they were both noticeably muted in our co-interview. We both identify ourselves within the middle class although we differ in our positioning within the finer gradations of that denominator, and our experiences of class are deeply structured by our nationalities. We share a political ideology and similar commitments to the oppressed, captured by the liberation theologian's "preferential option for the poor," (see, e.g., Martín-Baró, 1994) although these are differently expressed within local community and Left political organizing. Similarly, the common language of Spanish was very important to our individual and relational naming of self. For Amelia, encountering a professor and a mentor who is a Spanish speaker was very empowering. For Brinton, having a graduate assistant who speaks Spanish and who is Central American meant being able to work in a new way on her action research while far from the Guatemalan Highlands (see Lykes, 1996). There are some "categories of similarity" and much constructed commonalty.

In contrast, in listening to each other in the co-interview and in listening to how that conversation was reframed by the Culture Workshop, we discovered a number of differences in our self-understandings. These circled in and out of the language of race, ethnicity, color, and culture. We turn now to our conceptual analysis of the texts of the co-interview and the multiparty talk of the Culture Workshop to pry open some of the multiple meanings of these terms and the implications of our dialogue for thinking racially beyond or through white and Black. Our first category, *shifting social identities*, reflects the dynamic, changing, nonstatic nature of race and color.

SHIFTING SOCIAL IDENTITIES

In analyzing our co-interview and the multiparty talk of the workshop we discovered chunks of text that reflect differing experiences of being named and naming ourselves as "raced." We shared experiences of how we ourselves had been seen as oppressor (Amelia among the Miskito on the Atlantic Coast of Nicaragua; Brinton as white, upper-middle-class United Statesian) and oppressed (Amelia as brown Hispanic in the United States and as Nicaraguan, facing U.S. imperialism in the form of the Contra War; Brinton as a woman). Brinton's experiences as oppressor dominated the dialogue while Amelia's, of being oppressed, were most salient. More important than the fixed categories of oppressor or oppressed, however, are the ways in which we fill the categories with which we have been labelled as Other. Amelia noted several times that it was only in the United States that "I began to think about my skin color and I began to understand that part of my social identity . . ." (WK, ll. 182–184). This awareness of color was complex in that "you see I have choices; I am like a chameleon because some people perceive me as white; some people perceive me as brown; some people perceive me as a Hispanic which implies that I was born here and I am not—so they assume that I know their culture and I do not" (WK, ll. 192–196).

In the co-interview Amelia described the multiple impositions that fill this category, both those of the dominant group who label her as a "person of color" and a "Hispanic," even when she describes herself as a Latin American and an international student and those (including whites, Asian Americans, and African Americans) who "have a very negative stereotype of what a Hispanic is . . . lazy people, unskilled people, violent, drug addicts, pusher of all sorts of things . . . suddenly I felt that I was categorized with all that I didn't want to be . . ." (I, ll. 320–331).

Amelia appropriates this label and although "I do not have choices in terms of being treated as a minority with all its implications . . . my choice is to take a political stand in relationship to relations of power in the U.S." (WK, Amelia, ll. 630–636). She had described her understanding of the meaning of her choice in the co-interview:

I think that it is a very interesting thing about the self, a self that gives meaning to the context. The people in Boston have imposed an identity on me that I didn't opt for, but since their decision is already there and since I also have a choice of being open to Hispanics and I recognize that we come from the same culture or root experience and since I have chosen to work for the poor, in this case the Hispanic, I am giving meaning to that imposition, in my own way, so I am constructing it and giving it meaning. (I, ll. 376–384)

Brinton's experiences differ from Amelia's but have similarly been shaped by experiences of self "at home" and "abroad." When she began to work among Central Americans she can still remember "intense political situations in which I was very much defined as Other and excluded from discussions because of being from the U.S. and being white, that is, not an indigenous person . . ." (WK, Brinton, ll. 355–363). As one of the workshop participants commented,

there's no choice in defining your ethnicity, your race—you're white and that's it—but within that, the choice that you have is the political choice of being aware of . . . the power relations and where you want to be in that system of power . . . and thereby you can be seen as in solidarity . . . in contrast to Hispanics or Black Americans or probably Asian Americans or any other minority group going to Guatemala . . . [because they are from] the less powerful group [in the United States, they are automatically] perceived as in a position of solidarity. (WK, ll. 669–682)

Brinton characterized this positioning of herself as white and in solidarity earlier in the workshop in the following way:

How I define myself shifts, that is, what fills those categories takes on different meanings. . . . I'm a North American and the U.S. represents imperialism [for the folks with whom I work] but through how I position myself in struggle I show myself in solidarity with the Maya through my actions. The shifting sense of who I am is reflected, for example, in my recent introduction into a group of Maya I did not know. The Maya who presented me said: "most of her heart is here in Guatemala even though she's a gringa." So, for me it creates an understanding of whiteness and an understanding of my nationality in which I experience it as a constraint but also I experience it not as a boundary that's firm but a limit that is fluid, that is, creating of possibilities, a border around which different kinds of relationality can be constructed. (WK, ll. 328–370)

In that sense race and culture for both of us are not only stable categories which adhere to our bodily selves and in which others deposit multiple meanings. They are also subject positions that we construct and from which we take action. Those subject positions and actions are, of course, always constrained or facilitated by the social construction of those who "other us." Our shifting identities are thus bounded by time (history) and space (social context). Similarly, as we reconstruct our identities we are also reconstructing our herstories through political and ideological struggle. The social constructions of ourselves are deeply affected by relations of power within and beyond national borders.

WHITENESS AT HOME AND ABROAD

When we presented our co-interview to the Culture Workshop our colleagues questioned the extent to which we were talking about whiteness or race when we talk across cultures and nations. Some noted that Brinton's "otherness" in Guatemala was more reflective of her citizenship and her linguistic and cultural "otherness" than of her whiteness. Amelia indicated that she has been told that her experiences of discrimination are not due to her "brownness" but because she is not a U.S. citizen and speaks English with a noticeably foreign accent. The U.S. imperialist self overwhelms the context and color is submerged. However the dialogue in the workshop suggested otherwise. Our exchanges about whiteness at home and abroad evidence complex and diverging points of view. On the one hand, an Asian American participant suggested that

> the image that I get [about] what your dialogue is leading to, is that white is fixed to, in a sense, the essence of . . . what the U.S. is. Perhaps in Guatemala it is the imperialist U.S. but in other countries of the world, you know, it could be very different. But, somehow whiteness, in some sense, is and has appropriated the national, what the nation is, who the nation is—so that it sounds like the categories [of white, brown, etc.] have shifted away from race, you know, to nationality or ethnicity or culture.
> A Euro/white American participant added: . . . whiteness is perceived differently depend[ing] on which country you are in. Whiteness is power and it is [perceived as] power for oppression [in some contexts] or power for benevolent uses [in other contexts]. (WK, pp. 8–9)

These comments confirm the importance of the positionality of the perceiver and his or her context in making meaning of whiteness beyond the United States. Nationality and whiteness are seemingly collapsed into one when experienced beyond U.S. borders.

Our discussion suggested further that in many parts of the world U.S. Blacks, for example, are perceived by oppressed peoples in these countries as in solidarity with them, despite their nationality (i.e., U.S. citizens). In contrast, whites are the racist oppressor and also the colonizer (or neo-colonizer, the promoter of modernity). These complex interpretive schema are implicit in interracial, international, interethnic multiparty talk within a racialized U.S. context whether or not they are explicitly invoked. At some points the multiparty talk of the Culture Workshop engaged them more explicitly. A participant reported:

> I want to tell you also [related to] what Amelia said about this country being defined and perceived as white. But it depends [on] where you perceive it. Look at American marines that go overseas. I remember . . . when we went to visit the . . . white and Black American navy [stationed off the coast of Israel]. You see the Black, and the first reaction for somebody like me is, what is he doing there? Then you are reminded, one, that he or she is American. You think, of course. But your first reaction is that white people are coming.
>   Okay that's from my point of view, as a minority oppressed Palestinian. So what is he doing there? It's like, he is on my side. That's the simplistic, immediate reaction. (WK ll. 733–747)

Amelia concurred, describing her experiences of African American military in Nicaragua where, as she stated, "I feel the same thing, we are in the same boat. So what are you, [a Black], doing here [as U.S. invader]?" (WK, ll. 851–852). Another Euro/white American workshop participant reflected on Brinton's story stating that

> in the U.S. you simply—if you are white you are a person and, . . . whiteness does disappear. You know. [Beyond the U.S.] whiteness is the representation of the essence of U.S., and it's made very clear through the politics of the relationship. . . . But the absence of whiteness as a racial dimension in, domestically, here in the U.S., you know, is the dilemma that I hear. It's being discovered in the international context, and part of what's being discovered

is the essence of it as a privilege here, which is, that one is simply by virtue of that color, the essence, the center of the American way of life and one doesn't have to, it's not seen, and in the deepest sense it's privileged. (WK, ll. 953–958)

Our co-interview had suggested that in many countries a white United Statesian who wants to be perceived in ways that don't equate her or himself to privilege must self-consciously and intentionally enact or perform a different meaning of whiteness. This is possible, although complex, both within and beyond the United States. The workshop multiparty talk confirmed however that there are severe limits or constraints on how much redefining one can do within a broader set of national and international relations, particularly when the United States has historic, colonial relations with the "target" country. Those who argued that whiteness was less salient and somehow less relevant outside the United States struggled with those who saw it as more powerful precisely because it was less visible and equated with U.S. colonial power.

Engaging a conversation about whiteness across national boundaries raises important considerations for those concerned, for example, about the recent surges of anti-immigrant sentiment within the United States. The support for Proposition 187 among African Americans and Latinos in California suggests that citizenry, nationality, and race interact in complex ways that have not been sufficiently problematized. Our analysis of the perceptions of whites and Blacks abroad as oppressor or oppressed reveals a tendency to fix categories of race and color, a tendency that was resisted in the co-interview wherein we sought to destabilize categorical identity statements based on color. Reexamining the texts about race within the United States from beyond U.S. borders helped us craft our third category, *problematizing invisible privilege*.

MAKING THE INVISIBLE VISIBLE: RACE AND CLASS ACROSS CULTURES AND NATIONS

Class differences among the participants emerged in the multiparty talk of race beyond the borders of the United States. An African American participant suggested that United Statesians abroad are assumed to have money, thereby homogenizing racial differences in the U.S. population in terms of economic resources. Amelia defended the accuracy of this categorization, clarifying that relative to most Central Americans, most North Americans, including Blacks, are wealthy. Others in the workshop argued that this confirmed the invisibility of social class differences within the United States. Brinton suggested that her experiences in Latin America led her to conclude that many Latin Americans have a clearer analysis of social class and of economic power and privilege than do average United Statesians. In contrast, her Latin American mestizo colleagues are less likely to acknowledge racial or ethnic stratification within their own countries. Many are oblivious to the histories, cultures, and languages of their own indigenous populations. Amelia's experience, for example, of "racializing" the lens through which she now views Nicaragua is a consequence of having lived experiences of discrimination within the United States and of now viewing herself as "others," i.e., the indigenous of her country, have viewed her. Recent historical analyses of the designations "mestizo" and "Hispanic" and "Latino" describe the racialized nature of colonial relations.[5] Amelia now analyzes the taken-for-granted privilege of the majority "mestizo" population in Nicaragua in relationship to African descendants and indigenous groups in her country as analogous to McIntosh's (1990) critique of the invisible privilege of whites in the United States. In contrast the relationship between race and class oppression is analyzed with greater clarity by Latin Americanists[6] than by numerous United Statesian theorists (see, e.g., McIntosh, 1990; Helms, 1993; Terry, 1975).

Analyses of the co-interview and workshop talk suggest multiple intersections between race and class that are frequently submerged when we focus our attention exclusively on color and/or whiteness within U.S. boundaries.

Asian American participant: I think the white class is talked about in our society—but the middle class is the thing to which we aspire—so in cultural terms it's sort of—are you middle class, or are you not middle class? And [if not] are you working class?

I think that discussion sidetracks the more important question of class as an economic category. The real threat of elevating class analysis to social analysis in this society is that it goes to the core of how this country produces and reproduces itself—its economic system. . . .

It's the absence of that discussion, of making it a stark distinction between wealth and ownership in terms of the means of production—and all the rest . . . it's that discussion that is not in the public discourse. And in fact it's been increasingly . . . pushed even further and further away from the center of discussion, partly by the discussion of culture and race. (WK, ll. 1678–1701)

The workshop multiparty talk confirmed the absence of self-interest or solidarity links among the broad swath of the U.S. public that identifies as middle and working class as well as multiple meanings made of middle-class experience. Our struggle to be more nuanced about differing experiences of whiteness and privilege in relation to differing social classes might be interpreted by some as a "white move" to derail the analysis of racism and white privilege. Yet critiquing our own thinking about race and social class at home and abroad elucidated some blind spots in meaning making that reduce whiteness to privilege without acknowledging the complex variability in the access whites have to power and resources depending upon other social experiences, e.g., social class, gender, sexual identity. White United Statesians can fruitfully rethink these nuances through the lenses crafted by those beyond our borders. The structural understandings of social class that grow out of experiences of colonialism are particularly helpful for rethinking the meaning of white privilege. Similarly, rethinking social class privilege in Latin America through lenses crafted in dialogues with peoples of color and whites within the United States deepens our understanding of experiences of oppression and longstanding conflicts within these countries.

CONCLUSIONS

Through analysis of our co-interview and the multiparty talk, the root metaphor of color was reinscribed in place and time, and the limits and possibilities of appropriating and deconstructing the categories of race, color, and nationality were explored. Whiteness was identified as both a system of structural relations linked to privilege as well as a mobile self-identifier that changes through lived experience of race, gender, and social class and through praxis. At a number of points in our multiparty talk the need for whites to recognize whiteness as privilege *and* to deconstruct the meaning of privilege as essentially or exclusively white was articulated. This required that whites in the United States and mestizos in Nicaragua, among others, recognize how color and social class intersect and how we are both "of color" and, further, that as "whites" we are "one among many." If whiteness were to become simply one among many categories for describing white people (or whites were to become one among many diverse groups), that is, if whiteness were separated from the hierarchy of privilege to which it is now completely wedded, whites would not have access to privilege simply by virtue of their color. However, attempting to change the discourse of whiteness in the absence of structural change risks further confounding political struggles wherein peoples of color seek a more just and equitable redistribution of power and resources within the United States and beyond.

Activism is one resource we have found that challenges the experience of race, class, ethnicity, gender, and nationality as rigidly bounded categories that inscribe ourselves. As we struggle to deconstruct the language of white privilege, our experiences "in the field" warn us that meanings are made in historical and social contexts and can only be remade in context and through praxis.

Debate about whiteness offers important opportunities for forging solidarious relations within and across borders and creates contexts for exploring multiple meanings of whiteness and challenging current institutionalized practices of privilege. Only when this dialogue is forged in concrete struggles for more egalitarian social relations does it effectively challenge existing systems of power and privilege. Our dialogue emerged from and continues to inform multiple experiences of struggle whereby as racialized, privileged people we engage the power structures that institutionalize and sustain that privilege and press for change. We agree with Tessman (1995), who argues that "remaking ourselves in the coalition community does not decrease our differences; rather, it increases the degree of hybridity within all of us" (p. 80). In shared struggle for justice we celebrate the permeable border spaces we are developing, as we surface the multiple meanings of who we are as white/brown and gringa/mestiza within and beyond our national borders.

REFERENCES

Charmaz, K. (1988). The grounded theory method: An explication and interpretation. In R. M. Emerson (ed.), *Contemporary field research*: *A collection of readings* (pp. 109–126). Prospect Heights, Il: Waveland Press.

Gallardo, H. (1993). 500 años: Fenomenología del mestizo (violencia y resistencia) [500 Years: The phenomenology of the mestizo (violence and resistance)]. San José, Costa Rica: Editorial Departamento Ecuménico de Investigaciones (DEI).

Gould, J. L. (1993). "Vana ilusión!": The highlands indians and the myth of Nicaragua mestiza, 1880–1925. *Hispanic American Historical Review, 73* (3), 393–429.

Helmes, J. E. (ed.) (1993). *Black and white racial identity: Theory, research, and practice*. Westport, CT: Praeger.

Knight, A. (1990). Racism, revolution, and *indigenismo*: México, 1919–1940. In R. Graham, *The idea of race in Latin America, 1870–1940* (pp. 71–113). Austin: University of Texas Press.

Lykes, M. B. (1994). Terror, silencing and children: International, multidisciplinary collaboration with Guatemalan Maya communities. *Social Science and Medicine, 38* (4), 543–552.

Lykes, M. B. (1996). Meaning making in a context of genocide and silencing. In M. B. Lykes, A. Banuazizi, R. Liem, and M. Morris (eds.), *Myths about the powerless: Contesting social inequalities*. Philadelphia: Temple University Press.

Martín-Baró, I. (1994). *Writings for a Liberation psychology*. (ed.) A. Aron and S. Corne. Cambridge, MA: Harvard University Press.

McIntosh, P. (1990). White privilege and male privilege. In M. L. Andersen and P. H. Collins (eds.), *Race, class, and gender* (pp. 70–81). Boston: Wadsworth Publishing Company, and International Thompson Publishing Co.

McIntyre, A. (1995). Making meaning of whiteness: Participatory action research with white female student teachers. Dissertation Abstract International, 57–01A, 0175.

McMillen, L. (1995, September 8). Lifting the veil from whiteness: Growing body of scholarship challenges a racial "norm." *Chronicle of Higher Education*, p. A23.

Melville, M. (1993). "Hispanic" ethnicity, race and class. In T. Weaver (ed.), *Handbook of Hispanic cultures in the United States*: *An anthology* (pp. 85–106). Houston, TX: Arte Público Press.

Rodríguez, C. E. (1992). Race, culture, and Latino "otherness" in the 1980 census. *Latin American Perspectives*, 73 (4), 930–937.

Rosaldo, R. (1989) *Culture and truth: The remaking of social analysis.* Boston, MA: Beacon Press.

Skidmore, T. E. (1990). Racial ideas and social policy in Brazil, 1870–1940. In R. Graham, *The idea of race in Latin America, 1870–1940* (pp. 7–36). Austin: University of Texas Press.

Smith, L. (1949/1961). *Killers of the Dream.* New York: W. W. Norton.

Strauss, A., and Corbin, J. (1990). *Basics of qualitative research: Grounded theory procedures and techniques.* Newbury Park, CA: Sage Publications.

Terry, R. W. (1975). *For whites only.* Grand Rapids, MI: W. B. Eerdmans.

Tessman, L. (1995). Beyond communitarian unity in the politics of identity. *Socialist Review*, 24 (1 and 2), 55–83.

Trend, D. (1995). Representation and resistance: An interview with bell hooks. *Socialist Review*, 24 (1 and 2), 115–128.

NOTES

The authors thank the members of the Boston College Culture Workshop for their collaboration in thinking through whiteness, nationality, and race in our ongoing multiparty talk about psychology and/in/through culture, gender, and social class. We also thank Mary Coonan, Lisa Gonsalves, Sandra Jones, Ramsay Liem, Alice McIntyre, and Elizabeth Sparks for comments on an earlier draft of this chapter.

1. Ironically there is no adjective with which those of us who are citizens of the United States can easily describe ourselves. We call ourselves Americans but as Brinton learned in 1975 when working with Canadians the term "American" has been appropriated by United States citizens when it actually refers to citizens of all nations that make up the Americas—North, Central, and South. Since 1975 she has elected to refer to her nationality by the term United Statesian which, although linguistically awkward, is more accurate.

2. According to Gould (1993), mestizo/a is broadly defined as "the offspring of unions between Indians and whites" (p. 397). Gallardo (1993) argues that Ladino/a also refers to status and the praxis of submission of mixed people vis-à-vis the mainstream ideological discourse and the social class in power. Gould (1993) points out further that from 1930 to 1950, ideological discourse constructed mestizo as the social category that described the whole Nicaraguan society.

3. Amid this cultural, racial, class, and gender diversity a number of dimensions of possible difference have not been explicitly problematized by the group. These include age, sexual identity, and physical abilities/disabilities.

4. These narratives were excerpted from our co-interview. Bracketed words and punctuation have been added to clarify the narrative as written text. When the texts are quoted directly lines (ll.) and page numbers (pp.) refer to lines and page number(s) from transcript of the co-interview (I) and the multiparty talk of the Culture Workshop (WK).

5. Gould (1993) contends that between 1906 and 1920 the census of indigenous peoples in Nicaragua dropped from 30 percent to less than 4 percent. Knight (1990) reports a similar phenomenon in México at the beginning of the twentieth century that resulted by mid-century in the presentation of México as "a monoethnic mestizo nation" (p. 98). Skidmore (1990) analyzed the ideological discourse about race in Brazil around the same period wherein the social class in power was interested in "whitening" the racial image of Brazil by "importing" white Europeans.

6. Gould (1993) points out that the creation of the Nicaraguan mestizo had the purpose of fostering the disintegration of indigenous communities. Once the cultural ties and identity of the communities were destroyed, their communal land and autonomy were withdrawn. Without land and with the introduction of agricultural products for export necessitating land and a labor force, the indigenous people were proletarized. According to Gould (1993) and Knight (1990) the communal social organization of the indigenous peoples was supplanted by the stratification of social classes that presently prevails as the main schema of social categorization.

The White Girl in Me, the Colored Girl in You, and the Lesbian in Us: Crossing Boundaries

Medria L. Connolly and Debra A. Noumair

Medria L. Connolly, M.S.S.W., Ph.D. is a clinical psychologist in private practice in Santa Monica, CA. She is a consulting psychologist at Dorothy Kirby Center, Residential Treatment Facility for Adjudicated Youth and Assistant Clinical Professor at the University of California, Los Angeles, Department of Psychiatry and Biobehavioral Sciences. She is a Member of the A. K. Rice Institute and the UCLA Center for the Study of Group and Organizational Dynamics.

Debra A. Noumair, Ed.D., is Associate Professor of Psychology and Education in the Department of Counseling and Clinical Psychology at Teachers College, Columbia University. She is a psychologist in private practice of psychotherapy and organizational consultation. She is a member of the Board of Directors of the A. K. Rice Institute and the Executive Committee of the New York Center of the A. K. Rice Institute.

Writing this chapter is a political act. It is a dialogue between two women, one Black and one White. It is a deeply personal account of both our thoughts and feelings about race, gender, and sexuality as well as a description of the processes involved in exploring them, within ourselves and with each other. This dialogue is stimulated by the hope that if we can work with some of the differences between us as women then there is hope that we can collaborate in addressing the "isms" that are damaging to us all: racism, sexism, and heterosexism.

In our attempt to embrace the complexity involved in crossing boundaries, we turn to a Group Relations model because its theoretical roots in psychoanalytic and social systems theories allow for an understanding of both the irrational and unconscious forces as well as the group processes involved in creating a denigrated "other."

A Group Relations perspective maintains that differences such as race, gender, and sexual orientation of "others" are often used as receptacles for the unwanted aspects of oneself. The use of the other as a container for undesirable aspects of the self is accomplished in large part through splitting and projective identification, which are largely unconscious processes. Aspects of the self or the group that are disowned or rejected are projected onto others, so that desirable characteristics are contained entirely within the self or one's own group, and their undesirable counterparts are contained entirely in the "other." At the group level, this process is an important basis for stereotypes. Thus, projections and stereotypes are among the building blocks from which self-concepts and group identities are constructed. The "not me" and the "not us" are used to define "me" and "us."

It is with these ideas in mind that the process of a Black woman claiming her internal White girl, a White woman claiming her internal colored girl, and both of us as heterosexuals claiming our internal lesbian allows each of us to work across external group boundaries. As long as neither of us have to disown our "not me's" and use the "other" as a container, then we are free to work across real differences and see projection for just that—projection.

The reader should note that there has been no attempt to homogenize our voices in this dialogue. As a result, the reader may have a more difficult time integrating our voices because of the absence of connective tissue. Yet connective tissue may blur the boundary and make complex transactions appear simple and effortless. In order to preserve the complexity of our dialogue, we ask the reader to hold our different styles as well as take note of our individual and joint realities. We have found that these are prerequisites for collaborating across difference.

MEDRIA'S VOICE

The process of working on this collaborative project with Debra has been challenging for us both. It evoked, between us, reactions and responses which we hoped we could confront in a more detached, unaffecting way. The rather provocative title was my idea. It grew out of conversations that Debra and I had about the need to find parts of the "other" in oneself. As a Black, heterosexual woman, I thought it was time to speak openly about the white girl and the lesbian in me. At various times during my adulthood I have been accused of acting like a white girl, or being into things that white girls are into, so I thought I might as well just address the issue directly instead of getting defensive about it. Dealing with the lesbian in me presented a deeper challenge. I had to address my homophobia. But having a daughter whom I love deeply and feel very proud of and who is lesbian helped me begin this personal exploration.

As a White, heterosexual woman, Debra was already in the process of taking up more fully her "colored" parts. She had been confronted by too many light-skinned Black women who were wondering why she was busy identifying as a white girl when she is as dark-skinned as they are. So she knew it was time to do that work. And she was already in touch with her homoerotic energy, so she didn't have to work as hard as I did to free up her lesbian parts.

This is how our dialogue began.

As the implications of what we would be trying to discuss started to sink in, however, my enthusiasm began to fade and my anxiety began to rise. Initially, I carried the fear and anxiety. I worried that if I tried to talk about the white girl and the lesbian in me, it would generate contempt from Black women and men, and disbelief from lesbians. But it was hard for me to hold onto my fear and anxiety when Debra began to express similar feelings.

At first, Debra was also very enthusiastic about this work. But as the deadline for submitting the proposal approached, she became more anxious and ambivalent about doing it. Debra expressed fears similar to mine. She worried that if she tried to talk about the colored girl in her, it would generate contempt from Black women and White women. And, talking about the lesbian in her felt like she was "coming out." In addition, Debra was convinced that everyone would love what I had to say, and hate what she had to say. What initially felt like an exciting opportunity for her seemed to be rapidly degenerating into a win/lose situation in which I would be the winner and she would be the loser.

As we talked about our work, it became increasingly evident that Debra was getting loaded with vulnerability in the form of fear and anxiety. I was getting loaded with more powerful, idealized attributes, which of course runs quite contrary to the reality of my experience as a Black woman where I feel devalued in relation to White women, not idealized. So, what was going on here?

As we continued to talk about this, we thought that a projective identification dynamic was occurring between us, one which mirrors a dynamic that often occurs between Black women and White women. Debra was projecting her competence onto me which tended to inflate me, feed my narcissism, and provided me with a defense against my own feelings of vulnerability. In doing so, she was stuck carrying the vulnerability that I was not owning, as I was identifying with the more desirable aspects of courageous leadership.

Projective identification is a defense mechanism. For us it served as a defense against the more ambivalently held aspects of ourselves, my vulnerability, her fear of envy regarding her competence.

These defenses were mobilized in the service of protecting ourselves from a larger more painful dynamic, one that interferes with the collaboration of women across difference, the judgment and contempt that we often feel for each other. Of course, contempt for other women, those who look like us and those who don't, is often a defense against facing that which we are critical about in ourselves. But to get to that deeper experience of self, which is often unconscious, we must first deal with the conscious feelings of contempt and hatred for one another.

My reasons for hating White women are multidetermined. The most salient one is racism. White women are as racist as White men, if not more so. Being oppressed as women, White women have a lot of pent-up hatred of their own to carry which unfortunately finds an expression in racism. And when White women direct racial hatred at me because I am Black, I reflect racial hatred back at them because they are White.

Another important issue involves competition and envy. In American culture, White women represent the standard of beauty against which I cannot measure up as a Black woman. In this arena, I can compete with White women, but I can never win. Of course this beauty competition is in the service of attracting the attention of men, or women, depending on one's sexual orientation. But it is a competition that I will inevitably lose. I hate that!

White women also enjoy white skin privilege and access to power through their affiliation with White men. As a Black woman I am envious of this, but my envy turns to rage when White women refuse to acknowledge or try to deny their privilege and connection to power through their fathers, sons, and husbands.

I also hate what I refer to as the "weakness" of White women. My stereotype of White women is that they seem to whine all the time, stay scared and needy, and always seem to expect everyone to protect them and take care of them, including Black women. Envy is operating here too, because Black women in this country have never had the privilege of being protected and taken care of. Slavery taught us that we were equal to Black men (Black women worked as hard as Black men and were subjected to the same abuse); the legacy of slavery has taught us that we must take care of ourselves.

When I talk about hating White women, I am speaking in a general sense. In reality, I don't hate all White women. But I do approach White women with skepticism until I get to know them as individuals and we work through our historical relationship. If there is no opportunity to work through our troubled, collective past, there is no hope for a real, personal relationship in the present.

Denigration of the "other" to elevate oneself or one's reference group is a common psychological defense. It's a form of projective identification. But Black women pay a price for hating White women. That hatred spills over into our relationships with other Black women. Audre Lorde, a Black feminist and lesbian, spoke about our hatred in her essay "Eye to Eye: Black Women, Hatred, and Anger":

Racism and sexism are grown-up words. Black children in America cannot avoid these distortions in their living and, too often, do not have the words for naming them. But both are correctly perceived as hatred. Growing up, metabolizing hatred like daily bread. Because I am Black, because I am woman, because I am not Black enough, [because I am too Black], because I am not some particular fantasy of a woman, because I AM. On such a consistent diet, one can eventually come to value the hatred of one's enemies more than one values the love of friends, for that hatred becomes the source of anger, and anger is a powerful fuel. (p. 152)

Another important point is the fact that underneath all this hatred is a great deal of anger, and under that anger is hurt. As a Black woman I protect my hurt parts with my anger and my hatred. But this is double edged because while it allows me to have a voice, it also makes it hard to stay in touch with my more tender parts, which are needed to express love. Or as Audre Lorde states: "In order to withstand the weather, we had to become stone, and now we bruise ourselves upon the other who is closest" (p. 160).

Internalized racism and sexism are felt most profoundly in the contempt that Black women feel for each other. Sisterhood works conceptually, but does not begin to touch how angry, judgmental, and vicious we can be with each other.

It was this understanding about Black women that generated so much anxiety in me as I thought about writing this paper with Debra. I knew that, in part, I would have to speak from a place of woundedness and this revelation would make me appear weak and subject to the same contempt that I have for White women who seem weak.

My woundedness, however, is more a function of my relationships with Black women than with White women. I can manage the racism of White women. It makes me angry, but it doesn't touch my core. But I am vulnerable to Black women. What they think about me matters.

When I was a young girl, I was often taunted by other Black girls who threatened to "kick my ass" because they said I thought I was cute because I have long, straight hair (a vestige of my Native American heritage). I didn't think I was cute and their threats made me extremely self-conscious about my hair. As an adult I recognize this threatening behavior as envy. As a child, however, it felt like hatred. To this day I worry about drawing a negative reaction from Black women because of my hair.

As an adult, competition and envy from Black women comes in more subtle ways. It is less about physical appearance and more about competence and accomplishments. This is certainly true for me as well. I am most in touch with my feelings of competition and envy when I am around smart, high-achieving, successful Black women.

I had a dream which captures the essence of this struggle.

I enter a basement lounge at Teachers College, Columbia University, with my husband who is White. (In reality, this is where I completed my doctoral work.) He goes upstairs to do something with administration while I look for a quiet spot in the lounge, which is empty, except for three Black people, a man, a woman, and her child. I move to the back of the lounge, but as I do I realize that they are preparing to eat back there. To get out of their way, I try to move to the front of the lounge, but they have already taken their seats and I have to walk past them. The Black woman who is overweight, dressed in a uniform, and clearly works there, looks at me with contempt as I walk by. Quickly I try to assess what is generating the contempt—as if by naming or identifying the source of the contempt I can somehow protect myself from its impact. I run down a list in my mind: Is it because I'm with a White man? Is it because my hair is straight? Is it because I'm pretty? Is it because I'm well dressed? Is it because I have a role different than hers at Teachers College?

The dream describes the tension between Black women in general, and with me specifically. But, since I come from a working-class background, it also describes the tension between the me that has developed as an accomplished, professional Black woman and the working-class part of me left behind or differentiated from in the service of that development.

The price of my success is to be distanced by from those I feel bonded to, who see me as a race traitor, "a wanna be white girl." But there is some truth to this perception. While I am firmly rooted in my Black racial identity and do not identify with the race traitor label, graduate school did help me perfect my "white girl" behavior, while simultaneously increasing my range of knowledge. In fact, I am convinced that knowing how to act like a white girl contributed to my smooth passage through my graduate program.

As I understand it, white girl behavior can take various forms. It involves talking proper, that is, using standard English instead of Black dialect or patois. It involves presenting one's self with a neutral affect, instead of an impassioned or angry affect. It involves engaging through personal connections instead of being reserved and respectful of the sovereignty of the other. It involves acting as if one really needs the support of others, instead of acting in a self-sufficient and self-contained manner. It involves the avoidance of any discussion regarding race or racism, and lots of discussion about sexism.

Activating the white girl in me is a conscious process. She is particularly useful to me in situations where I am the only Black person present and I don't know the White people. Unfortunately, this is often the case in professional settings. When I'm feeling marginal around White people, the white girl facilitates my entry, helps me to connect, and allows me to be at least partially taken in by them. She also allows me to move comfortably in the company of White people. The white girl in me puts White people at ease. She knows how to make them comfortable. In my role as a therapist, the white girl in me allows me to genuinely and empathically connect with White and biracial clients.

The white girl in me broadens my social repertoire. She allows me to move across a wider range of cultural experiences. In this regard, I consider myself bicultural. There are times when it requires no effort to activate her. At other times it takes a substantial effort to mobilize her, and I feel resentful about having to work so hard. There are also times when I decline social engagements with White people (who are not good friends) because I don't feel like taking her out. There are even times when she gets on my nerves in the same way that White women get on my nerves. But in general I am grateful to the white girl in me. She really is a part of who I am.

The challenge for me is to integrate the successful, White-identified parts while remaining connected to my Black self. For only in this way can I maintain a sense of wholeness and not feel dismembered by the splitting dynamics present in American society, which values the white girl in me more than the colored girl.

Writing about the lesbian in me turned out to be a more difficult process than writing about the white girl in me. The word *lesbian* is so emotionally charged, implying something sexual and deviant. Within the Black community, lesbians are either ignored or attacked. Black people also devalue the significance of being a lesbian by construing it as a "white thang" or a phase that Black lesbians are going through. Most heterosexual Black women deal with lesbianism by being as rigid and closed about it as possible. Even Black lesbians who have no difficulty celebrating their lesbianism are often reluctant to declare themselves as lesbians (See Tate's article, p. 38). This is understandable since Black lesbians are already coping with racism and sexism. What good would it do to homophobia to the list?

The word *lesbian* is intensely charged for White heterosexual women and White lesbians too. In her essay "It is the Lesbian in Us" Adrienne Rich explains:

> the word *lesbian* has many resonances. Some of us would destroy the word altogether. Others would transform it, still others eagerly claim and speak it after years of being unable to utter it. Feminists have been made to fear that they will be discredited if perceived as les-

bians; some lesbians have withdrawn or been forced into nonfeminist enclaves (such as the "gay" movement) which reject and denigrate "straight" women. The word itself is frequently used by others loosely and pejoratively to imply that our politics and self-definition proceed first out of hatred and rejection. (p. 202)

It is not surprising that the distorted images associated with the word *lesbian* and the fear of homophobic attack prevents women from speaking about the powerful intellectual, emotional, psychic, and spiritual connection that is found in our same-sex pairing.

The voice of the lesbian in me is found in my relationships with women. This seems so simple. Yet the difficulty I had coming to this realization underscores the power of what I believe is the critical issue here. There is something dangerous and forbidden about the public pairing of women. And pairing across racial lines further heightens this tension. Of course private pairing among women occurs all the time. But the public pairing of women, especially Black and White women, is a political act and represents a disruption of the pattern of unequal power relations between women and men, and between Black people and White people.

I define the lesbian in me as the woman-centered part of myself. I realize that I am using the word lesbian in its broadest sense. In doing so, it is not my intention to minimize the lesbian culture, with all its joys, struggles, and complexities, but rather to emphasize a place of joining. Nor is it my intention to co-opt the term "the lesbian in me" and make it into a figure of speech. That would be yet another way of rendering the lesbian culture invisible. Finally, it would be disingenuous and contrary to the purpose of this paper to use "the lesbian in me" literally, while having access to heterosexual privilege. Conceptualizing the lesbian in me as woman-centered is my way of embracing the feminine and acknowledging the life-giving force found in powerful connections between women.

Since the voice of the lesbian is found in my relationships with women, it seems appropriate to describe how it operates in my friendship and co-authorship with Debra. I first met Debra when we were graduate students at Teachers College. But our relationship did not begin to flourish until she got more involved in Group Relations work within the A. K. Rice Institute and joined the faculty at Teachers College. Both occurred at about the same time. The beauty of the intimacy and affection we share is that it developed through our work together. We are open and honest with each other, including my "colored girl" and her "white girl" parts. It is deeply gratifying to connect with a woman who feels as passionately about these issues as I do.

Debra stimulates me both intellectually and erotically. She is smart, and smart women who are also authentic have always turned me on. And she is beautiful and sensual, which gets my erotic juices flowing. When I speak of the erotic, I am not just speaking of my homoerotic fantasies, I am also referring to Audre Lorde's definition of the erotic. In her essay "Uses of the Erotic," (p. 55) Audre Lorde explains:

The very word *erotic* comes from the Greek word eros, the personification of love in all of its aspects—born of Chaos, and personifying creative power and harmony. When I speak of the erotic, then, I speak of it as an assertion of the life-force of women; of that creative energy empowered, the knowledge and use of which we are now reclaiming in our language, our history, our dancing, our loving, our work, our lives.

It is this stimulation and trust in our capacity to collaborate that allows me to explore this sociopolitical territory with Debra.

Debra's Voice

Medria's rendition of our joining together in this enterprise accurately describes my experience. In the remarks that follow, I discuss my experience as having external trappings that allow me to identify as a White, heterosexual woman (albeit on the boundary between being White and being "of color" because of the shade of my skin) and having internal identifications as a colored girl and as a lesbian. These internal and external identifications alternately serve as "me" and "not me" containers, depending in part on the context in which I am operating. I am well aware of the privilege this boundary position affords me and will expound on the ways in which both White and heterosexual privilege have influenced me.

Both the external and the internal, the outside and the inside, have a relationship to me personally and are also related to the sociopolitical climate in which I and we exist. It would be a disservice to ourselves, to feminist thought, and to the tradition of Group Relations work to separate the individual from the contextual. One of the underlying premises of this work is that an individual's internal world is affected greatly by external reality. Moreover, who takes up what issue, when, and in what context has not only psychological but political relevance as well.

For example, in a Group Relations conference on diversity, it is the widely held assumption that race will be spoken about by people of color, that gender will be spoken about by women, and that sexual orientation will be spoken about by gays and lesbians. While I am well aware that there are Whites in the GR tradition who do work on race, men who do work on gender and heterosexuals who do work on sexual orientation, this is unusual. In the world at large, there are not a lot of Whites who address race, men who address gender, and heterosexuals who address sexual orientation. In fact, while writing this chapter, Medria and I have often been inhibited by what we imagined others might think of us for talking about our "inner parts" that are not represented in our "outer parts."

It is considered a given in group and organizational life that issues are taken up by whatever group is most affected by them; however, often that group is then accused of taking up only these issue for reasons of self-interest rather than for the benefit of the whole. The bind, however, is that if they do not bring them up, no one else in the group or organization will, and the status quo remains in effect. For the purpose of this work, the status quo refers here to the dynamic interplay of racism, sexism, heterosexism, and homophobia, persons of color, women, and gays and lesbians in the role of "other" and isolate them in the experience of oppression.

Toni Morrison, in *Playing in the Dark*, amplifies the concept of "othering." Morrison describes the ways in which African Americans have been used throughout American history to contain disowned aspects of dominant White society, a process she refers to as Africanism. Morrison states:

> Africanism is the vehicle by which the American self knows itself as not enslaved, but free; not repulsive, but desirable; not helpless, but licensed and powerful; not history-less, but historical; not damned, but innocent; not a blind accident of evolution, but a progressive fulfillment of destiny. (p. 52)

Morrison's central thesis is that for White Americans, the ideals and experiences of freedom, individualism, manhood, and innocence have depended on the existence of a Black population that is manifestly unfree, and which serves Whites as the embodiment of their own fears and disowned desires. Women (White women especially) have been used in a similar way to contain projections of being weak, passive, and powerless, as well as being seductive, manipulative, devouring, and castrating. Gays and lesbians have carried disowned projections of sexual nonconformity based on the fear that unbridled expression of sexual impulses will lead to the collapse of the institutions of family and society. Of course, it is *one's own* fears, desires, and sexual impulses, not those of others, that are the real source of terror (Reed and Noumair, in press).

In order to illustrate this point, I return to my experience of joining with Medria to write this chapter, since what we went through in order to coauthor is exactly the work that is involved in crossing group boundaries. My experience of Medria is that she is bright, wonderfully articulate and able to have access to her brain and her heart at the same time. And while I know there is reality to all of what I have just described, what I do with Medria is that I say it is the "colored girl" in her that allows her to be so out there. It is "the having fought for survival" that gave her permission to have voice. Maybe you, the reader, can guess that I put my competence regarding this work into Medria, and that by placing all that I admire in her colored girl and by disowning the colored girl in me, I am left vulnerable to silence. Until I can claim fully the colored girl in myself, I risk interacting with Medria as a container for my "not me." I ask her to be bold and courageous for me, in effect, to carry the provocateur in me and I miss out on the opportunity for an authentic exchange across our differences.

Perhaps, you the reader have also seen beyond this idealization of Medria and into a root of racism. By asking Medria to carry the provocateur in me, I am essentially asking her to carry my anger and for a White woman to ask a Black woman to carry her anger is to collude with the maintenance of parochial race and gender stereotypes whereby we construct "angry Black women" and "powerless White women." Moreover, by making Medria "other" I see her only as the "colored girl" and I lose the opportunity to take in the complexity of who Medria is and what she brings to our relationship. This loss, experienced acutely in our interpersonal relationship, is emblematic of the price we all pay for being unable to find the "other" in ourselves.

Disowning the "other," in this case the colored girl in me, involves a set of complex, interdependent maneuvers caused by racism. My racial/ethnic heritage is one half Italian and one half Lebanese, and while I have the looks of my father's family, my Lebanese heritage, I have always identified as White because of my connection to my mother's family and her Italian-European background. Thus, my internalized racism is based on my identification with my mother's values and the split in my family.

I can trace this to the moment of my birth. Upon seeing me as a newborn, my mother's father exclaimed "she looks like an Indian." This was not good news, I can assure you, because whenever the story is told, it always includes my mother's profound sense of injury. From that moment forward, the "dark" color of my skin was not a source of joy but rather an aspect of my body to be coped with, compensated for, and managed. My family's reaction to the color of my skin was an expression of racism and an expression of hatred for my father, the "denigrated other," who was held as "bad" in order for my mother to be the "idealized other" and held as "good." Thus, my inner life was characterized by my hatred of the "me" that was like my father, my dark skin and eyes, as well as my dark, curly hair. These parts became "not me," that is, identifying as White and not understanding why anyone would question my racial identity was an act of denial, an act of denigration, in effect, an expression of racism.

One consequence of my parent's divorce and the identification of my father as the bad object is that I held my Lebanese parts ambivalently. Until a few years ago, I always thought of myself as a "white girl" in spite of ongoing feedback to the contrary. Some people often thought I was anything but White. Folks would speak to me in foreign languages on the street. When seen with my mother, I was viewed as not belonging to her. My brother would tease me about being adopted, and I believed him. And since adolescence Black men have found me attractive.

Of all these occurrences, it was Black men's attraction for me that was most problematic because it influenced directly my relationships with Black women. I can vividly recall being chased down the street by Black girls in grammar school because of the attention I received from "their men." At the time I felt both fear and shame, fear that they would beat me up and shame that I could not protect myself or fight back. This behavior in grammar school shows a white girl who is timid, powerless, and in need of protection. It is exactly what Medria is referring to when she talks about her hatred toward White women. I understand her hatred because of my own contempt for that white girl in me. These attributes have not contributed to a healthy sense of self-esteem nor have they enhanced my relationships with others. Knowing that the price of Black men's desire for me was Black women's rage at me has had the deepest impact on my racial identity and on the relation between the white girl and the colored girl in me.

It was not until I actively engaged in Group Relations work that my sense of identity began to shift to allow more of my colored girl to emerge. First, there was an African-American woman senior to me who would ask angrily, "how could you identify as White, you don't look White, I can't take you in as White." Then I heard that the Black folks in the A. K. Rice Institute would inquire, "What's up with Debra, why does she identify herself as White?" And finally I worked with a senior African-American man whose challenge was, could I take him in? Could I find not just the colored girl in me but could I find the brother in me? In other words, could I find and embrace my father, the "not me" parts of myself? By no means is this process complete, however, I do experience my colored parts more readily, with more freedom, and with more pride than ever before.

In some ways, I wish the process of claiming all of my parts were that simple. On the contrary, finding the "other" in oneself goes against defensive projective processes, invites more complexity, and disturbs one's comfort and the exercise of various kinds of privilege. The internal tensions are as challenging as the ones found on the outside. Often what results in group life is that one identity is acknowledged while another is silenced. In fact, the presence of hatred between groups tends to erase aspects of oneself individually and to silence the voice of one group or the other, externally. For example, does it have to be that in order to authorize the colored girl in me, I must silence the white girl in me? What would it look like if they coexisted? How would they dialogue with one another? If White women were to stop having women of color carry their rage, their passion, in other words, their life force, what effect would this have on women of colors' identity? If I stop asking Medria to be my provocateur, what happens to her, to me, to our relationship, and to our individual representations of Black and White women? Would it lead to another bout of competition between Black and White women in service of preserving sexism and ultimately, racism?

The preservation of heterosexism and homophobia are also maintained through fueling the hatred rather than the erotic connections between women. Locating the lesbian in each of us can be a starting point for crossing various boundaries between women. As I will discuss, the complexity involved in negotiating a relationship between the colored girl and the white girl in me is reflected in my relationship with Medria and represents the third aspect of this chapter—the lesbian in us.

I engage in a similar set of maneuvers with the lesbian in me as I do with the colored girl in me, similar to Morrison's discussion of Africanism: lesbianism is the vehicle by which my heterosexual self knows itself as enslaved and not free, as object, not subject, and most profoundly as oppressed and quieted rather than as erotic and powerful.

The idea that the lesbian is where courage and power lie for me is not only related to my intrapsychic life but again to the issues of context and currency. This point is best illustrated by discussing my relationship with Medria. I first fell in love with Medria when I was a graduate student. I was pursuing my masters degree in counseling psychology and Medria was pursuing her Ph.D. in clinical psychology. We both did clinical work in the same clinic and attended case conferences together. On this particular day, Medria was presenting a case of a man she had been working with for some time. As I have come to know the norm for Medria, she was intellectually brilliant and emotionally available and she said things in public that, at the time, I would not have said in private. I was awed and mesmerized, and to this day, I can still remember the moment at which she stole my heart. It was when she spoke openly about her hatred for her patient in a way that I had never heard anyone speak. She was forthright, honest, and revealing. Her hatred seemed loving—it was compelling and *she* was compelling. Obviously, this experience is very consistent with my inner geography and the location of my colored girl and my white girl. However, tracing the path of falling in love with Medria also allows me to find the voice of the lesbian in me.

As I write this, I am aware that one could say that I am equating the idealization of someone of the same sex with homoerotic love. Earlier in this chapter, my idealization of Medria was a maneuver to "other" her, to encourage and admire her "colored girl" and to silence and hide my own, to ask her to carry my rage so that I can remain afraid of such passion. In this iteration, however, my love for Medria functions similarly to how Audre Lorde describes the erotic. What Medria and I share makes me feel powerful and what we do not share is less of a threat because of each of our understanding of the "other" in ourselves, such as her Blackness and my Whiteness.

It is true, however, that what I have just described is more about our interpersonal connection and less about what it means for us as White and Black women to give voice to the lesbian in us. This political struggle is best described by Adrienne Rich in *It's the Lesbian in Us*:

> I go on believing in the power of literature, and also of the politics of literature. The experience of the black woman as woman, of the white and black woman cast as antagonists in the patriarchal drama, and of black and white women as lesbians has been kept invisible for good reason. Our hidden, yet omnipresent lives have served some purpose by remaining hidden: not only in the white patriarchal world but within both the black and feminist communities, on the part of black male critics, scholars, and editors, and of institutions like the Feminist Press. Both Black studies and women's studies have shied away from this core of our experience, thus reinforcing the very silence out of which they had to assert themselves. But it is subjects, the conversations, the facts we shy away from, which claim us in the form of writer's block, as mere rhetoric, as hysteria, insomnia, and constriction of the throat. (p. 201)

Adrienne Rich saved Medria and me from what she refers to as "collaborating with silence" (p. 202). At various points in writing this chapter, we almost caved in to what I now understand as our fear of pulling the cover on patriarchy. The difficulty we encountered in locating the lesbian in us, in part, was our susceptibility to being rendered speechless by irrational forces that would prefer that we maintain our hatred for the "other" and never claim the erotic connection between us. Fueling hostility between Black and White women insures that women as a group remain splintered and therefore powerless to challenge the social order.

In order for Black women to trust White women and to cross what have been experienced historically as treacherous group boundaries, White women have to renounce their access to white male privilege, not only in word but in action. Symbolically, claiming the lesbian in me and my homoerotic feelings for Medria, shifts my relation to White male power and my access to white, heterosexual privilege. This is a catastrophic event, not only for me personally, but because White women have been used as a prophylactic against interrupting patriarchy. It is, however, this access to White, male, heterosexual privilege that allows me, as well as White women as a group, to permit this kind of use (and abuse). These arrangements are unlikely to change unless Black and White women can negotiate a different kind of relationship with each other. In *Ain't I A Woman*, bell hooks states:

> Women's liberationists, white and black, will always be at odds with one another as long as our idea of liberation is based on having the power white men have. For that power denies unity, denies common connections, and is inherently divisive. It is woman's acceptance of divisiveness as a natural order that has caused black and white women to cling religiously to the belief that bonding across racial boundaries is impossible. (pp. 156–157)

My experience in writing this chapter matches what bell hooks so eloquently describes. It has taught me that hatred, rather than erotic energy, between Black and White women, is nurtured in order to prevent finding the "other" in oneself.

CONCLUDING THOUGHTS

Projecting and stereotyping are insidious processes that do violence to all involved. These processes allow others to be used as "not me" containers, oppressed and powerless, so that "me" containers can be dominant and powerful. A solution lies in each of us claiming back our "not me's" so that we can have a fuller sense of integration and less use for "not me" containers. While it is clear that our external identifications organize much of our conscious lives, our internal identifications as a white girl, colored girl, and lesbian are where important aspects of ourselves live. The challenge remains to have the white girl, the colored girl, and the lesbian in dialogue with each other. Otherwise, we risk limiting ourselves as well as "others," and more importantly, we actively participate in perpetuating the institutions of racism, sexism, heterosexism, and homophobia.

REFERENCES

hooks, b. (1992). *Ain't I a Woman: Black Women and Feminism*. Boston, MA: South End Press.

Lorde, A. (1984). *Sister Outsider: Essays and Speeches by Audre Lorde*. Freedom, CA: The Crossing Press.

Morrison, T. (1992). *Playing in the Dark: Whiteness and the Literary Imagination*. Cambridge, MA: Harvard University Press.

Reed, G. M., and Noumair, D. A. (In press). The tiller of authority in a sea of diversity: Empowerment, disempowerment, and the politics of identity. In E. Klein, F. Gabelnick, and P. Herr (eds.), *New Paradigms of Leadership in the Twenty-First Century: Consultation and Diversity*.

Rich, A. (1979). On *Lies, Secrets, and Silence: Selected Prose 1966–1978*. New York: W. W. Norton & Company.

Tate, G. (June 13, 1995). The Black Lesbian Inside Me. *Village Voice*, pp. 35–38.

White Educators as Allies:
Moving from Awareness to Action

Sandra M. Lawrence and Beverly Daniel Tatum

Sandra M. Lawrence is Assistant Professor of Psychology and Education and Director of Middle and Secondary Teacher Education at Mount Holyoke College. She teaches courses on multicultural education and the impact of race, class, and gender in schools. Her research focuses on the influence of multicultural education courses on the attitudes and behaviors of white preservice students and practicing teachers. Her recent publications include "Feeling and Dealing: Teaching White Students about Racial Privilege" (coauthored with Takiema Bunche) in *Teaching and Teacher Education* (in press), and "Bringing White Privilege into Consciousness" in *Multicultural Education* (1996).

Beverly Daniel Tatum is Professor of Psychology and Education at Mount Holyoke College. She teaches courses on the psychology of racism and has lectured extensively on the impact of social issues in the classroom. Author of *Assimilation Blues: Black Families in a White Community*, Beverly Daniel Tatum is involved in research on racial identity development among African American youth, and the role of racial identity development in the professional development of teachers.

I am thirty-five years old and I never really started thinking about race too much until now, and that makes me feel uncomfortable . . . I just think for some reason I didn't know. No one taught us. That's what I tell my students.

—A white female teacher

Who teaches white teachers about the meaning of race? What do they need to know? How well prepared are white teachers to understand their own "whiteness" and the meaning it has when interacting with students and parents of color? How cognizant are they of their own racial socialization and how it may influence their perceptions of the performance potential of all of their students? Educators concerned about the increasing "whiteness" of the teaching force and the increasing racial diversity of the student population have begun to ask these and other questions. Even in schools with very small populations of color, educators are becoming more aware of the need to prepare white students to live in a multiracial society. Yet this is a world with which the current teaching force has limited experience. Most white teachers were raised and educated in predominantly white communities. Their firsthand knowledge of communities of color and their cultures and histories are quite limited. The secondhand information they have received through textbooks, media, and from friends and family has often been distorted by the negative, stereotypical attitudes about people of color which are so pervasive in American culture.

One way to address this deficiency in white teachers' experiences is to provide them with educational courses or programs that involve teaching about race and the impact of racism in American society. But while teacher education programs and school districts alike are struggling to address racial issues, the systematic study of the effects of antiracist educational efforts on the attitudes of teachers, either preservice or in-service, is limited. Existing studies involving white teacher education students enrolled in multicultural or ethnic studies courses reveal some positive changes in white students' attitudes about people of color (Baker, 1977; Bennett, 1979; Grant, 1981; Haberman and Post, 1992; Adams and Zhou-McGovern, 1994; Lawrence and Bunche, in press). However, fewer studies of the effects of in-service antiracist/multicultural programs have been conducted and the results of these studies are mixed (Redman, 1977; Washington, 1981; Sleeter, 1992). While some teachers do make fundamental changes in their thinking about race or redesign their teaching methods in positive ways as a result of this kind of formal instruction, many participants do not. As Carter and Goodwin (1994) suggest, we still have much to learn about the impact that effective antiracist professional development can have on teacher attitudes and teacher behaviors.

THE PROFESSIONAL DEVELOPMENT PROGRAM WE STUDIED

Given the paucity of formal studies on the effects of antiracist education for teachers and our belief that the professional development program we knew about was fundamentally different than others, we decided to conduct our own study on the effects of antiracist professional development for teachers. Our primary focus in conducting this study was to investigate the ways in which the course influenced white participants' perceptions about race and racism, and how those perceptions are manifested in schools. We were especially interested in whether white teachers' understanding of their own racial identity influenced their thinking and daily classroom practice.

In contrast to the commonly used one-day "flash and dash" in-service workshops, this professional development program extended over a period of seven months. Most of the sessions were three hours in length and took place immediately after school. The classes were scheduled approximately two weeks apart. The course was taught by a biracial team of instructors, one of whom was Beverly Daniel Tatum, an African-American woman and coauthor of this paper. Course activities included lectures, films, small and large group discussion, and in-class exercises. Between class meetings, participants were assigned reading material and asked to write reflection papers in response to the readings. The structure of the course experience encouraged ongoing reflection and integration of the course ideas into daily practice. Beginning with the first class meeting, the course content required participants to think about their own racial group membership and its meaning in the context of a race-conscious society.

In fact, helping educators to recognize the personal, cultural, and institutional manifestations of racism and to become more proactive in response to racism within school settings was one of the explicit goals of the course. Topics covered which were specific to this goal included an examination of the concepts of prejudice, racism, white privilege, and internalized oppression, an analysis of racial stereotypes in the media and in curricular materials, an explication of the process of racial identity development for both whites and people of color, and a discussion of the historical connection between scientific racism and common assumptions about the "fixed nature" of the intellectual capacity of students. In addition, participants were asked to chart their own growth through the use of a self-reflective taping exercise (described in Tatum, 1992) and to produce a case study or action plan based on actual school experience.

Since there was a significant number (30 percent) of participants of color in the course, voices which are often silent in predominantly white schools were frequently heard. The active participation of people of color in the classroom discourse was supported both by the leadership role of the African-American facilitator (an uncommon experience in these school contexts) and by the presence of so many of their colleagues of color.[1] All of the participants of color, including the one Latina, seemed to feel comfortable contributing to the dialogue and challenging white participants to look at their own assumptions and positions in the racial order. Though the impact of the course experience on the participants of color is also being investigated (Elliott and Tatum, 1995), we are intentional here in choosing to focus primarily on the effects of the course on white educators.

WHITE RACIAL IDENTITY DEVELOPMENT: A THEORETICAL FRAMEWORK

As indicated earlier, the focus of this paper is on the responses of the white participants to the course. In particular, we were guided in our thinking by Janet Helms's (1990) model of white racial identity development. As explained by Helms (1990, p. 3), "racial identity development theory concerns the psychological implications of racial group membership, that is belief systems that evolve in reaction to perceived differential racial group membership."

For whites, the abandonment of individual racism and the recognition of and opposition to institutional and cultural racism are central components to the development of a positive white racial identity. In the process, "the person must become aware of her or his Whiteness, learn to accept Whiteness as an important part of herself or himself, and to internalize a realistically positive view of what it means to be White (Helms, 1990, p. 55)." [For a further description of Helms's six-stage model, see Carter, "Is White a Race?" chapter 20 in this volume.]

Helms (1990) suggests (and we would agree) that individuals in the later stages of white racial identity development are better prepared to work effectively in multiracial settings than those in the earlier stages. Professional development programs which are intended to increase teacher effectiveness with multiracial populations should attend, then, to the impact that these programs have on the racial identity development of the participants.

THE CURRENT STUDY

Although it was our intention to include all white participants of the course in our study, some either did not complete the course assignments needed for data collection[2] or did not give permission to have their assignments reproduced. In all, 20 of the 28 white participants were included in this study. Of the 20 white educators, there were 14 women and six men, all of whom were in their mid-thirties or mid- to late forties.

The data we collected included essays and reflection papers participants wrote for the course, as well as pre- and post-course interviews conducted with four (three women, one man) of the teachers. The interviews were conducted by a white female interviewer, Sandra Lawrence (coauthor of this chapter), who had not been involved with the course instruction. The open-ended interviews were approximately one and a half to two hours in length, and focused on participant's prior racial history, teaching practices, educational philosophy, and course-related experiences.

We coded and categorized the transcribed interviews and the written documents qualitatively using Helms's theoretical framework. Specifically, we evaluated participant's statements about their own behaviors, attitudes, and beliefs and categorized them in terms of the characteristics outlined by Helms as typical of particular stages. For example, comments reflecting a desire to connect with other white people working against racism were seen as indicative of the Immersion stage, whereas comments reflecting a "color-blind" attitude, minimizing the social significance of

336

race, were seen as indicative of Contact Stage thinking. A profile of each individual's racial identity characteristics was constructed based on the pattern of responses they exhibited.

In addition, we identified themes across the profiles that illustrated the ways in which the course affected participants' thinking, classroom practice, and interpersonal interactions related to race. The profiles and themes, when considered together, provided information about the outcomes of the course in terms of participants' attitudinal and behavioral changes and their movement along a continuum of racial identity development.

RECOGNIZING PRIVILEGE: I NEVER THOUGHT OF MYSELF AS WHITE

Many of the participants had grown up in the sixties and considered themselves "liberal" in their thinking concerning political and social movements for equality. In relation to race, they were not "color-blind": they acknowledged the differential treatment that whites and people of color receive, and they were concerned about the racial oppression that people of color experience in this country. They were also aware that society in general and the educational system in particular had distorted, repressed, and silenced the voices and experiences of people of color.

But while all participants were aware of racial oppression and the differential treatment that whites and people of color receive, they tended to view this oppression as the result of individuals acting in racist ways rather than the combination of individual and long-standing institutional racist practices and policies. In addition, they had given little thought to the racial privilege and power that accompanied their own position in the racial order or the possibility of their own complicity in the racist practices they condemned. As Belinda wrote in her first paper, "I had been taught that racism was an individual act of meanness perpetrated against some minority group. I never suspected that it was an intricate system of advantage, of which I was a part." When asked about how they view their racial privilege, many participants, like Pam, were honest about the lack of consideration they had given to their racial positions: "I do admit that I have rarely thought of the position I hold because of my race. I have taken for granted the power and in most cases the security that my whiteness gives me." In reflecting back on the course, other participants explained how their avoidance of whiteness enabled them to perceive racism as external to their lives. Faith, in listening to an interview of herself taped at the beginning of the course, reflects on her pre-course thinking about her participation in the racial order, "I realize a certain naivete and white liberal smugness in my responses but without the depth of understanding of why racism exists and without the acceptance that I, as a white person, take an active role in perpetuating racism."

As exemplified here and throughout their writings, Faith and other teachers seemed to possess what Frankenberg (1993) has called a "power-evasive" orientation in regard to their racial privilege and racial dominance, having failed to notice the social power conferred simply by being white. From the perspective of Helms's racial identity theory (1990), most participants entered the course in a position characterized as the pseudo-independent stage of their white identity development, a stage consistent with "white liberal" thinking about race and characterized by avoidance of responsibility for racial inequality and injustice.

It was apparent in both the written documents and the interviews that the course had a profound impact on most of the participants in the study. Although each person's response was unique, there were areas of similarity which could be identified across responses. These three linked dimensions were 1) the knowledge they received about race and racism, 2) the ways in which their learning altered their thinking about themselves as racial beings, and 3) the manner in which their thinking moved them to change some of their behaviors regarding race and racism. The course was also instrumental in helping some of the participants to think about themselves as white persons in a white dominant society and in fostering the development of white antiracist identities.

NEW LEARNINGS—INITIAL MOVEMENTS

All participants related either in writing or during interviews that they learned more about racism as a result of the course. For some, this learning concerned new knowledge, such as definitions of racism and prejudice, the notion of "acting white," information about the cultural and institutional manifestations of racism, and theories of racial identity development. In addition to "new" learning, most participants mentioned that the course gave them a "heightened awareness" of existing knowledge: information they had some prior knowledge of, or thought they knew, but which the course "helped to bring more into consciousness." Anita's comments from the end of the course interview capture this view of learning which other participants experienced as well:

> I mean I thought that I had a pretty good understanding. I thought I was aware of what was happening, but there are lots of things that I had no conception of—that in a million years I would never even imagine! So, [the course] heightened my awareness. That was interesting because I did go [into the course] thinking, OK, this isn't going to be a problem for me because I already know a lot. And I did know a lot, but I certainly did not know as much as I thought I knew.

Participants had some prior knowledge of racist policies and practices within schools and other social institutions. They were aware of the negative impact of a legacy of distortions, stereotypes, and omissions concerning the lives and experiences of people of color; and they saw examples in their daily lives where whites and people of color were treated differently. But they were less aware of the pervasiveness of these occurrences. As a result of the course, Greg can now see the extent of the structural inequalities inherent in some school policies that he didn't see before the course.

> I think in general our education is structured to make white kids successful and we don't do those things that need to be done to make the Black kids successful. Some administrators see that the problem is with the kids: they're not as smart, they're not as good. It is not a problem with the school system. But I don't see things that way anymore. I see it that we, our culture, has done things for generations to depress the academic achievement of certain individuals in our society, and those happen to be people of color.

While relating his new thinking about the institutional practices that result in whites and people of color being treated differently, Greg also acknowledges, through pronouns such as "we" and "our," his membership in the dominant culture, a culture responsible for the inequities he describes.

As the course evolved, other participants also began to see their relation to the power structure in important ways. For example, nearly every participant reflected on her/his white privilege after reading Peggy McIntosh's (1989) *White Privilege: Unpacking the Invisible Knapsack* and for many that reflection was instrumental in forcing the white participants to think of themselves as racial beings. Evelyn, a woman who speaks frequently about gender oppression to her middle school students, relates the impact this reading had on her image of herself:

> Despite my keen awareness of the white male culture and its dominance and oppression over me as a woman, McIntosh's article put a new slant on privileges I had simply because I was white. I feel guilt associated with my unearned advantages because of my color, but I never closely examined the ease with which I can move within my world—how I do not have to be overly concerned with how I might be seen because of my color. After reading the article, I am more aware of being white.

These teachers, as well as others in the course, experienced a new level of awareness about systems of advantage that benefitted them as white persons, and this deepening awareness of their white privilege was for some a further movement within pseudo-independent thinking with a direction towards a more positive white racial identity.

Shifts in Thinking

When commenting about the course, teachers referred to their new awareness as something which caused a "shift" in their thinking, so that they viewed the world in relation to racism differently. Leslie describes this process as not just intellectual but personal as well:

> Before the course my thinking on racism, a lot of it was like how you learned how to think in schools. Like you think about things because you know they are the right thing to think about and you don't own them. From this course now, it is more a part of me, it's more just part of the lens I look out on the world with. It's just the way I look at the world.

Belinda also notices a change in her perceptions: "All around me I constantly see injustice and racism."

Participants began to notice not just the racist behaviors and practices of others, they also recognized their own racist attitudes and actions. Faith not only recognizes how her past and present ways of being are racist, she also sees how her actions maintain the racial order and her dominance as a white person.

> Throughout this course I have been coming to terms with my own personal and group responsibility in allowing racism to persist. It is not simply someone else's problem that I can step in and referee, it is my own problem as well. At this point, having confronted my own racism and learned view of superiority, I am teaching myself, through a constant state of processing events and feelings about people, that I can be genuine and truly understanding of the racism confronted by people of color.

The remarks of these teachers are typical of those in the course who began to realize that to be white meant to acknowledge the privilege that accompanied their whiteness. But rather than dwell on their white privilege as the primary defining aspect of their whiteness, they envisioned a more positive, less guilt-inducing definition of their white identity: one which might enable them to become "allies" (Tatum, 1994) in the struggle against racism. This search for a new, more affirming, antiracist white identity indicates entry into the Immersion/Emersion stage of Helms's racial identity model.

CHANGES IN PERSONAL AND PROFESSIONAL PRACTICES

While some participants were contemplating the need to take action, others felt ready to interrupt racist practices both in their personal lives and in their teaching. In their personal encounters, they challenged racist jokes and comments made by colleagues and family members and began to question those in authority about policies and procedures they suspected to be racist. Anita, for example, decided to tell the library director of her town that a sign in the children's room which read "Unattended children will be sold as slaves" was offensive.

As the course progressed, participants began to translate learning about their position in the racial order into classroom practices as a way to question the status quo or change "the ways things have always been." Prior to the course, teachers seldom brought up the topic of race with their students, even though they taught in racially mixed classrooms. While they acknowledged that "kids are hungry to talk about racism," some teachers were afraid to address the topic. They expressed fear about the emotions that students might express and felt inadequate to respond to students who might use racist language or who might become angry if racism was brought out into the open. However, as a result of the course, some teachers became more willing to bring the topic of race into the classroom. They integrated race and race-related topics into classes on social studies, language arts, and mathematics through lessons on stereotyping, Black history, and current events.

As a result of being more comfortable addressing the topic of race with students, some teachers altered their course content and made them more "inclusive" of the experiences and histories of people of color. For example, when team-teaching their middle school students the fundamentals of essay writing, Paul and Donald decided to model aspects of effective essay writing by having students read and discuss a newspaper article entitled, "Calling the Plays in Black and White," which dealt with the stereotypical language used by sportscasters and announcers. Through class activities, the teachers were able to illustrate to students how a clear focus, engaging introduction, descriptive examples, and a solid conclusion made for an effective essay. Paul and Donald were also able to use this essay to "start to raise students' awareness of racial stereotyping." They helped students to recognize the harmful implications of announcers' referrals to white players as intelligent strategists and African American players as only physically powerful athletes. These middle school teachers then continued to build several lessons on the article, one of which required students to watch athletic activities on television and critique the announcer's portrayal of Black and white athletes. Both Paul and Donald were pleased by the results of their lessons and felt that they had "broken the silence" by bringing issues of racism into the classroom.

Some participants changed their teaching practice in ways that did not involve curriculum. After a class discussion in which teachers acknowledged that they kept their distance from students of color in their classrooms and seldom communicated with parents of color, many teachers reflected on the negative effects of these behaviors. Once they realized how different communication patterns with students advantaged white students and disadvantaged students of color, some decided to step out of this pattern and take more initiative to interact with students and parents of color. Anita, writing for one of her reflection papers near the end of the course, chronicles her interactions with a student of color who was not doing well in her class.

My thinking throughout this course has prompted me to call Dwight at home one night just to see if he was doing his homework and to let him know that I was thinking about him and wondering if he needed help on the math problems. He was shocked that I called but I could tell that he was pleased to get the special treatment. Dwight has been a different student since that phone call. Things are far from perfect, but in general he's doing much better.

Anita has not stopped with this student, however. She has reached out to other students of color in her classes and feels more comfortable talking with their parents as well. Similarly, Kay and other white teachers also feel more comfortable talking with parents of color than they did prior to the course.

Nearly all participants (85 percent) reported taking a least one form of action to combat racism (some took four and five different actions) either in personal or professional spheres as a direct result of the course. While taking action is not necessarily characteristic of one particular stage in Helms's theory, it is indicative of persons moving towards more positive racial identities. Some took action as they moved more deeply within a pseudo-independent stage of white racial identity; others took action as they became more immersed in defining what their white identities meant to them. Though in most cases, there was no dramatic movement from one stage to the next it is important to point out that these participants, unlike the college students we have taught, were already in the second phase of Helms's model of development—developing an anti-racist identity—at the beginning of the course. They had been recruited for that reason. Yet even this group found they had things to learn and actions to take in creating a more inclusive learning situation for all their students. Whatever the stage, all "actions" represented positive moves out of the silence and complicity which have worked in tandem to maintain the cycle of oppression.

THE DYNAMICS OF TRUST

It is important to reiterate that the white educators participating in this pilot course were recruited because they were viewed as possessing some sensitivity to the needs of students of color and were willing to talk about race. They seemed eager to hear about the experiences of people of color, and actively sought out newspaper and magazine articles about the effects of racial oppression to share with each other. But that eagerness subsided when the discourse focused on the racial dynamics between themselves and people of color in the room. Most often the source of tension revolved around questions of trust.

For example, a Black male participant commented about using his "radar" to assess whether this racially mixed situation would be "safe" for him. When other African-Americans nodded their heads and exchanged knowing glances, many of the white people were taken aback that their colleagues would be suspicious of them, assuming that their very presence in the course would warrant the trust of the people of color. An excerpt from Anita's interview captures this puzzlement and the sense of insecurity that this information produced.

We somehow got on the topic of Black people's radars. . . . The African-American people in our group got talking about the radar that they feel goes off when they are around white people. And we just started getting into, well, what do you mean, radar? . . . Do you evaluate a person before you even know them?

The idea that white people were not assumed to be trustworthy unless proven otherwise was a recurring theme that consistently upset the white participants. This theme was sometimes brought into the discussion when white educators shared stories of their interactions with Black parents. During one particular session, a white teacher talked at length about his frustration that a Black mother had challenged his placement recommendation for her child. When Black participants spoke supportively of the parent's concern, placing it in the context of racist tracking policies, the teacher had difficulty accepting that his recommendation might be seen as part of that pattern.

In general, it seemed that many white participants were unprepared to acknowledge the legacy of racism that followed them into the room. This lack of acknowledgment, and belief that one could be seen only as an individual, was in itself a vestige of their white privilege. While white participants were troubled by the mistrust between themselves and people of color, participants of color understood it to be business as usual in a white-dominated, race-conscious society. Coming to terms with this reality was an ongoing source of tension for white participants, which for some remained unresolved.

STAYING OFF THE CYCLE?

Maintaining an opposition to racism in the face of societal pressure to "not notice" the racial order is difficult (Ayvazian, 1995). Our earlier studies (Tatum, 1992, 1994; Lawrence and Bunche, in press) examining the impact of courses on racism have highlighted the anxiety white undergraduates feel when "stepping off the cycle of oppression." The educators in this study expressed a similar anxiety. Some of them worried about returning to schools where racism is the norm, not antiracism. They knew they would find little support for continued dialogue about race in their buildings and questioned whether they would be able to maintain their commitment without a strong support network.

Creating a new identity, that of educator as ally, an advocate for students of color, and a much-needed antiracist role model for white students, is a long-term process. It means undoing years of "color and power-evasive" socialization (Frankenberg, 1993). Undoing racism in institutions which have historically perpetuated the racial order is a daunting task. The fact that this professional development effort was institutionally supported offered these participants a glimpse of hope that they might be able to make a difference in their districts. But more needs to be done to keep this hope alive. School systems like these, which have marshalled their professional development efforts into courses such as the one described here, need to create ongoing opportunities for follow up and establish peer support networks for educators to insure continued movement from awareness to action.

REFERENCES

Adams, M., and Zhou-McGovern, Y. (1994). The sociomoral development of undergraduates in a "social diversity" course: Developmental theory, research, and instructional applications. Paper presented at the American Educational Research Association annual meeting, New Orleans, LA.

Ayvazian, A. (October/November 1990). Being, not doing. *Fellowship*, p. 15.

Ayvazian, A. (January/February 1995). Interrupting the cycle of oppression: The role of allies as agents of change. *Fellowship*, 6–9.

Baker, G. C. (1977). Multicultural imperatives for curriculum development in teacher education. *Journal of Research and Development in Education*, 11, 70–83.

Bennett, C. T. (1979). The preparation of preservice secondary social studies teachers in multiethnic education. *High School Journal*, 62, 232–237.

Carter, R. T., and Goodwin, L. (1994). Racial identity and education. *Review of Research in Education*, 20, 291–336.

Elliott, P., and Tatum, B. D. (1995). Anti-racist professional development: What do Black educators have to say about it? Presentation at the National Association of Multicultural Education, Washington, D.C., February 18.

Frankenberg, R. (1993). *White women, race matters: The social construction of whiteness*. Minneapolis: University of Minnesota.

Grant, C. A. (1981). Education that is multicultural and teacher education: An examination from the perspectives of preservice students. *Journal of Educational Research*, 75, 95–101.

Haberman, M., and Post, L. (1992). Does direct experience change education students' perceptions of low-income minority children? *The Midwestern Educational Researcher*, 5 (2), 29–31.

Helms, J. E. (ed.). (1990). *Black and white racial identity: Theory, research and practice*. Westport, CT: Greenwood Press.

Jackson, Derrick (January 22, 1989). Calling the plays in black and white: Will today's Super Bowl be black brawn vs. white brains? *Boston Sunday Globe*, p. A25.

Lawrence, S. M., and Bunche, T. (in press, September 1996). Feeling and dealing: Teaching white students about racial privilege. *Teaching and Teacher Education*, 12 (5).

McIntosh, P. (July/August 1989). White privilege: Unpacking the invisible knapsack. *Peace and Freedom*.

Redman, G. L. (1977). Study of the relationship of teacher empathy for minority persons and inservice human relations training. *Journal of Educational Research*, 70, 205–210.

Sleeter, C. E. (1992). *Keepers of the American Dream: A study of staff development and multicultural education*. London: Farmer.

Tatum, B. D. (1992). Talking about race, learning about racism: The application of racial identity development theory in the classroom. *Harvard Educational Review*, 62, (1), 1–24.

Tatum, B. D. (1994). Teaching white students about racism: The search for white allies and the restoration of hope. *Teachers College Record*, 95, (4), 462–476.

Washington, D. T. (1981). Impact of antiracism/multicultural education training on elementary teachers' attitudes and classroom behavior. *The Elementary School Journal*, 81, 186–192.

NOTES

1. The high percentage of people of color in the course was especially significant because most of the educators present work in buildings where there are often only one or two educators of color, if there are any at all.

2. Though teachers attended the course voluntarily, many felt overwhelmed by the time commitment required in terms of after-school meeting time, reading assignments, and written work. Consequently, some participants did not complete enough of the assignments to be included in the study.

Interrupting Historical Patterns:
Bridging Race and Gender Gaps between
Senior White Men and Other Organizational Groups

THIRTY-ONE

Nancie Zane

Nancie Zane, Ph.D., is an organizational consultant with Praxis Consulting Group in Philadelphia, PA, an organization whose primary focus is assisting employee-owned businesses. The organization also works with organizational leaders interested in maximizing diversity and increasing employee participation. Nancie recently returned from a year abroad as a visiting lecturer at the University of Haifa, Israel, where she taught courses on race, ethnicity, and gender relations and organizational development. Recent publications include "When Discipline Problems Recede: Democracy and Intimacy in Urban Charters" in M. Fine's (1994) *Chartering Urban School Reform*, and "Theoretical Considerations in Organizational Diversity" in E. Cross, J. Katz, F. Miller, and E. Seashore's (1995) *The Promise of Diversity*.

Among the irrevocable consequences of recent events in a Los Angeles courtroom has been the heightened awareness about the complex role of race in interpreting reality. Ironically, while the media has only just discovered this issue of racial differences in perspective, these differences might be better viewed as a rediscovery of old truths. For example, organizational research focused as early as 1949 on white and black soldiers in the military revealed that whites and blacks perceive situations involving race quite differently (Stouffer, Suchman, Devinney, Star, and Williams, 1950, in Alderfer and Thomas, 1988). Research in the intervening years has confirmed these findings (Alderfer and Thomas, 1988; Alderfer and Smith, 1982; Zane, 1995).

The organizational research also reveals that the differences in perceptions that are rooted in the power disparity among racial groups are further complicated by the impact of gender on perceptions of social reality and justice (Kanter, 1977; Alderfer and Smith, 1982). The multiple identities [racial, gender, cultural, etc.] that all people bring to social and organizational life means that each person brings multiple perspectives on issues of power (Smith, 1982; Hill-Collins, 1990). For some people, these perspectives are in tension, while in other people they are mutually reinforcing. In the case of white men, for example, both racial and gender identity offer an integrated experience of membership in socially privileged or advantaged groups that hold certain degrees of power over white women and people of color. Consequently, for white men, challenging or overcoming a perspective that both feels "natural" and offers considerable benefits may be difficult.

These disparities in perceptions and experience raise important questions about the potential for successful cross-race, cross-gender communication and understanding. It also carries important implications about the obstacles to creating more just, equitable, and resourceful organizations. As a white female organizational researcher and consultant, I have become particularly interested in finding ways for whites to work more effectively and respectfully in heterogeneous settings. Most recently, I had the opportunity to do research in a predominantly white financial institution that I've called Eastern,[1] which was engaged in an organization-wide culture change process that included a commitment to becoming more diverse by race and gender. After documenting the senior managements' attempts to design and implement the first stages of a

"Diversity Initiative."[2] I have become convinced that change in the quality of race and gender relations and the development of acceptable notions of equity can only occur after people recognize the multiple, and often competing, social realities that exist among members of different race and gender groups. For whites in general, this means engaging in conversations about race in which we listen as members of a racial group as well as from our individual perspectives. It also requires hearing others' experiences about the race and gender biases which permeate meritocratic policies and practices as well as identifying (and ultimately changing) the organizational norms which maintain the dominant power relations. Being open to such systemic concerns is particularly critical for white men who tend to face less obstacles in accessing the rewards bureaucracies have to offer. As a consequence, they are over (and often exclusively) represented at the senior most levels (Wells and Jennings, 1983; Zane, 1995).

What might enable whites—and particularly senior white men—to be open to others' experiences that appear contradictory to their own? What might be the impact at the individual, group, and organizational levels if the senior white men positioned themselves to temporarily suspend their perceptual frames in order to hear the perception of others? *This chapter argues that there is a significant shift in senior level white men's conversations about race and gender when they have opportunities to have well-facilitated intra- and intergroup conversations about their organizational experiences in the context of a larger organizational change process.* Through the use of ethnographic and clinic research methods, I have found that as white men began to perceive themselves not only as *individual players* within the organization but also as *members of specific identity groups* which acknowledge race, gender, and organizational status, their understanding of themselves, race relations, and the distribution of organizational power changes. Not only do they change their beliefs about how white women and people of color are being treated within an organization, *they shift their analytic lenses* from blaming "flawed individuals" to understanding more about complex intergroup relationships and structural barriers. In addition, *they gain a perspective on the nature of white male privilege and their relationship to it.* In other words, as senior white men engage in "public talk" with other race and gender groups, they are able to construct new analyses about the problems and potential supports for and between themselves as white men and other race/gender groups. In addition, while I discuss how conversations (and even behaviors) among the senior white men and between the senior white men and other groups change as a consequence of structured race and gender/diversity workshops in which they have participated, I also attempt to contextualize white males' perspective by exploring the hidden *constructions of white masculinity within the postindustrial workplace* in the twentieth century.

THE SENIOR WHITE MALE DISCOURSES PRIOR TO THE DIVERSITY WORKSHOPS

In the six months preceding the Diversity Workshops, it was clear through various individual interviews and group observations that the majority of the senior white male managers had little interest in engaging cross-race or gender dialogues.[3] While aware that the CEO was supportive of the Diversity Initiative and that their attendance at the workshops was mandatory, there were two primary forms of talk that were most prevalent at the time which reflected their antipathy toward engaging such issues: the *Bottom Line* related to the financial problems associated with a Diversity Initiative and talk of the *Meritocracy* was a defense of the meritocracy against complaints of discrimination.

Undergirding the Bottom Line was the concern that engaging in a diversity initiative would mean that Eastern would either be ferrying race and gender tensions from the outside world into the organization or "stirring up" issues that would create intergroup problems within the organization. In either case, the white senior managers saw it as a distraction to the "real work" of making money and felt worried that the bank would loose control over the range of issues contained within its walls. As one senior Vice President, who felt that the organization already did too much to accommodate women and people of color, said, "If I had the authority, I'd change how the bank was doing things . . . not cow-towing to all these different groups . . . this isn't how the company used to run our business."

Other senior managers were less anxious about a diminution of organizational authority and thought that the changing demographics in the workforce required Eastern to acknowledge and consider the implications of race and gender for the workplace. As one EVP commented, "[Eastern] is just reacting to what's happening in the nation and we're interested in being a leader." Some even suggested that if there were resources available to invest in the issue, there could be some positive outcomes, "If it works, [Eastern] will be in the forefront as a "good citizen" and in 10 years we should see a significant rise of qualified people of color in management." Yet, many talked about it as an overextension of the organization's mission. In the words of one senior, "It seems like we're trying to be a social service agency, paternal and benevolent, but we're a business. [Eastern] is not going to solve the world's judgment." Another felt strongly that the organization would be unable to change intergroup patterns that were rooted in the external society.

While there were differences of opinion about whether diversity was an appropriate issue for the organization to engage, there was consensus that allocating considerable resources into a diversity program was a mistake—that the energy involved in highlighting race and gender issues and "becoming more diverse" would drain too much of the organization's resources and divert them from their primary task.

Perhaps the real bottom line was expressed by one of the Executive VP's when he said, "We have no evidence that diversity is actually economically valuable."

In addition to being concerned about the financial return on diversity, many white senior male managers believed that diversity or as they framed it—the concern for those who might be disadvantaged because of race or gender—was a false issue. Instead they believed in Meritocracy, which professed that anyone who worked hard and sought to self-improve could get ahead at Eastern. As one VP said,

I feel that anyone can make it to the top here if they're willing to put in the effort. I don't know if I was promoted because I was a white male but I sincerely believe that people are not judged here on the basis of race and gender.

Of course, there was some acknowledgment that "talent" and "best qualifications" were not necessarily just a matter of personality differences, that different groups had access to different academic opportunities which influenced employers' perceptions of "the best qualified." In one example, a white manager explained how a black student from a local university was perceived as lower quality when compared to a white student from Stanford, because of the status of the institution:

We need the best talent. If I'm choosing between a white from Stanford and a Black from [the local college] there's really no choice. The white student is more savvy. I feel that this in unfortunate, but who's responsibility is it to give Blacks the opportunity?

Even granting the possibility of differential opportunity, however, many of these senior managers were outraged about the oft-made accusation that employees at Eastern were being discriminated against by race or gender.

> Some people of color hide behind diversity issues when they are really performance issues. I don't have time to listen to people complain about racism if they're not performing. The [company] shouldn't prop you up just because you haven't had some opportunities in life.

For these white men, diversity was an issue based on false assumptions that belied the "reality" of fairness and equal opportunity.

THE WORKSHOP EXPERIENCE

For many of the senior managers with whom I spoke during and after the workshops, these workshops seemed to have a profound impact on its participants leading to attitudinal and discursive changes. What happened across these five days that so many of the members of the Management Committee believed "their eyes had been opened" around issues of race and gender?

While different individuals felt they had learned a variety of lessons from the structured exercises the Diversity Consultants took them through during the workshops, the overwhelming majority attributed their sense of opening up, taking in new information, and changing their perspectives—what Lewin (1948) might call "unfreezing"—to hearing the personal stories of white women and people of color. Although in the midst of one workshop, many white men reported that they could not relate to the kinds of experiences that members of different race/gender groups' shared, in retrospect, confronting the realities of these participants' painful work lives while sitting with the contrast of their own experiences was transformative. As Marv, an Executive VP who had little patience for the notion of discrimination in the organization, said:

> To me the biggest impact came from the personal stories that we heard in our two-day session. . . . intellectually, I thought I was aware of some of these issues, but when you actually hear the depth of emotion and general consistency in the stories, it made an impression on me that there is a problem here, and it is not just a couple of malcontents whining and complaining. . . .

In addition, the Diversity Consultants provided managers with new and broader frameworks for processing the data by distinguishing between individual, group, and institutional levels of analysis, a framework which for Evan, another Executive VP, meant he, like Marv, could "no longer dismiss individual concerns as idiosyncratic stories." Indeed, Marv and Evan's vision and understanding of some aspect of the world had been permanently altered.

As a way to try and capture some of the experience that led to a number of the senior white men's new outlook on race and gender issues at Eastern, I've tried to highlight a number of significant moments across several workshops in which the white men seemed to gain some significant insight into the dynamics of race, gender, power, and privilege.

Scene I

After talking in small homogeneous groups[4] about the some of the organization-wide data that had been collected at the beginning of the culture change process and categorically analyzed by race, gender, and level,[5] participants came back together to discuss the highlights of their conversations. People of color talked movingly about their pain of trying to "make it" in the organization and the systematic erosion of the psyche that takes place after continuously being exposed to racism.

> Elaine, a Chinese midlevel manager said: "It makes me sad that I'm always having to change myself . . . to adapt myself to others' expectations so they'll accept me."
> Carol Brown, the lead African-American Diversity Consultant responded: "What happens if they don't understand your perspective?"
> Elaine: "You take it in internally and I end up feeling like there's something wrong with me."
> Bob, an African-American midlevel manager added, "I'm used to being a minority . . . having to work hard to educate others . . . to make them understand that I'm o.k."
> Yvonne, an African-American senior level officer joined in as well: "I go home questioning my sanity, my intellect, my judgement . . . we hurt ourselves, put a lot of energy into saying, "I'm somebody, you can't make me feel like a nobody."

After hearing there comments, a number of white men asked the people of color in the group "Why do you take it?" "Why are you so docile?" "How come there isn't more activism in the streets?" With some impatience, different people of color talked about their fear of white violence and their fear for their children in the outside world—one in which their children could easily be killed by a cop or a gang member who sees their kid as "another nigger." Flora, an African-American midlevel woman manager elaborated:

> My son has everything going against him. The only thing he has is two intelligent parents. . . . I pray for him. . . . I know that if he gets an attitude he'll end up with a bullet in his ass . . . he's always suspect . . . he's already been asked by a white cop in our own neighborhood, "where do you live?"

While her story was quite gut-wrenching, the white men did not seem to relate to empathize with the emotionality. Yvonne, who was clearly angry about whites' assumption that blacks have choices about venting their rage, said forcefully:

> We put up with it because we have no choice. . . . we never get a leg up, we're still at the bottom . . . native people were wiped out . . . so we've learned to swallow hard. But you know what racism does to us? It destroys us systematically. . . . even with college degrees we can't find work . . . there are bright black men on street corners because there's no place for them in the system . . . they wait to die. Black men are an endangered species . . . you swallow until you can't take it anymore.

The white men begin to talk about their feelings of guilt and responsibility as well as their sense of powerlessness about changing the situation. Carol, the Diversity Consultant, asked people to move back into their same race/gender groups and identify their reactions to what they've heard. On newsprint the white men wrote:

> We often feel powerless or unaware of what to do to make a difference.

> We want and need feedback—we will make mistakes.

We have feelings of fear, guilt, anxiety.

We feel a lot of the burden is (appropriately) on us and we want/need to help.

During the next intergroup dialogue, a number of people of color responded with surprise, "I had no idea that white men had feelings of impotence or uncertainty."

Scene II

The group began with two white men acknowledging that they had been operating *only* from an individual perspective and did not understand group-level phenomena: "When I thought I 'had it' on an individual level I was most dangerous since I didn't get it on a group level."

Rosa, an upper-level Puerto Rican woman manager, went into depth about how, when she meets whites in power, she's either assumed to be stupid or, once seen as intelligent, assumed to be different than the "others" of her kind. This puts her in the position, if she wants to fit in and succeed, of having to choose to identify with those in power (whites) or her family, who are seen as inferior. "Every time it's a death that I die to think . . . my cousins are less than me. . . . its painful putting people behind the doors and making them invisible." Several other people of color and white women then told connecting stories related to this experience.

The white men appeared distant—again not connecting to Rosa's level of emotionality or her story. Finally one senior white man, Bill, admitted that "it's tough to hear this, because I can't relate to it." Initially some of the senior men tried to see it as a "people" story, but Donna, a white woman Diversity Consultant teaming with Carol Brown, quickly dispelled the notion that it was a universal story, and explained how it was different because of race and gender. She described how white men do not walk into a room and have to dispel negative stereotypes about themselves nor do they have to choose between themselves and their people to get into "the club." Essie raised the underlying issue, "How does it feel, that with the luck of the draw, you have the advantage? . . . You feel like you've earned your spot, but haven't recognized the group advantage."

Slowly, some of the white men began to let in the possibility that they have been privileged in certain ways. Chaz, an executive V.P., says, "You're saying that we got where we are because of who we are . . . you're putting down a life that's been hard to come by . . . that hurts my self image." John, a black man on the Diversity Consultation team asked, "Why do you hear her negating your hard work?" Chaz replied, "Well, most of us think we did it through hard work . . . but hard work or not we had an advantage."

As the conversation continued a few white men then described some of their resistance to being race and gender conscious—that they felt uncomfortable and awkward about having to be so conscious of what they say and how they say it: "Wouldn't it be better if we could all be comfortable?" Donna framed it as, "How does change occur and who's responsible for change? . . . We're willing to tell you about our experience but, you do have to change your behavior . . . to be more sensitive . . . to realize you didn't get there just by merit . . . it's uncomfortable to see this stuff and acknowledge it . . . over time you will feel more integrated."

Scene III

During a large group session, Bill began to discuss his newfound belief about race, gender, and self-esteem—i.e., that while it takes a lot of energy for individuals to maintain their self-esteem, it must take more energy for white women and people of color given the daily psychic assaults with which they are confronted. He said, "As a white man, I carry a one-pound weight; not the 100-pound weight that women and people of color do. Self-esteem is everyone's issue, but for women and people of color it's worse." Bob, another white man, built on that idea and made the connection between self-esteem and power. "Some of us use our positions of power to feel good. . . . If you don't have self-confidence, you don't want to give up the power . . . and lots of us don't have it."

The conversation then moved to the question of what would motivate white men to share the prize/power/privilege. "I think it would be decency," said Bob. Tim responded in a matter-of-fact tone, "We know that doesn't work . . . we've been able to wall off others from getting their hands in the cookie jar . . . the system isn't working."

The white men began to problem-solve about how they should address these issues. "The only way to get out of this is to correct inequities . . . and go the other way . . . that means we should be hiring blacks that are less qualified and training them." Brown quickly intervened and reframed the issue: "The issue is not about less qualified blacks, but less qualified whites. . . . What does it do to his self-image and your relationship to him?" A senior white man mused that unknowingly, white men have, in the name of objectivity, "built in a whole lot of prejudice into the judgment tools and check marks." A middle-level white woman and black man both responded, "We don't understand what the check marks are that signify qualifications . . . we think some are subjective and about seeing yourself in others." A white man then linked the nature of the organizational structure to its function. "Structures have become invisible to protect white men's self-image." Donna then connected his comment to the question of change and responsibility: "White men's responsibility is to get people to say that the invisible structures which maintain inequity have to change."

UNRAVELING THE WORKSHOP DISCOURSE

In reflecting on these scenes from the Diversity Workshops, I was deeply moved by the power of the workshop dialogue; of the generosity of the white women and people of color to share at such emotionally meaningful levels—revealing their pain, vulnerabilities, and strengths;[6] and of the willingness of the white men to reveal their anxieties about their own limitations and failures. In regard to the white men, I was also struck by the psychological and cognitive leaps many of them demonstrated, in which they not only took in others' experiences as a valid expression of reality, but chose to work with this "new" information in a way that yielded fresh insight into their own perspectives.

The significance of the white men's openness became more impressive as I began to unravel the embedded discourses about work, organizational structures, maleness, and white privilege that underlied their conversations. For example, one tension that was evident in the workshop dialogues related to the credibility of the meritocracy, and the relationship between achievement at work and self-esteem. The senior white men were clearly invested in the notion that their hard work, ingenuity, and skills had won them their senior-level positions. As others talked about the fact that there were obstacles to their getting ahead, white men heard it as a condemnation that they somehow didn't "deserve" their position. During the diversity workshops, the consultants tried to assure the senior men that the implications of discrimination did not reflect a diminution of their hard work, but rather a statement about the structural barriers which certain others faced, disabling them from demonstrating or being recognized for their equally meritorious efforts. As the consultants and a number of white men ultimately acknowledged, one consequence of these impermeable barriers was that the pool of competitors that white men were vying against was smaller than it might have been.

But rather than simply framing the senior white men's anxiety about the legitimacy of their organizational status or their uneasiness about the discriminatory nature of the system as merely self-serving or a desire to maintain double standards, it is important to contextualize their reactions by examining the historical discourses which have permeated white middle-class worklife during the last two centuries.

In *American Manhood*, Rotundo explained that only at the turn of the nineteenth century, as the market economy emerged and the interconnected web of relationships between home, community, religious affiliation, and work disappeared, did white mens' work take on heightened meaning and "provide the chief substance of their social identity" (Rotundo, 1993, p. 167). With the shift from a more communal to individualistic social context, white men and women's lives became more distinctly divided into private versus public spheres, in which men dominated the more powerful public or work sphere. From Rotundo's perspective this separation had important political implications:

> From the hierarchy and assigned social status of colonial society to the doctrine of the spheres . . . [the latter] enshrined individualism as a male privilege, making men's sphere the locus of individualism and women's sphere the place where a woman submerged her social identity in that of her husband . . . (Rotundo, 1993, p. 290)

However, while white men's power was heightened, so were their anxieties about their work lives as the association between male work and self worth as a "male human" became pivotal. On the one hand, "Work could serve to reassure a man about his manhood and about the freedom and power that manhood beckoned" (Rotundo, 1993, p. 177). On the other, the thought of failure plagued the psyches of many middle-class white men. After all, not only did a man's individual achievements serve as a reflection of his character, but it also served to mark the social status of his whole family. Supported by an ideology of denial, in which white men were taught to deny their fears and forge ahead regardless of their feelings, there was great social pressure for men to exhibit individual initiative to get ahead within their chosen professions (Rotundo, 1993; Doyle, 1995). Over time, sports and relaxation became extensions of the work world as well, so socializing in all (white) male lodges, restaurants, and athletic clubs in which competition and fraternization were intermingled were critical components of male work life.

During the twentieth century three major shifts occurred which impacted white middle-class men's work world. The first two related to gender relations: 1) women demanded and won the right to vote as well as the right to work, invading the boundaries of the male workplace, and 2) Darwinian theory shifted the negative judgment on the "primitive passions of men" into a more positive one. So while white women had been the keepers of the domestic and more contained, civilized sphere, as they moved into the workforce, white men reclaimed their right to define the elements of civility—despite/in spite of the judgments of women. The notion now included self-expressions of male passion—combative strength, ambition, and boldness. These characteristics, which in the workplace were tempered by virtues of cooperation and connection as it related to accomplishing the aims of the larger organization, became the marks of an independent, successful man. So at the time white women were gaining access to the workplace, white men were changing the rules about the kinds of behavior that would gain individual acclaim and recognition. Ultimately, white men continued to define and dominate the workplace. As Rotundo explains it:

As we have seen historically . . . the middle-class workplace was constructed by men according to shared male values and customs that are culturally alien to women. In recent years, women have made statistical inroads in the world of the team player, but as yet there is little change—culturally or statistically—at the level where most power is wielded.

The third trend that affected the interiors of white men's organizational life pertains to race relations and civil rights. Prior to the 1960s, race and ethnicity were rarely overt topics of conversation within organizational settings (Alderfer and Thomas, 1987) and concerns about systemic barriers that prevented access to primarily white institutions were trivialized and denied. Maintaining an advantage over people of color, particularly blacks, was a reflection of the natural order of social and organizational relations—individuals with less skills, education, and/or motivation remained at the bottom of the hierarchy. Their place in the pecking order was the very justification for their being positioned there. Since whites tended to see the world in individual rather than group terms, patterns of discrimination and dominance were made invisible. However, the emergence of the civil rights movement highlighted racial differences and the myths of social and organizational mobility. The passage of the Civil Rights Act and the development of the notion of affirmative action forced organizations to confront the issue of racial discrimination.

However, even with people of color and their white allies pressing the legal and moral issues, middle-class whites—and white men in particular—have maintained their aversion to thinking in group-level terms, invested instead in asserting the myth of the "color-blind" meritocracy—a stance that allows white men to resist marking themselves as white and as dominant. Taking such a stance, according to Ruth Frankenberg, "is itself an effect of its dominance. Among the effects on white people both of race privilege and of the dominance of whiteness are their seeming normativity, their structured invisibility" (Frankenberg, 1993, p. 6).

With notions of masculinity, whiteness, and self being inextricably intertwined with the dominant ideologies of individualism and meritocracy, it is not surprising that the senior white men at Eastern would cling to the images of themselves and their white male colleagues as hard-working, deserving employees. However, when they were no longer insulated from the pain that the white male bureaucratic culture imposed on "others," these men acknowledged the ways their own vision had been obstructed by the very systems they relied on to help them know their world. They could no longer deny the flaws in the meritocracy and the resulting patterns of institutional discrimination. Further, the jarring experiences of the Diversity Workshops and the cross gender/race relationships that were established may have forced a wedge in the tightly constructed historical web of white male privilege.

DISCUSSION

In listening to the conversations that took place during the Diversity Workshops as well as the reflections of the senior white men after the event, the senior white men seemed to have undergone a rather striking metamorphosis. Rather than maintaining a stance towards diversity characterized by negativity, they began to move towards a postion of openness and genuine interest. How did this evolve? By participating in dialogue in which white women, women of color, and men of color spoke candidly both from their personal as well as their group-level experiences within the organization, the senior white men were confronted with collective data which was categorically different from their own. This exchange, facilitated by well-seasoned Diversity Consultants, provided a window into certain systematic patterns which could no longer be comfortably labeled as the specific problems of whiny individuals or undeserving minorities. In acknowledging the gaps between their and others' realities, many of the white men were able to hold previous assumptions at bay and hear old information in new ways. This served as a basis for constructing new, more complex critiques about others, themselves as a group, and their relationships to the organization. It also provided the foundation for the emergence a new set of organizational discourses in which there was an embracing, rather than negation of, race and gender differences, as well as an eschewing of discriminatory policies and practices.

In reflecting on the Diversity Workshops and the experience of these senior white men, I feel privileged to have witnessed their process over time. I am also heartened by the notion that carefully structured, well-facilitated dialogue offers tremendous possibilities for bridging intergroup relationships and building more equitable organizations. It feels critical to point out, however, that expert facilitators and good faith on the part of individuals and groups is, unfortunately, not enough. In this experience, while the diversity workshops created an environment in which the senior white men began to listen and hear others in ways that altered some of their own perspectives, the context for this transformational process was not neutral, nor was managers' participation voluntary. The Diversity Workshops themselves took place in the context of a larger culture change process within the organization that was being championed by the CEO. Although mandatory participation in the Diversity Workshops could not guarentee that the senior managers would change their perspectives, recognizing that their boss was quite serious about creating a more humane, diverse organizational climate—in which he was willing to commit financial and human resources as well as his own time—created a set of expectations about the managers' openness to new organizational and relational possibilities. Further, as conversations about the importance of developing policies and practices that support "diversity management" came to the fore, discussions about strategies for holding managers accountable to a new set of prodiversity behaviors were not far behind. The prospect of having the formal (and informal) reward and punishment systems linked to a new way of doing business certainly raised the ante to at least begin "talking the talk." Finally, although no senior manager had been guarenteed a senior position at Eastern, there was some acknowledgment that they had already "made it" within the organization and had little to fear if policies changed in a way that expanded the pool of competitors for various upper-level jobs. Thus, supporting, rather than resisting, a climate of change may have been perceived as less costly—and even advantageous—to the senior managers. Ultimately, while facilitated talk may be a prerequiste to altering white male discourse, a larger institutional context that supports change guided by a powerful champion is required as well.

REFERENCES

Alderfer, C., and Smith, K. (1982). "Studying Intergroup Relations Embedded in Organizations," *Administrative Science Quaterly 27.*

Stouffer, Suchman, Devinney, Star, and Williams (1950) in Alderfer, C., and Thomas, D. (1988). "The Significance of Race and Ethnicity for Understanding Organizational Behavior." In *International Review of Industrial and Organizational Psychology*, eds. Cary L. Cooper and I. Robertson. (New York: Wiley).

Frankenberg, Ruth. (1993) *The Social Construction of Whiteness: White women, Race Matters.* Minnesota, MN: University of Minnesota Press.

Hill-Collins, P. (1990). *Black Feminist Thought.* (New York: Routledge).

Kanter, R. (1977). *Men and Women of the Corporation.* (New York: Basic Books).

Lewin, K. (1947). "Group Decision and Social Change." In T. N. Newcomb and E. L. Hartley (eds.) *Readings in Social Psychology*. (Troy, MO: Holt, Rinehart, and Winston).

Smith, K. (1982). *Groups in Conflict*. (Iowa: Kendall/Hunt Publishing Company)

Wells, L., and Jennings, C. L. (1983). "Black Career Advances and White Reactions: Remnants of Herrenvolkk Democracy and the Scandalous Paradox." In D. Vails-Webber and W. N. Potts (eds.) *Sunrise Seminars*. (Arlington, Va.: NTL Institute).

Zane, N. (1996). "The Multiple Discourses of Diversity: The Links Between Language, Culture, and Structure." Unpublished manuscript.

NOTES

1. Both the name of the organization and the names of individuals quoted in the text have been altered to protect confidentiality.

2. In the beginning of Eastern's culture change process, diversity was defined as a desire to value individual differences and encourage a range of perspectives in an environment of respect. Two years later it was cast as eradicating oppression at the institutional level and harnessing the talents and contributions that all bring to the organization.

3. There were approximately twenty-four senior white managers who were most responsible for top-level decisions.

4. There were four small groups: white women, white men, women of color, and men of color. The women of color were not racially homogeneous in that there were Asian-American, Hispanic-American, and African-American women present. The "men of color" group consisted of African-American men.

5. As a way to create some benchmarks for the culture-change process, the ad hoc committee responsible for designing and overseeing the process hired a consulting group to construct an organizationwide employee satisfaction survey. The survey was used to get an initial pulse of the organization. The data indicated that there were significant differences in how various race and gender groups felt about organizational practices as it related to recruitment, retention, and promotion of employees. Tower and her associates had participants in the workshop discuss the survey findings as a way to begin the conversation about differential experiences among groups at Eastern.

6. The question that remains unexplored is the cost (and gain) to white women and people of color for their self- and group-disclosures. For example, some of the women of color at Eastern reported in interviews with me after the workshop that they had continued to feel emotionally drained and exposed because they had discussed situations in which not only was the content upsetting, but it was about things they usually repressed in order to function. Consequently, they felt "left hanging" and "used." For others, the experience was cathartic—they felt heard and responded to. Many also felt that they had learned things about white men's experience and perspectives which they hadn't known before and which provided new understanding about certain racial differences. In addition, several white women and people of color mentioned that the workshops had given them an opportunity to get to know and network with senior white men that they hadn't known before. One result was that they found themselves gaining access to situations from which they were previously excluded. The flip side, of course, was that they found themselves being tokenized in a variety of situations as well because now they were the one "black person" or "white woman" that was known by the senior manager who was trying to be more inclusive. While it is beyond the scope of this paper to address this issue in depth, it is a critical one, particularly since many diversity workshops (otherwise known as multicultural, race, or human-relations workshops) use this model of intergroup dialogue in which white women and people of color "spill their guts" as a way to do consciousness-raising with white men about discrimination and institutional oppression.

Home/Work:
Antiracism Activism and the Meaning of Whiteness

Becky Thompson and White Women Challenging Racism

Becky Thompson, Ph.D., teaches sociology at Simmons College, is the author of *A Hunger So Wide and So Deep: American Women Speak Out on Eating Problems* (University of Minnesota Press, 1994), and coeditor with Sangeeta Tyagi of *Names We Call Home: Autobiography on Racial Identity* (Routledge, 1995) and *Beyond A Dream Deferred: Multicultural Education and the Politics of Excellence* (University of Minnesota Press, 1993).

In the summer of 1994 two Italian-American white women friends, Patti DeRosa and Angela Giudice, who had worked together for many years at a community multicultural project in Boston, put a call out to other white women they knew who had been doing some form of antiracism activism for at least ten years. They pulled together about a dozen women—working, middle, and mixed class, lesbian, heterosexual and bisexual, Jewish and Christian-raised—who ranged in age from 35 to 53.

Through our initial meetings, the group, "White Women Challenging Racism," identified two priorities.[1] First, we wanted to document our existence and the history of other white antiracist activists as we organize against racism as it is manifested locally, nationally, and internationally (evident, for example, in policies on immigration, welfare, the death penalty, and crime). Second, we hoped to create a "home base" where we could rejuvenate and push ourselves forward in our continuing work. This article became a piece of our first agenda item—a way to try to document white antiracist activism in the 1990s—and a means to engage with a central topic in this book: namely, what it means to live as white people who are attempting to unravel racial hierarchies.

WHAT IS ANTIRACIST ACTIVISM?: OR, WE ARE MORE THAN WHAT WE OPPOSE

In general, popular imagery about activism is limited to holding placards at demonstrations and climbing into police vans after civil disobedience arrests. While these are vital forms of protest, the bulk of the work that many of us do to oppose racism occurs in more mundane, subtle, and circuitous ways. This, in and of itself, is part of what makes white anti-oppression work invisible. This dynamic has been coupled with widespread, historical amnesia regarding progressive politics in general, including white antiracist politics. While many sports stars, Hollywood actors, and cartoon characters are household names, few of us could name even five white antiracist activists—in this generation, decade, *or* century. The effects of this historical amnesia is that few white people have roles models or ways of knowing what has worked before—and not.

Given these realities, we realized that we needed to spell out what antiracism means to us. During our first meeting together, in 1994, we spoke about white people we have looked to for guidance, including Lillian Smith, Muriel Rukeyser, Tillie Olsen, Mab Segrest, Morris Dees, Anne

Braden, Linda Stout, and those people in our own families and communities who have taught us to oppose oppression.[2] As group member Elly Bulkin noted, most of the antiracist activists we could think of were people who had *written* about their activism. We rarely find out about the many white people outside of local communities who are doing grassroots organizing but don't have the time, resources, and/or inclination to write about their work. The consequences of class and access to higher education often help determine who becomes widely recognized as "leaders."

Although we all acknowledged the real threat that a visible national movement of white antiracist activists could pose to white supremacy, we found less obvious the way in which our own socialization as white people perpetuated our invisibility. When we first began meeting, many of us weren't sure if we really "belonged" in the group: perhaps we hadn't done "enough" or were not "really" qualified, and we certainly knew of others whose contributions exceeded our own. When we realized how many of us shared such feelings, we began to try to piece together the reasons behind them.

Our hesitance in claiming a *right* to be among other antiracist white women partly stemmed from our lacking a definition of antiracism. Very few venues are available for white people to know and learn from each other collectively. For example, hardly any of us had been in a group before where we had been able to talk openly about our antiracist activism. Our anxiety about whether we belonged also clearly reflected our constant awareness of how much more needs to be accomplished—particularly in the 1990s—as racial injustice continues to escalate. In addition, as group member Meck Groot pointed out, by worrying about our credentials and right to claim a seat among the others, many of us were doing a real "girl" thing—distancing ourselves from our accomplishments and abilities. What became curious though—to group member Patti DeRosa— is why women who had talked with her individually for years about their antiracism then got shy and self-deprecating in the group.

This apparent contradiction actually reveals several characteristics about how whiteness is gendered. First, socialization for white women in this society involves learning to be competitive with and distrustful of other women. This competition is fed by compulsory heterosexuality—which teaches women that competing with each other is a necessary part of "getting a man."[3] In addition, one of the worst accusations that can be leveled against white girls/women is a claim that we are self-promoting, proud, or overtly self-confident. Third, white female socialization involves learning to disown one's privileges and power.[4]

Once we were able to claim our right to be there—and unpack how our hesitations related to whiteness—it became easier to begin to define antiracism. Over the years, our antiracism has included: organizing protests on a range of progressive issues; working in activist multiracial organizations, on political campaigns, in progressive Jewish organizations, and for curriculum transformation and academic institutional change; teaching about racism, imperialism, and other forms of oppression in community and campus settings; supporting welfare rights and fair housing; participating in lesbian-feminist antiracist groups;[5] and serving as draft counselors and testers in discrimination cases. In most cases, our activism against racism has been linked to opposition to other forms of oppression.

Building a national antiracism movement partly depends upon defining in an expansive way what constitutes antiracism. As Patti DeRosa explained,

> The work that I get paid to do in the 1990s—antiracism trainings—is the same work we called teach-ins in the 1960s. If I need to call it training and education, because that is the current vernacular, I'll use that language. For me, the point is to take advantage of any available vehicle for talking about antiracism to a wide range of people.

For Patti, it is problematic when people imply that working with corporations is less valuable than working with nonprofits and social service agencies. As she sees it, "training and education is a form of political education and a way to not only get to those who are already questioning racism, but also to get to those in the great middle who haven't even thought of the questions yet."

For many of us, our antiracism has often been done outside of our paid work.[6] Some of us have had the class and educational privilege to be able to choose paid work that gives us the flexible schedules and geographical locations that facilitate our continued organizing. Identifying one's activism solely by one's paid job title has other limitations as well. For example, someone might be an affirmative action officer (a position that connotes opposition to racism in employment) and yet might be pressured to rubber stamp white-biased hiring strategies. On the flip side, although group member Barbara Bond is currently in a position—as a social worker on an oncology unit of a major medical center—that is not explicitly about race, she defines her job so that struggling against exclusionary practices in health service becomes key. In other words, antiracism is often less about people's job titles than it is about how we use our power and expertise within and outside of our paid work. Recognizing a range of ways people do antiracism work does not mean that everything goes—that anything counts. But the narrow way antiracism has been popularly defined is one of the many impediments to seeing ourselves and others as active change agents and to naming our accomplishments accordingly.

Because doing antiracism work has been so deeply connected to all aspects of our lives, it is hard to separate out what is "just doing our jobs and living our lives" from being antiracist. For example, when group member Angela Giudice described her public and private life she said,

> Being antiracist and multicultural *is* my life. It is what I do and who I am as a white Italian American lesbian involved in a ten-year relationship with an African American and Cherokee woman. We have just recently become the parents of a biracial child who's also African American and Italian and we live in Roxbury (a historically Black community in Boston). I work in a multiracial, multiethnic organization that was founded by and is predominantly run by African American women.

For Angela, working against racism predated her involvement in her long-term relationship—an order of events that she is careful to clarify when people assume that her motivation for opposing racism stems from her relationship with her lover. At the same time, being antiracist and living and working in a multicultural environment has become so much a part of her being that she often feels "bicultural." She is wary of describing herself as "bicultural" however, because of historical and present attempts by white people to minimize the difference our whiteness makes in the world. When white people cross cultural borders, that does not necessarily mean this crossing is done in a nonexploitative way. At the same time, Angela wants to claim and validate the work that she has done and celebrate the rich, complex life she leads.

Since, for many of us, our paid work, political commitments, and personal relationships are deeply intertwined, we are seeking terms that not only show what we are against but also speak to what we affirm and who we are becoming. Part of the problem with the term "antiracist" is that it only says what we are *against*. In fact, for many of us, our antiracism involves creating multicultural spaces in which we live and work. The absence of terms that fully describe the antiracist/multiracial lives many of us have created underscores the potential subversion of living such lives. Making multiracial alliances at work and through organizing, working in white communities to push affirmative action forward, raising white children in an antiracist way, or being part of a multiracial family—all are ways of refusing to buy into white supremacy. Being part of multiracial families that are working and loving flies in the face of common notions that interracial relationships are deviant, abnormal, and inherently vexed.[7] For many group members, making conscious choices to raise their white children in communities that are mixed by race, ethnicity, culture, and socioeconomic status subverts the common assumption that the "best" communities and schools are white and wealthy. Subversion, in these and other instances, includes defying often unspoken barriers to cross-cultural communication, funneling resources to support multicultural education and antiracist organizing, and doing the bridge work needed to make political links between progressive struggles.

WHAT IS WHITENESS?: "WHAT CHOU MEAN 'WE' WHITE GIRL?"

Much of what whiteness has meant and constituted in the United States historically and currently has been intertwined with death, destruction, arrogance, and unearned privileges.[8] We came together partly because of our collective realization that doing antiracism work effectively with other white people requires understanding that it is possible to be white and *not* buy into racial hierarchies and intentionally exert power over others. One of the challenges facing those of us interested in understanding (and theorizing about) whiteness is to create a language of whiteness that does not rely upon simple equations between color and the abuse of power.[9] Patti DeRosa teased out the components of whiteness by making distinctions between whiteness as description, whiteness as experience, and whiteness as ideology. As a *description*, whiteness identifies those who are light-skinned, with Western European physical features. As a physical description, this label is fairly self-evident. The *experience* of whiteness in the United States is one of unearned privileges which all white people receive in various ways due to racism. A light-skinned "white" person who experiences race privileges may or may not buy into the *ideology* of whiteness as a system of exploitation based on white supremacy. However, that person can not separate her/himself from the experience of being white, since we live and breathe the privileges every day.

Whiteness is confusing and complex partly because white people are symbols and individuals at the same time.[10] Because it is possible to oppose white supremacy and still receive unearned privileges as a white person, some of the group members refer to ourselves as "antiracist racists"—women who have journeyed from being unconscious about our own racism to being activists who continue to challenge our own racism and white supremacy in general.

Because whiteness is both a description and a symbol, white antiracist activists may often feel as if we are living schizophrenic lives: we both identify that we are white (as a description) and that we experience privilege (based on racial hierarchy) as we confront the absurdity of an invented ideological system that bases power on descriptive differences. We must claim a reality (that we have white skin) and deal with unearned privileges as we show that the hierarchy is, itself, an invention. To not claim our whiteness for reasons of shame, guilt, lack of awareness, or denial effectively reinforces the invention, since we are then unable to oppose the ideology of whiteness (based on white supremacy).

Our challenge, then, is to claim our whiteness as a physical description and acknowledge white privilege as we reject what whiteness means ideologically. As Barbara Bond explained,

There is absolutely no reason not to embrace being who we are physically. Lillian Smith and others have understood that historically. They were able to step outside of their context and say, "I am fine. It's the system that's been set up around this construct of race that isn't fine."